Findlaters—
The story of a Dublin merchant family
1774–2001

Findlaters—
The story of a Dublin merchant family 1774–2001

Alex Findlater

A. & A. Farmar
2001

British Library cataloguing in Publication Data
A CIP catalogue record for this book is available from the
British Library

Editing by A. & A. Farmar
Cover design by Tony Colley
Text designed and set by Image Creation Technologies
Index by Helen Litton
Printed and bound by Estudios gráficos Zure S.A.

ISBN 1-899047-69-7

Published by
A. & A. Farmar
Beech House 78 Ranelagh Village
Dublin 6 Ireland
Tel: +353 1 496 3625
Fax: +353 1 497 0107

Email: Publisher: afarmar@iol.ie
Author: alex@findlaterbook.com

Web: Publisher: farmarbooks.com
Author: findlaterbook.com

Contents

Preface

This book is about my family, the Findlaters, who have been merchants in Dublin over the past 175 years. I try to give as full a picture as possible of the lives and times of members of the family, at work and at play, in politics, religion, business and our parts in the shadow of historic events. I encompass as wide a family circle as possible to cover the full spectrum from grocer to doctor, from merchant to soldier. The text is enriched by reminiscence from customers and staff. The story itself is not one of rags to riches, nor riches to rags. We were neither ascendancy nor peasantry. We were the new merchant and professional class in-between—first Presbyterian and then Church of Ireland—through this period.

In his memoir, *Dublin Made Me,* Todd Andrews, one of the architects of the present state, recalled his childhood in the inner city in the first decade of the 1900s: 'From childhood I was aware that there were two separate and immiscible kinds of citizens: the Catholics, of whom I was one, and the Protestants, who were as remote and different from us as if they had been blacks and we whites. We were not acquainted with Protestants but we knew that they were there.' [1] And later he wrote: 'Considering that I rarely met and never mingled with Protestants and only saw them when they paraded on Sunday mornings in great style to Findlaters' Church—the Presbyterian Church in Rutland Square—it is strange that from earliest childhood I seem to have been aware of their presence and influence in the community.'[2]

Contrary to Andrews' impression, 'Protestants' were not a single type, but extremely varied. Tony Farmar, in his history of Craig Gardner, probably hit the nail on the head: 'Protestants did not however form the homogenous social and political group imagined by Catholic polemicists. There was a considerable difference in political and social attitudes between the Church of Ireland's adherents and other groups.' There was the unionist, land-owning, Church of Ireland tradition, there were the Presbyterians, staunch defenders of their position against both Catholics and Church of Ireland, leading participants in 1798, not to mention numerous other groups such as Methodists, Quakers and Moravian Brethren.[3] And their range of occupations was as wide as their beliefs: they were farmers, merchants and commercial men, labourers, soldiers and police—any stereotype, however well loved, is bound to be a simplification. I have written this book partly to show how different one group of Protestants, the merchant and professional class, was from the pre-conceived image.

I only deal with issues that come naturally into the text. This means that, for example, the *Ne temere* decree of 1907, which caused intense stress in other

Protestant families, does not arise. Under that decree, both partners in a Roman Catholic–Protestant marriage had to give an undertaking that all children of the marriage would be brought up Roman Catholic. The book illustrates that the lot of the southern Protestants since independence has, in many ways, been a happy one. There was surely a lot of insecurity as they moved from being part of a British Isles religious majority to an island minority. This is illustrated by the delegation dispatched by the General Synod of the Church of Ireland on 12 May 1922 to wait on Michael Collins to inquire: 'if they were permitted to live in Ireland or if it was desired that they should leave the country'.[4]

This sensitivity caused the vast majority of Protestants to keep their heads well below the parapet and refrain from stating any views on Church and State, even in the privacy of the family. We were mum about the great power of the Catholic Church in the middle of the 20th century and did not have any strong political allegiance. As a result the research into this book has been a voyage of discovery. For instance, I had no idea that Billy Findlater, when MP for Monaghan, had supported Gladstone in formulating the Land Act 1881 giving the tenant-farmers rights of tenure, nor that his cousin Adam had played a part in securing local government for the country. It was a total surprise to find a letter from Michael Davitt suggesting that should Adam stand for the Nationalists in the 1906 election, he would doubtless win. I was interested to discover that my maternal grandfather took the surrender from both Michael Collins and Seán Lemass, as well as most of the Rising leaders in 1916, and none of the family had any idea that my father Dermot had helped the anti-TB league to get its voice heard in 1943.

I am the product of my history. It has shaped me and it is recorded here. I have presented the events as they appeared to me. My Aunt Sheila, at ninety-eight the senior member of the family, and my mother Dorothea, have fully supported me in this task. I hope that it acts as an encouragement and an inspiration to the readers and in particular to my nine nephews and nieces and my many cousins.

Alex Findlater

June 2001

Notes and references

1 C. S. Andrews, *Dublin Made Me* Dublin: Mercier Press 1979 p 9

2 Op. Cit. p 20

3 Tony Farmar *A History of Craig Gardner & Co, The First Hundred Years* Dublin: Gill & Macmillan 1988 p 65

4 Terence Brown *Ireland, A Social & Cultural History 1922–1985* Glasgow: Fontana p 109

Acknowledgements

As Tony Farmar handed back my twelve hundred pages of research and agreed that the book should be written, I rather naively inquired of him who should write it. He replied that there were only two people in the room—and he knew who was not going to do so. As I left, he lightly mentioned that of course the manuscript should be delivered on disk. So I bought a computer, and four months later arrived back with a beautifully typed script of 273,000 words which has acted as our basic quarry ever since.

The fun was only beginning. I had compiled it thematically, with all the churchie stuff in one chapter, the business confined to a single chapter and all the interesting 'I remembers' together in another. Unfortunately, Tony had not told me that, on the whole, he thought that history should be written in chronological order. As the unscrambling progressed, Tony spotted the hundred or so dusty ledgers in my study. I dismissed them with a wave of the arm as being purely filled with uninteresting columns of figures. To Tony they were a treasure-trove. So I set to work, and uncovered the most wonderful archive. We may not have had a wealth of letters, but it was all here in figures. It was the DNA of the business. We were able to reconstruct the entire 19th century—business profits and activity, personal spending and donations to charity and a lot more in addition. This provided us with much interesting analysis, and a whole new way of questioning the handed-down family stories. What exactly did Alexander the founder sell from his premises on Burgh Quay in 1828? Was his nephew John a steady religious man, or a risk taker—or perhaps it was John's son Adam who propelled the firm into music-halls and hotels?

Gradually the text took shape. It passed to and fro as we came to agree the text. Conscious that the book was long, every paragraph came under scrutiny. The word count came down to 193,000. Nothing too serious has been cut—except, sadly, my research into the Irish wine trade over the same period which has to be held over for a later publication. Having access to my editor's extensive knowledge of 19th- and 20th-century business and social history has greatly enhanced the book and to him and Anna I am very much in debt.

But getting the text in order was only half the job. All the original pictures in our museum had been carefully copied and much in addition. The librarians in Trinity College were unbelievably helpful in permitting us to copy all the Findlater material in their archive of *The Lady of the House*, a publication once owned by the family.

The credit for the miracle of getting me up and typing the manuscript within twenty-four hours goes to Maria Gageby, and I am also in debt to herself and

Val McCullagh for typing the multitude of research from old documents and crumbly newspapers. My nephew Axel Dahl and my neighbour Marcus Gageby take credit for keeping me and the machine in harmony and seeing that nothing was lost through faulty backups or crashes or being eaten by bugs.

Thanks also to Ciara Farrell for helping me prepare the manuscript in a professional format for the editor and to John Sherlock for the master classes on the writer's craft. And that's how the book came into being.

On behalf of the family, I must make a disclaimer: the story in the book is my story, my translation of events over the past two centuries; they have not read the text and may not be in agreement with every word that I have written. That's the risk I take. However they have been fully supportive of the project and contributed an immense amount of material and left me alone for days at a time to get on with the task. To my Aunt Sheila, my mother, my brother John and my sisters, most sincere thanks. To Suzanne and Grania an additional embrace: many years ago Suzanne set about capturing the atmosphere of old Findlaters by conducting interviews with former staff and customers. These now form some of the best 'I remembers' dotted throughout the text. And credit to Grania for discovering and editing Auntie Do's letters from India describing the tiger shoot in fascinating detail.

On the Wheeler side of the family Desmond, Grattan, George, Richard (Horace) and Frances and of course my mother have contributed most of the stories told in Chapters 9 and 10. Also a thank-you to Pat de Courcy-Wheeler in London. My editor attempted to cull the stories but I wasn't having it. In fact I may have embellished them a bit. To them all, thank you.

I am also in debt to Sylvia Findlater of Dorset, A. J. M. Findlater in Somerset, June Mitchell in Reading and cousins Beatty McGrath and Frances Bunch in San Antonio, Texas, Pat Findlater in Edinburgh, the late Alexander Napier Findlater in Dunedin and Mary Herbert in New South Wales.

Moving away from the family, I very much appreciate the contributions from two of my father's oldest friends, Ptolomy Roberts and Alf Delaney. And thanks to long term friends of Doris and Sheila: Rita Rutherfoord on gardening and the country markets, Mary Simpson again on gardening, Seán McCann on roses, the Very Rev. Victor Griffin on the Irish Protestant faith and Jane Wilson on the Friends of St Patrick's Cathedral.

A special thank you to Robert Marshall for guiding me through the complexity of late 19th- and early 20th-century law and politics; to Feargal Quinn on the development of the Irish supermarket industry, Charles Benson, Keeper of Early Printed Books and Shane Mawe of the Berkeley Library, TCD, for access to *The Lady of the House* collection, Dr Máire Kennedy and her team in the Gilbert Library, Pearse Street and Daniel Gillman and Peter Pearson for access to their wealth of knowledge of the city and county.

Thanks to Wilfred M.Weir of the United Commercial Travellers Association and for entrusting me with custodianship of the Association's Jewel in our Museum.

To Martyn Turner, Terry Willers, Uto Hogerzeil and Mrs Marie Fannin, widow of the late Bob Fannin, for permission to use the best of their illustrations from our Christmas lists in the 1980s and 1990s and to Pat Liddy for the watercolour of our old shop on the Upper Rathmines Road.

The following librarians were also a wonderful help:

John Gibson, of *The Irish Times*, Patrick Yeates of the ESB archive, Mary Heslin of the AIB library, Margaret Byrne of the Law Society, Alex Ward, curator at the Masonic Hall, Aoife Dineen of Dublin City Archives, South William Street and Mary Clark, Dublin City Archivist, on the history of the Dublin Guilds, Mary O'Doherty of the Mercer Library, Royal College of Surgeons in Ireland, the staff in the Institute of Chartered Accountants Library, the National Library of Ireland, the Irish Architectural Archive and the National Archive.

I needed some expert advice on some of the trickier accountancy issues and am in debt to Adrian D'Arcy, on the 19th-century ledgers, Robin Simpson on the 1899 flotation, Andrew Knowles of Arnotts on the excess C P Tax 1941–6 and Paul McCleary on the accounts 1899–1969.

The brewing and distilling industry is a study on its own and particular thanks go to Tom Halpin, brewery industry historian and Frank O'Reilly, who untapped the mystery of the Banagher distillery and other useful information and to Andy Bielenberg whose book on Locke's distillery provided such a useful source.

For helping me find my way around the Presbyterian labyrinth my thanks to Harry Barr and to Rev. Alan Boal, Abbey Presbyterian Church and to Finlay Holmes of the Presbyterian College Belfast and Stephen Gregory, librarian of the Union Theological College Belfast.

Thanks to Senator David Norris, Ken Monaghan and Bob Joyce in the Joyce Centre.

And on the discovery that Ireland had another patented invention in addition to the tyre my thanks to David Eccles and his wife for details of Bindon Blood's tricycle patent.

Thanks to all my friends whose material I have not used and to those who have answered my queries or checked over particular pieces of text, lent me books or given me useful advice: Ruairi Quinn TD, Professor R. B. McDowell, Professor Louis Cullen, Henry McDowell, Charles Guinness, Walter and Lavinia Greacen, Morgan Dockrell, Jim Quinn, Marisi Lalor of the Embassy of Brazil, Frank Callanan SC, Lord Roy Jenkins, Lawrence Warner on my ancestors' handwriting, Senator Trevor West on Sir Horace Plunkett, Peter J. Foss on the Bog of Allen, Pat Loughrey on the lager market, Dan Donnelly on Darley's brewery, Dave Hosgood for access to the church records at All Saints, Blackrock, Daire Hogan of McCann FitzGerald on early 19th-century solicitors' training, Judith Faraday, Partnership Archivist of the John Lewis Partnership, and Christopher Rowe of Findlater Mackie Todd, London, on their illustrious history, Fiona Fitzsimons, TCD, for deciphering correspondence, Patrick Carroll and Noel Ross on the poet's sister in Dundalk, Deirdre Heapley, archivist of the Overends'

Trust, Brian Smith of Dún Laoghaire on Findlater Street Glasthule, Richard Roche, Paul Hamilford, Clare Hamilton, Richard Hewat, Hugh Grogan, Jack Phelan and last but not least Caroline and John Hamilton.

For the loan of special texts thanks to Derek Turbett (*St Catherine's Bells* by Walter Thomas Meyler 1870), Hilary Pratt (*W. E. Wylie and the Irish Revolution 1916–1921* by Leon Ó Broin), Christopher Pringle (*Erris in the Irish Highlands and the Atlantic Railway* by P. Knight, 1836), Cormac Lowth (*Modern Irish Trade* by E. J. Riordan, 1920), Harry Hannon (*Whigs on the Green* by Cornelius Smith and Bernard Share 1990).

Thanks for the 'I remembers' to Ned Kelly, Enniskerry, on the Trojan vans, Linda Browne on Mr Willie in Sackville Street, Eric Fenelon on the mercy flight to London, Mary Kane on Mr Vaughan's helpfulness in Blackrock branch, Rosalind Matthews, Killiney, on Dún Laoghaire branch in the good old days, Anne Cronin on van deliveries in Dorset Street, the late Johnny McDermott on his fascinating experiences as a messenger and canvasser in Baggot Street branch, Marie Lock on the Royal Hotel Bray in 1922, Mary Gunning for permission to quote from *Lady Fingal*, the Joyce estate for permission to quote from *Ulysses* and *Finnegans Wake*, J. P. Donleavy for permission to quote a passage from *The Ginger Man*, the late Pauline Russell for her interesting passage on Findlaters Howth, Bob Montgomery for use of his research on the Gordon Bennett race, Maureen Haughey for details of the Findlater service in the 1960s, Dr Garret FitzGerald for his recall of the post-war wine merchants, Aidan Kelly for his amusing story of the fun had in O'Connell Street, Godfrey Fitzsimons on Regal Lager in the 1930s, Ann Gaskin on the helpfulness of our staff in Bray, Irene Lawless on the bumble bee in Malahide and Joe Murphy on the difficult start of Tayto.

I also apologise to all my friends in the trade for the exclusion of the chapter on the history of Irish wine merchants. We hope to use this research in a later publication. My appreciation for the contributions.

Thanks to Tony Colley, for the cover design and other design work, who, in the course of researching this book, discovered that among his other great ancestors is Gilbert Burns, and to his son Jeffrey Colley for rewrites of some of the early research, to Axel Dahl for developing the web site and to Redmond Power, Declan Ryan and Joanne Birmingham of ICT for their sterling work in the production of this opus. To Bob Sharpe, Master Printer in the National Print Museum, Beggar's Bush, for the impression of old Findlater's on the title page.

And finally to my colleagues in Findlaters, who were delighted when I volunteered to relinquish my executive responsibilities and take a sabbatical to research and write this book, and to my neighbours Douglas and Dorothy Gageby for the encouragement to record this story and their support throughout.

Alex Findlater
June 2001

Money

Throughout this book I have indicated the approximate equivalent of historical sums of money in today's Irish money (i.e. 2000). The equivalents are enclosed in [parentheses]. The equivalents are calculated according to the long-run cost of living index (1914 = 100) compiled by the Central Bank.

Euro

On 1 January 2002 Irish currency converts to euro, and the Irish conversion rate is €1 = IR£0.787564. There are no euro currency calculations in the book.

Map to the Book

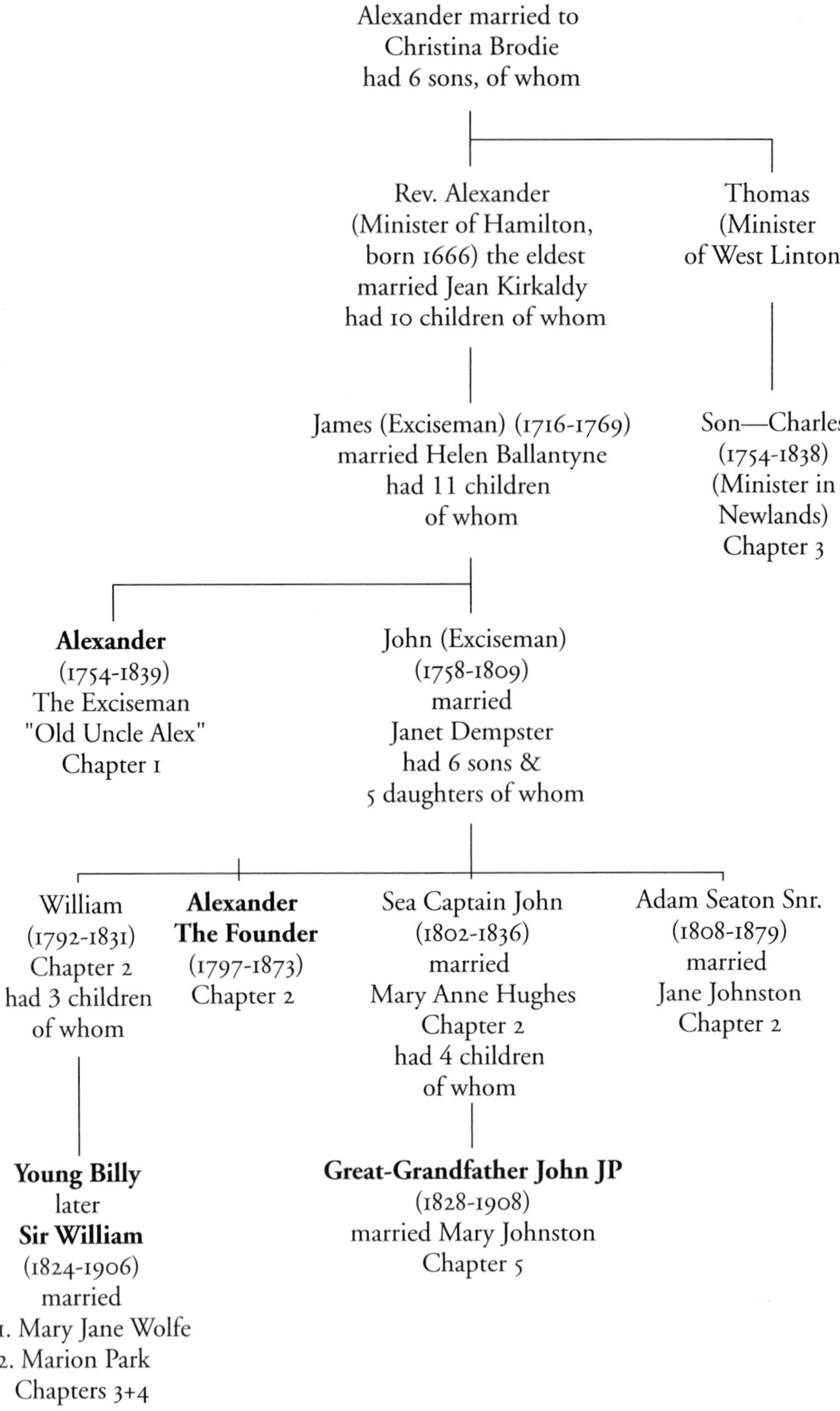

Alexander married to
Christina Brodie
had 6 sons, of whom
Rev. Alexander
(Minister of Hamilton,
born 1666) the eldest
married Jean Kirkaldy
had 10 children of whom
Thomas
(Minister
of West Linton)
James (Exciseman) (1716-1769)
married Helen Ballantyne
had 11 children
of whom
Son—Charles
(1754-1838)
(Minister in
Newlands)
Chapter 3
Alexander
(1754-1839)
The Exciseman
"Old Uncle Alex"
Chapter 1
John (Exciseman)
(1758-1809)
married
Janet Dempster
had 6 sons &
5 daughters of whom
William
(1792-1831)
Chapter 2
had 3 children
of whom
Alexander
The Founder
(1797-1873)
Chapter 2
Sea Captain John
(1802-1836)
married
Mary Anne Hughes
Chapter 2
had 4 children
of whom
Adam Seaton Snr.
(1808-1879)
married
Jane Johnston
Chapter 2
Young Billy
later
Sir William
(1824-1906)
married
1. Mary Jane Wolfe
2. Marion Park
Chapters 3+4
Great-Grandfather John JP
(1828-1908)
married Mary Johnston
Chapter 5

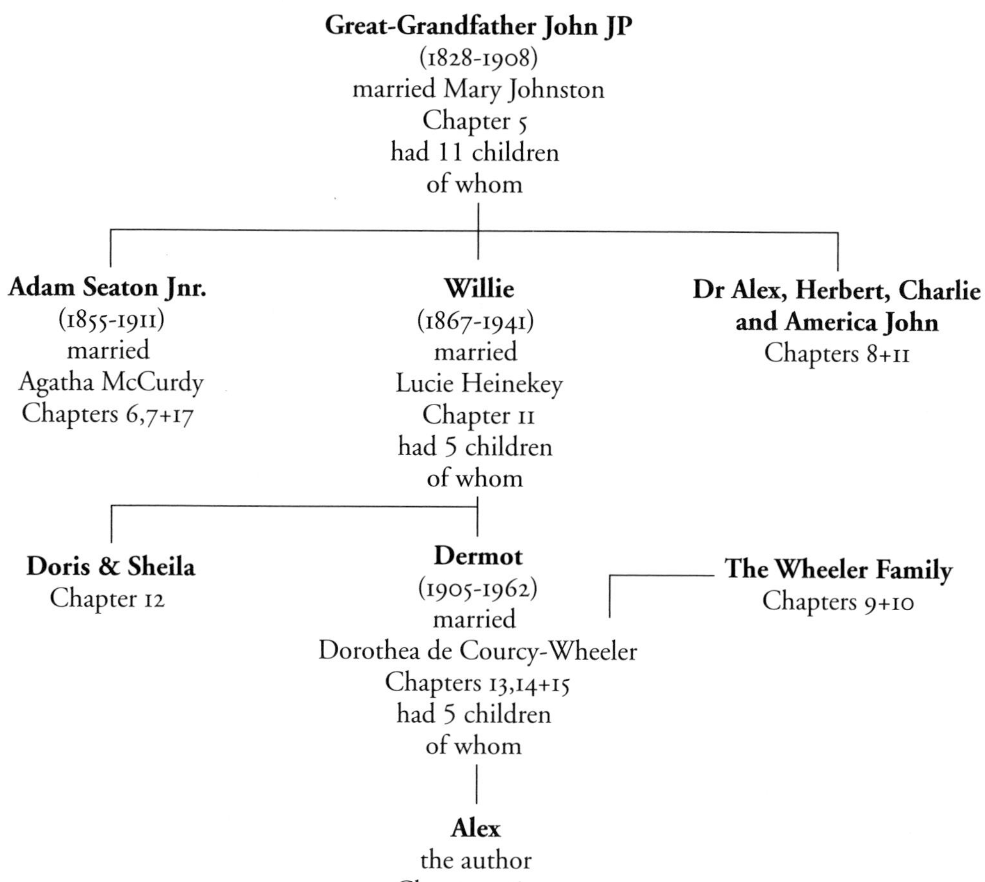
Great-Grandfather John JP
(1828-1908)
married Mary Johnston
Chapter 5
had 11 children
of whom
Adam Seaton Jnr.
(1855-1911)
married
Agatha McCurdy
Chapters 6,7+17
Willie
(1867-1941)
married
Lucie Heinekey
Chapter 11
had 5 children
of whom
Dr Alex, Herbert, Charlie and America John
Chapters 8+11
Doris & Sheila
Chapter 12
Dermot
(1905-1962)
married
Dorothea de Courcy-Wheeler
Chapters 13,14+15
had 5 children
of whom
The Wheeler Family
Chapters 9+10
Alex
the author
Chapters 16+17

Main Personages

Alexander, the Exciseman (Old Uncle Alex) and his friend Robert Burns, the Scottish poet [Chapter 1]

Alexander the Founder and his brother **Adam Seaton (Senior)** [Chapter 2]

Billy, later Sir William, eldest nephew of Alexander the Founder [Chapters 3 and 4] (His father was William, brother of Alexander)

John, second nephew of Alexander the Founder and great-grandfather of Alex, the author [Chapter 5] (His father was Captain John)

Adam Seaton (Junior) eldest son of John [Chapters 6, 7 and 17]

John's sons **Dr Alex, Herbert and Charles** who fought in Gallipoli [Chapter 8] and **America John** who settled in Texas [Chapter 11]

Harry de Courcy-Wheeler, the author's maternal grandfather [Chapters 10 and 11] and his daughter Dorothea, the author's mother

Surgeon Wheeler, father of Harry and great-grandfather of the author and his sons Billy (Sir William Ireland de Courcy-Wheeler), George, Diamond (Robert) [Chapter 11]

Willie, fourth son of John and the author's paternal grandfather [Chapter 11]

Doris and Sheila, daughters of Willie, and aunts of the author [Chapter 12]

Dermot, son of Willie, and father of the author [Chapters 13, 14 and 15]

Alex the author [Chapters 16 and 17]

1. Alexander the Exciseman and Robert the Poet

Alex. Findlater & Co. was founded in Dublin in 1823 by Alexander Findlater who came, like many other successful Dublin businessmen, from Scotland.

The name Findlater is ultimately Norse, *fyn* being white and *leitr* cliff, so called because of the quartz in the local rock of a district on the coast of the parish of Fordyce in Banffshire where the name originates. The family of Ogilvie of Deskford held the title of Earl of Findlater, after the district, from 1683 to 1811. The earldom became extinct on the death of James, the seventh earl.

In the 7th century the then Earl of Findlater built a castle near Cullen, a small seaport town in Banffshire. The castle stands on a rock overhanging the sea, and is now a picturesque ruin, slowly crumbling into the sea. Once a place of power, playing its part in the feudal wars, it was one of the places that joined the Gordon rebellion against Mary Queen of Scots in 1562. The story goes that when the Queen sent to Findlater Castle to demand the keys the occupant, one Sir John Gordon, refused to receive her. He took a party of her soldiers unawares and massacred all of them. The Queen issued a royal decree commanding Sir John to deliver up the castle to her officers on pain of treason. He refused and moved towards Aberdeen where he attacked the Queen's forces at the Battle of Corrichie. He was captured and three days later beheaded at Aberdeen. (Some four hundred years later I was in a cottage on an island off the West of Ireland

The ruins of Findlater Castle, painted in oils by A. Perigal RSA 1874

Rev. Alexander and his wife Jane Kirkaldy

and, by chance, was recounting this story. My host, Derrick Gordon, looked at me quizzically and declared himself to be a descendant of those Gordons!)

Another legend of Findlater Castle has it that

> while the nurse of the infant son of the lord of Findlater, was walking on the sea-battlement already mentioned, or standing at an open window, on a genial summer day, singing and dandling the child, he, all of a sudden sprang from her arms in his glee, and disappeared in the gulf below, not, however, without a wild and vain attempt on the part of the nurse to save him. She, too, rushed headlong into the water and perished. The baron, overcome with grief, left the castle never to return.[1]

A Findlater from the area assured me recently that the ghost of the nurse haunts the ruins to this day.

More substantially, an old family bible records that our Findlaters are descended from Alexander Findlater who married at Dyke, in the County of Moray, Christina, daughter of David Brodie of Brodie, on 5 November 1665. She was the sister of Sir Alexander Brodie of Brodie, Lord of Sessions and one of the Commissioners who negotiated Charles II's Restoration in 1660. They had a large family of six sons, of whom some settled in the North of Scotland and others went to the West Indies.

Their eldest son, from whom the characters in this book are descended, was the Rev. Alexander Findlater, born at Dyke, and baptised on 3 November 1666. He was the first minister of Hamilton after the Revolution in 1688. He married Jean, daughter of Rev. Thomas Kirkaldy, the second son of the laird of Grange. Jean was the grandniece of Sir William Kirkaldy of Grange, brother of the great soldier, Sir James Kirkaldy, whose defence of Edinburgh Castle, in the cause of Mary Queen of Scots, is one of the most heroic episodes in Scottish history.*

* After the eventual surrender, Sir William was hanged on a scaffold in Edinburgh's High Street, in August 1573, with his brother Thomas and two counterfeiters.

Old Uncle Alex 1754–1839.
The friend of Robert Burns in life and vindicator after death.

Alexander and Jean had four daughters and six sons, one of whom, Thomas, became a minister in West Linton. He, in turn, had a son, Charles, also a minister at Newlands, near Peebles. Alexander and Jean's youngest son, James, was born on 7 March 1716. He married Helen, daughter of Ronald and Janet Ballantyne, she born a Nisbet. They had five daughters and six sons, one of whom, Alexander (Old Uncle Alex), became the friend and defender of the poet Robbie Burns; another son, John, born on 10 May 1758, became Supervisor of Excise at the booming seaport of Greenock and married Janet Dempster on 12 August 1769. He was the father of the Alexander who was to land in Dublin in 1823.

Old Uncle Alex was born in August 1754 and joined the excise service in 1774. Two years later he was stationed at Coupar Angus as a gauger—measuring the strength and volume of excisable goods—and in 1786 he became acting supervisor in Dumfries and in 1791 full supervisor. He eventually reached the top of his profession in Scotland when he became Collector of Excise in Glasgow, a position he held for eleven years before retiring in 1825 at the age of seventy-one.

At that time, before direct income taxation was introduced, all the money required to finance the long series of wars that built the British Empire came from customs and excise. For most of the century Britain was engaged in a fierce (and expensive) war with France for military and economic predominance from India to South America. Excise duties were levied on a range of goods, from luxuries to necessities, including salt, tea, coffee, soap, starch, candles, paper, hides, skins, printed goods, glass, bricks, and of course beer, spirits, wine and tobacco.

In Scotland, France's financial support for the Jacobite cause (patriotically represented by Burns' songs), and a growing anti-English feeling lent respectability to the natural disinclination to pay tax. Smuggling was rampant. Beer was illegally brewed and spirits illicitly distilled all over Scotland. The population as a whole evaded or disregarded the revenue laws in spite of the draconian penalties, including execution, incurred for flouting the law. Not surprisingly the revenue officers of the period, personifying as they did the tax regime, were unpopular.

In 1789 a new recruit was posted to Old Uncle Alex's division, one Robert Burns, now Scotland's best-loved poet, author of 'Auld Lang Syne', 'Comin' Through the Rye', 'The Banks of Doon', 'Tam O'Shanter', 'To Mary in Heaven', 'Scots Wha Hae' and a multitude of others. He was already a poet of note. Alexander wrote many years later of their friendship: 'I believe I saw more of him than any other individual had occasion after he became an Excise officer' and on another occasion, 'few people, I believe, were more frequently in his house, particularly after he came to reside in Dumfries, and in the latter days of his life.' [2]

Robert Burns (1759–97) was born near Ayr, the son of a small farmer. His first poems were published in 1786 and were at once successful. He bought a 100-acre farm at Ellisland and it was on this farm, where Alexander was a frequent guest, that he wrote many of his great verses. Indeed, according to John Sinton, one of Burns' biographers, 'The three-and-a-half years that he spent there, in his triune capacity of farmer, gauger, and poet, were said to be the happiest and busiest of his life. In the prime of early manhood, idolised at home, beloved abroad, full of energy and love of life, he galloped along the country lanes and mountain paths, humming sweet melodies, and dashing off immortal lines and poems that shall continue to delight and instruct mankind in ages yet to come.'[3]

Burns' Cottage, where the poet was born in 1759

Burns' farm at Ellisland
Engravings by D.O. Hill RSA of Dumfries

As an exciseman from 1789, Burns was in charge of fourteen circuits, technically named 'rides'. He had to own his own horse, and every two months his supervisor, Alexander, had to certify that he was well mounted. On his grey mare called Jenny Geddes he travelled at least thirty miles a day surveying licensed traders and inspecting dirty ponds for sprouting bags of barley as well as 'yeasty barrels' intended to be used in the illicit distillation of mountain dew. His farming venture eventually failed and he moved, with his wife and family, into a house in Dumfries where they occupied the first floor.

Alexander spent time training and supervising his new officer. For example, on 11 June 1792 they spent the whole day together and visited twenty-five tax-payers—a brewery, eight wine and spirit dealers, eight victuallers, three chandlers, two tanners, two tawers (preparers of white leather) and a tea dealer—in a tiring ten-hour period. However, Alexander discovered that his new officer had some

Dumfries at sunset (D.O. Hill)

shortcomings, and noted one or two instances: at one victualler's he had failed to record the stock properly and was formally admonished.[4] On another occasion he had not surveyed a brewery as his instructions required, and again recorded the stock incorrectly.

Burns seems to have been upset by being admonished and tried to shift the blame:

> I am both surprised & vexed at that accident of Lorimer's Stock.–The last survey I made prior to Mr Lorimer's going to Edin^r I was very particular in my inspection & the quantity was certainly in his possession as I stated.–The surveys I have made during his absence might as well have been marked 'keys absent' as I never found any body but the lady, who I know is not mistress of keys, &c. to know anything of it, and one of the times it would have rejoiced all Hell to have seen her so drunk.–I have not surveyed there since his return.–I know the gentleman's ways are, like the grace of G—–, past all comprehension; but I shall give the house a severe scrutiny tomorrow morning, & send you in the naked facts.–I know Sir, & deeply regret, that this business glances with a malign aspect on my character as an Officer; but as I am really innocent in the affair, & as the gentleman is known to be an illicit Dealer, & particularly as this is the single instance of the least shadow of carelessness or impropriety in my conduct as an Officer, I shall be peculiarly unfortunate if my character shall fall a sacrifice to the dark manoeuvres of a Smuggler.[5]

Burns included in his letter, below his signature, 'I send you some rhymes I have just finished which tickle my fancy a little'. He was given the benefit of the doubt and that is the last that was heard of the matter.

Excisemen had unpopular laws to enforce, and had to deal with the people who suffered as a consequence of prohibitive taxation. People being people, ways were discovered of working outside the laws, making the excise officer's work more difficult. Robert was of the opinion that it was not the officers, whose duty it was to execute the laws, who were to blame, but those who made them, and subsequently squandered the money at home and abroad. He recorded his opinion in these lines:

Ye men of wit and wealth, why all this sneering
'Gainst poor excisemen? Give the cause a hearing;
What are your landlords' rentrolls? Taxing ledgers:
What premiers, what? Even monarchs' mighty gaugers;
Nay, what are priests these seeming godly wisemen:
What are they, pray, but spiritual excisemen? [6]

Burns was a zealous officer, but several anecdotes are related which show he was understanding and sympathetic to those widows whose misdemeanours were of a petty nature. For instance on a fair day in 1793 Burns called at the door of a poor woman named Kate Watson, who was doing some business of her own that day.

> With a nod and a movement of the forefinger Burns brought her to the door:
>
> 'Kate,' said he, 'are ye mad? The supervisor and I will be in on ye in half an hour; gude bye ti ye at present,' and with that he disappeared in the crowd.
>
> On another occasion, a woman—Jean Dunn of Kirkpatrick, who had been brewing beer duty–free for the fair, observed Burns and another officer, Robinson, coming towards her house. Jean slipped out at the back door, and left her servant and young daughter to face the gaugers.
>
> 'Has there been any brewing for the fair here to-day?'
>
> 'Oh no, sirs, we hae nae licence for that', replied the servant girl.
>
> 'That's no true,' exclaimed the wee lassie, 'the muckle kist'* is fu' o' the bottles o' yill that ma mither sat up a' nicht brewin for the fair.'
>
> 'We are in a hurry just now,' said Burns, 'but when we return from the fair we will examine the muckle black kist–come along Robinson.'[7]

Burns' behaviour was noticed by the authorities. At a meeting of the district justices, one of them asked: 'Let me look at the books of Burns, for they show that an upright officer may also be a merciful one.'

On the other hand, Burns showed no mercy to regular smugglers.

> One of the fraternity, not knowing Burns personally, offered one night to sell him some smuggled whisky. 'You've lichted on a bad merchant,' said the Bard, 'I'm Robert Burns the gauger.' The smuggler stared, then impudently replied 'Aye, but ye're likewise Robert Burns the poet; I mak sangs too, sae ye'll shurely ne'er ruin a brither poet.'
>
> 'Why, friend,' said Burns, 'the poet in me has been sacrificed to the exciseman, and I should like to know what superior right you have to exemption,' and sangs or no sangs, the seizure was made then and there.[8]

* A muckle kist is a large chest, trunk or press.

However, working as an excise officer often involved more than dealing with small-time smugglers. A story is told about one of the big smuggling operations which Burns encountered on the Solway Firth. Walter Crawford, the excise riding officer for Dumfries, operated a patrol along the coastline between Dumfries and Gretna. His work involved finding out when a smuggling run was going to take place and which route it would take. On this occasion, in February 1792, a smuggling schooner had slipped into shallow waters, and Crawford and another officer were waiting for it with a party of thirteen dragoons. Armed only with pistols, they made a first attempt to board the ship, but were forced to withdraw when they found themselves threatened with fire. Crawford was then permitted to board, and was able to find out the number of armed men on board. He disembarked and sent for reinforcements, and next morning had a force of forty-four dragoons, 'fully accoutred and on horseback'.

Robert Burns 1759–1796

Ellisland 28th Oct. 1789

Sir

I believe I mentioned something to you yesternight of the character that Mr Corbet told me you had given of me to our Edinr Excise folks, but my conscience accuses me that I did not make the proper acknowledgements to you for your goodness. — Most sincerely & gratefully do I thank you, Sir, for this uncommon instance of kindness & friendship. — I mean not by this as if I would propitiate your future inspection of my conduct. — No, Sir, I trust to act, and I shall act, so as to defy scrutiny; but I ~~trouble you with~~ send this as a sheer tribute of gratitude to a Gentleman whose goodness has laid me under very great obligations, and for whose character as a Gentleman I have the highest esteem. — It may very probably never be in my power to repay, but it is equally out of my power to forget, the obligations you have laid on, Sir, your deeply indebted & very humble servt

Robt Burns

In this letter Robert Burns expressed his gratitude for Alexander's support. The last few lines read: 'I send this as a sheer tribute of gratitude to a Gentleman whose goodness has laid me under very great obligations, and for whose character as a Gentleman I have the highest esteem.– It may very probably never be in my power to repay, but it is equally out of my power to forget, the obligations you have laid on, Sir, your deeply indebted and very humble serv. Robt Burns'.

However, overnight the schooner had drifted a mile down the firth under a strong current, which made it impossible to get at it either by foot or on horseback. The logical answer was to row out, but the crafty locals, who thrived off smuggling, had holed all the boats, while the schooner in the meantime kept up a fire of 'grape shott and musketry'.

The only thing to do was attack the ship from land, but quicksand by the water's edge prevented the use of horses, so there was nothing for it but to make an attempt by foot. Crawford divided his forces into three groups, with the intention of attacking the ship fore and aft, and broadside. The third party was commanded by Burns, who waded sword in hand to the brig, and was the first man to board.

> Our orders to the Military were to reserve their fire till within eight yards of the vessel, then to pour a volley and board her with sword & Pistol. The vessel kept on firing though without any damage to us, as from the situation of the ship they could not bring their great guns to bear on us, we in the mean time wading breast high, and in Justice to the party under my Command I must say with great alacrity; by the time we were within one hundred yards of the vessel the Crew gave up the cause, gott over side towards England which shore was for a long way dry sand.[9]

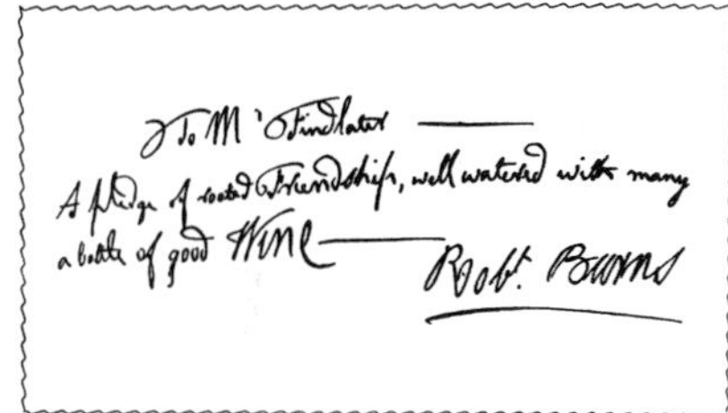

Inscription in music book presented by Robert to Alexander

The next day the vessel, with all her arms and stores, was sold by public auction at Dumfries. Burns purchased four of her rusty carronades for £3 and despatched them to the French Legislative Assembly, with a letter requesting them to 'accept them as a present, and as a mark of his admiration and sympathy'. The customs confiscated them at Dover.[10]

It was this type of incident that brought Burns under scrutiny by the Excise Board. At this time the colonies in America had achieved their independence, the French Revolution was in full swing, the cry of 'Liberty, equality, fraternity' was striking chords in excitable hearts, at least until the Terrors of 1793 and 1794. Throughout 1792, Burns was vocal on the subject of civil and religious liberty. But as a paid servant of the Crown, it was unwise of him to be so public in his sympathies with the French Republicans. (The long expected war between France and Britain finally broke out in February 1793, a few days after the French had shocked the world by executing Louis XVI.)

Most of the commissioners thought he should be dismissed 'without so much as a hearing, or the slightest intimation'. However, the chairman decided to send a senior inspector to Dumfries to investigate. Here, Alexander, his supervisor, affirmed that Burns was exact, vigilant, and sober and was one of the best officers in the district. Burns never allowed his patriotic sentiments to interfere with his public duties. His survey books and business papers were examined, and deemed correct. He was found to be an efficient officer—but then it was not a question of his efficiency but rather of his loyalty. The investigations worried him greatly. His character was at stake and his prospects in life appeared to be blasted. He wrote:

> In naked feeling and in aching pride,
> He bears the unbroken blast from every side.

Interior of Burns' house in Dumfries

The inspector reported favourably. Burns was acquitted of misconduct, and his chances of promotion were unaffected. His job was secure but the message sent to him must have annoyed him intensely: 'His business was to act not to think; and that whatever might be his opinion of men or measures, it was for him to be silent and obey.'

By 1794 Burns' mind was set on promotion and on 29 December he wrote to Mrs Dunlop of Dunlop: 'I have been appointed to act temporarily as supervisor in place of Mr Findlater, who is absent on sick leave. I look to an early appointment as full supervisor. My political sins seem to be forgiven me.'[11] When Alexander resumed business, Burns returned temporarily to his own station. He had a very high opinion of his supervisor, as we learn from a letter to Mr Graham, Chairman of the Excise, when he referred to Alexander as 'not only one of the first, if not the very first of excisemen in your service, but also one of the worthiest fellows in the universe.'[12]

However, the poet's health started to deteriorate in the autumn of 1795. His letter to Mrs Dunlop, on 15 December 1795, was more alarming: 'If I am cut off, even in all the vigour of manhood as I am, gracious God, what will become of my little flock . . . But I must not think longer on this subject, so I shall sing with the old Scotch ballad: "Oh, that I had ne'er been married".'[13]

In the spring of 1796 Burns became seriously ill with rheumatic fever. On 4 July he was brought to the seaside to see if sea bathing would help. There the excruciating rheumatic pains tortured him. He knew that he was dying. On 12 July he returned in a small spring cart to Dumfries to die. He wrote his farewells. On 21 July 1796 the illness, from which he had suffered so long, 'terminated his earthly career'. Scotland's great poet was only thirty-seven years of age. Alexander wrote: 'On the night, indeed immediately preceding his decease, I sat

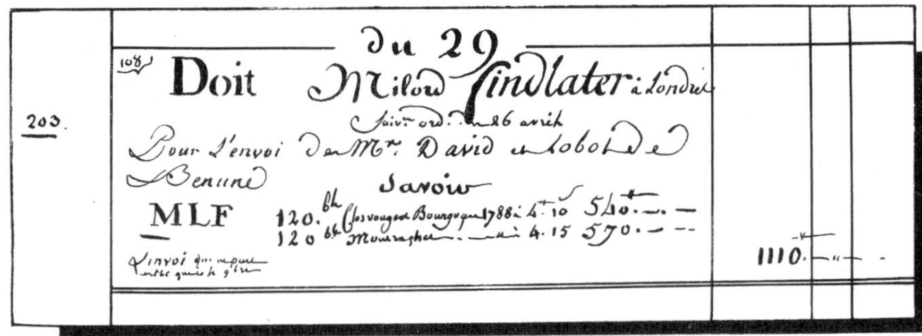

203. Du 29

Doit Milord Findlater à Londres

Pour l'envoi de Mr David ... Beaune

Savoir

MLF 120 bt ... 1788 à 4.10 540.—.—

120 bt ... à 4.15 570.—.—

1110.—

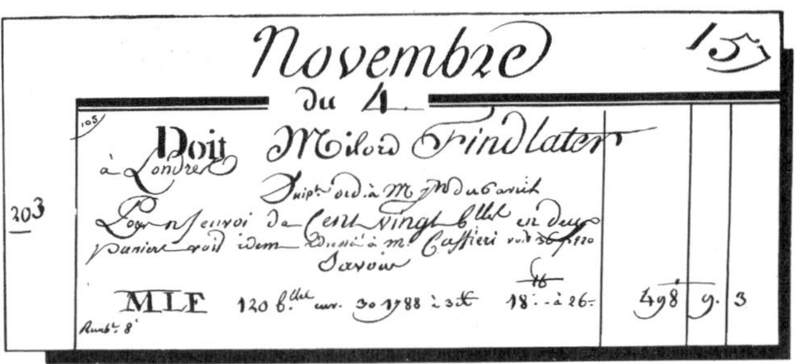

Novembre 157

Du 4

203 Doit Milord Findlater à Londres

Pour l'envoi de cent vingt bt ... Cassiers ...

Savoir

MLF 120 bt ... 1788 ... 498 | 9 | 3

Purchases in 1789 by Milord Findlater (MLF) James, 7th Earl (who died without issue in 1811) from Jean Remi Moët, co-founder of Moët & Chandon in 1807. The top picture shows MLF purchasing 120 bottles Clos Vougeot and 120 bottles of another wine. The lower illustration is for a purchase of 120 bottles champagne, vintage 1788. Mr Moët first produced champagne in 1741 and the first Irish purchase was made in 1788 by the Hon. John Butler of Molesworth Street, Dublin. Source: Henry Vizetelly '*Facts about champagne*' 1879 London, Ward, Lock & Co.

by his bedside and administered the last morsel he ever swallowed, not in the form of medicine or of the cordial of romance, but what was better fitted to allay his thirst and cool his parched and burning tongue.'[14]

After the poet's death exaggerated stories, imputing drunkenness and dissolution, were spread concerning him, and were credited by many people who might have known better. What Alexander described as 'Burns' convivial habits, his wit and humour, his social talents, and his independent spirit' inspired these tales. One does not need to read between the lines to realise that these very traits of Burns' character were what endeared him to a broad-minded, intelligent man, such as Alexander undoubtedly was.

For the next forty-three years Alexander defended Burns' honour in the leading publications of the day. Dr Currie, the first, official, biographer of the national bard accepted as true much of the gossip about the poet's habits and character, but fourteen years later Alexander Peterkin, who was editing Burns' works, invited Alexander to commit to paper his testimony for inclusion in his appreciation of the poet. It appeared in Peterkin's *The Works of Burns* and is dated 10 October 1818. Alexander wrote:

> His convivial habits, his wit and humour, his social talents, and independent spirit, have been perverted into constant and habitual drunkenness, impiety, neglect of his professional duty, and of his family, and in short every human vice. He has been

branded with cowardice, accused of attempted murder, and even suicide, and all this without a shadow of proof, proh pudor!

Is there nothing of tenderness due to the memory of so transcendent a genius, who so often delighted even his libellers with the felicities of his songs, and the charms of his wit and humour?—And is no regard to be had to the feelings of those near and dear relatives he has left behind; or, are his ashes never to 'hope repose'?—My indignation has unwarily led me astray from the point to which I meant to have confined myself, and to which I will now recur, and briefly state what I have to say on the subject.

My connection with Robert Burns commenced immediately after his admission into the Excise, and continued to the hour of his death. In all that time, the superintendence of his behaviour as an officer of the revenue was a branch of my especial province, and it may be supposed, I would not be an inattentive observer of the general conduct of a man and a Poet so celebrated by his countrymen.

[Robert Burns] was exemplary in his attention as an excise-officer, and was even jealous of the least imputation of his vigilance; . . . and I will farther avow, that I never saw him, which was very frequently while he lived at Ellisland, and still more so, almost every day, after he removed to Dumfries, but in hours of business he was quite himself, and capable of discharging the duties of his office; nor was he ever known to drink by himself, or seen to indulge in the use of liquor in a forenoon, as the statement, that he was perpetually under its stimulus unequivocally implies.

. . . but permit me to add, that I have seen Burns in all his various phases—in his convivial moments, in his sober moods, and in the bosom of his family; indeed I believe I saw more of him than any other individual had occasion to see, after he became an Excise Officer; and I never beheld any thing like the gross enormities with which he is now charged. That when sat down in an evening with a few friends whom he liked, he was apt to prolong the social hour beyond the bounds which prudence would dictate, is unquestionable; but in his family, I will venture to say, he was never seen otherwise than attentive and affectionate to a high degree . . . the virulence indeed with which his memory has been treated, is hardly to be paralleled in the annals of literature.

In *Johnston's Edinburgh Magazine* of February 1834 he wrote: 'Had Burns been subject to a Board's recorded censure, I must ex-officio have known of it, as it could not have been concealed from me. I say without hesitation, that Burns would, had he lived, have been promoted in due course, and that at a shorter period of service than any of his predecessors.'

Old Uncle Alex strove long and hard to protect the name of his friend. He finally succeeded in quashing all the exaggerated and invented stories put about by Burns' enemies and critics, and his ill-informed biographers. It was now undisputed that Burns was a zealous and thoroughly efficient officer the whole of his career. As late as 1923, eighty-four years after his death, Old Uncle Alex was commemorated by the Sandyford Burns Club, Glasgow, who, in recognition of his defence of the poet's honour and reputation, erected a gravestone in the form of a boulder of silver-grey Creetown granite over his burial place. The inscription reads 'The friend of Robert Burns in life, his vindicator after death.'* The Corporation of Glasgow then voted £15,000 [£500,000] for the foundation of a Chair of Scottish History and Literature in the University of Glasgow in Alexander's memory.[15]

The friendship between the poet's family and the Findlaters survived long after Burns' death. His nephews, William and Gilbert Burns, went to Dublin and, as we shall see, were founding partners, with Old Uncle Alex's nephew, in the establishment of various business houses in Dublin. Burns' eldest sister Agnes also crossed the sea and married William Galt, a land-agent in Stephenstown near Dundalk.†

Old Uncle Alex was married twice. While stationed at Coupar Angus he wed, in 1778, Susan Forrester, daughter of John Forrester, a writer from Falkirk. She died in 1810, not long before Alexander's appointment as Collector of Excise at Glasgow. There were four sons and a daughter from this marriage.

His second marriage was to Catherine Anderson and they had one son and two daughters. The family lived for the greater portion of his remaining twenty-eight years in Glasgow. After his death his furniture and personal belongings were auctioned, and there was much interest in one of the pieces of furniture, an organ, originally made for St Andrew's Church, Glasgow. This instrument, a large chamber finger organ, with six stops and a swell, was bought or hired from a Glasgow music seller for the church, but was only played once, so great was the popular wrath at the innovation. It was four years afterwards, apparently, that Old Uncle Alex acquired it from the music seller.

Old Uncle Alex left the excise in 1825 and lived in retirement for a full fourteen years before he died. At the time he retired his nephew Alexander had been in Dublin for two years, and was establishing himself in the business community there.

Piper Findlater VC of the Gordon Highlanders, 1897

Piper Findlater was one of the great heroes of late-Victorian society, and a man with a canny modern sense of how to turn his fame into cash. 'Sporran' tells the story of his great deed.‡

The Gordons have come. Listen to the crashing music, the lilt of the pipes, and the rolling tap of the lead side drummer, which

* The graveyard was closed down some years ago.

† This association with the town led the well-known tobacco company P. J. Carroll & Co., who enjoyed a good trade with Scotland, to name a new brand of their cigarettes 'Sweet Afton' after one of Burns' poems, 'Flow gently, sweet Afton'. With the head of the poet prominent on the front of the packet, the brand became popular with millions of smokers in both islands for several generations.

‡ Piper Findlater's story has been told many times. This one was written under the pen-name 'Sporran'. A fuller account is in *The Wonder Book of Daring Deeds—True Stories of Heroism and Adventure* (London: Ward Lock nd) printed between Scott of the Antarctic and Lawrence of Arabia.

Piper Findlater playing the Gordon Highlanders to victory on the Dargai Heights in 1897

increases to a great volume of sound as all the drums throb in staccato thunder. The band swings by, the music into the distance recedes.

A regiment is proud of its drums and band, while it is said that the worth of a regiment or battalion is gauged by the smartness of its bandsmen, drummers and pipers. If that is so, then, the Gordon Highlanders must surely be among the leaders of the army. It was a piper of the Gordon Highlanders who won the highest and most coveted of all awards for exemplary courage in action. That was Piper Geordie Findlater, who won the Victoria Cross in the Tirah Campaign of 1897.

The incident took place at the small Indian station of Dargai, which is situated on the Afghan border, and which is now the most northerly railway station in India. Dargai is on a range of hills, which overlooks the strategical Malakand Pass and the Swat Valley. In the Tirah campaign the British forces were of necessity, through scarcity of water, forced to evacuate the post. It was decided that it should be retaken, and the Gordon Highlanders were chosen for the attack, for the regiment was noted for its dash and courage. Highland regiments always take their pipes into action with them, and it was to the skirl of Scottish music that the lines of kilted men leaped forward with bayonets flashing in the bright Indian sunlight. The keen eyed and fanatical enemy greatly outnumbered the attackers, and the long barrelled jezails, accurately aimed, picked off the charging Highlanders by the score. The attack was repulsed, but with blood aflame at their setback, the Gordons once again leaped forward, while the pipes wailed above the din of war. The defenders fought valiantly, and it seemed as if once again the Highlanders would be driven back. Men fell by the score, and pipes fell to the parched earth, with tartan ribbons in the dust, as their players closed their eyes in death.

Piper Findlater was with his company, playing lustily as he leaped over the rocky ground. Suddenly he fell, shot through both of his legs. With indomitable courage, and although suffering agonies through his wounds, he again took up his pipes, and propping himself with his back against a rock began to play the regimental march—the Cock o' the North. The men seeing Findlater fall, wavered, but, as the wild music again rose and fell across the Indian hills, they sprang forward with a rush. Nothing could stop the hurricane charge, and with a yell of triumph, Dargai was taken. On all the battlefronts where Highlanders have been called for service in all parts of the world, the Gordon Highlanders have upheld the glorious traditions of the Scottish clans.*

For his gallantry Piper was awarded the VC, and became an instant celebrity.† After the war he had to earn his living. He accepted an engagement at twenty-five guineas per night to play the pipes at one of the London music halls. His debut as a music hall artist was a great success. However his performance came to the attention of the War Office who looked upon it with disfavour and advised him that Queen Victoria herself was not amused. The Piper later wrote: 'I, being without anyone to depend on for advice and having been only a common soldier, agreed that the engagement should be cancelled.' There were suggestions that a post might be found in Her Majesty's Balmoral household. He commented: 'A few questions were asked—if I was educated, etc. I had been a farm servant before joining the army and I was only fifteen when I enlisted, so I had not the advantages of a good education.' He was then twenty-five.

However this contretemps did not inhibit his music hall career in the provinces, and he appeared regularly in Glasgow, Dundee and the Findlater-owned Empire Theatre Belfast. A piquant interest was

* The first battalion of the Gordon Highlanders was raised in 1787. Recruitment to the second battalion was stimulated by the beautiful Duchess of Gordon, who promised each man who enlisted a kiss and, in case that might not be sufficient, a shilling.

† Never ones to miss a commercial opportunity, we in Dublin immediately marketed a bottled sauce called 'Dargai Dash', described by the *Irish Figaro* as 'a full-bodied sauce of very pleasing flavour, and one which will be found by connoisseurs to greatly add to the qualities of fish, soup or meat. The proprietors of this admirable sauce,' wrote the journalist, 'in adopting the title "Dargai Dash" have done wisely, for the slightest reference to the heroic conduct of our troops at Dargai arouses the blood much in the same way as a "pick-me-up" of this stimulating sauce does when taken as such.' (*Irish Figaro* 3 September 1898)

added to his fame by the appearance on the stage (in a bridal gown) of Miss Mary Gellatly, a former sweetheart, who it was reported he was going to marry. But soon the couple fell out, and the marriage was off. She sued him for breach of promise and got a settlement equivalent to two years' wages for a skilled worker. Luckily her heart was so little broken that eleven days later she married another former lover.

Piper died on his farm near Turriff in Aberdeenshire in March 1942 at the age of seventy. His medals were purchased at auction by the Gordon Highlanders Regimental Museum in 1995.

Notes and references

1 James Spence *Ruined Castles–Monuments of Former Men in Vicinity of Banff* Edinburgh: Edmonston and Douglas, 1873, p 3
2 Extract from a letter from Old Uncle Alex to Alexander Peterkin of Edinburgh and first published in Peterkin's edition of Burns. Cited in Wilson *The Works of Robert Burns* Glasgow: Blackie & Son CCCLIX
3 John Sinton *Burns Excise Officer & Poet* 2nd edition, Glasgow and Edinburgh: J. Menzies, 1895, p 12
4 Ian McIntyre *Dirt and Deity: A Life of Robert Burns* London: Flamingo 1996, pp 292-3
5 McIntyre *op. cit.*, p 282
6 Quoted in Sinton *op. cit.*, p 9
7 Sinton *op. cit.*, p 10
8 Sinton *op. cit.*, p 11
9 McIntyre *op. cit.*, p 293
10 Sinton *op. cit.*, p 13
11 Sinton *op. cit.*, p 18
12 *Burns Chronicle & Club Directory*, January 1924, p 72
13 Sinton *op. cit.*, pp 20–21
14 Sinton *op. cit.*, p 21
15 *Burns Chronicle and Club Directory* January 1924, pp 80-3

The Abbey Church, Parnell Square, donated by Alexander the founder and popularly known as Findlater's Church, copy of the original watercolour by Andrew Heiton of Perth, the architect of the church.

2. *Alexander the Founder (1797–1873) and his Brothers*

To young men entering upon business, no life is calculated to give more encouragement or better counsel than that of Alexander Findlater.
The Irish Times, 14 August 1873

Alexander Findlater, the founder of the business in Dublin, was born in Glasgow, on 9 March 1797, the second son of John Findlater, Supervisor of Excise at Greenock (brother to Old Uncle Alex). His father died at a comparatively early age, leaving a widow with a large family in circumstances requiring that Alexander should soon begin to earn his own living. A letter to Alexander from his brother Joseph describes their mother as 'not overloaded with money'. To supplement her income she had a lodger: 'We have a Mr Bennet in the house at present, he is a very fine young man—he has the parlour and bedroom for half a guinea.' (This gentleman, who became Alexander's business contact in Glasgow, struck up a friendship with the youngest daughter, Janet, born in 1804; the couple were married at the Manse, Newlands on 6th August 1834 by Rev. Charles Findlater (see chapter 3). She died of typhus in Glasgow in 1850, aged 46.)

Scotland's industrial revolution was under way in the 1820s and people were flocking to the towns; in the country the old farming patterns were changing. The population of Glasgow, which in 1780 was 42,000, was to reach 274,000 by 1840. As usual, there was a human cost. The tenement slums were (at the time) said to be far worse and more squalid than in Dublin, with their occupants existing in frightful degradation. In towns all over Scotland, merchants and industrialists were laying the foundations for the shipping and industrial empires of the latter part of the nineteenth century. Glasgow was establishing its great industries, mainly shipbuilding and cotton. There was an increasing concentration of business power in a few families: to achieve efficiencies shipping was consolidated into a small number of large firms. Successful industrialists amassed colossal fortunes, and lawyers, doctors and small businessmen also did well. However, Scotland, at the height of its industrial success, was a most unequal society.[1] It is easy to imagine that an ambitious young man whose family connections were more with the excise than the great shipping or industrial firms might explore options outside the country.

Alexander began his career in his early teens in the office of his elder brother William, a shipbroker in Greenock, where a large portion of Clyde shipping then berthed. William was born in Glasgow in 1792. In 1813, aged twenty-one, he was the hero of a remarkable incident in Greenock; the story, told by George

Williamson, another participant, gives a good impression of the young man's mettle.

The following circumstance occurred in the year 1813, about the time I was appointed Procurator-Fiscal of the town of Greenock. I happened one day to go down the quay (now the Steamboat or Customhouse Quay), when I saw a great crowd of persons assembled at the corner of the harbour, west of where the Customhouse was afterwards built. It was low water at the time, and I observed two lads, having the appearance of apprentice seamen, standing up to the waist in the water, having hold of a woman, who was also in the water, and whose head they were attempting to put under water, with the evident intention of drowning her. At the same time I observed also in the water, a young gentleman whom I knew to be Mr William Findlater, a clerk in a counting-house in town, doing his best to protect the woman. I did not hear any words uttered by the persons in the water. As I could not bear the sight, I resolved to endeavour to rescue the woman. I learned that the offence was that she had given information to the Press-gang against some sailors.

A war with France was then raging, and every effort was being made by the Government to procure men for the navy. The vulgar supposed that certain persons gave information where sailors were to be found, and that the Press-gang somehow or other got hold of these men more readily than those of whom they had no information. I am not aware that this was the case, for I do not remember hearing anything said of the gang having gone to houses to pick up men. They used to prowl about the quays and shipping to catch men, and I have seen them myself do so. Be that as it may, the name of Informer was odious, and it was supposed that every insult might be offered to such as bore the character, and that even life might be forfeited, as seemed likely to be the case in the instance I am now detailing.

I have said that I resolved to endeavour to extricate the woman from her very dangerous position. A stair at that time led down to the water, but as the parties were at some distance from the stair, I did not think it prudent to go into the water. Luckily, or, I should rather say, as a special Providence directed, I observed a boat belonging to Allan M'Lean, pilot, coming into the West Harbour, with M'Lean on board. The boat came alongside a vessel at the Quay, not far from the spot where the people in the water were. I leaped directly into M'Lean's boat, and desired him to push her over to where the woman was, but he at first peremptorily refused to do so, fearing, no doubt, that he would participate in the odium attached to the name of Informer, if he gave any assistance. He afterwards yielded, and came ashore, saying he would hold me responsible for the safety of the boat.

I took an oar, and pushed the boat over without any resistance from M'Lean. On reaching Mr Findlater, I gave him my hand, and he got into the boat. Before I had this done, the young sailors had got the woman out of Mr Findlater's hands, and put her into another boat, into which they themselves also went, and proceeded out of the harbour. We followed in our boat. At the harbour mouth, as the wind drove the boat out into the river the young men used all their force [trying] to throw the woman into the sea. Mr Findlater and I got our boat alongside of the other, on which one of the young men lifted an oar, and aimed a blow at me with it, but I warded it off with the oar I held, and then stretched out my hand, and called to the woman to give me hers.

She was lying in the bottom of the boat with her hands grasping the gunwale, and her feet firmly pressed against the opposite side. One of the young men was in the act of beating her fingers with a thole pin to make her let go her hold, when our boat got alongside. Had a few more minutes, or perhaps seconds, elapsed before we reached her, she would without mercy have been thrown into the sea, and a foul murder would have been committed in presence of hundreds of men, women, and children, who stood on the Quay, idle spectators of what was going on. When I held out my hand, the woman eagerly grasped it, and I drew her into our boat. I then addressed myself to a number of persons who were standing on the end of the West Quay, and implored them to assist me in landing the woman, and protecting her from further violence. I knew some of the persons I addressed, particularly a ship master of the name of L . . . n, but he would not interfere, and my appeal was answered by a volley of stones from the crowd.

We let our boat drift out of reach of the stones into the river, and proposed to row down to Mr Scott's building-yard, and there put the woman on shore. On getting abreast of the yard, the carpenters were all assembled (it being dinner hour), and I made an appeal to them, but they would not allow the woman to land. There appeared, therefore, no alternative but to row alongside the Press-tender, then lying at the Tail of the Bank, which we did, put the woman on board, and left her there. Mr Findlater and I returned to the harbour with the boat.

Had the police of the town done their duty, a scene so disgraceful could not have been witnessed. I had the principal actors apprehended and imprisoned, but so little account was made of the offence, that no conviction followed. One of the young men apprehended was under indenture to a tradesman in town. Mr Reid, hardware merchant, a decent, sober, religious man, who was his cautioner, appealed to the magistrates, who ordered his liberation to prevent his forfeiting the penalty in the indenture. Such was the state of the police of the town, and such the state of public feeling, that persons who had attempted a deliberate murder were allowed to escape without any trial or punishment. There was no Sheriff in the place then, nor for two years afterwards, and there were only two or three police officers. I remember shortly before that seeing a man who was said to be an informer driven about the streets, all besmeared with mud and blood, then thrown down and abused, and no one dared to interfere to rescue him from the band of miscreants who were following him.

Outrages and homicides were of frequent occurrence, and little account was made of them. My predecessor in office paid no attention to such matters. No notice was taken of the above occurrence in the *Greenock Advertiser*. It was passed over as a thing unworthy of notice. I heard nothing of the woman for a month or six weeks after this. One day, while I was sitting at my desk, a woman came in and inquired if my name was Davidson. On my saying it was Williamson, she instantly dropped to her knees, pulled off her cap, and implored God's blessing on me for having saved her life. I did not at first recognise her as the woman whose life had been attempted, as above. I inquired how she got on shore from the tender. She told me the people of the brig had landed her where some boats lay turned upside down on the beach, and that she had crept under one of the boats, and concealed herself for several hours, and then had found her way to a friend's house, where she lay for several weeks, bruised and hurt all over by the cruel treatment she had received. I forget what she called herself. She was a little, short-made Irish woman, about thirty years of age. On reviewing this narrative many years after the occurrence, I feel some pleasure in reflecting that I was instrumental in saving the life of a fellow creature.[2]

Alexander in Newfoundland

After some years with his brother, when he was in his sixteenth year, in 1813, Alexander accepted an assignment to the island of Newfoundland from the firm of Shannon, Stewart & Co. He was to operate as clerk, storekeeper and book-keeper to the shipping company. The contract was not over-generous: he was sent out steerage, and was initially to be paid less than 10s a week (all found), for which he was 'not to absent himself from said service day or night'. He was not to deal on his own account. The carefully indited contract survives in pristine condition.

At this time the economy of Newfoundland was undergoing a mini-boom, 'brought on mostly by the reopening of the Spanish market for salt cod, on exceedingly favourable terms, two years earlier'. The boom conditions attracted immigrants, especially from the Waterford area who quickly became a dominant group, so that by 1815 it was estimated that three-quarters of the population of the capital, St John's, were Irish Catholics.[3]

As far as I can deduce from surviving letters, Alexander was stationed on Newfoundland's Atlantic coast, in a fishing village called Ferryland, about fifty miles south of St John's.* The principal product traded in was dried cod. Alexander's role seems to have been to organise the catching and drying of an appropriate amount of fish, and to serve as a 'feeder', preparing cargo for the brig Bennett to take north to St John's. It must have been a somewhat lonely period and he seems to have taken a bit of time to find his feet. In January 1814 his principal wrote bleakly: 'I hope and trust that you will conduct yourself in a way to prevent fault being found.' A year later the principal wrote again, when Alexander's colleague in Ferryland had slipped away to St John's: 'I must remark my surprise at his appearance here leaving only yourself in charge of all our concerns at Ferryland, a circumstance that cannot fail to be taken notice of by everyone.' However, Alexander steadily proved his worth, and in March 1816 he was appointed official Agent and Manager in Ferryland, with the power to bind the partnership.

This success was, however, short-lived. The Newfoundland economy had been hit a serious blow when Spain subjected its dried cod to 'rapid and enormous tariff increases'. After the end of the Napoleonic wars in 1815, other European countries followed, and French fishermen began to provide increased competition. By late 1815 nervous creditors were demanding immediate payment, and the domino effect set in, with one bankruptcy causing another. 'By mid December there were 700 writs issued and nearly forty insolvencies'.[4] The local journal provided a 'dismal record of insolvencies, dissolutions of partnerships, notices from merchants quitting the fishery or withdrawing from business in outposts, notices of sheriff's sales and other bleak testimonials of failure'.[5] Shannon, Stewart were not immune. A month after Alexander's appointment as

* St John's, at that time, was the centre of the region's fishing industry, with a population of 10,000 in 1815 (up from 5,421 in 1806).

manager, his principal wrote: 'It is with the most heartfelt sensation that I have to communicate to you of Shannon, Stewart & Co having stopped payment about 10 January.' The firm was bankrupt, and his contract of employment, which still had a year to run, was worthless. (The outcome throws a different light on Alexander's careful preservation of the contract among his papers.)

He was sent a notably pompous, and cool, testimonial from his principal–'I consider myself in duty bound in justice to your character to take this method of expressing my sentiments of your having acted during the whole of your servitude to my entire satisfaction.' Alexander's superior was probably in no mood for pleasantries. Bankruptcy was taken extremely seriously in Newfoundland: there was nothing abnormal about whipping civilians 'for debt'. Thirty-six lashes on the bared back was not an unusual sentence.

It appears that nineteen-year-old Alexander went from Newfoundland to Quebec, in Canada, in July 1816, and later to Montreal, where a letter from William suggests that though he had work, it was very hard. (The winter of 1816–17 was one of the coldest the locals could remember.[6]) Alexander had evidently asked his brother what he should do. William could only suggest that if the work was endangering Alexander's health, he should leave immediately. The advice was the more poignant because the original purpose of the letter was to announce the death of their brother—poor James, of a fever in St Croix. (Another brother, Charles, had died the year before, aged seventeen, at sea near New Orleans.) St Croix, a tiny island in the West Indies, was a Danish colony. James evidently had a rough time, as the letter says. 'There is no telling what hardships he may have lived through . . . as he had no friends on the island his effects were confiscated by the Danes.'

Years later, on his death, one newspaper reported that Alexander had later been involved in a distillery in Canada, until a great fire led to the winding-up of the business. Returning to Scotland he worked for some years for Messrs Blarvey, eminent distillers, before deciding to set up on his own account in Dublin in 1823. In 1822 William, having married Sophia Huffington of Fahan, Donegal, settled as a shipbroker in Londonderry. They had one son and three daughters. No doubt reports from William led Alexander to believe that Ireland offered a field for energetic commercial enterprise. Contacts already in Dublin would have promoted the decision. His friend William Burns, thirty-one-year-old nephew of the poet, was busy laying down business roots there and was later joined by Gilbert Burns, another nephew of the poet. Alexander himself was well connected; he would have had an introduction from Old Uncle Alex, the Collector of Excise in Glasgow, to his opposite number in the Custom House Dublin. After all they were both employees of branches of His Majesty's revenue service and co-operated on such items as smuggling and illicit distillations.[7]

Dublin in the 1820s

Alexander was twenty-six years old when in 1823 the ship on which he was a passenger slipped into a berth on George's Quay on the opposite side of the river

The Custom House and River Liffey as it would have been when Alexander arrived in Dublin in 1823

Liffey to the Custom House. George's Quay and Rogerson's Quay were spectacular, the home of mariners, shipbuilders, ship brokers, rope and sail makers and ships' chandlers.

Ireland in the first quarter of the nineteenth century was a much more populated country than Scotland. The 1821 census shows that the population of Ireland was almost seven million, compared to Scotland at two million and England and Wales at twelve million, giving Ireland one-third of all the people in the British Isles.* However, in 1823, Dublin was a busy place, with plenty of activity and potential. There was a still-thriving industrial sector but decline was setting in as a result of the withdrawal of protective duties following the Act of Union. Dublin was still the 'second city of the Empire' but its pre-eminence was rapidly to be overtaken by industrial towns such as Manchester, Liverpool and Belfast. Its 200,000 population lived between the canals that embraced the city centre. In 1830, although many of the aristocracy had removed to London, there were still twelve hundred nobility and gentry in the city, five thousand merchants and traders, supported by nearly two thousand lawyers, six hundred medical men but only twelve dentists. The Catholic merchant and professional classes were steadily growing in prosperity.

For visitors, Dublin was an impressive city, described by Walter Scott as 'splendid beyond my expectations'. Karl Marx's collaborator Frederick Engels was also impressed, but characteristically saw a little deeper: 'The traveller to Dublin finds the approach as imposing as when he visited London', he wrote. 'Dublin Bay is the most impressive in the British Isles . . . the city itself is most attractive and its aristocratic quarter is laid out in a more tasteful manner than any other

* Ireland's position was to change dramatically under direct rule from Westminster, as the census figures for 1901 illustrate. By then the population of Ireland had been overtaken by Scotland, and was down to four and a half million and declining. In the year 2000, the thirty-two counties represent only one-tenth of the total population of the two islands.

British town. By contrast the poorer districts are among the ugliest and most revolting in the world.'

The peaceful invasion by Scottish merchants was in sharp contrast to all the warring factions that had invaded the land over the previous nine centuries. The new invaders were welcome, and quickly integrated into their adopted land, became citizens and contributed to its institutions. They did not crave after their roots, nor hold property elsewhere to depart to. Their commitment was total. As Walter Thomas Meyler noted in his 1870 autobiography *St Catherine's Bells* 'instead of investing in the funds to lie idle and useless, they [the Scottish merchants] expended their profits in enterprises valuable to the country of their adoption, extending employment and circulating the wealth they have acquired amongst the community from whose support they derived it.' [8]

Seals with brass heads for branding the wax that seals the cork into the bottle

Foremost among them was John Jameson from Alloa who established his distillery in Dublin in 1780. Thomas Heiton followed in 1818 and served his apprenticeship in his brother-in-law's coal and steel business before setting up on his own. John Arnott set up his first store in Cork in 1834.*

Other great names survive into the twenty-first century: for instance, Dunlop who re-invented the pneumatic tyre;† Millar who came over on the invitation of the Jamesons and opened a wine, spirit and cordial business in Thomas Street, then very much the hub of brewing and distilling; Mackey the agriculturist and horticulturist;[9] Alexander Thom of *Thom's Irish Almanac and Official Directory* who ran the leading firm in the printing industry of that time; Weir the prestigious Grafton Street jeweller and Johnston the Ballsbridge miller, one-third of the 1889 amalgamation that became Johnston Mooney and O'Brien.

As far as I can ascertain Alexander came to Dublin to trade in whiskey. He may have held the agency for the Glasgow Distillery Co. or represented a spirit merchant called Thomas Harvey in Glasgow. He arrived at an opportune time in the spirit business. In 1823 the duties on spirits, in Ireland and Scotland, were reduced by 56 per cent to 2s 4d per imperial gallon, a change, the commissioners observed, 'the beneficial effects of which, in the great object of suppressing illicit trading, by enabling the legal distiller to carry on his trade in competition with the illegal trader, were found in both divisions of the kingdom to surpass

* John Arnott financed, engineered, owned or partially owned Arnott & Co., Belfast; Arnott & Co., Dublin; Cash & Co., Cork; Baldoyle and Cork Park Race Meetings; the City of Cork Steam-Packet Company; Arnott's Brewery, Cork; the Passage Docks Shipbuilding Company, the Bristol Steam Navigation Company and *The Irish Times*.

† Dunlop came from the village of Dreghorn in Ayrshire in Scotland. The story of Boyd Dunlop who re-invented the pneumatic tyre is told in the *Dublin Historical Record* Spring 1996.

the most sanguine'.

In 1821 the quantity of spirits produced in Ireland on which duty was paid was 3.6m gallons, in 1825 it had increased to 8.8m gallons, and in 1836 to 11.9m gallons; certainly a good trade for Alexander to embark upon. Brewing, distilling and shipbuilding industries were in fact the only industries to increase as a result of the Act of Union.[10]

Alexander was to develop his business around family and trusted associates, mainly those with Scottish roots. His brother William was in Londonderry, and so was the eldest of the family his sister Helen, who was married to a merchant there, Robert Corscaden. In Glasgow William Bennet (who married Alexander's sister Janet) acted as a general broker, assembling a wide range of produce, in particular rum, sugar and coffee which were shipped there from the Bahamas and Latin America. In Liverpool his brother John and his brother-in-law John Snowden, married to sister Susanna, were both ships' captains. The youngest brother, Adam Seaton, went to Brazil at the age of sixteen to engage in trade.

From the beginning Alexander and his brothers set their sights high; in 1825 he received a letter from his brother Joseph in Glasgow, addressed to his lodgings 'at Mrs Catherine Dawes, 5 Gardner Street (lower)'. As well as discussing the type of merchandise to be sent to Adam in Brazil, Joseph wrote:

> 'You will have heard no doubt of the great failures amongst Banking Houses in England. They have created considerable distress amongst the lower classes in that quarter, the circulation of a number of them being small notes—I am much afraid there will be a few here [Glasgow] sharing the same fate . . . [he adds] James Johnston has got a fine situation in a Bank at Londonderry. His salary I believe is £250.'

Alexander certainly moved quickly to establish himself. In 1826, maybe earlier, he, with William Burns, was trading, across the river from the Custom House, as The Irish & Scotch Whiskey Stores at 7 Burgh Quay. By 1828 he had added Hawkins Street, North Wall, High Street and North King Street to his premises as well as recording sales for a 'Spirit account', which must have been wholesale. The North King Street premises had a store around the corner in Halston Street. By 1830 a branch at Kingstown (Dún Laoghaire) had been added (four years before the opening of the Dublin–Kingstown Railway), first trading as The Irish and Scotch Whiskey Stores, and in 1832 Hawkins Street was combined into the Burgh Quay operation, the former acting as the stores for the wholesale. From this date he traded under his own name 'Alex. Findlater'.

This was an opportune location. Alexander's arrival in 1823 had coincided with the foundation of the first Catholic Association, the focus of Daniel O'Connell's campaign for Catholic emancipation which eventually culminated in the Act of Parliament passed in 1829 granting Catholics the right to sit in parliament and in 1832 the right to vote. Conciliation Hall, later the Tivoli Theatre (and in the twentieth century the *Irish Press* headquarters), was nearby and was the rendezvous for Daniel O'Connell and the foremost politicians of the day. Another of Alexander's Scottish friends, William Todd, had set up business just across the river, in the drawing-room of 10 Eden Quay, dealing in carpets.

The goods he traded in

The very earliest ledger entries in the Findlater archive are dated July 1826, three years after Alexander's arrival in Dublin.* He is already in a reasonable way of business. He buys 20 puncheons of malt (whiskey) from Shaw & Turbett and 13 puncheons from William Burns. A puncheon was a large barrel containing 126 to 130 gallons—so he has bought the equivalent of nearly 40,000 modern bottles. This is over-proof whiskey, which requires to be diluted to bring it to normal sales strength.

Over proof whiskey

Whiskey is always distilled over-strength. A strength between 11 and 25 per cent over-proof as against the then standard resale strength of 25 per cent under-proof (75 per cent proof) requires the merchant to increase the total volume by 40 per cent by adding pure water. Once the dilution process was complete, the contents of the barrels had to be bottled, corked and labelled. Alternatively the whiskey was despatched to publicans and small traders throughout the country in five and ten gallon earthenware jars now used as display pieces in pubs.

A perfect specimen of a Findlater Whiskey jar

Alexander made several small sales of both Scotch and best Irish in that year to his landlady Catherine Dawes, charging 10s per gallon and pro-rata for half and quarter gallons. A Henry Major got much better value—he must have been a trader—paying 8s 6d per gallon for his supplies of 11 per cent over-proof Scotch. On another occasion a gallon of best rum was sold at 12s a gallon and a dozen Cape wine at 20s.

The first record of purchases of Guinness and Jameson (James) was in February 1827. Shop bills and lists of prices were used for promotion, 7s 6d was paid for 1,000 in February 1827, 4s in December 1827 and 5s in 1828. 6,000 bottle labels cost 12s, 20 gross corks £1 10s and bottles were charged out at 2s a dozen. The bottles came from the Dunbarton Glass Co., William Burns being

* Details survive of our trading for all but the first three years in the span of old Findlaters from 1823 to 1968. These are in bound ledgers, journals and cash books and form a wonderful archive with a wealth of information.

their Irish agent here. Our main source for Scotch was the Glasgow Distillery Co. Alexander's salary for the twelve months to June 1827 amounted to £80 [£4,400] and £150 [£8,250] for the eighteen months to December 1828, plus his share of profits.

The business was faring well: on 30 June 1827 the retail account was showing a net profit of £465 [£25,600] and the spirit account (wholesale) £134 [£7,400]. Stock on hand for spirits was £700 [£38,500] and on the retail account £585 [£32,000]. In February 1828 the fine (today we would call it key money) for the North King Street lease was £50 [£2,750], and £250 [£13,750] for the North Wall premises. There was a match tax of £1 4s, two years' pipe water cost £2 15s 5d, the Chamber of Commerce subscription was one guinea and he gave a 7s 6d [£20] donation to the Catholic church in Halston Street. On another occasion the minister received 16s 8d and the priest 5s.

Wages varied between 11s (a porter) and 17s a week; some of those employed were later to be partners of Alexander in his ventures here and across the water, Todd, Gladstone, Carmichael and McKie (or Mackie). There was a couple, Mathew and Mary, who worked in Hawkins Street; he earned 7s and she 5s, making 12s for the week; by 1828 this was up to 14s.

Interest on £1,000 [£55,000] for the North King Street branch was £2 12s 1d and duty on 4 puncheons containing 440 gallons came to £77 18s 4d. By 1829 annual sales were £8,900 [£465,000]. The inventory in January 1830 for the four outlets amounted to £2,740 [£145,000], wholesale accounting for £2,276 [£119,000] of the total. In May 1830 the new premises in Kingstown was stocked up with a wide variety of goods: ale, malt, Cape wine, sherry, port, rum, soap, sealing wax, a coffee roaster, coffee mill and imported Dunlop cheese. This was followed by raisins, figs and tobacco, the latter at 3s per lb.

In Dublin the bulk, one-off nature of some of the purchases suggests that Alexander was doing a substantial ships' stores or export business from the North Wall premises on the north side of the river, from the Burgh Quay/Hawkins Street premises on the south side of the river and in Kingstown from his premises there. For example, in October 1830 Hawkins Street handled 2 loads of English meat, 2 loads of East country meat, 103 hams, 2 barrels of Dunlop cheese, 1 barrel of red herrings, and 5 bags of barley while across the river they handled in one particular instance 40 cwt of yellow soap and 20 cwt of white soap. But the main commodity was whiskey.

In January 1831 Alexander purchased 10 puncheons of malt and 20 puncheons of grain whiskey from the Glasgow Distillery and these sorts of purchases were made at regular intervals. They were not exclusively Scotch—for example, 5 puncheons were purchased from John Jameson in 1833. Sugar was bought in cone-shaped loaves. In August 1833 he bought 44 loaves of refined sugar totalling 12 cwt 1 qtr and 15 lbs at 86s per cwt; thus each loaf was 31½ lbs and 1lb of sugar cost about 10d.

Monthly sales for his outlets in Burgh Quay, Kingstown, North King Street, High Street and the North Wall rose from under £1,000 a month in 1828

[£54,000] to over £1,500 in 1830 [£81,000] and £2,400 by 1834 [£130,000]. This is the equivalent of annualised sales in the year 2000 of £500,000, £1m and £1.6m respectively and this was only the start of his great commercial career.

By 1830 Alexander, now thirty-three, was laying the foundation of a substantial commercial empire. He was able that year to bring his mother over from Glasgow together with a manservant, John Harries. The following year his brother William died, leaving a widow and four children, for whom Alexander took responsibility. Joseph had died in Glasgow three years earlier, at the age of twenty-one. He had not married.

In 1831 there was a revolution in Brazil, and Don Pedro I abdicated. Adam, Alexander's younger brother, who had been in Brazil for eight years, was by then in partnership trading as Miller & Findlater. During the riots in Rio de Janeiro the firm's premises were burned down. The firm relocated in Bahia (today called Salvador) and operated as both shipping agents and merchants dealing on their own account. Made-up fabrics and textiles were shipped out to Bahia and sugar and cotton back to Europe. Ships plied to and from Liverpool, Falmouth and Hamburg. In 1834, for example, silver coins were consigned to London and gingham, handkerchiefs, hair cords, shirtings, Indian books, book folds and Verona handkerchiefs, and special cloths such as madapottams, pullicates and osnabergs, went back out to Bahia.

The ledgers of the company, Miller & Findlater, 1830–1839, have survived in almost pristine condition. The most surprising discovery from these books is the export of large quantities of bottled porter during this period. The porter was brewed by Arthur Guinness, then bottled, corked, and labelled and packed in straw into barrels by Findlaters for despatch. The porter was sold as Findlater's Pure Dublin Porter—in January 1832 10,000 porter labels were printed. In 1835 we consigned 45 barrels of bottled porter from Burgh Quay to Miller & Findlater in Bahia, each barrel containing 3½ dozen quart bottles. In another consignment there were 108 casks containing 3½ dozen each, making 378 dozen, and 75 casks each containing 6 dozen pint bottles, making 450 dozen.

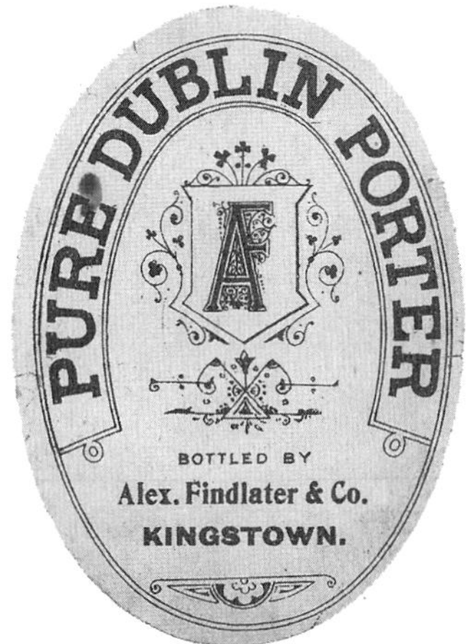

A good quantity of ale was shipped; for instance, in September 1834 Burgh Quay purchased 20 barrels of Cairns and North Wall 10 barrels. There were also purchases of 6 guinea ale from an Andrew Roy at £6 6s per hogshead less 7½ per cent. This compares with Guinness porter at £2 2s 3d and Cairns ale at £1 18s a barrel,* suggesting that Roy's ale was of a much

* Guinness hogshead = 52 gallons (54 gallons in the industry generally), Guinness barrel = 32 imperial gallons until 1881 (36 gallons in the industry generally), Irish barrel = 42 Irish gallons = 32.96 imperial gallons (S. R. Dennison and Oliver MacDonagh *Guinness 1886–1939* Cork: Cork University Press 1998 Appendix pp 271-2)

Todd Burns 47 Mary Street after rebuilding following the very extensive fire that occurred in the early part of 1902 destroying the main structure; fortunately the premises and stock were insured.

superior quality. It is probable that this ale came from John Roy & Co., ale and table-beer brewers who in 1822 were at 28 North Anne Street, just around the corner from Alexander's outlet in North King Street. In 1836 the street directory shows John Jameson as the brewer at this address.

In 1834 Alexander formed one of his best partnerships, that with William Todd and Gilbert Burns, in Mary Street, trading as the department store Todd Burns. Alexander seems to have funded the development. His ledger accounts for the workmen's weekly wages at around £22 10s, and with, a nice touch, drink money for labourers 2s 2d; 11 tons of slates from Dockrells cost 62s 6d per ton, 14 iron pillars £32, nails £1 10s and rubbish cartage 21s 4d. He also paid for the slaters, plasterers and £40 on account for mahogany.

The store proved one of the most profitable of his investments. He had a quarter-share in the profits from 1838 to 1848 and one-fifth from 1849 to 1873; he also received interest on loans and undrawn earnings. Dublin was obviously ready for a new department store.* Profits climbed from £9,296 [£450,000] in 1838 to £13,000 [£800,000] in 1843. In the years of the Famine, 1847–9, profits were down three-quarters, but rose again in the 1850s to an average of over £10,000 [£600,000] and increased to over £20,000 [£1.2m] in the 1860s, finally standing at £21,765 [£1.2m] at the time of his death in 1873. The highest was £27,870 [£1.6m] in 1866. These were superb profits.

A brig

In 1835 the builders and shopfitters were again at work for Alexander, this time in Sackville Street, where he had taken a lease at the upper end of the street. He began trading here as Findlater Lennox & Co.,

* In 1838 John Switzer set up at 91 Grafton Street as a woollen draper. In 1843 John Arnott started trading at 14 Henry Street and in 1848/9 Hugh Brown and James Thomas, both previously buyers in Todd Burns, set up as 'general drapers and haberdashers' at 16 and 17 Grafton Street.

tea merchants, Robert Lennox having learnt his trade in one of his other outlets. The 165-year-old monopoly of the East India Company had been abolished in 1833 and Charles Bewley, the most enterprising of his family at that time, had chartered a small schooner named *Hellas*, capable of carrying no more than two hundred tons, and imported the first cargo of free tea from Canton to Dublin in 1835. The ledgers record our first purchases for the new outlet in 1835 as: 4 chests of Bohia (414 lbs) at 1s 8¼d; 6 chests of Congou (484 lbs) at 1s 9¼d; 6 cases of Congou (493 lbs) at 1s 10½d and 5 boxes of Caper (105 lbs) at 1s 11d—total £134 18s 6d.

Tea was still an expensive luxury. In 1834 popular tea retailed at 4s per lb., good Congou 4s 6d, strong Congou 4s 8d, fine full 5s, Pekoe 5s 8d and finest Pekoe 7s (5s represents about £14 in today's money—by comparison, 1lb of Bewley's breakfast tea in the year 2000 cost about £3.70). From then Findlaters' tea business grew apace, in line with the rapidly growing Irish taste for tea, as we shall see in subsequent chapters.

I made some interesting discoveries while looking through the old ledgers. Wine imports, for instance, were by no means all from France. Among the more obscure wines we shipped was 'Bene Carlo' (7s 6d a gallon in 1827) from Valencia, 'Bucellas' from Portugal, 'Calcavella' from Italy and 'Constantia' from the Cape, all in general circulation in this period. In 1830 good Cape wine retailed at 1s 2d a bottle, fine Cadiz sherry and fine port at 2s 3d bottle, Calcavella 2s 4d, old port 2s 6d, prime claret 3s 4d; but here's the catch: were these quart or pint bottles? Most likely the former.

Shrub, which sold at 5s a gallon, was a drink made from sweetened fruit juice and spirit, typically rum or brandy. 'Raspberry' featured prominently; we had 2,000 labels printed in August 1827 at a cost of 4s and it sold at 7s to 8s a gallon which suggests it had an alcoholic content. Malt whiskey was 8s and 9s an imperial gallon which equals 6s 4d and 7s 2d an Irish gallon (1 gallon = 6 x 75 cl. bottles). Old Jamaica rum was advertised at 17s 6d an imperial gallon, 14s for an Irish gallon. In 1841 we were advertising best old Irish at 9s a gallon, Scotch at 8s 8d, and Islay at 10s an Irish gallon. White currant and ginger cordial of superior quality were also 10s a gallon. Later, rich raspberry vinegar was 9s a gallon; Guinness double stout porter 3s 10d per dozen quarts, Drogheda ale 4s and Cape wine of very special description 18s a dozen, again presumably quarts. In 1843 quarts of Guinness were 3s 6d and pints 1s 10d a dozen (2s in 1827), Drogheda ale 3s 8d and 1s 11d respectively, light bitter ale 2s 9d per dozen. Cider first appeared in 1827, but not very frequently afterwards.

In February 1836 there was an extension of porter exports to Quebec: 290½ dozen quarts and 156 dozen pint bottles, packed as usual in barrels; this consignment also included ale, 129½ dozen quarts and 54 dozen pints. In September there was a shipment to New York, in October to New Orleans and in November to Pernambuco, in Brazil. In January 1837 Guinness paid us a Christmas allowance on 630 hogsheads, 60 barrels and 36 half barrels of porter; I'd say that we were a valued customer. 1836 seems to have been the peak of the

Sackville Street in the early days of Findlater's trading

exports to the Americas.

In that year Alexander's brother John (my great-great-grandfather) died at sea, aged just thirty-four. He was Master of the brig *James Laurie* which went down off the Bahamas with a total loss of life. We rely on the *Nassau Royal Gazette* for the sparse information we have on the disaster, in an article entitled 'Melancholy Shipwreck':

> The early part of the 25th of March last was somewhat squally and threatening. Nevertheless, Captain Findlater was anxious to get out of the harbour without delay, as the wind was fast veering to the westward, which might detain the vessel in port for several days. The passengers, with their luggage, hurried on board. The bar was passed, only a few minutes before the wind had come round to north-west. By two o'clock it blew a strong gale from that quarter but being so far fair as to allow a course to be shaped out to sea from among the islands. The brig made sail and was soon out of sight of the town. The weather throughout the night was wild and stormy and in the morning fears were expressed for the safety of the *James Laurie;* and those fears were, some days afterwards, increased by several articles which had been on board being found on the shores of Abaco. No less than thirteen passengers, beside the master and crew, were hurried into eternity, it must be presumed, in a very short time after their departure from hence who, it is reasonable to believe, perished that night or the day after.

John had married twenty-year-old Mary Anne Hughes in Liverpool on 18 April 1827. They had four children: John (my great-grandfather) born in 1828, Helen in 1829, Joseph in 1831 and Elizabeth in 1833. A year after John's death Mary Anne died of consumption (tuberculosis). The orphaned children were brought up with their Findlater aunt, Susanna Snowden and by their uncle Alexander who looked after the expenses.

Also in 1836 Alexander was associated with other prominent merchants in the establishment of a steam packet service between Dublin and Glasgow, as recorded in *The Story of the Burns & Laird Lines.*

It was in the year 1836 that the new shipping company, the Dublin and Glasgow Sailing and Steam Packet Company, began to trade. The new line began under auspices that could not well have meant other than success. The articles of association bore the signatures of great merchant princes of the Irish city, including Benjamin Lee Guinness and Arthur Lee Guinness; John Jameson [distiller]; John D'Arcy [D'Arcy's brewery]; Alexander Findlater; Wm. Todd and Wm. Burns [Todd, Burns & Co.]; Alexander Maguire [wholesale linen and muslin commission agent] and Robt. Gatchell

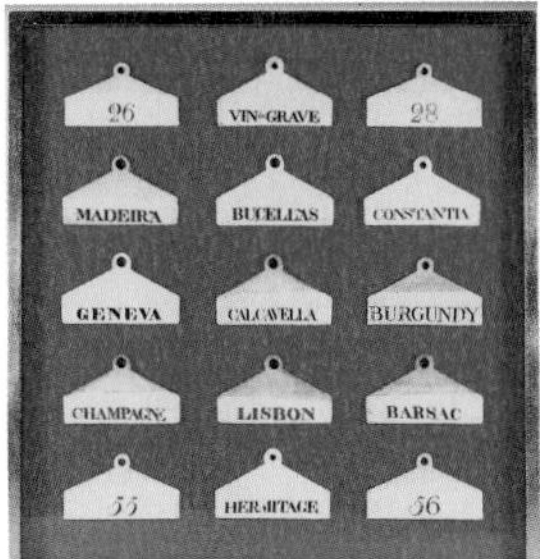

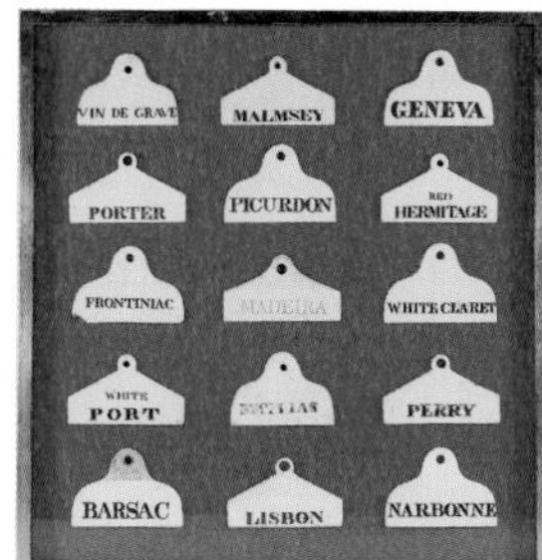

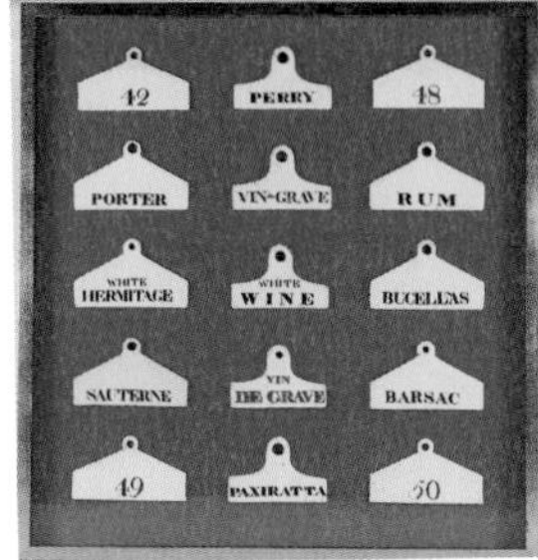

Ceramic bin labels used in the cellars in Alexander's time

[hardware and ironmongery merchants]; Alexander Ferrier and Andrew Pollock [wholesale haberdashers]; J. and H. Campbell and Company [wine merchants]; Daniel Miller [coppersmith and brass founders]; William Hopkins [carpenter and builder]; John North [hardware and ironmongery]; and John Thwaites [chemist and importer of mineral waters].[11]

This shareholding was held for a number of years.

The wine trade in England

In 1838 Alexander ventured into the large and lucrative English wine market. With Ivie Mackie he set up Findlater & Mackie in Manchester and Findlater Mackie & Co. in the Strand, London. In the Manchester partnership he had a half share from 1846 to 1859, a quarter share from 1860 to 1869 and one-fifth to 1873. Profits averaged £5,200 [£300,000] from 1846 to 1850; £7,000 [£400,000] from 1851 to 1860 and over £8,500 [£500,000] from 1861 to 1873. In the Strand in London he had 25 per cent to 1858, 66.6 per cent to 1866, 50 per cent from 1866 to 1869; the partnership profit averaged over £4,500 [£250,000] over the previous twelve years. In 1870 he generously parted with the goodwill of his share for £1,000.

In the meantime, in 1856, realising that London could take more than one outlet, Alexander established another wine merchants Findlater Mackie Todd & Co. with premises in Dooley Street until 1863 and then under the railway viaducts at London Bridge, known as Findlater's Corner (replicating the name used for the premises in Sackville Street, Dublin). It was said that this position was probably passed or seen by more persons every day than any other spot in London. In this venture there were five partners: Ivie Mackie, a merchant of Manchester and thrice Mayor there, Bruce B. Todd, of the Dublin drapery family, Thomas Gordon of Warrington, near Liverpool, and John Findlater Corscaden, Alexander's nephew. One of the partners dropped out from 1858. In 1864 profits in this partnership overtook the other London outlet and averaged £6,000 to 1873 [£350,000].

John Findlater Corscaden owned a couple of ships and was a member of various of Alexander's partnerships including Findlaters in Brighton—at number 19 Black Lion Street. (Alexander had a one-fifth share in the profits of this tidy earner which averaged over £4,000 [almost £250,000] in the five years to 1872.) In 1853 John married his own niece Helen, daughter of Captain John. They had no children and John died in 1887. Helen's younger brother Joseph was also in the London partnerships; he also had no heirs and died in 1912.

Findlater Mackie Todd

Findlater Mackie Todd have had an illustrious history since the 1870s, mainly under the ownership of the Todd family. The firm was responsible for the worldwide sales of Findlater's wines and spirits, the best known being Dry Fly sherry and Findlater's Finest Scotch. In 1924, head office moved to 92 Wigmore Street W1, known as Findlater House. The firm at one time had fifty wine shops in and around London, Oxford, Cambridge and Cirencester. In 1968 the Todds sold the firm to their old friends the Bulmers of cider fame in Hereford. To clear the decks for a public quotation, Bulmers passed it on to Beechams, the pharmaceutical giant, in 1970, when it was fashionable for large international firms to diversify outside their core business. In 1987 it was subject to a management buyout and moved its headquarters to Great Queen Street in Covent Garden and then to Merton Cellars, south of London, which had been built in 1959. It is now a thriving part of the John Lewis Partnership concerned mainly with the mail order of wine. Findlater Scotch is distilled and marketed by Invergordon Distillers, under the banner of Findlater Scotch Whiskey Limited. The Chairman of Findlater Mackie Todd, Christopher Rowe, was President of the Royal Warrant Holders Association in 1998.

Adam returns from Bahia

Adam returned to Europe in 1839 and became Alexander's main partner in Dublin, a partnership that endured for thirty-four years, until Alexander's death. Adam set up in the centre of Rathmines as S. Findlater & Co., at 9 Rathmines Terrace, later renumbered 302 Rathmines Road, a premises recognised until recently by the large clock at the junction of Lower and Upper Rathmines Road and the Rathgar Road. We traded from that premises for 130 years in all, until 1969.

Originally Adam lived in the commodious premises over the Rathmines property. The area was then surrounded by green fields and countryside. 'In those

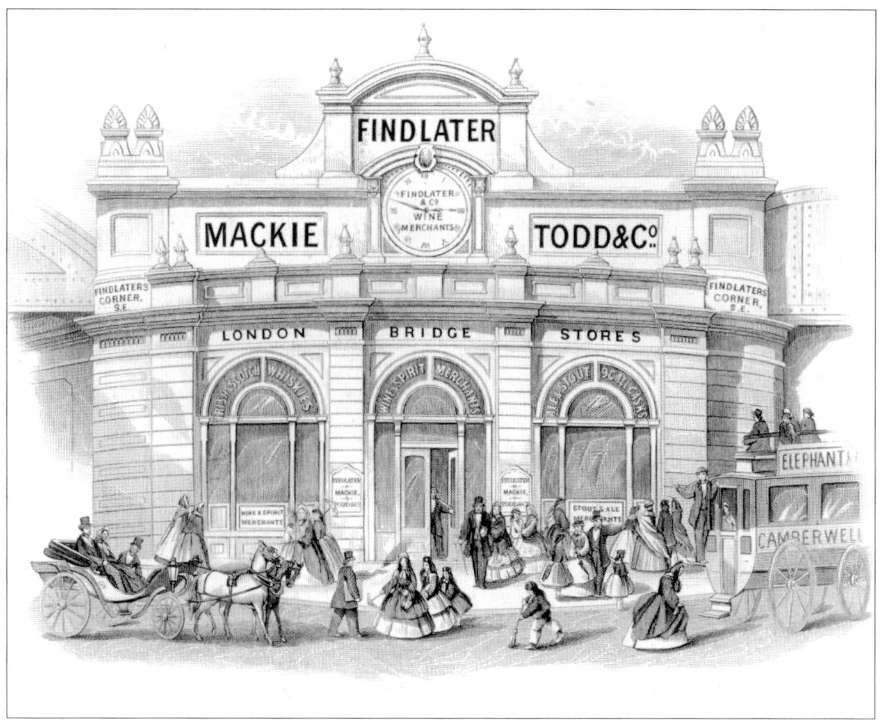

Findlater Mackie Todd head office at London Bridge, 1862

days Rathmines village commenced opposite Rathgar Road. The whole district was laid out in meadows and dairy fields. Rathgar Road was not formed, and the passage to Roundtown [Terenure] was by Old Rathmines. Leinster Road, then part of Mowld's Farm, was formed to Harold's Cross, in 1840.'[12]

In 1840 Alexander dropped out of the North Wall lease and the Irish and Scotch whiskey stores there were managed by Mackie and Gladstone. In 1842 Alexander's ledgers show Mackie and Gladstone active in Liverpool, the home base of the Gladstone family. Another commercial offspring, although Alexander was not a member in the partnership, was that of Dunlop Mackie & Co. of Bristol, established in 1846. Their centenary catalogue records that Matthew Dunlop, Bruce Todd and Tom Gladstone, of Scottish stock, gained their early experience in the Irish capital with Alexander and then went on to be associated with Ivie Mackie in Mackie & Gladstone of Manchester. Robert Gladstone was a partner of Alexander's in the Mountjoy Brewery (see Chapter 4). Robert and Tom were of the Scottish Liverpool Gladstone family of which W. E. Gladstone, the Prime Minister, was also a member.

In 1848 Alexander ceased to sell groceries through North King Street, confirming the family understanding that Alexander was himself primarily a wine and spirit merchant with some dry goods, and that the main thrust into groceries was for the next generation.

In November 1847, at the time of the arrival of the first colonial settlers, Alexander became one of the original purchasers of a section of land in Dunedin, Otago, New Zealand. This distant colony was gradually being taken from the Maori; the Free Church of Scotland sponsored the New Zealand Land Settlement Company in its offer for sale of land sections to prospective migrants in Scotland. The purchase price for a mixed lot of town and country land amounting to sixty acres was £120 10s [£6,000]. Alexander's town section became the site of the Bank of New South Wales, Princes Street, Dunedin. His suburban section was located at Deborah Bay, on the Otago Harbour near Port Chalmers, and his farm section was located at East Taeiri, Otago. The farm property at East Taieri was located in swamp land and under water, and situated next to a property on higher land owned by Andrew Todd, the location of the first recorded sod to be turned by plough in Otago.

Original partners in the London firm of Findlater, Mackie, Todd. Standing, l-r; J. Findlater Corscaden, Bruce B. Todd, Thos. Gordon. Seated, l-r; Ivie Mackie, Alexander Findlater

While Alexander himself never visited the colony his namesake, a cousin from Edinburgh, arrived in Otago with his wife and five children in March 1850. They brought with them much essential equipment, small items of furniture, musical instruments, pictures etc., including a full-sized grandfather clock. Their first home was made of fern trees—'bungis' as they were called—a material which was much used locally for home making in the early days before there were organised timber sawing outfits operating. The nearest Maori settlement was located near the mouth of Otago Harbour twenty miles away, where there was a whaling station.[13]

However that was not the end of our Alexander's involvement in that far away country. His niece Sophia, daughter of his brother William, married for the second time Henry Morse of Otago and settled there. She was one of the beneficiaries of Alexander's will. It appears that the town section of his property in Otago was transferred to Gilbert Burns and the farm property to Andrew Todd. By 1849 Alexander's second eldest nephew, Captain John's son twenty-one-year-old John (my great-grandfather), was well enough versed in the trade to be entrusted with an outlet of his own. He was set up in South Great George's Street in the centre of Dublin and took up residence overhead. It was John's lot to provide the succession that kept the Irish trading arm of Alexander's empire in business into the 21st century.

All was not easy in Dublin at this time, as the effects of the Great Famine had hit trade hard, and caused many food merchants and traders to fail both in Ireland and in Britain. As Walter Thomas Meyler, in 1870, records in his autobiography *Saint Catherine's Bells:*

> The great commercial failures in Ireland in 1847, after the terrific famine, and again

> in 1852, in Dublin, brought on by great mercantile collapse . . . decimated hosts of highly respectable and honourable merchants, who were swept off the lists by the occurrences, and many of whom disappeared from the stage.

(To add insult to injury, in 1853 Gladstone extended the income tax to Ireland for the first time. It started at just 3p in the £.)

The fact that laws for Ireland were enacted in the Westminster parliament at this time was frustrating for the Dublin merchants who found themselves remote from the centre of power, and so had great difficulty in getting appropriate legislation through the imperial parliament (this was to be a continuing grievance to the very end of the century). In January 1851 Alexander was one of two hundred merchants who put his name to the following:

> To the Right Hon the Lord Mayor of the City of Dublin [Benjamin Lee Guinness] we, the undersigned, request your Lordship will be pleased to convene a meeting of Citizens of Dublin, on an early day, for the purpose of taking into consideration the propriety of petitioning Parliament to establish a Transatlantic Packet Station at some suitable port in Ireland, and to appoint a deputation to wait on his Excellency the Lord Lieutenant, to request the exercise of his influence with her Majesty's government to accomplish this great national object.*

Roe's Distillery in Thomas Street

Roe's 15 year-old whiskey in the unique bottle shape

On another occasion in the same month Alexander signed his name to the great campaign to take tax off paper, whose brilliant slogan was that a tax on paper was a tax on knowledge: 'We the undersigned request your Lordship will be pleased to convene a meeting of Citizens on as early a day as may meet your Lordship's convenience, for the purpose of petitioning Parliament for a removal of the Excise duty on paper.' This was signed by sixty Dublin merchants. The tax on paper was finally removed in 1861.

Alexander was well aware of the tremendous success being enjoyed by the Guinness brewery in St James' Gate and, as we have seen, he and Adam had sold large quantities of porter and ale in the Americas during the 1830s, as well as through the outlets in Dublin. It was thus only natural that he should entertain the

* As early as 1835 it had been proposed to a select committee of the House of Commons that a great Atlantic railway should be constructed across Ireland as a step to connect England with America. The Erris area of Co. Mayo was suggested as the ideal location both on account of its seaward position and its magnificent natural harbours. It was said that it was capable of holding the whole British navy and a vast number of other vessels at safe anchorage afloat. It was also said that 'it will create a spirit of improvement in Ireland, which will ultimately develop the great resources of a hitherto neglected country'. (P. Knight Erris in the *Irish Highlands and the Atlantic Railway* Dublin: Martin Keane & Son 1836.)

The Findlater épergne

possibility of building his own brewery. When he first came to Dublin whiskey was the drink of choice in Ireland. But over the century there was a significant decline in spirit drinking, and an equally significant rise in the consumption of beer. Contemporaries were well aware of these trends, and ascribed various reasons. Some said it was the temperance movement, notably Father Mathew's campaign between 1838 and 1847, that started the shift; others looked more to rising educational standards, even the new enthusiasm for athletics and sports generally. However this may be, in 1852 Alexander built a brand-new brewery which quickly became a major force in the burgeoning Irish porter and stout market. The brewery story is told in Chapter 4.

On 29 May 1857, fifteen of Alexander's partners, prominent amongst whom was Adam, gathered together and presented him with a magnificent silver épergne. It was made by Hunt & Russell of London in 1856 at a cost of 250 guineas [£16,000 in 2000]. The inscription and names of the donors are as follows:

> Presented to Alexander Findlater, Esq., of Johnstown House, County Dublin, by his 15 partners whose names are hereon inscribed as a token of their respect and esteem for his many excellent qualities.
>
> William Todd, Bruce Todd, Robert Gladstone, John Carmichael, John Blood, Gilbert Burns, John Findlater, Ivie Mackie, William Williamson, Adam S. Findlater, John Smith, John F. Corscaden, W. T. McConkey, Thomas Gordon, Henry W. Todd.

It was said that Alexander was an exceedingly good judge of character, an attribute that enabled him to place implicit trust in all those whom he selected, and at the time of his death he had, it was computed, no fewer than twenty-two partnerships in various businesses. I asked a graphologist[14] to examine his handwriting for clues to his character. His judgement was that Alexander was 'zealous in approach to everything, he could motivate others with his enthusiasm. It was important that he be in charge. His sharp mind would ensure that he understood the rationale behind what was told to him. There was a strong element of generosity in his character. His emotions were always close to the surface.'

Family responsibilities

Although he was to remain unmarried, Alexander had many family responsibilities, especially for the children of his deceased brothers, William and John. Straight away after William's death in 1831 he was paying for seven-year-old Billy's 'teaching' and did a good job judging from the letters in Chapter 3. He also contributed to the education of Billy's sisters—Janet known as Jessie, Sophia and Margaret, a baby in arms. He paid his mother a regular allowance and in 1836 became responsible for Captain John's four young children. They lived with his sister Susanna who was married to sea captain John Snowden. And then, as if that was not enough, his sister Helen, married to Northern Ireland merchant Robert Corscaden, was widowed in 1841 and he contributed to the upkeep and education of her two sons. Thus it is not surprising to find him investing in a larger house when in 1842 he paid £1,000 fine [£58,000] for the lease of Johnstown Farm, at the top of Knockmaroon Hill in Chapelizod, just outside Dublin. It was probably some 45 acres. The farm was well stocked with 26 Kerry heifers, 2 milch cows, 2 fillies, 2 mares, 4 pigs, and 1 donkey plus implements and feeding bringing the total value to over £500 [£30,000] in 1846. The house has, alas, now been demolished.

There was quite a little Scots community around there. His associate Gilbert Burns, who was married to Jemima Ferrier, lived nearby in Knockmaroon Lodge,* and her father Alexander Ferrier lived at Belvue Park. William English lived nearby in Farmley. (This house, now Farmleigh, was bought in 1870 by Edward Cecil Guinness, First Earl of Iveagh, and extensively remodelled as a spectacular Victorian neo-classical mansion. It was acquired by the state in 1999.) Another of Scottish ancestry, James W. Mackey, lived in Clonsilla House.

Alexander's ledger records family expenditure. The annual account for groceries from Findlaters in 1848 was £81 6s 1d [£5,000], the man servant's wages were £3 for three months. Catherine, the cook, received £2 10s, presumably also for three months, a dress for his niece Sophia cost £3 8s, Kelly the shoemaker got 10s, life membership of the nearby Zoological Gardens for the children's pleasure and education cost £10 [£630], and in November 1849 for a family holiday, the passage cost £71 2s [£4,500] and he took £25 [£1,500] for expenses.

In 1852, 11 tons of coal from Thomas Heiton cost £7 13s [£550], the Chamber of Commerce was still £1 10s, the cook's wages had increased to £3 for three months, he paid £21 for a new car with an old one in exchange. In 1855 he bought a brougham from the reputable coach builders John Hutton & Sons for £146 4s [£8,700] and in 1859 sold his old one for £75 [£4,700]. In 1868 he spent £68 18s 6d on repairs to one of his broughams. In 1853 he gave two of his nieces £500 [£31,500] each and in 1858 he took on the cost of his Blood grand-nephew's schooling. The Scottish genre painter Erskine Nicol received the enormous sum

* Gilbert Burns lived here until his death on 9 October 1881 aged seventy-seven; he is buried in the Church of Ireland graveyard in Castleknock. His brother William died in Portarlington on 11 June 1878 aged eighty-six, and is buried in Mount Jerome.

Alexander 1797–1873

of £105 [£7,000] for a painting called 'The Chiropodist'. He also gave his nephew Billy a present of £500.

Charitable donations

Alexander was now well-off, despite all his family obligations. This enabled him to fulfil the Presbyterian ideal of donating substantial sums of money to charity. His most conspicuous contribution to Dublin was his offer to finance a splendid new place of worship for the Presbyterian congregation of St Mary's Abbey.

It is a curious feature of Dublin's 19th-century history that in 1865 the brewer Benjamin Lee Guinness financed the refurbishment of St Patrick's Cathedral; the distiller Henry Roe, in 1870, underwrote the reconstruction of Christ Church Cathedral, at a cost that staggered even his large fortune.* For a lesser, but still significant sum, Alexander, the wine merchant, built the Presbyterians a fine new place of worship in the city centre. The soda water manufacturer, Henry Bewley, proprietor of Bewley and Draper of Mary Street, in 1862, contributed a generous sum towards the completion of another place of worship, the Merrion Hall in Merrion Street[15], now the Davenport Hotel.

The Rev. W. B. Kirkpatrick DD in 1865 told the story of Findlater's Church:

> It had been for some time a subject of friendly discussion amongst the members of the congregation of St. Mary's Abbey whether they should continue to worship in the old church or build for themselves a new church in some more prominent position in the city. The difficulty was unexpectedly solved by the generous proposal of Mr Findlater, a member of the Presbyterian congregation of Kingstown, to build a church for the people of Mary's Abbey at his own sole expense, so soon as they obtained a suitable site. An admirable site was selected in Rutland Square, [now Parnell Square] for which the congregation paid the sum of £2,600 [£150,000].†

The foundation of the new building was laid in November 1862, and the work was completed in October 1864. It was in the newly fashionable 'Gothic' style, richly decorated. The church cost '£13,394 9s. 11d. and included £1,000 alleged additions, the builder Samuel Bolton having claimed that he lost by the contract'–or so Alexander recorded in his private ledgers! The following description

* It was said that this munificence cost Roe his distillery and he died in poor circumstances. The industry attributed another reason: he imported a substantial shipment of barley from Russia that was not sweet and sound and affected his whiskey thus destroying his market.

† On this site formerly stood Headford House, the town house of the Earl of Bective; and an even earlier occupant was Thomas Cobbe, son of Charles Cobbe, Archbishop of Dublin 1743-65 (M. D. C. Bolton, *Headford House* Dublin: The Fieldgate Press 1999).

of the building was given in *Saunder's Newsletter* (19 November 1864):*

> The church is in the early English style–a modification of the Gothic. It is built of Dalkey granite, dressed with Portland stone; and its carved ornamentation and lofty spire, wrought out in this material, form an object of peculiar beauty.
>
> The frontage towards Frederick Street is 142 feet, and that towards Rutland Square [now Parnell Square] is 60 feet. The former or longer side of the edifice is divided into three bays, each having a pointed roof, and a large five-light window richly traceried at the head. The bays are divided by massive buttresses. The end towards Rutland Square has the principal entrance to the church. The light window, or rather series of windows, light a vestibule within, approached by the main entrance. Above these vestibule windows is the grand window of the building, twenty eight feet in height by fourteen in breadth.
>
> This is a 'Memorial' Window, erected by the congregation.
>
> It contains, at the centre, the arms and monogram of Mr Findlater, and on blue glass at the bottom are the words: 'To commemorate the munificence, and to perpetuate the name of Alexander Findlater, the founder and donor of this Church'. The entire window is filled with beautifully stained glass, presenting texts of Scripture on a variously ornamented ground.
>
> Amongst these are the following cautionary lines:
>
> *Behold the heaven of heavens cannot contain thee*
> *Much less this house that I have built*†
> *God forbid that I should glory*
> *Save in the cross at our Lord Jesus Christ.*‡
>
> The centre of the church is lighted by six handsome mediaeval coronas of thirty lights each, suspended from the roof. They were made expressly for the church, to the design of the Architect, Mr Heiton of Perth, by Messrs Edmondson and Co., of Capel Street, to whom the whole gas-lighting was entrusted. The effect is very good—quite in keeping with the building, and when lighted the whole church is brilliantly illuminated. The galleries and staircases are lighted by massive brackets, and the lobbies and vestibules by handsome circular lanterns, with mediaeval brass mounting. The pulpit and reading desk and choir, of stained woodwork, carved in Gothic style, form per-

The Church.

SERVICES AND ANTHEMS.

A deputation of the parishioners of St. Andrew's waited upon Alexander Findlater, Esq., J.P., on Tuesday last, for the purpose of presenting to him an address, acknowledging his generous donation of £1,000 towards the completion of the parish church. They were very kindly received by Mr. Findlater, who expressed strongly the gratification which he felt in helping forward so good a work. The address will be found in another column.

MISCELLANEOUS

TO ALEXANDER FINDLATER, Esq., J.P.

11TH FEB., 1869.

DEAR SIR,—

We, the undersigned members of the Building Committee of St. Andrew's Parish, desire to express to you our grateful sense of the generosity which prompted you to contribute the munificent sum of £1,000 towards the completion of our new Church, and of the liberality of spirit thus manifested by you as a member of a different Christian denomination, for which you had previously shown your full appreciation by building for them, entirely at your own cost, a noble House for the worship of Almighty God. This did not hinder you from giving us assistance in our similar work. We are also deeply sensible of the kind consideration with which you consented to pay the amount at once (when you heard that we were pressed for funds to carry on the work), and thus to forego the important condition specified in the first intimation of your generous intentions.

We remain, dear Sir,
Your's faithfully and obliged,
CADW. WOLSELEY, Adn., Vicar.
FRANCIS C. HAYES, } Curates.
CHAS. EDWD. WRIGHT, }
J. MARSHALL MURRAY, } Churchwardens.
CHAS. R. TROUTON, }
JAS. F. WRIGHT, }
ALEX. COMYNS.
CHAS. ALLEN.
FREDK. LEWIS.
THOS. PETTIGREW.
JEREMIAH SWITZER.
HENRY HAYES.
HENRY ANDREWS.

Public appreciation of Alexander's contribution to St. Andrew's church in Suffolk Street, now Dublin Tourism Offices

* Samuel Bolton established the Rathmines Road Works in 1852, located on the corner of Lower Rathmines Road and the Grand Canal. Among the notable works he built were the Ulster Bank in College Green, Christ Church, Leeson Park, and the Iveagh Buildings, Patrick Street. The firm closed in 1929 and the premises were sold to Mr G. A. Brittain for the assembly of Morris cars.

† Based on King James version Kings 8 verse 27.

‡ King James version Galatians 6 verse 14.

haps the chief embellishment of the interior. The seats are of red deal, carved and stained in imitation of oak, and constructed on the modern longitudinal plan, each being decorated with fleur de lis at the ends. The accommodation is sufficient for 850 persons. It is heated with hot air pipes. There is a suite of rooms at the end of the church, and a schoolroom underneath it. All the windows, it should be mentioned, are filled with richly stained glass, which has been supplied by Mr Ballantyne, of Edinburgh. The plans were prepared by Mr Heiton of Perth, Architect; and the contract was entrusted to Mr Samuel Bolton, of Richmond Street.

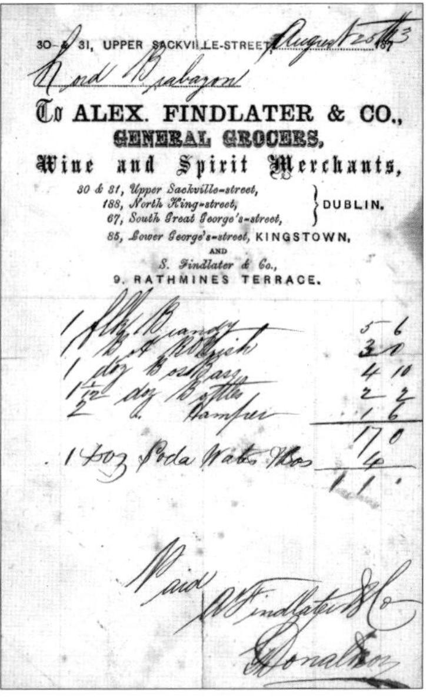

30 & 31, UPPER SACKVILLE-STREET, August 20th 1873

Lord Brabazon

To ALEX. FINDLATER & CO.,
GENERAL GROCERS,
Wine and Spirit Merchants,
30 & 31, Upper Sackville-street,
188, North King-street,
67, South Great George's-street, DUBLIN.
85, Lower George's-street, KINGSTOWN,
AND
S. Findlater & Co.,
9. RATHMINES TERRACE.

Paid
A. Findlater & Co

A sole surviving invoice from 1873—for the account of Lord Brabazon

Alexander's munificence did not end with the Abbey Presbyterian Church, nor was it limited to the Presbyterian congregation. In 1869 he subscribed £1,000 [£60,000] to the completion of St Andrew's, the Church of Ireland parish church in Suffolk Street (now Dublin Tourism's main tourist information centre).* His regular donations to charity were sizeable and are all recorded in his ledgers. From 1860 to 1865 they averaged £750 per annum [£45,000]. In 1860 he made a £100 [£6,000] donation to the new Presbyterian Church in Rathgar. The Greenock Academy received £50 [£3,000] and the Scots Church in Kingstown £1,017 [£61,000]. From 1866 to 1869 he averaged over £1,000 [£60,000] per annum. For the subsequent four years to his death in 1873 his donations amounted to £2,796 [£170,000]; £4,807 [£300,000]; £4,796 [£270,000] £3,750 [£200,000] per annum. He selected his charities carefully. He looked after the Dublin hospitals generously; he was on the investment committee in the Royal Hospital for Incurables in Donnybrook with Frederick Stokes and William Digges La Touche. Dr Helen Burke, in the history of the hospital, writes:

> They proceeded to plan the investment of legacies and donations and to change the hospital's investments in accordance with their knowledge of the stock market. Under their stewardship the hospital's annual income from investments went up from £583-0-4 in 1862 to £1454-14-7 in 1872 [£83,000]. Very often stockbrokers who were friends of these men would carry out transactions for the hospital without charging any fee . . . Thanks to the commitment of these men the hospital got sound financial advice during this crucial decade.

In 1866, during a time of rapid expansion in the hospital, two new wings were added and the new wards furnished through the gifts of donors, Alexander contributing £250 [£15,000].

He gave £1,000 [£60,000] for a Findlater scholarship in Glasgow university

* This confirms my Aunt Sheila's story that whenever she was in that part of town with her father, he would point up to the steeple and say: 'That's ours!'

Adam Seaton—Alexander's brother and partner in Dublin

and £100 [£6,000] to Monkstown Roman Catholic Church, £100 to a Methodist Chapel and £25 to the Lord Mayor of London's fund for Persian famine relief. As many as one hundred and fifty separate charities benefited each year and almost all the Dublin hospitals benefited in his will as they had in his lifetime.

His brother and partner, Adam, was equally active in charitable donations. In 1866 he was quietly dispensing £3,000 per annum [£180,000], in his latter years divided between some three hundred beneficiaries. Since he was a busy man, it seems likely that most of these donations were as a result of solicitations, which implies a formidable correspondence.

Alexander and Adam were particularly generous to the new Presbyterian theological college in Belfast. In 1870 Alexander gave them £1,000 [£60,000] of railway stock to provide for two scholarships with an annual value of £25 each [£1,500]. The following year Alexander was written to concerning the 'bankrupt condition' of the college. In due time he promised £1,500 [£90,000] on condition that another £3,500 [£200,000] be raised to reach £5,000 [£300,000] in all. There was a distinct possibility that this condition would not be fulfilled until a Mrs Gamble undertook to contribute a sum equal to Alexander's. In addition to this he gave £300 [£18,000] for the purchase of books.*

In 1876, three years after Alexander's death, the college approached his brother Adam about a professional endowment fund to increase the remuneration paid to the staff. After some reflection, Adam indicated that he would contribute £1,000 [£60,000] towards the fund on condition that four other donations of the same amount were forthcoming. They found these conditions exacting and just as his offer was in danger of lapsing owing to the non-fulfilment of the conditions, there was a turn of events. I quote from Robert Allen's history of the Presbyterian College

> In a conversation between him [Professor J. L. Porter] and Findlater there was some discussion regarding the buildings still required for the College—three more staff residences, a chapel and additional student chambers. 'How much are these likely to cost?' inquired Findlater. 'About ten thousand pounds, I should estimate,' replied Porter. 'Very well,' said the Dublin merchant, 'let the Church raise the ten thousand pounds

* The library, opened in 1873, is now one of the country's main theological libraries.

Stock of Whiskey in Bond April 21, 1860

Recapitulation

	P	B	H	Qr	Total Puns
John Jameson & Son	,	29	51	16	58½
Henry Roe & Sons	18	75	67	7	128¼
Jameson & Robertson	"	18	3	-	19½
John Busby & Sons	5	33	6	-	41
M. McFarlane & Co	5	99	38	"	123
John Gourlay & Co	"	5	"	"	5
Norman Buchanan	2	"	"	"	2
J & R Mutter	4	"	"	2	4½
Bankier Distillery Co	7	"	"	"	7
	41	259	165	25	388¾

Findlater's stock of whiskey from various distilleries in bond, April 1860. 'A year later the stock of John Jameson at 172 Puncheons surpassed that of Henry Roe at 63½ Puns and by 1877 our stock of Jameson had risen to 407 puncheons out of a total of 692' [Puncheon = 130 gallons held at 20 per cent over-proof in bond as against a resale strength of 25 per cent under-proof].

already agreed by the Assembly for the Professional Fund and I undertake, at my own expense, to complete the buildings. But I must insist on two things—that the money be raised by 30 June 1878, and that my name be not disclosed, at least for the present.' . . . This was a bold and generous gesture on the part of Findlater. At one step, and in order to stimulate the Church to greater activity, he had increased his original offer eleven-fold, and the total sum now within the grasp of the trustees was twenty thousand pounds [£1.2m], one half of which was to be to the Endowment Fund, and the other half to the new buildings. This was the most munificent offer yet made to the College, and when it was stated in public that an 'unknown friend' had acted with such vision and altruism there was much speculation as to his identity; and, with a new sense of urgency, fresh efforts were put forth . . . The goal was reached at the eleventh hour.

The chief addition to the college, made possible by the increased endowment, was the chapel with the adjoining facility room. The windows of the chapel, which were donated by three families, including Adam's widow who generously donated £500 [£30,000] towards the erection of two of them, were to be the cause of some controversy. The original plan for these had been to include religious symbols on these windows, but this raised purist hackles among the Presbyterian community, who feared ritualistic influences. The upshot was that two of the windows displayed the coat of arms of the college's great benefactor. However during a renovation some years ago all the memorial windows were mysteriously removed from the chapel.

The association of the scholarship with Findlater's drinks business was to cause more trouble. In 1927 controversy in connection with temperance and the Church entered what a newspaper called 'a new and regrettable phase'. The Presbyterian Church was accused of condemning the drink traffic while enjoying the fruits of the Findlater scholarships in the Assembly's college—benefactions drawn from alcoholic liquors. So intense had feeling become that it was suggested in certain influential quarters that the Church should discontinue these particular scholarships altogether; but in that case what would become of the trust funds? Give them to charity? Happily the scholarships are still being awarded as we enter the 21st century.

Growth in wines

All this time the business was flourishing in wines, spirits, beers and tea, both in Dublin and through the London outlets. A measure of that success can be seen from the duty paid on wine at the port of Dublin in 1867. There were 77 merchants on the complete list. Surprisingly Gilbeys, whose Irish branch was opened in 1859, are missing from the list.

Importer	*Duty £*
R. J. Turbett	7,423
J. & G. Campbell	3,937
T. W. & J. Kelly	3,549
Wm. & P. Thompson	2,996
J. McCullagh, Son & Co.	2,599
A. Findlater & Co.	2,523
Bewley and Draper	2,175
Thompson, D'Olier	2,143
Kinahan & Sons	2,047
Drake & McComas	2,006
T. Bewley & Co.	1,965
H. Brennan	1,912
G. F. Brooke & Son	1,912

Note: £1 in 1887 is equivalent to £60 in 2000

Growth in teas

As we have seen, we first sold tea in the 1830s when all tea came from China. By the 1860s the firm had considerably increased the volume of tea handled. In April of 1859 year we held 407 chests in stock, of which 349 were held in bond, i.e. the duty had not yet been paid on them. A chest held approximately 100 lbs of tea. The duty rate was 1s 5d per lb on a wholesale cost ex duty of between 1s 2½d per lb to 2s 10d per lb, quite some duty rate! Teas were advertised at 3s 8d for breakfast tea, 4s 0d for black tea and 5s 0d for orange Pekoe. The earliest arrival of Indian that I can trace was on 31 May 1861 when it is recorded in the cash book that we paid duty on 6 chests—528 lbs—of Assam which was shipped

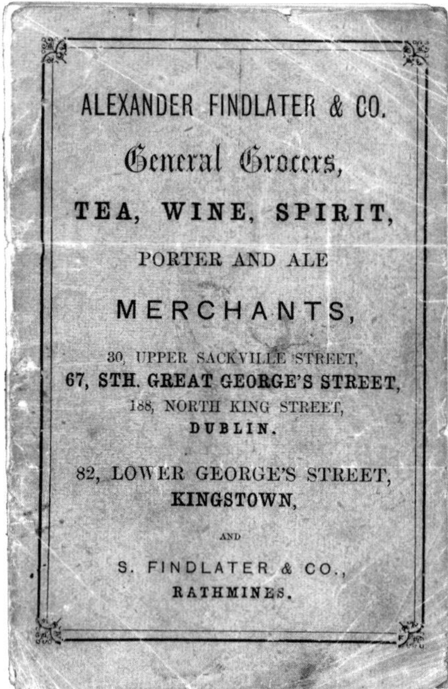

ALEXANDER FINDLATER & CO.

General Grocers,

TEA, WINE, SPIRIT,

PORTER AND ALE

MERCHANTS,

30, UPPER SACKVILLE STREET,
67, STH. GREAT GEORGE'S STREET,
188, NORTH KING STREET,
DUBLIN.

82, LOWER GEORGE'S STREET,
KINGSTOWN,

AND

S. FINDLATER & CO.,
RATHMINES.

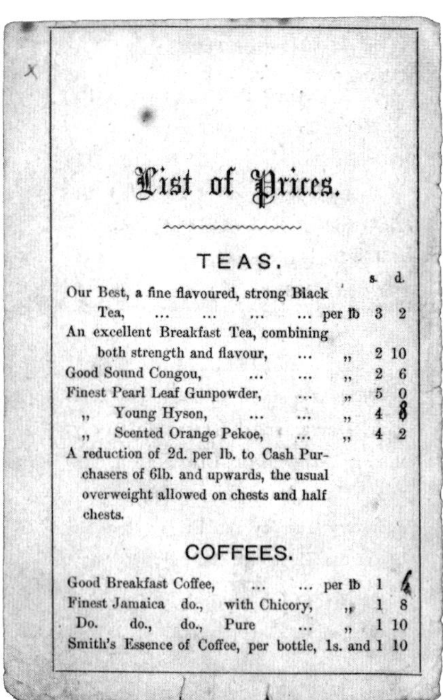

List of Prices.

TEAS.

		s.	d.
Our Best, a fine flavoured, strong Black Tea, ...	per lb	3	2
An excellent Breakfast Tea, combining both strength and flavour, ...	„	2	10
Good Sound Congou, ...	„	2	6
Finest Pearl Leaf Gunpowder, ...	„	5	0
„ Young Hyson, ...	„	4	8
„ Scented Orange Pekoe, ...	„	4	2

A reduction of 2d. per lb. to Cash Purchasers of 6lb. and upwards, the usual overweight allowed on chests and half chests.

COFFEES.

		s.	d.
Good Breakfast Coffee, ...	per lb	1	4
Finest Jamaica do., with Chicory,	„	1	8
Do. do., do., Pure ...	„	1	10
Smith's Essence of Coffee, per bottle, 1s. and		1	10

8 ALEX. FINDLATER & CO.'S

SUNDRIES.

		s.	d.
Finest Java Rice, ...	per stone	5	0
„ Patna „	„ „	3	6
„ Arracan „	„ „	3	0
„ Ground „	„ „	4	6
„ Pearl Sago, ...	„ „	4	6
„ Tapioca „	„ lb.	0	8
„ St. Vincent Arrowroot, ...	„ „	1	2
„ Italian Maccaroni, ...	„ „	1	0
„ „ Vermicelli, ...	„ „	1	0
„ French Maccaroni, ...	„ „	0	10
„ „ Vermicelli, ...	„ „	0	10
„ Russian Isinglass, ...	„ oz.	1	4
„ Pearl Barley, ...	„ stone	3	0
„ Split Peas, ...	„ „	2	6
Fine Mustard, ...	„ lb.	1	2
Superfine „	„ „	1	6
Double Superfine, 1, ½, and ¼ lb. tins,	„	1	10
Refined Table Salt, in drums, ...	each	0	2
Saltpetre, ...	„ lb.	0	8
Carbonate of Soda, ...	„ „	0	3
Italian Liquorice, ...	„ „	1	6
Carraway Seeds, ...	„ „	0	8
Patent Gelatine, per packet, each, 5d. and		0	10
Swinborne's Patent Refined Isinglass, in 1 oz. packets, ...	each,	1	0
Prepared Barley and Groats, in 6d. packets, & 1s. tins.			
Keiller's Dundee Marmalade, ...	per doz.	8	0
„ Jams, ...	„ „	12	0
Calf's Foot Jelly, ...	per quart	2	6
„ „	„ pint	1	6
Orange Jelly, ...	per quart	2	6
Lemon „	„ „	2	6

10 ALEX. FINDLATER & CO.'S

SPIRITS AND CORDIALS—*con.*

		s.	d.
Ginger Wine, ...	per dozen,	14	0
Hollands Geneva, per Case (as imported)		32	0
Orange Bitters, ...	„	36	0
Finest Cognac Brandy (as imported)	„	60	0
Do, do., ...	„	52	0
Ginger Brandy, ...	„	42	0

WINES:

		Per Dozen Quarts		Pints	
		s.	d.	s.	d.
Port,	New bottled, ...	28	0	15	0
	Good Old, ...	36	0	18	0
	Fine do., ...	42	0	21	0
	Superior Old, ...	48	0		
	Very Choice Old, ...				
	Vintage, ...				
Sherry,	Fine Light Dinner, ...	20	0		
	Good, ...	24	0		
	Do. Pale or Golden,	30	0	15	0
	Superior Pale or Golden,	36	0	18	0
	Choice do. do.	42	0		
	Amontillado, ...	42	0		
	Solera, ...	42	0		
	Oloroso, ...	48	0		
	Manzanilla, ...	42	0	21	0
Madeira,	Fine Old E. India, ...	72	0		
Bucellas,	... ...	28	0		
Calcavella,	... ...	26	0		
Lisbon,	Dry or Sweet, ...	26	0		

Extracts from an 1865 price list. Finest Java rice, at 5s per stone, works out at £1.10 per pound in today's money, almost exactly today's price. The bottle sizes are quarts and pints. (A quart contains 1.13cl and a pint .60cl. Today a wine bottle holds .75cl and a spirit bottle .70cl.)

6 ALEX. FINDLATER & CO.'S

PICKLES AND SAUCES.

		s.	d.
West India Pickles, ...	per doz.	18	0
Mixed, quarts	„	18	0
„ pints	„	10	6
Girkins, „	„	10	6
Onions, „	„	10	6
Walnuts, „	„	10	6
Piccalilli, „	„	10	6
Essence of Anchovies, ...	„	10	0
Do. do., pints ...	„	16	0
Essence of Lobster, ...	„	12	0
Harvey's Sauce, ...	„	12	0
Do. do., pints ...	„	22	0
Worcester do., ...	„	14	0
Do. do., pints ...	„	24	0
Reading do., ...	„	14	0
Tomato do., ...	„	12	0
Do. do., pints ...	„	24	0
Mushroom Ketchup, ...	„		
Do. do., pints ...	„	12	0
Chilli Vinegar, ...	„	8	0
Do. do., pints ...	„	14	0
French Capers, (2 oz.) ...	„	8	0
Do. do., (4 oz.) ...	„	12	0
Gorgona Anchovies, ...	„	14	0
Olive Oil (in bottles), ... 30s., 16s., and		10	0
Do., (in flasks), ...	„	10	0
French Vinegar, ...	per gal.	3	0
Spanish Olives, ...	per doz.	18	0
French do., ...	„	14	0
Oriental Pickle, ...	„	18	0
India Soy, ...	„	10	0
Tarragon Vinegar, ...	„	8	0

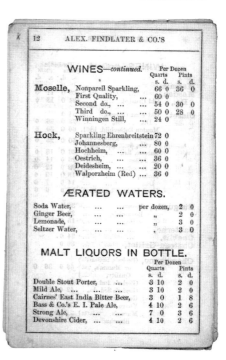

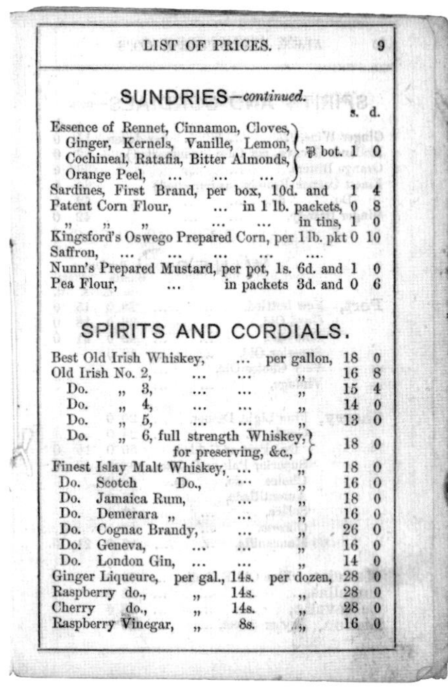

LIST OF PRICES. 9

SUNDRIES—*continued.*

	s.	d.
Essence of Rennet, Cinnamon, Cloves, Ginger, Kernels, Vanille, Lemon, Cochineal, Ratafia, Bitter Almonds, Orange Peel, ... ℔ bot.	1	0
Sardines, First Brand, per box, 10d. and	1	4
Patent Corn Flour, ... in 1 lb. packets,	0	8
„ „ „ ... ... in tins,	1	0
Kingsford's Oswego Prepared Corn, per 1 lb. pkt	0	10
Saffron, ...		
Nunn's Prepared Mustard, per pot, 1s. 6d. and	1	0
Pea Flour, ... in packets 3d. and	0	6

SPIRITS AND CORDIALS.

		s.	d.
Best Old Irish Whiskey, ...	per gallon,	18	0
Old Irish No. 2, ...	„	16	8
Do. „ 3, ...	„	15	4
Do. „ 4, ...	„	14	0
Do. „ 5, ...	„	13	0
Do. „ 6, full strength Whiskey, for preserving, &c.,		18	0
Finest Islay Malt Whiskey, ...	„	18	0
Do. Scotch Do., ...	„	16	0
Do. Jamaica Rum, ...	„	18	0
Do. Demerara „ ...	„	16	0
Do. Cognac Brandy, ...	„	26	0
Do. Geneva, ...	„	16	0
Do. London Gin, ...	„	14	0
Ginger Liqueure, per gal., 14s.	per dozen,	28	0
Raspberry do., „ 14s.	„	28	0
Cherry do., „ 14s.	„	28	0
Raspberry Vinegar, „ 8s.	„	16	0

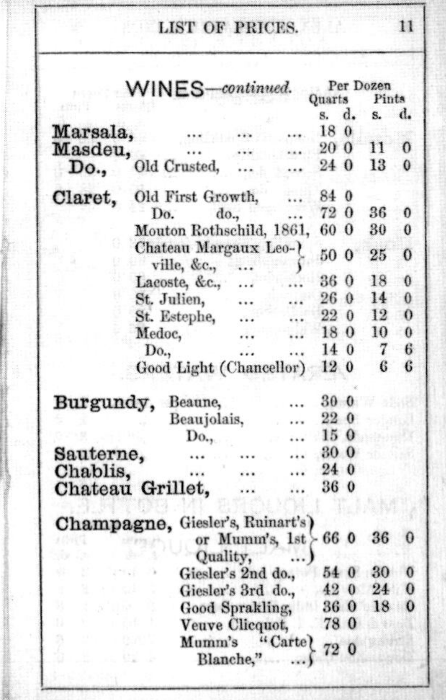

LIST OF PRICES. 11

WINES—*continued.*

		Per Dozen Quarts s.	d.	Pints s.	d.
Marsala,	... ...	18	0		
Masdeu,	... ...	20	0	11	0
Do.,	Old Crusted, ...	24	0	13	0
Claret,	Old First Growth, ...	84	0		
	Do. do., ...	72	0	36	0
	Mouton Rothschild, 1861,	60	0	30	0
	Chateau Margaux Leoville, &c., ...	50	0	25	0
	Lacoste, &c., ...	36	0	18	0
	St. Julien, ...	26	0	14	0
	St. Estephe, ...	22	0	12	0
	Medoc, ...	18	0	10	0
	Do., ...	14	0	7	6
	Good Light (Chancellor)	12	0	6	6
Burgundy,	Beaune, ...	30	0		
	Beaujolais, ...	22	0		
	Do., ...	15	0		
Sauterne,	... ...	30	0		
Chablis,	... ...	24	0		
Chateau Grillet,	... ...	36	0		
Champagne,	Giesler's, Ruinart's or Mumm's, 1st Quality, ...	66	0	36	0
	Giesler's 2nd do.,	54	0	30	0
	Giesler's 3rd do.,	42	0	24	0
	Good Sprakling,	36	0	18	0
	Veuve Clicquot,	78	0		
	Mumm's "Carte Blanche," ...	72	0		

12 ALEX. FINDLATER & CO.'S

WINES—*continued.*

		Per Dozen Quarts s.	d.	Pints s.	d.
Moselle,	Nonpareil Sparkling,	66	0	36	0
	First Quality, ...	60	0		
	Second do., ...	54	0	30	0
	Third do., ...	50	0	28	0
	Winningen Still, ...	24	0		
Hock,	Sparkling Ehrenbreitstein	72	0		
	Johannesberg, ...	80	0		
	Hochheim, ...	60	0		
	Oestrich, ...	36	0		
	Deidesheim, ...	20	0		
	Walporzheim (Red) ...	36	0		

ÆRATED WATERS.

		s.	d.
Soda Water, ...	per dozen,	2	0
Ginger Beer, ...	„	2	0
Lemonade, ...	„	3	0
Seltzer Water, ...	„	3	0

MALT LIQUORS IN BOTTLE.

	Per Dozen Quarts s.	d.	Pints s.	d.
Double Stout Porter, ...	3	10	2	0
Mild Ale, ...	3	10	2	0
Cairnes' East India Bitter Beer,	3	0	1	8
Bass & Co.'s E. I. Pale Ale,	4	10	2	6
Strong Ale, ...	7	0	3	6
Devonshire Cider, ...	4	10	2	6

via London from Maxwell in Calcutta. We later claimed to have been the first Irish firm to import Indian tea. In that month we also paid duty of £443 18s 3d on 53 chests of China tea brought through brokers Thomas Bewley & Co. By the end of the century India had replaced China as the main source of tea. In 1863 Gladstone halved the tea duty from 1s to 6d per lb and Findlaters were receiving regular shipments from Calcutta, often shipped on *The City of Poonah.**

The family

In 1860, with the family educated, Alexander sold his leasehold interest in the farm for £740 [£44,000] and paid £2,000 [£120,000] for a fine house called The Slopes in the fashionable Monkstown area by the sea in south county Dublin. There he was joined by his widowed sisters Helen and Susanna. Susanna managed the household and he paid her a regular sum. On 20 April 1846, Adam married Jane Martin Johnston–she was known as 'The Aunt Jane'. (Her sister Mary was later to marry John, my great-grandfather.) His mother, whom Alexander had brought over from Glasgow in 1830, died in Rathmines two months later on 14 June 1846, and was buried in the family vault in Mount Jerome cemetery.

In the 1860s Jane and Adam lived near the 'Scotch' Church in Adelaide Road. Around 1870 they moved to a house called Melbeach in Monkstown, which, I am told, was specially designed for them, perhaps by the noted architect, John McCurdy, whose daughter was shortly to marry into the family.

By 1865 Alexander's net worth was over £220,000 [£13m]. He was a director of the Royal Bank of Ireland and as we have seen an active contributor to the city's main charities. In June 1865 his niece Elizabeth, sister of John, married Rev. William Clarke and Alexander paid Todd Burns £90 13s 6d [£5,500] for her outfit. His wedding present, a canteen of cutlery, was chosen in West & Son Jewellers in Grafton Street at a cost of £43 13s [over £2,500].

His niece Jessie had married Joseph Taylor of Melbourne, Australia in 1859 and in 1865 Alexander paid her expenses for a visit to Paris £22 17s 9d [£1,000]. Also in 1865 he paid Todd Burns £51 13s 2d [over £3,000] for goods despatched to Otago in New Zealand where his niece, one of Billy's sisters, had taken Henry Porson Morse as her second husband. He paid £2 15s to W. H. Smith for *The Times,* £4 [£240] annual membership of the Royal Irish Yacht Club, £14 [£840] for a twelve-month rail ticket to and from town and £10 [£60] for his church seat in Kingstown. He purchased his groceries from Findlater's Kingstown and wines from Findlater's Sackville Street and discharged the accounts annually in December and January respectively. The grocery bill for 1866 amounted to £59 15s [£3,600] and wines £97 [£5,800]. The 1869 figure for groceries was £97 17s 5d. Vegetables were obviously grown at The Slopes and the gardener, James

* Tea had long been a favourite with the taxman. The first British tax on tea was in 1660, when it was taxed in liquid, made-up, form, and accordingly had to be prepared in advance before being assessed by the exciseman. This could not have done much for its flavour. By 1689 tea was being taxed on the leaf. A duty of 5s per lb nearly killed the trade, but the rate was brought down to 1s in 1692. A further 1s per lb was added in 1695 to pay for expenses incurred a few years earlier 'for the reduction of Ireland'.

The family in 1869. *Left to right:* Adam, Susanna, Alexander, Helen

Barret, was paid 21s a week. (He was left £150 [£9,000] in Alexander's will.)

After his sister Susanna died in December 1871 he employed a houseman, David Cantillon, who was paid 20s a week with a £4 Christmas gratuity and left £25 in Alexander's will [£1,500]. The cook also received 20s a week and the housemaid 15s. There were also payments to a laundress. David noted sundry expenditure in the house book which Alexander discharged regularly. He continued to entertain and travel. On 27 February 1872 the account for dinner for fourteen amounted to £15 13s 2d [£900]. He liked his cigars and on this occasion paid £3 12s for six boxes of cigars, that is 12s a box. In October 1871 he took £35 [£2,000] cash for a trip to England, and in March the following year £17 10s. A trip to the continent required considerably more and in June 1873 'cash at starting for continent' was £230 [£13,000]. But Susanna's death hit him badly and visits to the health resort of Harrogate became more frequent. His well-worn bible showed him to be, as might be expected, a regular reader of the scriptures, and his expenditure in December 1872 of £146 [£8,800] on the granite monument over his vault in Mount Jerome cemetery showed some intimations of mortality. Although there are now sixteen interred there, not all are family, and the inscription simply states: 'The family burial place of Alexander Findlater'. I may well join them there.

In July 1873 Alexander made his last entries in the ledgers which he had assid-

The first show held at Ball's Bridge, Dublin, in 1871, by the Royal Agricultural Society of Ireland. Th
four provinces. Among the personalities portrayed in this typical Victorian panora

uously written up through his life: £1 16s for 3 boxes of cigars and £1 [£60] for the poor of York Street church. On Friday 8 August 1873, aged seventy-six, he died while taking the waters in Harrogate in England. His death was copiously noticed in the newspapers. One obituary is worth quoting at length as it not only remembers Alexander's fine character, but also paints a vivid picture of his funeral:

> It is with the most extreme regret we announce the demise of Alexander Findlater, Esq., J. P., of 30 and 31 Upper Sackville Street, and of The Slopes, Kingstown. The melancholy event took place yesterday morning at Gascoigne's Hotel, Harrowgate, where the lamented gentleman had gone for the good of his health, which had been failing for some time past. He had for a long series of years occupied a leading position amongst the merchants of our city, and was besides for several years a director of the Royal Bank. All classes thronged at the funeral and around his grave to do honour to the memory of a man distinguished as an enterprising merchant, a useful citizen, a public benefactor, and a generous friend and employer. The merchants and traders of Dublin—amongst whom the lamented gentleman occupied for years a foremost place—members of the learned professions, the clergy, members of the Municipal Corporation, of the Chamber of Commerce, the Dublin Port and Docks Board, Commissioners of the Kingstown and Rathmines and other townships, directors of banks and other public and mercantile institutions and companies attended in large numbers, and formed a funeral cortege not exceeded in extent and influence for many years in this city . . .

ows, the forerunners of the RDS Spring and Horse Shows, were held during August alternatively in the
ere the Prince of Wales, numerous lords and a few commoners, including Alexander Findlater.

It was announced that the funeral would leave The Slopes at nine o'clock this morning, but long before that hour a large number of carriages had arrived bringing gentlemen from Kingstown and Dublin and intermediate places. The funeral started at 9.15 and went slowly along the Rock Road to Ball's Bridge, then by the Clyde Road, Leeson Street, Adelaide Road, Circular Road, Clanbrassil Street on to Mount Jerome Cemetery. Along the route there were constant accessions of carriages so that by the time the cortege reached the South Circular Road it was composed of over 200 carriages.*

The remains were enclosed in a leaden coffin, surmounted by one of polished oak, on the breastplate of which was the simple inscription:

Alexander Findlater,
Died August 8, 1873

The Irish Times (14 August 1873) also wrote fully about the death of Alexander:

Today the grave closes over the remains of one of the most enterprising, spirited, and successful merchants of this city. Although Alexander Findlater was a Scotsman born, once he settled amongst us he became as Irish as the Irish themselves. He firmly adhered to the belief and the Church of his native land, but he was not merely tolerant but generous to the charities of all creeds. If he erected, at a cost of more than £13,000 the tasteful Church in Rutland Square, and presented it to his fellow worship-

* There were 239 private carriages at Benjamin Lee Guinness' funeral. (Michèle Guinness *The Guinness Spirit: Brewers and Bankers, Ministers and Missionaries* London: Hodder and Stoughton, 1999, p 140).

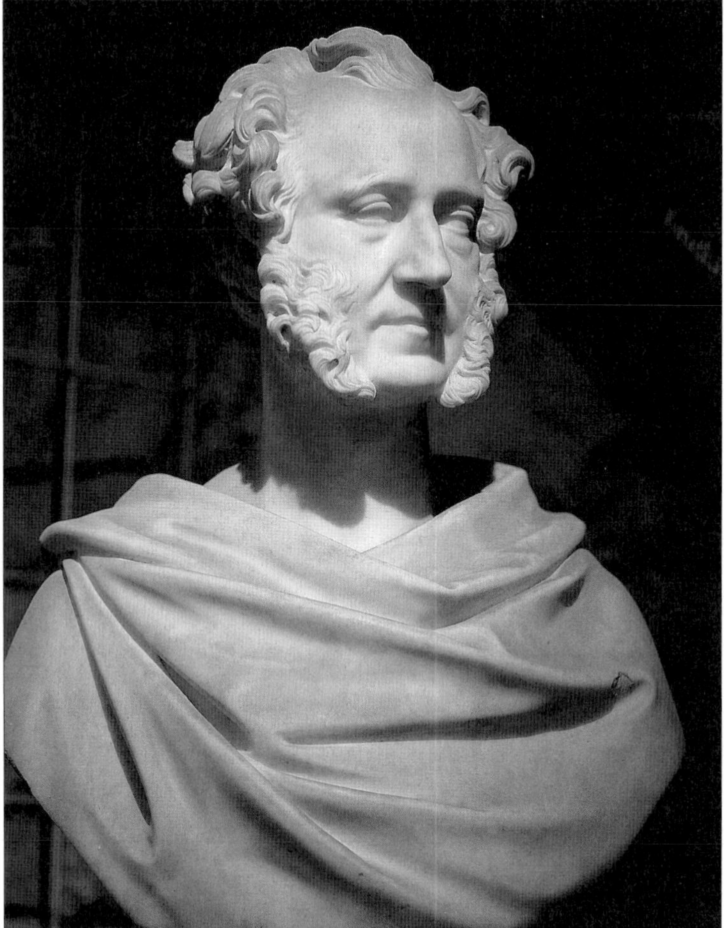

Bust of Alexander, in marble, executed in 1857, the work of Dublin sculptor John Edward Jones (1806–1862)

pers, he also gave most liberally to aid of Episcopalian communities. His name was constantly found in the lists of every subscription for any worthy public or charitable purpose.

Mr Findlater exhibited a wonderful ability—indeed almost an intuitive power—in the selection of his employees, many of whom, as time passed on, became his partners, and realised large fortunes. So early as 1834, in conjunction with Mr William Todd and others, he founded the well-known firm of Todd, Burns & Co., in which firm he continued to be a partner until death removed him. The Mountjoy Brewery, in Russell Street, is another of the numerous undertakings which the indomitable energy of Mr Findlater originated. At the time of his decease he was a partner, and that to a considerable amount in firms carrying on extensive business in London, Manchester, Brighton, Dublin and Kingstown. All of them are prosperous and flourishing . . . The biography of such a man must produce rich fruit, for example always is more impressive than precept. Fortunately for the future of this country, it is no longer considered to be outside the pale of gentility to engage in commerce or mercantile speculations. Industry is honoured and generally rewarded. The idle son of an indolent squire is no longer respected, and the excellence of the rule that what a true man finds to do he should do with all his might, is held by the autocracy itself. To young men entering upon business, no life is calculated to give more encouragement or better counsel than that of Alexander Findlater.

After Alexander's death Adam and Jane moved into The Slopes and nephew John and Mary to Melbeach. Adam lived on until 1879. On his passing at the age of seventy-one, it was reported: 'Adam was a kindly, genial man of unobtrusive manners, but genuine ability for business. Like other members of the family he was a liberal contributor to all our charitable institutions, and his private benevolence was never withheld from any real claim brought under his notice.'

In 1881, two years after Adam's death, his widow Jane was married again, to Dr John Blythe of Fitzwilliam Square, notwithstanding that her annuity from her late husband would halve to £400 a year [£24,000] in the case of that eventuality. However she was independently wealthy, not only as a Johnston of the milling family, but also through a slip-up by her late husband Adam. He failed to rewrite his will following the death of his brother Alexander in 1873, thus leaving many anomalies. In compliance with the Statutes of Distribution she became entitled to half the estate in addition to the fund set aside to provide her with an annuity. Thus in 1881 she had investments worth £89,000 [£6m] and was well able to buy The Slopes from the estate and live there in some style.

What the Blythes of Fitzwilliam Square drank 1880-99

A ledger recording, inter alia, purchases of wines from 1880 to 1899 gives a wonderful insight into the drinking habits of a well-off household in the late 19th century. During those years the Blythes bought over forty cases a year, and sometimes as many as sixty cases; they were obviously entertaining well. They usually bought six or seven cases of Champagne a year, vintage and non vintage, and half bottles, at prices between 74s and 90s a dozen; the same quantity of pale sherry at 24s to 36s a dozen, but port was the favourite at fifteen to sixteen cases. They paid 44s and 48s a dozen with the occasional vintage at 54s. This puts their consumption of fortified wines, ports and sherries, at over 50 per cent of all wines compared with the modern average of 2½ per cent.

Claret was in favour in the 1880s, averaging fifteen to sixteen cases a year, but later the 18s a dozen quality they were buying began to cloy and they moved on to a better standard of Burgundy—Beaune and Pommard, at 30s a dozen and got through some ten cases a year between 1892 and 1899. The only claret they bought in the 1890s were Chateau Margaux at 54s, 60s and 65s a dozen and Léoville Barton, mainly 1877, a well-rated pre-phylloxera vintage, at 60s a dozen. From 1880 to 1890 hock was the favoured white wine when it averaged four and a half cases, at 30s a dozen. Spirit purchases were modest at six bottles of brandy,

Adam and his wife Jane

six bottles of VSO whiskey and the occasional Islay malt; maybe Dr Blythe received generous Christmas boxes of spirits from his patients. Bottled water was an occasional purchase: Oberselters, Carrara and Zoedone.

Alexander's fortune

The values of Alexander's assets were updated annually in his ledgers. They rise from £7,675 [£400,000] in 1838 to £354,996 [£21m] in 1873. After 47 of his 50 years in trade, in 1870, his commercial partnerships were valued at £77,494 [£4.65m], 4.7 times his income from them; bonds and loans were £13,927 [£836,000]; bank and gas company shares (queer combination!) were £19,227 [£1.15m]; leasehold properties £13,550 [£813,000] and railway investments, some 25, had a value of £171,448 [£10.3m]; making a total in 1870 of £295,648 [almost £18m].

Of his commercial partnerships totalling £77,494, investments in the brewery £44,796 [£2.7m] and Todd Burns £17,711 [£1.06m] accounted for over 80 per cent. The brewery gave him a poor return on assets at 4.5 per cent, and from time to time generated actual losses, as in 1868 and 1869 and again in 1872. Todd Burns was satisfactory at 18.5 per cent and the wine and spirit firms both here and in England gave excellent returns on account of their low capital base.

The combined wealth of Alexander and Adam amounted to some £550,000, the equivalent of £30m in the year 2000 values; not a bad sum for two of modest origins and who had been so generous in life. By comparison, Benjamin Lee Guinness, who died in 1868, left an estate of £1.1 million [£66m], the largest at that time,[16] and from another great Irish wine dynasty Hugh Barton in Bordeaux estimated his wealth at £650,000 [£39m] in 1845.

So what happened to the fortune that Alexander created in his lifetime? The answer is that he dispersed it among his fourteen nephews and nieces, who were spread across the world, in Australia, New Zealand, England, the North of Ireland and of course Dublin. His residuary legatees and largest beneficiaries were his senior nephews Billy and John.

On the death of Adam, Billy, who was a solicitor, became sole proprietor of the brewery. Todd Burns and the English wine firms continued with their surviving partners. The Dublin business based around the Sackville Street shop (a mere 7 per cent of his total assets, but generating profits of £8,000 a year) went to his nephew John. We shall see how Billy and John fared in subsequent chapters.

Notes and references

1 T. M. Devine *The Scottish Nation 1700-2000* London: Allen Lane 1999 pp 134, 334, 263
2 George Williamson *Old Greenock from the Earliest Times to the Early Part of the Nineteenth Century 2* Paisley and London: Alexander Gardner 1886. The story was also published in *Greenock Herald*, 22 October 1881
3 Patrick O'Flaherty *Old Newfoundland: A History to 1843* St Johns: Long Beach Press 1999 p 122
4 Op. cit. p 127
5 Op. cit. p 127
6 Op. cit. p 128
7 See *The Digest of the Reports of the Commissioners of Inquiry into Excise Establishments and the Management and Collection of the Excise Revenue through-out the United Kingdom, 1836*
8 Walter Thomas Meyler, *Saint Catherine's Bells* Dublin: Cowen and Thomson 1870, Part Two p 271
9 Op. cit. Part 2 pp 64-5
10 E. J. Riordan *Modern Irish Trade and Industry*, London: Methuen 1920, pp 32, 33
11 Ernest R. Reader *The Story of the Burns & Laird Lines* Glasgow: Burns & Laird Ltd 1951
12 Meyler op. cit. vol. 1, p 43-4
13 This information is based on a letter from Alexander Napier Findlater of Dunedin, New Zealand dated 27 January 1971 and his subsequent research
14 Lawrence Warner, Personality Assessment Consultancy; he was certainly right in respect of his generosity. As we see later in the chapter he contributed large sums to charity
15 Meyler, Part Two p 14
16 Michèle Guinness *The Guinness Spirit: Brewers and Bankers, Ministers and Missionaries* London: Hodder and Stoughton, 1999, p 139

3. Billy, later Sir William, Findlater 1824–1906

Alexander the founder's eldest brother, William the ship broker, had four children. His only son, Billy, later Sir William, was born in 1824. In 1831, when Billy was seven years old, the senior William died in Londonderry at the age of thirty-nine, and as a result Billy and his three sisters spent much of their childhood in Dublin with their Uncle Alexander. Billy later made a successful career in the legal profession and for four years was a Liberal Member of Parliament for Monaghan, sitting as a moderate unionist. He took an active part in the passing of Gladstone's 1881 Land Act, which gave tenants the famous three Fs: fair rent, fixity of tenure and free sale. In 1879 he became proprietor of the Mountjoy Brewery (see Chapter 4).

The Scottish connections were still strong while the children were growing up, and young Billy's elderly cousin, the Rev. Charles Findlater from his parish in Newlands in Scotland, took a keen interest in his welfare. Surviving letters show a pleasant intimacy. The first was sent in 1834, when young Billy was ten.

> For Little Billy alias the Admiral.
>
> How do you do, Billy? And how is Gran Mamma? I trust this finds you both in good health. I doubt not that Grand Mamma is as kind to you as ever—and that you repay her kindness by endeavouring to please and oblige her.
>
> What are you learning at present? Do you continue at the Latin? I trust you are also becoming expert at writing and counting, with English, Geography, or probably also some swatch of civil or natural history—you cannot however attend to everything at once.
>
> What amusements and diversions have you? Do you sometimes regret the want of the Newlands schoolboys with whom you used to romp or have you got Irish little Teagues to supply their place?
>
> The Whitefords are all well—and since you left us there is an addition to the family of a bold, squalling little brat named James, after his father. We had an examination of the school last week—I made G. Williamson (who seems inclined to become a doctor) translate upon a slate a paragraph of Celsus from the Latin—and Aitkin to translate a paragraph from the French—and made both extract the square root—and both performed their tasks to satisfaction—and all the rest acquitted themselves well. Mr Whiteford's school is much increased, the one at Goldiesmill being given up.
>
> Mr Gladstone* goes out to Demerara, the beginning of May, to oversee schools upon a large estate belonging to Mr Gladstone of Liverpool and to preach to and cate-

* The Rev. William Gladstone was ordained in Newlands in April 1834 to go to Demerara as Minister of the gospel at the request of John Gladstone, owner of plantations there and of Fasque in Kincardineshire in north east Scotland not far from Aberdeen, and also of Liverpool. John Gladstone's fourth son, William Ewart, a Liberal, was Prime Minister in the latter half of the 19th century. The eldest son, Thomas, born 1804, was, as we have seen, a partner of Alexander Findlater.

Billy, 1824–1906, Solicitor, Brewery proprietor and M.P.

chise his Negroes. How did Grand Mamma pass the winter? Did she get a party made up for whist?

Write to me or your aunt and tell us all about it–and give my best wishes to your Uncle and Grand Mamma and Aunt Snowden.

Yours truly Chas. Findlater
Newlands 14 April 1834

PS. A newspaper came addressed to me in your hand, as your Aunt thought. Tell your Uncle the whiskie arrived safe—having escaped the various laws of the Excise, altho neither permit nor account came along with it. It seems very good, and we prefer it even to the Inneschonian.

A year later, a certain schoolmasterly facetiousness enters the correspondence:

To Billy Findlater
August 1835

Dear Sir,

I was well pleased to receive your letter—in which I have nothing to remark excepting your display of extreme modesty—so becoming in a young man–for, when speaking of yourself in the third person, instead of pushing yourself forward with a bushy cropped head and slender waist as an (I) I find you creep modestly forward with a most humble (i).

I delayed writing, endeavouring to procure for you Rupells popular lectures on natural philosophy, which I saw lately advertised, but of which I could not procure a copy either in Glasgow or in Edinburgh—the whole I presume having been bought out by those attending mechanics institutions—I therefore now send you a book which, tho' I consider it as in no way so useful, may nevertheless serve as a showbook – I consider it as the first stereotype publication edited in France—which country got the start of us in applying this cheap mode of printing to such books as seemed calculated to defray the expense by an extensive and continual demand. I trust you are now attending more to things than to mere words.

My parishioners, as a testimony of their regard, have subscribed for a marble bust of me–to be placed I presume in the Church—as there is no other place of public resort but the change house—and I presume you'll agree with me that it would be rather out of character to set me to preside over drunken orgies—I sat to the Sculptor eight different days in Edin. and am now returned.*

You may consider this as of the date of your receiving the book—I leave some empty space for your Aunt to speak a word in season to you if the spirit shall so move her.

Meantime, with best wishes to your Grandmother and uncle and aunt.

Yours truly, Chas. Findlater.

* This bust may be seen in the art gallery in Peebles.

Mary Jane Wolfe, Billy's first wife

Charles Findlater, born in 1754, graduated from Edinburgh University in 1770 and in 1777 was ordained assistant to his father, the Rev. Thomas Findlater. In 1790 he moved to the neighbouring parish of Newlands where he lived until 1835. He died in Glasgow in 1838, aged eighty-four. Charles was a scholar and an author; in 1802 he wrote *Findlater's Agriculture of the County of Peebles* and in 1830 published his *Sermons, or Essays as the reader shall choose to design them, upon Christian Duties.* In his retirement, in the winter of 1835–6, he translated *Roman Nights at the Tomb of the Scipios*[1] from Italian/Latin. His intention had been to give the translation to a publisher gratis, but alas upon so offering it, it was found that he had been anticipated by a London translator.

Charles then sent the two handwritten leather-bound manuscripts to young Billy in Dublin—'I doubt not but the work will afford you amusement as it has done to me.' Billy was then eleven years old. Charles wrote to him in November 1836 to reproach him for failing to thank him for the gift, forgetting perhaps what might be expected of a lad of that age—'little rogue that you are, you never have had the grace to thank me yet'.

Billy was apprenticed to a solicitor in 1840. From a letter written to Billy by his mother Sophia in Derry in November 1840, it is clear that his Uncle Alexander paid his apprenticeship fees. He also acted as his guarantor at the King's Inns. This was clearly not taken for granted, as she writes 'your uncle's truly noble and generous conduct to you and myself, I cannot express in as grateful terms as I would wish, but I must just repeat your own words and say as long as we live we can never forget?' The letter finishes 'let us ever rejoice with trembling and leave every thing in his hands who will never forsake those who trust in him.' Sophia died in 1870.

Billy was admitted as a solicitor in 1846, starting his professional career just at the beginning of the Great Famine of 1845–9.

Billy's first partnership was as Findlater & Lee. In 1851 he practised with Matthew Anderson, Chief Crown Solicitor for Ireland and father of Sir Robert Anderson, one-time Chief of the Criminal Investigation Department in England. He then appears to have joined John Wolfe, solicitor of Ormond Quay and Fitzwilliam Street as his junior partner. In 1853 he married Wolfe's daughter

Mary Jane. In 1856 he became a full partner and subsequently took over the practice on Wolfe's retirement. In 1863 we find him as Findlater & Collins from the same address (35 Ormond Quay) before practising on his own account as William Findlater & Co., ultimately taking his nephews Edward Neptune Blood and Adam Lloyd Blood into partnership. The practice continued until 1956, finally closing on the death of Ken Lloyd Blood, son of Adam Lloyd Blood.

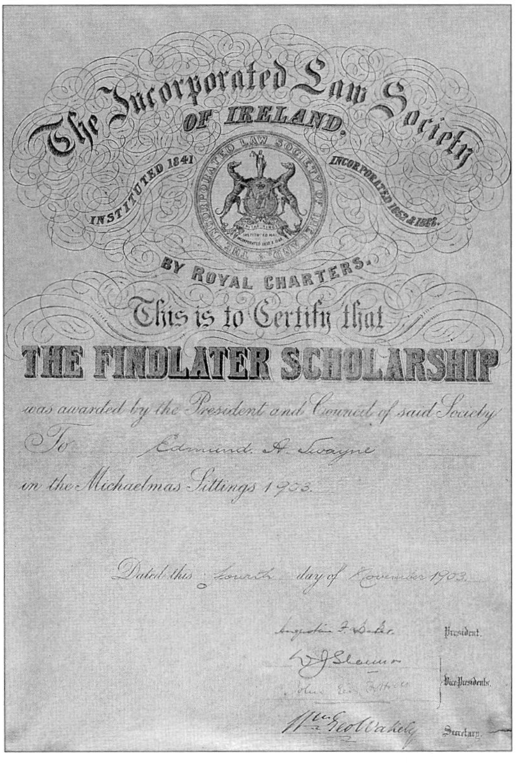
The Incorporated Law Society of Ireland.
Instituted 1841
Incorporated 1852 & 1888.
By Royal Charters.
This is to Certify that
THE FINDLATER SCHOLARSHIP
was awarded by the President and Council of said Society
To Edmund A. Swayne
in the Michaelmas Sittings 1903.
Dated this fourth day of November 1903.
President.
Vice-Presidents.
Secretary.

The Findlater Scholarship

John Wolfe died in 1871 and his daughter followed not long after, in 1877. She and Billy had no children. In 1878 Billy married Marion Hodges, daughter of Lt Col. Archibald Park, son of Mungo Park, the celebrated African explorer. She had two sons and a daughter by her first marriage, and she and Billy then had three children. The first, William Alexander Victor Findlater, was born in 1880, when his father was fifty-six. He was educated at Harrow and Trinity College, Dublin before joining the Royal Irish Rifles, where he was awarded the DSO during the First World War. In 1904 he married Leila Blackwell, daughter of Thomas Blackwell of Merrion Square, and then settled in Kent where they had two sons and three daughters. Billy and Marion's second son was Percy (Percival St George) of the Royal Army Services Corps, who was killed in action on 28 March, 1918. His memory is recalled on the memorial plaque in the Kildare Street and University Club in Dublin. Billy and Marion's only daughter Muriel was born in 1884 and died in 1896 at the tender age of twelve.

In 1852 when he was still in partnership with Matthew Anderson Billy joined one of the Dublin freemason lodges, Victoria Lodge.* It is possible that he was introduced to freemasonry by one of the Blood family, whose members were prominent in various Dublin lodges. Towards the end of his life he joined more

* Adam and Willie Findlater (of the next generation) were both masons. Willie was affiliated to several lodges in the 1920s, including the Lodge of Research, and he progressed to the 18th Degree, implying some interest. Dermot Findlater became a mason in 1938, when Frank Lowe, Chairman of *The Irish Times* and deputy Grand Master was on the Board of Findlaters.

specialised lodges, working his way through the higher degrees. In 1892 he achieved the 28th degree (out of 33) of the Ancient and Accepted Order, an elevation that implies simultaneous membership of various lodges, each with their regular monthly meetings.

Although well-known in business circles, Billy's Uncle Alexander did not attempt to enter politics. Billy, or Sir William, as he eventually became, certainly had aspirations in that direction, as did his cousin Adam. Billy started his public career, as many do, in the organisation of his profession, becoming a member of the Council of the Law Society in the late 1850s. He was elected President of the Incorporated Law Society in 1877/8 ten years after it had been entrusted with the task of training solicitors' apprentices. In the same year he endowed the Society with the Findlater Scholarship at a cost of £1,000 [£62,000] and in 1900 added to its value by transferring £700 [£50,000] Dublin, Wicklow and Wexford Railway Company 4 per cent debenture stock, and £165 [£2,000] 4¼ per cent debenture stock in the same company, to the Society to be held on the same trusts as his original gift. The scholarship is awarded annually to the top scoring apprentices in the second and third Law examinations.[2] According to Charles Gamble in *Solicitors in Ireland 1607-1921* it 'continues to be the blue ribbon of the Society's educational awards, which stamps the successful candidate as the first of his class amongst his contemporaries'. The scholarship is currently awarded for the best overall performance in the professional and advanced courses. In 1919 another President of the Law Society, Trevor Overend of Overend,[*] McCarron and Gibbons, added further funds so that all three law examinations were covered. A few highly talented apprentices have won both the Overend and the Findlater scholarships.

The Dublin Artisans' Dwellings Company

The state of Dublin housing had actually improved during the first part of the 19th century as the poorest families moved into the abandoned houses of the rich. But as jobs became scarce, the houses decayed, and more and more people crammed into less and less space. The notorious Dublin tenements were created. As an early response to the poor state of working-class housing, the Dublin Artisans' Dwellings Company was founded in 1876. The venture was supported by the great and the good of the day, including the Earl of Pembroke, the Guinness family, the Earl of Meath, and most of Dublin's top lawyers, doctors and businessmen. It set out to provide decent housing for the city's respectable working families at manageable rents. Its initial capital was £50,000 in 5,000 shares of £10 each [£3m]. The original directors were Sir Arthur Edward Guinness (later Baron Ardilaun) Chairman, Richard Martin (timber merchant), Deputy Chairman, Richard Armstrong (a land agent), William Findlater,

† Father of Letitia and Naomi Overend of Airfield, Dundrum. The celebrated sisters, famed for their 1927 Rolls Royce, were founding members of the Children's Sunshine Home in Stillorgan, much involved with the St John's Ambulance, and, in 1993, left their home and farm, including Jersey herd, in a private trust as an educational facility, open to the public.

Edward Kinahan (a wine and spirit merchant), Frederick Stokes and Robert Warren.[3]

The company's first building included a tenement block in Upper Buckingham Street and cottages in Upper Dominick Street. After that the emphasis was on cottages and terraced houses for which there was an excess demand. Cottages were built in the Manor Street area in 1880 and at the end of the year a scheme was started in the Coombe which involved 210 houses housing 1,100 people, six shops and premises for two caretakers. The earliest cottages built in Upper Dominick Street cost £120 [£2,700] and were let at 5s 2d per week. This was too much for the average un-skilled labourer, being approximately 40 per cent of his wages, so the houses were let to skilled workers and those with steady earnings. By 1914 the company had built a total of 3,081 dwellings housing a total of 13,938 tenants. The company was profitable. Dividends averaged 4 per cent during the 1880s, by the 1890s they had reached 4½ per cent and were at their maximum level of 5 per cent from 1899.

The Irish Builder of January 1881 reported:

> Although the operations of the Artisans' Dwelling Company in Dublin are small compared with the wants of the city, a little improvement is better than none at all. The Corporation of Dublin can clear sites, but it is not empowered to build; and even in the clearing of sites there are difficulties in this city when it is borne in mind that there are upwards of 10,000 tenement houses, inhabited by more than 120,000 persons, who are living in dwellings practically unfit for habitation, and yet, if suddenly dispossessed, have no better houses in which to seek a home.
>
> And if the public authorities can not build under some wise restrictions, at any cost, we fear they will be compelled for the public safety to pull down thousands of rookeries which are a constant danger and menace to the public health . . . the Corporation, as the sanitary authority, is called upon to compel landlords to do their duty in keeping a number of the houses from which they draw large incomes in a clean and habital condition. It is a notorious fact that a great number of the owners of tenement houses in Dublin will not lay out a penny on the repair of their property if they can avoid it and particularly there is a class of landlords who, anticipating a scheme of strict improvement, will do nothing at all, and yet are ready to prefer preposterous claims for compensation . . . [these landlords] should be promptly and summarily dealt with by bringing them before the magistrates, and inflicting heavy penalties for their continued defiance of the law.

Findlaters themselves owned a small number of tenement buildings, behind their premises in Upper Sackville Street, and the records show that year after year as much as half of the rent was spent in refurbishment. At another level, the Guinness family set up the Iveagh Trust with a benefaction of £50,000 [£3.95m] in 1890; it built 586 tenements (flats) to a high specification. The emphasis was on smaller properties more in tune with the needs of the city's unskilled workers, and rents were more modest than those in the Artisans' Dwelling Company.

At least two streets developed by the Artisans' Company were given the Findlater name. The first is off Infirmary Road, near the Phoenix Park on the outskirts of the city, and the other is in south county Dublin, just beyond Dún

Laoghaire in Glasthule, named in respect of Adam Seaton Findlater Junior, who was Chairman of the Kingstown Commissioners at the time. And there's another. On perusing the records of Dublin's Municipal Council for 1881 I came across an interesting entry:

Findlater's tenement buildings: the nearest first floor window is the one from which Cathal Brugha is reputed to have been shot in 1922.

> An application was before your committee from Messrs A. Findlater & Co., stating that they had been endeavouring to improve the condition of Gregg's lane by erecting Artisans' Dwellings but found it difficult to get a respectable class of persons to occupy the houses on account of the name, Gregg's lane. A letter was also received from Alderman Gregg, suggesting that the lane might be called Findlater Street, and a sub-committee were requested to call on Messrs. Findlater on the subject; and your committee, having fully considered the matter directed that in future this place be called Findlater's Place.

And there it is to this day beside Cathal Brugha Street but alas, the tenements, in which I once had a flat and a lot of student fun, were knocked down in the 1970s.

MP for Monaghan

In the 1874 general election Billy acted as 'conducting agent' for the winning Liberal candidate in South Londonderry. With his Presbyterian background he was firmly on the side of the modernisers in opposition to the economic and political power of the Church of Ireland ascendancy.

The 1880s were a political watershed period, not just for Ireland, but for the British Isles as a whole. The decade saw the beginnings of the great Liberal attack on the landed interest that resulted in what David Cannadine, in *The Decline and Fall of the British Aristocracy,* called 'a territorial transfer rivalled only by two other landed revolutions in Britain this millennium: the Norman Conquest and the Dissolution of the Monasteries.'[4] Estates in Wales, in England and to a lesser extent in Scotland, were broken up and dispersed, so that by the 1920s the rural landscape was completely transformed.

In Ireland the process started with failing harvests. The tide of agricultural growth turned in 1877; 1878 was wet and 1879 was disastrous—prices were down 30 per cent on 1876 levels. Tenants, better-off and better organised than the generation of the 1840s, began to combine to demand rent reductions. Small reductions were often granted, but landlords had their own problems (mortgages, pensions to mothers and sisters, and hunters to maintain) and were happy to think that the distress was exaggerated. ('Why,' complained a Clare magistrate, 'the people appear to me to be well-off. The son of one said his father would not sell a cob to which I took a fancy.'[5])

Protest activity grew more and more threatening. On one side evictions and re-letting; on the other speeches and demonstrations which quickly turned into rent strikes, boycotts and ultimately violence. Landlords, land agents, bailiffs and process servers were attacked; sometimes they were killed, sometimes merely beaten, occasionally mutilated. The Liberals, led by Gladstone, responded by a new Land Act which conceded the famous 'three Fs' thus effectively redefining the relationship between landlord and tenant. In a telling attack on the 'rights of property' it enabled any tenant to apply to have his rent fixed by legal arbitration. A kind of dual ownership of the land was established, the first step that eventually led to the complete buying-out of the landlord interest and the establishment of an agricultural economy based on small (and very small) farms. The political lesson was clear too, for it did not take long for people to associate the absence of landlords with the absence of any British connection.[6] The Tories of course opposed any diminution of the landlords' legal position.

Early in 1880 the Catholic lawyer Charles Russell was invited to stand for the Liberal interest in County Monaghan. Russell was born in 1832 near Newry, Co. Armagh. He attended Castleknock College, and afterwards became a solicitor, practising in Belfast. He later decided to join the Bar in London, and was a striking success. A notable feature of his persona was his strong and public Catholicism. Indeed he strongly suspected that a move to nominate him as Liberal candidate for Durham in 1874 was thwarted by anti-Catholic feeling. He had stood unsuccessfully in the Liberal interest for Dundalk in 1868 and 1874. He accepted the invitation from County Monaghan on condition that they thought him 'the best man to fight the battle'. The prominent Liberals in the constituency, however, ultimately came to the conclusion that he would not win the seat because though the Catholics were willing to support a Presbyterian Liberal candidate the Presbyterians were not willing to support a Catholic on any terms. The Catholic bishop accepted the *realpolitik* of the situation, as was revealed in a telegram from James Riordan, Monaghan, to T. A. Dickson, MP for Dungannon.

> House of Commons, Feb. 1880: Have just seen the [Catholic] Bishop. He is strongly of opinion that starting a Catholic candidate would lose both seats. I am sorry to have to say that I concur with him. See to this at once.

Accordingly, Russell was passed over, and two Presbyterian solicitors, John Givan and William Findlater (Billy), were selected, despite the somewhat unpopular image that profession had as agents of the law. Socially, of course solicitors were looked down on by the Anglo-Irish ascendancy; according to Elizabeth Bowen, a writer typifying that caste, solicitors were not people one invited to dinner.

The two solicitors were elected.* Although he was elected for Dundalk, Russell was bitter about the experience.† As he told his biographer:

> The Catholics of the county out-number Episcopalians and Presbyterians combined, and yet they were not manful enough to make a stand against the Presbyterians. The meeting at which the candidates were selected was held in a Catholic chapel. Almost all present were Catholics, and the meeting decided unanimously to reject the Catholic candidate and to adopt the two Presbyterians. The Catholics were, in my judgement, too timid; but what they did they did on public grounds, and were not swayed by religious prejudices. But the case illustrates the narrowness and bigotry of the Presbyterians, who are always talking of their Liberal principles.

After his election, true to his principles, Billy threw his weight behind the rights of the tenant farmers. At Monaghan, on 21 November, a massive meeting was organised by T. A. Dickson, the two Liberal MPs Givan and Findlater, William Ancketell (a Liberal landlord) and Canon Smollen, parish priest of Clones. Henry Overend, a Carrickmacross Orangeman, opened the meeting by proposing a resolution that tenant right did not provide protection against eviction or unjust rents, and Canon Smollen went through the situation in Monaghan where tenant right had virtually ceased to exist. The objectives of the meeting were indicated by Dickson in a speech which clearly demonstrated that it was a new departure for Ulster liberalism.

> When in March we canvassed you for support, we advocated fixity of tenure at fair rents and free sale with the creation of tenant proprietary . . . But we were regarded as visionaries. But what is our position today? We don't recede nor take one step backwards. The force of circumstances has driven public opinion up to our platform and today we see the farmers' three Fs and a tenant proprietary . . . recognised by leading statesmen as the true and only solution of the Irish land question . . .
>
> The coming Land Bill will meet with tremendous opposition. The men whose only remedy for Ireland's miseries is coercion and Peace Preservation Acts, failing in their dastardly attempts to frighten the Executive into suspending the liberties of the people will, in the Houses of Commons and Lords . . . endeavour to fritter away the Bill and by cunning amendments, to render its clauses ambiguous and negating. Then will be the time for Irish members, North and South, to stand by the government and resist insidious compromises and thereby prevent the disastrous mistakes and blunders of the Land Act of 1870 from again being repeated.[7]

* Votes polled: Givan (Liberal) 2,818, Findlater (Liberal) 2,545, Leslie (Conservative) 2,117, Shirley (Conservative) 2,009.

† In the 1880 election Russell was finally elected to represent Dundalk, and when that seat was abolished in 1884 he was returned for a London constituency. He sucessfully defended Parnell at the Special Commission where he was charged with complicity in the Phoenix Park murders. He was twice Attorney General in Gladstone's Home Rule governments, and finally in 1894 became the first Catholic Lord Chief Justice of England since the Reformation. R. Barry O'Brien, *The Life of Lord Russell of Killowen,* London: Smith, Elder & Co., 1901.

In the House of Commons Billy actively participated in the debates on Gladstone's historic Land Act of 1881 and the Arrears Act of 1882. The landlord class quite correctly saw these Acts as an attack on their long-established position, and so fought tooth and nail to resist. They saw Gladstone as the villain of the piece. Cartoons of him were hung in the WC and there were chamber pots with his portrait leering up from the bottom. More seriously, many in the ascendancy believed that his speeches were active encouragements to tenants and others to shoot landlords. At the same time, while the landlords cried that the Act would spell ruin, they realised that if the government fixed the rate of compensation, at least that compensation was secure.[8] Aided by the Protection of Person and Property Act, and the fair wind of economic recovery, the agitation died down, at least for a time.

One of Billy's more important contributions to the debate in the House of Commons on 13 June 1881 was reported in Hansard, as follows:

> The result of the discussion upon the Amendment was looked forward to with the deepest interest in the county he had the honour to represent (Monaghan). His Catholic constituents looked with great suspicion upon any provision which would enable the landlord to become possessed of his tenant's holding for any amount less than the fair market competition price. He was sorry to say a very strong and bitter sectarian feeling existed in the county; and as the great majority of the tenants were Roman Catholics, they naturally and properly entertained the greatest dread, from their experience of the past, that if the landlords got possession of their holdings upon easy terms they would be removed, and replaced by a solely Protestant tenancy. They had no confidence whatever that fair play would be afforded to them, and therefore he hoped his hon. Friend would press the Amendment to a division. As the Government would not deprive the landlord of the right of preemption altogether, they should press that that privilege should be only exercised at the same price as an ordinary purchaser would pay in the open market. They were, in his humble opinion, entitled to that protection, and on their behalf he should insist upon it.[9]

After the passing of the Acts Billy addressed the tenant farmers of Monaghan at Carrickmacross, in the Barony of Farney and County of Monaghan on Wednesday 27 September 1882:

> Men of Farney
>
> When I promised you if you elected me to represent you in Parliament, I said I would, to the best of my ability, with the assistance of my excellent colleague, fight the battle of the down-trodden tenants of this noble County, and endeavour to emancipate them from the unworthy bondage in which the representatives of feudal landlordism held them shackled and confined.
>
> What I promise I like to perform, if in my power, and here, in your presence, I fearlessly aver that I have spared no effort to carry out and perform every undertaking I ever made or gave to you. I have said many changes have taken place since we first met—Is not this true? You are no longer the land serfs you then were, uncertain as to how long you would be permitted to retain your homesteads, dreading continual increases of rent if you ventured to expend your money or your labour on the improvement of your holdings, and unable to realise their full value if you were obliged to part with them by sale.

The terror of landlordism and its powers was upon you, and no wonder, when you knew that if your landlord discovered that you had recorded your vote for any one who did not meet with his approval all the engines of that unjust law which was placed upon the statute book of the realm by him and his privileged class would be set in motion to oppress and ruin you.

Your clergy, as they always do, did their duty well, and encouraged you by their presence in the polling booths to brave the watchful eyes of the bailiffs and sub-agents who were planted in official capacities there at the instance of alarmed and prying landlordism.

You have got substantially under the tenure clauses of the Land Act of 1881 the fair rents, fixity of tenure, and free sale, you longed and struggled for, if you choose to seek for them under its beneficent provisions. Look at the splendid position occupied by the yearly tenant at the present moment. If he thinks his rent greater than a fair rent he is at once entitled to apply to the Land Commission or the County Court Judge to determine what is a fair rent. In ascertaining this fair rent the Court is bound to exclude from its consideration all improvements made on the holding by the tenant or his predecessors in title, unless they have been paid or compensated for by the landlord or his predecessors . . .

You can form a very inadequate idea of what the great man [Gladstone] had to contend with, but my colleague and I who saw every step of the contest, and how bravely he won success in the face of the bitter opposition of open foes, and the withholding of assistance by lukewarm and weak-kneed supporters, cannot refrain from expressing, as your representatives, our warm and hearty recognition of his generous services. I hope—I know you will be equally grateful, and mark your appreciation of the benefits he has conferred upon you, by availing of them without delay.

To return to the position of the yearly tenant. The moment the judicial fair rent is fixed by the Court the tenant forthwith becomes entitled to his holding for fifteen years, subject to statutory conditions, and during the continuance of this term his rent cannot be increased, and he cannot be evicted unless for violation of those statutory conditions.

Again, although the tenant is entitled to this perpetual tenure, if he desires, the landlord has no power of compelling him to hold on for the fifteen years if he finds it unprofitable to do so, even at the fair rent which has been fixed. He can surrender at any time he chooses, thus being in a far better position than if he had a lease which would bind him irrevocably to his holding during the term . . .

Further legislation became necessary, and on the 18th day of August 1882, after a prolonged struggle with the Upper Chamber, which is now matter of history, the Arrears of Rent (Ireland) Act, 1882, became law. By its enactment the Land Commission are authorised to advance money to discharge arrears due by Irish tenants, either by way of gift or loan . . .

I have now, I trust, as briefly as the nature of the case would admit, explained to you the most important provisions of the Land Act of 1881, and the Arrears Act of 1882. They hang together, and explain each other, and I do not well see how they can be treated separately, or the provisions of the one expounded without a reference to, and explanation of the other. The importance of the subject must prove my excuse for trespassing upon your indulgence at such length. No measure, where so many different interests are concerned, and have to be considered, can be framed and passed in such a form as to satisfy every one.

Men of Farney, in conclusion, allow me to express my earnest hope that a bright and happy future is before you.[10]

When the second reading of the Land Purchase (Ireland) Bill was proposed, Billy spoke again in the House of Commons; as reported in Hansard he

> most heartily approved of the Bill which, in his opinion, would confer a great boon upon the people of Ireland. Its provisions were good, and with some slight but necessary Amendments it might be made a good working measure. In the belief that it would be a boon to both parties, he desired to see it pass as soon as possible, and so far as he was concerned, he would aid its passage by making it as perfect as possible. With that object he should make several suggestions to the Government when the Bill reached the committee stage.[11]

As a staunch Liberal, Billy supported Gladstone in these momentous changes, but like most Presbyterians, he was not prepared to go down the home rule path. Billy was out of parliament by the time Gladstone brought in his first Home Rule Bill in 1886, but it is very unlikely he would have been happy with it. For Presbyterians an ascendancy of members of the Church of Ireland was bad enough—an ascendancy of Roman Catholics was quite unthinkable.[12] However, Billy was an active parliamentarian, intervening on a variety of Irish affairs, mostly those with a legal tint. In 1882, for instance, he spoke on the Poor Law, on bankruptcy, on the mail service between Dublin and London, on the grand jury system, on the sale of army rifles, on Trinity College leases, on patent registration, on the registration of deeds, on police pay and on the prevention of crime generally. As a modern, no-nonsense Victorian he was a supporter of the loop line across the Liffey connecting the south and north railway systems 'for the acceleration of the mails'. He had no truck with the 'sentimental objection with regard to the beauty of the view from Carlisle Bridge [O'Connell Bridge].'

In 1883 Billy's fellow-MP for Monaghan, John Givan, was appointed Crown Solicitor for Meath and Kildare and resigned his seat. Tim Healy, representing the new home rule party, was elected in the ensuing by-election and joined Billy in the House of Commons. Ominously, the Liberal vote, represented by Henry Pringle, was decimated.* Perhaps as a result, in the general election of 1885 Billy decided to stand for South Londonderry, where he had been born and brought up. He stated he was leaving Monaghan 'solely because his constituents had got ahead of his views'. He canvassed for his Liberal unionist stance hard throughout the county but was beaten into third place by none other than Tim Healy,† the Home Rule candidate, and polled less than Col. McCalmont for the Conservatives.‡ Healy actually stood for both South Londonderry and for Monaghan in the election, won both, and elected to sit for South Londonderry. Bad feeling arose between Billy and Col. McCalmont and after the election Billy refused to shake hands. Healy's success was the first time a nationalist had won

* Votes polled: Healy (Home Rule) 2,376, Moore (Conservative) 2,011, Pringle (Liberal) 274.

† Timothy Healy, barrister, later a leading anti-Parnellite. Governor-General, Irish Free State 1922-8.

‡ Votes polled: Healy (Home Rule) 4,723, McCalmont (Conservative) 2,342, Findlater (Liberal) 1,816.

a seat in Londonderry.

As an active parliamentarian, Billy involved himself with issues of social reform, such as housing. The *Londonderry Standard* of 23 November 1885 reported his views: 'He would like to see the working man well housed in a comfortable dwelling, with good sanitary applications, and as an earnest of his efforts in that direction, he mentioned what he, in conjunction with others, had done for the working man in Dublin, where they caused to be erected a large number of most comfortable dwellings, which were let at the low rent of one shilling per week.' He was also a founder member of the Ulster Reform Club* but took no further part in its affairs after his departure from politics. In his time he would have been remembered by members of the Bar as the principal promoter of the Act of Parliament, (called Findlater's Act[13]), which was passed in 1883, and which facilitated appeals from County Court Judges to the Judges of Assize. Undoubtedly his main political contribution was his part in the bloodless revolution that by 1910 saw the old landlord class virtually eliminated from Ireland, and the land in the hands of small farmers.

Inaugural dinner of the Institute of Chartered Accountants

As a leader of his profession, Billy was a guest speaker at the dinner to celebrate the formation of the Irish Institute of Chartered Accountants in 1888.[14] The first president of the new institute was Robert Gardner, who was founder of the firm of Craig Gardner,† and, by marriage, a connection of the Findlaters. These dinners were done with style, as Tony Farmar, the historian of Craig Gardner, relates:

> On the evening of the first General Meeting (19 November, 1888), over eighty gentlemen sat down to dinner at the Shelbourne Hotel, Dublin to a repast served 'in the most recherché style' as *The Accountant* characteristically put it. The relationship of accountants and lawyers and the dependence of accountants on the legal profession in those days were clearly shown by the choice of guests at the first dinner.
>
> The first toast after the Queen's health had been drunk, was 'The Legal Profession' proposed by Robert Gardner as President. This was replied to by Mr Carton, QC on behalf of the Bar of Ireland and William Findlater, J.P., on behalf of the Solicitors of Ireland. Findlater's speech is interesting as it paints a picture of Robert Gardner which explains much that followed in the next few years. He was glad to see that his old friend, Robert Gardner, had been chosen as the man who could most fitly fill the presidential chair. 'To be sure he found their worthy President a little impetuous now and then (laughter, and a voice 'impossible') but then this was a trifle'. Later he referred to Gardner as a 'despot' much to the approval of *The Accountant* who considered that his despotism would be approved by sensible men everywhere. Gardner's despotism and impetuosity were unfortunately to separate him before long from the Institute he was

* The Reform Club was under discussion from 1880 and officially opened in 1885. It was formed to advance the Liberal unionist cause in Ulster, which was under threat from a strong Conservative strategy attempting to establish the identity Unionist = Conservative. To counter this, in November 1885 a meeting of the Club required that every Liberal candidate pledge himself to the maintenance of the union, declaring that 'the establishment of an Irish Parliament would be inconsistent with the maintenance of the Union and fraught with danger to the Empire.' In 1982 it merged with the Ulster Club and is completely non-political.

† Now PricewaterhouseCoopers.

Leaders of the Ulster Liberal Party 1880. *From left, standing:* Mr John Givan MP; Rt Hon Andrew Marshall Porter; Mr James Dickson; Sir Thomas Lee MP; *Sitting*: Mr William Findlater MP, Sir Thomas McClure MP; Rt Hon T.A. Dickson MP and James Richardson. The party was wiped out in the election of December 1885, but soon became merged in the new Unionist Party.
Belfast Telegraph

so largely responsible for forming.

The toast of The Institute of Chartered Accountants in Ireland was proposed by Maurice Brooks, J.P* who, as a merchant of Dublin, recalled the time when the presence of an accountant in a place of business was looked upon in much the same light as the visit of an undertaker or a coroner would be.

Besides the lawyers, the permanent heads of 'those Government Departments which deal with accounts,' the editors of the Dublin newspapers, and of *The Accountant*, some English accountants, representatives of the banks, and even some Dublin merchants attended that first dinner. Rather wickedly, *The Accountant* pointed out 'the peculiarity which could not but strike any visitor' that probably every single guest was a man of direct practical and daily importance to the accountants of Ireland.

President for the second time

In 1896 Billy was elected president of the Law Society for the second time, despite a special resolution of the society passed twenty years before that no one would be eligible for re-election. The council declared that it took this unusual course in recognition of the many and valued services rendered by him to the profession, as well as to mark their appreciation of the fact that his name was to

* Maurice Brooks 1823-1903, glass merchant and later Brooks Thomas & Co; Lord Mayor 1874–5, Liberal MP for Dublin.

be found as one of the members of the council for nearly forty years. A Mr Falls, in putting the resolution, hoped the society would long enjoy the benefit of his great experience. They should also bear in mind that this was the fiftieth year of his professional career, and he looked as fresh today as, he ventured to say, he did thirty years ago, and with as much 'go' in him.

The Irish Law Times thoroughly approved:

> We have the greatest pleasure to announce that the Council of the Incorporated Law Society of Ireland at their meeting, on Wednesday last, elected Mr William Findlater, J.P., D.L., as their President for the year 1897—an office which has been worthily filled by a long succession of men of the highest intellectual stamp, and of great social and personal influence. The Council's choice will, we are sure, be most heartily endorsed by the public . . .
>
> Mr Findlater is permanent Chairman of the Solicitors' Benevolent Association, a member of the Council of the Royal Dublin Society, member of the Council of the Dublin Chamber of Commerce, and of various other public and charitable Boards in Dublin; in all which various capacities his valuable assistance and advice are eagerly sought . . .[15]

The Statistical and Social Inquiry Society of Ireland

Billy was elected president of the Statistical and Social Inquiry Society of Ireland for 1891-92.[16] At the meetings of the society papers on statistics, jurisprudence, political economy, and social science were read and discussed. This was before mathematical statistics were current and the papers tended to stress information rather than analysis—modern developments of statistics such as mathematical tests of statistical significance were hardly known. No discussion was allowed of subjects likely to introduce religious differences or party politics.

In his presidential address in May 1892, Billy presented a paper on 'Statistics'—covering their origin, history, status as a science, uniformity, use as a proof and value. On other occasions during his presidential year papers were read on such subjects as 'Co-operative Agricultural Societies in Germany' (presented by Rev. T. A. Finlay, a great supporter of Plunkett and the Irish co-operative movement), 'Self-help *v.* State help', 'Legislation on behalf of Neglected Children in America and Elsewhere', and 'The Fusion of the Two Branches of the Legal Profession'.

Knighthood

In present-day Ireland the granting of honours is wisely left to the universities (honorary doctorates) and city corporations (city freedoms)—woe be the day that a national honour is re-introduced. However in Victorian Dublin such honours flowed from the Crown, and were (generally) highly regarded. A mark of social distinction sometimes conferred on solicitors (but never on barristers and very rarely on judges) was that of being knighted.[17] A number of presidents of the Law Society were so honoured, including Sir Richard Orpen (who was president between 1860 and 1876 and was knighted in 1868, perhaps as much for his services to the Liberal Party as for his services to the profession), Sir William Fry,

Sir William Findlater, Sir George Roche (president in the year of the Coronation of King Edward VII), Sir John Lynch, and, in Ulster, Sir Samuel Black, Sir Charles Brett, Baronet, and Sir Alexander McDowell.

Billy's second wife, Marion Hodges née Park

In 1896 Billy received a letter from the Lord Lieutenant offering him a knighthood, and he was happy to accept—he enjoyed the ceremonial and trappings that accompanied the honour. The *Irish Law Times* reported the event:

> We are delighted to find the name of the President of the Incorporated Law Society of Ireland included in the list of the recipients of New Year's honours. In conferring a Knighthood on such a distinguished member of their body, the entire Solicitors' profession in this country will feel honoured. Long may he live to enjoy his well-merited distinction![18]

The knighthood of the great historian of Dublin Sir John Gilbert, the benefactor of the Gilbert Library in Pearse Street, was noted in the same issue of the *Dublin Gazette.*

Old age

For the last years of his life Billy was in poor health, and did not appear much in public. He spent his time in Fernside,* his Killiney home where he and his family had so often decamped for the summer. Dr Blood of Enniskerry, of the closely intertwined Blood/Findlater/Inglis/Wolfe families (see pages 90–1) remembers Sir William in his old age:

> I knew Billy very well and owing to my double relationship I was always welcome to stay at any time as long as I liked, especially when they went down to Fernside, Killiney, as they did each summer. I recount great kindness from them all. Percy Findlater, who was 3 years older than myself, was my best friend—he was killed in the 1st war.
>
> My great uncle kept a large stable—2 carriage horses—one cob (for himself)—2 ponies for the children—a pony for the luggage cart. He rode every morning before breakfast until he got too old for it. My father rode with him, if he was staying. He

* Completed in May 1862 to the design of architects Deane and Woodward, who designed Queen's College Cork, the Museum Building Trinity College Dublin, the Oxford Union and the old Kildare Street Club. Frederick O'Dwyer *The Architecture of Deane & Woodward* Cork: Cork University Press, 1995 pp 467–71.

drank nothing but Scotch Whiskey and smoked cigars.

In April 1906 Sir William died quietly in Killiney at the age of eighty-two. *The Irish Times,* as befitted such a prominent citizen, wrote an obituary and report of his funeral:

> With much regret we announce the death of Sir William Findlater, J.P., D.L., which took place last Monday morning at his residence, Fernside, Killiney, Co. Dublin. Sir William had been in failing health for a considerable time, and during the last few years was rarely seen in public. On Sunday night he retired to rest apparently as well as usual, but on Monday morning he complained of weakness, and death ensued almost immediately.

After mentioning the Findlater Scholarship and the Artisan Dwelling company the obituary went on:

> The deceased also took part in the management of many charitable and other public institutions in Dublin. He was the chairman and trustee of the Solicitors' Benevolent Association that he had founded 23 years earlier, and a member of the Dublin Benevolent Society of St Andrew. He was for 31 years associated with charitable work for The Royal Hospital for Incurables in Donnybrook. He was a member of the Royal Irish Yacht Club, the Stephen's Green Club and the Devonshire and Reform Clubs. Deputy Lieutenant of the County of Dublin, 44 years Council Member Incorporated Law Society.*

He was buried in Mount Jerome, some distance beyond his uncle Alexander's vault. With him is his first wife Mary Jane Wolfe who died in 1877, his daughter Muriel who died aged twelve in 1896 and his second wife Marion, who died in 1916 aged seventy-two. The grave is also a memorial to his second son Percy (Captain Percival St George Findlater) who was killed in action on 28 May 1918, aged thirty-six.

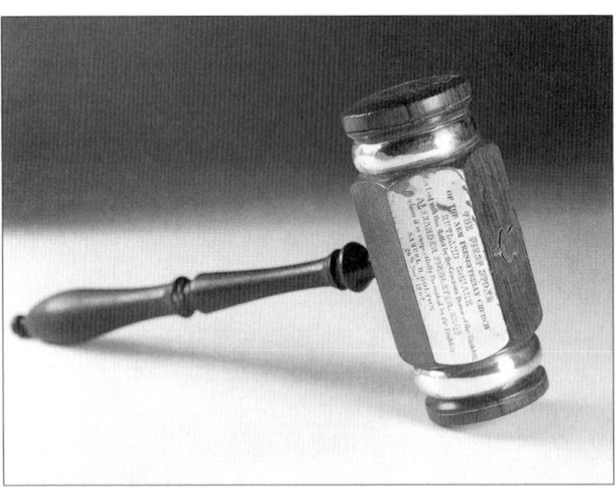

'The first stone of the Presbyterian Church, Rutland Square was laid with this mallet by the Gracious Donor of the building, Alexander Findlater Esqr, to whom it is respectfully presented by the builder Samuel H. Bolton. 26th November 1862'
The mallet, with the above inscription, was retrieved from the cellar of Sir William's house where it was being used to bang corks into bottles. †

* *The Irish Times* 17 April 1906. Sir William's deep involvement in Freemasonry is not mentioned in the obituary—but this is surprising rather than sinister or secretive. Next to the report of his funeral, on 20 April, is the description of the funeral of a prominent mason Dr J. G. Byrne, whose masonic activities are reported in detail.

† Billy himself laid the memorial stone of the Presbyterian church at Hanley in Staffordshire. I have no idea what the circumstances were.

Notes and references

1 The original *Notti Romane* is from the press of Francesco Bertini Lucca mdccxiv (1814)
2 Jacinta Morris, Education Office, The Law Society, in the Society's *Gazette* March 1981
3 Mary Daly *Dublin's Victorian Houses,* Dublin: A.& A. Farmar 1998; also the archives of the Gilbert Library, Pearse Street, Dublin 2, *The Irish Builder* 1 Jan 1881, *Thoms Directory* 1877, 1878
4 D. Cannadine *The Decline and Fall of the British Aristocracy* London: Picador 1992 p 89
5 S. Clark *Social Origins of the Irish Land War* Princeton University Press 1979 p 233. The echoes of Penal legislation, under which no Roman Catholic was supposed to own a horse worth more than £5, are unmistakable
6 P. Bull *Land, Politics and Nationalism* Dublin: Gill and Macmillan 1996 pp 91-3
7 Frank Wright *Two Lands on one Soil, Ulster Politics before Home Rule:* Dublin: Gill and Macmillan 1996
8 Peter Somerville-Large *The Irish Country House* London: Sinclair-Stevenson 1995 p 315
9 Hansard 13 June 1881 p 392
10 Findlater family records
11 Hansard 4 August 1885 p 1112
12 Finlay Holmes *The Presbyterian Church in Ireland* Dublin: Columba Press 2000, p 119
13 45 & 46 Vict., c.29
14 The inaugural dinner is described in detail in *The Accountant* for 1 December, 1888 and in Tony Farmar *A History of Craig Gardner* Dublin: Gill and Macmillan 1985
15 *The Irish Law Times* 5 December 1896
16 *Journal of the Statistical & Social Inquiry Society of Ireland* vol IX August 1892 pp 636-648
17 Daire Hogan *The Legal Profession in Ireland 1789-1922* Dublin: The Incorporated Law Society 1986
18 *Irish Law Times* 2 January 1897

The memorial window in Findlater's church erected by the congregation in appreciation of their benefactor, Alexander Findlater. (Photo: Paul Oatway)

4. *Findlater's Mountjoy Brewery*

On 13 January 1852 six businessmen sat around the table and signed an indenture which brought an exciting new venture—Findlater's Mountjoy Brewery—into being. They had agreed to establish the brewery on land between Russell Street and Portland Street, on the north side of the city of Dublin. In the grandiose style of legal documents of the day they were identified as:

> Alexander Findlater of Sackville Street in the City of Dublin, Merchant;
> Ivie Mackie, of the Town of Manchester in the United Kingdom of Great Britain and Ireland called England, Merchant;
> Henry Walter Todd of Mary Street in the City of Dublin, Merchant;
> Robert Gladstone of the Town of Liverpool of the said United Kingdom and called England, Merchant;
> Adam Seaton Findlater [Senior] of Sackville Street in the said city, Merchant; and
> John Brown Johnston of Balls Bridge in the County of Dublin, Merchant.

No accountants or lawyers!

Alexander and Adam must have been planning the building of a brewery for some time. They were well aware of the export potential of porter following their successes in the Americas in the 1830s. They may have had to bide their time until sufficient financial resources had been accumulated, and of course the late 1840s, the time of the Famine, was not a good time for such a venture. Alexander

The Mountjoy Brewery, Russell Street (across the road from Croke Park)

would have been conscious that various causes had driven down the national consumption of whiskey, with production halving from 11.9m gallons to 5.3m gallons between 1838 and 1843.[1] Between 1850 and 1880 there was a further 30 per cent drop. The slack was taken up by beer drinking, which rose from 575,000 barrels in 1841 to 1,298,000 barrels in 1861. By 1890 annual production had risen to 2,490,000 barrels and in 1900 some three million barrels of beer were being brewed, a good deal of which was exported.*

This major shift in drinking habits meant that it was an opportune time to emulate Guinness' success and establish a brewery—this is what Alexander and his partners did.

They were entering a competitive market; it is interesting to look back on the brewing industry over the previous century. In 1750 the city had 35 brewing alehouses, producing an estimated 4,400 barrels a week.† (The Irish barrel then contained 42 gallons, equalling 32.96 imperial gallons.[2] This difference of course complicated matters in the assessment of duties and statistics.) One of Dublin's oldest brewing families then, the Leesons (after whom Leeson Street is named), gave up their mercantile pursuits in order to enter the nobility of the time. Dublin wit was quick to remark that they had 'traded their beerage for a peerage'. The Leeson burial place is a feature of the small graveyard in Camden Row, off Camden Street.

The Sweetmans were another great brewing family of the mid-1700s, producing, between them, 800 barrels per week in five different breweries, one in St Stephen's Green and another on Aston Quay. Two of the other brewing families, the Lawlesses and the Clinches, became associated with the Sweetmans through marriage. There was also a Sweetman connection with a brewer called Val Brown, who was brewing 260 barrels a week in 1756, but he had dropped out of the scene by the 1766 excise returns. Richard Phepoe was another large brewer who produced 360 barrels a week and the smallest was a Matthew Reilly, who brewed 40 barrels a week in Francis Court. The only female brewer then was a Mary Donovan, producing 100 barrels a week.

Alderman Taylor then ran the famous Ardee Street brewery, located on the monastic site of St Thomas in the Liberties, with an output of 300 barrels, slightly less than Richard Phepoe. Ale at that time cost 19s per barrel (less than 1d per pint) and had to be brewed from malt and hops imported from England, although they could be sourced cheaper elsewhere. Competition from imported beers grew from a mere 4,000 barrels in 1750 to 40,000 in 1768. Arthur Guinness, ale brewer, first appears in the excise list of 1768, amongst 42 other brewers. At that time Sir James Taylor's brewery had become the largest in Dublin, paying £4,300 in excise. Guinness paid £1,500 which was about 2 per

* T. W. Grimshawe 'Statistical Survey of Ireland 1841-1881' *Journal of the Social and Statistical Society of Ireland* vol ix pp 322 ff and T. W. Grimshawe *Facts about Ireland* (1893). Dr Grimshawe was Registrar-General for Ireland and a regular contributor to the *JSISSI*, of which Billy Findlater became President in 1891.

† Historical information from Tom Halpin, brewery industry historian, and from his article in *Food Ireland* July 1984.

cent of the total returns of the Dublin brewers.

By 1820 the number of breweries was down to 22. The top five were exclusively porter breweries headed by Arthur Guinness at 600 barrels per week. Next came Michael Sweetman with an output of 450 barrels from his location on St Stephen's Green. Then came the Ardee Street brewery, now owned by Watkins, with a production of 300 barrels per week. One of the smaller breweries was Darley and Guinness in Brewery Road, alongside the Lepers Stream, in Stillorgan. Peter Pearson's *Between the Mountains and the Sea* shows it to have covered an extensive area either side of Brewery Road.

The establishment of the Findlater brewery was a sizeable investment. Alexander's initial share in the investment was £13,000, for which he got one-fifth of the profits. This suggests that the full cost of the brewery was £65,000 [£3.9m], although from Alexander's ledgers we can see that it absorbed further capital in the ensuing years. Land was bought in Russell Street, between the Royal Canal and the North Circular Road—it was said that the brewery had far more picturesque surroundings than any other in the capital. A generation before a magnificent orchard had grown there, and the place had been a favourite summer resort for Dubliners. The Behans were later inhabitants of Russell Street, long after Findlaters had sold their interest in the brewery; Dominic Behan remembers 'the native industries of Russell Street were drink and cleanliness, represented respectively by the Mounjoy Brewery and the Phoenix Laundry. The aroma from this mixture was, as you would expect, of alcohol brewed from carbolic.'[3] The new brewery was named after nearby Mountjoy Square, then still quite a grand address, and not after the prison, as wags often suggested. The premises of the brewery covered an area of 3 acres, 1 rood and 7 perches statute, and had a frontage of 320 feet to Russell Street, and also to the North Circular Road, and Portland Street. At the Portland Street side a large plot of ground was available for further extension. The Royal Canal bounded the premises on the north side.

When completed the brewery buildings comprised a porter's lodge, counting-house, brew-house hop stores fitted up on best and most modern principles with elevators, etc., malt stores, vat houses, cooling houses, malt house and kiln, racking store, pump house, fining stores, large and spacious racking house, and large scalding shed with steam machinery for cleansing barrels. There was also a red brick chimney shaft, engine and boiler houses, branding house, stabling for 20 horses, stable man's house, cooperage and two fitter's shops, one furnished with forge and lathe. In total, 120 men were employed. There were two wells on the premises, and the brewery was, in addition, supplied with Vartry water, and from the Royal and Grand Canals. All the buildings were erected in a most substantial manner with limestone, ashlar and chiselled granite dressings. The brewer's residence adjoined the brewery in Russell Street, with stables and coachhouse attached.

As would be expected of a venture of this size, the new brewery did not come into profits until 1857. It made comfortable profits for most of the 1860s, peak-

A selection of the Mountjoy brewery labels

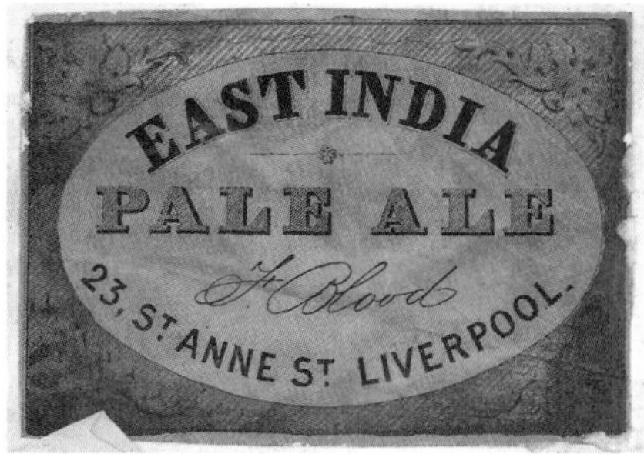

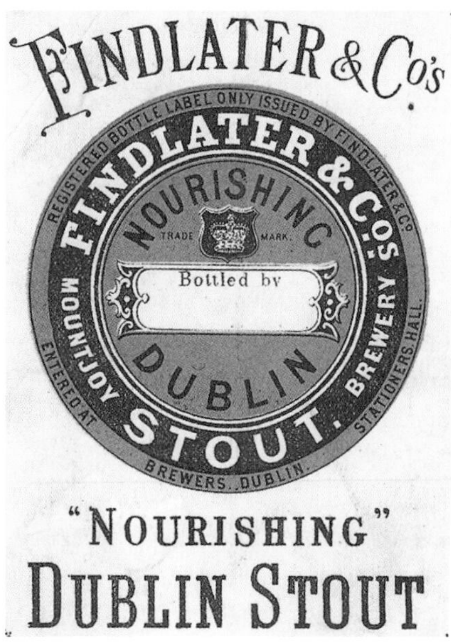

More labels from the Mountjoy collection

ing at £13,785 in 1866 [more than £800,000 in 2000]. It excelled in export markets as is illustrated by the export statistics for 1865.

Table 4.1 : Porter exports in 1865 (hogsheads)

Guinness	99,239	Watkins	14,352
Findlaters	27,925	Phoenix	8,890
Manders	26,526	Sweetman	7,881
D'Arcy	23,806	Caffrey	1,761
Jameson, Pim	19,107	All others	3,187

Note: A hogshead contained 54 imperial gallons

In 1866 Guinness' exports rose to 107,000 hogsheads (an increase of 8 per cent), and Findlater's to 35,000 hogsheads (a gain of 25 per cent). Findlater's share of the export market rose from 3.2 per cent in 1854, just after the bewery was established, to 13.9 per cent in 1866. In the same period Guinness' share fell from 49 per cent to 42 per cent. (Statistics do not seem to be available for subsequent years or for the domestic market.)

After the deaths of Alexander and Adam, their eldest nephew Billy became sole proprietor. His nephews and cousins Francis R. Wolfe, Frederick Blood, John Redmond Blood, Alexander Findlater Blood, Adam Lloyd Blood, and the accountant, John Jennings, all had an input into the running of the brewery. (See page 87 for the colourful history of their ancestor Colonel Blood, who attempted to steal the British Crown Jewels in the 17th century.)

In 1888, twelve years after Alexander's death, the brewery was visited by an English journalist who left a detailed description of his outing.

> Only stout and porter have ever been brewed at the Mountjoy Brewery, which is sold principally in Ireland and England. The firm, however, ships a considerable quantity to Gibraltar, Malta, and Cyprus, where they have a connection of many years standing. The stout is specially brewed for these hot climates, and to stand the long sea voyage. The brewery is of neat and lofty elevation, and is mainly constructed of granite. The buildings have a frontage to the highway of 240 feet, and the brewhouse is 65 feet high. The maltings, great vat-houses, cooperages, etc., are situated at the rear, the whole being enclosed by a lofty stone wall and numerous buildings. In a line with the front of the brewery there is a terrace of handsome houses, one of which belongs to and adjoins the brewery property. It is occupied by Mr J. R. Blood, the head brewer, and nephew of the original proprietor, who conducted us through the establishment.
>
> We commenced our inspection at the maltings, a block of stone buildings adjacent to North Portland Street, and bounded on the right by the Royal Canal. They are four storeys high, and extend, with the yard, a distance of 130 feet. The top floor, which is devoted to the storage of barley, contains, at one end, a metal steep, or cistern, some 8 feet wide, which is capable of wetting at one time 100 barrels of grain. The other three storeys are devoted to the process of malting, the floors therein being laid with a concrete considered most suitable for germinating purposes.

When the malts have been duly worked on these floors, they are removed to the kiln to be thoroughly dried. This building forms the north end of the structure, and is approached from the yard, but is loaded from the malting floor through iron doors. The kiln floor is laid with Irson's perforated Worcester tiles, and heated underneath by open furnaces.

From the kilns the malt is delivered by shoots into small wagons, running on a miniature tramway through one of the long racking-stores to the malt bins, which occupy a large building to the north of the brewhouse. Of course, Messrs Findlater & Co. make but a small portion of the malt consumed in their brewery, and they therefore purchase considerable quantities from English and Irish maltsters. All the roasted malt used is manufactured by themselves, in a house built for the purpose, which we afterwards visited.

Crossing the large yard we entered the brewhouse by the south door, and found ourselves in an extensive lobby, running through the premises, from which springs a wide stone staircase reaching to the top of the building. The engine-house, which is near the centre of the edifice, is a handsome paved apartment, containing two powerful engines, one a beam, the other a horizontal one, each of thirty horsepower, also a battery of pumps for wort, liquor and porter, and each in duplicate.

Passing the Excise office, we made our way upstairs to the head brewer's office, which faces the road and overlooks the pleasant fields which stretch to the plains of Clontarf. Here we were shown samples of barley and hops, also the various apparatus for testing the gravity and quality of the various stouts. From this place we made our way to the topmost storey of the brewery to reach the top of the malt bins. Before giving them our attention, we stepped out on the staging which crosses the great reservoir, from which position we obtained the finest view of Dublin we had yet witnessed, including Dublin bay and mountains, also Glasnevin and the Botanical Gardens. Near us on the left, is the great DWD, with its new windmill and towers rising among the trees. DWD stands for the Dublin Whiskey Distillery Company, where the native wine of the country is produced—a fit companion for the drink manufactured at Mountjoy, which has been described as the poor man's meat and drink combined. Both of these celebrated and national drinks are made from the waters of the Dublin Canals, and Messrs Findlaters store it in this great tank after it has passed through two of Rawling's patent filters, fixed outside the reservoirs. Besides this, the firm has three other supplies, all equally important in their way, viz., the Vartry, another canal, and a well, the latter 70 feet deep. The water is pumped from this last source, to a reservoir, by means of a powerful set of three-throw pumps, having rods over 20 feet long, and, at the bottom, in addition, a five-inch double rain pump. Our guide next conducted us, by a gangway off the copper-head, to the malt lofts, which form the upper portion of the great porter stores, hereafter mentioned. It contains ten spacious bins, each capable of holding 2,500 barrels. The malt is screened from dust and combings and then conveyed by elevators to the mill hoppers.

The special store for black or roasted malt is adjacent to this floor. At the bottom of each bin there is a trap slide, which, on being lifted, drops the malt on to an elevator, by which it is conveyed to the screening room, where it is screened and weighed. On

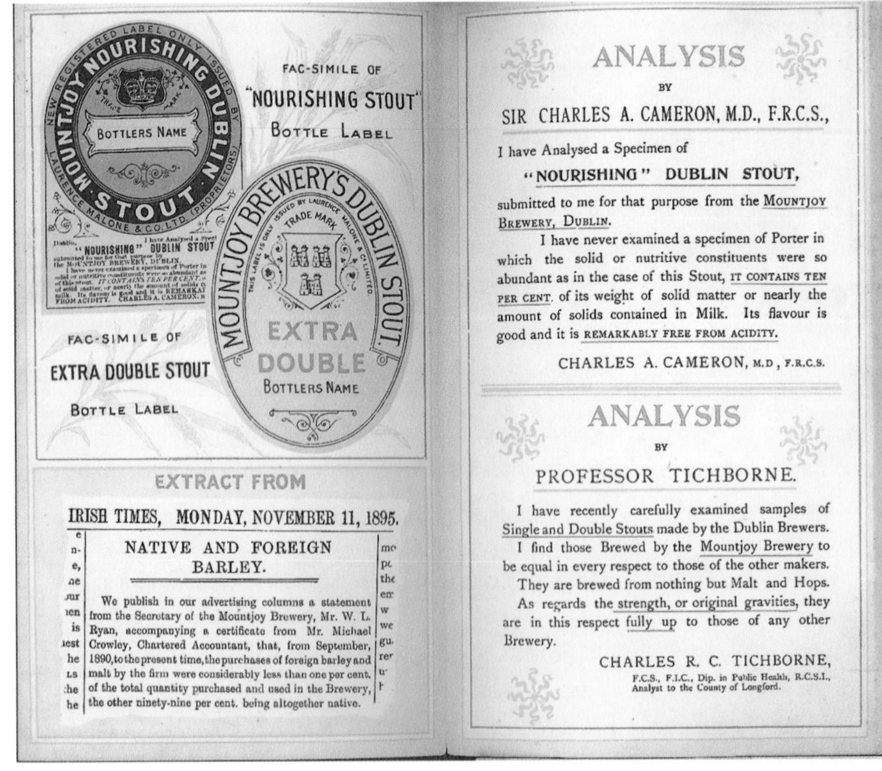

FAC-SIMILE OF "NOURISHING STOUT" BOTTLE LABEL

FAC-SIMILE OF EXTRA DOUBLE STOUT BOTTLE LABEL

EXTRACT FROM

IRISH TIMES, MONDAY, NOVEMBER 11, 1895.

NATIVE AND FOREIGN BARLEY.

We publish in our advertising columns a statement from the Secretary of the Mountjoy Brewery, Mr. W. L. Ryan, accompanying a certificate from Mr. Michael Crowley, Chartered Accountant, that, from September, 1890, to the present time, the purchases of foreign barley and malt by the firm were considerably less than one per cent. of the total quantity purchased and used in the Brewery, the other ninety-nine per cent. being altogether native.

ANALYSIS

BY

SIR CHARLES A. CAMERON, M.D., F.R.C.S.,

I have Analysed a Specimen of

"NOURISHING" DUBLIN STOUT,

submitted to me for that purpose from the MOUNTJOY BREWERY, DUBLIN.

I have never examined a specimen of Porter in which the solid or nutritive constituents were so abundant as in the case of this Stout, IT CONTAINS TEN PER CENT. of its weight of solid matter or nearly the amount of solids contained in Milk. Its flavour is good and it is REMARKABLY FREE FROM ACIDITY.

CHARLES A. CAMERON, M.D., F.R.C.S.

ANALYSIS

BY

PROFESSOR TICHBORNE.

I have recently carefully examined samples of Single and Double Stouts made by the Dublin Brewers.

I find those Brewed by the Mountjoy Brewery to be equal in every respect to those of the other makers.

They are brewed from nothing but Malt and Hops.

As regards the strength, or original gravities, they are in this respect fully up to those of any other Brewery.

CHARLES R. C. TICHBORNE,
F.C.S., F.I.C., Dip. in Public Health, R.C.S.I.,
Analyst to the County of Longford.

An endorsement from Charles Cameron, the well-known Medical Officer of Health for Dublin

Right: 'Lily', a grey mare, 1st Class Prizewinner at the RDS Spring Show 1894. Left: 'Beaumont', a brown gelding, 2nd Prizewinner also at the 1894 Spring Show

descending to the second landing of the staircase, we reached the mill room, containing a powerful set of mill-rolls, capable of grinding 100 barrels per hour. The grist falling therefrom is conveyed by a shoot into the two grist cases that supply the mash tuns. Our steps were next directed to the kieve stage, a large saloon running through the building, the floor of which is laid with grooved iron plates. Here are to be seen two cast-iron mash tuns each capable of mashing fifty quarters, and both containing revolving mashing gear and a set of automatic sparging apparatus. They are both commanded by Steel's mashing machines, and possess wooden covers, raised or lowered by balance weights. It is in these vessels that the actual process of brewing commences, for here it is that the malt first comes into contact with the water. The mashing operation occupies about one hour, if the wort after the tap is set, comes down to the satisfaction of the brewer.

We were much struck with the underback, a handsome copper vessel, holding 100 barrels. It is fitted with a steam jacket to keep up the temperature of the wort. To reach the copper head, which is over the brewing room, we remounted the staircase to the top of the building, this time branching off to the left, where we found ourselves on a floor of great extent. Here there are four splendid coppers, two of them capable of boiling 300 barrels at one time. Two of them are used for liquor and two for wort. All of them possess the usual rousers, driven by steam power, for stirring up the hops from the bottom of the coppers. As soon as the brewer has got this wort into these vessels, he adds the hops, and then boils it sharply for a couple of hours. The all-pervading odour of the hop was supreme as we crossed the floor to take a peep at the operations.

The copper hearth is 60 feet long, and all the coppers are heated by 'Allare's' patent furnaces. Contiguous, there is a fine large metal hop back, covering the entire floor of a large room, the interior of which is laid with slotted draining plates. It is into this vessel that the porter runs from the coppers to be separated from the hops, which remain behind as it is drawn off to the coolers. Before returning downstairs we inspected the hop loft, which occupies the top storey of the malt stores, and contained, at the time of our visit, some 2,000 pockets of English hops.

In a wing of the central block, built out into the courtyard, is the cooling house, a bright and handsome place. The wall on one side is louvered from floor to ceiling, and is ventilated in the roof. It measured 75 feet by 32 feet, and is covered by an open cooler, constructed of Dantzig pine, bound with iron, holding 200 barrels. In the centre of it there is a large four-bladed fan, of the newest description, to hasten the cooling, by Grendon, of Drogheda. On a large space, at a slight elevation at the east end of this building, there are four of Morton's horizontal refrigerators, capable of cooling forty barrels per hour. Messrs Findlater and Co. were the first brewers in Dublin to adopt the now famous Morton's refrigerators.

Passing through the engine-room, we made our way to the fermenting-department, where we saw six fermenting tuns with an average capacity of 250 barrels each. Peeping into one of them, where fermentation was actively commencing, we observed that the surface of the dark liquid was covered with bubbles; as we watched, we noticed that these bubbles, by the power of attraction, were drawn to the sides of the vessels. At first they were small and few, but they soon increased in size and number till, at last, they spread over the whole surface.

From a gallery in this department, we watched the next interesting process, that of eliminating the yeast from the porter. It is carried on in seven large shallow metal vessels, placed on the floor below and extending into the next building. Following our guide we descended to the ground floor to see the slate reservoir referred to. Here, also, we saw the operation of barm-pressing being carried on by a number of men, by means of a Johnson and a Ritchie's patent yeast-pressing machines.

The yeast is turned out of the machines in a semi-solid state, then packed in bags and sold to the distillers and barm merchants.* From the settling tanks the porter is pumped to the distant vat-houses, through an enormous main 200 feet long, whither we followed it. These houses, three in number, together with a large open building running parallel with them, comprise a second block between the maltings and brewery. Some idea of the enormous size of the vat-houses may be gathered from the fact that each house measures 100 feet in length with a breadth of sixty feet, and that they contain together twenty-seven vats, averaging 600 hogsheads each.

We commenced our inspection at the No. 1 house, a lofty and well-lighted building with an open roof. From the concrete floor rise an array of massive iron columns, which support fifteen ponderous vats, all constructed of English oak, beneath which we walked. The floor of this and the other houses is slightly graduated down to the centre where there is a channel laid, to convey the water away used in flushing the floors, which is done every hour in summer, it being absolutely necessary to keep the place sweet, cool and clean at this season of the year. In the second house, which is of enormous height, there are nine large vats, similarly arranged, with a space of 15 feet beneath them, used for storing stouts in barrels, if required. Following our guide, we reached the third house. Here are to be seen four vats holding 60,000 gallons of old stock stouts for the foreign market. Their top is reached by an iron ladder 40 feet long.

All these houses open into the great building referred to, where the racking operations are conducted. Along the centre is laid a double line of rails, one for conveying the malt-laden trunks from the malthouses to the bins, the other for rolling away the

* Quote from a former chairman of Powers distillery: 'It was always considered important to have some yeast from Mountjoy Brewery in the fermentation of our whiskey, and this was done until the closure of that brewery.'

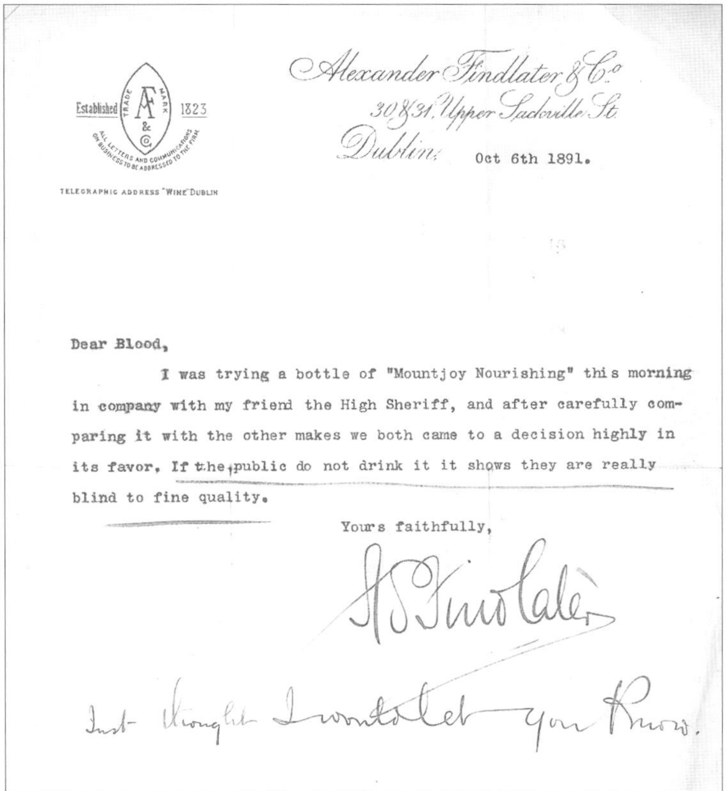

Established 1823 TRADE MARK AF & Co.

All letters and communications on business to be addressed to the firm.

TELEGRAPHIC ADDRESS "WINE" DUBLIN

Alexander Findlater & Co.
30 & 31, Upper Sackville St.
Dublin. Oct 6th 1891.

Dear Blood,

I was trying a bottle of "Mountjoy Nourishing" this morning in company with my friend the High Sheriff, and after carefully comparing it with the other makes we both came to a decision highly in its favor. If the public do not drink it it shows they are really blind to fine quality.

Yours faithfully,

A. S. Findlater

Just thought I would let you know.

filled casks into the extensive porter stores, to which place we next bent our steps. They spread out under the malt stores and brewery, and are capable of holding 70,000 casks. To keep a regular temperature in winter, these vast stores are heated by a system of steam pipes.

Returning to the larger yard, we crossed over to the cask-washing sheds, constructed principally of iron with tiled roofs. The first operation is to clean the outsides of the barrels, which is accomplished in the open. They are then rolled into these sheds, filled with hot water, and placed on Dawson's patent cradles, worked by an engine, then placed over steam jets and dried by hot and cold air. Three thousand casks can be turned out of these sheds daily, and thirty men are employed at the work. Facing these sheds there is a space of ground, upwards of an acre in extent, which is covered with casks, and adjacent there is a blacksmiths' forge, carpenters', joiners', engineers', and painters' shops. Opposite, in a detached building, is the No. 1 engine (horizontal) of thirty-horse power, for driving the cask-washing apparatus, the drying machinery, malt-roasting cylinders, chaff and fodder cutters, etc.

The cooperage next claimed our attention, where the casks are repaired before being sent to the washing sheds. It occupies the southern end of the yard, near the stables, and is well arranged for the conduct of this important department. After this, we made our way to the malt-roasting house, a brick building constructed for the purpose. Messrs Findlater & Co. were the first brewers to take advantage of the new Act in Ireland, which enabled the brewers to roast their own malt.

A short distance from this are the stables and dray sheds. The former, consisting of seventeen stalls, is a neat and well-ventilated building. Also two sick boxes and a large fodder and hay store. Then we made our way to the wheelwrights' shop. This is an important place, as the firm manufacture all their floats, waggons, and carts, and paint them besides.

We then walked through that building, which contains a spacious counting house, where fourteen clerks are employed, private offices, waiting rooms, etc. This brewery can easily turn out 100,000 barrels per annum. There are five houses on the estate, occupied by the head brewer, assistant brewer, head maltster, head stableman, and gatekeeper. Over 120 men are employed on the premises. In conclusion, it may be added that the Mountjoy Brewery is now a Limited Company, of which William Findlater, Deputy Lieutenant of the County of Dublin, and senior nephew of Alexander Findlater, the founder, is the Sole Director.[4]

Although (as we have seen) Billy had numerous other interests, he kept a close eye on the brewery. Every week there was a minuted meeting between himself

FINDLATER & CO.,

BREWERS OF

CROWN, XXX, XX, & X STOUTS,

Mountjoy Brewery, Dublin.

Messrs. FINDLATER & CO. desire to call attention to their **CROWN & XXX STOUTS**, which, for strength, richness of flavour, and good keeping quality, cannot be surpassed, and are especially suitable for private families and invalids. They can be had in 9-gallon casks, and also in bottles, guaranteed by their labels from their Agents, in most of the leading towns in Great Britain.

Messrs. FINDLATER & CO. are the ONLY Dublin Brewers, who send out all sizes of Casks in English Measure or equal to Four Gallons per Barrel more than the Irish Measure of the other Dublin Brewers.

AGENTS IN MOST OF THE LARGE TOWNS IN GREAT BRITAIN.

"The Estimation in which DUBLIN STOUT is held, evidenced by the increasing demand from England, Scotland, and Wales, renders it as celebrated as either Burton or Edinburgh Ales. Messrs. FINDLATER'S Brewery was built in 1853, and their shipments from the Port of Dublin in 1855 were 2,808 hhds., they occupying the seventh place in the list of shippers; last year, however, (1866), their shipments were 31,818 hhds., they taking the second position, thus showing that Messrs. FINDLATER AND Co. have enjoyed more than a proportionate share in the increasing trade of Dublin Stout."
—*Historical Review*.

and the head brewer (who was also his nephew) John R. Blood, at which the number of barrels brewed was reported, as well as other key figures. At this time sales were steadily dropping to less than three hundred barrels a week, having been four hundred a week in the 1860s. In July 1889 he notes that he is going to be abroad for his health for six weeks, but that the minuted meetings should continue in his absence.

By 1889 Billy was disturbed by the drop in profits shown in accountants' Craig Gardner's annual audit results. The management committee minutes record:

> Mr Findlater requested that a separate report by each of the managers as well as the Accountant Mr Jennings be prepared and submitted to him. Mr Findlater desired that Messrs Redmond, Hyland and Ewing, representatives of the company, should each send in a statement of their opinion as to the cause of the falling off in the trade of the Brewery from 1884 to 1888 inclusive, and submit their ideas of how the business could be increased.

One answer that came back was the difficulty of selling the firm's beers and ales to tied houses (pubs owned by brewers), and it is possible that this influenced Billy in his later decision to sell his interest a year or so later to a man who had much better connections with the trade.

At the meeting of 12 June 1889 Billy reported that he had telephoned the brewery between two and three in the afternoon, and was unable to get an intelligible response from a workman who answered (telephones were then very new, of course, and this was perhaps the first time he had ever picked up the contraption). By bad luck all of the clerks were either at the bank, on holiday or out to lunch. Billy, who had not long since complained about loss of profitability, evidently blew his top, complaining that 'such an easy-going system is unsuited to the exigencies of the present times'. Why couldn't the clerks bring their lunch to work with them? He was very doubtful of the wisdom of allowing the clerks to have a heavy meal in the middle of the day. The hours were nine to five, and he could not see why they could not be covered. In their defence the Blood brothers explained to their uncle that firms such as Guinness and Findlaters provided hot dinners free to all their clerks between one and three every day, and noted that 'the system is in full swing all over England and Scotland'. They maintained that the fact that by bad luck all the clerks were out had nothing to do with 'the success or non-success of the Brewery', and that anyway this was not an opportune moment to make changes, being 'the busiest time of year'.

Even though profits were down, Billy got some side benefit from his interest in that the debt collecting business went to his law firm, W. Findlater & Co. In October 1889 the Blood brothers complained about the very high charges that Billy's firm was deducting for this service, amounting, they claimed, to 20 per cent of the debt. Next week they were obliged to revise this to 9½ per cent, although this was still regarded as high. A year later, with sales continuing to decline Billy (being now in his mid-sixties), decided to sell his interest in the brewery. The land, buildings and machinery were valued at £60,000 [£3m] and the cash, stocks and debtors at a further £20,000 making a total of £80,000 [£4m]. There was no valuation placed on goodwill. The purchaser was Laurence Malone, a distiller. In the prospectus offering the trade an opportunity of taking an interest in the company Malone wrote: 'The price must be admitted to be extremely modest, and my directors consider the bargain a most advantageous one.'

I suspect that Billy was more at home in his law practice, and lacked the commercial charisma of his Uncle Alexander. Moreover, the surviving minute book shows the Bloods as rather under the thumb of their Uncle Billy. Malone as good as alluded to these points when he wrote: 'There is every reason to believe that with energetic management and the increased business which will be added through the connections and customers of Laurence Malone & Co., it will soon become as prosperous as ever.' On quality, he added: 'The first consideration of the directors will be the production of an article which will be second in quality to none in Dublin, and such as will on its merits alone deserve the support of the Trade.' As the brewery traded for another sixty years, we must take it that his was a successful formula.

Malone was president of the Dublin Chamber of Commerce in 1907/8 and had good trade connections that enhanced the distribution of Mountjoy Stout and Joy Ale. Malone died around 1917. His widow remained the largest shareholder for many years. In the 1920s and 1930s the chairman was D. J. Healy of Drogheda who controlled the firm of W. and L. Ryan and Co., wine merchants on Ormond Quay. The head brewer at this time was Michael Read and the Malone shares eventually passed to the Read family. About 1935 Frederick Ryan joined the board and succeeded D. J. Healy as chairman, remaining there until his death in 1955. The company was liquidated a year or so later and there is now very little left of the magnificent buildings that once graced the site, diagonally across the road from Croke Park.

By 1900 only six breweries remained in Dublin, of which Guinness was by far the largest. A son of Daniel O'Connell had bought the Phoenix Brewery situated in what is now the Guinness powerhouse, in 1820. He was not a good businessman and the company went bankrupt. John Brennan, who had been the manager, came to the rescue and made a big feature of O'Connell's Dublin Ale. This brewery advertised itself as 'the largest brewery in Ireland—but one'! It closed in 1906. When the brewery closed the franchise for brewing the ale went to D'Arcy's Anchor Brewery on Usher's Island which John D'Arcy had purchased in 1818. It prospered on its stout brewing. It closed in 1926.

The brewing of O'Connell's Ale was then handed over to Watkins, who, in addition to their brewery in Ardee Street, had acquired Roy's Brewery in North Anne Street from whom Alexander bought Six Guinea Ale for export in the 1830s. In doing so they became Watkins, Jameson and Pim. They owned some Dublin pubs which they called 'Taps'. They also had a good export trade and were undoubtedly one of Dublin's finest brewers, outlasting their competitors. Sadly they closed in 1939.

A Mountjoy advertisement—a play on the famous 'His Master's Voice' gramophone slogan

The two hundred year shrinkage in the number of breweries continued. By the middle of the 20th century there remained but two breweries in Dublin, Guinness at St James's Gate and the Mountjoy Brewery in Russell Street. Alas, the latter's days were numbered. As an exporter of Irish stout it had enjoyed considerable success and, for many years was second only to Guinness through the port of Dublin. For a city once famous for the art of brewing, by the late 1950s Guinness was the lone Dublin brewery until the welcome arrival of the craft breweries in the last decade of the 20th century.

Colonel Blood–the Irishman who stole the British Crown Jewels An ancestor of the Bloods of Findlater's Mountjoy Brewery

I loved this story as a child and, like distant cousin Brian Inglis, I used to boast about this relative when at school in England.

Thomas Blood was born in Ireland, probably in Dublin, somewhere round the year 1620. His father had an iron works and was reasonably well-to-do. Of Thomas Blood's education and early life we know nothing. When Cromwell became Protector of England Colonel Blood, like other leaders in Cromwell's forces, was given land in Ireland and might even have been content to settle down and become one of the landed gentry. But with the Restoration, which put Charles II on the throne, Colonel Blood's lands were confiscated. They were given to the Duke of Ormonde, and from then on Colonel Blood pursued a blood feud against the Duke, twice attempting to murder him.

The first of these plots was to seize Dublin Castle, the seat of the

Duke, by tricking the guards into scrambling for loaves of white bread while Blood's men forced their way in. But the plot failed and Blood fled to Holland. The next attempt came seven years later when, after a fugitive life in England, Ireland and on the Continent, often in disguise and with a price on his head, Blood attacked the Duke in St James's Street. With five cut-throats, he way-laid the Duke's coach and the Duke was overpowered. Blood's plan was to string his old enemy up on Tyburn gibbet, but the coachman raised the alarm and after a tremendous struggle the Duke escaped.

The Royal proclamation went out offering £1,000 for his capture, but this, far from daunting Colonel Blood, seems only to have encouraged his next and most daring adventure. Early in May 1671 Blood, dressed as a Doctor of Divinity in a false beard and accompanied by a woman whom he pretended was his wife, visited the Tower of London to see the jewels. The woman feigned a faint and the kindly old keeper of the jewels, Talbot Edwards, took her upstairs in his home, gave her a drink and allowed her to rest on a bed. Parson Blood was very grateful and three days later returned to the Tower with a present—four pairs of white gloves for Mrs Edwards.

The keeper and he became quite friendly and Blood let it be known that he had a handsome young nephew with a substantial income who would be a fitting match for Talbot Edwards' pretty daughter. The details were arranged there and then and Blood agreed to bring the nephew early on the morning of 9 May. Miss Edwards was peeping out of the window, hoping to catch a glimpse of her possible husband-to-be when Blood with three other men called at the Jewel House. Two of the men went with Blood to call on Talbot Edwards, and the third, whom Miss Edwards assumed was the shy lover, remained some distance away. In fact, he, like the other two cut-throats, was one of Blood's confederates. All had rapiers in their walking sticks, daggers in their belts and pistols in their pockets. Blood explained to Talbot Edwards that his wife had been slightly delayed and suggested that while waiting for her they fill in the time by having a look at the Crown Jewels.

Talbot Edwards took them upstairs and as he led the way into the room where the jewels were kept they attacked him, struck him with a mallet, threatened him that if he shouted they would kill him, and then began putting the Crown Jewels into the swag bag. The crown had to be bent almost flat to get it in and in doing so the Black Prince's ruby fell from its setting. The sceptre was so long that they had to saw it in two.

What would have been the greatest robbery in history was all but complete when, by an amazing stroke of ill fortune for Blood and his men, Talbot Edwards' son, who had been abroad, arrived home at that very moment. He raised the alarm. There was a chase, a running fight, and in the end Colonel Blood was captured. It seemed certain that he would be executed, but Blood's behaviour was astonishing. He refused to say who was with him in the plot, and he presumptuously demanded a private audience with the King. Only to him, he said, would he tell all. And most surprisingly, the King agreed to see him. The door was shut behind them, the courtiers kept outside, and Blood and the King were left together. Shortly afterwards the King announced that he had pardoned Colonel Blood, had restored to him his lands in Ireland and had invited him to attend the Court.

One explanation is that Blood threatened the King, saying that the rest of the gang would murder him if Blood were executed. But the chances of the King being attacked were remote. Another theory is that hidden inside the sceptre was a copy of the secret treaty of Dover which Charles had made with Louis XIV and that the King knew that Colonel Blood must have seen it when it was sawn in half and that he saved Blood's life in exchange for his silence. But the most likely theory of all is that King Charles was so short of money that he was in the plot to steal the crown jewels, was in fact the instigator of it. The timely arrival of young Edwards seems too much of a coincidence and old man Edwards and the son were afterwards given grants of £200 and £100. Was old Edwards, who was seventy-seven at the time, as badly injured by mallet blows on his head as he pretended? He lived on until he was eighty-one.

It seems possible that Charles II, Blood and the Edwards were all in the plot together, but that the young Edwards panicked for some reason and gave the alarm. His grant could have been in payment for his silence. Whatever the reason for the King's strange clemency Blood became a very powerful member of the Court, and for a while seekers after favours made their applications through him. No one seems to have trusted him and even when he died rumour had it that he had staged a disappearance and that the corpse was not his. To prove it his body was dug up from its grave in Tothill fields and then identified at an inquest before being finally reburied.[5]

William – eldest brother of Alexander, the founder (Chapter 2)

Billy, later Sir William (Chapter 3)

Married
1 Mary Jane Wolfe, daughter of John Wolfe, solicitor.
(No issue)

2 Marion, daughter of Archibald Park, son of Mungo Park, the African explorer. They had issue (Chapters 3 & 8); Victor, Percy, Muriel

Janet (Jessie)

Married
Joseph Taylor of Melbourne, Australia.
(No issue)

Sophia

Married
1 Henry Geoghegan, Solicitor and had daughters Jessie and Helena. (Helena married twice
a) to Max. J. d'Elsa
b) to Adam Lloyd Blood who was the fourth son of Sophia's younger sister, Margaret. (Col. 4)

2 Henry Porson Morse of Otago, New Zealand.
(No issue)

3 Francis Johnston

Margaret

Married
John Lloyd Blood who was previously married to Margaret Wolfe, sister of Mary Jane (Col. 1). They had four sons and two daughters, Susanna and Lucy

1 Alexander Findlater Blood KC who married Rachel Park, younger sister of Marion (see left hand column)

2 William Findlater Blood, artist

3 John Redmond Blood, head brewer whose eldest daughter Vera married (Sir) Claud Inglis, parents of Brian Inglis, author

4 Adam Lloyd Blood, solicitor, who married Sophia's daughter Helena and parents of Ken Lloyd Blood last partner of William Findlater Solicitors

Keep it in the family

In 1842 and 1855 the brothers John Lloyd Blood and Frederick Blood married the sisters Margaret Wolfe and Isabella Susannah Wolfe, both daughters of John Wolfe, solicitor. Margaret died in 1851 and John Lloyd Blood then married Margaret Findlater, third sister of Billy. They had four sons and two daughters. John became a brewer in Findlater's Mountjoy Brewery of which Billy was proprietor. (JLB's eldest brother Neptune was a partner in William Findlater, Solicitors.)

The eldest son, Alexander Findlater Blood KC (born 1853) married Rachel Park, daughter of Lt Col. Archibald Park of the 29th Bengal Army, a younger sister of Marion, second wife of Billy. Alexander was called to the Irish Bar in 1877. He practised in New Zealand between 1878 and 1883, was called to the Irish Inner Bar in 1899 and was a member of the Senate of Dublin University and a bencher of King's Inns. (His son Dr Blood of Enniskerry (born 1885) was the author of the letter to me in the previous chapter about Billy in his old age.) The second son was William Findlater Blood (born 1854). He was a journalist, author and artist and had two marriages. The third son, John Redmond Blood (born 1858), was head brewer in Findlater's Mountjoy Brewery until 1913 having started there in 1874 at the age of sixteen. He married Sophia, daughter of Andrew Armstrong JP of Malahide. Their eldest daughter Vera married Sir Claud Inglis FRCSI, son of Sir Malcolm John Inglis* and Carrie Johnston. She was sister of Jane Johnston, married to Adam Seaton Findlater and of Mary Johnston, married to his nephew, John Findlater, JP (see Chapter 5). Sir Claud and Vera's son was Brian Inglis, journalist, broadcaster and author of a number of books including *West Briton*.

The fourth son was Adam Lloyd Blood, partner in William Findlater, solicitors. He married Billy's niece Helena, daughter of his sister Sophia. (Helena had previously been married to Max J. d'Elsa.) Their son, Ken Lloyd Blood, who died in 1956, was the last family member in William Findlater, Solicitors. Sophia married three times: in 1852 to Henry Geoghegan, solicitor, with whom she had two daughters, Jessie and Helena; then to Henry Porson Morse of Otago, New Zealand—there were no children. Her third marriage in 1877 was to Francis Johnston, perhaps a member of the Johnston family mentioned above and in Chapter 5.

* Chairman of Heitons 1896-1902; of Scottish stock, being the second son of William Inglis of Falkirk.

Notes and references

1 Andrew Bielenberg *Locke's Distillery, a History* Dublin: Lilliput Press, 1993
2 S. R. Dennison and Oliver MacDonagh *Guinness 1886-1939,* Cork: Cork University Press, 1998 pp 271-2
3 Dominic Behan *Teems of Times and Happy Returns* London: Heinemann, 1961, p 55
4 Condensed from *The Noted Breweries of Great Britain and Ireland* by Alfred Barnard London: Joseph Causton & Sons 1889
5 For more on the Blood family see *Burke's Irish Family Records* 1976 pp 142-52

Activities in Findlaters Sackville Street

Vatting and bottling in the Whiskey House

The Grocery Department

Loading outside Sackville Street

Beer bottling in the cellars

5. Great-Grandfather John, Head of Findlaters 1873–1908

*Shopping should always be done by the mistress herself. It is extremely unwise to send servants with money to buy what is required, as, however honest they may be, a temptation to pilfer is put in their way which a mistress has no right to subject them to. A good housekeeper will never run short of anything, and so will have no occasion to send off in a hurry at the last minute to try and obtain what should have been ready to hand. A strict account of all money spent each week should be kept by all housekeepers who wish to attain efficiency and economy, and those who have never done so will be surprised how many entries are made, and how the most trifling expenditures amount very quickly to large sums. (*Findlater's Ladies' Housekeeping Book *for 1890)*

Great-grandfather John was forty-five when he inherited the Dublin-based organisation, with their headquarters in Sackville Street. He had been in the business since he was fourteen. But as with other members of the family, his education could have been on-going. There is no record of his schooling but cash transfers suggest that part was in Belfast. The Sackville Street operation was only part of Alexander's empire, but was to be the mainstay of the Findlater family business for the next century.

Smells and aromas

It was in this era that Findlaters became part of the everyday life of the citizens of Dublin. When asked to recall old Findlaters many start with the wonderful array of smells and aromas. This can be attributed to the great variety of produce being handled and processed, as one scribe put it:

> great wines of the world arriving in cask and leaving years later matured to perfection; barrels of over-proof whiskey maturing in bond, before blending and despatch to the nation's licensees; porter, stout and ale, kegs by the dray load, from Mountjoy, Bass and Guinness, awaiting bottling by hand, maturing, (yes, beer), before distribution to the city's enormous and thirsty workforce; sacks of rice, barley, oats and semolina in the 'Lofts' where Barney with his needle and bodkin, repairs the holes made by a meandering mouse over night; piping hot cakes and scones, crisp from our own Bakery up in Thomas Street and Bread by the van load, horsedrawn of course, brown and unwrapped from our cousins, the Johnston's, of JM&O'B in Balls Bridge; boxes of raisins, sultanas and cherries; sacks of brown sugar; all-spice and mixed spice, all ready for weighing into brown Kraft bags, by the stone, by the pound or by the ounce at customer command; freshly roasted coffee; smoked bacon, eggs, butter, potatoes and cabbages all fresh from the farms of Dublin, Wicklow, Meath and Kildare. And last

but not least, to add to the aromas are those fine dray horses, tired but fit, after a day of good service in a city bustling with activity, safely stabled around the corner, in Findlater Place.'

By the time he became senior partner, John had worked in the firm for some thirty years. In 1854 he married Mary Johnston of the milling and baking family that was to become part of Johnston, Mooney & O'Brien whose sister Jane was married to his Uncle Adam. She was the fourth daughter of John Johnston of Ballsbridge. John and Mary were to have a large family—nine sons and two daughters.

Household expenditure 1854-1862

Remembered in the family as 'a nice old gentleman, who sat on the top of the tram, and always had sweets in his pocket for the children', John was small and dapper. He was also clearly meticulous and conscientious. (His handwriting is wonderfully clear.) From his reading matter we can deduce that he identified with his ancestral homeland of Scotland, and with the union. He was a pious Presbyterian, regularly attending sermons and giving donations to various churches and Protestant charities. On the other hand he was not puritanical—he bought playing cards and whiskey, went to the theatre and the pantomime, and subscribed to *Punch*. All these details are decipherable from the detailed cash book that he kept in the early years of his marriage, in which he recorded all his personal expenses.

At the start of the cash book, John was earning a modest salary of £200 a year [equivalent to £12,000 after tax in 2000], but on his marriage in 1854 he was made a junior partner with a small share in the profits and his income jumped to £471 [£27,000 after tax]. In the 'personal' category of the cash book he records the purchase of toothbrushes (two for himself, one for his wife, in the normal order) collar studs and haircuts, and under 'sundry' his presents ('jet bracelet to wife 22s 6d'), entertainments ('season ticket Royal Hibernian Academy 2s 6d') and holidays ('rent of cottage at Kingstown 15 May to 30 Sept £23 10s').

The early pages record John's share of the costs of getting married—Mary's family would of course have paid for the wedding. Here is '1 plain gold ring, with guard 14s 6d' [£45]; a marriage licence 6s [£18] and numerous white kid gloves from Todd Burns £8 5s [£240]–the great drapery emporium in which his uncle Alexander was a partner. Then there is a payment to his cousin Billy the solicitor for preparing the marriage settlement (£2 3s 8d) [£60], various presents to the bridesmaids and others, wedding cards £3 16s 6d, hire of carriages on the big day £1 5s 6d [£75], expenses of the wedding tour 20 April to 5 May £40 [£2,400] (plus 10d for 'key to carpet bag', and 8s 6d for a copy of Tupper's *Proverbial Philosophy** to while away the tedious hours of travel).

* Martin Tupper's *Proverbial Philosophy* was rather unkindly described in the *Oxford Companion to English Literature* as 'presenting maxims and reflections couched in vaguely rhythmical form . . . the favourite of millions who knew nothing about poetry. It remained a best-seller in Britain and America for more than a generation.'

Findlater's Corner, 28–32 Upper O'Connell Street, 1835–1969

84 and 85 Lower George's Street, Dun Laoghaire, 1830–1969

On their return the newly married couple faced the task of setting up home. They started in 20 Eglinton Terrace, Seville Place (rent £42 pa) [£2,500] and moved to Anna Ville, Upper Leeson Street in 1858 (rent £52 pa) [£3,300] and then again to Wellington Place, also off Leeson Street, in 1862 (rent £70 pa) [£4,200]. Typically of the time, they rented rather than bought, and spent only a year or two in each house. Just over 7 per cent of his expenditure went in rent.

John and Mary now started to invest in furniture. They found a sofa to their liking, for seven guineas [£450]; '1 mahogany Albert bed £9 15s' [about £600], and '1 spring mattress £6 15s' [£400]; a set of dining room chairs ('12 balloon back chairs £15' [£900]), and a 'rosewood loo table, ten guineas' [£630].

I am always interested in my ancestors' drinking preferences. John tended to drink spirits, especially whiskey, and fortified wines such as port and sherry. (This was normal of the time, fortified wines representing more than half of total wine consumption.) In March 1855, for instance, he bought a dozen pints of claret, 1½ doz. sherry and 1½ doz. port, plus two bottles of whiskey and a 'flask' each of Geneva, London gin and rum. He bought two gallons of 'Best Irish' in May, and then nothing more until November, when he bought 2½ dozen pints of beer, from Findlaters of course, with six bottles of whiskey and three bottles of port—all quite modest in comparison to his uncle's household, but then he was only twenty-seven at the time.

As well as the housekeeping, John gave Mrs Findlater—as he refers to Mary in his ledgers—an allowance for her personal expenses and those of the children. At first this was quite modest, a mere £15 [£900], but as the family prospered, it crept up, becoming £40 [£2,500] a year in 1859 and 1860, and jumping to £50 {£3,000] in 1861 and £65 [almost £4,000] in 1862. Although Mary's allowance represented the annual wage of a skilled man by 1861, it is likely that this was not the whole of her income. A later cash book (from the 1880s) records her receiving half-yearly dividend income of £80 [over £5,000] from a trust fund.

John's expenditure on books and magazines (and later prints), on the garden and on a wide range of entertainments and 'treats' is interesting. In 1855, for example, he subscribed to *Saunders Newsletter*, to the *Illustrated London News*, the *Advocate*, and he bought a pictorial bible, and *Chambers' History of the Russian War*, the *Christian Treasury* for 1855, and *Marriage–Why so Often Unhappy*. A keen gardener, he bought various bits of garden equipment, and splashed out three guineas [£190] for a man to help him restructure the fences to his satisfaction. He went to the opera (2s [£6], including car hire), the theatre and the pantomime, attended psalmody classes at Zion Chapel, Kings Inn Street, and bought a pack of playing cards (1s [£3]) and '4 cigars for use of friends' (also 1s).

The following year he spent a further £6 (equivalent to nearly £400 in current terms) on his garden, and later a copy of Joseph Paxton's *Cottager's Calendar of Gardening Operations*. He bought more books, continuing *Chambers History of the Russian War* and the 1856 edition of the *Christian Treasury*. With his first child just born, he bought a copy of *The Home School, or Hints on Home*

Education, and a copy of Johnson's dictionary; also a cheap reprint of Susan Ferrier's novel *The Inheritance,*[*] originally published in 1824. He subscribed to *The Economist*, and rented a cottage in Kingstown for the summer months. This cost him £23 [£1,380] for 4½ months. Presumably Mary and the children retreated there. From 1858 he started to fill the house with prints. He became a keen subscriber to art unions in Dublin, Glasgow and Edinburgh.[†]

As time went on his reading tastes broadened: he took in *Punch*, which at this period was notably anti-Catholic and anti-Irish—an entertaining, topical and humorous publication but hardly reflecting his own views as a successful liberal businessman in a Catholic country. He bought *Shirley* and *Jane Eyre*, and Griffin's *The Rivals*. In August 1858 he and Caroline Johnston (his sister-in-law) went to hear Charles Dickens read *The Christmas Carol*[‡] (he was a regular subscriber to Dickens' newspaper *Household Words*). In the same month he bought Caroline a 'steel petticoat' for 10s [£30]. (This oddly intimate present is a crinoline, a fashion introduced by Princess Eugenie in Paris in 1856 to conceal the signs of pregnancy, or so it is said.)

In 1856 John bought a book called *The Scriptural Duty of Giving a Stated Portion of Income to Charitable Purposes*. Whether by coincidence or not, for his personal circumstances did become easier at this time, from 1857 he began a regular programme of charitable donations. Over the eight years of the cash book, John gave away 18 per cent of his expenditure to charity and worthy causes. He gave in small sums, and often, unlike his Uncle Alexander who tended to give large donations to a few recipients but his uncle was then head of the family and considerably wealthier; however, John's time would come.

In a typical year, for instance, John made over a hundred separate payments totalling £146 [£9,000].[§] In 1857 he gave £3 each to two advertisers in *Saunders Newsletter*—a 'respectable family in great distress', and 'a gentleman in bad health with a wife and six children'. There were numerous church-related subscriptions: to the Young Men's Christian Association, to the Presbyterian congregation in Clonakilty, to building the new Presbyterian church at Rathgar (£10—his uncles also subscribed), to Bray Presbyterian church, to the Dublin City Mission, to the annual sermon at the Scots church at Kingstown, and the Adelaide Road church, to the Protestant Orphan Society, to the collection at Sandymount church towards the General Assembly's Foreign Mission, to the 'Home Mission', to the Jewish Mission and to the Roman Catholic Mission, to paying the debts of the Presbyterian church Ormond Quay, and towards the rent of the Gloucester Street church, where two of his children were baptised. Other payments included a donation 'per Miss Duffy towards sufferers by accident in

* Described by *The Oxford Companion to English Literature* as having 'an improbably complex plot told with much good humour'.

† Subscribers to an art union entered a lottery for a named painting—the successful one got the painting itself, all the others got a print. Subscriptions were one guinea per share.

‡ Dublin was the first stop on Dickens' first provincial tour with his readings.

§ Although £1, a typical payment, does not now seem much, we should remember that it is equivalent to almost £60 in modern purchasing power.

Christmas circular and price list 1881

' Can't catch me' 1888

'Wild roses', after a painting by Fred Morgan exhibited at the Royal Academy in 1889

'Grandfather's birthday' 1891

Calendars given to customers with the compliments of Findlaters

'First swan' 1892

'Little Miss Vanity' 1894

Baggot Street', to the Adelaide Hospital, the Hospital for Incurables, the Coombe, the City of Dublin Hospital and Whitworth Hospital.

Of the sons of their marriage, six survived into adulthood, all characters, and are subjects of chapters in this book. As they grew, John required a sizeable residence for this lively lot and, in 1866, the family became the first occupants of Clyde House in Clyde Road. This was in easy reach of The High School at the top of Harcourt Street and Trinity College where the boys were educated. His neighbours in the newly-built road included: Robert Gardner, John B. Johnston, William Henry Bewley, the Italian Consul and several members of the legal profession.

In later years John, as senior partner in the firm, became increasingly wealthy, and his personal expenditure and his donations to charity went up. In 1873, on the death of his uncle Alexander, he moved into his Uncle Adam's house, Melbeach in Monkstown, Adam having moved into Alexander's house, The Slopes. John now kept a stable, with a number of carriages, including a splendid brougham brought over especially from England. Among his other conveyances at Melbeach were a landau, a Victoria, a barouche, a hooded gig and an outside car. There were three horses in the stables.

Before reverting to the Findlater business I will bring you on a tour of our Inglis and Johnston cousins. First, Malcolm Inglis, born in Dunfermline in 1837, who came to Dublin in 1859. He started his public life in the 1860s by becoming involved in various main drainage, gas and water schemes. In 1874 he was elected to the Blackrock town council. When Thomas Heiton, the coal importer, died in 1877 Malcolm Inglis and William Hewat purchased the business. Thomas Heiton was born in Melrose, Scotland in 1804.

According to a senior member of the family, Malcolm was always known in the family as John, but when he was knighted as President of the Dublin Chamber of Commerce in 1900 he said 'Sir Malcolm' sounded better (or more original!) than 'Sir John' and so he was knighted 'Sir Malcolm'. Actually, the family story was that he was offered a baronetcy, but said that his eldest son was a bit of a problem, and was not worthy of inheriting a title, thus he refused the baronetcy and accepted a knighthood. Malcolm married Caroline, another of the Johnston sisters. She was known in the family as 'The Aunt Carrie'. They lived for a time (1897 to 1905) in Montrose, Donnybrook, now the headquarters of RTE. Montrose had been built in about 1836 for John Jameson, the distiller. The Findlaters were frequent visitors to the Inglis', thinking nothing of making the journey on foot from Blackrock along the unlit and spooky roads.

Jennie Johnston who married Robert Gardner in 1880

Malcolm's youngest son Claud, a civil engineer, became director of the Indian Waterways Experimental Station in Poona, India and was knighted for his pioneering works on tides, currents, rivers and harbours. He became the first director and head of research at the experimental station, Howbery Park in Wallingford, Oxfordshire. Another son, Malcolm, married Vera Blood (daughter of John Redmond Blood, who ran the brewery).* My aunts, Doris and Sheila, were good friends of Claud and Vera and used to stay with them in Oxfordshire, and they with Doris and Sheila in Glensavage, Blackrock. Claud and Vera had one son, Brian, the broadcaster, journalist and author of *West Briton* and *Downstart* and numerous other books.[1] His difficulties with my father Dermot are noted in Chapter 13.

Mrs Jury, who had bought Clyde House from John and Mary in 1873, sold it to John B. Johnston,† whose daughter Jane, known as Jennie, married, in 1880, the accountant and co-founder of Craig Gardner, one Robert Gardner of Ashley,

* He had a brother Johnston Inglis, known as Johnsie, who was an artist and settled in America. I have a painting of his, of the eel weir at Lareen, the fishing lodge in County Roscommon where they holidayed in the West of Ireland.

† And if that's not enough on Johnstons, John Findlater's cousin Sophia's third marriage was to a Francis Johnston on 31 July 1877. Talk of approved families, three Johnstons to three Findlaters!

Clyde Road, Ballsbridge. This was Robert's second marriage and there was a marriage settlement, the trustees being John and his eldest son, Adam. The original settlement document, still preserved in our archives, included £2,000 [£130,000] Russian bonds, £1,500 [almost £100,000] stock of Eastern Telegraph Company, $9,000 New York Central Railway Currency bonds and stock in the Mexican Railway Company. Robert Gardner bought Ashley for £3,000 [almost £200,000] in 1878 at a time when his average earnings (after tax) from the accountancy firm were £3,000 a year. Not so bad!

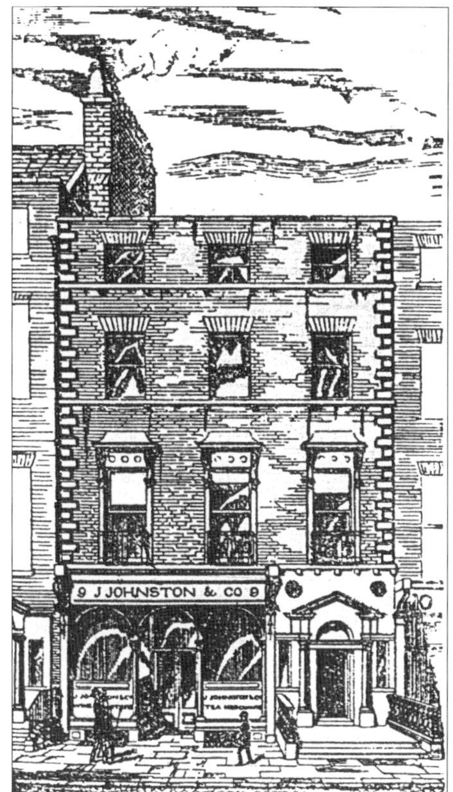

J. Johnston & Co. in Leinster Street which became the sixth Findlater branch in 1893

These connections were turned to good use when Robert's wife Jennie inherited a share in the Johnston milling and bakery business in 1883 on the death of her father John Brown Johnston. In 1889 John Findlater and Robert Gardner brought together William O'Brien, baker, of Ailesbury House, Merrion, with his brother Joseph, and John Mooney, miller and baker, of 42 Elgin Road, Ballsbridge to form the well-known firm of Johnston, Mooney & O'Brien. The first directors were: John Findlater (chairman), Robert Gardner, John Mooney (managing director with a salary of £1,200 [£80,000]), Joseph and William O'Brien, Joseph Todhunter Pim (a member of the Quaker business family and Deputy Governor of the Bank of Ireland) and John Malcolm Inglis (a few years later another Pim, Frederick W., became one of the first directors of Thomas Heiton & Co. when it was incorporated in 1896).

There is, as it happens, no direct connection with our Johnstons and the family of Francis Johnston (1761–1829), one of Ireland's most celebrated architects and founder of the Royal Hibernian Academy, who died without issue. That branch of the Johnstons was also of Scottish descent, a William Johnston having been sent to Ireland by the government as an engineer or architect to re-build public works after the 1641 rebellion, and settled in Armagh. It was descendants of the Armagh Johnstons who became wine *negoçiants* in Bordeaux from 1734 and are now celebrated, with the Bartons and others, as the wine geese. During John Findlater's stewardship of Findlaters (1873–1908) wine was purchased from Nathaniel Johnston & Fils, Quai des Chartons, Bordeaux, still to this day under

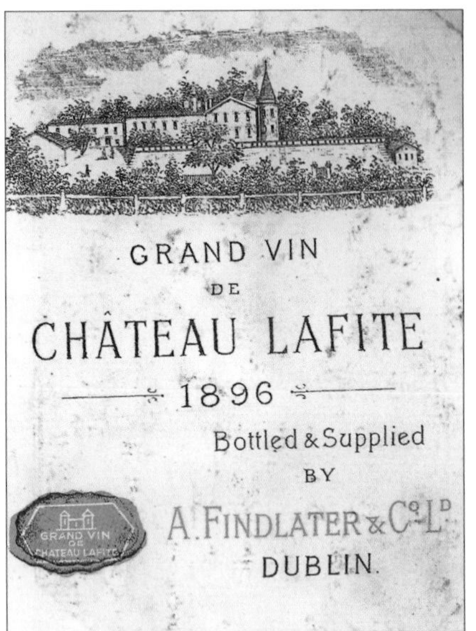

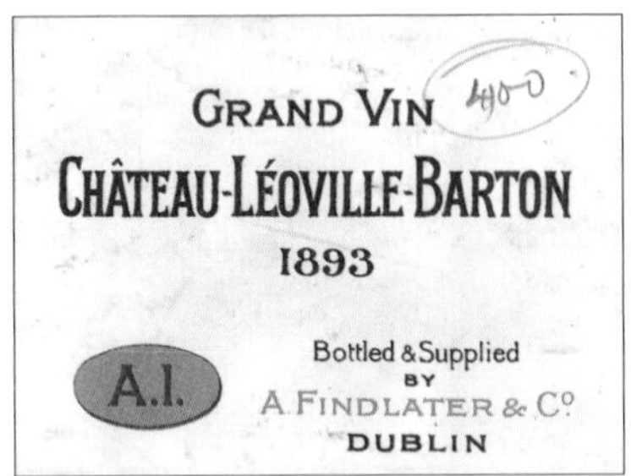

The great wines of Bordeaux were shipped in casks and bottled in our Sackville Street cellars

Johnston ownership. Barton wines, principally Château Léoville Barton, have been on Findlater lists since the early days of the company—the Bartons of Enniskillen, Tipperary and later Straffan were *negoçiants* in Bordeaux since 1725 and are there to this day.

There was a Johnston & Co. wine shop in Dublin at 9 Leinster Street, trading as 'Grocers, Tea Merchants, Wine & Spirits and Bottlers of Dublin Whiskey'. It was established in 1868 and achieved a high reputation for the quality of their Dublin bottled whiskey, and commanded a large trade all over Ireland and in England and Scotland. The publicity states that the firm only dealt in John Jameson & Sons Old Dublin Whiskey. This shop belonged to the Ballsbridge Johnstons and became Findlaters' sixth branch shop in 1893, trading as Findlaters until 1967. (William O'Brien, the baker—later of Johnston Mooney & O'Brien—occupied Nos. 7 and 8 and the rere of 6 and 9 Leinster Street, all beside Findlaters at No. 8.)

Buying wine

Four years after becoming senior partner, John, Mary and their twenty-two year-old eldest son Adam visited Bordeaux on a trip to the continent. He obviously intended to enjoy the holiday, since he took with him 'probable expenses of trip to continent £150 [£10,000]'. Later in October he required further funds, and received £50 'remitted self to Rotterdam, further costs of trip with Mrs JF and Adam junr' as he recorded in his cash book.

In October he wrote home, vividly describing conditions in the Bordeaux vineyards of the day:

> Hotel de Nantes
> Bordeaux, October 5 1877
>
> We started for Bordeaux that evening at 8 o'clock. Our intention had been to have stopped at Tours and so break the length of the journey, but as the night was pleasant we travelled on and reached Bordeaux early the next morning. Having refreshed ourselves by a bath and breakfast, we strolled through the town and called on our friends. They were, of course, anxious to pay us all the attention in their power and in the afternoon we took a drive through the town, under the guidance of Mr Calvet's representative Mors Visquis (pronounced Whiskey). The town itself is uninteresting, the only objects worth a visit being the Cathedral (Gothic, reminding me somewhat of St Ouen, Rouen), the theatre which until the building of the Grand Opera House Paris, was considered the finest and most convenient in France.
>
> . . . Next day the business of our visit was commenced and we set ourselves in earnest to learn all we could about claret and the claret districts. Bordeaux as your geography will tell you is situated on the Garonne and the claret districts extend along the right bank of the estuary, almost to the sea, with an average width of several miles. The land is level and uninteresting as regards scenery and almost without trees of any kind except a few formal poplars ranged in lines as so many soldiers. We started early in the morning by train and in a quarter of an hour or so began to get into the midst of the vineyards. We arrived at St Estèphe which is the farthest distant of the important

districts in about an hour and a half, where a carriage and horses were waiting for us.

Hotel de la Poste

Angouleme, Octr. 9, '77

In this district the vines are planted in long lines and are tied to wires that stretch along from end to end of the vineyards at about a height of three feet to three feet six. At the top most of the foliage is located, any lower down being removed to allow the sun to fully ripen the grapes. These generally cluster where the new wood springs from the old stump of the vine which is about 18 inches high. The vines are esteemed better the older they are and reach sometimes sixty to one hundred years of age.

In comparison with our English hothouse vines the quality of the grape for eating purposes is poor, the skin being thick and the juice having little flavour. The quantity on each vine is also small, ranging usually from 3 to 6 poor sized bunches of berries about the size of a sixpence. But in grapes as in everything else one must not judge by appearances, the poorer grapes very often making the best wine. In a similar manner, with regard to the soil, that of some of the finest vineyards being full of round shingle and so dry and dusty in form, and hard and unyielding in others that to the uninitiated it would appear fit for nothing.

The roads in this, the Medoc district, from whence nearly all the high-class wines come, have no fence of any kind and any passer-by can pluck the grapes. That is, of course, if he is not seen. Having now to some extent given you a description of the country I will endeavour to give you some idea of the mode of making the wine. This is as primitive as possible, being that which is transmitted from father to son from generation to generation. This was strikingly shown by Baron Sarget, the owner of Chau. Larose, one of the largest and highest class of the vineyards, who to our query of why he did not use machinery for certain operations, replied that 'the wine was good in his father's time and that this was the way his father taught him to make it'.

To commence at the beginning, the plucking or gathering of the grapes of course comes first. This is generally performed by boys and women who collect the bunches in small baskets. When these are filled a man comes round with a large flat tub on his back to collect from the gatherers. This tub is again emptied into big tubs which stand on a cart ready for carriage to the wine presses. These carts are drawn by two bullocks and have large wheels. They are very narrow and long and are constructed to carry three tubs of grapes, which I would say is about half a ton. The oxen are enormous powerful animals and altho' extremely slow are able to draw a much greater weight than horses. They are particularly suitable for the vineyards where horses, on account of the uneven ground, would likely 'baulk'.

The grapes are then forwarded to the places where they make the wine which I shall describe. The building of which I speak and take as typical of the class is that Chau. Pomys, one of the fifth growths of the St Estèphe district. As a rule the systems followed differ but little from each other, altho' some have a slightly more modern appearance. Imagine a long building of say twenty feet wide, on one side half a dozen vats, each containing say 400 gallons each, on the other half a dozen windows opening about 3½ feet from the ground. These are the openings through which the grapes are delivered. Ready to catch the grapes are large wooden troughs or rather one large wooden trough divided, extending the whole length of the building.

This is constructed of large beams of about six inches in thickness. The first operation is to separate the grapes from the stalks which is done by rubbing the grapes over a sieve of a perforated piece of zinc by the hands or a rake until the grapes have fallen through and only the stalks remain. When the trough is sufficiently full of separated grapes the sieve is removed and the process of trampling is commenced.

I should have said before that the building is full of vintagers in the usual picturesque garb of the country. To them the Vintage is a time of feasting and revelry and altho' there is plenty of hard work they make up for it by hard eating at the expense of the proprietor of the farm. These men, having removed their boots, and I need hardly say taking little heed of the state of their feet, jump into the trough and having heaped the grapes into the centre and having formed themselves into a circle, commence trampling the grapes, keeping step with the sound of a fiddle.

The juice of the grapes escapes through a hole in the side of the trough into a tub ready for it, and from thence is conveyed in long shaped tubs with a pole through them, into the vats on the other side of the room. When the grapes are sufficiently trampled, they are also conveyed in a similar manner to the same vats. This is then allowed to remain for some time on the vats until it has gone through the fermenting process and is then wine—although it has still to go through many purifying processes, such as racking, fining, etc. etc. The skins, stones etc. after the fermentation rise to the tops of the vats and separate from the wine and then the vat is run off into hogheads. They are left behind to be squeezed in the press for whatever may be in it, but this is not considered so good and is not mixed with the more natural wine.

Unfortunately the balance of the correspondence has not survived. John's cash books make it clear, however, that the extravagance continued. In Paris he spent the equivalent of over £20,000 on various pieces of statuary and a pair of Sèvres vases. Back in London he again indulged his wife and bought 'Mrs JF' a diamond ring for £80 [£5,000] and a pair of ear-rings for £155; also more statues and another pair of Sèvres vases.

The Vartry Waterworks Banquet 1892

Our position as one of the premier wine and food merchants in the city of Dublin occasionally exposed us to notoriety, as was demonstrated by the Vartry Waterworks Banquet of 1892.[2] Soon after the waterworks on the Vartry were completed in 1870, members of Dublin Corporation adopted the convention of mounting an annual tour of inspection. For the 1892 tour, catering was organised by the firm, in such a princely style that the local government auditor Mr Drury decided to disallow some of the expenses claimed. Among the items disallowed was a sum of £51 16s 8d [almost £4,000] spent on the expedition to Roundwood with

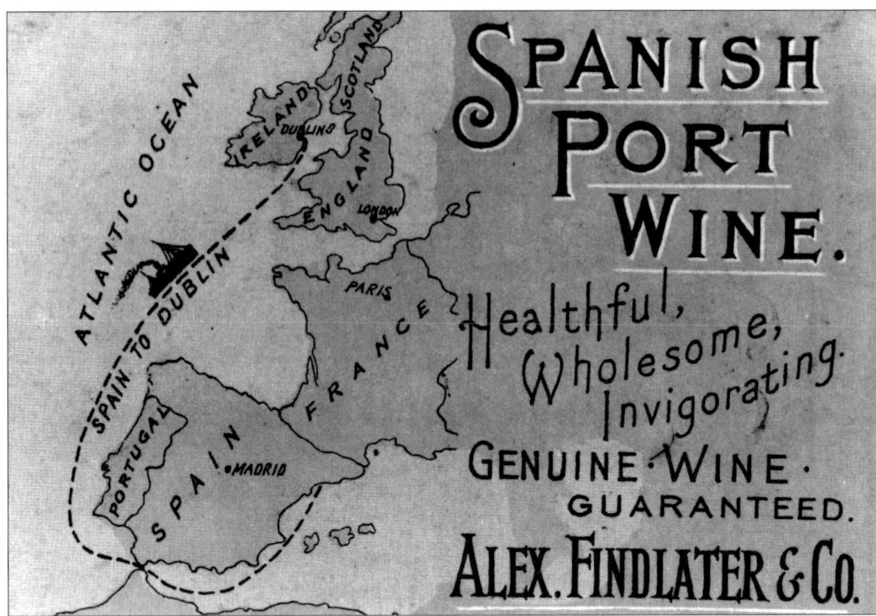

A 19th Century Spanish Port wine, but I can't find any evidence that we ever sold it.

accompanying luncheon and refreshments. On appeal, the Queen's Bench Division affirmed the auditor's decision. The Lord Chief Justice, Lord O'Brien, concentrated on the day's arrangements, in particular those made for the lunch:

I now come to deal with the expenditure in respect of the lunch. This is the most interesting item with which we have to deal . . . I have before me the items in the bill. Amongst the list of wines are two dozen champagne, Ayala, 1885—a very good brand—at 84s. a dozen; one dozen Marcobrunn hock—a very nice hock; one dozen Château Margaux—an excellent claret; one dozen fine old Dublin whiskey—the best whiskey that can be got; one case of Ayala; six bottles of Amontillado sherry—a stimulating sherry; and the ninth item is some more fine Dublin whiskey! Then Mr Lovell supplies the 'dinner' (this was a dinner, not a mere luncheon!) including all attendance, at 10s. per head [£38]. There is an allowance for brakes; one box of cigars, 100; coachmen's dinner; beer, stout, minerals in syphons, and ice for wine. There is dessert, and there are sandwiches, and an allowance for four glasses broken–a very small number broken under the circumstances.

In sober earnestness, what was this luncheon and outing? It seems to me to have been a picnic on an expensive scale. What authority is there for it? No statutable authority exists. By what principle of our common law is it sustainable? By none that I can see . . . this is a question of providing a sumptuous repast for the members of the Corporation in the Wicklow Hills. It is not certain-

Hock.

LABEL.	STILL.	Per Dozen. Bottles	Half-Bottles.
"*Laubenheim*"	Laubenheim ..	18/-	
"*Deidesheim*"	Deidesheim ..	24/-	12/-
"*Oestrich*"	Oestrich	36/-	18/-
"*Liebfraumilch*"	Liebfraumilch ..	48/-	24/-
"*Rudesheim*"	Rudesheim	53/	27/-
"*Marcobrunn*"	Marcobrunn ..	59/-	30/6
"*Hochheim*"	Hochheim	60/-	31/-
"*Johannesberg*"	Johannesberg ..	72/-	38/-
	SPARKLING.		
Black, "*Hock*" ..	Sparkling, recommended ..	45/-	24/6
White, "*Ehrenbreitstein*"	" Ehrenbreitstein ..	65/-	34/6
" "*Johannesberg*"	" Johannesberg-Brut ..	60/-	32/-
" "*Cabinet Sect*"	" Cabinet	66/-	35/6

Moselle.

LABEL.	STILL.	Per Dozen. Bottles.	Half-Bottles.
White, "*Winningen*" ..	Winningen ..	24/-	12/-
" "*Bocksteiner*" ..	Bocksteiner ..	42/-	22/-
	SPARKLING.		
Black, "*Moselle*"	Sparkling, recommended	45/-	24/6
" "*Nonpareil Moselle* ..	Finest Nonpareil ..	65/-	34/6

ly for the benefit of the property of the Corporation, or of the rate-paying citizens of Dublin, that the members of the Corporation should lunch sumptuously. I asked for statute or for case, but neither was cited.

The Solicitor-General in his most able argument—I have always to guard myself against his plausibility—appealed pathetically to common sense; he asked, really with tears in his voice, whether the members of the Corporation should starve; he drew a most gruesome picture; he represented that the members of the Corporation would really traverse the Wicklow Hills in a spectral condition, unless they were sustained by lunch. I do not know, whether he went so far as Ayala, Marcobrunn, Château Margaux, old Dublin whiskey and cigars. In answer to the pathetic appeal of the Solicitor-General, we do not say that the members of the Corporation are not to lunch. But we do say that they are not to do so at the expense of the citizens of Dublin. They cannot banquet at their expense in the Mansion House, and, in our opinion, they cannot lunch at their expense in Wicklow.

The *Ladies' Housekeeping Book*, which was first published in 1890, enables us to see another side to the story. It was published for us by Crawford Hartnell of Wilson Hartnell and Co. of the Commercial Buildings, Dame Street, Dublin who also 'conducted' our monthly magazine *The Lady of the House*. The book was bound in terracotta cloth and ran to some 100 pages of text plus a week to view diary. It was liberally supported by advertisers, some in colour. The *Dublin Daily Express* in 1896 described it as a 'most practical and excellent publication'.

It contained a full set of housekeeping accounts and a diary with each page interbound with blotting-paper. There were articles on the details of Victorian living, including food and cookery, household management, home dressmaking (illustrated), decorative arts, house furnishing, domestic medicine, nursery notes, the laundry, gardening for ladies and a host of other useful topics. It was certainly full of advice, though one wonders how many of the readers really lived in such style! It forms a fascinating insight into the aspirations (if not necessarily the realities) of the rising professional and merchant class.

Household Management

Attention to Detail is of the utmost importance. No mistress can hope to have her house in order, her servants under command, her wishes promptly attended to, and yet leave herself plenty of time for the prosecution of the social duties which is demanded by society of the present day. The house must be conducted like a business—with the same order and regularity that is observed in her husband's study, office or factory. The successful wife and housekeeper is the one who, had circumstances demanded it, would have made a fortune as a manufacturer or a name as an inventor.

The Engagement of Servants requires an amount of tact and hence the frequent dismissals which afford so large a fund for conversation. It is necessary not only to satisfy oneself that the person about to be engaged holds credentials from his or her last mistress, wholly satisfactory with respect to honesty, sobriety, and cleanliness, but the thought–'Is this person suitable for my situation,' should be uppermost in the mistress' mind. It is more than usually imperative that a round worker should not be put into a square hole in the matter of household servants.

Our Attitude towards Servants requires also a word. The mistress who at one time verges almost upon familiarity in her conversations with her servants, is almost as bad as the one who habitually treats all dependants with the disdain which one would hardly have for a beggar. Both these modes are the fruit of ill breeding, and we subject ourselves to unnecessary and frequent discomfort by adopting either the one or the other. The mistress who wishes to command respect, will observe towards her dependants an easy, kind, but even temper upon all occasions.

The Duties of a Cook should be carefully indicated at the outset, so that both mistress and servant will be agreed as to the duties for which the one is hired and the other is hiring. The time of rising having been decided upon, a cook should be expected to prepare the kitchen for the cooking of breakfast. (If there is a scullery maid, of course much of this would be done by her.) She should then make the front door of the house, the steps and immediate approaches clean for the day, the hall and the doors leading into the various rooms should receive attention, the hall furniture be carefully dusted, and the mats, curtains and carpets shaken. By this time breakfast should be prepared, while that meal is in progress (the servants' breakfast all being cleared away) she should visit the larder, put all in order, and make a list of anything likely to be wanted. The mistress having made her morning visit, such cooking as can be done, without immediate connection with a meal, should be taken in hand. All utensils should be cleaned immediately after using. They are then ready when next required, and do not take so much cleaning as when left for some time. Lunch having been prepared, cook will be at liberty to clean up her kitchen, put all in order, and, having dressed herself for the afternoon, she may do sewing until afternoon tea is required, or until it is time to prepare dinner.

Housemaids and Parlourmaids are expected to prepare the sitting rooms, breakfast-room, dining room, library, etc. for the reception of the family. The staircase, too, must be carefully cleaned before anyone leaves the bedrooms. If anyone desires hot water the housemaid should take care to provide it. As soon as cook announces the breakfast to be ready, it should be placed upon the table and the gong sounded. The housemaid should then proceed to the bedrooms, while the parlourmaid remains to attend to the family at breakfast. The general cleaning of the rooms devolves upon the housemaids, while the parlourmaid is occupied more particularly with the china, silver, and glass and the dusting and arranging of the sitting rooms. In the case of a butler being kept the silver would pass into his hands; but if only a youth as page, it is better to let the parlourmaid take this in charge. Putting the table linen in the press, keeping the sideboard in order, and placing any ornaments about the room in their respective places all falls to the parlourmaid, while the housemaids will be occupied with keeping the bedrooms ready for use, and the lavatory and rooms generally, in a proper state of cleanliness.

The Visitors' Bell should be answered by the page, if one is kept, or by the upper housemaid, if only female servants. In any case this should be done with the greatest speed, not only as a convenience to the caller, but as a mark of respect. The page would also assist the parlourmaid if waiting at table, and would be responsible for

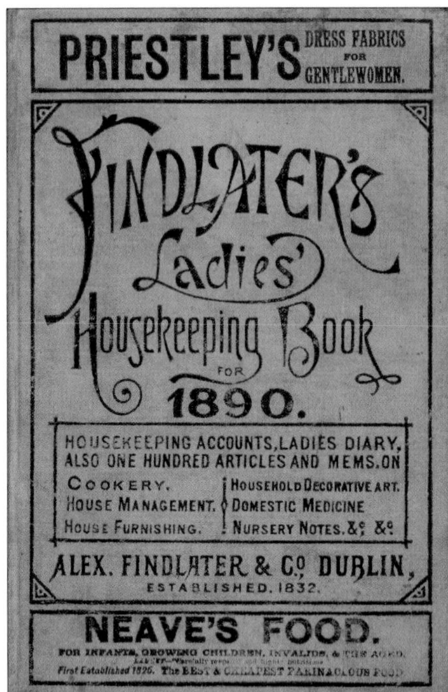

keeping the fires properly mended in the winter.

The Servants' Meals should be expected to be taken with the same regularity as you desire for your own. Unless a servant, who knows her work, can depend on her time not being broken in upon up to a certain hour, she cannot do her best.

The Prevention of Waste is, perhaps, the most difficult thing a wife can set herself to accomplish. It is well known that those who have little of their own are least careful of the goods of others, and the persons whose diet is of the most spare character when provided by themselves, are the most fastidious when it is provided for them.

To exact obedience it is essential that the orders given should be reasonable, and some degree of thoughtfulness for the convenience of others shown. The master or mistress who consults only his or her own convenience may obtain what they require for the moment, but it will be at the expense of the neglect of some other duty.

Punctuality must be observed to be obtained. The hour at which the servants' bell is rung for them to rise must not vary. You cannot complain that servants do not rise at the proper hour if you yourself are unable to awake at that hour to call them. If you order dinner for seven, but do not arrive in the dining-room until half-past, you need not be very surprised if the next time you bring a friend home you have to wait till eight o'clock before dinner is announced.

A time for everything is absolutely needful if you wish to be able to get through life easily. Certain rooms should receive special attention upon certain days. Every portion of the day should have its allotted duty and the person to perform it. If the whole household work with regularity, ample time for recreation for each will be found, instead of servants always appearing busy each will have leisure and, indeed, fewer will be required. People take away impressions of their friends from the appearance of the maid who opens the door to them. A plain print uniform dress should be worn by the servant or servants in the morning, and black in the afternoon.

Definite instructions should be given every morning concerning the work of the day. Subsidiary orders must necessarily be given as occasion arises, but, if possible, they should be given each morning at a stated time. This will allow servants, who have any head upon their shoulders, to do their work with intelligence, and will be easier for themselves, while the work will be more efficiently performed.

Visits to various parts of the house should be made at stated times, for if it is made capriciously and with the view of catching the servants, a mutual lack of confidence

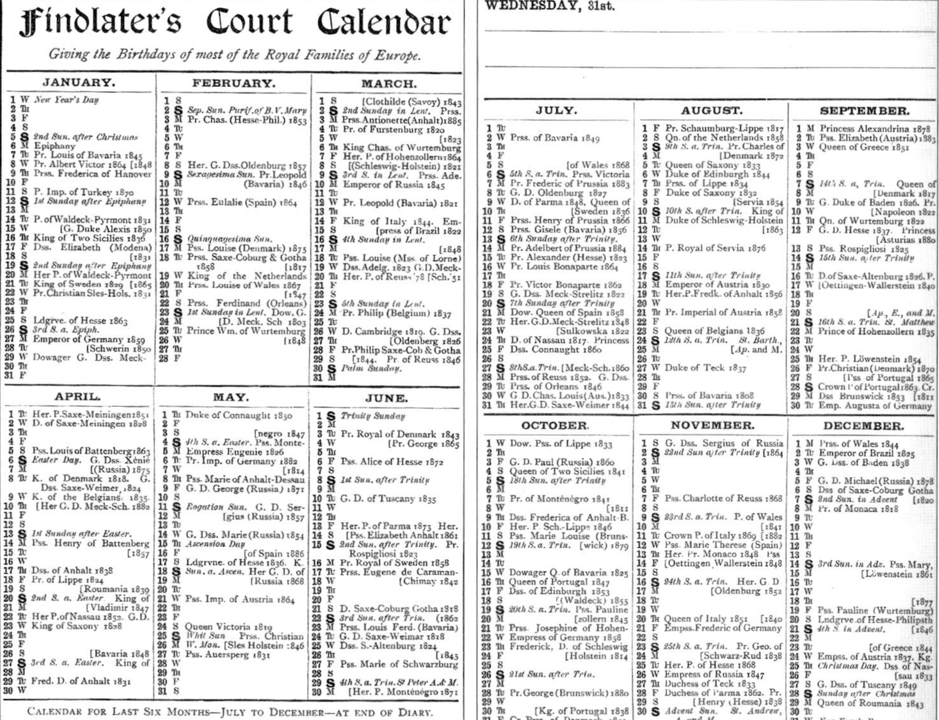

Findlater's Court Calendar

Giving the Birthdays of most of the Royal Families of Europe.

JANUARY.

1	W	*New Year's Day*
2	Th	
3	F	
4	S	
5	S	*2nd Sun. after Christmas*
6	M	Epiphany
7	Tu	Pr. Louis of Bavaria 1845
8	W	Pr. Albert Victor 1864 [1848
9	Th	Prss. Frederica of Hanover
10	F	
11	S	P. Imp. of Turkey 1870
12	S	*1st Sunday after Epiphany*
13	M	
14	Tu	P. of Waldeck-Pyrmont 1831
15	W	[G. Duke Alexis 1850
16	Th	King of Two Sicilies 1836
17	F	Dss. Elizabeth (Modena)
18	S	[1831
19	S	*2nd Sunday after Epiphany*
20	M	Her P. of Waldeck-Pyrmont
21	Tu	King of Sweden 1829 [1865
22	W	Pr. Christian Sles-Hols. 1831
23	Th	
24	F	
25	S	Ldgrve. of Hesse 1863
26	S	*3rd S. a. Epiph.*
27	M	Emperor of Germany 1859
28	Tu	[Schwerin 1850
29	W	Dowager G. Dss. Meck-
30	Th	
31	F	

FEBRUARY.

1	S	
2	S	*Sep. Sun. Purif. of B. V. Mary*
3	M	Pr. Chas. (Hesse-Phil.) 1853
4	Tu	
5	W	
6	Th	
7	F	
8	S	Her. G. Dss. Oldenburg 1857
9	S	*Sexagesima Sun.* Pr. Leopold
10	M	(Bavaria) 1846
11	Tu	
12	W	Prss. Eulalie (Spain) 1864
13	Th	
14	F	
15	S	
16	S	*Quinquagesima Sun.*
17	M	Pss. Louise (Denmark) 1875
18	Tu	Prss. Saxe-Coburg & Gotha 1858 [1817
19	W	King of the Netherlands
20	Th	Prss. Louise of Wales 1867
21	F	[1847
22	S	Prss. Ferdinand (Orleans)
23	S	*1st Sunday in Lent.* Dow. G.
24	M	[D. Meck. Sch 1803
25	Tu	Prince Wm. of Wurtemburg
26	W	[1848
27	Th	
28	F	

MARCH.

1	S	[Clothilde (Savoy) 1843
2	S	*2nd Sunday in Lent.* Prss.
3	M	Prss. Antionette (Anhalt) 1885
4	Tu	Pr. of Furstenburg 1820
5	W	[1823
6	Th	King Chas. of Wurtemburg
7	F	Her. P. of Hohenzollern 1864
8	S	[(Schleswig-Holstein) 1821
9	S	*3rd S. in Lent.* Prss. Ade.
10	M	Emperor of Russia 1845
11	Tu	
12	W	Pr. Leopold (Bavaria) 1821
13	Th	
14	F	King of Italy 1844. Em-
15	S	[press of Brazil 1822
16	S	*4th Sunday in Lent.*
17	M	[1848
18	Tu	Pss. Louise (Mss. of Lorne)
19	W	Dss. Adelg. 1823 G. D. Meck-
20	Th	Her. P. of Reuss '78 [Sch.'51
21	F	
22	S	
23	S	*5th Sunday in Lent.*
24	M	Pr. Philip (Belgium) 1837
25	Tu	
26	W	D. Cambridge 1819. G. Dss.
27	Th	[Oldenberg 1826
28	F	Pr. Philip Saxe-Cob & Gotha
29	S	[1844. Pr. of Reuss 1846
30	S	*Palm Sunday.*
31	M	

APRIL.

1	Tu	Her. P. Saxe-Meiningen 1851
2	W	D. of Saxe-Meiningen 1828
3	Th	
4	F	
5	S	Pss. Louis of Battenberg 1863
6	S	*Easter Day.* G. Dss. Xénie
7	M	[(Russia) 1875
8	Tu	K. of Denmark 1818. G. Dss. Saxe-Weimer, 1824
9	W	K. of the Belgians 1835.
10	Th	[Her G. D. Meck-Sch. 1882
11	F	
12	S	
13	S	*1st Sunday after Easter.*
14	M	Pss. Henry of Battenberg
15	Tu	[1857
16	W	
17	Th	Dss. of Anhalt 1838
18	F	Pr. of Lippe 1824
19	S	[Roumania 1839
20	S	*2nd S. a. Easter.* King of
21	M	[Vladimir 1847
22	Tu	Her P. of Nassau 1852. G. D.
23	W	King of Saxony 1828
24	Th	
25	F	
26	S	[Bavaria 1848
27	S	*3rd S. a. Easter.* King of
28	M	
29	Tu	Fred. D. of Anhalt 1831
30	W	

MAY.

1	Th	Duke of Connaught 1850
2	F	
3	S	[negro 1847
4	S	*4th S. a. Easter.* Pss. Monte-
5	M	Empress Eugenie 1826
6	Tu	Pr. Imp. of Germany 1882
7	W	[1814
8	Th	Pss. Marie of Anhalt-Dessau
9	F	G. D. George (Russia) 1871
10	S	
11	S	*Rogation Sun.* G. D. Ser-
12	M	[gius (Russia) 1857
13	Tu	
14	W	G. Dss. Marie (Russia) 1854
15	Th	*Ascension Day*
16	F	[of Spain 1886
17	S	Ldgrvne. of Hesse 1836. K.
18	S	*Sun. a. Ascen.* Her G. D. of
19	M	[Russia 1868
20	Tu	
21	W	Pss. Imp. of Austria 1864
22	Th	
23	F	
24	S	Queen Victoria 1819
25	S	*Whit Sun* Prss. Christian
26	M	*W. Mon.* [Sles Holstein 1846
27	Tu	Pss. Auersperg 1831
28	W	
29	Th	
30	F	
31	S	

JUNE.

1	S	*Trinity Sunday*
2	M	
3	Tu	Pr. Royal of Denmark 1843
4	W	[Pr. George 1865
5	Th	
6	F	Pss. Alice of Hesse 1872
7	S	
8	S	*1st Sun. after Trinity*
9	M	
10	Tu	G. D. of Tuscany 1835
11	W	
12	Th	
13	F	Her. P. of Parma 1873 Her.
14	S	[Pss. Elizabeth Anhalt 1861
15	S	*2nd Sun. after Trinity.* Pr. Rospigliosi 1823
16	M	Pr. Royal of Sweden 1858
17	Tu	Prss. Eugene de Caraman-
18	W	[Chimay 1842
19	Th	
20	F	
21	S	D. Saxe-Coburg Gotha 1818
22	S	*3rd Sun. after Trin.* [1862
23	M	Prss. Louis Ferd. (Bavaria)
24	Tu	G. D. Saxe-Weimar 1818
25	W	Dss. S.-Altenburg 1824
26	Th	[1845
27	F	Pss. Marie of Schwarzburg
28	S	
29	S	*4th S. a. Trin. St Peter A. & M.*
30	M	[Her. P. Monténégro 1871

CALENDAR FOR LAST SIX MONTHS—JULY TO DECEMBER—AT END OF DIARY.

WEDNESDAY, 31st.

JULY.

1	Tu	
2	W	Prss. of Bavaria 1849
3	Th	
4	F	
5	S	[of Wales 1868
6	S	*5th S. a. Trin.* Prss. Victoria
7	M	Pr. Frederic of Prussia 1883
8	Tu	G. D. Oldenburg 1827
9	W	D. of Parma 1848, Queen of
10	Th	[Sweden 1836
11	F	Prss. Henry of Prussia 1866
12	S	Prss. Gisele (Bavaria) 1856
13	S	*6th Sunday after Trinity.*
14	M	Pr. Adelbert of Prussia 1884
15	Tu	Pr. Alexander (Hesse) 1823
16	W	Pr. Louis Bonaparte 1864
17	Th	
18	F	Pr. Victor Bonaparte 1862
19	S	G. Dss. Meck-Strelitz 1822
20	S	*7th Sunday after Trinity*
21	M	Dow. Queen of Spain 1858
22	Tu	Her. G. D. Meck-Strelitz 1848
23	W	[Sulkowska 1822
24	Th	D. of Nassau 1817. Princess
25	F	Dss. Connaught 1860
26	S	
27	S	*8th S. a. Trin.* [Meck-Sch. 1860
28	M	Prss. of Reuss 1852. G. Dss.
29	Tu	Prss. of Orleans 1846
30	W	G. D. Chas. Louis (Aus.) 1833
31	Th	Her. G. D. Saxe-Weimer 1844

AUGUST.

1	F	Pr. Schaumburg-Lippe 1817
2	S	Qn. of the Netherlands 1858
3	S	*9th S. a. Trin.* Pr. Charles of
4	M	[Denmark 1872
5	Tu	Queen of Saxony 1833
6	W	Duke of Edinburgh 1844
7	Th	Prss. of Lippe 1834
8	F	Duke of Saxony 1832
9	S	[Servia 1854
10	S	*10th S. after Trin.* King of
11	M	Duke of Schleswig-Holstein
12	Tu	[1863
13	W	
14	Th	P. Royal of Servia 1876
15	F	
16	S	
17	S	*11th Sun. after Trinity*
18	M	Emperor of Austria 1830
19	Tu	Her. P. Fredk. of Anhalt 1856
20	W	
21	Th	Pr. Imperial of Austria 1858
22	F	
23	S	Queen of Belgians 1836
24	S	*12th S. a. Trin. St. Barth.,*
25	M	[*Ap.* and M.
26	Tu	
27	W	Duke of Teck 1837
28	Th	
29	F	
30	S	Prss. of Bavaria 1808
31	S	*13th Sun. after Trinity*

SEPTEMBER.

1	M	Princess Alexandrina 1878
2	Tu	Pss. Elizabeth (Austria) 1883
3	W	Queen of Greece 1851
4	Th	
5	F	
6	S	
7	S	*14th S. a. Trin.* Queen of
8	M	[Denmark 1817
9	Tu	G. Duke of Baden 1826. Pr.
10	W	[Napoleon 1822
11	Th	Qn. of Wurtemburg 1822
12	F	G. D. Hesse 1837. Princess [Asturias 1880
13	S	Pss. Rospigliosi 1825
14	S	*15th Sun. after Trinity*
15	M	
16	Tu	D. of Saxe-Altenburg 1826. P.
17	W	[Oettingen-Wallerstein 1840
18	Th	
19	F	
20	S	[*Ap., E., and M.*
21	S	*16th S. a. Trin. St. Matthew*
22	M	Prince of Hohenzollern 1835
23	Tu	
24	W	
25	Th	Her. P. Löwenstein 1854
26	F	Pr. Christian (Denmark) 1870
27	S	[Pss of Portugal 1865
28	S	Crown P. of Portugal 1863. Cr.
29	M	Dss Brunswick 1853 [1811
30	Tu	Emp. Augusta of Germany

OCTOBER.

1	W	Dow. Pss. of Lippe 1833
2	Th	
3	F	G. D. Paul (Russia) 1860
4	S	Queen of Two Sicilies 1841
5	S	*18th Sun. after Trinity*
6	M	
7	Tu	Pr. of Monténégro 1841
8	W	[1811
9	Th	Dss. Frederica of Anhalt-B.
10	F	Her. P. Sch.-Lippe 1846
11	S	Pss. Marie Louise (Bruns-
12	S	*19th S. a. Trin.* [wick) 1879
13	M	
14	Tu	
15	W	Dowager Q. of Bavaria 1825
16	Th	Queen of Portugal 1847
17	F	Dss. of Edinburgh 1853
18	S	[(Waldeck) 1855
19	S	*20th S. a. Trin.* Pss. Pauline
20	M	[zollern 1845
21	Tu	Prss. Josephine of Hohen-
22	W	Empress of Germany 1858
23	Th	Frederick, D. of Schleswig
24	F	[Holstein 1814
25	S	
26	S	*21st Sun. after Trin.*
27	M	
28	Tu	Pr. George (Brunswick) 1880
29	W	
30	Th	[Kg. of Portugal 1838
31	F	Cr. Prss. of Denmark

NOVEMBER.

1	S	G. Dss. Sergius of Russia
2	S	*22nd Sun after Trinity* [1864
3	M	
4	Tu	
5	W	
6	Th	
7	F	Pss. Charlotte of Reuss 1868
8	S	
9	S	*23rd S. a. Trin.* P. of Wales
10	M	[1841
11	Tu	Crown P. of Italy 1869 [1882
12	W	Pss. Marie Therese (Spain)
13	Th	Her. Pr. Monaco 1848 Pss
14	F	[Oettingen Wallerstein 1848
15	S	
16	S	*24th S. a. Trin.* Her. G. D.
17	M	[Oldenburg 1852
18	Tu	
19	W	
20	Th	Queen of Italy 1851 [1840
21	F	Empss. Frederic of Germany
22	S	
23	S	*25th S. a. Trin.* Pr. Geo. of
24	M	[Schwarz-Rud 1838
25	Tu	Her. P. of Hesse 1868
26	W	Empress of Russia 1847
27	Th	Duchess of Teck 1833
28	F	Duchess of Parma 1862. Pr.
29	S	[Henry (Hesse) 1838
30	S	*Advent Sun. St. Andrew, A. and M.*

DECEMBER.

1	M	Prss. of Wales 1844
2	Tu	Emperor of Brazil 1825
3	W	G. Dss. of Baden 1838
4	Th	
5	F	G. D. Michael (Russia) 1878
6	S	Dss of Saxe-Coburg Gotha
7	S	*2nd Sun. in Advent* [1820
8	M	Pr. of Monaca 1818
9	Tu	
10	W	
11	Th	
12	F	
13	S	
14	S	*3rd Sun. in Adv.* Pss. Mary,
15	M	[Löwenstein 1861
16	Tu	
17	W	
18	Th	[1877
19	F	Pss. Pauline (Wurtemburg)
20	S	Lndgrve. of Hesse-Philipsth
21	S	*4th S. in Advent.* [1846
22	M	
23	Tu	[of Greece 1844
24	W	Empss. of Austria 1837. Kg.
25	Th	*Christmas Day.* Dss. of Nas-
26	F	[sau 1833
27	S	G. Dss. of Tuscany 1849
28	S	*Sunday after Christmas*
29	M	Queen of Roumania 1843
30	Tu	
31	W	*New Year's Eve*

From Findlater's *Ladies' Housekeeping Diary* 1890. Did we expect our customers to send greetings cards to European Royalty on their birthdays?

will be established, and the servants will hurry over the parts most likely to catch the eye, hoping thereby to avoid censure. Endeavour to establish between yourself and your servants a feeling of confidence, a knowledge of certain censure if work be ill done, and of praise if satisfactorily performed.

Amusements are necessary for servants as for other human beings, and they undoubtedly do their work better for an occasional change. It has not been found a bad plan to take seats for as many as can be spared at concerts which may be given, or at theatres for plays which are approved, a few times in the course of the year. It is better that servants should attend such amusements as you can approve, than that they should gain access to places of amusement of which you strongly disapprove.

A Night Out is another question most mistresses have to come to some decision about, and, no doubt, a great deal may be said upon both sides of the question. In the country, servants get plenty of fresh air and exercise, and do not need extra time, nor, indeed, ask for it. But in the town one can well understand how strong the wish for change and, indeed, how physically necessary it is. But this change and exercise is not best obtained at night. A whole day shall be granted to them once a month, which they shall be allowed to spend exactly as they wish.

The Children's school hours ought on no account to be broken in upon. The nursery should, indeed, never be visited, except for urgent reasons, while lessons are in progress. The governess cannot hope to obtain their attention if they are distracted by other members of the family passing to and fro. Young children should never be expected to do lessons in the morning, that being the time when the air is most important for them. Both their brains and bodies will be invigorated by outdoor exercise when fine.

The Children's Meals, if taken in the nursery, must be arranged with due regard for the age of the children, and the time must be strictly adhered to by both the cook and the nurse. Punctuality on the part both of the cook and the nursemaid is of the utmost importance, or the health of the little ones will suffer.

Dusting the Drawing-room should be the special care of the mistress. Valuable articles of vertu are frequently placed there, and much damage may easily be done through ignorance if left to a servant, besides which, the arrangement of flowers and ornaments have not that air of taste which can only be imparted by the touch of the lady who takes an interest in her surroundings.

Furniture Polish should be kept under lock and key if you wish to keep your furniture in good condition. If it is kept where servants can get it when they wish they will inevitably use it, but, eventually, the cabinet-maker will have to be called in to explain how it is the furniture looks so bad.

The General Cleaning Day should be a day unknown in a properly ordered house. There should be no day in the week on which visitors or friends cannot be seen should they call. If the various rooms are carefully attended to every day, all the furniture rubbed as well as dusted, there will be no accumulation of dust and dirt leading up to a grand cleaning day, which throws all the usual arrangements out of gear, and thoroughly disorganises the maids.

Window cleaning is in many houses very difficult. Architects seldom give a thought as to how the persons who will live in his house will accommodate themselves in his vagaries. The state of the Coal Cellar is a sure indication of the way in which the general management of the house is conducted. Show me a coal cellar with the blocks neatly packed and the small swept into a heap apart, and I will undertake to say that the rest of the house is in equal order. A coal-cellar with the blocks and small coal intermingled, with no clear place upon which to break the blocks, is a guarantee that if you examine the corners of the rooms or the top of the beading round the doors dust and dirt will be found in abundance.

Servants' Work: to plan it out

I have often heard of the necessity for making out a list of work for the servants to follow every day and every week, and I consequently have decided to give one for daily work that has worked well, and also append a list for a fortnight's work, for a family of four, where a cook and house-parlour-maid are kept. A copy of each, written out distinctly on a strong card, is given to each new maid when she enters the service. This is the cook's daily card:

- 6.30 Light kitchen fire, and make the water hot for baths. Sweep and dust dining-room, opening windows, and lay kitchen breakfast.
- 7.45 Dining-room and kitchen breakfast.
- 8.30 Clear breakfast table, and take up crumbs in dining-room.
- 9.00 Settle with mistress about arrangements for lunch, dinner, and next morning's breakfast.

9, Leinster Street, 1893–1969

9, Rathmines Terrace, 1839–1969
(Later renumbered 302, Rathmines Road)

9.30 Clean doorsteps and hall.
10.00 Special work of day.
1.30 Dining-room lunch and kitchen dinner.
2.15 Wash up.
4.30 Kitchen tea.
7.30 Dinner.
9.00 Kitchen supper.
10.00 Bed-time.

Housemaid's Daily List

6.30 Open windows in drawing-room; sweep & dust that room and stairs.
7.00 Take bath-water to bedrooms, and call everybody.
7.15 Lay breakfast table.
7.45 Dining-room breakfast and kitchen breakfast.
8.30 Go to bedrooms, open windows, turn down beds, and empty basins.
9.00 Make the beds, dust the rooms, afterwards do special work of day.
1.00 Be dressed for afternoon, and lay luncheon table.
1.30 Lunch and kitchen dinner.
2.15 Clear away lunch, and wash glasses and silver.
4.30 Kitchen tea.
5.00 Drawing-room tea.
7.00 Lay dining-room cloth.
7.30 Wait at dinner.
8.30 Wash up glasses & silver, dessert plates, ice plates & finger glasses.
9.00 Kitchen supper.
10.00 Bed-time.

This list is not exactly as the laws of the Medes and Persians, but can be altered to suit varying circumstances. Only on very few days are there ice plates to wash up, for instance, but they are included in the list, so that when they are used the house parlour-maid may know that it is her business to wash them.

Cook always answers the hall-door up to lunch-time, but on the day when she turns out the servants' bedroom, the housemaid, who is on that morning cleaning plate in the kitchen, is 'on' the hall-door. The following list shows an arrangement that has worked fairly well in one household, and may be of use to inexperienced young wives:

Housemaid's Work List

First Week:

Monday	Turn out best bedroom and dressing-room.
Tuesday	Turn out second best bedroom and dressing-room.
Wednesday	Turn out drawing-room, with cook's help.
Thursday	Clean plate.
Friday	Do stairs down thoroughly.
Saturday	Clean all brasses, door-handles, chests of drawers etc. all through house.

Second Week:

Monday	Turn out two smaller bedrooms.
Tuesday	Turn out two more bedrooms.
Wednesday	Help cook with dining-room.
Thursday	Clean plate.
Friday	Do stairs down thoroughly.
Saturday	Turn out third sitting-room.

Cook's Work List*:

First Week:

Monday	Wash towels, socks, and flannels.
Tuesday	Mangle, air, and iron washing.
Wednesday	Help housemaid turn out drawing-room.
Thursday	Turn out her bedroom.
Friday	Clean down hall and kitchen stairs.
Saturday	Clean kitchen and scullery.

Second Week:

Monday	Wash towels, socks, and flannels.
Tuesday	Mangle, air, and iron washing.
Wednesday	Turn out dining-room, with housemaid's help.
Thursday	Clean all the cupboards.
Friday	Clean down hall and kitchen stairs.
Saturday	Clean kitchen and scullery.

This plan of work, it will be seen, is arranged to suit a family where early rising is the rule. Breakfast at a quarter to eight leaves a nice long morning wherein to accomplish the daily task of cleaning necessary for keeping a house in order. With the meal even an hour later, it would be difficult to fit it in, and to leave the afternoon free for servants to rest, and have a little time for themselves, to darn their stockings, mend their clothes, write letters, or otherwise amuse themselves in their own way.

This leisure time should be spent in the kitchen and it should be made a rule that the maids should both be dressed and tidy before they settle down to enjoy their time of rest. They cannot go on working all day, and it is far better to arrange a little off-time for them than leave them to snatch it when they can. It is more comfortable for them, and it saves friction.

A household in which the afternoons are given to the servants for their own occupations is almost sure to be one where they remain long, and do their best to please, for they know very well that such consideration is not always meted out to them. And they appreciate it. How can they fail to do so?

I have seen so many unsatisfactory servants turned into satisfactory ones by having their work planned out for them, and their time measured out to it, that I am con-

* In addition of course to the actual cooking.

Harbour Road, Howth, 1898–1969
'The starting gun for each race will be fired five minutes after the first gun, the time to be taken by Findlater's clock', from W. M. Nixon, *Howth—a Centenary of Sailing*

67 South Great George's Street 1849–1969

28 and 30 Upper Baggot Street 1890–1969

> vinced it is the only way to make the household machinery work smoothly. The servants soon begin to like it. They find that if they are thrifty with the flying minutes in the mornings, they have good, solid blocks of time all for their own use in the afternoons. If cook is firmly, though gently, induced to get all her preparations for meals made as soon as possible after breakfast, she will soon find that it is to her own advantage to do so, and she begins to fall into habits of regularity that are a joy to her mistress and a pleasure to herself.

Incorporation and flotation

John and his eldest son Adam had expanded the firm rapidly during the latter part of the century. Branch houses were opened in the city and suburbs: 1879 in Blackrock, 1890 in Baggot Street, 1893 in Leinster Street near Lincoln Place, 1896 in Thomas Street, 1897 in Sandymount, 1898 in Howth and Dalkey, around 1900 three hotels, the St Lawrence in Howth and the Royal Hotels in Bray and Howth. Then in 1901 a branch house in Bray, 1904 Foxrock, known as The Gables, and in 1906 Dorset Street.

The 1890s saw the zenith of John's career. From a modest yet significant inheritance he had built up an organisation which was now poised for a flotation on the stock market. His shops were prominent landmarks throughout the city and suburbs and were part of the citizens' everyday lives. The city's main social journal was backed by the company and often contained Findlaters' full price list. The family were foremost amongst the merchant and professional class. Billy was at the top of the legal profession, the brewery was second only to Guinness, Adam junior was a recognised public figure as chairman of Kingstown Town Commissioners and a prominent Southern unionist. He was also newsworthy as chairman of two variety theatres and a distillery, as well as being managing director of Findlaters. John's son Willie was also in the news, as president of the Grocers Federation of the United Kingdom, whose annual conference was held in Dublin for the first time in 1898. Sons Herbert and Charles were young men about town, Herbert a solicitor and Charles as an engineer and prominent in the bicycle and early motor trade.

The headquarters in Upper Sackville Street, nos. 29 to 32, was a large establishment, a great hive of activity, incorporating wine cellars, whiskey bottling, beer bottling, dry grocery storage, account handling, and stabling for a large team of horses. All that in addition to the retail departments. In 1897 the trade paper, *The Grocer and Oil Trade Review* (27 February 1897) described a conducted tour:

> The commodious and extensive premises of the head office are replete with every luxury and managed with the utmost ability. The ground floor is occupied by the counting house, order counters and retail departments. At the rear of this building are the extensive stores from which are supplied the various branch establishments. In all these departments are to be seen a large staff all working as busy as bees, and three large hydraulic lifts are kept in perpetual motion connecting the cellars with the store lofts.

> All the premises are lit throughout with electric light which is supplied from plant on the premises. The stables and harness room of this establishment are well worthy of a visit and a model of perfection. There are to be seen more than thirty well-bred horses that are always on the road delivering goods in the surrounding districts.

However all this expansion was demanding on capital, and the minute book of the firm's bankers, the Royal Bank, records that John Findlater had a series of interviews with their managing director in 1898. The bank estimated the firm's capital value at £85,000 [£6.6m], and raised their overdraft limit to £10,000 [£2.3m] to enable three shops to be added to the existing seven.

At this time the firm was still a partnership, and the new organisational form of limited liability was becoming increasingly fashionable, having lost its earlier rather dubious image.*

There were two strong reasons why Findlaters should have considered this route. The first was to fund the rapid expansion of the branch network. They had negotiated a facility with the bank, but the preferable option was to raise finance through the stock market, so it was decided to incorporate and float the company. The prospectus noted that 'the branches at Thomas Street and Sandymount were opened about the latter end of 1896, and that of Howth about the middle of 1897, and the losses arising in connection with these Branches, and an exceptional loss in another Branch, have all been charged against Revenue for the year ending 28 February 1898'. Further branch openings were contemplated after the flotation. The other reason was that John was getting on in years and there would be inevitable estate problems.

On top of this the firm seemed to act as financial managers for various members of the extended family. Money was deposited with the firm, and interest paid, usually at the rate of 4¼ per cent; this was quite a normal source of corporate finance at the time. Findlaters' ledgers show deposits by Sir William Findlater, Sir John Nugent and others, including 'Young Men', presumably staff actually working in Findlaters who deposited their savings with the firm. This practice extended over time to the firm performing various tasks for the depositors. For instance Mrs Blythe, Adam's merry widow, was sent regular lengthy accounts showing her income from investments and deposits, John's son, his namesake in America, got advances (all carefully accounted for) for oil exploration, and young Dr Alex, who had just taken up a post in Edgeware and played a good game of polo had his own accounts:

> Paid to P. Rogers for Bay Mare, 5 years old £50 [£3,900]
> paid to P. Rogers for livery of Black Gelding 43 nights @ 3s £6. 9s
> and for 2 sets shoes 10s and clipping 4s
> freight on horse to Euston £3 12s; and from Middlesex £3 12s

Dr Alex's account was debited with two cash orders totalling £500 [£38,500]

* When limited liability was first made possible, conservative businessmen regarded it as no more than a declaration in advance that the promoters had no intention of paying their debts!

34

Dr. Sackville Street

1895			Advertising	Goods	House Expense	Annual Expense	Total
Feby	28	To Stock					64,148 12 2
Mar			161 12 10	5053 17 1	74 1 11	511 19 8	5801 11 6
Apl			80 2 9	6626 2 2	82 · 9	565 18 4	7354 4 ·
May			125 6 4	7000 15 1	80 14 1	755 5 9	7962 1 3
June			117 19 11	4621 15 7	66 19 3	724 12 5	5591 7 2
July			79 1 9	6738 5 ·	77 10 8	665 7 3	7560 4 8
Aug			219 17 ·	5191 16 8	71 16 4	624 7 7	6107 17 7
Sep			162 11 6	4561 13 1	82 5 10	506 6 4	5312 16 9
Oct			182 · 7	7358 9 8	76 8 6	644 1 11	8261 · 8
Nov			388 4 ·	8491 5 11	94 · 11	777 3 11	9750 14 9
Dec			137 3 ·	8366 12 ·	88 1 7	512 4 7	9104 1 2
1896 Jan			359 7 2	5900 3 5	76 13 2	714 9 5	7050 13 2
Feb			76 · 8	4792 11 7	86 3 6	686 16 ·	5641 11 9
			2089 7 6	74763 7 3	956 16 6	7688 13 2	149,646 16 7

To J.H. Harris £478 10 5 H.W. Browne £325.15.9 — 804 6 2
Mr Patterson — 50 · ·
rent of rear of 76 Gt Britain St £15 rent of 77+78 Gt Britain St £15 — 30
Depreciation in value of Horses 242 19 8
" " Vans 224 11 1
" " Harness 104 2 4 — 571 13 1
Net Profit – Interest on Account 3025 7 4
" " Leasehold 1200 · ·
Surplus Profit 2525 · · — 6750 7 4 — 8206 6 7
Advertising — 2089 7 6
House Expense — 956 16 6
18941 3 9 — 157,853 3 2

Gross Profit £18941 3 9 or £47.16.7 % on sales
Net " £2525 or £6.7.6 %

34

29th February 1896 Cr.

Keep of Leinster St Hand	Keep of Georges St Hand	Goods supplied to Branches	Wholesale	Retail Sales	Total
1 3 9	13 6 8	3709 2 1	794 1 1	2442	6959 13 7
1 3 9	13 6 8	3038 15 8	1262 6 7	3493	7808 12 8
1 3 9	13 6 8	3174 13 2	1242 8 7	3369	7800 12 2
1 3 9	13 6 8	3215 14 7	392 3 ·	2983	6605 8 ·
1 3 9	13 6 8	4071 17 2	789 18 1	3538	8414 5 8
1 3 9	13 6 8	2849 13 6	1685 18 1	3315	7865 2 ·
1 3 9	13 6 8	3087 6 3	1183 · 10	3237	7521 17 6
1 3 9	13 6 8	2767 10 4	877 1 10	3040	6699 2 7
1 3 9	13 6 8	5534 18 ·	1098 3 7	2921	9568 12 ·
1 3 9	13 6 8	4257 18 ·	1217 6 5	4251	9740 14 10
1 3 9	13 6 8	2259 17 10	1706 13 4	3656	8237 1 7
1 3 9	13 6 8	3350 · 11	1745 19 1	3355	8465 10 5
14 5 ·	160 · ·	41917 7 6	13995 · 6	39,600	95,686 13 ·

By Cartage & hirage horses vans & harness — 289 14 ·
refund re J. Tanner — 7 · ·
Rent of upper portion of No 29 Up. Sackville St. — 12 · ·
Stock viz Bonded 33,416 11 ·
Wine cellars 12,490 16 6
Groceries 5705 18 11 — 51,613 6 5
Debts 12,419 11 9
less credits 90 15 7
" bad 154 2 11 — 244 18 6
12,174 13 3
less 10% on £5779.15.9 — 577 19 6 — 11596 13 9
Cash on hands, or Stock money — 150 · ·
63,360 · 2
Less unpaid a/cs — 1508 10 4 — 61851 9 10 say 61,857 16 2
157,853 3 2

Twelve months retail sales £39,600.

Profit and loss analysis 1896

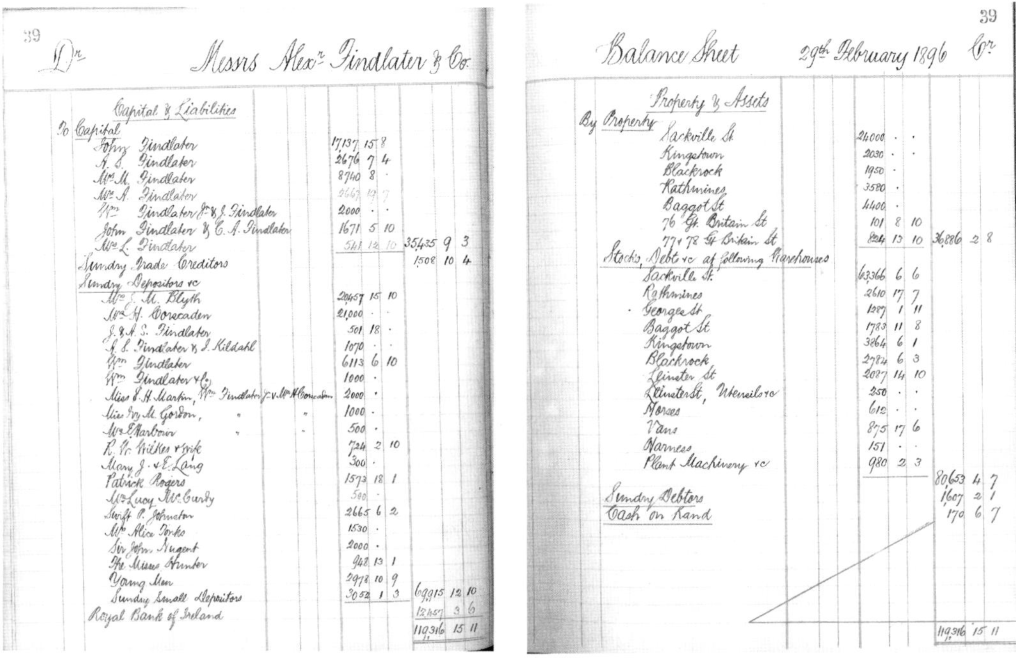

39

Dr. Messrs Alexr. Findlater & Co.

Capital & Liabilities

To Capital			
John Findlater	17,137 15 8		
A. S. Findlater	2676 7 4		
Mrs M. Findlater	8740 8 ·		
Mrs A. Findlater	2667 19 7		
Wm Findlater Jr & J. Findlater	2000 · ·		
John Findlater & C. A. Findlater	1671 5 10		
Mrs L. Findlater	541 12 10	35,435 9 3	
Sundry Trade Creditors		1,508 10 4	
Sundry Depositors &c			
Mrs E. M. Blyth	20,457 15 10		
Mrs H. Corscaden	21,000 · ·		
J. & A. S. Findlater	501 18 ·		
A. S. Findlater & I. Kildahl	1070 · ·		
Wm Findlater	6113 6 10		
Wm Findlater & Co	1000 ·		
Miss E. H. Martin, Wm Findlater Jr & Mrs H. Corscaden	2000 ·		
Miss Ivy M. Gordon, " "	1000 ·		
Mrs E. Harbour " "	500 ·		
R. W. Wilkes & wife	724 2 10		
Mary J. & E. Lang	300 ·		
Patrick Rogers	1573 18 1		
Mrs Lucy McCurdy	500 ·		
Swift P. Johnston	2665 6 2		
Mrs Alice Tonks	1530 ·		
Sir John Nugent	2000 ·		
The Misses Hunter	948 13 1		
Young Men	2978 10 9		
Sundry Small Depositors	3052 1 3	69,915 12 10	
Royal Bank of Ireland		12,457 3 6	
		119,316 15 11	

39

Balance Sheet 29th February 1896 Cr.

Property & Assets

By Property		
Sackville St.	24000 · ·	
Kingstown	2030 · ·	
Blackrock	1950 ·	
Rathmines	3580 ·	
Baggot St	4400 ·	
76 Gt. Britain St	101 8 10	
77 & 78 Gt Britain St	824 13 10	36,886 2 8
Stocks, Debts &c of following Warehouses		
Sackville St.	63,366 6 6	
Rathmines	2610 17 7	
Georges St	1287 1 11	
Baggot St	1783 11 8	
Kingstown	3864 6 1	
Blackrock	2784 6 3	
Leinster St	2087 14 10	
Leinster St, Utensils &c	250 · ·	
Horses	612 · ·	
Vans	875 17 6	
Harness	151 · ·	
Plant Machinery &c	980 2 3	80,653 4 7
Sundry Debtors		1,607 2 1
Cash on hand		170 6 7
		119,316 15 11

Balance Sheet 1896—note that two–thirds of the capital before the flotation was contributed by 'Sundry Depositors'

The Gables, Station Road, Foxrock, 1904–1969

2, The Green, Sandymount, 1897–1969

and debited with interest to date, at 5 per cent per annum. He later redressed the balance on the account by selling one of his mares, Ruby, to P. Rogers for £65 [£5,000]. The establishment of a limited company meant that the non executive members of the family had in future to manage their own affairs, as John was obliged to remind America John some years after the flotation. All in all it was a propitious time for the company to float.

This period was an explosive time for the Dublin stock exchange. The quoted capital on the exchange rose from £7.25m [£580m] at the beginning of the decade to £17.2m [£1376m] at the end of the decade.[3] 145 new companies sought listings in 1897 alone. It is interesting to reflect on the profits reported by well known firms in 1899, and in particular the prominence of, for instance, department stores, in the listings. The net profit is as reported in the *Irish Investor's Guardian* and is before dividend, reserve funds and depreciation reserves.

Company	*Profit*	*Modern Equivalent*	
Arthur Guinness	812,699	[65.0m]	Brewer
Royal Bank of Ireland	45,226	[3.60m]	Bank
Irish Times	28,062	[2.24m]	Newspaper
Johnston Mooney & O'Brien	19,705	[1.57m]	Millers/bakers
Alex. Thom	14,551	[1.16m]	Printer/publisher
Thomas Heiton	14,082	[1.13m]	Coal importer
Arnotts	13,175	[1.05m]	Department store
Pims	12,572	[1.00m]	Department store
Bolands	11,625	[0.93m]	Millers/baker
Todd Burns*	11,050	[0.88m]	Department store
Findlaters	**10,087**	**[0.81m]**	**Wines, spirits, grocer**
A. Millar	9,926	[0.79m]	Tea, wine and spirits
Thomas Dockrell	9,736	[0.78m]	Builders providers
Brooks Thomas	9,521	[0.76m]	Builders providers
Hely's	8,842	[0.71m]	Stationers/printer
Switzers	8,808	[0.70m]	Department store
Cannock	8,478	[0.68m]	Department store
J. G. Mooney	8,164	[0.65m]	Licensed vintners
A. & R. Thwaites	7,774	[0.62m]	Mineral water
Crowe, Wilson	7,084	[0.56m]	Clothing warehouse
McBirney	5,781	[0.46m]	Department store
H. Williams	5,755	[0.46m]	Grocers/tea merchant
Merchants Warehousing	5,363	[0.43m]	Corn stores
Dolphin Hotel	4,038	[0.32m]	Hotel

*1900 figures. They had an exceptional loss in 1899.
Source: *Irish Investor's Guardian* 1899/1900

The company was floated on the stock market on 17 March 1899, St Patrick's Day. Stokes Bros. & Pim, chartered accountants, reported in the prospectus that the net profits for the central establishment in Sackville Street and the branches in South Great Georges Street, Blackrock, Leinster Street, Thomas Street, Sandymount, Howth, Rathmines, Kingstown and Baggot Street were as follows, as at 28 February:

1894	£12,936	[£1.03m]
1895	£13,555	[£1.08m]
1896	£12,756	[£1.02m]
1897	£11,562	[£0.925m]
1898	£10,087	[£0.807m]

The statement continued: 'in arriving at the above-mentioned profits no charge has been made for interest on Capital, or for remuneration of the Partners for their services; but all other charges, including, in our opinion, a sum sufficient to cover depreciation, have been included.' Interestingly, the company was floated on falling profits arising from the costs of opening new branches.*

The new company acquired the property and business of Alex. Findlater & Co. from the family. The prospectus, which was a much simpler document than would be acceptable today, gave the reasons for forming the company as 'for many years the business has been actively managed by Mr Adam S. Findlater, assisted for several years by Mr William Findlater. Owing to the advancing years of the Senior Partner of the firm (Mr John Findlater) and for other family reasons, it has been considered desirable to convert the business into a limited liability company.' The newly formed company acquired the business and assets for £175,000 [£14m]. The vendors (i.e. John, Adam and Willie) guaranteed the value of the stock book debt, but any surplus over valuation was to be refunded to them. The properties were valued by two well-known valuers Battersby's and North's, and fixed at the average of the two. The price comprised:

Assets—freehold and leasehold				
Freehold and leasehold premises			£52,228	[£4.178m]
Fixtures and fittings			£7,334	[£0.587m]
Horses and vehicles etc			£2,081	[£0.166m]
			£61,643	[£4,931m]
Assets—floating				
Stock in hand	£64,000	[£5.120m]		
Book debts	£20,000	[£1.600m]	£84,000	[£6,720]
Total			£145,643	[£11.651m]
Goodwill			£29,357	[£2,349m]
Total assets acquired			£175,000	[£14.0m]

The acquisition of the Findlater family interest was financed by the following:

11,000 ordinary shares @ £5	£55,000
11,000 preference shares @ £5	£55,000
13,000 4 % debenture in £5 units	£65,000
Total	£175,000

* Craig Gardner tendered for the flotation work in 1894 at a fee of £2,750 [£220,000], but were obviously not accepted, despite the family connection with Robert Gardner. Stokes Bros & Pim are now KPMG and Craig Gardner are PriceWaterhouseCoopers.

As was common with flotations at that time, the ordinary shares continued to be held by the founding family. Preference shares and debenture stock were offered to the public and quoted on the Dublin stock exchange. In the event the family held a sizeable number of preference shares and some of the debenture stock.

So far, so good, but the first decade as a listed company was not so easy. In 1905 a further tranche of debenture stock had to be issued. In 1909 and again in 1914, the capital of the company had to be written down.

Staff conference 1902

'You cannot sell unless you know what you are selling' Adam Findlater 1902

At the beginning of the new century, the company held a staff conference. The speeches of John's sons, Adam and Willie, then managing director and assistant managing director respectively, give an insight into the style and concerns of the company. Opening the session, the forty-seven-year old Adam observed that such a meeting was common practice in America, but not on this side of the Atlantic: 'I learn with some surprise that a meeting such as ours, though novel in this country, is quite common in America, and in the latter country it is a very usual practice indeed for the heads of firms to meet their employees and exchange ideas. I need scarcely point out to you that the system is one which is well calculated to result in advantage to both employer and employed.'

The conference was held in the Gresham Hotel on 28 November 1902. Adam took the chair and opened the meeting:

> The first thing I wish to say to you is to express my very deep regret that my father—the Chairman of the Company, Mr John, is not here to-night. When we recollect that he is seventy-five years of age, and has been at the business for sixty-one years, I think you will agree with me in saying that it would have been very interesting to have heard some reminiscences from him of the periods when he was apprentice, assistant and manager of Alex Findlater and Co., without the 'Limited'.

He then got down to business, starting with the crucial customer contact:

> You cannot sell unless you know what you are selling, and nothing looks more awkward or miserable than an unfortunate man who has neglected to learn his prices, squirming like a worm behind a counter when a customer asks a simple question, and displays more knowledge of the goods than the individual who is there to sell them.
>
> It is also most important that counter hands should learn the correct names and addresses of the customers, as nothing is so annoying to old customers as to be asked their names continually and treated generally as if they were strangers in the house.
>
> I propose to adopt a system which will weed out those who do not know the prices. On this day week an examination will be held on the price list, and sealed papers will be sent to each branch. We will settle on a set of prizes for good work, and we hope that bad work will not exist. Every person dealing with retail figures will have to go in for this examination.

(The no-nonsense tone and sharp sales orientation would undoubtedly have dismayed some of the firm's more genteel customers.*)

If you enter upon your day's work with zeal and enthusiasm and make up your mind to learn your business, there is no fear but that you will get on, and that you will be sure of promotion in our firm.

When I look back and remember coming almost as a small boy in the year 1870 to Sackville Street, and think how I have seen the business of the firm growing bigger and expanding, year after year, it does seem to me that Alex. Findlater & Co. have plenty of vacancies for men on their staff. The man who is fit for the position is the man who will obtain it, and who is bound to get on well in life.

I intend now to go through our wine list and give you some reasons why Alex. Findlater & Co. can cater for the public more successfully than a great number of firms.

You are aware that a circular was issued a short time ago to the public with the information that Alex. Findlater & Co. were the largest bottlers of Bass and Stout in Ireland. If asked why the bottled porter is the best, you can give as reasons—good corks, clean and reliable bottles, and reliable stuff that has been properly treated. What I say of Guinness's Stout applies very much more to Bass. If there is one thing more than another that needs care and watchfulness, and requires years upon years of experience it is the proper treatment of beer. The beer-drinker quickly recognises the difference between a bottle of beer thick and muddy and that which is sparkling and fresh. I think it is easy to explain these points to the public, and to speak of our undoubted success in this branch of our trade. As you know we import our cargoes of Bass's April and October brewing regularly to Kingstown Harbour.

You are also aware that about two years ago I visited Oporto. I went up the Douro for a couple of hundred miles and saw all the different vineyards. Through the fact of going up the country away from the shippers in Oporto, and getting into touch with the owners of the vineyards on the banks of the Douro, we succeeded in saving a very large intermediate profit. The result is that, at the present moment, I really believe no firm in Ireland, and few in England, have bought port wine so advantageously as we did. We bought direct from the vineyard—from the grower—and then the casks of wine came direct here from the country, only passing through Oporto for the purpose

* There was often a piece of innovation and gamesmanship in the firm's quest to publicise itself. In 1903 the newspapers reported that sandwichmen advertising Findlaters had been prosecuted for infringing the regulations. 'Messrs. Findlater & Co. for an infringement of a regulation of the Dublin Traffic Regulation Act which provided that no advertisement board should exceed 4ft. by 3ft. The defendants explained that instead of advertising their tea on two boards on a sandwichman's chest and back, they now used four boards so as to form a square inside which the man walked. Neither board exceeded the prescribed limits, but the police contended that as the boards did not remain rigidly at right angles they were entitled to measure diagonally from the end of one board to the end of the next. They submitted that rival traders had put the police in motion because Messrs. Findlater paid the men 6d. a day more than they did. Messrs. Findlater had made the things absolutely rigid, and then no matter how it was looked at or measured, it could not be over 4ft. by 3ft. Inspector Kiernan suggested the advertisement might still constitute an obstacle. The defendants undertaking not to offend in the same way again.'

Pictures from the Port Country.

From Photographs by our Managing Director.

A STREET FOUNTAIN IN OPORTO.

PORTUGUESE FLOWER SELLERS.

PEASANT VISITORS TO OPORTO.

THE VINEYARDS OF THE DOURO.

Pictures taken by Adam on his visit to Oporto in 1900

of shipping. Speaking of our thirty-six shilling (36s) Invalid Port, I am glad to tell you that we have been able to give a very large advance in quality. We have also secured large quantities of tawny wine, the same as that supplied to the King of Portugal for which our price is 48s shillings to the public, fresh from the wood. If the customer wants a fuller-bodied port, let him go to the vintage ports. The 1887 port, for which we charge fifty-four shillings, is the same as that supplied at the King's table. We have a large stock of it.

At this point Adam gave a tasting to illustrate the different qualities of wines. His expertise in this matter was well recognised; in 1908 he was one of the jurors appointed by the Wine and Spirit Association as the only Irish representative sampling between five and six thousand wines, spirits, beers and aerated waters for the Franco-British Exhibition.

He then continued:

The draught wines are the most economical for the customer, as they leave no glass of 'muddy' wine behind, but for the connoisseur who wants a very old wine, and one which retains a considerable amount of bouquet, old bottled wine may be more what he requires.

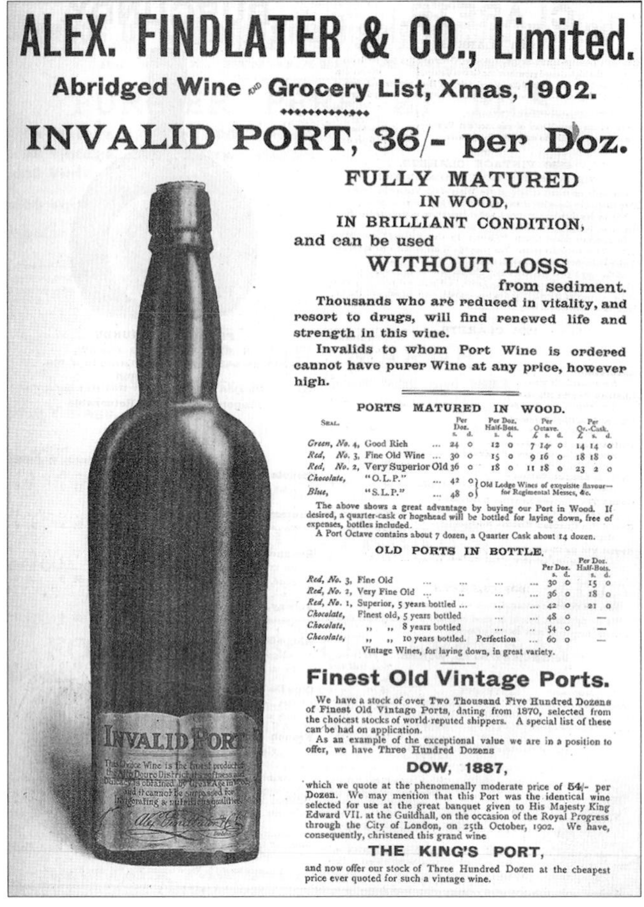

ALEX. FINDLATER & CO., Limited.

Abridged Wine AND Grocery List, Xmas, 1902.

INVALID PORT, 36/- per Doz.

FULLY MATURED
IN WOOD,
IN BRILLIANT CONDITION,
and can be used
WITHOUT LOSS
from sediment.

Thousands who are reduced in vitality, and resort to drugs, will find renewed life and strength in this wine.

Invalids to whom Port Wine is ordered cannot have purer Wine at any price, however high.

PORTS MATURED IN WOOD.

Seal.		Per Doz. s. d.	Per Doz. Half-Bots. s. d.	Per Octave. £ s. d.	Per Qr.-Cask. £ s. d.
Green, No. 4,	Good Rich ...	24 0	12 0	7 14 0	14 14 0
Red, No. 3,	Fine Old Wine ...	30 0	15 0	9 16 0	18 18 0
Red, No. 2,	Very Superior Old	36 0	18 0	11 18 0	23 2 0
Chocolate,	"O.L.P." ...	42 0	Old Lodge Wines of exquisite flavour—for Regimental Messes, &c.		
Blue,	"S.L.P." ...	48 0			

The above shows a great advantage by buying our Port in Wood. If desired, a quarter-cask or hogshead will be bottled for laying down, free of expenses, bottles included.

A Port Octave contains about 7 dozen, a Quarter Cask about 14 dozen.

OLD PORTS IN BOTTLE.

		Per Doz. s. d.	Per Doz. Half-Bots. s. d.
Red, No. 3,	Fine Old	30 0	15 0
Red, No. 2,	Very Fine Old	36 0	18 0
Red, No. 1,	Superior, 5 years bottled	42 0	21 0
Chocolate,	Finest old, 5 years bottled	48 0	—
Chocolate,	,, ,, 8 years bottled	54 0	—
Chocolate,	,, ,, 10 years bottled. Perfection ...	60 0	—

Vintage Wines, for laying down, in great variety.

Finest Old Vintage Ports.

We have a stock of over Two Thousand Five Hundred Dozens of Finest Old Vintage Ports, dating from 1870, selected from the choicest stocks of world-reputed shippers. A special list of these can be had on application.

As an example of the exceptional value we are in a position to offer, we have Three Hundred Dozens

DOW, 1887,

which we quote at the phenomenally moderate price of 54/- per Dozen. We may mention that this Port was the identical wine selected for use at the great banquet given to His Majesty King Edward VII. at the Guildhall, on the occasion of the Royal Progress through the City of London, on 25th October, 1902. We have, consequently, christened this grand wine

THE KING'S PORT,

and now offer our stock of Three Hundred Dozen at the cheapest price ever quoted for such a vintage wine.

Port had two images in 1902: as a toper's tipple leading to gout, and as a valuable part of the pharmacopeia. Invalid Port as such was first marketed by Gilbeys in 1889.

Hocks and Moselles are frequently stated to be summer drinks, but Moselle is a very much more refreshing drink than Hock. Indeed, for a refreshing drink Moselle is the proper one. Sparkling Moselle and Still Moselle are as different as chalk is from cheese, the Sparkling Moselle being flavoured with Muscatel.

On the question of so called 'New World Wines' he advised:

The difference, for instance, between our French Burgundies and the Australian and Californian wines, largely depends upon the fact that Australia's and California's virgin soil is so rich that it makes wine of such a nature as to be too rich. There is one point about wine which holds good all round, and it is this, wine is never good if it cloys the palate. Then you know there is something that will disagree with your stomach.*

In the old days the grapes were picked by women and children, who emptied them

* Two years after this, the *Daily Mail* noted a growing trend in favour of claret: 'Is it the entente that is doing it? Claret, so people in the wine trade tell you, is a returning vogue, and is elbowing on one side other wines—more particularly Moselles and Hocks—which for a season threatened a serious rivalry with the beautiful wine of Bordeaux . . . a few months ago "The Lancet," pointed out the benefits that would accrue from the more general consumption of sound wines of this kind. The family doctor who would nowadays suggest Hocks or Moselles in place of a good claret of even the humbler growths would be hard to find.' October 25th 1905.

into baskets. They were then carried on the backs of men to bullock carts, which conveyed them to the pressoir. Then you would see men with their trousers tucked up, treading the grapes until the juice drained out into the vats. And in my apprentice days it was the custom to carry the coopers of wine from the cellars—in fact, do porters' work—label, bottle, cork, in fact, go through all the departments.

On the question of stocks to back up trade he continued:

Just remember that our stock of John Jameson is worth about £50,000 [£3.75m], and with wines the total of our cellar stock in Sackville Place reaches about £80,000 [£6m] of bonded stock. When you go over our cellars and consider that the wine is lying there maturing, I think you will admit that Alex. Findlater & Co. are in a grand position to supply the public properly.

We have lately, as no doubt you have observed, introduced a new whiskey—our 'eight-year-old' John Jameson. That is, to some extent, a departure, as we used to prefer to sell our John Jameson whiskey without John Jameson's name, simply because we felt that there was a great deal of difference in John Jameson's whiskey distributed by other merchants in opposition to us according to the casks it has been stored upon. 'Fine sherry' casks mature old whiskey, and the result of us having a large quantities of sherry casks is that the whiskey matured in them is worth cent per cent more than whiskey matured in other casks. Owing to our supply of good casks, and the treatment the whiskey receives in that way, our eight year old John Jameson, our 'V.S.O.' and our 'A1' are cent per cent better than many whiskies I see around me. I do not say we have a monopoly of good whiskey, but I do say that we have consistently good whiskey always, and that is a very handsome monopoly to have. John Jameson's have introduced a three star label, and any man down the country who sells Jameson's whiskey can get the label. The casks may be good or bad, but the label is put on as long as the whiskey is the proper age and year. When we have a cask which has not matured properly, that cask is sold by public auction. John Jameson's whiskey bearing our name and our labels is a guarantee of a different article from whiskey matured on poor and unsuitable casks.

Now we come to our old A1 Whiskey. It was introduced and started on its career by my late Uncle Alexander, and the quality has always been kept up to the very highest standard. We have had appreciations of our AI on many occasions, and in a spirit of business conservatism we have declined to label it with John Jameson's name. Many who knew good whiskey, as whiskey, blessed it and swore by it. You need never be doubtful about inviting the attention of customers to it.

Twin-brother to the 'A1' is our 'Best Old Irish', on which you can always rely. If a man wants other than 'A1' you can sell him, at 21s, our Black Label, a six year old John Jameson, Findlater's Bottling. This whiskey is in competition with Gilbey's six year old J. J. Castle Brand.

Just let me give you an illustration of how you can push business. Suppose a man comes in to you, and returns an empty bottle in exchange, and you notice that it has a Gilbey's label (one of the most honourable of our opponents), or any other bottler. You should ask him, 'why don't you try our John Jameson eight year old?' If he were a

Findlater's Irish whiskey advertising 1902

pleasant fellow you can engage him in a chat, and gradually induce him to take a bottle of Findlater's Jameson.

The man in our branch house, who sells Hennessy's brandy when brandy is merely asked for, will know that there will be a black mark against his name. Our pink wrapper brandy is 20 per cent better than Hennessy's Three Star. It is an old brandy matured in casks. Hennessy's Three Star is, no doubt, well-known in public-houses, and if, for example, one was down the country and not sure of the drink, one would be on the safe side to take Hennessy's.

Branded groceries

Mr Willie, William Findlater, the thirty-five-year old assistant managing director, then addressed the meeting on the question of proprietary or branded groceries. This was the period when the great manufacturers of the twentieth century laid the foundations to their success. Foremost in Ireland were H. J. Heinz (then a premium priced brand) who had a comprehensive display of products in Findlaters Sackville Street as early as 1899. Our price lists included other branded goods, such as Nestlé, which only had a listing for condensed milk, Lazenby's for chutney, pickles, sauces, potted meats and fish. The biscuit manufacturers were well represented by W. & R. Jacob & Co., Huntley & Palmer, McFarlane Lang, and chocolates by Carrs, Rowntree, Fry, Cadbury, Suchard, and Meunier. Kelloggs were not to arrive until the late 1920s when the cereals gradually grew in popularity.

But by far the largest brand was Findlaters, which basically pre-dated all the major brand owners. The Findlater label was affixed to teas and coffees imported, blended and pack by ourselves, over sixty varieties of cakes manufactured in our Thomas Street factory, and as many varieties of sugar boilings also made there; squashes, cordials, vinegar, salad oil, and olive oil were bottled in the cellars and honey and golden syrup decanted into cans; herbs, spices, mustard and Indian curry powder were packed in the spice room in the lofts, as were baking powder, com flour, shell cocoa and marrow-fat peas; and our pickles (mixed, piccalilli, cauliflower, Chow Chow, walnuts, etc) were 'prepared in wooden vessels, and with the finest malt vinegar', as the catalogue put it. On canned and bottled foods we stated that 'we derive our supplies from the source of production, thereby avoiding all intermediate and unnecessary expenses'.

The Findlater name was also on anchovies, capers, ten varieties of fruits in bottles, four available in magnum bottles; jams bore our name only, fifteen varieties in 4 oz and 8 oz pots, and in 2 1b and 7 1b jars. Jellies were Findlaters and Lazenbys, lime juice Findlaters and Roses, and Marmalade Findlaters and Keillers, In the non-food section ammonia, boot creams, black lead, furniture polish, knife powder, starch, varnish stains and soaps all had the Findlater branding. With the exception of the top Bordeaux chateaux and Champagnes almost all wines and spirits were bought in cask and sold under the Findlater label and guarantee.*

But for many years to come many basic commodities were distributed to the branches in bulk and weighed out at the counter. This survived as far as the 1950s because a pound loose was always cheaper than a pound pre-packed, and that mattered for many of our customers. In this group would be sugar, flour, rolled oats, rice, dried fruits for Christmas baking, and basics such as semolina, tapioca, and barley.

Willie had this to say:

> I would ask you all to push Findlater's Goods—first on account of their quality. We buy the very finest quality of goods obtainable, and as we buy in bulk we get them at fair prices, but quality is our first consideration.
>
> One of the great alterations that have taken place in our trade is the number of proprietary articles that have been introduced of late years. There are many things to be said for and against this, but, as a rule, it does not tend to benefit the grocer or the customer. It does not mean that the customer is getting better value than if the selection of the brand is left to the grocer. When a demand is created for the goods by

* Over ninety years later one celebrated supermarket proprietor, on seeing ALFA Rolled Oats in the company museum, commented: 'I see that you were very early into own brands.' To which I replied: 'Not so, what you see are the original brands and not own brands.' The goods sold under the various Findlater labels were the origin of the species!

Findlater's claimed to be the largest bottlers of Bass and stout in Ireland in 1902.

advertising the manufacturer is able to fictitiously raise the price of the article.

Let us take the example of packet oats: Quaker Brand. A 6d. packet weighs about 2 lbs and is sold at 5½d. If a customer orders 2 lbs of our Flake Oatmeal he gets what I would consider a better article, fresher and made from Irish Oats, and would only pay 4d. and the profit to us is about the same. In the latter we are anxious to give the very best article in the best condition.

This brings up the question of packet goods, which is one of the curses of the trade, unless they bear our own brand. If this is encouraged much further it will mean the passing of the grocer, and he will be replaced by a mere hander-out of packet goods, or, we will have nothing but girls behind our counters, which may be unpleasant to many of the young men present! It is also a question whether the customer is getting better value as he must pay for the package; also packet goods are sold at so much a packet, not a lb. or 2 ib; in other words, in many cases there is short weight to make up for the extra cost.

The core of the grocers' goods v manufacturers' brands debate was firstly a question of profit, and secondly a question of de-skilling. Men who had served a seven-year apprenticeship, learning the many skills of the trade, did not relish

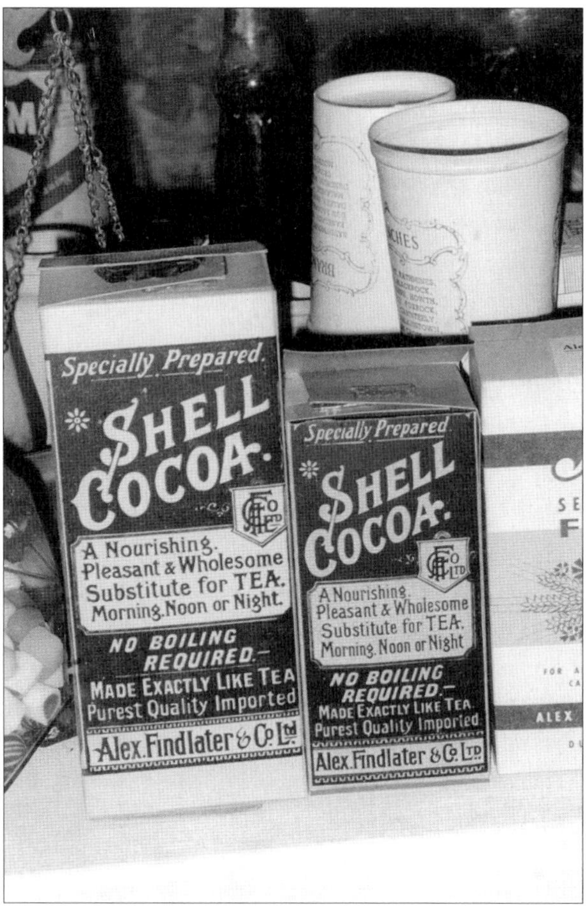

Packets made up and filled in the grocery lofts in Head Office

being turned into stackers and servers of packets.

Fifty years ago proprietary articles were comparatively unknown, for then goods of every class were bought by bulk, and the grocers and their assistants handled, tested, weighed, and parcelled every article, gaining knowledge and expertness to their own and their customers' advantage. But in the present day their shops are stocked with proprietaries, which deprive them of the interest, experience and profit which would be theirs were they packing the goods in the old way from bulk . . . grocers should seek to sell all goods that they stocked as their own, and not as if they were agents of those from whom they bought. In his opinion grocers should not sell packeted or specially put up goods without in the first place having a satisfactory knowledge of their contents and quality, and in the second place unless such lines afforded them a proper margin of profit. (Applause)

Adam went on to stress what we now call the bottom line:

Do not forget that we are doing business for the purpose of making a profit. It is the net profit that decides the success of an enormous business such as ours. If we get a farthing extra for every 2s 1d, a halfpenny for every 4s 2d, or a penny for every 8s 4d worth of goods sold, that sum at the end of the year would amount to £1,500 per annum [£114,000], equal to a dividend of 3 per cent on the Ordinary shares of the firm. It is my intention to revive the practice of the firm before it was a Limited Company, (1899), and charge each branch 5 per cent against your profits on the capital you require for the carrying on the business.

I am proud of the firm, and it seems to me that I see more of Findlater's delivery carts around Dublin than those of any other firm. An efficient organisation for delivery depends to a great extent on the care that is taken of horseflesh, and that is indeed

Findlater's grocery department 1899—the first display of Heinz goods in Ireland

Findlater's original jam labels 1904

a most serious part in our business. Much waste is often caused by sending out men on unreasonable runs. I remember when I was an apprentice being put into delivery work and getting a map of Dublin and studying it thoroughly. I remember, with some friends in business, going around the whole city to learn where all the various places were.

It is an old rule of the firm that we have a fixed price for each article and that it can be had at the same price at any of our houses. This is an advantage to the public and prevents them being overcharged. I am told that the system of charging different prices holds with some of our large rivals, where the counter hand is instructed that if a well-dressed customer comes in, that he or she is to be charged an extra halfpenny or pence, whenever the opportunity arises.

Willie then wound up the conference:

You are working for a firm that is likely to be heard of in Ireland for many years to come. You are working for a firm that is determined to succeed, and that will do its duty to those who help it to succeed. Even on a Sunday when I call to see the Boss [Adam] he is always sitting at a table surrounded by the weekly returns.* I am immediately cross-questioned about the goings-on at one of our branches, or the behaviour of one of our staff. Let us all then join for the purpose of working for the firm while we are in it.

Two years later the staff made a presentation to John and Mary in celebration of their fiftieth wedding anniversary. John wrote a rather wistful thank-you letter to each of the staff, personally addressed and signed: 'I am now 76 years of

* One wonders what Adam and Willie's Presbyterian ancestors would have felt about this use of the Sabbath.

age, and I entered the service of AF & Co as an apprentice when I was about 14 years old. Verily it is a long time to look back upon . . . I am glad to think that AF & Co is showing enterprise and push, I realise how much the firm is indebted to its able and intelligent staff in this regard. I thank you again and trust you may have a long and prosperous future before you when business shall have long ceased from troubling me, and I shall be at rest.'

John in 1880

John the risk taker

John is an enigma. Was he simply the kindly old man remembered by my aunts, the charitable, religious man who carefully recorded every jot of expenditure, the safe pair of hands who took over the business from his entrepreneurial uncle, and carefully built it up? He undoubtedly took his trade seriously: in 1882 he presented a long paper to the Presbyterian Youngmen's society in Belfast on 'Free trade, protection and fair trade', in which he described at length the origins and background to the grocery business. The text began at the Norman Conquest of England and came right up to the nineteenth century.[†]

But the surviving ledgers suggest that he also had a bit of the gambler in him, engaging in a series of more or less risky investments.

In 1880 John, at the age of fifty-two, had assets of £106,000 [£6.9m]. These were spread between the firm, the distillery, George West and Daniel Lowrey (property and theatre), premises for the firm and investments, fifteen railway stocks and £3,000 [£200,000] in the Dublin Sugar Refinery. In the subsequent years he received a further inheritance from his Uncle Adam and sold his brewery interest to his cousin Billy for £20,000 [£1.4m], making a book loss on the transaction. In fact, if we are to read into an entry in Sir John Power's diary of 27 August 1883, he felt a little hard done-by. His uncle Adam did not rewrite his will after the death of his brother Alexander, resulting in a court direction as to the distributions. Adam's widow was doubly provided for, first by a sum set aside for a generous annuity and then by 50 per cent of the residual. The balance went to Adam's fourteen nephews and nieces spread world-wide. John's gripe, confid-

† Subtitled 'A Sketch of the rise and fall of some of the restrictions imposed on Trade and Traders in England' the text ran to 52 pages. It was published by Marcus Ward, London and Belfast 1882. John's views are summed up on p49: 'Free Trade is an attempt to follow the laws of nature; Protection, an attempt to improve on those laws—hitherto, as far as I can judge, an unsuccessful attempt'.

ed to Sir John, was 'he had to pay out of the Sackville St. concern to the family, half of which he thinks old Mr Adam would have left him had he made a will'.

However, let's not cry for Great-Grandfather John, he was well enough off. In 1876 he started the risky journey with George West and Daniel Lowrey, the subject of Chapters 7 and 14. In 1880 he invested in the Dublin Sugar Refinery; it folded later in the decade but his son Adam made money selling it on to the Dublin City Distillery, and then lost heavily when the distillery went into liquidation in 1905. Such can be the roller-coaster of the risk taker.

Another investment has a salutary lesson for investors in mining both then and now. In John's investment portfolio of 1889, in addition to the customary railway stocks, he held stocks in various mining companies: the Bonnie Dundee Gold Mining Co., the Sheba Gold Mining Co., the Eastern Mysore Gold Co., the Mosman Gold Mining Co., Goldfields of South Africa, and various copper mines. His portfolio in railways and mines amounted to some £40,000 [£3m] in 1889. He reviewed them annually and recorded the increases and decreases in value. In 1889 he took a heavy fall in the value of his Mexican railway stock and in most of the mining stocks.

It is every entrepreneur's aspiration to be in at the start of a good venture, to be an original participator, rather than a passive investor when it gets quoted on the stock market. And so it happened for John and his son Adam in 1888. In that year, with Malcolm Inglis, the director of Heitons and brother-in-law of John's wife Mary, John Jameson, head of the distillery and two members of the Tedcastle family, they invested in the Isle Royal Land Corporation Limited. The corporation was formed in London to purchase large tracts of

Presented to John & Mary by the staff on the occasion of their golden wedding, 20 April 1904

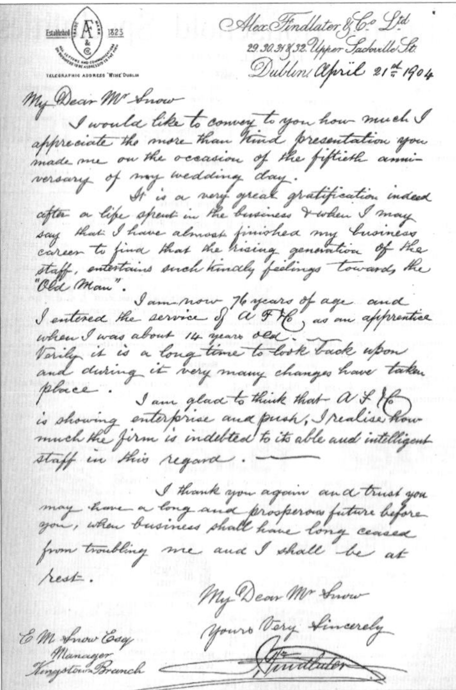

Established 1823 A F & C Trade Mark
All letters and communications to be addressed to the firm
Telegraphic address 'Wine' Dublin

Alex Findlater & Co Ltd
29.30.31 & 32 Upper Sackville St.
Dublin April 21st 1904

My Dear Mr Snow

I would like to convey to you how much I appreciate the more than kind presentation you made me on the occasion of the fiftieth anniversary of my wedding day.

It is a very great gratification indeed after a life spent in the business & when I may say that I have almost finished my business career to find that the rising generation of the staff, entertains such kindly feelings towards the "Old Man".

I am now 76 years of age and I entered the service of A F & Co as an apprentice when I was about 14 years old. Verily it is a long time to look back upon and during it very many changes have taken place.

I am glad to think that A F & Co is showing enterprise and push, I realise how much the firm is indebted to its able and intelligent staff in this regard.

I thank you again and trust you may have a long and prosperous future before you, when business shall have long ceased from troubling me and I shall be at rest.

My Dear Mr Snow
Yours Very Sincerely
Jno Findlater

E M Snow Esq
Manager
Kingstown Branch

Letter of appreciation from John to the staff

land on Isle Royale, State of Michigan, USA, amounting to 83,314 acres. The land was specially selected for its copper-bearing qualities, but the island turned out to have other potentially lucrative assets, as one of the directors reported in 1889: 'We possess many magnificent harbours on the island, all of which possess good anchorage ... and the expense of erecting steamboat wharves or piers would be trifling'. Even more optimistically he adds 'I believe we shall be able to turn the great natural beauties and health giving properties of our harbours with their lovely wooded islets to great advantage, and that we shall make the island one of the great American summer resorts.' He talked of building a first class hotel and selling building lots for summer residences.

John, taken at Bloemfontein, South Africa, November 1895

In 1890 The Wendigo Copper Company Limited was formed in London to purchase a large tract of land from Isle Royale 'to prosecute mining and the development of its mineral and other resources'. Adam (Findlater) and Malcolm Inglis were directors. The following year Isle Royale reported that it had to take the entire consideration in fully paid shares, as Wendigo shares had not been fully subscribed for. The report also mentioned that Wendigo had purchased additional land from the State of Michigan at $10 an acre as against Isle Royale's original purchase at $3½ an acre, which augurs well for the future. Wendigo commenced with a working capital of £40,000 [£3m] and in May 1891 Isle Royale raised an additional £15,000 [£1.1m] through a mortgage debenture. So far, so good.

From here on the mood turns more sombre. In November 1894 Isle Royale shareholders were informed that 'Owing to the financial difficulties in the United States, the company has been unable to deal with the timber referred to in the last report', and added that for the same reason 'the negotiations entered into for the erection of the hotel . . . and the sale of land for summer resort purposes, have been unsuccessful.' And at the same time the Wendigo shareholders were informed: 'I found the financial position of the company so involved through the inability of Mr Hay to realise on the dock property and consequently to pay the outstanding liabilities. The fact of having no money to work with, and the severe depression in all branches of trade here—much aggravated by the big railway and other strikes—have very much handicapped me in the work of developing our property'. And remember the lovely wood that was to be such a bonus: 'the forest fires commenced, and, as a result of an unusually long spell of drought, spread with such alarming rapidity, and over such vast areas, that timber speculators drew back in alarm.' Furthermore the timber merchant who was to erect a large saw mill was unable to raise sufficient capital.

On the main *raison d'être* of the company, copper mining, he reported 'nothing has been done in this direction'! Mr Houghton, who had an option to commence the mining, reported that he could find no one with courage enough to go into mining ventures with trade and mining so disorganised and depressed.

On agriculture he reported that 'only very little fresh land was cleared this year, as none of the horses were left on the island this winter.' When they were returned to the island the following spring, they were 'in such miserable condition that they could do no work for some weeks. Consequently our farming operations were limited.' He then talks optimistically of the excellent hay and vegetables they grow and there being a good market for them. 'Our potatoes, turnips and carrots are equal to the finest I have ever seen.' They also anticipated good revenues from fishing but alas had not the capital to acquire large enough nets for it to be successful.

The next Wendigo report to hand is for the year ended 31 December 1896.

> The company being without funds with which to prove the mineral deposit, confidently believed to exist on your property, and Mr Houghton having returned the option to do so at his own expense, this very desirable operation has had to be abandoned. Under these circumstances Mr Feldtmann has devoted his energies in trying to make a satisfactory sale of the timber. It is much regretted that his efforts have been unavailing but he still holds out hope etc.

In 1900 the Isle Royale directors in their report for the year to end December 1899 said that their efforts to dispose of the property had been unsuccessful and the parties with the option on the timber had declined to proceed. The efforts to raise further funds through a second debenture had been unsuccessful 'and the result is that the company have been without funds to pay either the US government taxes or the interest on the debentures.'

So ends the sad story of Wendigo and Isle Royale. I am sure that Adam visited the Isle as we know he travelled to Canada and America on business. John must have queried the loss of his investment since he received the following from the company [Isle Royale]: 'In reply to your letter the object of the proposed scheme of reconstruction is to provide funds for paying off the debentures and other liabilities so as to give the Directors an opportunity of continuing their efforts to find a purchaser for the property. It is, of course, quite impossible to say what the prospects of success in this direction are. It may be sold at once or years may elapse before anything can be done. It is entirely speculative.'

How these investments affected John's estate is not clear. We can however see his net worth fluctuating considerably during the 1880s. Starting in 1880 his cash book records his worth at £106,000 [£6.9m]; by 1882 it had climbed to

35 Castle Street, Dalkey 1898–1969

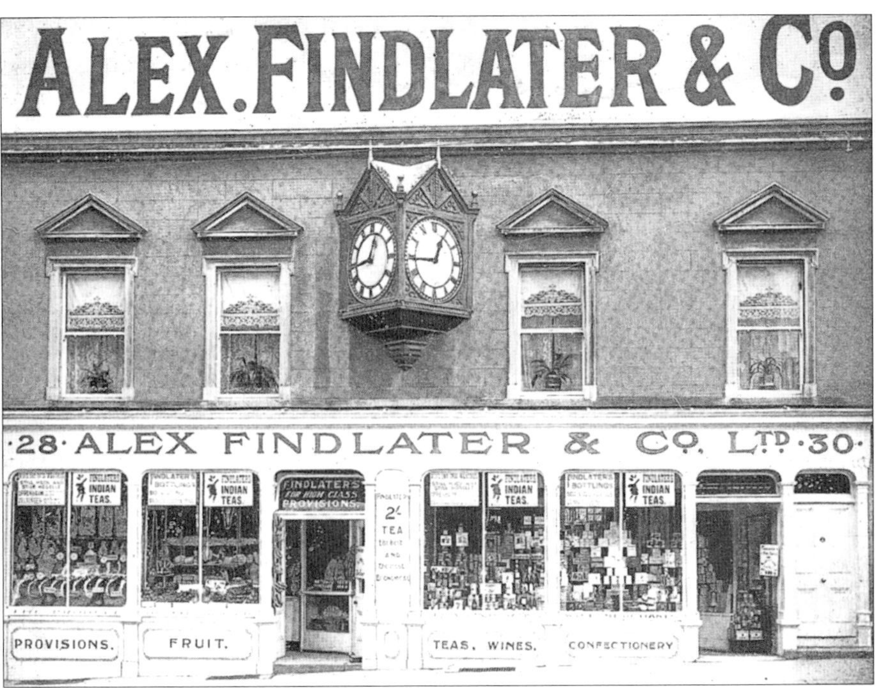

28 and 30 Main Street, Blackrock, 1879–1969

£128,000. Then it takes a downturn, sinking to £99,000 in 1887, reviving slightly in 1888 and ending the decade at £95,000.

Early electricity

Telephone and electricity were the great practical marvels of the day. In 1880 John, William Martin Murphy* and others participated in the flotation of the Dublin Electric Light Company with a paid-up capital of £15,000 [just £1m].[4] The company had a small experimental station in Schoolhouse Lane from which Kildare Street, Dawson Street and part of St Stephen's Green were lighted with arc lamps on wooden posts and overhead wires. There was a station in Fade Street to supply the southside and one in Liffey Street to supply the northside of the city including Henry and North Earl Streets. The first electric light in Ireland was an arc lamp outside the office of the *Freeman's Journal* in Princes Street, erected in 1880. By 1881 the company had 17 arc lamps in circuit and by 1882 this had increased to 114 with thirty customers. Supply of current was exclusively for lighting and the new service was, as yet, seen to offer little challenge to gas, even though a number of major companies, including Pims and Jacobs, and the School of Surgery, were linked up. (Lighting by gas is much older, of course. The Dublin Gas Light Company was instituted in 1821 and the Mansion House was lit by gas in 1824.)

Unfortunately the Electric Light Company was not a business success. In 1882 the Westminster parliament passed the Electric Light Act which limited the concession of supply by private enterprises to a maximum of seven years where the local authority granted the licence. This period was too short to justify the investment of further capital. The company was already electrically overloaded and only just paying its way. The directors put it in the hands of a liquidator who sold the plant to the Alliance Gas Co. who claimed that they were entitled to produce electricity under one of their own enabling Acts. Dublin Corporation disputed this. John lost £400 [£32,000] on this venture.

Early golf

As we enter the 21st century, we live in exciting times, but so did John and his sons a century earlier. The internal combustion engine, pneumatic tyres, telephones, electricity and golf were all new. And John had his input. Let's take golf

* It is interesting to see John and William Martin Murphy in partnership. Murphy was a staunch Catholic from Cork and one of the great entrepreneurs of the day. His empire included the Dublin United Tramway Company, electrified in 1896, Clery's departmental store and the Imperial Hotel, both in O'Connell Street Dublin and the *Irish Independent* newspaper. His wealth came mainly as a tramway and railway contractor in Britain, Africa, South America and of course Ireland. He was President of the Dublin Chamber of Commerce in 1912-13 and led the counter-attack against the growing labour militancy of James Larkin's Irish Transport & General Workers' Union in the 1913 lockout. He was a good employer, provided housing for his workforce and above average wages. He was a man of tremendous vision and energy and in 1885 was elected MP for St Patrick's Division Dublin. He was a director of the Hibernian Bank. See Thomas Morrissey *William Martin Murphy* Historical Association of Ireland 1997.

Dublin tram in Fry's model railway exhibition in Malahide Castle
(Photograph by Pat Langan *The Irish Times*)

first. The pioneer of modern golf in Ireland was Thomas Sinclair of Belfast. During frequent visits to Scotland he played at St Andrews as early as 1872 and became determined to introduce serious golf to Belfast. Golf had been played before this, by Scottish regiments' officers based at Athlone and Limerick, but the course could only have been private grounds extemporised.

John was a founding member of the Royal Belfast Golf Club, as were the Right Hon. Thomas Sinclair, a Belfast provender merchant and the leading liberal Unionist and later Privy Councillor, Sir Edward Porter Cowan, William Q. Ewart, C. K. Cordener, Dr W. F. Collier, W. Murphy-Grimshaw, W. S. Johnston, John G. Brown and George L. Baillie. Sinclair was the first captain. The first meeting was on 9 November 1881 and thus the Royal Belfast Golf Club was born. The annual subscription was fixed at one guinea. The committee in Belfast got to work immediately and a six-hole course (later nine) was laid out.

The first competition was held on Boxing Day 1882 and even after allowing for the primitive clubs and golf balls of the period, the standard of play must have been somewhat less than spectacular. In the 18-hole stroke competition the three top prizes were won by players returning net scores of 121, 130 and 131 and the tail-enders came in at 200 and an incredible 228. This latter player is said to have been so 'delighted' with himself that he never played again. He quite clearly made the right decision! We have no record of John's prowess on the course.

The game in Dublin was started by John Lumsden, of the Provincial Bank of Ireland's office, College Green. The object, Lumsden said, would be to foster the good old Scotch game in Dublin where, he was sure, it would quickly become popular. The Dublin club was initially based in the Phoenix Park, moved to Sutton in 1886 and in 1889 established the famous links course on the North Bull Island, some four miles from the centre of Dublin. On 24 October 1885 the first golf match took place between the Royal Belfast Golf Club and the (Royal) Dublin Golf Club.

Early telephones

The Dublin Metropolitan Police had their own primitive telephone system from 1882. The system was called ABC; it was simple to operate, but costly to provide and maintain and required a high degree of skill in its adjustment. Two examples show that it did not give universal satisfaction. In November 1878, when a fire occurred at Maynooth College, a messenger was dispatched to the local post office to telegraph for the assistance of the Dublin Fire Brigade, but as a journalist wrote: 'As is only too frequently the case when the wires are earnestly needed, they are found to be utterly useless . . . The instrument is out of order, Sir, and I cannot send your message was the reply of the fair operator at the Maynooth Post Office. The instrument was an ABC, the most worthless construction in the postal service and one which even when in apple-pie order, is not deserving houseroom in any office of a civilised country. The messenger had to go to Celbridge to get his message through.'[5]

Another occasion on which the ABC was found wanting was in July 1883. Findlaters had ABC circuits connecting the Sackville Street head office with branches at South Great Georges Street and Rathmines. A complaint was made about the working of the latter instrument and Mr Burge of the Post Office investigated. Mr Findlater complained that, 'It has never given satisfaction and he would like to get rid of it if the Post Office could allow the contract to be broken'. On the previous day, the call bell had been ringing even though Sackville Street was not calling, and shortly afterwards they were unable to use the line for about a half-hour. Mr Burge pointed out that rapid and impatient working was most detrimental to the well working of the apparatus. Finally, he laid the blame at the door of the telephone company's workmen. Findlater agreed to have the ABC circuit replaced by a Gower-Bell telephone connected with the telephone exchange, as the Sackville Street branch already was. Findlaters was subscriber No. 152 in the corporation list. In spite of these difficulties the ABC remained in service for many years, until 1928, at least. In that year what were probably the last two circuits were converted to telephone.

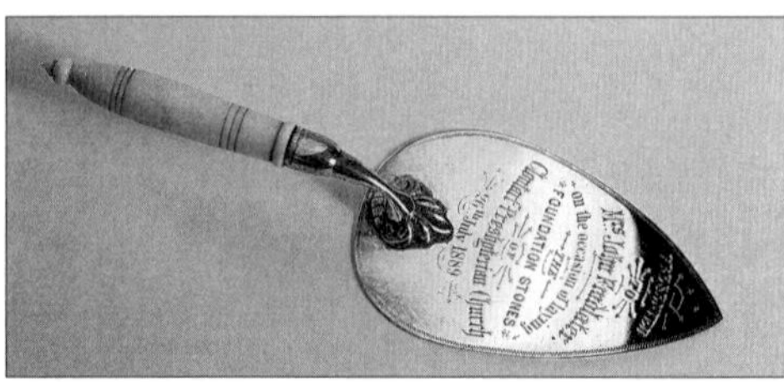

John wife Mary laid the foundation stone of Clontarf Presbyterian Church in July 1889

John's generosity

John Findlater died on 8 January 1908 at the age of eighty. As so often, the newspapers carried obituaries which revealed the man behind the business leader. In an obituary, an author in the *Belfast*

John and Mary in old age.

Witness told this story:

A few years ago I received a short private letter from him, in which he stated that he would like to see me for a few minutes any day I chanced to be passing his place of business. My acquaintance with him at the time was slight, and I wondered very much what he wanted to see me for. In a day or two I called upon him, and he received me with the quiet and undemonstrative courtesy which marked the gentleman. He took me into his own private office, and after the ordinary inquiries about health, etc., Mr Findlater said to me—I notice that you have been expending a great deal of money on your church premises, and I thought I would like to help you if you would allow me.

I thanked him and explained in detail what we had expended, and what were our liabilities, and also told him that my present frame of mind was pre-eminently receptive. He then took his cheque book and wrote me out a very handsome cheque, and handing it to me across the table said—I am sorry it is not twice or three times as much, but if you are hard driven to liquidate the whole of your liabilities come back and tell me.

I accepted the gift, and I think it only right to add that during a long life of hard work in the Kingdom of Christ this incident stands out along with only three or four more as among the most Christ-like I have met with. It was not the amount of the subscription which most impressed me, although that was handsome. Neither was it the spontaneous way in which it was given. It was something more. It was the modest, unostentatious spirit in which the thing was done; the beautiful way in which Mr Findlater made you feel that he was not conferring a favour in giving so much as receiving a favour in my accepting; and the pleasure it seemed to be to him to be able to do something to lighten another's burden, and to take a small part in work that might be useful. . . .

After that incident Mr Findlater and I became what might be called friends. In this imperfect world we meet with few so genuine and so modest. If he did not draw his life from the unseen Head of the Church he loved I do not know where he found it. His death removes one whose character I greatly loved and honoured, and I have no hesitation in saying that both our Church and our city are distinctly the poorer by reason of his departure.[6]

John's will is brief; he leaves his house, Melbeach in Monkstown, to his wife Mary. There is no mention of his commercial concerns and investments and no executor's account of his assets. His widow died in November 1917, and the contents of Melbeach, the house they had built up together, were auctioned by North's. At this time the First World War was still in progress, and in Ireland Sinn Féin was noisily flexing its muscles prior to the shooting campaign which began in January 1919. This was therefore not a good moment to auction such items. Of his pictures, for instance, the top value was achieved by Erskine Nicol's 'Guinness' best' which fetched £75 [£2,500]. He had bought this painting in 1877 for £115. The total contents actually realised about £3,000 [£100,000] –top item was a 'massive six-light glass chandelier' with cut bowls and Waterford drops which achieved £129 [over £4,000].

Mary's will gives us some idea of the tangle of her sons' finances: 'I have equal love for all my sons and in making the following distributions I am anxious that they and their families shall be dealt with equally as far as possible and I am bearing in mind their father's request that I should remember the younger sons as he had done the elder ones. I bequeath to my son William the sum of eight hundred pounds [£30,000]. The following three amounts I direct to be liability of my estate: the eight hundred pounds owing by my son William to the estate of my son Herbert, the six hundred he owes to the Provincial Bank [£23,000] and for which some of the stocks of my son Herbert are lodged as security, and the eight hundred and fifty pounds he owes to Alex. Findlater & Company Limited for which I am security.'

She then divided the residue in seven equal parts between her surviving sons and the widows of Adam who died in 1911 and Herbert who was killed in Gallipoli in 1915. The legacy bequeathed to the estate of Adam was conditional on no claim being made by his estate against her estate, her late husband's estate or her son William's estate. In the event of such a claim she bequeaths Adam's share to William. What are we to read into that? And so ended the great wealth created by Alexander and his brother Adam Seaton Senior and to a degree sustained by their nephew John. From here on the family are comfortable but not affluent.

Notes and references

1 Brian Inglis, *Downstart* London: Chatto & Windus 1990 p 69
2 Queen *v* Drury Queens Bench and Exchequer Divisions, vol 11, 1894. The case is discussed in W. N. Osborough, *Law and the Emergence of Modern Dublin* Dublin: Irish Academic Press 1996
3 Tony Farmar *A History of Craig Gardner* Dublin: Gill and Macmillan 1985 p 71
4 Maurice Manning and Moore McDowell *The History of the ESB,* Dublin: Gill & Macmillan 1984 p 1; and P. Harkin, 'Electricity Supply in Dublin 1880-1930', paper read 16 January 1940, ESB library; and ESB archive department, Harold's Cross, Dublin
5 Eircom archive
6 'Our Dublin Letter' *The Witness,* Belfast 17 August 1908

6. *A Southern Unionist Businessman: Adam Findlater (1855–1911)*

Adam was born on 25 January 1855, the eldest son of John and Mary. He attended High School, then situated at the top of Harcourt Street. In 1872 he entered Trinity College and graduated in 1876 with a first class honours degree in Logic and Ethics. He got his MA in 1889 and was called to the Bar in 1906.

When he died, a friend wrote of Adam:

> To the Dublin public he was more than the managing director of the great business which bears his name, and which was founded by his forefathers in the early years of the last century. That was but one of the many commercial and industrial interests with which he was directly connected. Nor was the esteem in which he was held based upon his rare personal qualities or upon his conspicuous service to the public. It was the combination of exceptional qualities of head and heart in one commanding personality that rendered him a notable figure in the Irish capital. For instance, while pursuing his studies in Trinity College he was also learning in his father's counting-house the principles of commerce and their application to every-day work. He made himself thoroughly acquainted with economics, science, and equally with modern business methods. By the time he took his degree of MA he was already prominent in the mercantile community.
>
> The wholesale business of the firm, covering all Ireland, and the branch establishments in the townships adjoining Dublin, such as Howth, Rathmines, Kingstown, Dalkey, Bray and Foxrock, would have sufficed to engross the attention of any ordinary merchant. Their administration and direction formed but one of his many activities. As chairman of the Kingstown Commissioners he rendered invaluable service to that prosperous township, which in a few years was transformed by his enterprise and ability. During one term of his tenure of office there occurred the disaster in Dublin Bay, when the entire crew of the Kingstown lifeboat, attempting to rescue Russian sailors from a wreck were drowned outside the harbour. Within six hours Adam had organised a relief fund for the families of the lost men, and in a fortnight had raised a sum amply sufficient to satisfy the needs of all their dependants.
>
> In a similar spirit, when the licensed trade was threatened some years ago by novel extractions under a valuation scheme at the instance of the Treasury, Adam aroused public opinion on the subject, led the opposition, gave evidence before a Select Committee of the House of Commons dealing with the subject, and defeated the hostile project. About the same time he drafted, promoted, and obtained the passing into law of the General Dealers' (Ireland) Act—usually referred to in the law courts as Findlater's Act—by which an effectual check was put on the operations of receivers of stolen goods, especially goods handled in the licensed and allied trades.[1]

Adam and Agatha (Agatha in fancy dress)

As an index of his prominence in the day, Adam drew mentions in both *Ulysses* and *Finnegans Wake,* more so the latter, which was not finally published until 1939, nearly thirty years after Adam's death.

In 1881 Adam married Agatha McCurdy; she was the only daughter of John McCurdy of Chesterfield House, Blackrock, a well-known architect. McCurdy himself was married to Lucy Heinekey, aunt to Adam's sister-in-law Lucie, brother Willie's wife. Among other buildings, John McCurdy designed the Shelbourne Hotel (1865), the Masonic Girls' School (1882), now Bewleys Hotel on the Merrion Road, the Royal Marine Hotel in Dún Laoghaire (1863/6), the Salthill Hotel at Seapoint (now demolished), St Helen's in Stillorgan (1863), now the Radisson Hotel and All Saints Church of Ireland in Carysfort Avenue, Blackrock. He was also architect to Trinity College. He died in 1885 at the age of sixty-one and is buried in Dean's Grange.[2]

Adam and Agatha had a son Seaton and a daughter Wanda, both of whom eventually settled in England. Seaton was sent to school at Harrow. Wanda pursued a career on stage and married in England. I quote from *The Lady of the House* of January 1912:

TO MY CHILDREN.

MY DEAR S——N. AND W——A.

I GIVE YOU THIS LITTLE BOOK, IN REMEMBRANCE OF OUR MANY HAPPY EVENINGS IN THE TWILIGHT, WHEN YOU ASKED ME TO TELL YOU A STORY.

PERHAPS IN THE TIME TO COME, WHEN YOU AND I ARE PARTED, YOU WILL LOOK AT THE WELL-KNOWN PAGES, AND LET YOUR THOUGHTS DWELL ONCE MORE ON THE DEAR OLD DAYS WHEN THE "RED HEN" WAS A THING OF REALITY, AND FAIRYLAND VERY CLOSE TO YOU; ALSO, YOU WILL, PERHAPS, REMEMBER THAT THESE TALES WERE WRITTEN SO THAT YOUR SMALL MINDS COULD UNDERSTAND THEM WITHOUT BIG WORDS OR LONG SENTENCES BY

YOUR LOVING

MOTHER.

Agatha was a prolific writer of children's stories many of which were published in *The Lady of the House*

Wanda is the young Irish lady who has made such a success as a dancer at the Victoria Palace, London. She is the first pupil of M. Mordkin, who took London by storm in the Russian Ballet. 'Wanda' otherwise Miss Findlater, dances a suite of dances arranged for her by Miss Rosina Filippi and Miss Eileen Allen. Her 'Amazon' and 'Autumn', danced to the music of Schubert and Sibelius, aroused great enthusiasm. Wanda was again and again recalled and left the stage laden with floral trophies.

Agatha, her mother, died in 1927 aged sixty-nine and is buried in her father's plot in Dean's Grange. Her mother, Wanda's grandmother, died one year later, aged ninety-two and is also buried in this plot.

Despite the wide range of interests mentioned by his friend's encomium, Adam was first of all the managing director of Findlaters, with a tight grip on trading realities. In 1896, for instance, Adam entered into a ten-year contract with the powerful Mazawattee Tea Company, London, which appointed Findlaters their sole agent in the city and county of Dublin for packet and tins of tea. He agreed to purchase at least 500 chests during the first year, and during the remainder of the agency a minimum of 1,000 chests each year, some for the Findlater blends. In seconding the motion at the 1903 AGM of Mazawattee

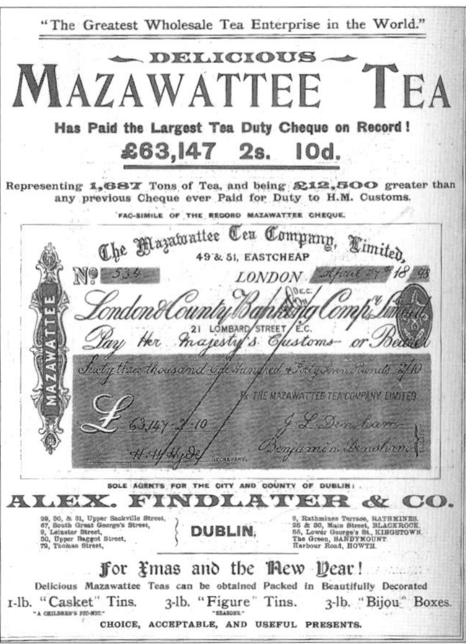

In 1900 Mazawattee claimed a new world record duty cheque of £85,862 and if the cups and saucers were put side by side they would reach 30 times around the world!

in London Adam mused that he thought he had 'the largest power of distribution in the trade in Ireland' and reported that in the first year of his agreement his tea turnover almost doubled to a level equivalent to just under £1m in year-2000 values. Adam's careful choice of words reflected that at the time Baker Wardell & Co. and Adam Millar & Co. were No. 1 and No. 2 tea wholesalers in the country.

To finance the Boer War (1899-1902) the duty on tea was raised to 8d. However this was followed by a spirited Anti-Tea-Duty campaign which succeeded in persuading the Chancellor to take first 2d and then a further 1d off. In an interview he gave to a journalist of the *Evening Telegraph* on 1 May 1906, Adam expressed his disappointment at the size of this last reduction:

'Then, the penny reduction is a disappointment to the trade?'

Mr Findlater: 'Undoubtedly it is. So small a reduction as a penny is most unsatisfactory. And for this reason: in sales of a quarter of a lb. the consumer can get a farthing reduction; but look at the countless purchases made of tea in ounces and two ounces by the poorer classes in our towns and all over the country, and how can they get a proportionate benefit or reduction? The retailer simply cannot do it.'

'Then, the small shopkeeper would reap all the benefit in that case—that is what you mean?'

Mr Findlater: 'Yes, the shopkeeper would have the advantage in that case. But the consumer may get an indirect benefit in this way. He may be enabled to get a better tea at 1s a pound (or 1d an ounce) than he does at present; but, on the other hand, if the consumption of 1s 4d tea increased, the tea growers might endeavour to absorb a portion of the penny by increasing the price to the market.'

'I suppose the largest trade is done in teas about 1s 4d per pound?'

Mr Findlater: 'Yes, in teas ranging from 1s 4d to 2s a pound.'

'Summing up the question, what do you think the effect of the remission will be to the poorer people?'

Mr Findlater: 'On the whole I am satisfied that the poorer classes will benefit by the remission of the taxes even though it may not be apparent in their purchases of small packages. And while on that subject I would like to say that it is a great pity the poorer classes don't always recognise the fact that a higher priced tea is really more economical than the lower priced article.'

'That is a most interesting statement, Mr Findlater, so interesting that I would like you to enlarge upon it,' said our representative.

Mr Findlater: 'The reason of that is that the higher priced tea goes further, the resultant brew is much more refreshing, and for my part I don't know anything more refreshing than a good cup of tea. Hence I say that teas from 1s. 10d to 2s 4d a pound are really more economical than the lower priced article.'

'I suppose your trade is to a great extent in the higher priced teas?'

Mr Findlater: 'Yes, our business is largely in the latter class of teas.'

'I would assume that China tea has now but a slight sale?'

Mr Findlater: 'Yes, the sale of China tea is small, indeed. Indian and Ceylon teas are those in great demand for some-time past. I would also like to say a word or two in conclusion, and to this effect. I am glad to see that there is a growing inclination among the better class of people to recognise the value of fine teas. In the old days I have known men who would not give you a bad glass of wine or anything but the finest whiskey in the way of refreshment, but very often if you sat down to have tea at these men's tables you would get anything but a good cup of tea. Now, at 5 o'clock teas you will get a really fine tea, and, as I have already said, a good cup of tea is a great luxury—an excellent thing.'

FINDLATER'S

SPECIAL BLEND TEAS.

	s.	D.	
Strong Tea	1	2	per lb.
Useful Blend	1	4	„
Strong Flavouring and Wonderful Value	1	6	„
The Best Value that can be bought in Tea at the Price	1	8	„
Wonderful Fine Tea at a Moderate Price	1	10	„

THE TEA OUR REPUTATION HAS BEEN BUILT ON - 2/-

This Tea has an even leaf, free from dust, and gives a lovely colour in the cup both before and after milk is added.

Our Special Five o'clock Tea	2	4	„
The Tea of Luxury	2	8	„
Connoisseur's Tea	3s. and 3	4	„

Findlater's Special Blend Teas

Fancy Teas.

We also stock various Teas which are not in general consumption, including :—

Finest Golden-Tipped Assam	4s.	6d.	per lb.
Finest Pearl-Leaf Gunpowder	3s.	0d.	„
Finest Young Hyson and F'oo Chan Pekoe	3s.	0d.	„

Scent with Delicate Orange Perfume.

Tea prices in 1905

However, as well as his responsibilities as managing director, Adam was chairman of two theatres, the Star in Dublin, from 1897 known as the Empire Palace Theatre, and the Empire Theatre of Varieties in Belfast, both of which he took over from Dan Lowrey. He was chairman of the ailing Dublin City and Banagher Distillery. He was also involved in hotels, with interests in the St Lawrence in Howth and the Royal Hotels in Bray and Howth. He was an active member of both the Dublin Port and Docks Board and the Dublin Chamber of Commerce. He was chairman of the Commercial Travellers' Benevolent Institute and raised considerable funds for those who had fallen on hard times. But perhaps his most interesting role was as a vocal proponent of the views of liberal Southern unionists in Dublin, particularly when he was speaking of things he himself knew from his personal or business experience.

The election which saw Billy bowing out of parliament in 1885 marked a turning point in Irish politics. It was in this year that a formal unionist organisation began to emerge as a counter-weight to the increasingly well-organised Home Rule party. A more representative franchise, combined with Gladstone's first Home Rule Bill (1886), meant that the unionists had plenty of work to do. In the early years, unionism was dominated by Southern unionists—typically landed

Tea packs designed early in the 20th century. These designs were used until the mid 1960s. The actual packs were strong silver foil which ensured a perfectly fresh and aromatic cuppa.

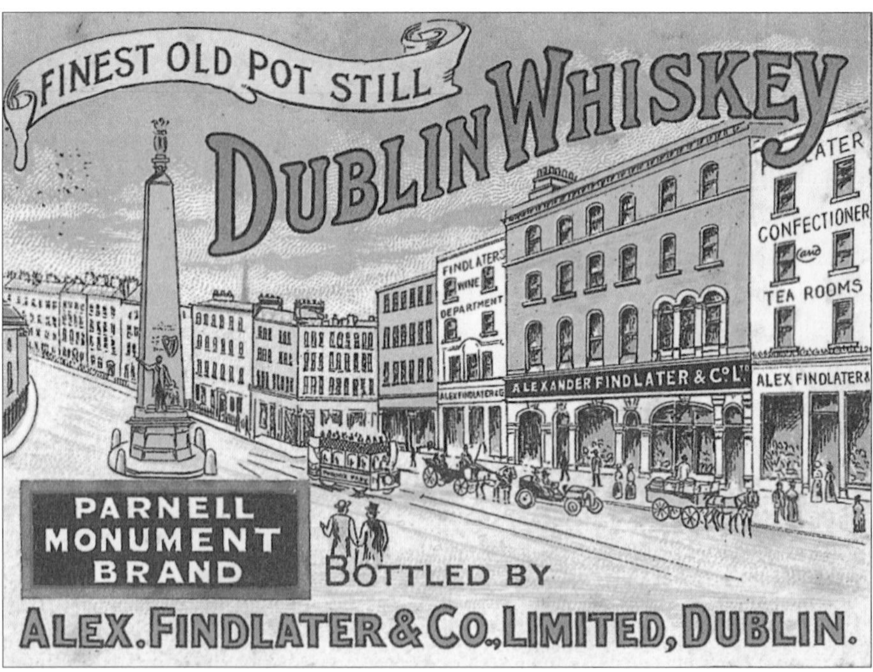

A prototype label based on Findlater's proximity to the Parnell monument erected in 1911 and showing that grandfather had no qualms in associating the firm with the great Irish nationalist.

FINDLATER'S PURE INDIAN TEAS.

A glance at the following figures for the past ten years will show that China Teas continue to give way to Indian. The falling off in the delivery of the former, and the increase in the latter, have been more marked in the past year than in any previous one, and it seems only a question of time ere Indian will take the precedence :—

HOME CONSUMPTION OF INDIAN AND CHINA.

	Indian.	China.	Total.	Percentage of Indian.
1883	59,097,000	114,953,000	174,050,000	34
1882	50,497,000	115,569,000	166,066,000	30½
1881	48,836,000	112,156,000	160,992,000	30⅓
1880	43,807,000	111,307,000	155,114,000	28¼
1879	35,243,000	125,576,000	160,819,000	22
1878	36,776,000	120,192,000	156,968,000	23½
1877	28,013,000	123,012,000	151,025,000	18⅔
1876	26,735,000	126,004,000	152,739,000	17½
1875	23,275,000	126,508,000	149,783,000	15½
1874	17,756,000	121,622,000	139,378,000	12¾

We send 6 lbs. of our Pure Indian Teas, per Parcel Post, Carriage Free, to any part of the United Kingdom.

Prices 2s., 2s. 4d., 2s. 8d., 3s., 3s. 4d.

ALEX. FINDLATER & CO.,

30 UPPER SACKVILLE STREET, DUBLIN.

and Anglican. However, between 1881 and 1907 a series of Land Acts eroded their power base and unionism became more and more a Northern phenomenon, as it is today.

Very little is now spoken of Southern unionism. It is as if the word unionist is a soiled word, and one which refers exclusively to the uncompromising wing of Northern unionism. Yet my great-uncle Adam was a Southern unionist businessman and was highly regarded by, and on good terms with, the moderate nationalists. As well as running a thriving wine, spirit and grocery business, with (as his speech to the 1902 staff conference has shown) a very detailed and hands-on control, Adam was also a political activist. He fought for reforms in local government, land law, as well as financial and fiscal reforms–in fact he concerned himself in most facets of the economy. Happily, his political activities did not affect the popularity of his businesses which relied on the custom of a large cross-section of the population.

The Kingstown Programme

Adam's first appearance on the political stage was the occasion of the presentation of an address to the Lord Lieutenant by the town commissioners of Kingstown. Adam was chairman of what was then a separate local authority, completely independent of Dublin Corporation. There were seven such townships, as they were called, in the Dublin area: Kingstown being established in 1834, Rathmines 1847, Blackrock 1860, Pembroke 1863, Dalkey 1867, Clontarf 1869 and Drumcondra in 1879. After Adam was elected chairman of the

Kingstown Commissioners in 1895 he used the position to involve himself in both local and national issues and to campaign for legal and social reforms. He did this by addresses, speeches, booklets, letters and lobbying of MPs at Westminster, although he never actually stood for parliament.

When Lord Cadogan, the incoming Lord Lieutenant of Ireland, landed at Kingstown on 22 August 1895, Adam, then chairman of the Kingstown Board, and his colleagues on the Commission, presented an address of welcome. The contemporary commentator Michael J. McCarthy described this address as 'breaking through the silly veil which is supposed to hedge in viceroyalty from the realities of Irish life.* The town commissioners, led by Adam, laid down a programme of 'wants' in simple and straightforward language:

> Many matters that are absolutely necessary to stimulate industry and produce peace, prosperity and contentment among our people, will demand the immediate consideration of Parliament.
>
> A system of Local Government, similar to that now enjoyed by the people of Great Britain; an extension of the principle of the Land Purchase Acts, so as to spread amongst us the conserving influences of peasant proprietorship; an Act to provide for leaseholders in towns that security which is at present possessed by agricultural tenants; the re-adjustment of the financial relations between the two Islands, so that Ireland will not be compelled to contribute more than her fair proportion to the Imperial revenues; an Act to facilitate Private Bill legislation, so as to obviate the necessity for the excessive expenditure which, under existing circumstances, must be incurred in inquiries on the other side of the Channel before any useful improvement requiring the sanction of Parliament can be effected; are all measures so indispensable to a good condition of affairs here, that they may be considered as outside the range of party politics. We have, therefore, no hesitation in pressing them upon the attention of your Excellency and, through you, upon the attention of Her Majesty's Government.[3]

In the heated political atmosphere of the day, even unionist Kingstown had nationalists on the Commission, and they 'decline[d] to join in the presentation of any address to or any public demonstration in honour of Earl Cadogan or any other Viceroy, until an adequate measure of Home Rule has been passed for this country, and evidence has been given of improvement in the disposition of the English people by the restoration of the evicted tenants to their homes, and of the political prisoners to freedom.'[4]

* The Lord Lieutenant was the representative of the Queen, and strictly speaking not a political appointment, though in practice the appointment had political overtones. The senior political figure was the Chief Secretary who was a cabinet member. The 'silly veil' comment is from Michael McCarthy *Five Years in Ireland 1895-1900* Dublin: Hodges Figgis 7th ed 1902 p 51. R. B. McDowell writes in *Crisis and Decline* (Dublin: Lilliput Press 1997 p 42): 'Protestant antagonism to Irish Catholicism was nourished by the writings of discontented Catholics, such as *Priests and People in Ireland* by M. J. E. McCarthy and *Father Ralph* by G. O'Donovan, which depicted Catholic ecclesiastics as domineering, intellectually unprogressive and oppressive, determined to control as much of Irish life as they could and excessively eager to obtain financial support for Church purposes'. See also T. West *Horace Plunkett: Co-operation and Politics* Gerrards Cross: Colin Smythe p 72.

ALEX. FINDLATER & CO., LTD., DUBLIN.

Wine Connoisseurs!

The Wine Connoisseur invariably selects his wines from big stocks held by Merchants of high repute and extensive dealings. He is aware that the small trader, buying his little lots from hand to mouth, cannot compete in variety, quality, or price with the great wine house backed by large capital, ripe judgment and vast cellarage. Accordingly the Connoisseur goes where the conditions exist in the best way for supplying his wants.

Alex. Findlater & Co., Ltd.,

Offer the public interested in Old Bottled Wines their choice from immense stocks such as no Wine House in this country has at any time accumulated. These stocks at present consist of over TWENTY THOUSAND DOZENS, including :—

3,500 Dozens Fine Old Ports, 5 to 30 Years Bottled.
9,500 ,, Vintage Clarets, 1888 to 1900.
7,500 ,, Burgundies, 1895 to 1903.
1,500 ,, Hocks and Moselles, Old in Bottle.

One Hundred and Fifteen Thousand Pounds

Is the value of these immense stocks of Wine, as above stated, together with the Stock of JOHN JAMESON & SON'S Dublin Whiskey in our Bonded Stores, from which the Purchaser, whether it be of a Single Bottle or a Dozen, can draw with the assurance of obtaining the very finest article of its class at the most reasonable rates.

An Invitation.

We cordially invite the Public to inspect the above immense Stocks in our Cellars and Bonded Warehouses. We can offer a variety and value, absolutely authenticated, which is not elsewhere obtainable by the Purchasers of Old Bottled Wines and Fine Dublin Whiskey.

FINDLATER'S EXCISE BONDED STORES

ALSO CONTAIN

120,000 Gallons of Fine Dublin Whiskey

(JOHN JAMESON & SON'S OWN MAKE),

Specially Bonded in Findlater's High-Class Sherry Casks, Mellowed and Matured by Age Only.

ALEX. FINDLATER & CO., LTD.,

Head Offices, Cellars, and Duty-Paid Stores—

29—32, UPPER SACKVILLE STREET, DUBLIN.

Bonded Stores and Bottlings—

FINDLATER PLACE, DUBLIN.

30

December 1906:
Even by today's standards these are very large stocks

Despite nationalist rejection, the address gained public attention, with The *Freeman's Journal* commenting sadly: 'There is, we fear, little hope of the Kingstown Programme [as the address was referred to] from the present Government'.[5] But Adam did not leave things there: he wrote a magisterial letter (of 3,000 words!) to the London *Times* (12 October 1897) entitled 'Ireland under Unionist Government' arguing the case for the reforms. On the subject of local government he wrote:

> The system of county government in Ireland is an anachronism. It is entirely in the hands of a body called the grand jury, selected (except in the county of Dublin) by the sheriff by a tortuous method . . . It is hardly possible to over-estimate the benefits conferred upon any community by the establishment in its midst of a peasant proprietary. Experience all the world over has shown that there is no greater guarantee for the maintenance of law and order, that it promotes thrift and industry among the working classes, fosters a spirit of true nationality, and diffuses among the masses a sense of freedom and independence.

As McCarthy notes, 'it had not been heralded by any series of promises or by any flourish of trumpets whatsoever', but three years after their accession to power the government, 'having no doubt, by inquiry and investigation, thoroughly satisfied themselves that the time for action had arrived',[6] passed the Local Government Act 1898. This new Act replaced the abolished grand jury system, (in so far as it was responsible for the administration of local government), and transferred all the fiscal and administrative business of the counties to county councils, whose members were elected on the parliamentary franchise. In general, nationalists and moderate unionists welcomed the new Act, though the dying landlord class quite clearly saw the Act as yet another nail in their collective coffin—and this verdict has been confirmed by historians. As Conor Cruise O'Brien put it: 'the Southern unionists were of course mainly, though not exclusively, Protestant. Their decline from what was once a position of exclusive domination may date from the Tory Government's Local Government Act of 1898.'[7] By 1911 it was reported that of 707 county councillors in the three Southern provinces only 15 were unionists.

Land Acts

Over a period of a quarter of a century, from 1881 to 1907, the Land Acts transformed landholding in Ireland. By the end of that period, the old landed ascendancy had been bought out, in effect by the government, and a local small farmer proprietorship had been put in its place. (Ironically, the triumphs of the 19th century caused one of the worst headaches of the 20th, as the resulting fragmented structure made the modernising of Irish agriculture very difficult.) The process was in its early stages in 1896, when Adam and his fellow commissioners, though without land or pretensions to land themselves, were in favour of the change. In the address to the incoming Lord Lieutenant they requested an extension of the principle of the Land Purchase Act, 'so as to spread amongst the peo-

CHOICE
OLD
HIGHLAND WHISKY
TRADE MARK
AF
&
Co
LTD
ALEX. FINDLATER & Co. LTD.
DUBLIN &
BRANCHES

1798
The
"Irish
Standard"
Whiskey.
STRENGTH 30° UNDER PROOF.

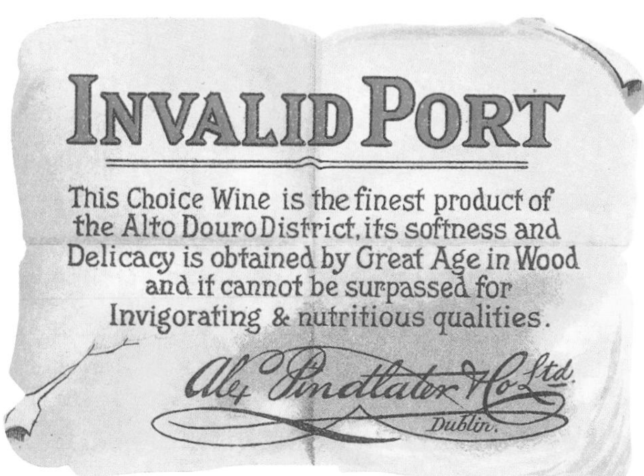
INVALID PORT
This Choice Wine is the finest product of
the Alto Douro District, its softness and
Delicacy is obtained by Great Age in Wood
and it cannot be surpassed for
Invigorating & nutritious qualities.
Alex Findlater & Co. Ltd.
Dublin.

ple the conserving influence of a peasant proprietorship'. In his great letter to the London *Times*, he is critical of the efforts of the present government save the introduction of 'several clauses intended to render somewhat easier the annual instalments payable by tenants who have been fortunate enough to buy out the interests of their landlords and root themselves permanently in the possession of their holdings'.

Agriculture

On the question of agriculture Adam wrote in the London *Times*: 'The staple, and indeed almost the only, industry in Ireland is agriculture, and the backward state of that industry is but too well known.' He commented that the Recess Committee, a body composed of Unionists, Gladstonites (Liberal Home Rulers), and Parnellites had strongly urged the appointment of a Board of Agriculture and Industries for Ireland. Just as it seemed the labours of the committee were about to bear fruit, the Chief Secretary announced his intention to bring in the necessary Bill, and the subject was quietly withdrawn. Adam concluded that there should be 'some central department to collect statistics, afford information to the local bodies, and superintend the working of the various Acts of Parliament relating to agriculture and kindred subjects. The Privy Council, in which most of these powers are at present vested, has proved wholly inadequate to this work'. As it happened, the Department of Agriculture and Technical Instruction for Ireland was established two years later, in 1899. This resulted mainly from the efforts of Horace Plunkett, pioneer of the agricultural co-operative movement in Ireland, with Father T. A. Finlay, George Russell (Æ) and R. A. Anderson.*

On 21 November 1903 Adam wrote to *The Irish Times*, supporting Plunkett generally, and revealing the rapid shifts of political allegiances of those days, and the distance of his own views from the standard conservative unionist line:

> Sir, As one who was until three years ago—until after the last election in South County Dublin—a fairly active member of the Council of the Unionist Registration Association, I must candidly say that I rejoice at the action of the Right Hon. Jonathan Hogg, P.D., Sir John Nutting, Mr Hamilton Drummond, Mr Elrington Ball, and others in severing their connection with that body . . . For my part, I trust that this decisive action of the influential gentlemen who have seceded from the Association indicates the opening of a new era in Irish public affairs, when there will be a better understanding amongst us all who find that we can agree upon questions that affect the material interests of the country. It is hopeful from another point of view. Without recalling errors of judgement in the past I do not think I am unkind in

* Plunkett, a Unionist MP for South Dublin in 1892, was the first president of the Irish Agricultural Organisation Society, in 1894. He subsequently became an adherent to home rule and founded the Irish Dominion League to keep Ireland united within the British Commonwealth. He was appointed to the new Irish Senate in 1922. His house Kilteragh in Foxrock was a centre where people of all creeds and political persuasions used to meet and discuss the new emerging Ireland. He also acquired 90 acres around Kilteragh, which he used for practical agricultural instruction, but his spirit was broken when the house was burnt down during the Civil War in 1923, and many fine records, pictures and furniture lost.

saying that some, at least, of these gentlemen strove hard to procure the defeat of Sir Horace Plunkett (as he is now) in South Dublin. I can readily understand that they now regret the disastrous success of their labours.

Their ostensible reason for driving that hard working, practical, patriotic Irishman from Parliament and the Ministry was his avowed liberality of thought, and among other matters, regarding the University question.* I am sure that Mr McCann's views are not more illiberal. Therefore I assume that we may congratulate ourselves upon this unexpected proof that even Conservatives may be progressive. It is not the least interesting of latter-day developments in Irish politics.

Yours etc. A. S. Findlater, Primrose Hill, Kingstown. 20th November, 1903.

The overtaxation of Ireland

One of the great controversies of the late 1890s was the question of the relative tax burdens of England and Ireland. Towards the middle of the 19th century successive British chancellors had adopted the view that a policy of 'fiscal equality' between the two countries should be adopted. Gladstone initiated this policy in the 1850s. He imposed income tax on Ireland, and equalised excise duties, declaring that he could not see how the rights of man demanded that 'an Irishman should get drunk more cheaply than an Englishman'. Nationalists argued strongly that, given the relative national incomes, this was unfair. It was regularly pointed out that Ireland contributed one-eleventh of the imperial revenue, when her capacity was believed to be about one-twentieth. In 1896 a Financial Relations Commission established by the Liberal government substantially supported their view. In the furore that followed, the standard unionist view was that since at least three-quarters of the tax paid was excise on tobacco and whiskey, a remedy for any apparent injustice was clearly in the Irish people's own hands. Adam, with other progressive unionists, took the other view.

In his letter to the *Times* he wrote:

> A Commission composed of men of the highest repute, all of them possessing considerable ability, some of them experts, representing every interest and every shade of political opinion, came, after patiently hearing the evidence of witnesses most likely to give full, reliable, and impartial information on the subject, to the conclusion that, for the purpose of taxation, Ireland was entitled to be treated as a separate entity; that the Act of Union had imposed upon her a burden which, as events turned out, she was unable to bear; and that during the forty years from 1853 to 1893 she had been compelled to contribute much more than her fair proportion to the Imperial revenues.

* The university question was one of the most sensitive and intractable problems of post-Famine Ireland. The core of the problem was that the Roman Catholic hierarchy, following papal guidelines, insisted that nothing less than a fully-Catholic, state-financed university was adequate to meet the spiritual and intellectual needs of the country. The (Protestant-backed) British government were reluctant to endorse that. Caught in between were the rising Catholic middle class, wanting their sons to receive third-level education, and yet anxious to respond to their bishops' views. Complicating the issue was the fact that since the 1850s the Catholic hierarchy had forbidden their flock to attend Trinity without specific permission from the bishop—which, at least until John Charles McQuaid's time, was normally granted.

ALEX. FINDLATER & CO., LIMITED.

FINDLATER'S SPECIALITY IN FINE DUBLIN WHISKEY.

JOHN JAMESON & SON'S

EIGHT-YEARS-OLD WHISKEY.

Matured in Findlater's Bondings, under the supervision of HIS MAJESTY'S EXCISE OFFICIALS.

One of the many Chambers in Findlater's Bonded Stores, showing the Bottling of John Jameson & Son's Fine Old Dublin Whiskey after it has been Mellowed and Matured in the Original Casks.

A Connoisseur's Whiskey at a Popular Price.

This, the Finest Old Dublin Whiskey of

John Jameson & Son's Own Make,

specially filled at Bow Street Distillery, Dublin, into our High-Class Sherry Casks in the year of Distillation, 1894, and thereafter Mellowed and Matured by Age Only in Findlater's Bonded Warehouses, Findlater Place, Dublin, is now submitted to the Public at a Popular Price, viz.: **3/9 per Bottle** (Six Bottles to the Gallon. This Fine Old Dublin Whiskey is **Certified Eight Years Old**, and is the Finest Dublin Whiskey procurable.

Being the Largest Importers of really Fine Sherries into Ireland, we have had available a constant succession of High-Class Sherry Casks in which the finest wine has been imported.

These were the casks used for maturing this EIGHT-YEARS-OLD WHISKEY, to which they have imparted colour, character, bouquet, and vinosity, rendering this Grand Whiskey the

Choicest Bottling of John Jameson & Son's Own Make now before the Public.

BOTTLED ONLY AND GUARANTEED BY

Alex Findlater & Co Ltd

TO BE HAD ONLY FROM **ALEX. FINDLATER & CO., LTD.**

The Bottle must bear our Signature, Guarantee, and Special Capsule, otherwise it is Not Genuine.

31

1902—Whiskey bottling in our Sackville Street cellars

Adam referred to the Act of Union as 'a system of taxation under which the poorer country is unfairly treated and further impoverished.' Indeed, he stated that 'The members of the present government have, however, refused to hold out any hope of redress. Nay, we know, and, what is worse, we feel, that under the provisions of the Finance Acts passed since 1894 the injustice to Ireland has been immensely aggravated.' He put his finger on the major defect of the Commission's report—it had pointed out a grievance, but had suggested no remedy. It did not take much imagination for home rulers, and others, to think their way through that problem.

The issue was also confused with the great debate on free trade going on in Britain, in which Joseph Chamberlain was one of the most public protagonists.* Adam was very much in favour of the use of fiscal means to protect Irish industries. On 20 November 1903 he took the chair at the inaugural meeting of the Irish Tariff Reform (Central) Association in the Gresham Hotel. Adam explained to those present that the meeting was in the nature of an informal conference and that they came there to put their heads together, to think out the question of whether they should not take advantage of the present movement in England to promote the interests of Ireland. He pointed out that this was one of the questions upon which Irishmen of all classes and creeds were agreed and that the purpose of the meeting was to consider what was the best for Ireland and Irishmen. He was also keen to clarify that this association would be an Irish association, independent of any English organisation.

During the meeting the members passed the following resolution: 'That the object of this association shall be to support the reform and modification of the present Fiscal system by the imposition of tariffs directed to the assistance of agriculture, the development of existing industries, and the creation of others, for which this country is suited, and thus, by enabling our population to live and thrive at home, to turn backwards the flow of emigration that menaces every material interest of Ireland.'

Adam followed up this meeting with a letter to *The Irish Times* published on 28 November 1903:

> Sir, . . . I, for one, believe that Protection would help what industries we have, would enable others to be started, and thus by opening up sources of employment check the dreadful flow of emigration. With the tariff utilised only as a bond between the Colonies and Great Britain, Irishmen cannot grow enthusiastic, but on the question of protective tariffs as beneficially affecting Ireland, as well as the Colonies, we can all consider the economic question from an Irish standpoint. If we cannot agree as to the respective merits of Protection and Free Trade, we can discuss it in an atmosphere free from disturbing elements.
>
> That in certain circumstances Protection as a national policy is not an economic heresy, but an economic truth, is admitted by all thoughtful men, who have studied

* Chamberlain, who had been a Liberal under Gladstone and was now a Conservative, was an early advocate of a partial return to policies of protection.

the science of political economy . . .

Yours etc. A. S. Findlater.

On the same day the *Pall Mall Gazette* carried an interview with Adam, as President of the Irish Tariff Reform Association:

> The first thing that he told me was that the association will work entirely on Irish lines. It has nothing to do with Mr Chamberlain's association, and will be run exclusively from Dublin, and exclusively in the interests of Ireland and of Irishmen. It was a mistake, he said, to think as some people thought that the cases of Ireland and of Great Britain were the same.
>
> He pointed out that Ireland is a separate entity, not merely from the point of view of administration and legislation, but also from that of taxation.

In fact Chamberlain specifically declined to become involved in the Irish situation. He wrote to Adam on 11 December 1903: 'I have said all along that my own personal feeling was in favour of an entirely independent and National committee in Ireland on the fiscal question . . . there are so many complications in the politics of Ireland that I do not feel justified in offering advice or suggestions.'[8]

In the same year, 1903, in the mood of the time, the first Industrial Development Association was established in Cork, followed immediately after by similar bodies in Limerick, Dublin, Belfast, Galway and Londonderry. Its aim was the advancement of Irish industries and in particular the defence of the Irish market from increasingly predatory British manufacturers. Between 1841 and 1901, while the population declined by 46 per cent the number employed in manufacturing industry fell by 60 per cent. The new association set about organising direct shipping facilities between Ireland and the countries abroad as well as assisting in finding foreign markets for Irish goods. It also devised an Irish national trade mark, the first instituted by any country in the world, to help identify for the consumer goods of Irish manufacture. To be licensed to display the symbol the cost of labour had to represent more than 50 per cent of the total production cost of the article.

The association was fortunate to have as its chairman for its first fifteen years George Crosbie of the *Cork Examiner* family. It was due to his interest and assistance that the movement progressed so rapidly in its early days. He exerted his influence with the owners and editors of the other leading newspapers.*

Adam clearly identified Findlaters with the movement and at the staff meeting of 1903 said: 'We are only too anxious to encourage Irish manufacture as much as possible, and give it our preference, as we feel that living in Ireland and making our living here, we are bound to do what we can in this direction'. He

* E. J. O'Riordan (first Secretary of the Irish Development Association) *Modern Irish Trade and Industry*, with an introduction by George O'Brien Litt.D. MRIA London: Methuen 1920 pp 265-279. It is interesting to see how the theme of Free Trade crops up again and again: John wrote his paper discussing it, Adam chaired meetings about it, Willie took it up at the time of the Treaty, and Dermot expressed different views, during the Economic War and then in the post-Emergency period.

ALEX. FINDLATER & CO., LIMITED.

Findlater's Speciality in Fine Dublin Whiskey.

John Jameson & Son's

EIGHT-YEARS-OLD WHISKEY.

Matured in Findlater's Bondings, under the supervision of HIS MAJESTY'S EXCISE OFFICIALS.

A Connoisseur's Whiskey at a Popular Price.

This, the Finest Old Dublin Whiskey of

JOHN JAMESON & SON'S OWN MAKE,

specially filled at Bow Street Distillery, Dublin, into our High-Class Sherry Casks in the year of Distillation, 1894, and thereafter Mellowed and Matured by Age Only in Findlater's Bonded Warehouses, Findlater Place, Dublin, is now submitted to the Public at a Popular Price, viz.:

3/9 per Bottle

(22/6 per Gallon, Six Bottles).

This Fine Old Dublin Whiskey is

CERTIFIED EIGHT YEARS OLD,

and is the Finest Dublin Whiskey procurable.

Being the Largest Importers of really Fine Sherries into Ireland, we have had available a constant succession of High-Class Sherry Casks in which the Finest Wine has been imported. These were the casks used for maturing this EIGHT-YEARS-OLD WHISKEY, to which they have imparted colour, character, bouquet, and vinosity, rendering this Grand Whiskey the

Choicest Bottling of John Jameson & Son's Own Make now before the Public.

BOTTLED ONLY AND GUARANTEED BY

Alex Findlater & Co Ltd

TO BE HAD ONLY FROM

ALEX. FINDLATER & CO., LTD.

The Bottle must bear our Signature, Guarantee, Special Capsule, and Branded Cork, otherwise it is Not Genuine.

32

1902—Note the 'season' at the bottom of the bottle. 3s 9d is the equivalent of £14.25 in 2000 money, not so very different from today's price. The content however was 75cl at 25° under proof compared with 70cl at 30° under-proof today. Eight-year-old was a Findlater speciality; most other bonders sold Jameson at seven or ten years of age.

Labels in use in 19th and early 20th centuries

did, nevertheless, caution that quality and value had to be the equal of the alternative product. We shall see Willie and Dermot identifying with the Association in subsequent chapters.

Findlater's Act

The fifth item on the Kingstown Programme called for 'an Act to facilitate Private Bill legislation, so as to obviate the necessity for the excessive expenditure which under existing circumstances, must be incurred in inquiries on the other side of the Channel before any useful improvement requiring the sanction of Parliament can be effected.' Adam explained that

> the procedure with respect to Irish Private Bill Legislation is most fitly described by the word 'disgraceful': The house fees alone are prohibitive; but when to these are added enormous fees to English counsel, or, worse, the cost of bringing over to Westminster Irish counsel, fees to English experts, fees to Parliamentary agents, fees to solicitors, and expenses of witnesses, one cannot wonder at the excessive cost furnished for the promotion of even unopposed and unimportant Bills. Then, after all these have been incurred, the Bill is often brought before a committee not a single member of which has any knowledge of the locality or the interests affected by it, has ever been in Ireland, or even learned to pronounce the names of the places or the persons that will be mentioned in the course of the evidence.

On top of this, English parliamentarians were complaining 'of the unreasonable extent to which the attention of that Parliament is monopolised by the inevitable Irish problem.' Adam refutes this by pointing out the small amount of Irish legislation passed into law. However, I presume the campaign was successful as we find Adam promoting a Bill in 1903.

In 1903 Adam took the initiative to draft and promote the General Dealers' (Ireland) Act—usually referred to in the law courts as Findlater's Act—by which an effectual check was put on the operations of receivers of stolen goods, especially second-hand metal goods and 'bottles, syphons, tools, bags, packing cases, boxes, articles of pottery or glass'. (These were also known as 'Marine Stores'.) Among the provisions was one prohibiting such a 'general dealer' from buying from or selling to 'any person apparently under the age of fourteen years'. Findlaters may have had a problem with returnable cases, bottles and syphons finding their way into unauthorised hands, but the problem was deeper than that and required legislation.

On Wednesday 3 June 1903 Adam presided over a meeting of the Dublin Merchants' Committee held at the Gresham Hotel to consider the Bill. Four months later, *The Irish Times* reported on the importance of this act:

> At the recent Criminal Sessions a case was heard which brought out very conspicuously some of the good points of the Marine Store Dealers Act, which will come into operation on the first day of next year. The Act, which in the language of the official draughtsman is entitled 'An Act for regulating the business of Marine Stores Dealers and Dealers in Second-hand Goods in Ireland,' was rechristened by Sir Frederick

Interesting Facts about Light Summer Beverages.

ALEX. FINDLATER & CO., LTD.,

DUBLIN, RATHMINES, SANDYMOUNT, BLACKROCK, KINGSTOWN, DALKEY, BRAY, & HOWTH.

The Relief of Thirst in Summer Weather.

LIGHT SUMMER WINES.

THE HOCK AND MOSELLE DISTRICTS.
THE GERMAN NATIONAL MONUMENT AT RUDESHEIM.

HOCKS AND MOSELLES

FOR WARM WEATHER.

"Of light alcoholic strength, and yet almost imperishable through their purity, and with marked fragrance of the true vinous character, the Rhenish Wines are the Wines for intellectual gaiety They increase appetite, they exhilarate without producing heaviness and langour afterwards, and they purify the blood." . . .
"The higher class of Rhenish (all of which are called 'Oc' by our men servants) differ remarkably in their flavours, but, as a rule, are all very useful in cases in which we want to support the nervous system, clean the tongue, quench thirst, and oxidate the blood."— Dr. Druitt.

Hocks.

The demand for "White Wines" has been steadily increasing for some years both in England and this country, and as far as can be judged from actual statistics, the consumption of this class of wines has grown considerably. In that direction no more suitable wines could be recommended than Hocks and Moselles—their delicacy, freshness, and low alcoholic strength seem to make them particularly suitable for present requirements. Although these wines of course have been known in this country for many years, they have come to the front more particularly within the last few years, and their merits seem now to be generally acknowledged.

ALEX. FINDLATER & CO., LTD.

1902—German wine: 'For intellectual gaiety'!

Falkiner [the Recorder of Dublin] 'Findlater's Act,' which is at once handy as a title and a very excellent recognition of the part which was taken by Mr Adam Findlater in carrying it through Parliament. He initiated the movement which gave birth to the measure, and in the most indefatigable manner forced members and Ministers to legislate in the direction which he advocated.

The case which inspired the Recorder to supply the 'short title' was typical of the class of cases which the measure is designed to meet. An unoccupied house was raided by a number of youths. They pulled down iron fittings, lead piping, a kitchen range, and other fixtures, and sold some of them to a marine store dealer. The price paid by the latter was altogether out of proportion to the value of the goods, and was of itself sufficient to indicate that he, at all events, strongly suspected that the articles had not been come by honestly. He asked one of the boys who brought him the goods where they had been got, and was content with the reply that they had been found in a field at Ringsend. Of course the transaction was, on the part of the buyer, dishonest from the beginning. He must have known that such goods are not picked up by boys in fields on the outskirts of the city, and that he was certain that they were the outcome of a fraudulent enterprise was quite apparent from the fact that he acquired them immediately for fourpence.

The police inspector in charge of the case mentioned that there was no record of the transaction in the books of the dealer, and it is in that connection that the Recorder referred to the Act which he will have to administer after the first of next January. The Act makes it an offence for marine store dealers not to register such transactions in books kept for the purpose. The section is very precise—'Every general dealer shall enter in a book, to be kept by him on his premises, the particulars of each transaction in his business, including (a) a proper and distinctive description of each article purchased or received by him; (b) the name and place of abode of the person from whom he purchased or received the article; (c) the date and hour of the day of each transaction; and (d) the price paid, or agreed to be paid, for the article.' Nothing could be more complete in the way of drastic legislation; but when the ever-recurring frauds of the class which the Recorder had to investigate last Monday are taken into account it cannot be considered by any means too severe.

The section will not press hardly upon honest traders, and it will facilitate the police and the Courts in dealing with those dishonestly inclined. The Act, however, contains other provisions which are eminently calculated to reduce the possibility of the disposal of stolen goods, and for that purpose the licensing provisions will probably be found most effective. Some of the sections are exceedingly strong; for instance, those limiting the hours of business and prescribing the age of customers; but it can scarcely be denied that a vast deal of the minor crime of Dublin has resulted owing to the non-existence of some such safeguards.[9]

The Irish *Figaro* commented:

The Marine Store Dealers' Act will come into force in a little while, and the 'rag and bones man' will be pulled up on a short halter. Mr Adam Findlater has rendered the public many big services; but I question if he ever did a better stroke than when he

ALEX. FINDLATER & CO., LIMITED.

FINDLATER'S BOTTLINGS

PRESENT

Bass's Pale Ale and

Guinness's Extra Stout

In the Most Perfect Condition.

EXTRA STOUT.

Per Dozen Reputed Pints.

GUINNESS'S XX

Buff Label - - 1s. 10d.

Guaranteed by Alex. Findlater & Co., Ltd.

ALE.

BASS & CO.'S

Pale Ale - - 2s. 4d.

Guaranteed by Alex. Findlater & Co., Ltd.

Important Notice!

ALEX. FINDLATER & CO., LTD., give their personal guarantee that the above EXTRA STOUT and PALE ALE are supplied pure as received from the Breweries, and bottled in perfect condition.

34

1902—Note the emphasis on Findlater's bottling

started the subject and conceived and drafted that Act. Meanwhile, let us feel thankful that the Recorder has determined to make the punishment fit the crime at last.[10]

Of course, Adam did not claim to have done this by himself. In a letter to *The Irish Times* (16 December 1903), complaining that he, a private citizen, had to get this Act to check the receiving and disposal of stolen goods, not to mention 'the infinitely worse trade of the Fagin-like training of young thieves', he freely acknowledges the help given by friends such as J. P. Nannetti, MP for College Green and John Atkinson KC, the Attorney General for Ireland, in formulating the Act.

Adam *v.* Dublin Corporation

The Kingstown Programme had sought redress for the position of the urban tenants, a matter in which, as a large property holder throughout the town, Adam had a close interest. In 1899 he came into direct conflict with the Corporation in respect of the rent of the shop in South Great George's Street. The kernel of the problem was that the lease had fallen in, and the Corporation proposed to charge eight times what the previous rent had been. In an aggressive pamphlet called *A Tale of Municipal Landlordism*,[11] Adam described this as 'rackrenting a tenant on his own improvements', and a 'monstrous extraction'. After vigorous representation by the firm, the Corporation's finance committee eventually reduced the proposed rent to £7.80 per foot lineal frontage. Not appeased, Adam pointed out that the large department store Pim's, next door, had just been granted a similar lease for £4 per foot. Failing acceptance of this final rent, the company had to face eviction.

Adam complained bitterly about this conduct, which he described (rather melodramatically) as 'a deliberate policy of rackrenting and eviction which could not be paralleled in the woeful history of the relations between landlord and tenant in Ireland'. It was 'an exemplification of the truth of the proverb that a Corporation had neither a body to be kicked, nor a soul to be damned'. He alluded to the fact that the family had owned the house for over fifty years. 'In that house, 67 South Great George's Street, my father, now a man of seventy-two years of age, played as a child; and there in my turn, I learned as an apprentice, working behind the counter, what knowledge I possess of my business.' Adam declared (in print) his determination 'to permit the severance of cherished ties, and to allow the evicting corporation to do its work rather than endure to the end of my days the humiliating consciousness of having weakly yielded to the extravagant extortion—not to call it blackmail—which the Corporation of the City of Dublin would levy upon me as the price of peaceful enjoyment'. As the firm remained in South Great George's Street for another seventy years, it is likely that the finance committee made some concession.

The valuation of licensed premises

We have seen that the Local Government Act of 1898 gave new powers to the Irish boroughs; among these was the right to demand a revaluation of their districts. Both the Belfast and the Dublin Corporations applied for revaluation, but as Belfast had applied first the commissioner for revaluation, Sir John Barton, began work on that city. At the same time, Barton introduced for the first time into Ireland the English principle of valuing the licenses attached to public houses as well as the properties themselves. Previously, the sale of a public house would fetch much more than a non-licensed house and Barton did not see why both should be valued at the same amount.

When Adam heard of this move, he was alarmed because it was obvious that the same principle would be applied in Dublin. Taxation and licensed duties would be increased by a large amount.

His first step was to organise a meeting in February in the Mansion House with the Lord Mayor in the chair. *The Evening Telegraph* stated that 'Mr Adam Findlater opened with a stirring speech, and gave his views in lucid fashion'. The speech of Mr A. S. Findlater JP, it stated, 'is well worthy of careful perusal. It does not profess to give an exhaustive explanation of the economic problems involved in the revaluation of Ireland, but it is pregnant with suggestions and facts, and is calculated to enlighten the public regarding the dangers of revaluation and the effects that would follow if the principles enunciated by Sir John Barton before the Select Committee of the House of Commons were adopted'.[12] The meeting was very representative, the largest ratepayers in the city being present. However, not everyone was on Adam's side. The aggressively nationalist political weekly *The Leader* attacked Adam and the other 'Mr Bungs' in this entertaining article.*

> Mr Bung, of course, was indignant, for his taxation and licence duties were very largely increased under the new principle. Of course, too, when Mr Bung in Dublin saw what had happened to Mr Bung in Belfast he began to grow mightily alarmed, knowing that in the revaluation of Dublin, for which the Corporation had applied, the same principle would be introduced. All unconscious of the fate in store for him, he had allowed the Corporation to take this fatal step, but, at all cost, he made up his mind to try and avert from himself the disaster that had befallen his brother Bung up in the Black North.
>
> So he cast about him for a means. He rushed across to London and bitterly complained to the Parliamentary Committee that was enquiring into this subject of valuation. He roundly abused Sir John Barton. He sought to raise a great outcry about increased Imperial Taxation. Then a brilliant idea occurred to him. He would get the

* *The Leader*, edited by D. P. Moran (1871-1936) had a great influence in drawing people into the national movement in the first decade of the 20th century. It deployed an aggressive, name-calling rhetoric to great effect—Plunkett was called Sir Horace Shallow, and Protestant unionists were called Sourfaces. 'Mr Bung' was the favourite expression the teetotal Moran used to express his contempt for the powerful liquor trade. In this article the author (Richard Hazleton, also a total abstainer) comes perilously close to identifying Adam as *the* Mr Bung.

FINDLATER'S BOTTLINGS.

FINDLATER'S BOTTLINGS

Are carried on in hygienic stores under the best conditions. The beverages are untouched by hand, the entire process of bottling being carried out by costly machinery and appliances.

ALES.

	Per Doz. Reputed Pints. s. d.	Per Doz. Snipes. s. d.
Bass & Co.'s Pale Ale (Findlater's Bottling) ...	2 4	
Allsopp's Pale Ale	2 4	
A. F. & Co.'s Pale Dinner Ale	1 6	
Bass & Co.'s No. 1 Ale	2 9	1 10
Lager Beer, Tuborg	2 4	
Pilsner Beer, Tuborg	2 4	
Munich Beer, Tuborg	2 7	
Allsopp's Lager Beer	2 6	
,, ,, per doz. ½ pints ...	2 0	

CIDER.

Finest Devonshire or Hereford	2 4	
Finest Irish Cider (Blackwater)	2 4	

PORTERS.

Guinness's Export Stout, blue label (Findlater's Bottling)	2 0	1 4
Guinness's XX Stout, salmon label (Findlater's Bottling)	1 10	1 3
Mountjoy "Nourishing"	2 0	1 4
Mountjoy Medium	1 6	
Watkin's Crown Stout		1 4

NOTE.—We give our *personal* guarantee that the above Ales and Stouts are supplied without admixture, and labelled identically as received from their respective breweries.

Egan's Irish Hop Bitters ...	per doz. bottles	1 2
Wheatley's Hop Bitters	per doz. bottles	1 2
Wheatley's Ginger Stout	per doz. bottles	1 2
Extract of Malt—Hoff's ...	per doz. bottles	18 0
Johnston & Co.'s	per doz. bottles	3 6

This latter has been recommended by the most eminent medical men for its strengthening and nutritive properties, and is therefore specially adapted for invalids.

IN WOOD.		Half Brl. s. d.		Qr. Brl s. d
Guinness's XX Stout	(16 gals.)	22 6	(8 gals.)	11 6
Guinness's X Stout ...		15 6		8 6
Mountjoy "Nourishing" Stout		24 6		13 6
Mountjoy Extra Double Stout		21 6		11 0
Mountjoy Medium Stout		18 6		10 0
Bass & Co.'s Pale Ale ...	(18 gals.)	30 0	(9 gals.)	15 0
S. Allsopp & Son's Pale Ale	(18 gals.)	30 0		15 0
S. Allsopp & Son's Pale Dinner Ale	(18 gals.)	21 0		10 6
R. Perry & Son's Light Bitter Ale	(16 gals.)	16 0	(8 gals.)	8 0
R. Perry & Son's East India Ale	(16 gals.)	24 0	(8 gals.)	12 0

Ales and Porters, 1903

Lord Mayor to call a 'citizens' meeting of protest in the Mansion House, and, having packed this meeting, he would get it to appoint a 'citizens' committee to oppose Sir John's proposals before Parliament. And so a requisition was got up and presented to the Lord Mayor. Mr Bung kept himself in the background, and tried to hide the real meaning of this move, with the result that many unsuspecting citizens put their names to the requisition. However, out of over 300 names on this document nearly 150 were those of Bungs.

Things went merrily on. The meeting was boomed in the Press, and Mr Bung cocked himself up in the happy belief that everything was so cleverly managed that he was going to have a complete walk over. Indeed, so sure was he of this that he wrote up to Belfast, and imparted the good news to his brother Bungs of the Belfast and Ulster Vintners' Association, for in the report of the monthly meeting of that great body it was officially stated that 'it was learned from a letter from Dublin that steps were been taken to hold a great meeting of merchants in the Mansion House with the view to arousing the country to the danger which Sir John Barton's proposals threatened.'

But alas for poor Mr Bung's hopes! All the time there were those who were silently watching this secret intrigue to subvert the interests of the citizens to those of the licensed trade.

On Thursday last the 'great' meeting was held. The Lord Mayor presided, and from all sides of the city, and from outlying districts, such as Kingstown and Blackrock, Bungs of every description swarmed to the Mansion House. There were Bungs on the platform; Bungs to the right, Bungs to the left; Bungs in front, and Bungs behind. Never was seen such an array of Bungs. Aldermen, Councillors, P.L.G.'s–the Great Ones of Dublin were there. There, too, were the lesser Bungs, and Bungs in embryo, down even to the very pot-boys. And as Mr AI Findlater [AI was a much publicised Findlater whiskey brand] rose in his might and smote Sir John Barton, and drivelled on and on for more than one mortal hour, they rubbed their greedy hands together and thought what a fine meeting it was, to be sure. The resolution which Mr AI Findlater proposed was a clever one—exceedingly clever. In fact, it was too clever, for, as *The Irish Times* remarked next morning, it was too obviously framed in the interests of the licensed trade, winding up, as it did, by declaring that what Dublin wanted was readjustment 'without any introduction of any new principles of valuation hitherto unknown in Ireland.'

Then a thing happened that gave the Bungs their first fright. Mr T. W. Russell, MP, was seen to get up, take off his coat, and step on to the platform to address the meeting. Worse still, he got a good reception. Would he open out on them? Would he expose the intrigue? At first he agreed with some remarks of Mr AI Findlater; then he went on to differ from him, but he did not attack 'the Trade.' The Bungs heaved a sigh of relief as he sat down. The worst was over, thought they. But, horror of horrors, here was another Temperance crank getting up who dared to face them at their own meeting. It was Mr John Gore. In a speech of great force, clear, ringing, and eloquent, he put the case forward for the new system of valuing publicans' licenses, and declared, in concluding, that he would divide the meeting on the last part of Mr AI Findlater's res-

FINDLATER'S CLARETS

FOR SUMMER, 1902.

PETIT VILLAGE
1ER CRÛ POMEROL.

Splendid Wine, with very full body and colour, excellent bouquet and flavour.

Per Doz. Bots., **20/-**
Per Doz. Half-Bots. **10/6**

THE CLARET VINTAGE IN THE BORDEAUX DISTRICT.

GATHERING THE GRAPES.

GRAND VIN
CHÂTEAU LANGOA-BARTON.

A very stylish Wine, with great bouquet and flavour.

Per Doz. Bots., **24/-**
Per Doz. Half-Bots **12/6**

1902—Clarets for summer drinking

olution. His attack was as effective as it was utterly unexpected. Bung was aghast. The seriousness of the position was at once realised, for Mr Gore's speech had created a profound impression upon the disinterested section of the audience, which, however, was but too small. A hasty and anxious consultation was held near the door by the big Bungs, who, taken by surprise, were utterly unprepared for this opposition, and did not know how to meet it; but before they had time to decide upon any course of action an appalling catastrophe occurred on the platform. Mr T. W. Russell intervened, and Mr Al Findlater surrendered unconditionally! Absolutely and unreservedly he withdrew his carefully-prepared resolution—the resolution that the meeting was called together to pass; in its place he accepted a resolution drafted by Mr T. W. Russell approving of the introduction of the English system of valuation! This resolution was seconded by Mr Gore, put to the meeting, and carried unanimously! So 'flabbergasted' were the Bungs that they had not enough spirit left in them to say 'No.'

The citizens of Dublin have reason to congratulate themselves on this signal defeat of the publicans. It will probably mean a substantial reduction in their burden of local taxation, as they have all along been paying rates for 'the Trade.' The defeat, also, has its moral for the citizens, because it proves that the publicans have only to be faced boldly in order to be put in their proper place. With over thirty of their number members of the Corporation they think that they own the city of Dublin, and can use the citizens, the Council, and the Mansion House for any selfish purpose they like. But they may yet find that they have gone too far, and that a reaction may set in which will sweep them and their hangers-on from the position of power which they have abused and degraded.[13]

Despite this defeat, Adam pressed on and four months later, on 22 June 1903, gave evidence to a Select Committee of the House of Commons agreeing with a revival of the revaluation of Dublin, but calling for great care to be taken so as not to hamper enterprises or local improvements.

Robert Gardner, JP, of Craig Gardner and Co., accountants, Dublin, was asked about the question of valuing licensed premises.

From his experience he was able to state most positively that in Ireland there was nothing in the profits accruing from the carrying on of the licensed trade to justify exceptional treatment. On the contrary the profits in many other businesses were greater. For the information of the Committee he had carefully gone into the accounts of firms carrying on various businesses, and had found the following percentages of profit: drapers, 8¼; cabinetmakers, 9⅓; ironmongers, 9⅓; iron merchants, 7; carriage builders, 22½; manure merchants, 6⅞; seed merchants, 5; corn merchants 18; chemists 8⅔; maltsters, 13; bakers, 10; confectioners, 5¼; printers and paper merchants, 8; mineral water manufacturers, 10; bottle manufacturers, 14⅓.[14] [There is unfortunately no record of vintners' earnings.]

Adam continued to press the issue, as can be seen from a 1905 article in the *Irish People* entitled 'Plea for combined action: Views of a Prominent Unionist':

Mr Findlater strongly believes that the policy which has taken greatest hold of the Irish public at the present day is that of seeking points of agreement, and, while

> engaged on practical beneficial work, forgetting that differences exist on other matters. For instance, the re-valuation question, which is being investigated by a Committee at present, may, according to the evidence cited by Mr Findlater before the Committee, lead to an increase of £28,000 [£2.6m] of Imperial taxation on the City of Dublin alone. That is a matter which affects all classes alike, and in order to resist successfully the imposition of a fresh burden of this kind, there should be hearty co-operation among all Irishmen.[15]

Although Adam's efforts were successful in this case, there was a sting in the tail when an extra licence duty was imposed not long after.

Temperance magistrates, May 1903

In 1903 Findlaters came into conflict with various magistrates, claiming that they had been refused a licence as a result of the judges being members of the temperance association. Findlaters appealed, as the *Grocer and Vintner* reported on 29 June: 'Seldom has there been such an array of eminent counsel engaged in connection with the one case as was seen in the King's Bench No. 2 of the Four Courts'.

Temperance societies and organisations in Ireland had struggled since the 1820s to reduce the consumption of whiskey, particularly illicit whiskey and poteen. The sterner type of nationalist promoted temperance with the slogan 'Ireland sober is Ireland free'. For others the temperance movement was part of a wider attempt to discipline and control the working class; one of its early triumphs had been the abolition of Donnybrook Fair in the 1850s. In 1898 the Pioneer Total Abstinence Association of the Sacred Heart was established by Father James Cullen.[16] Initially the association was an elitist devotional organisation, not a populist crusade. It did not aspire to a mass following nor did it aim to reclaim drunkards. The Pioneers were to be small bands of devoted

PUBLISHING OFFICES, 69, LOWER GARDINER STREET, DUBLIN. ALL REMITTANCES TO BE MADE PAYABLE TO H. E. HUDSON, MANAGER.

Illustrograph

A MONTHLY ILLUSTRATED PAPER.

No. 6.—Vol. 1.] DUBLIN, JUNE, 1894.

FINDLATER'S A1 WHISKEY

ONLY GOLD MEDAL FOR DUBLIN WHISKEY,

DISTILLERS & BREWERS' EXHIBITION, AUGUST, 1892.

ALEX. FINDLATER & CO., SACKVILLE STREET, DUBLIN.

CONYNGHAM'S

T. R. SCOTT & Co.,

The Grosvenor Furnishing House,

Medals from trade fairs were an important marketing tool then as now.

Findlaters' Kingstown shop, pre–1900

Catholics, setting an example of piety and asceticism for others. However, it was the right instrument for an increasingly puritanical and Roman Catholic society. Its success exceeded all expectations. By the 1920s it had some 300,000 members and in 1999 celebrated its centenary with a gathering of some 40,000 in Croke Park.

The group that confronted Adam in 1903 was the Irish Association for the Prevention of Intemperance, established in 1878, and dominated by Quakers, Presbyterians and members of the Church of Ireland. One prominent member, Charles Eason, chairman of Eason's booksellers, insisted that the Association had no axe to grind, and stated, conforming to traditional Protestant thinking, that they merely wanted to see the country 'sober, industrious and happy'. Their membership was not large, but it was influential.

In 1903, a gentleman named Moynihan purchased a public house next door to the Roman Catholic church at Kingstown for a sum of £1,900 [£177,000]. However, this public house was considered an eyesore in Kingstown, so much so that the community jointly subscribed a sum of £900 [£84,000] to extinguish it. Findlaters agreed to contribute a sum of £500 [£47,000], making £1,400 [£131,000], and Mr Moynihan was public-spirited enough to agree to sacrifice the balance in the general interest of the people of Kingstown, he himself being a county councillor.

Findlaters had agreed to give the sum of £500 on condition they were allowed to extend the existing licence they had in Lower George's Street, Kingstown, a few doors round the corner, a house, which was really a grocery, but which had a licence attached to it. It was not used at all on Sundays, and on ordinary days the house closed at six o'clock. Findlaters wanted to add the house next door to their existing premises, and, therefore, there was an application by them for a new licence. The licence was refused, and Adam, believing that members of the temperance association had affected the result, appealed.

The Legal Terms

The various parties were represented by the following: Messrs Ignatius O'Brien KC, A. F. Blood KC and J. M. McAuley (instructed by Mr Gerald Byrne) appeared for Findlaters. Mr O'Shaughnessy KC, and Mr A. M. Sullivan (instructed by Mr H. J. McCormick) appeared for Mr Henry J. Allen JP. Mr D. S. Henry KC and Mr Michael J. Dunn (instructed by Mr H. J. McCormick) appeared for the Rev. C. S. Laird and Rev. T. Guy Rogers, objectors in the lower court. Mr J. O. Wylie KC, and Mr James Henry (instructed by Messrs D. and T. Fitzgerald) appeared for Messrs Eason, Booth, Jacob and Wallace, Justices of the Peace. Serjeant Dodd and Mr W. A. Fitzhenry (instructed by Mr W. Geoghegan) appeared for Professor Barrett JP. Messrs. John Wakely KC and Cecil Atkinson (instructed by Sir Patrick Coll, CB, Chief Crown Solicitor) appeared for the Crown.*

The Irish Times outlined the court case, in which so many big legal guns were involved on both sides:

* Ignatius O'Brien was subsequently Solicitor General 1911, Attorney General 1912-13, Privy Councillor Ireland 1912, Lord Chancellor of Ireland from 1913 to 1918, when he retired and was created Lord Shandon. O'Shaughnessy KC subsequently became Recorder of Dublin and was sworn a Privy Councillor in 1912. In 1924 he was appointed a judge of the High Court of the Free State and was knighted following his retirement in 1926. A. M. Sullivan subsequently became a Serjeant at Law. He defended Roger Casement and later practised in England. He was the last of the Irish Serjeants, the order being abolished on independence. He was the author of two books, *Old Ireland* and *The Last Serjeant.* Henry KC was elected MP for South Londonderry in 1916 in the Unionist interest, although a Catholic; he became Attorney General in 1918 before being appointed upon partition, under the Government of Ireland Act, as the first Lord Chief Justice of Northern Ireland. James Owens Wylie was the uncle of Judge William Evelyn Wylie (Chairman RDS etc). J. O. W. was a liberal and became Land Judge, a position which he held from 1906, being succeeded by his nephew in 1920. Sergeant Dodd was also a liberal who failed to win Londonderry South in 1895 but was subsequently elected for North Tyrone in 1906. He never served as Attorney General but was appointed to the Bench in 1907. He was created a Privy Councillor in 1913 and served on the Bench until 1924 when, being eighty, he was not reappointed on the establishment of the Free State Courts. John Wakely became a County Court Judge and was re-appointed in 1924 to the Circuit Court. Cecil Atkinson was the second son of Lord Atkinson who had served the Tory administration of 1892 and 1895 to 1905 as Attorney General in Ireland. He was appointed as Lord of Appeal in ordinary in 1905, shortly before the fall of the Tory government. The Chief Crown Solicitor instructed the Attorney General's son as junior counsel to represent the Crown. Cecil Atkinson died in 1919.

HIBERNIA

A Monthly Popular Review.

ol. I.—No. 2. WEDNESDAY, FEBRUARY 1, 1882. [Price Sixper [All Rights Reser

There have been four *Hibernia's* from the first which started in 1764 to the most recent which closed in 1980. This version began in 1882 and was edited by Count Plunkett whose son Joseph was one of the leaders of the 1916 Rising. Findlater's vigorous support of the early edition must have been most welcome.

Yesterday, June 17th 1903, in the King's Bench Division No. 2, before the Lord Chief Baron (Christopher Palles), Mr Justice Johnson, Mr Justice Barton and Mr Justice Wright, the case of the King (Findlater) *v.* the Recorder of Dublin came on for hearing.

Mr Ignatius O'Brien said this was a very important case. The affidavit of Mr Gerald Byrne, solicitor for Mr Findlater, stated that when it was announced by the Clerk of the Crown that the licensing application list was about to be called on behalf of his client, Mr Findlater, he (Mr Byrne) called the attention of the Recorder, who was chairman on the Bench, to the fact that several of the magistrates were subscribers to the Irish Association for the Prevention of Intemperance, which had for its object the diminution in the number of licensed houses, and that this association paid out of its funds and instructed their solicitor, Mr McCormick, to appear at the licensing sessions to oppose all applications for new licences, and he objected to these magistrates taking any part in adjudicating upon the several licensing cases about to be called; and he produced a copy of the annual report of the society with the names of the magistrates then present as subscribers, and some of them members of the Executive Committee.

Professor Barrett took a very active part in the proceedings on the bench in opposition to the applications, and so did Messrs. Eason, JP; Allen, JP; Booth, JP; Jacob, JP and Wallace JP.* He was informed that the secretary of the association sent circulars to the magistrates who subscribed to the association informing them of the applications for hearing and requesting their attendance on the bench. Notwithstanding his objection that those magistrates were disqualified to act they did act, and the applications were refused. He charged that the bench of magistrates was biased, and that their decision should not be upheld.

Mr Wallace, JP, made an affidavit stating that he was not a subscriber to the association, but that he had this year learned that his firm subscribed 10s. to it. He was not aware that the firm had so subscribed until his attention was drawn to the fact at the licensing sessions. There were no grounds on which he could be charged with bias.

Mr Moriarty, secretary of the association, made an affidavit, in which he stated that meetings of the executive council took place before each licensing sessions with a view to making suggestions as to licensing business. They did not oppose all licences. It was the Rev. Caleb Laird and Rev. T. Guy Rogers that communicated with him to oppose the licences. The magistrates impugned also made affidavits stating that they were in no way biased, and only acted according to their judgement.

Mr O'Shaughnessy said he proposed to argue that it would be necessary to prove real bias, not the mere suspicion of bias regarding the decision given under these conditions.[17]

A few months later Findlaters were back in the licensing court. *The Evening Telegraph* reported on 29 September:

Messrs. Findlater applied for a new six-day licence for No. 84 Lower George's Street, Kingstown, being premises attached to the present licensed premises, 85 Lower

* These were all prominent businessmen in the city and members of the Chamber of Commerce, as was Adam.

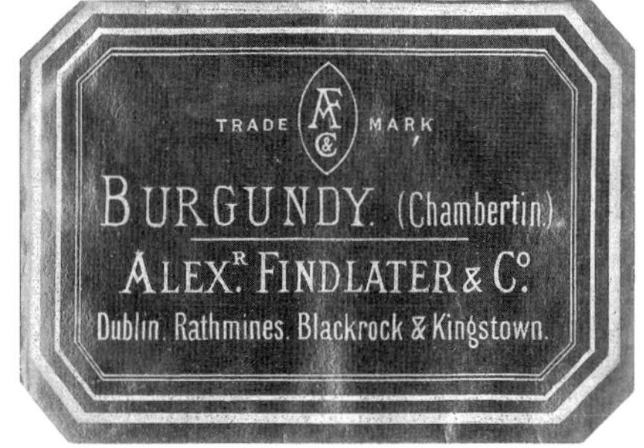

⅛OHN 1870s

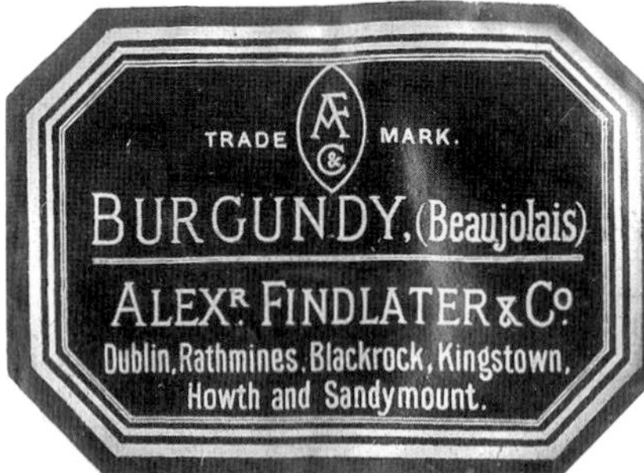

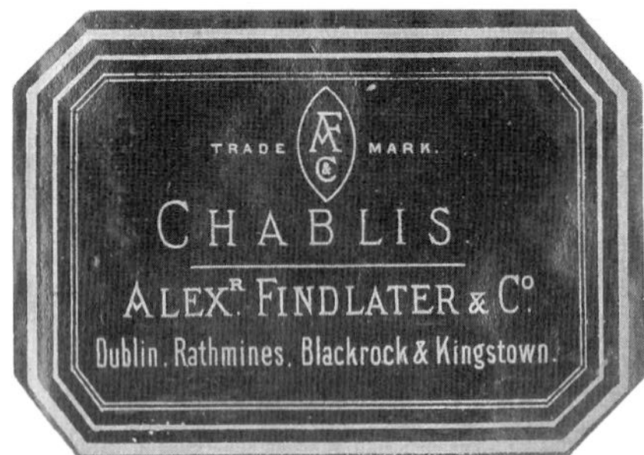

19th century wine labels—the branches named enable us to date the labels to within a year or two.

George's street, in order to render the licence more suitable for the business.

Mr T. W. Russell, MP, one of the magistrates, said it was an extraordinary thing to ask for at a time when a great reduction in the number of public houses was recommended. Were the premises to be used as a public house?

Mr Healy–No; Lord De Vesci and Lord Longford had refused to renew the leases if the premises were to be used for the purpose.

Mr O'Shaughnessy said his client owned a large public house in Kingstown, and had paid a large fine; but he was not anxious to continue his opposition to the present application, the object of which was to turn the whole place into one shop. But his client desired that an undertaking should be embodied in the lease.

The case was eventually resolved. After argument Mr Adam Findlater gave an undertaking to surrender the seven-day licence of No. 85, and to apply for a six-day licence for it and the adjoining premises. Both premises to be used as one shop, with one licence for the business of a family grocery heretofore carried on at No. 85, the business of an ordinary public house not to be carried on therein. Only on these terms was the licence granted.

The importance of the first case can be seen from the line-up of lawyers: interestingly, save for Crown Counsel they are all Liberals. For some reason the unionists kept their heads down, with the exceptions of Cecil Atkinson and D. S. Henry KC, who appeared for the Rev. Laird. The Licensing Act, 1902, which still stands as a key piece of the licensing law of Ireland, became law shortly before the case. The policy of the Act was to reduce the number of licenses, which were then more prolific than today. Obviously, given the interest of the Findlaters, they were anxious to establish the parameters of the new legislation and not to find the off-licence trade restricted in the same way as public houses.

The Irish temperance associations did not propose Prohibition, but there was a precedent in the State of Maine which had been 'dry' since the 1850s, and the trade kept a wary eye on such movements. Years later, Findlater Mackie Todd put stickers on their correspondence warning that 'the indifference of the public resulted in America going dry; use your vote and influence against "local option" which is the thin end of the wedge of Prohibition'.

After all this trouble, Findlaters eventually managed to expand their Kingstown branch, one of the oldest in the chain. The press celebrated the new premises:

The Kingstown house, which has been under the management of Mr Edward Snow, a gentleman of great experience, for the past 27 years, is situated in Lower George's Street. New premises have just been built beside the old establishment so as to enable the management to cope with the large and growing business with which they are favoured. The old establishment has been in the hands of the Findlaters since 1839, and was formerly known as the 'Irish and Scotch Whiskey Stores', there being a large bar attached.

During the last 25 years the business has increased considerably under the managing directorship of Mr Adam S. Findlater. The firm has got no less than twelve establishments in the city and surrounding towns, and of these that at Kingstown may be said to be the most important of all the branches, as it is favoured with the patronage of a big percentage of the leading residents of South Dublin. Needless to state that everything in the way of high-class groceries can be supplied at Findlater's without delay, and all orders received by post have the immediate attention of the management.

Mr Findlater pays particular care to the selection of the goods he supplies, believing as he does that the genuine article is the best at any cost.

In connection with the opening of the new premises it is the intention of the firm to have the confectionery department considerably enlarged, and to have a special counter for provisions, of which they are making a speciality. They have now a special department devoted to vegetables, fruits, and flowers, an innovation which is sure to find favour with many of the customers. From this branch all the customers residing in Kingstown, Monkstown, Killiney, Cabinteely, Foxrock, Carrickmines, Shankill, etc., are supplied, vans being sent to each place daily.[18]

General Election 1906

In 1905 Adam presided over a citizens' testimonial banquet and presentation to J. P. Nannetti MP for the College Green division of Dublin, and Lord Mayor of Dublin 1906-7. The evening was reported in the *Freeman's Journal* on 3 May 1905, and reveals something of how Adam was regarded by others in the political arena.

Last night, Mr J. P. Nannetti, MP for the College Green Division of Dublin, was the recipient of a handsome presentation at the hands of his fellow-citizens as a token of the esteem and regard in which he is held, and as a recognition of his services to Dublin, both in his capacity as a member of Parliament and the Corporation. Mr Adam Findlater, J.P., presided.

Mr Nannetti, MP, on rising to reply, said—I am wholly unable to express my thanks for the kindness of which this night's proceedings are the culmination (applause). My political convictions are to serve my fellow workers, to serve Dublin—to serve all Dublin, without regard to distinction of class or creed or political conviction—within the measure of my ability, while steadfastly faithful to my own opinions and my own party, was my ambition (applause).

Mr Chairman, you [Adam Findlater] by your presence here tonight and by your most kind and encouraging words have given a character to this presentation and this compliment that they would not otherwise possess. The casual observer might think that you, Mr Chairman, and I could never have established such a relationship as your presence indicates. You are a respected representative of the commercial interests of the city; your political convictions are not mine—between the Unionist merchant and the Nationalist Labour member there might seem a gulf that could not be bridged. But we have found a bridge in common devotion to the well-being of the city, and I venture to add, to the well-being of the nation (applause). We cannot all be of one view—I doubt whether it would be good for Dublin, or good for Ireland, if we were all of one view. The discussion, the consideration, the forethought that are compelled by differ-

I imagine the three–in–hand was used for long distance deliveries deep into the Kildare and Meath countryside.

Blackrock branch in the late nineteenth century, before the days of window displays.

Adam caricatured (*Ireland* August 1905)

ences of opinion are good things and necessary to the well-being of every community (applause). They are only bad when we allow them to prevent united action for common interests when these are in danger or have to be promoted. You are one who has recognised that there are such interests, and you have not feared to trespass beyond the party hedges in order to promote common action (hear, hear). You will agree that there is need of it in Dublin, not merely in reference to industrial and commercial matters that lie outside the province of Government, but in semi-political matters also (hear, hear).

You, Mr Chairman, have also been busy on a question that is beset with difficulty—the valuation question—a problem in the solution of which we may suffer severely if we do not unite to secure that revaluation shall take place under proper safeguards (applause). I merely indicate these as matters that deserve our attention. There are many more. They affect us all, commercial men and non-commercial men, employers and employed. It should be our aim to develop a union of good and patriotic citizens in reference to such matters; and should I be attaching too much meaning to this occasion if I said it showed in its own way the possibility of such a union (applause).

The chairman then proposed the toast of 'Our Native Land', which was honoured.[19]

In 1906 this regard was very nearly translated into a seat in parliament for Adam. In those days the process of an election lasted two weeks. This meant that a candidate defeated in one constituency had a chance, if he moved quickly, of standing in another. This happened to Walter Long, Chief Secretary, the cabinet member with responsibility for Irish affairs, who was defeated in South Bristol, and now presented himself as unionist candidate for Adam's home base of Kingstown. Many nationalists felt that they had little or no chance of a seat in the solidly unionist constituency of South Dublin, even against a British candidate hunting for a safe seat. Walter Long was identified with uncompromising unionism, and so was doubly unwelcome to the nationalists, as an English carpet-bagger and as a unionist. The idea was floated by the influential leader of the United Irish League, Michael Davitt*, that Adam, as a sympathetic Liberal unionist, should stand and combine the nationalist and the moderate unionist votes against Long. However, the established nationalist candidate, Richard

* Michael Davitt (1846-1906) founded the Land League in 1879 with Charles Stewart Parnell. The League's agitation was a crucial element in persuading Gladstone to introduce the 1881 Land Act. Davitt died in May 1906.

Hazleton—a devoted abstainer, and author of the 'Mr Bung' article in *The Leader*—and his supporters insisted that they should fight the seat, expecting that the strongly nationalist spirit of the day would carry them through (in the event this was the only non-university seat outside Ulster to elect a unionist). Davitt wrote sadly to Adam:

Private to Adam Findlater
United Irish League
39, Upper O'Connell Street, Dublin, Jan. 17th 1906
Dear Mr Findlater,

I find that the Nationalist candidate, Mr Hazleton and his friends, are not inclined to any compromise, and as H. is to go forward, I could not dream of asking you to stand merely to reduce Long's majority.

It appears that our leaders here were committed to the Hazleton candidature before they had known of my proposition about yourself. I regret this decision, as I think it a foolish one. I am satisfied that you would win if you went forward.

Yours very truly, Michael Davitt

Despite his disappointment, Adam took a prominent part in the election debate, which spanned eight days. He proved a determined foe, with his moderate unionist views being seen by all sides as a kind of middle ground. It is interesting to see how the anti-home rule parties were at this stage no more united than the pro-home rulers, a situation that was to change as the issues became more tightly defined. The style of debate is typical of a time when set-piece speeches rather than soundbites were the order of the day.

Monday

22 January 1906 *Irish Independent*

Mr Long's entrance into the arena in South Dublin has not been acclaimed with much enthusiasm by the Unionist electors of the constituency. The letter from Mr Adam Findlater which we publish today gives utterance to an opinion widely held that it is 'a terrible admission of their own incapacity' on the part of Unionist Irishmen and Mr Long has been shoved forward for this position over the head of an Irishman who had, at all events, an intimate knowledge of our country and its needs.

'UNIONIST DISCONTENT. PROTEST BY MR FINDLATER'

We have received the following letter for publication:

Sir, The *Freeman's Journal* of today rightly prints my name as one of those attending Mr Hazleton's meeting at Kingstown last evening, but in such a way as to make it appear that I had formally identified myself with the Nationalist cause. As a matter of fact, I was at that meeting as an ordinary listener in the body of the hall, anxious to make myself acquainted with Mr Hazleton's capabilities and views, and also to hear what Mr Redmond had to say after the extraordinary electoral revolution which has taken place all over the Three Kingdoms. I hold that it is the duty, as well as the right, of every voter to listen to both sides, and then to judge between them. I have not ceased to be a Unionist, as I understand the term. I believe that separation from

ALEX. FINDLATER & CO., LIMITED.

Racking and Bottling John Jameson & Son's Old Dublin Whiskey at Alex. Findlater & Co.'s Duty Paid Bottling Stores.

The Bottling Vats (capacity of the one Vat shown, 1,037 gallons) in the Duty Paid Bottling Stores

These Vats are equipped with an ingenious attachment which automatically measures and bottles the Whiskey.

FINDLATER'S Bottling of John Jameson & Son's Fine Old Whiskey, Mellowed and Matured by Age only, Presents the FAMOUS OLD DUBLIN WHISKEY in its Finest Form.

30

1902—The bottling vats in the whiskey house

England is undesirable in our own interests, and most level-headed men, I am persuaded, share my view.

But I confess that I am profoundly discontented with the legislation, and particularly with the administration of the Unionist Government in this country during the last twenty years . . .

A. S. Findlater

22 January 1906 *Freeman's Journal*

The possibility that Mr Walter Long, the rejected of Wiltshire, Liverpool, and Bristol may, as the result of the industrious manufacture of bogus votes in the constituency, be foisted upon South Dublin as its representative, is proving so humiliating to the electorate that the feeling of the people of the constituency has been thoroughly aroused. The sense of humiliation seems to be spreading from Nationalists to Unionists. We welcome the letter which we publish today from Mr Adam Findlater, though it is written to correct the impression that he had become a Home Ruler and had made up his mind to vote for Mr Hazleton. He has taken no definite resolution; but wants to hear both sides before deciding.

This state of open-mindedness on the part of intelligent Unionists is all that the opponents of Mr Long should desire. For they may safely leave it to Mr Long himself to determine in the right way the judgement of the open and liberal-minded Unionists, especially commercial men like Mr Findlater, whose interests are identified with the prosperity of their country and of the people among whom they live . . . Mr Findlater was one of the Unionists who joined with the late patriotic Protestant Archbishop of Dublin, Lord Plunket, and with the former Conservative member for the County of Dublin, Lord Holmpatrick, in the remarkable protest against the overtaxation of Ireland when the Financial Relations Commission's Report had revealed the facts . . . how are they going to swallow Mr Long's declaration that 'the less said about the three millions overtaxation the better,' and that 'the advantage which Ireland derived from her share in the Imperial Exchequer was a very real advantage.'

Again, Mr Findlater is a business man. He believes in getting value for his money and in the principle of a fair day's work for a fair day's wage. Does he think that Ireland gets value for the money spent upon the Irish establishments? Take the police. Lord Welby, a former Secretary of the British Treasury, has pointed out that though Ireland is freer from crime than Great Britain the police in Ireland cost £700,000 a year more, relatively to the population. Mr Arnold White has just been pointing out to the readers of the 'Daily Chronicle' that while in 1903 there were only 1,169 convictions in Ireland for serious offences, there were 2,114 in Scotland; yet the cost to Ireland of her police is £1,569,214 a year, while Scotland, with twice as many criminals, pays only £539,196. Mr Wyndham recognised the extravagance, and proposed to save £250,000 a year to provide part of the bonus to the Irish landlords.

Now what has Mr Long told the Unionist businessmen of Dublin? 'There had,' he said, 'been a reduction in the police force, which he regretted. He had stopped it, and he hoped that no man would be so unwise as to again attempt the reduction of the force.' Now we put it to Mr Findlater as a sensible business man that such a perfor-

ALEX. FINDLATER & CO., LIMITED.

BURGUNDY.

"In neglecting Burgundy Wine, we ignore a most powerful agent in disease of the nervous system. If any one of my readers will do me the honour to be advised to study this Wine, let me entreat him not to begin with a cheap sort, but to select a good specimen, in which he will find the peculiar excellences well marked." . . . "I am satisfied that, although out of a million drinkers, fewer would find anything possibly disagreeing in Bordeaux than in Burgundy, yet, for a large class of people who want support Burgundy has in it materials which Bordeaux has not." . . . "What Bordeaux is to the blood, that is Burgundy to the nerves." . . . "Burgundy is pre-eminently a full-bodied Wine; but its body is aromatic, not alcoholic." . . . "Whoever would add an innocent pleasure to his Christmas festivities, let him hand round a bottle of Volnay or Chambertin with the roast turkey."
—Dr. Druitt.

IN SCREW STOPPERED FLAGONS,

Which can be Re-Stoppered during Connsumption of Wine.

2s. per Flagon.

Containing One Quart Imperial, equal to a Bottle and a Half of Wine.

RED BURGUNDY.

	Per Dozen Bottles. s.	d.	Half Bots. s	d.
Fleurie Beaujolais A full yet Soft Wine	18	0	9	6
Santenay. Cote d'Or Very full, with good bouquet	24	0	12	6
Beaune. Cote d'Or An excellent specimen of fine Burgundy, soft round, with great bouquet and flavour ...	30	0	15	6
Volnay. Cote d'Or Splendid body, yet very elegant and delicate ...	36	0	18	6
Aloxe-Corton. Cote d'Or A high-class growth, celebrated for its tonic properties, recommended for laying down ..	42	0	21	6
Clos De Vougeot. Premier Cru Cote d'Or One of the finest wines of the Cote d'Or, excellent body and flavour, with perfect bouquet ..	48	0	24	6

French Burgundy, in flagons, a Speciality—24/- doz.
Flagons 6d. each, returnable.

WHITE BURGUNDY

Label					
White, "*Chablis*"	Chablis	24	0	12	0

SPARKLING RED.

Pink, "*Sparkling Red Burgundy*"	Extra Quality ...	59	0	31	6

Burgundy bought in Wood bottled free, and saves 3/- a dozen.

PORT.

"As a gentle corrective and tonic compensation to restore the equilibrium of the constitution; as a safeguard against organic disturbuance; as a soothing refreshment where vitality is feeling exhausted; and as a means of giving energy and strength when man has to struggle against the various ills that flesh is heir to—Wine cannot be surpassed by any product of Nature or Art."—Baron Liebig.

WINES MATURED IN WOOD.

Seal.	Prices Per doz. s.	d.
G. een, No. 4, Good Rich	24	0
Red, ,, 3, Fine Old Wine	30	0
Red, Invalid	36	0

These fresh bottled Ports being dry and of a ruby color, from being a long time in wood, have the characteristics of old bottled wines, and can be used immediately, not being crusted.

Invalid Port Wine

36/- Per Doz.

INFLUENZA.

The Lady says.—"In the greatest modern work on Influneza, that of Dr. Theophilus Thompson, in which he has compiled, for the Sydenham Society, a vast mass of information from all sources concerning outbreaks of this disease for more than three centuries, we find him quoting these words: 'Those drinking Port Wine in moderation, and living much in the open air, appeared less liable to the infection.'"

Dr. MORTIMER GREVILLE writes:

"Port, which has been long enough in the wood to be thoroughly matured before bottling, I regard as not only permissible, but to be recommended, particularly in the cases of those who are much subjected to mental worry, etc."

After-Dinner Wines.

OLD LODGE PORTS.

Any Connoisseur requiring fine after-dinner Wine cannot have anything finer. They show a beautiful ruby shade in the glass, and are bright as crystal in condition. There is no waste in decanting.

Seal.	s.	d.
White, "O.L.P." (Old Lodge Port)	42	0

RARE OLD TAWNEY.

S.L.P. (Superior Lodge Port.)

Blue, "S.L.P."	48	0

This Wine has been twenty-one years in Lodge in Oporto, and five years in our own Bonded Stores in Dublin. No finer Tawney Wine can be procured.

For full and detailed Catalogue apply to

ALEX. FINDLATER & CO.,

LIMITED.

1902—Burgundy and Port listings. Note the use of screw-stopped flagons for Burgundy mance is not merely fatal to the cause of public economy, but that it is making hash of the true interests of the Unionist Party in Ireland. There is Unionism and Unionism. And surely if the Unionist cause is to thrive it ought not to permit itself to be identified with the cause of overtaxation, and gross and wasteful expenditure. Surely Ireland wants that extra million now spent upon an idle police force, and can find uses for it more advantageous to every man in Ireland, Unionist or Nationalist, than supporting an unnecessary army of strapping men in enforced idleness?

Tuesday
23 January 1906 *Freeman's Journal*

For a 'bluff, straightforward, honest Englishman' Mr Walter Long has developed with surprising rapidity a serpentine facility of wriggling. He found himself at Kingstown last night among a community whose progress has been paralysed by the exactions and confiscations of urban landlordism . . . The apparition of Mr Findlater has convinced Mr Long that those Irish Unionists who are Financial Reformers are not to be put off with 'bluff' of this transparent character. Mr Walter Long, we venture to say, never opened the Report in question, any more than his leader, Mr Balfour, before he denounced its conclusions in 1896 . . .

We print as a supplement to the report of the Kingstown meeting the questions to which Mr Adam Findlater seeks an answer. They are a suggestive catechism; and are a valuable indication of the questions that are troubling the Unionist business men of Dublin just now. Mr Findlater wants an explanation of the contemptuous treatment of the Financial Relations Report by the late Government. He will not receive the explanation we venture to prophesy. He seeks light as to the refusal of the Government to enable the Irish local authorities to save the people whom they represent from having their Imperial Taxation increased by the very simple device of using the Castle Valuation Department to increase the valuation of Irish property upon every opportunity, without regard to circumstances. The oracle is so far silent on that question. 'Does Mr Long,' asks Mr Findlater, 'consider that the general government of Ireland, as a whole, should continue to be in the hands of the bureaucracy of many Boards nominally presided over by the Chief Secretary, and appointed haphazard by successive Governments?' The answer is that he does, for he assured the Rathmines Unionists of the fact. Mr Findlater wants Mr Long's attack upon Lord Dudley supplemented by a statement of his own Irish policy . . .

Mr Findlater is evidently nettled by the application of the word 'traitors' to those Irish Unionists who refuse to be made pawns of in the place-hunters' game which brought Mr Long to Ireland. He should change the form of his question on that point, and ask Mr Long why he wrote to the electors of Greenwich to knife the son of his old leader, Lord Salisbury, who was the official Unionist candidate, with the result that a Home Ruler was elected owing to the divided Unionist vote. Who is the greater 'traitor' to his Party and his cause? The Unionist who refuses to allow his cause to be identified with a policy of pure negation and stagnation, or the cabinet Minister that turns on the son of the man who appointed him, and assists a dissentient Unionist to defeat that cause in an English constituency?

ALEX. FINDLATER & CO., LTD., DUBLIN.

Summer Wines,

Of Very Low Alcoholic Strength,

For use in Hot Weather.

The Wines Drunk in Tropical Climates.

STIMULATIVE AND COOLING.

STILL HOCKS.	STILL MOSELLES.
Oppenheim, 15/- per doz.	Zeltinger, 17/- per doz.
Laubenheim, 18/- ,,	Winningen, 24/- ,,
Deidesheim, 24/- ,,	

PURE

FRENCH BURGUNDY,

IN SCREW STOPPERED FLAGONS, which can be re-stoppered during consumption of wine.

WHAT DR. DRUITT SAYS:—"In neglecting Burgundy Wine we ignore a most powerful agent in nerve troubles. For a large class of people who want support, Burgundy has in it materials which Bordeaux has not. What Bordeaux is to the blood, that is Burgundy to the nerves."

2/- per Flagon, Containing One Quart Imperial, equal to a Bottle and a Half of Wine. **1/- per Half Flagon.**

Eau Des Carmes,

THE GREAT FRENCH NERVE RESTORATIVE, Price **1/-** and **2/-**

Alex Findlater & Co., Ltd.

33

1908—Note the ubiquitous 'medical' note—'what Bordeaux is to the blood, that is Burgundy to the nerves'!

23 January 1906 *Dublin Daily Express*

ENTHUSIASTIC MEETING AT KINGSTOWN

Long: 'Some of the things which have been told about me are very remarkable' (laughter) . . . It is alleged that people interested in temperance should not vote for me because I am the chairman of a brewery company. I hope that those people interested in temperance will not think that I am unworthy of their support when I am obliged to confess with profound regret that I am not the chairman of a brewery company, or anything like that (laughter). I don't know much about the position of chairman of companies . . .'

Wednesday

24 January 1906 *The Irish Times*

From A. S. Findlater, St Albans, Albany Avenue, Monkstown.

Dear Mr Long I think it only fair and courteous on my part that, before your meeting commences, I should hand you the questions I would like to ask. If you deal with them in the course of your speech it may save me the unpleasantness of having to more directly invite your reply.

Yours faithfully, A. S. Findlater

Walter Long: Well, now gentlemen . . . the writer of that letter was present close to me on the right of the platform during the whole of the meeting. He was there at the end. I had his letter in my hand and his questions, and I expected he would ask one or two or three of them. He never asked me one of them.

(A Voice—'He was frightened.') . . .

But, gentlemen, what an interesting reflection there is to be drawn from this. I am not worthy to be the member for Dublin South because it is alleged that I am chairman of a brewery company, while the candidate who stands against me is a professed and, I believe, an earnest abstainer. Now, gentlemen, do not let us whisper even to ourselves this horrible suggestion. Is it conceivable that this earnest, devoted, life-long abstainer is going to receive political assistance from one who is even remotely connected with an industry which, though not actually brewing, is first cousin to it? (Laughter and applause). Why, gentlemen, wherever I go about the City and County of Dublin I see magnificent pictures which invite me to partake of whiskey which bears a particular name, pronounced 'A one', Findlater's leading brand of whiskey. But by what curious methods are some results achieved! (Laughter)

The Nationalist candidate is apparently to receive the co-operation of one who, amid many other calls, finds time to devote himself to the manufacture and production of a very excellent and valuable article of consumption, provided it is not consumed unduly. (Laughter) This gentleman is not ashamed to take advantage of this assistance, and he is to be helped by questions addressed to me, it is said, but which have never reached me, except in the form that I have described to you. Gentlemen, do you know the meaning of the word 'farce?' because if you do, I say this is a solemn farce. (Hear, hear, and a Voice—'A contemptible farce.') I say a conspiracy of this kind is one which ought to be exposed, and I am here tonight to say what I said last night

Our Findlater's A1 whiskey label, we believe, pre-dates the very similar Guinness label.

in Kingstown—you can elect me if you will; you can, if you like, elect somebody else; but one thing I declare to you, as I declared last night at Kingstown—that if I can help it you shall never elect me on false pretences . . .

24 January 1906 *Freeman's Journal*

On the subject of needful reforms, Mr Long is tricky and evasive. Of the injustice done to Ireland by over-taxation, he thinks the less said the better. He wants no change. The financial system which provided him monthly with a fat cheque is good enough for him. He has contrived so far to evade the searching questions put to him by Mr Adam Findlater, but any person who has studied Mr Long's political career can supply the answers for himself. He is a reactionary of the reactionaries, opposed to all reforms. One fact he cannot evade. He voted against the Irish Town Tenants Bill, which even the Orangemen supported. It shows courage of a kind in Mr Long, with this achievement to his credit, to demand the votes of a constituency where the town tenants question is with so many a question of reform or ruin.

24 January 1906 *Freeman's Journal*

By Special Wire, From our own correspondent London, Wednesday morning

The agents of Mr Walter Long appear to be in a bad funk over the prospects of his election for South Dublin. They have sent a circular to the editors of the London Tory papers appealing for their aid in rounding up the outvoters of the constituency who are resident here in order that they should go over and record their votes for the rejected of South Bristol on Friday next. In this delightful document, Mr W. W. Seddall, in whose name it is issued, writes: 'There are a very considerable number of people residing in various parts of England who have leasehold or freehold votes in the South

ALEX. FINDLATER & CO., LTD., DUBLIN.

CHAMPAGNE.

NON-VINTAGE WINES.

	Per Dozen. Bots. s. d.	Per Dozen. H. Bots. s. d.	Extra Old Landed. Per Dozen. Bots. s. d.	Extra Old Landed. Per Dozen. H. Bots. s. d.
Ayala & Co.—Extra Quality, Extra Dry	79 0	42 0	86 0	45 6
Furcier, Pere et Fils—Extra Quality	60 0	32 6	65 0	35 0
Giesler & Co.—Extra Superior, Very Dry	38 8	42 0	88 0	46 6
Pommery & Greno	90 0	47 6	94 6	—
Viardot Freres—Special Cuvee	48 0	26 6	53 0	29 0
Fontanel & Cie	36 0	21 0	40 0	22 6

VINTAGE WINES.

	Vintage.		
Rittscher & Co.—Cuvee de Choix	1898	86 0	45 6
Furcier, Pere et Fils—Extra Quality	1900	65 0	35 0
Giesler & Co.—Extra Superior	1900	90 0	—
Perrier, Jouet & Co.—Extra Quality	1900	—	55 0
Pommery & Greno	1900	—	65 0
Roederer, Louis—Extra Dry	1900	115 0	60 0
Ruinart, Pere et Fils—Carte Anglaise	1900	90 0	—
Viardot Freres	1900	—	29 0
Rittscher & Co.—Cuvee de Choix	1900	—	45 6
Ayala & Co.—Extra Quality	1904	95 0	50 0
Bollinger—Very Dry	1904	120 0	62 6
Giesler & Co.,—Extra Superior	1904	85 0	45 0
George Goulet & Co.—Extra Quality	1904	95 0	50 0
Charles Heidsieck—Extra Quality	1904	85 0	45 0
Heidsieck & Co.—Dry Monopole	1904	102 0	53 0
Duc de Montebello—Max Sec	1904	80 0	42 6
Moet et Chandon—Dry Imperial	1904	96 0	50 6
G. H. Mumm & Co.,—Extra Dry	1904	100 0	—
Perrier Jouet & Co.—Extra Quality	1904	95 0	50 0
Pommery & Greno—Nature	1904	123 0	64 0
Roederer, Louis—Extra Dry	1904	95 0	50 0
Ruinart Pere et Fils—Carte Anglaise	1904	82 0	43 6
Veuve Cliquot—Dry	1904	120 0	65 0
Deutz et Geldermann	1904	85 0	—

Subject to being unsold, and to market fluctuations.

CHAMPAGNE IN QUARTER BOTTLES.

	Per Dozen
Furcier, Pere et Fils—Extra Quality	21 3
Giesler & Co.—Extra Superior	23 6
Ayala & Co.—Extra Quality, Extra Dry	23 6
Fontanel	12 0

FURCIER PERE ET FILS
EXTRA QUALITY
DRY CHAMPAGNE.

FURCIER, PERE ET FILS, AND VIARDOT FRERES.

We are sole Proprietors of these Brand as quoted above, and we have every confidence in recommending them as better value at their respective prices than any of the so-called "fashionable" brands.

We court a comparison with the Wines of any other Shipper, no matter how high priced, stipulating only that it be made on the merits of the Wines, without reference to the labels beforehand.

	Per Dozen Bots. s. d.	Per Dozen Hf Bots. s. d.
Furcier, Pere et Fils. 1900 Vintage	65 0	35 0

We strongly advise our customers to lay down a stock of this Wine at present prices, as they will have to be advanced before long.

SAUMUR CHAMPAGNES.

	Per Dozen. Bots. s. d.	Per Dozen. Half Bots. s. d.
Brut Saumur	36 0	20 0
Extra Quality	33 0	18 6
Dry Royal (Ackerman—Laurance)	54 0	29 0
Brut Royal (Ackerman—Laurance)	54 0	29 0
Cremant du Roi (Veuve Amiot)	48 0	26 6

Do. **do.** in baskets of 12 quarter bots. 15/-

ALTAR WINES.

These Wines are specially adapted for sacerdotal purposes, being perfectly pure and free from spirit :—

"Vino Sacro." The Perfect Church Wine—

		s. d.
Single bottles, not carriage paid	each	2 6
Single Half-bottles, not carriage paid	,,	1 6
12 Ordinary Wine Bottles, carriage paid		30 0
6 Ordinary Wine Bottles, carriage paid		16 6
24 Ordinary Wine Half Bottles, carriage paid		33 0
12 Ordinary Wine Half Bottles, carriage paid		18 0
One Bottle per post, to include box and postage		3 6
Malaga—As recommended by Bishops	per doz.	20 0
Creaderias—As used in Spanish churches	,,	21 0

AUSTRALIAN WINES.

	Per doz. flagons. s. d.	Per doz. bots. s. d.
Tintara, Burgoyne & Co.	38 0	27 0
Harvest, Burgoyne & Co.	26 0	19 0
Carbinet	—	21 0
Emu Burgundy	26 0	19 0

Flagons, 6d. per doz. extra.

SUNDRY WINES.

Vibrona	per bottle	3 9
Vibrona Sherry	,,	2 9
Calcavella	per dozen	26 0
Masdeu		24 0
Tarragona	,,	25 0
Valencia Wine	,,	18 0
St. Raphael, Tannin Wine	,,	29 6
Quinine Wine	,,	27 0
Hall's Coca Wine	per bottle 2/- and	3 6
Coleman's Wincarnis	per bottle, 2/3 and	3 6
Lemco Wine (Carvine)	per bottle	3 0

28

1911—The relative prices of champagne brands are much as today. Veuve Clicquot vintage 1904, at 10s a bottle, is the equivalent of £35, more or less in line with today's price.

County division of Dublin, and it is of the utmost importance that every pressure should be brought to bear on them to come to Dublin on the 26th inst. (the polling day) to record their votes, as I need hardly point out the very great importance to the Unionist Party of winning this seat. I have been requested by Mr Walter Long to write to you and request you to be good enough to publish in your columns an appeal to such electors to be sure to attend to register their votes, as we have no doubt that this would have a very good effect.'

Thursday

25 January 1906 *The Irish Times*

It is said that speeches have little effect on the results of elections. Even if this statement be generally true, we confidently make an exception of the series of speeches which Mr Walter Long brought to a conclusion last night at Dalkey. Unlike the Russellite candidates who are now being swept out of Ulster, Mr Long does not woo the Nationalist vote. He appeals to the unionist electors of South Dublin on the straight issue of the Union versus Separation.

25 January 1906 *Freeman's Journal*

AN OVERFLOWING MEETING IN RATHMINES

Last evening a splendid meeting of the supporters of Mr R. Hazleton was held in the Boys' Brigade Hall, Richmond Hill, which, owing to the refusal of the Rathmines Commissioners, was the only building in that Division at the disposal of the Nationalists. The action, however, of the Commissioners led to a most remarkable outburst of National feeling, for while the Hall was filled to its utmost capacity, a huge crowd assembled outside, and had to be addressed by several speakers, so that instead of one meeting there were two going on contemporaneously.

A few persons usually regarded as of the student class turned up with the evident intention of creating a disturbance. They marched into the hall armed with sticks, and with their caps well pulled down over their foreheads, and, lining up, they looked daggers and, pantomime fashion, their visages all seemed to proclaim, 'Beware! We are the Trinity Desperadoes.' The chaps were quickly recognised, and the crowd laughed them out of the place. Inside the Hall the meeting commenced at eight o'clock sharp, when, on the motion of Mr Sheehy Skeffington, the chair was taken by Mr D. J. Gibnew, CE . . .

Mr Skeffington, MA, who was received with loud cheers, said they were fighting against overwhelming odds, but the fight was nevertheless an inspiring one. The spirit and earnestness of the people were putting their opponents in a blue funk (cheers). He was opposed to Unionism in any shape and form; but the policy of Mr Long could not command the approval of any intelligent unionist (cheers). It was a policy that would not command the support of any intelligent unionist, from Mr T. W. Russell to Mr Adam Findlater (applause).

Mr Hazleton: What was Long but a bird of passage, a brief stay in Wiltshire, a still briefer stay in Liverpool, a brief stay in Bristol, and no stay at all in South County Dublin (loud applause). Why had he not answered Mr Findlater's questions? Mr

ALEX. FINDLATER & CO., LTD., DUBLIN.

"A Goblet of Sherry."

"Never in my life had I such medicine."—THOMAS CARLYLE.

SIR JAMES CRICHTON BROWNE on THOMAS CARLYLE, and a certain Goblet of Sherry which might fitly be termed Historical.

In the course of an article recently contributed to a leading daily paper, Sir James Crichton Browne strongly pleads the case for Alcohol as a Restorative, and especially as a Potent Remedy for some of the most dangerous effects of Exposure to Cold. Whilst heartily condemning Intemperance, he asks the Total Abstinence zealots to remember that Alcohol has Virtues as well as Vices, and that its Goodness can be utilised to good effect. He gives an instance relating to Thos. Carlyle and a Goblet of Sherry. It forms a little story which may be read with interest and profit.

Few of us can escape the many circumstances which reduce one to the state of chill and exhaustion in which Thos. Carlyle arrived home—and the moral of the story is obvious.

Sir James Crichton Browne says:—"When, after exposure to cold, there is stagnation of the blood that has been driven from the chilled surface to the internal organs, a judicious dose of alcohol will re-establish the equilibrium of the circulation and ward off dangers both immediate and remote."

The eminent Physician goes on to say:—"**Thomas Carlyle,** I recollect, bore testimony to the benign action of alcohol under such circumstances. He had journeyed from Liverpool to London forty or fifty hours on the outside of a stage-coach, in cold and wet weather, and arrived in London 'half-dead.' I landed at the door in Cheyne-row,' he says, 'more like mad than sane, but my darling was in the lobby, saw at a glance how it was, and almost without speaking brought me to my room, and with me a big glass, almost a Goblet, of the best Sherry. 'Drink that, dear, at a draught! Never in my life had I such a medicine. Shaved, washed, got into clean clothes. I stepped downstairs quite new-made, and thanking Heaven for such a doctor.'

"Who shall say that it was not to that Goblet of Sherry that we are indebted for the 'French Revolution' or the 'Lectures on Heroes.' Any medical man who in like case declined to sanction a Goblet of Sherry or its equivalent, would incur a very grave responsibility."

SPANISH MEDICAL MEN

Says "Medicus" in the *Lancet*, order Sherry in preference to Brandy; my own experience is that it is far more easily assimilated by those who are very ill. In pneumonia, when fever is beginning to overtax the strength, I give a light Sherry such as Manzanilla every four hours; if there is any sign of heart-failure, I increase the quantity to a wine glass every hour. The effect of such wines is to steady the pulse, to clear the head, to clean the mouth, and, perhaps for this reason, to help the appetite.

The Virtues of Sherry, although well known to many, may not be known to all, and it will perhaps be permissible to enumerate a few of them.

Of all Wines, red or white, **Sherry** is the most tonic, and contains the greatest proportion of iron. For this reason it is the only Wine used by the Pharmacopœia (under the name of Vinum Xercicum) in the manufacture of medicinal Wines. **Sherry** contains almost double as much tonic vinosity as any other Wine. This fact was endorsed by the Commission sent to Jerez in 1897 by *The Lancet*. This quality no doubt accounts for the general use by Spanish doctors of Sherry as a restorative in cases of collapse. **Sherry** is the only Wine that can be taken equally well before, during, or after a meal. **Sherry is the** Wine the flavour of which can be appreciated while smoking.

Sherry has a most attractive taste, and has been used for centuries as a flavouring in cooking. With all this flavour, however, Sherry is cleaner to the palate than any other Wine, as is testified by those of the old school always taking a glass "as a whitewash" at the conclusion of a dinner. **Sherry** is the most economical Wine for the household; unlike other Wines, the contents of the bottle remain good after having been opened many days. This to the man of means may appear a small thing, but to those who are not plentifully possessed of this world's goods, it is a great thing to be able to open a bottle of good wine one day, and to find that it is not in the least deteriorated the next, nay even a week after.

We have the following qualities in Pale, Golden, and Amber colour—Dry, Mellow, and rich flavour.

Seal		Per Doz. s. d.	Per Doz. Half Bots. s. d.
Black,	Nice Light Lunch Wine	20 0	—
Green,	**Recommended** (real good value)	**24 0**	**12 0**
Red,	Superior Fine Wine	30 0	15 0
Yellow,	**Very delicate**	**36 0**	**18 0**
Chocolate,	Choice Old Solera	42 0	—
White,	A connoisseur's Wine	48 0	—

In addition to the above Wines we have acquired the monoply of the following two rare old Vintage Sherries, which we are sure will be appreciated by our customers for their exquisite and delicate taste and most unusual bouquet:—

Rare Old Vintage 1874 (Maria) Amontillado Pasada ... 54/- Per Dozen.
" " 1860 (Lord Roseberry) Amontillado 60/- "

32

1908—'Any medical man who declined to sanction a goblet of sherry would incur very grave responsibility'

Findlater was an Irishman who worked for the welfare and progress of Ireland, and he was not prepared to see South County Dublin made a dustbin for the rubbish of Irish politics. Why did Mr Long only take a single ticket from Bristol to Dublin; was it not because he knew that returned empties always had to go back carriage paid (loud laughter).

25 January 1906 *Irish Independent*

MR FINDLATER AND MR LONG: STRAIGHT ANSWERS DEMANDED

We have received the appended letter from Mr A. S. Findlater:

Dear Sir, As Mr Long has thought it proper to give his Blackrock audience of last night my letter of Monday evening, covering certain questions on matters of high public importance to the electors in general that I wished him to answer at his Kingstown meeting, my tongue is loosed as regards some of what preceded the writing of that brief and not very important note. His suggestion that he got the covering letter, but not the contents, I dismiss with the remark that here in Ireland, even in times of election excitement, such mistakes rarely occur. The letter and its contents were brought by my secretary to the Shelbourne Hotel at six o'clock on Monday evening, and there delivered personally to Mr Long's private secretary. I did not wish to take Mr Long at a disadvantage.

Now for a few facts:

On Monday morning last, the morning of the Kingstown meeting, Mr Long, in company with Mr Arthur Samuels, KC, and Mr Percy Bernard, called upon me, and I think almost the first word that was spoken between us was my assurance that I was quite as good a Unionist as either Mr Samuels, Mr Bernard, or himself. But I went on to explain to him that I thought many Unionists were, as I had stated publicly, discontented with the action of the Conservative Government when they were in power. I explained to him also that his attitude with regard to the Town Tenants Bill would alienate a considerable number of votes from him unless he stated straight-forwardly what his opinions were.

Mr Long told me that he had not clearly understood, until he came to Ireland, the position of the town tenants, and that he quite saw that, whatever the merits might be in England, Ireland has a very much stronger case. I also stated to him that I thought his remarks on the Financial Relations question at Earlsfort Skating Rink might be interpreted adversely to himself, to which he replied that what he meant to convey was that the question was asked him as to the £3,000,000 over-taxation very late in the evening, and there was not time to go into the question; but he promised that he would make his view clear on both the Town Tenants and the Financial Revelations questions at the meeting in the evening—that is to say, the Kingstown meeting.

We then discussed Mr Long's own Valuation Bill as regards England and the Irish law, and I urged him to say that he would be prepared to give the same legislation to Ireland that he had proposed for England, Scotland and Wales. I am satisfied that in advocating equal legislation for all parts of the United Kingdom I was taking a stronger Unionist position than Mr Long. At the end of the interview Mr Long assured me that he would deal with the Irish question in his speeches in a more constructive manner, and he left, thanking me for my suggestions. Those who were present can deny or

ALEX. FINDLATER & CO., LTD., DUBLIN.

The Wine of Marsala.

A PURE PRODUCT OF THE GRAPE.

SICILIAN MARSALA BOAT
Loading Marsala for Conveyance to Steamer.

Ancient history tells us that the Wines of Sicily were famous so long ago as the time of the Punic Wars, but they were not known as

"MARSALA WINE"

until about the year 1773 A.D.

The soil from which they are grown is highly calcareous in nature, and also contains sulphur, owing, no doubt, to the volcanic character of the island.

The Wine is absolutely the pure product of the grape, and has always been considered most wholesome and anti-rheumatic. It is one of the best and most reliable Wines imported, and as Lord Nelson said in 1800:—"It is so good that any gentleman's table might receive it."

The Wine is of a low alcoholic strength, and it improves greatly with age in bottle, while it blends well and makes a refreshing and an invigorating beverage with water—aerated or mineral.

"IN CELLAR COOL." MARSALA AWAITING SHIPMENT.

ORDINARY WINES.

Seal.			s. d.		s. d.	
Black,	——	Gold	15 0	Per Doz.	—	Per Doz. ½ Bots.
Red,	Jubilee	Gold	18 0	,,	9 0	,, ,,
Red,	Jubilee	Pale	18 0	Per Doz.	9 0	Per Doz. ½ Bots.
White,	Virgin	Nutty	20 0	,,	—	,, ,,
Blue,	Montilla	Dry	24 0	Per Doz.	—	Per Doz. ½ Bots.

SPECIALITIES.

	s. d.	
Choice Italian, dry and full bodied	22 0	Per Doz.
Fino type, dry and delicate	24 0	Per Doz.
Choice Madeira style, rich and generous	26 0	Per Doz.

29

1908—Nelson's fleet, based in the Kingdom of the Two Sicilies, during the Napoleonic war, took to Marsala in place of Sherry.

affirm the accuracy of this account of our interview.

Mr Samuels came back and asked me would I give a list of my questions to him in the afternoon. It so happened that I was unable to formulate them before 6 o'clock in the evening, but at that hour my secretary, as I have already said, drove to the Shelbourne Hotel and brought a full list of my questions to Mr Long. I sent an absolutely identical copy to the Press. What was wrong in that? This is a matter of public interest. My object really was that every chance of disunion or 'heckling' should be eliminated from the Kingstown meeting. I observe that Mr Long and his friends think that I should have created a disturbance. Well, I think better of my Party than to take such lessons from even its leaders.

At that meeting Mr Long was not quite candid. He told us what he had done for Wicklow Harbour—a matter of spending some thousands of pounds to repair the former blunders of an Irish Government Department, and he talked of the Belmullet Railway. But he passed over, and he has carefully avoided in his subsequent meetings, the more important matter of the £3,000,000 per annum by which admittedly Ireland was over-taxed ten years ago, a sum that has increased substantially in the interval. Why not state that he considered this a rank injustice to Ireland? Instead, at the Kingstown meeting and since then, he has simply said 'it is a subject for investigation.' The subject has been investigated, and a verdict formed by a jury not selected for partiality to this country.

Had Mr Long taken my questions and answered them straightforwardly, which he has not done up to this, he possibly would have induced a large number of Unionists who are doubtful at the present moment, to vote in his favour. These questions were honestly meant, and should have received explicit answers. They dealt with matters that trouble betimes the conscience of the Irish Unionist who asks himself whether his politics are for or against the best material interests of the country. They referred mainly to the excessive cost and the inefficiency of the Irish administration. Surely we are all concerned with these matters, and we are entitled to know where stands the representative of South Dublin in regard to them. It is not my fault if Mr Long and the Unionist Press agree between them that ignoring these questions will get rid of the feeling that is behind them in the minds of thousands.

I refrain, for the good of the Unionist cause, from criticising Mr Long's pronouncements, but let me say that I believe if he does not even now abandon his claim that South Dublin should take him on trust merely as an Englishman and a Unionist, he will be beaten at the poll. Let him, before Friday, give a straightforward answer to my questions, or it will be taken that he and his friends are unable to do so.

Yours faithfully, A. S. Findlater.

PS Talking of the Town Tenants' question: it is interesting to find Mr Long speaking soft words of sympathy to the holders of terminable leases in South Dublin while his active election agent, Mr Seddall, solicitor, is busily engaged in whipping up the South Dublin voters who possess the franchise as lessors and who, after the manner of their kind, live in England.

ALEX. FINDLATER & CO., LTD., DUBLIN.

SCOTCH
(Highland, Islay, and Lowland)
WHISKIES.

Our firm's long connection with Scotland has enabled us to supply these wonderful Whiskies in a way no other Irish firm can approach:—

FINDLATER'S

Finest Liqueur
(10 YEARS OLD),
26/6 per Gal.; 53/- per Doz.

Cream of Scotland,
25/6 per Gal.; 51/- per Doz.

Barley Bree,
22/6 per Gal.; 45/- per Doz.

Highland Dew,
20/6 per Gal.; 41/- per Doz.

Long John, Dew of Ben Nevis,
20/6 per Gal.; 41/- per Doz.

Islay Malt,
18/6 per Gal.; 37/- per Doz.

Scotch Malt,
16/6 per Gal.; 33/- per Doz

SCOTCH HIGHLAND DEW
20s. 6d. per Gal.
41s. per Doz.

CANADIAN WHISKEY.

	s.	d.
Canadian Club—Gold Capsule	49	0

RUM.

	Imperial Gal. s.	d.	Per Doz. s.	d.
Jamaica, very fine—Pine Apple flavour	18	6	37	0
Demerara	16	6	33	0

GIN.

	s.	d.	s.	d.
London	14	6	29	0
London Old Tom (sweetened)	16	6	33	0
Plymouth	16	6	33	0

GENEVA.

	s.	d.	s.	d.
Hollands	16	6	33	0
Hollands (De Kuyper's)	—		30	0

BRANDY.

For centuries Brandy was considered to be the pre-eminent spirit—in fact, the *Eau-de-Vie* it was popularly named. It maintained this position against all attacks until the destruction of the vines in the Charente by the phylloxera some ten years ago. So dreadful were the ravages of these insects that within an incredibly short space of time whole vineyards were laid waste, and, to make matters worse, it was the best vineyards that suffered most. Over thousands of acres, where once there was nothing but smiling vineyards, there is now not a vine to be seen! Not in our time, certainly—perhaps never—will Charente produce the Brandy that made it famous. *Sic transit gloria mundi.* In other countries and other parts of France attempts have been made to distil fine Brandy, but none has yet been able to compare with the old Cognac.

Fortunately we possess a considerable stock of the finest quality which we imported before the vine plague visited France; and as the taste for Brandy has largely given way to that for whiskey, we can with confidence rely on our ability to supply our customers for many years with genuine Charente Brandy of as fine quality as was ever exported from that district.

		Per Gallon. s.	d.		Per Doz. s.	d.
White Wrapper	Good Cognac	24	6		49	0
Yellow Wrapper	Old Pale Cognac	28	6		57	0
Pink Wrapper	**Choicest Old Pale Cognac, 14 Years Old**	33	6		67	0
Blue Wrapper	Findlater's "Liqueur" 15 ,,	36	6		73	0
Green Wrapper	Findlater's "Curious Old" 20 ,,	42	6	Light	85	0
Red Wrapper	Findlater's "Eau d'Or" 25 ,,	48	6	Brown	97	0

FOREIGN LIQUEURS.

	Per Bot. s.	d.	Half Bot. s.	d.
Benedictine	7	6	3	10
Benedictine Bijou Bottles	0	9	—	
Maraschino di Zara—Luxardo's	4	3	2	3
Curaçoa, White, Orange, and Dry	5	6	2	9
Curaçoa, White, Stibbe's Triple Sec.	5	6	2	9
Noyeau, White and Pink	7	0	3	9
Cherry Brandy, Heering's Copenhagen	3	9	2	3
Kummel	4	3	—	
Grand Chartreuse, green (from Monastery)	10	0	5	3
Grand Chartreuse, yellow (from Monastery) ...	8	6	4	6
Liqueur d'Or	7	0	4	3
Trappistine, green	8	3	4	6
Monastine	7	9	4	3
Lerina	7	3	4	0
Angostura Bitters	—		3	0
Apricot Brandy	6	6	—	
Peach Brandy	6	6	—	
Vermouth	3	3	—	

BRITISH LIQUEURS, &c.

	Per Gal. s.	d.	Per Doz. s.	d.
Ginger Liqueur	18	0	36	0
Grant's Cherry Brandy (Sportman's)	—		42	0
Grant's Cherry Brandy (Queen's)	—		36	0
Cherry Whiskey	—		42	0
Raspberry Cordial	18	0	36	0
Raspberry Vinegar	10	0	20	0
Ginger Wine	—		14	0
Ginger Wine, rich	—		24	0
Orange Wine	—		18	0
Orange Brandy	—		48	0
Ginger Brandy	—		42	0
Orange Bitters	—		36	0
Peach Bitters (half bottles)	—		18	0
Quinine Wine	—		27	0
Sloe Gin	—		36	0

Send to ALEX. FINDLATER & CO., LTD., for FULL DESCRIPTIVE ILLUSTRATED PRICE LIST, containing attractive Pictorial articles on

WINE AND THE WINE COUNTRIES,

including a Fine Series of Views of Oporto.

35

1903—Inflation adjusted, whiskey is about the same price as today, gin cheaper and liqueurs a bit dearer. A shilling in 1903 = £4 to-day.

25 January 1906 *Irish Independent*

All other topics relating to the elections, however, are dwarfed in interest by the controversy which Mr Long's candidature for South Dublin has provoked. Indeed, a straight answer to a plain question is the last thing that is expected from him. Mr Findlater's exposure of Mr Long's hedging and doubling is damning in its completeness. Decidedly Mr Long is not a man to be taken on trust.

His explanation of his reasons for abolishing the extra fees for the teaching of Irish in the National schools, too, was as disingenuous as anything of which he is accused by Mr Findlater. Mr Long was in quite a merry mood last night over what he chose to regard as the complete discomfiture of the Irish Reform Association. He may possibly find that he has been a little previous in his exultation.

25 January 1906 *Evening Telegraph*

Last night Mr Long, at his Dalkey meeting, referred to South Dublin as 'South Bristol'. It was a slip of the tongue, to be sure, but as a straw shows how the wind blows, it is a most illuminating flashlight on the mental attitude of the man towards Ireland and Irish matters. Mr Long is not only a stranger in South Dublin personally; he is a stranger politically. He told Mr Adam Findlater as we find from that gentleman's excellent letter published this morning, that he did not understand the question of Town Tenants 'until he came to Ireland,' and that he now 'quite saw that, whatever the merits might be in England, Ireland had a very much stronger case.' This is the gentleman who has asked the electors of South Dublin to take him on trust!

THE CANDOUR OF MR LONG

'I am not chairman of a brewery company or anything like that.'–Mr Long, Kingstown, January 22, 1905.

'I am chairman of the Bath Brewery and receive my fees as such. I believe the statement as to the tied houses (that 90 such houses are in the possession of the Bath Brewery) to be correct.'–Mr Long, in the House of Commons on June 20, 1900.

Friday

26 January 1906 *The Irish People*

The useful intervention of Mr Adam Findlater and Mr Lindsay Crawford in resenting the self-degradation of Irish Unionists who are crawling to the feet of Mr Walter Long to beseech him to become their leader, are a pleasant reminder how much ground has been travelled since a few months ago.

Monday

29 January 1906 *Freeman's Journal*

MR LONG ELECTED

The result of the poll for South Dublin was declared in the Courthouse, Kingstown, shortly after one o'clock on Saturday. The counting took place in the Town Hall. It commenced at half-past eleven, and occupied about an hour and a half. For a considerable time before the figures were announced a large crowd had assembled in the

ALEX. FINDLATER & CO., LTD., DUBLIN.

Is Tea Like Whiskey?

One wouldn't think so. For silliness the question seems above the average. But there's just one resemblance all the same—the *common kinds* of both are bad for you. Common whiskey hurts—you admit it. In smaller degree common tea does harm too, but this time you don't realise it. The tea that hurts the nerves, that damages digestion (though something else gets blamed), is the sort that brews these strong, bitter, black infusions (see it before the milk and sugar are added). The difference between common tea and "**Keemun Congou**" China Tea is just the difference between your doctor's condemnation and recommendation. They all advise Findlater's "Keemun Congou," because it is real tea—good tea. It is a choice *China* brand, which means tea with its *native* soothing and healthful properties, with its native delicate taste—without an atom of foreign hurtfulness in it. The tonic effects of **Findlater's "Keemun Congou"** China Tea compete with its fragrance as a beverage. Its subtle aroma charms the palate, while its quality soothes the nerves. All the richness of the old *home* soil of the tea plant is embodied in Findlater's "Keemun Congou." Among infusions it ranks as exquisite. Messrs. Alex. Findlater and Co. import and sell it at 3/-, 2/6, and 2/- per lb. Try it. It has

A FLAVOUR REMEMBERED.

FINDLATER'S

KEEMUN CONGOU

CHINA TEA,

3/-, 2/6, and 2/- per Lb.

26

1908— Findlater's China Tea 'without an atom of foreign hurtfulness in it'!

street outside, and the result was awaited with intense interest. Before the actual result was announced it became known that Mr Long had received a big majority of the votes, and the anxiety of the people manifested itself in a desire to learn the exact figures. When the news reached the crowd of the return of Mr Long there was cheering and counter-cheering. A large number also assembled in the Courthouse, and awaited the declaration of the poll there for a considerable time. Among those who were present at the counting of the votes, and who rendered valuable assistance to Mr Hazleton in his candidature were Mr William Redmond, MP; Mr Redmond, jun.; Mr J. M. McDowell, solicitor*; Mr T. M. Kettle, and Mr Sheehy-Skeffington.†

The High Sheriff announced the result as follows:

Mr LONG (C.) 5,269 Mr HAZLETON (N.) 3,926

Majority for Mr Long 1,343

The announcement of the result was received with cheers and boos. Mr Hazleton, speaking from an outside car, said: We have won a moral victory (cheers)–and I am not discouraged (cheers). I say that even if we were beaten by a greater majority than 1,343, we would not be discouraged here today. We know that it is due to the neglect of registration, and that there is no change in the opinions of the people of South Dublin.

Mr William Redmond, MP, who was loudly cheered, said–We can afford to discount the result of this election, because we know perfectly well that the votes cast do not represent the majority of the people of South Dublin (cheers). I was yesterday in the Rathmines Town Hall, and saw the people who were coming to vote, and I can upon my word of honour declare that numbers of the young men could not possibly have been twenty-one years of age, and during the last hour the Town Hall was like a railway station, because of the hundreds of men from across the channel who came up with their trunks and baggage to vote for Mr Long. There is no doubt we are partly to blame ourselves, because we neglected the register. We will never do that again (cheers), and we will do what Sir Thomas Esmonde did when he was a member for South Dublin. We will win this constituency by 2,000 votes for the National cause (cheers). I don't know what the Liberal Government is going to do, but if they are true to their word the Liberal Government must alter the registration law and give every honest man a vote (cheers). . . .

We beat them in Belfast (cheers for Devlin); we beat them in Stephen's Green (cheers), we beat them all over Ireland (cheers), we have beaten them in England, and if we lost one seat here today, I say it will not be long until we have Home Rule for our country (cheers). Some said this was a fight about religion. It was no such thing

* Grandfather of Michael McDowell, Attorney General at the time of going to press.

† William Redmond was the party leader's brother. With the rank of Major, he was killed at Messines in 1917. Francis Sheehy Skeffington was assassinated in Portobello Barracks in 1916 by a demented British officer named Bowen-Colthurst. Skeffington's brother-in-law Tom Kettle was called to the Bar in 1905. In 1906 he was elected to Westminster via a by-election in East Tyrone with the paper-thin majority of sixteen. He was re-elected in 1910 with a greatly increased majority of 118. In 1909 he became Professor of Economics in the National University. In the same year he married Mary Sheehy. Tom Kettle was killed by a sniper's bullet at Ginchy in France on 8 September.

DUBLIN HORSE SHOW ANNUAL, 1907.

FINDLATER'S SPECIALITY

John Jameson & Son's

Alex. Findlater & Co. are the Largest Holders of any Irish Firm of John Jameson & Son's Famous Old Dublin Whiskey.

One of the many Chambers in Findlater's Bonded Stores, showing John Jameson & Son's Fine Old Dublin Whiskey Mellowing and Maturing in the Original Casks.

THE NEWSPAPER PRESS OF DUBLIN ARE FOR ONCE UNANIMOUS!

The Irish Times says:—A unique specimen of really fine Dublin Whiskey which has attained first place among high-class stimulants by reason of its rare flavour, delicate tone, and great age.

The Freeman's Journal says:—This Old Dublin Whiskey ranks amongst the finest products of the old Dublin pot-still process that it is possible to obtain, and it has acquired the maturity and mellowness which long storage in wood before being bottled can alone confer. It is in this maturing stage that the œnanthic and other æthers which the spirit contains are developed, and these æthers are all-important, as to them the liquor owes its distinctive character and fragrance. A bottle of Findlater's fine whiskey when uncorked gives forth an aroma and bouquet which is an important evidence that all the grain products contained in the whiskey have undergone decomposition, and that their elements have been rearranged into fresh combinations of a kind analogous to those vinous æthers which are among the most exhilarating and perfect of all stimulants.

The Daily Express says:—Medical science and the taste of the present day public have alike chosen Old Dublin Whiskey of known excellence and purity, and without admixture, such as the specially selected whiskeys bottled by the well-known firm of Mr. Alex. Findlater & Co., Dublin.

The Irish Daily Independent says:—This whiskey is one of the finest products of the Dublin pot stills that it is possible to secure, and it is distilled from the choicest home-grown barley malt, potable water, possessing special powers for dissolving vegetable matter and retaining vegetable aromas.

The Dublin Evening Mail says:—This whiskey is produced in the old pot stills of Dublin, from a mash of the finest barley malt, and is then stored for long periods in sherry casks to be matured by time alone, the only method by which the pungent product of the stills is converted into the fragrant and wholesome liquid so dear to the Celtic race.

The Evening Telegraph says:—To this whiskey Shakespeare might fitly have applied his famous line: "A rarer spirit ne'er did steer humanity"

The Evening Herald says:—This whiskey, after distillation, is stored in Messrs. Alexander Findlater & Company's extensive bonded stores, where it remains for six years, undergoing maturation by age only. The firm is thus, from facts within its own knowledge, able to absolutely guarantee the purity, quality, and age of this popular Dublin Whiskey.

1907—The large casks in front are waiting to be trundled into the duty-paid sector of the cellar (The Whiskey House)

> (cheers). All we want is fair play for all. We want no ascendancy of Protestant or Catholic (cheers).
>
> At this stage a van belonging to the firm of Findlater and Co. passed through the crowd.
>
> Mr Redmond–You might as well give a cheer for old Findlater now (loud cheers). I am glad that this election has shown that there are plenty of liberal-minded Protestants—men like Mr Crosbie and Mr Crawford and Mr Findlater (cheers). It has shown that the day is soon coming when, with God's help, we will all be united for freedom and fair play in Ireland (cheers). I say that Richard Hazleton (loud cheers) has fought a noble battle. He is entitled to the thanks of all Ireland for the struggle he has made (loud cheers).*

Long's biographer tells us that he did not stay long in the hectic atmosphere of Irish politics, but soon retreated; 'On 2 February 1908 Long resigned as chairman of the Irish Unionist Party and began actively searching for a seat in the London area from which he could safely wage the fight for the union while playing his part in Westminster politics. Long knew that South County Dublin was a marginal seat for the unionists. If he stood for it again there was a grave risk he would be beaten. Thus, in early June, after much backroom negotiation, Long was adopted as a candidate for the Strand, a safe London seat. He wrote immediately to the South Dublin association informing its members of the decision'.[20] In his letter of resignation Long declared that he was not of course abandoning his unionist principles.

A few years later John Redmond† was invited into the Findlater boardroom after he unveiled the monument in Sackville Street erected in honour of Charles Stewart Parnell on 1 October 1911. The event was attended by a truly enormous crowd from all over Ireland. After a cheerful lunch Willie (since Adam's death ten months before, managing director of the company) invited Redmond to sign his name on the chair on which he sat, which he did. The chair, with his somewhat unsteady initials, remains with us to this day. One wonders if Willie, reading the signs, was moving away from Adam's liberal unionism to a more constitutional nationalist position. The Home Rule Act for which Redmond's constitutional Irish Parliamentary Party had struggled for so long eventually received the Royal Assent in September 1914—and was immediately suspended for the duration of the First World War.

Findlater's profits

While these political excitements were going on, Adam was managing director of a major Irish company whose profits put it in the front rank. However, progress over the few years after the flotation was to come under heavy scrutiny

* In the election as a whole, the Liberal-Unionists and the Conservatives suffered a disastrous defeat, losing 215 seats. They returned to the House with a mere 157 seats against a Liberal, Labour, and Irish nationalist total of 513. Long's triumph in Dublin South was the only non-university unionist victory in Ireland outside Ulster. Hazleton became MP for North Galway.

† John Redmond (1856-1918) was leader of the Irish Parliamentary Party 1900-1918.

ALEX. FINDLATER & CO., LTD., DUBLIN.

DO YOU WANT
AN EXTRA CHOICE
BOTTLE OF PORT
FOR THE
XMAS SEASON?

Choice Old Crusted

VINTAGE, 1887.

14 YEARS IN BOTTLE.

50/- per Dozen.

One of the Finest Vintages
of the Century.

The Public are, for various reasons, using fresh Bottled Wines.
But to have a Bottle of Port in perfection
for the Connoisseur,
AGE IN BOTTLE IS A GREAT DESIDERATUM.

ALEX. FINDLATER & CO., LTD.

70

1901—Vintage port for Christmas—'Age in bottle is a great desideratum'!

Jameson floats delivering casks of whiskey to Findlater's bonded warehouse under the tenements in Findlater Place.

by the *Irish Investor's Guardian,* a publication that didn't mince words if it felt all was not going well. In 1902 everything seemed fine:

> The directors can be fairly congratulated on the successful results for the past year's operations. The prospectus profits averaged £11,468 a year [£0.92m] for three years, and the year before floating were £10,087 [£0.80m]. In 1900 the trading amounted to £9,552 [£0.76], in 1901 to £9,121 [£0.73m]; and for the year ended 28 February last to £10,665 [£0.85m]. Only the £65,000 in 4 per cent Debenture Stock and £55,000 in 5 per cent Cumulative Preference Stock are in the hands of the public, while the vendors hold all the Ordinary Shares. The general conditions of trading have been, admittedly, unfavourable since the company was floated. When the Shareholders consider the difficulty of making profits just now, and the unfavourable trading results of most other kindred concerns during the past few years, they will admit the above record of Alexander Findlater & Company is both satisfactory and encouraging.[21]

In 1904 profits were reported at £9,131 [£0.73m], and the *Investors' Guardian* comments:

> There has been a considerable increase in the debts due to the company and in the stocks held, owing to a large increase in the volume of trade, and the new departments added, due to larger premises accommodation. The development of the business has been continuous for years past, but it is evident from the large sum due that the capital issued is insufficient, seeing that so much has had to be spent on new buildings which the company had to undertake.

These sound like warning signs.

In 1905 a small decrease in profits is reported, to £9,017, and an issue of £20,000 [£1.6m] in 5 per cent second debenture stock was made to replace the working capital that had been depleted by the additions and rebuilding since the

ALEX. FINDLATER & CO. LTD., DUBLIN.

IRISH OATMEAL

is far superior in every way to that made in America, the home-grown oat being larger, better developed, and more succulent and nourishing than the dried-up American grain.

FINDLATER'S IRISH OATMEAL.

Findlater's Finest Quality Pinhead, per 5 lb. linen bag, **1/-**

" Finest Flake, per stone, **2/4**

" " Pinhead, " **2/4**

ALEX. FINDLATER & CO., Ltd.

39

1905—1s per 5lb in today's money is equivalent to £1.64 per kilo. In 2000 Odlum's oatmeal sold at 84p per kilo.

company had been floated. The paper commented hopefully:

> The company's operations now cover every principal district in and around Dublin, and a largely increased trade has been done. The prevailing stagnation of trade, which is now believed to be passing away, should have a good effect on the trade and profits of this company.

However

> By the regrettable death of Sir Henry Cochrane, Bart, DL, JP, the company lost an able and sound business man, but it is satisfactory to find his son, Sir Ernest Cecil Cochrane, Bart, has been co-opted in his place.
>
> The company has a valuable business which is worked energetically, and now that the capital expenditure has practically been closed, we look forward to seeing the net profit in future reflect volume of trade that has followed the extensions and increased facilities provided for the firm's many and ever growing clientele.

Sir Henry was a true friend to Findlaters. The second debenture stock was in fact subscribed for in its entirety by Cantrell & Cochrane* Ltd, 'Aerated and Mineral Water Manufacturers in Dublin, Belfast, London and Glasgow.' Sir Henry, one of the great entrepreneurs of the 19th century, once related that he started his career as a 'doffer' in Chartres Mills on the Falls Road at 7s a week, and made his entry into Dublin as a barman at half-a-sovereign weekly with a publican named James Weir, who kept the Scotch House, the tavern on Burgh Quay, which he leased from Alexander from 1840.

The results for 1906, 1907 and 1908 were around the £10,000 mark [£800,000], and all was well. But the *Investor's Guardian* of July 1909 was severe about that year's results: 'There is no gainsaying the fact that the results . . . were in every respect unfavourable in the extreme'. Profits had fallen to £5,879 [£0.47m] before provisions. The directors commented that they 'regret that owing to the depression in the Trade during the past year, the exceptional losses in some departments of the business and in connection with undertakings which have in the past been the means of largely increasing the Company's output, the results . . . have not been satisfactory.' The directors took the necessary action and reduced the value of the ordinary capital, which was held entirely by the family, from £55,000 to £25,000. This enabled them to reduce the goodwill by £10,000.

The *Investor's Guardian* dealt with the subject at length in its February 1910 issue.

> To write down the Ordinary Capital [was necessary] to cover the heavy depreciation losses that accrued in con-

* Cantrell & Cochrane was founded in 1852 by Dr Thomas K. Cantrell to market their unique Irish soda water which rivalled natural sparkling waters such as Appollinaris. In 1868 Alderman Henry Cochrane of Dublin joined Dr Cantrell and from then the company never looked back. Cantrell retired in 1884 and Henry Cochrane became head of a business which is still a major force in the Irish drinks industry.

The Royal Hotel, Bray

> nection with undertakings which, admittedly, in the past increased the company's turnover, but which, in recent years, had become a serious and increasing burden on the entire business, owing to the exceptional wave of depression in the trade, and particularly in the Hotel extension business, which had been entered on at a time when these properties were considered in the trade a more or less desirable investment. [The hotels referred to were the St Lawrence in Howth and the Royal Hotels in Bray and Howth.] We always considered the Hotel extensions injudicious and risky at the best of times, but the conditions that have overtaken the trade since then rendered these investments, to a large extent, a total loss to the company, and it is to meet and cover the deficiency that has arisen that the Board now find themselves obliged to make good, by writing down. After the unfortunate and bitter experiences accruing from these enterprises, we doubt not the board will, in the future, stick to the legitimate business of the company . . .

What the journalist was not saying, but could well have had in mind, was that Adam was diversifying and employing his energies on too broad a front. He was chairman of two quoted theatres, one in Dublin and one in Belfast, he was a prominent voice in southern unionism and he was primarily the full time managing director of a quoted company. He was also chairman of the ailing Dublin City Distillery Co. Ltd.

John and Adam had entered the distilling business in 1888 when they joined a consortium of English spirit merchants to purchase the Banagher Distillery Co. Ltd which was in receivership. The new company had a capital of £200,000 [£15.6m]. After two years in business the directors were able to report that the whole of last season's output had been sold and that they had present orders which would absorb a large portion of their manufacture for the coming season. They declared a profit of £9,201 [£700,000] and, with a lack of prudence, paid a dividend of 8 per cent on the ordinary capital, a payout of 57 per cent of profits.

Flush with this initial success they bought the defunct sugar refinery at 111 Great Brunswick Street, now Pearse Street, not far from the Grand Canal Docks. The sugar refinery had been built by two Dublin merchants, Thomas Bewley and Henry Moss, in about 1860, to recapture their extensive sugar business which had ceased almost altogether after the introduction of refined crushed sugar from Britain. Adam turned a profit of £5,000 [almost £400,000] on the purchase and resale of the refinery and obviously impressed his father with his business prowess. The formidable premises were converted into a distillery and the company renamed the Dublin City and Banagher Distilleries Ltd.

However, the early promise was not to develop. Whiskey needs to be matured in bond for several years before it is marketable. The English trade investors had taken up their initial commitments but the established Dublin distillers, mainly Powers, Jamesons and Roes, had defended their strong position in the Irish market. Thus the new entrant had to finance the build-up of large stocks of maturing whiskey. This was to be their eventual downfall. The attraction from Findlaters' point of view was a cheaper source for their popular house brands. In 1891 Findlaters held 28,676 gallons of Banagher whiskey at an under bond cost of 3s a gallon in comparison to 43,000 gallons of Jameson at 4s 11d a gallon. Findlaters' total value of whiskey in bond at 28 February 1891 was £20,284 [over £1.5m] and the total bond stock, including wines, amounted to £30,440 [£2.3m].

The Dublin City Distillery had a short and chequered career; the *Freeman's Journal* of 20 April 1909 reported that its original shareholders were 'an English set of spirit merchants who had little concern for the business relations with the Dublin mercantile world, and its failure was due in part to that, and in a measure to the slump the sale of Irish whiskey suffered in the English market.'

The Dublin City Distillery

The family story is that Adam was called in to help sort out the distillery and fared badly, the only thing he salvaged being the roll-top desk that I have to this day. The desk passed to me from my father with the moral 'never back a cheque', which in today's language must mean never give a personal guarantee. However the ledgers make it clear that John and Adam were financially involved from 1888 and by 1892 to the extent of £9,696 [£750,000].

The Banagher Distillery

The distillery went into liquidation

in 1905 when they defaulted on the payment of interest on the mortgage debentures secured on the assets of the company including the stocks of whiskey. There was a large crop of law suits. In 1909 the bankruptcy court put it up for auction and it was bought by Mr Gallagher, the Belfast tobacco manufacturer, for £20,000 [£1.46m]. As a distillery it was doomed and from 1914, and for the most of the century, the site was occupied by the Hammond Lane Foundry.

In contrast to his grand-uncle Alexander, whose great legacies had passed into history, these diversifications were a drain on Adam's resources, and left his estate in poor shape when he died in 1911 at the early age of fifty-six. The same was to happen some fifty years later, during the last years of my father's custodianship of the company. The moral must be 'stick to the knitting!' or 'diversify at your peril'. Today, as we enter the 21st century, we are in but one trade—wine—and with no ancillary activities.

Motoring

By 1906 there were just over 2,000 motor cars registered in Ireland, of which 269 were based in Dublin. One of these was Adam's new Stanley steam car, in which he took the intrepid reporter of the *Evening Herald* for a spin around the branches just before Christmas of that year.[22] They set off from Sackville Street: 'the day was ideal, and with customary businesslike and clockwork regularity Mr Findlater had the car outside the great concern in O'Connell Street just at the moment arranged. There was no waiting about while some strong man "wound up" the car. We got in, took our seats, and directly we were careering off in the direction of Blackrock'.

In these days of highly accurate and cheap wrist-watches, it is difficult to imagine the service that Findlaters famous clocks supplied to sleepy suburbs. The *Evening Herald* reporter was of course aware of their usefulness: 'A fine public clock, a delightfully clean, smart frontage, and an air of prosperity are the characteristics of all the Findlater branches. When you deal with Mr Findlater, or whether you do not, you have a constant bonus from him in the shape of the correct time, and this is a distinct boon in some of the suburbs, where policemen are scarce and watches much the same.'*

They dashed through the Blackrock shop and then roared off to Kingstown, where the reporter duly admired the shop's bustle. Then off to Dalkey, Foxrock, Dundrum, Rathmines and Baggot Street.

> We got back in record time to O'Connell Street, where the big parent establishment was increasingly active. Verily, this 'A1' business is a monster one, and that it is conducted on the right lines is obvious to the least intelligent member of the community. The best of everything, the goods well set out in clean, attractive, and well-maintained shops, and a keen desire to give general satisfaction, are the objects which are before the Messrs Findlater, all of whom work hard and set the example of industry and cheeriness to those around them. Mr Adam S. Findlater, MA, JP, who directs the great

* For further information see also J. Curtis *Times, Chimes and Charms of Dublin A unique guide to Dublin and its clocks* Dublin: Verge Books 1992 pp 20, 96

Adam is in the centre looking towards the camera with his son Seaton most likely in the driving seat. His car is probably a 1906 Daimler.

> enterprise, is a firm believer that the inert life is bad. He avails of all good opportunities and he often, with a smile of satisfaction, quotes the following:
>
> Work and the world works with you
> Sit down and you sit alone.

Adam's son Seaton clearly inherited his father's dashing motoring style. In 1904 (when there were only 140 cars in the whole of the city and county of Dublin) he was before the court at the Bray Petty Sessions for having failed to stop his motor car when motioned to do so; and also for not having his licence with him. The complainant said that on the occasion in question he raised his hand for Mr Findlater to stop. He did not stop then, but pulled up for petrol, where the complainant asked him why he did not stop, and he said:

> 'You saw my identification number. I did not think it necessary'.
>
> The defendant said that he was proceeding slowly, and thought the constable was merely saluting him; and as he was pulling up for petrol he did not think that the constable's motion was for the purpose of making him stop. The constable, on being asked why he wanted the defendant to stop replied: 'To inspect his licence'. The Court imposed a fine of 2s 6d and costs for not having his licence and £5 and costs for not stopping when motioned to do so by the constable. The defendant said he would pay the fine for being without his licence, but would appeal against the other. [£365 plus costs in 2000].[23]

Nelson's Pillar

To the traders of Upper Sackville Street, among whom Findlaters was predominant, Nelson's Pillar was a grievance. The enormous base of the column split the street in two, making it difficult for traffic to flow north, and also to flow east-

ALEX. FINDLATER & CO., LTD., DUBLIN.

THE SALAD SEASON.

SOME FACTS ABOUT

Findlater's Pure Olive Oil,

WHICH IS IMPORTED DIRECT FROM LEGHORN.

Guaranteed Absolutely Pure, no admixture of Cotton Seed Oils. It Preserves all the Full Flavours of the Olives. . . .

As a Remedial Agent Findlater's Olive Oil has few Equals and no Superiors.

Within its amber recesses lies stored a wealth of healing that produces vigour and elasticity of the body, aids digestion, strengthens the nerves, promotes suppleness, and helps the brain to attain the best possible development. It has been observed for centuries that those who treat Olive Oil as a common article of food and use it as such are generally healthier and stronger than those who do not.

The Housewife has yet to learn that there are many ways of using the Oil besides in Salads.

It may be used with good effect as a substitute for butter in compounding the ordinary brown or white sauce. A tea-spoonful of oil added to every quart of split pea, bean, potato, or other soup, lacking fat, just before taking up, greatly increases its richness as well as flavour.

As a Frying Medium it has no Equal, and is not Extravagant,

As a little goes a great way. Fish or game that is to be boiled should be brushed over first with a little of the oil.

In all Invalid Cooking, Findlater's Olive Oil should be used in place of Butter.

A child soon learns to prefer it on its bread, and should be encouraged to eat all it likes. Any cold meat that is to be recooked is improved by having a little oil poured over it at least an hour before heating.

FINDLATER'S PURE OLIVE OIL

Per Large Bottle	...	...	**1s. 11d.**
,, Half Bottle	...	...	**1s. 1d.**
,, Quarter Bottle	...	...	**0s. 7d.**

27

1908—It has taken over a hundred years to get the nation to appreciate the health qualities of pure olive oil. A large bottle cost the 2000 equivalent of £7.50.

west (say from Amiens Street station to the law courts). The busier the streets got, especially once the trams began to use the pillar as a terminus, the more significant an obstruction it became.

Eventually the IRA blew up the top half of the pillar on the night of 7 March 1966, leaving the Army to complete the destruction. Thus was achieved something that the traders of Upper O'Connell Street, led by Adam and then by his brother Willie, had sought for seventy-five years.

In 1891 Adam, with book publisher Henry J. Gill, a fellow-trader in O'Connell Street, and another, promoted a private bill to remove the pillar from its position just north of the GPO and to place it less obstructively at the top of Sackville Street.

T. D. Sullivan, the MP for College Green, Dublin, during the second reading the Bill on 13 February 1891, explained that

> the simple object of the Bill is to remove an obstruction from the middle of Sackville Street, and re-erect it at one end of the street. At present the pillar intersects four thoroughfares, and prevents free communication from Earl Street to Henry Street. The O'Connell Monument is a large and handsome erection, but if placed where Nelson's Pillar is, it would undoubtedly be an obstruction. The Bill proposes to move the pillar further down the street, where it will be no obstruction, and provision is contained in the measure for the re-erection of the monument within one month after it has been taken down. This will improve the City of Dublin, and it would be a hard thing if the House of Commons, in such a local matter should interfere with the carrying out of a reform which has been long desired in the ancient capital of Ireland.[24]

Tim Healy, representing Longford North, took up this latter point:

> Although I am in favour of the Bill I sincerely hope that the House will reject it, for if an argument in favour of Home Rule is wanted it would be found in the refusal of the House to allow this matter to be inquired into by one of its own Committees.

He then went on with a more stirring thought:

> Monuments in a public street are a public nuisance, and I should be prepared to support a Bill not only for the removal of this monument but also for those to O'Connell, Father Mathew and Sir John Gray. If it is desired to commemorate the memory of the great dead the statues ought to be placed somewhere where they will not be in the way of the living.

The main opposition came from 'a little knot of Northern Representatives' who, Sullivan claimed, 'lose no opportunity of supporting everything that would tend to disfigure the City of Dublin and opposing everything that would beautify and improve it'. As we have seen nationalists voted for this postponement, pointing out that the imperial parliament was discussing an issue relating to a Dublin street on which Dublin opinion had not been asked. In his autobiography *Letters and Leaders of My Day* Tim Healy described the events of February 1891:

A farseeing contemporary cartoon anticipating the traffic chaos caused by the Parnell monument. *The Leprachaun* June 1908.

That day a Bill was promoted by a Dublin Conservative named Findlater to enable Nelson's Pillar to be removed from O'Connell Street, Dublin, as being an obstruction to the thoroughfare. The Government opposed it, but it was carried by a majority of five. Parnell strolled in as the bells rang. Knowing nothing of what was going on he voted with us. Finding that we had beaten the Government, he approached Justin McCarthy with a smile, saying, 'Allow me to congratulate you on the first great victory of your new Party!'[25]

Despite this victory, nothing actually happened, and Nelson remained secure in his place. However, Adam continued to concern himself with the welfare of O'Connell Street and on Friday 22 May 1908, in a letter to the *Freeman's Journal*, he vented his alarm over the siting of the monument commemorating Charles Stewart Parnell:

Dear Sir, It is with feelings of the utmost alarm that the residents of Upper Sackville Street view the position selected for the Parnell Statue, namely, the centre of the intersection of Sackville street and Britain street [now Parnell Street].

It was generally understood that the Parnell Statue would be placed in the position at present occupied by the Coffee Palace, where it would have formed a most useful resting place for those crossing the street.

If the Corporation adhere to their present decision the result will be, with the quick traffic from the Broadstone and Rutland Square, to make the place a most dangerous one, and to interfere greatly with the cross traffic along the two Great Britain Streets and across Sackville Street. The block which will ensue can be best illustrated by the separation caused by Nelson's Pillar as between Henry Street on the one side and Earl Street on the other. Undoubtedly the obstruction will not be as great as that at present existing at Nelson's Pillar, but still it will be very serious.

The proper position for the Parnell Statue is where the Coffee Palace now stands. I have been in communication with many of the residents in this neighbourhood, and, without exception, they agree with my views. I will be glad to hear from others who are of the same opinion, and who would be in favour of respectfully submitting the matter to the reconsideration of the Dublin Corporation and the Parnell Statue Committee.

Yours faithfully, A. S. Findlater.

The Corporation paid no attention. However, the campaign to move Nelson was not over. In 1931 Willie drafted a letter to the Minister of Local Government:

We, the undersigned, representing the Residents, Ratepayers and Shopkeepers in the

ALEX. FINDLATER & CO., LTD., DUBLIN.

The Bacon Cutters of the Past and Present Day.

In cutting under the Old System, the meat received a considerable amount of handling, which is most objectionable. Even when cut by experienced men, the rashers were uneven, and not thin enough These were distinct drawbacks.

Now, by means of our special machinery, the Bacon is sliced into rashers—all of exactly uniform thickness, and without bone. Each rasher can be shaved off as thin as a Bank note, or of any thickness desired. Handling is reduced to a minimum.

Notice the curious effect!—The Rotunda, though a hundred yards away, is reproduced in the window reflection.

PROVISIONS.

We have opened Provision Departments at our Head Offices, and at the Leinster Street, Rathmines, Howth, Sandymount, Blackrock, Dalkey, and Bray Branches.

We stock only the finest quality goods, and guarantee everything to be as described.

It is impossible to quote prices, as they are constantly changing with the fluctuation of the market. Latest quotations will be sent immediately on receipt of an enquiry. Amongst other goods we stock :—

Matterson's Hams & Bacon	Picnic Hams	New-laid Eggs	Finest Gloucester Cheese,
Shaw's Hams and Bacon	Limerick Hams	Matterson's Sausages	Cheddar, Gorgonzola,
Canadian Hams and Bacon	Jowls	Black and White Puddings	Gruyère, Stilton, & other
American Hams	Cleeve's Creamery Butter	Palethorpe's Sausages	varieties of Home and
Boiled Hams	Best Cool Butter	London Brawn	Colonial Cheese, &c., &c.
Spiced Hams	Cooking Butter		

SPECIALITIES:

"A.S.F." IRISH BACON AND HAMS, Specially Cured and Smoked for Ourselves.
CANADIAN PEA-FED BACON AND HAMS.

ALEX. FINDLATER & CO., Ltd.

The strategic move into provisions must have taken place during 1903 as there was no mention of the department at the staff conference in 1902. Departments were set up in each branch on the left hand side inside the door. We remained a force in that trade for the following 65 years.

North side of the City in and adjoining Upper O'Connell Street, and the citizens generally respectfully desire to say that for very many years the question of the removal of the Nelson Monument has occupied public attention, and in recent years, the desire for its removal has increased with the passage of time. We respectfully submit that the time is now opportune to carry out what has been so long agitating the public mind.

It is generally recognised that for upwards of forty years the effect of the retention of this obstruction in the heart of the chief street of the Metropolis has been to injure property of all kinds in the North side of the City. Anybody in middle life can bear testimony to the great damage to business and property that has taken place in the upper half of that thoroughfare, even in his own time; while nobody will deny that from the aesthetic point of view this monument destroys the beauty and harmony of what has often been described as one of the finest streets in Europe.

Forty years ago a Bill was passed through the British House of Commons endorsing the removal of the Monument, and the extension of Gloucester Street to O'Connell Street, but owing to the political situation then existing and the sentimental feeling against removing the pillar, the former project was never carried out. In recent years Gloucester Street has been extended and linked up with O'Connell Street, but the Pillar still remains.

The political or sentimental aspect of the problem is now removed and there is really no argument whatever for its retention any longer in the heart of our most beautiful street, while all the arguments point the other way. We therefore pray that the necessary steps will be taken without any further delay to carry out what has long been the desire of the overwhelming majority of the citizens.

O'Connell Street is the natural thoroughfare for the increased traffic which will result from the extensive building schemes which are being carried out in the northern part of the City from Glasnevin and Whitehall to Marino, and now that Gloucester Street could facilitate the traffic from the Northern area, Howth and Malahide, as was intended, the project is nullified by the non-removal of the Pillar.

The recent opening of the General Post Office has enormously increased traffic in this area, and is an added argument in favour of our request, otherwise the congestion at this particular point will reach a dead-lock as well as becoming a menace to life and limb.

We are Sir, Your Obedient Servants etc.

Later that year Dublin Corporation decided unanimously to remove Nelson's Pillar since 'the flower sellers and loungers as well as the ordinary crowds were always in danger of traffic',[26] but once again, nothing happened.

Letters to the Editor

Adam was a vigorous writer of 'Letters to the Editor', on a wide range of topics, from the decorations for royal visits to re-arming the RIC. He favoured, for instance, the widening of lower Grafton Street, so that the Bank of Ireland could be seen from Nassau Street, proposing: 'the removal of the high blank wall that shuts off the Provost's House from Grafton Street. It is an unsightly structure, a

ALEX. FINDLATER & CO., LTD., DUBLIN.

WE HAVE NOW COMPLETED ARRANGEMENTS WITH THE PRINCIPAL POULTRY BREEDERS THROUGHOUT IRELAND FOR OUR SUPPLY OF
TURKEYS AND GEESE.
ALL HAVE BEEN CAREFULLY SELECTED AND ARE OF EXCELLENT QUALITY.

Our Special Show

OF THESE BIRDS WILL BE HELD ON **MONDAY, DECEMBER 19th,** UP TO WHICH DATE WE ARE PREPARED TO BOOK ORDERS AT THE FOLLOWING PRICES:—

COCK TURKEYS.

10 lbs. ...... **1/-** per lb. 12 lbs....... **1/0½** per lb. 14 lbs. ...... **1/2** per lb. 16 lbs. ...... **1/2½** per lb.
18 lbs. .... **1/3** per lb.

SELECTED HEN TURKEYS

From 8 to 12 lbs. .... **11½d.** and **1/-** per lb.

GEESE.

6 lbs. and upwards .... **8d.** per lb.

TURKEYS AND GEESE ARE SOLD BY WEIGHT WHEN KILLED.

CLEANED AND TRUSSED **6d.** PER BIRD EXTRA

OUR CELEBRATED PORK SAUSAGES .... **8d.** per lb.

HUGON'S BEEF SUET—Block or Shredded .... per lb., **10½d.**; per ½ lb., **5½d.**

SPICED BEEF ROUNDS, only Finest Quality, weight from 5 lbs. upwards .... **9d.** per lb.

HAMS.

We have secured some of the Finest Limerick and American Hams. Full Selection on view 6th December.

	PER LB.		PER LB.
Matterson's Limerick, 10 lbs. to 12 lbs.	**1/3**	A. F. & Co., Ltd., 10 to 12 lbs.	**1/-**
Matterson's Limerick, 12 lbs to 14 lbs.	**1/2**	A. F. & Co., Ltd., 12 to 14 lbs.	**11½d**
O'Mara's Limerick, 10 lbs. to 12 lbs.	**1/3**	Unbranded, 9 lbs. to 11 lbs.	**1/-**
O'Mara's Limerick, 12 lbs to 13 lbs.	**1/2**	American, 10 lbs. to 12 lbs.	**1/-**
Denny's Limerick, 12 lbs. to 14 lbs.	**1/3**	York, 14 lbs. to 18 lbs.	**1/2**

Hams weighing not more than 10¾ lbs. can be forwarded per Parcels Post. They make a suitable present for friends in Great Britain and Continent.

CHEESE.

	PER. LB.		PER LB.
Stilton, Whole	**1/4**	Gorgonzola, Whole, about 14 lbs	**10½d**
Stilton, Cut	**1/6**	Gorgonzola, Cut	**1/-**
Cheddar, Cut	**11d.**	Roquefort	**1/6**
Loaf Cheddar, about 10 lbs.	**1/-**	Edam, red	**8d.**
Double Gloster	**1/-**	Gouda Cream, small	**9d.**

27

1910—Poultry and cheese were an extension of the provision departments and at Christmas time we developed an enormous trade in fresh turkeys. A shilling is equivalent to £3.75 in 2000.

veritable eyesore, and why it has been so long allowed to disfigure one of the most important thoroughfares of the city is inexplicable. A prison wall is all right in its own place, for it is appropriate to its purpose, but surely its place is not in Grafton Street . . . *(Freeman's Journal* 21 July 1904).

In 1903, ahead of a royal visit to Dublin he wrote on the subject of the city's decorations, revealing an intriguing insight into the organisation of the royal family's visit across the empire: 'Are you aware that these decorations I speak of follow Royalty from city to city, and from town to town, and I am sure most of the crowned heads of Europe (including our King and Queen), know every one of these decorations by heart.'[27]

On 18 December 1903 he was a member of a committee of regular railway users on the line between Dublin and Kingstown who proposed a Christmas gratuities fund to recognise the courtesy and attention they had received from the employees. 'It has been suggested that a small subscription from a large number, properly divided amongst the Guards, Ticket Collectors, and Porters, together with the Signal Men, Engine Drivers and Stokers, would be the best method to show this general appreciation.'

And in the same year he wrote a considerate letter to the Dublin *Evening Telegraph* concerning his employees' Christmas holidays, by way of a public announcement of the firm's opening hours over the Christmas holiday.

> Dear Sir, Recognising the pressure of the season on the workers in our various establishments, we have decided to grant an extra holiday, and to close from the Thursday evening, 24th inst., until the following Tuesday morning. The great majority of our assistants come from far away parts of the country, and the absence of a train service on the Sunday would prevent many being back to their duties in time on Monday morning, unless indeed they returned on the Saturday, and in so doing break up the 'welcome home party' all too soon. Under the circumstances we feel certain our friends and the public generally will heartily co-operate in the matter, and by purchasing sufficient supplies prior to Christmas enable us to grant this concession without inconvenience to themselves.
>
> Yours faithfully, Alex. Findlater and Co. Ltd.[28]

To which the staff replied:

> The Assistants of Alex. Findlater and Co., Sackville street, and Branches, take this opportunity of publicly thanking the directors for their thoughtful consideration in allowing them Monday the 28th inst., as an extra holiday. Were it not for this generous concession a visit to home and friends would be impracticable for many.

Adam was a shareholder in the railway, and had taken some interest in the affairs of the company. By 1909 the Dublin and South Eastern railway was making substantial losses, which they claimed was due to effective competition from William Martin Murphy's electric trams which had been re-organised in 1896. Adam rejected this reasoning.[29]

ALEX. FINDLATER & CO., LTD., DUBLIN

Revolution in House Cleaning

BY THE USE OF

THE VACUUM CLEANER.

Carpets do not need to be taken up. . . .
Curtains can be cleaned. . . . .
Every particle of dust abstracted from furniture. .
House Cleaning rendered a pleasure instead of a worry.

AT WORK.

Terms of Hire for	**One Day**	...	**5/-**
„ „ „	**Two Days**	...	**7/6**
„ „ „	**Three Days**	...	**10/6**

ALEX. FINDLATER & CO., LTD.,

DUBLIN and Neighbourhood.

27

1909—Powered by boy-power not electricity—this advertisement declared that housekeeping would be a pleasure instead of a worry! Rental charges about £20 a day in 2000 money.

ALEX FINDLATER & CO, LTD, DUBLIN.

HAVE YOU TRIED

FINDLATER'S

SELL THEM

. . AT . .

9d. per Dozen !!

NOTICE.

There being so much difficulty in handling Bananas when they are ripe, we strongly recommend our Customers to buy them when on the turn of ripening. A day or two in an even temperature will bring them to perfection.

ALEX. FINDLATER & CO., Ltd.

38

1905—Ripening plants came in very much later

> Dear Sir, The case put forward by Mr Pim for years past is that the unfortunate financial position of the Dublin and South Eastern Railway is principally caused by the loss of traffic brought about by the construction of the Electric Tram between Dublin and Kingstown.
>
> When the recent Bill was before Parliament the Secretary of the Company, in answer to the chairman of the Committee, stated that the annual loss resulting from the competition of the electric trams was at the rate of £25,000 [£1.8m] per annum . . . The directors of the company have not revealed the fact that although the tramway has diminished the passenger receipts, it has largely increased those from parcels, a traffic which has become of a most remunerative character, as the receipts the Wicklow Company derive from this traffic are practically net receipts, the collection and delivery being performed by the Tramway Company.
>
> The foregoing facts will be sufficient, I trust, to impress my fellow-shareholders of the importance of taking an interest in the management of their property at this critical stage, to decide whether, under the circumstances, new blood on the Board is required or not.
>
> I am, yours faithfully, A.S. Findlater.

While at Trinity in the 1870s, Adam had no doubt rowed and so had learned the late-Victorian lesson of the moral and social value of sport. He put some of these views in a letter[30] in which he attempted to calm ruffled feathers in the rowing world:

> I think it is very pitiful that there should be any conflict of interest between the old Metropolitan Regatta at Ringsend, known to us all and endeared to us by many pleasant recollections, and the University Regatta at Chapelizod.
>
> No doubt there is room for both, I would say that there is occasion for both. Every man who has rowed in a racing boat—who has learnt to catch his water quickly and feather his oar cleanly—knows well the difference between taking a boat through the usually lively but bumpy water at Ringsend, and through the dull placid stretch of the Liffey from Chapelizod to the weir. Here you have absolutely two sets of conditions . . . Rowing is more than a pastime, a sport, or way of ascertaining which one of a number of crews may be the best. It is a real educational influence, teaching lessons of self-restraint, self-denial, hard work, and co-ordinated effort such as no other form of physical training affords so fully. The man who breaks away from his fellows and, even under extreme pressure, indulges in some thing that may have the effect of stopping his boat by half a canvass is rightly regarded as a traitor. He knows as much, and the knowledge is a deterrent against such treachery . . . The Liffey can support two Regattas if their Committees work in harmony, friendship, and good-fellowship. It cannot, and will not, support one at all if the rivals continue their late policy of throat-cutting.
>
> Yours faithfully, A. Findlater.

The Commercial Travellers Association

As we have seen, Findlaters had a nation-wide wholesale business, mainly to the licensed trade, and key to its success was the now-forgotten men of the road, the

FINDLATER'S

HALLOW EVE!

The Children's Festival.

APPLES, GRAPES,

NUTS AND CRACKERS

BARMBRACKS

AND FRUIT CAKES,

Rich with Sultanas and Vostizza Currants,

1/- EACH, also 6d. & 2d.

The Best Quality and Size ever offered for their respective prices.

N.B.—In each of our Branches we are giving in one Barm Brack a

REAL GOLD RING.

BUY AT

FINDLATER'S, DUBLIN

Halloween fully identified with children, *Irish Independent* 30 October 1906 commercial travellers. These men often spent six months or more a year travelling the country seeking orders from small and large stores, promoting their brands by supplying samples to the retailers, and generally acting as the eyes and ears of the business in the country. Hotels had special rooms set aside for their accommodation, places where they could write up their orders, and generally sort out their samples.

The United Kingdom Commercial Travellers Association, later the United Commercial Travellers Association of Great Britain and Ireland, looked after the interests of salesmen/company representatives in the days when there was no stigma to the word 'Traveller'. The Dublin branch, founded in 1903, had an average membership of 550 out of a total in 115 branches of close on 24,000. Its aims were to look after all the interests of its members, those who spent six months or more travelling the country. This involved everything from better deals on the railways and in the hotels (sometimes the only business in the winter came from the commercial travellers), to legal assistance, liaising with other professional bodies and legislators in the interests of its members, and managing a fund for those who had fallen on hard times.

Adam was chairman of the Benevolent Institute in 1904 and reported that 'since its foundation in 1841 it had relieved 834 persons, at a cost of over £260,000 and at the present time it afforded relief to 429 annuitants, amounting to over £13,000 [almost £1m] a year'.

It is sometimes difficult for us to sense the impact of historical changes, particularly those before the profound turmoil of the 20th century. Adam, however, had no doubt he was living in revolutionary times. In his chairman's speech he alluded to

> the fact that they must realise they had passed through a social revolution. It was very serious, and changeful in its consequences, owing to the land legislation of the past twenty-five years, and also owing to the Local Government Act of 1898. The position, however, was not as deplorable as some people said it was. He believed that the position was very hopeful indeed (hear, hear). There must in the transition stage be difficulties, but he had a strong hope that things would work for the good of the country (hear, hear).[31]

The family continued to take a keen interest in the Association, not only having commercial travellers of its own but also because of the large number of travellers canvassing for business at Findlaters. Adam's brother Willie was both Dublin and national president for 1919/20 and in his presidential speech on 28 December 1918, he 'gave an eloquent address congratulating the Branch upon its continued progress. He surveyed the state of trade and commerce during the year, stating he thought the government and the control Boards had hampered businessmen very much, especially the Commercial Traveller; and he exhorted every CT to watch very carefully for changes which are bound to arise, and not to fail to make their voices heard when opportunities present themselves.' He concluded by drawing attention to the benevolent activities of the association.

In his speech on 20 December 1919 his advice to every member, in the troublesome times that were possibly ahead, was to 'sit tight, and always play the game'! It must have been very difficult for 'the men of the road' whose livelihood depended on travelling from town to town seeking orders.

Dermot, Willie's son, when chairman of Findlaters, filled the position of president of the Dublin branch for five years between 1946 and 1951. He presented back to the Association the presidential jewel that had been presented to his father Willie when he presided over the only international conference of the UKCTA held in Dublin in 1902/3. This now resides in the Findlater museum.

Lifeboat disaster 1895

Sir Thomas Robinson*, a member of the Kingstown Urban District Council and chairman in 1900, wrote of Adam:

> Those who had the privilege of working with Adam would recollect the extraordinary ability and energy that he brought to bear on his labours for the benefit of Kingstown. During one term of his tenure of office there occurred the disaster in Dublin Bay, when the entire crew of the Kingstown lifeboat, attempting to rescue Russian sailors from a wreck, were drowned outside the harbour. Mr Findlater had organised a relief fund for the families of the lost men, and in a fortnight had raised a sum amply sufficient to satisfy all the needs of the widows and families who were left penniless.

This disaster occurred on 24 December 1895 and was described in detail in the *RNLI Journal:*

> Gales blew without moderation for the entire month. In the final week the ferocity increased bringing disaster around the entire coast with a great number of shipwrecks on the shore or sunk at sea. At 10 am on the 24th December, the ship 'Palma' of Finland, a wooden three masted full rigged sailing ship, which had come to Kingstown for shelter, was observed dragging her anchor off Kingstown Harbour, while a strong gale was blowing from the ESE with a heavy sea. The Kingstown No. 2 Lifeboat proceeded to her assistance under sail, but when about 600 yards distant from the vessel, the 'Palma' went aground in 15 foot of water surrounded by a rough, short and confused sea. Just as the Lifeboat was manoeuvring into position, a huge wave capsized her throwing the entire crew into the water. The lifeboat failed to self right and the entire crew perished. The Kingstown No. 1 Lifeboat was following and she also partially capsized but with no loss of life. The crew of the 'Palma' were rescued on St Stephen's Day by the Irish Lights tender 'Tearaght'. The 'Palma' was subsequently sold as a wreck.[32]

The *Evening Mail* reported the disaster on Christmas Eve. Adam, as chairman of the Kingstown Commissioners, had a letter in the issue calling a public meeting in Kingstown at 8 pm that night to consider what could be done.

At the meeting a fund was inaugurated 'for the immediate and permanent

* An original partner in the firm of Hayes, Conyngham and Robinson, the chemists, established in 1897.

ALEXANDER FINDLATER & CO., LIMITED.

EVENTS OF THE PAST MONTH.

Alex. Findlater & Co., Ltd., Kingstown, supplied

THE GERMAN SQUADRON (10 SHIPS) AT KINGSTOWN, WHILE IN COMMAND OF H.I.H. PRINCE HENRY OF PRUSSIA.

THE DINING ROOM "GIGAS" BAZAAR, DUBLIN.

Wines, Spirits, Beer, and Mineral Waters supplied by Alex. Findlater & Co., Ltd., Dublin.

35

The German squadron visited Kingstown in May 1902. Prince Henry and his officers were invited to dine at the *Royal Irish Yacht Club* and he was made an honorary member. (*Lady of the House,* June 1902) relief of the families of the brave men who perished in the ill-fated lifeboat'. The attendance was large and sympathetic. Adam, in the chair, first apologised for being late owing to the congested state of the traffic at Westland Row which had prevented him from being there as early as he had intended. He continued:

> When at 2.30 o'clock that day he had heard of the deplorable accident, or act of God—at all events—the fact that sixteen of the bread winners of Kingstown had gone, and that sixteen families, with their relatives, their wives, their children, were now in the position, in many cases, he believed, of trusting to public charity for their support (hear, hear). It would be a dreadful thing to think that when they were all going into town that morning by the ten o'clock train, smoking their cigarettes and thinking of nothing but of going into their business, at that moment men were struggling in the sea near by between life and death, and that now they were gone. He was glad that he had the opportunity to get this meeting to gather together to do what they could in the smallest way to give some solace to those who were afflicted, and to do something to support those whose bread winners were gone (applause). They were joined there together for that purpose, and really the enthusiastic and hearty answers which they had received, the telegrams they had from the Lord Mayor and from the different institutions in town, showed that, after all, there was a common spirit of humanity amongst them (applause) and that really somehow or other there was something good left yet in the world (applause). Let them make up their minds to do what they could for these poor distressed people that had lost what was to them the dearest thing in the world.
>
> Kingstown was a seaport town, so was Howth, so was Malahide, Baldoyle, Dalkey and Bray. He would suggest that the secretaries should write to the most representative men in those places asking them to do something to help them. Representative men of enterprising spirit were also to be found in the other towns. There were also a large number of wholesale firms in Dublin, such as Guinness' and Jameson's, and the steam packet and railway companies, including the London and North Western, all of whom, if properly approached, would, he thought, be only too willing to do what they could to see that the widows and orphans of those poor fellows, who behaved as heroes that day, would not be forgotten, and would not be in want (applause).[33]

There was an amazing public response to this appeal. All of the leading commercial firms contributed as did smaller firms and very many citizens. It was said that there was not a firm, a parish or a citizen with a copper in his pocket who did not contribute. Mayors of different English towns opened subscription lists and the members of the London stock exchange contributed generously. The Royal National Lifeboat Institution contributed £2,200 [£180,000 in 2000] to which Adam acknowledged: 'Doubly grateful for your magnificent donation which will be well administered. The donation was announced publicly at the Mansion House luncheon to-day after the inauguration of the new Lord Mayor, signed Findlater.' The RNLI contributed a further sum 'to defray the costs of the funerals and also the purchase of graves, in perpetuity, in Dean's Grange Cemetery, for the families of those men who lost their lives in the melancholy

38 ALEXANDER FINDLATER & CO.,

THE KINGSTOWN BRANCH

OF

Alex. Findlater & Co.

HAS FOR YEARS SUPPLIED THE

OLD ROYAL MAIL BOATS,

AND THE FIRM ARE NOW THE CONTRACTORS FOR ALL SUPPLIES TO THE

NEW ROYAL MAIL STEAMERS

(KINGSTOWN & HOLYHEAD).

Some 65 years after this appeared, I was about to re-run it, with two extra ships added, when we reluctantly gave up the supply contract. (*Lady of the House,* August 1897)

catastrophe'. A public funeral was held on Friday 27 December which started from the town hall at 1 o'clock.

On 4 January Adam received a letter from the Lord Lieutenant: 'Dear Mr Findlater, I have received a communication informing me that Her Majesty has been graciously pleased to forward a donation of £30 [£2,500] towards the Kingstown Disaster Fund. I am yours faithfully, Cadogan.'

All the contributions were acknowledged in the press and many by Adam personally. When the fund was closed in the middle of January a total of £ 17,000 had been contributed, the equivalent of £1.4m in 2000 currency. This period was tough for Adam. In addition to the relief fund which he dealt with on a daily basis, there was a fire in the Belfast theatre of which he was chairman, reported in the press of 27 December. Also on the 27th he had to chair a difficult and extraordinary meeting of the Star Theatre Dublin where it took two hours to scrutinise the votes concerning a sacked director. As if that was not enough, on the 28th, as chairman of the Dublin and Banagher Distillery, he had to face a rough AGM on account of a loss of £5,000 [over £400,000] and directors' subscription of £11,000 [£900,000] towards a second mortgage (it gave them only temporary respite). Adam appears to have been a tough and resilient character.

Companions of St Patrick

In December 1906 a representative committee of Dublin's citizens, under the chairmanship of the Lord Mayor J. P. Nannetti, gathered for the purpose of establishing a society analagous to St Andrew's in Scotland and St George's in England. The aims and objectives of the Companions of St Patrick were: the promoting of social intercourse between Irishmen, irrespective of political or religious creeds; the development of a spirit of mutual sympathy and practical goodwill among its membership; and the accumulation and application of benevolent funds.

The chairman stated that they wished to make the society a broad platform on which Irishmen could stand, and enable them to meet both socially and in other ways, thus letting the world see that there was a body of men in Ireland who could band themselves together independent of class and creed. It was proposed to establish companionships in towns and cities of Ireland, and in various parts of the world where Irishmen congregated. They had also taken powers to form a benevolent fund, and they had set by at least 50 per cent of the income for benevolent purposes. Amongst the founders were J. P. Nannetti, Sir James Talbot Power, distiller, who was first President, Adam Findlater, E. A. Aston,* Hon. Sec., Dr W. Lombard Murphy, son of William Martin Murphy, Thomas Myles FRCSI†, Dr Edward Magennis, Alderman Cotton, Thomas Macardle, Surgeon McArdle and Sir John Irwin, a paper mill owner who did a tremendous amount

* Aston: journalist, engineer, pioneer of Irish planning.(see J. Anthony Gaughan (ed) *Memoirs of Senator James G. Douglas* Dublin: UCD Press 1998 p 160)

† Sir Thomas Myles was an eminent Dublin surgeon. In 1916 he ran guns into Wicklow on his yacht 'Chotah', at the same time as Erskine Childers ran the Asgard into Howth

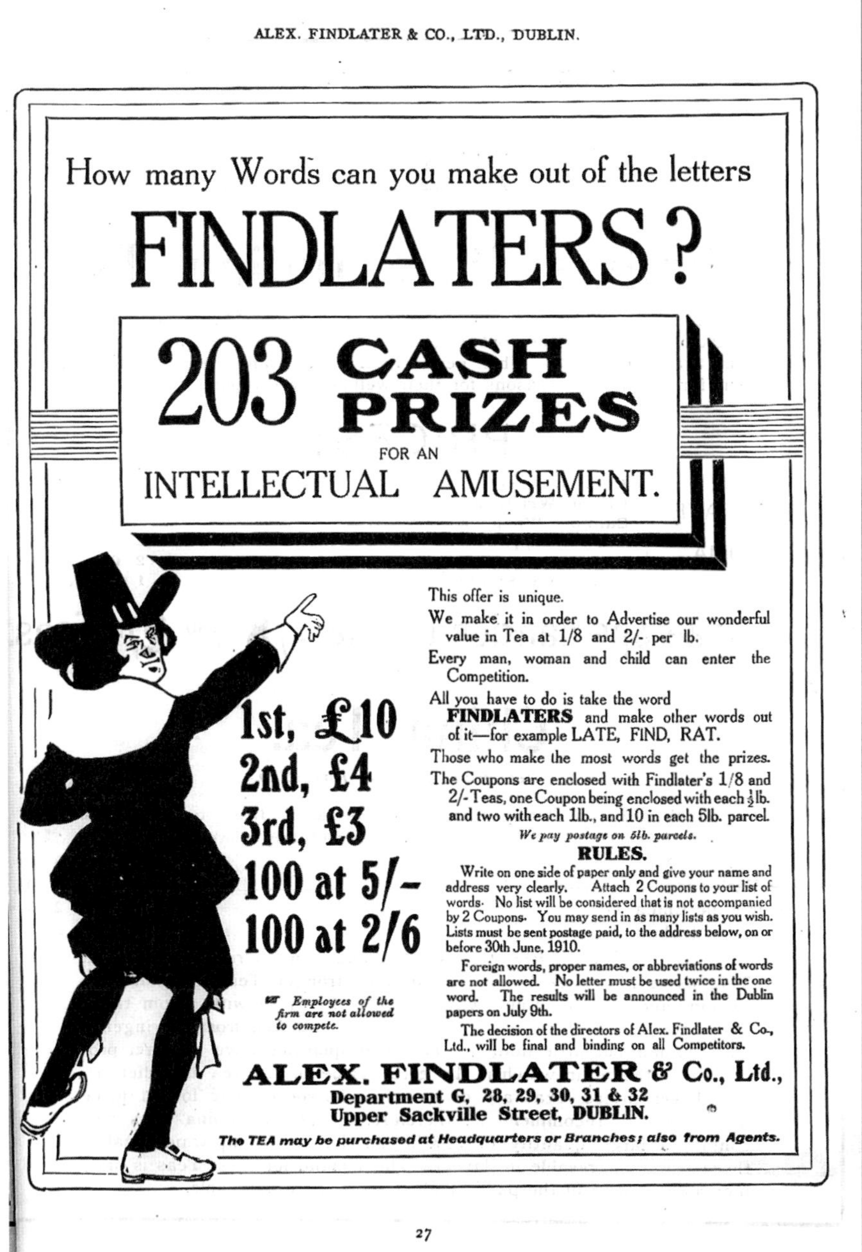
ALEX. FINDLATER & CO., LTD., DUBLIN.

How many Words can you make out of the letters

FINDLATERS?

203 CASH PRIZES

FOR AN

INTELLECTUAL AMUSEMENT.

1st, £10
2nd, £4
3rd, £3
100 at 5/-
100 at 2/6

Employees of the firm are not allowed to compete.

This offer is unique.

We make it in order to Advertise our wonderful value in Tea at 1/8 and 2/- per lb.

Every man, woman and child can enter the Competition.

All you have to do is take the word **FINDLATERS** and make other words out of it—for example LATE, FIND, RAT.

Those who make the most words get the prizes.

The Coupons are enclosed with Findlater's 1/8 and 2/-Teas, one Coupon being enclosed with each ½lb. and two with each 1lb., and 10 in each 5lb. parcel.

We pay postage on 5lb. parcels.

RULES.

Write on one side of paper only and give your name and address very clearly. Attach 2 Coupons to your list of words. No list will be considered that is not accompanied by 2 Coupons. You may send in as many lists as you wish. Lists must be sent postage paid, to the address below, on or before 30th June, 1910.

Foreign words, proper names, or abbreviations of words are not allowed. No letter must be used twice in the one word. The results will be announced in the Dublin papers on July 9th.

The decision of the directors of Alex. Findlater & Co., Ltd., will be final and binding on all Competitors.

ALEX. FINDLATER & Co., Ltd.,
Department G, 28, 29, 30, 31 & 32
Upper Sackville Street, DUBLIN.

The TEA may be purchased at Headquarters or Branches; also from Agents.

27

1910—First prize was won by a prisoner in Derry prison. On another occasion the winning entry by Georgina Allen of Londonbridge road consisted of 2,817 words and more than fifty entries exceeded 1,000 words!

of good for his city.*

Adam, in seconding the motion to adopt the constitution said that he would not be surprised if it bore very reproductive fruit in the future of the country. They did not desire flunkeyism in the society. Everyone should be the same as everybody else.

Thomas Myles, speaking at the third annual banquet in the Gresham Hotel, on St Patrick's Day said:

> Wherever the Irishman went he carried with him not only his brogue, but an undying love for the land which gave him birth. Their society was founded not in the hope that they could ever do anything to add to the devotion of their countrymen to their beloved country, but to give expression in a coherent manner to the feelings which animated the great mass of Irishmen on this national festival. St Patrick's Day used, in times gone by, to be celebrated by only a portion of Irish people, but it was now the anniversary of every Irishman without distinction of politics or creed.(Applause)
>
> The desire of the Society was to make every one of the 365 days of the year a St. Patrick's Day for Ireland. The success with which the Society had met in the early stage of its career gave them a promise of a fair and happy future. They hoped as time went on that their countrymen would see that although they might differ they might yet esteem each other and tolerate each other's differences, and unite in the common purpose of elevating their country and countrymen. (Applause)

Companionship was to be a little strained when the issue of the royal toast came up. However, they arrived at a suitable compromise. But such difficulties in Dublin were as nothing to those Adam met in Belfast where 'an inaugural banquet, raised to fervour by the patriotic eloquence of Adam Findlater, was followed by Press warnings against any kind of association with Dublin citizens whose "loyalty" was open to suspicion. The result, of course, was inevitable, and the social bridge builders found their structure without adequate supports at its northern end; and so collapsed one of many well-intentioned efforts to forge human links across the Boyne'.[34] However that was seen as 'hope deferred'!

The society prospered in Dublin and remained true to its ideals. It 'managed to survive the storms and stresses of the last thirty years', as *The Irish Times* put it in April 1935. The big event of the year was always the St Patrick's Day banquet. Adam's brother Willie, also in since the foundation, was still a vice-president in 1930. One can only surmise that it faded away with the passing of the early members. Willie died in 1941.

Adam dies

At the height of his influence, when his voice as representative of a moderate unionist opinion might have been increasingly important, Adam died on 18

* Sir John Irwin founded the Mansion House Coal Fund. He was one of the original members of the Council of the Dublin Industrial Development Association and was, during and after the Great War, chairman of the National Relief Fund. He was also chairman of the Visiting Justices and Committee of the Dublin Prisons. He was outspoken in his demand for fair treatment of political prisoners.

January 1911, of carcinoma of the larynx, at the early age of fifty-six. The disease had been with him for some time, and he had spent an extended visit to Egypt, presumably in the hopes that the climate might help his throat.

The *Evening Telegraph* wrote generously:

> Liberal in all his opinions, hating all humbug and bigotry, and qualified by his attainments to judge questions of moment to the community with broad impartiality, Adam was eminently a desirable representative on public boards. Here his presence and co-operation were always welcomed, as well by those who differed from his opinions as by those who shared them. He had deservedly the reputation of being a model employer, but only his closer friends knew his kindliness of disposition and the genial graces of his hospitality. None could ever know the extent of his benevolence, which knew no distinction of creed or country.[35]

Only his closer family knew that his wide range of activities and interests, from theatre to politics, from hotels to distillery, caused his eye to wander from the core activity of the firm. In the end Adam did not die a rich man.

There was an unexpectedly warm tribute in *The Irish Orchard and Forest Glade:*

> Adam Findlater is dead, and we are downright sorry. Where shall we begin in trying to describe the nature of a man whose personality was an embodiment of all the splendid qualities and characteristics, and even of those minor yet sensitive bonds of human feeling that make a man beloved by his kind? Is there a man who knew him who cannot recall countless manly acts of courage, generosity, breadth of view, and intellectual intrepidity that made his example, as it will make his memory, an inspiration and a source of genuine encouragement. He was our friend—hearty, cheery, forceful, true—and we never had, nor wish to have, a man to work with or to work for in any walk of life who could better blend in his own person all the best and bravest qualities of heart and brain.
>
> Mr Findlater was, in fact, a lawyer, and a member of the Irish Bar, although he never practised. As a public speaker he was effective, because he thought clearly and spoke plainly. No man was a more genial host or a more welcome guest, whether at the festive table or in the hunting field; wherever men met in social relations he was a 'prince among good fellows'.

Tributes of respect to Adam's memory came from all sides, for, as a Dublin evening newspaper, opposed to his political views, wrote on the day of his death: 'Fine qualities as a man and the bigger civic virtues distinguished him.' His friend, writing in the *Wine Trade Review,* described having the privilege of his friendship and companionship for many years; he had accompanied him on several holiday and business trips over Europe, Canada, and the United States, and on his trip to Egypt a few months ago. It was, he wrote, an education to travel with him.

Perhaps Adam's contemporary Alfred Manning, with the touch of exaggeration suitable to an obituary, best sums up Adam's vibrant character:

> Adam was a man of many parts, a man who filled a great part in the life of his coun-

try; he was an Irishman to the backbone, and a very able and clever man. He had a great heart, was a great fighter, and he only wished they had a hundred such men in Ireland. He was a contemporary of Adam as a student in Trinity College, and since that time he had known him as a sincere and true friend. He had been told by one of the most powerful Irish members of Parliament, a great orator, and a great Irishman, that if Adam, years ago, had liked to go the whole hog and take off his coat in the fight for Home Rule he would have stepped into the shoes of the most illustrious Irishman that ever lived, Mr Charles Stewart Parnell. He was one of the few men that could have taken that position.[36]

Notes and references

1 *The Wine Trade Review* 15 February 1911
2 In *Dublin's Victorian Houses* Dublin: A. & A. Farmar 1998 pp 160-1, Mary Daly gives details of three houses in Belgrave Square built by McCurdy. When his daughter married Adam, these houses provided the security for the annuity of £100 [£7,000] a year he settled on her
3 Minutes for the year 1895 of the township of Kingstown, pp 112-113
4 *Idem.* pp 110-111
5 Quoted in M. McCarthy *Five Years in Ireland* Dublin: Hodges Figgis 7th ed. 1902 pp 52-3
6 Quoted in McCarthy *Five Years in Ireland* p 364
7 *Sunday Independent* 5 April 1998
8 Findlater archive
9 *The Irish Times* 15 October 1903
10 *The Irish Figaro* 17 October 1903
11 Pamphlet distributed by Adam: *Corporation of Dublin v Alexander Findlater & Co., Ltd., A Tale of Municipal Landlordism, illustrated by the acts of Dublin Corporation*
12 *Evening Telegraph* February 1903
13 *The Leader* 2 February 1903
14 *The Irish Times* 21 February 1905
15 *The Irish People* 14 October 1905
16 Diarmuid Ferriter *A Nation of Extremes, The Pioneers in Twentieth-Century Ireland* Dublin: Irish Academic Press 1999 pp 120-1, 150
17 *The Irish Times* 18 June 1903
18 *The Saturday Herald* 5 September 1903
19 *Freeman's Journal* 22 June 1906
20 John Kendle Walter Long, *Ireland and the Union 1905-1922* Dublin: Glendale 1992 p 40
21 *Irish Investors' Guardian* August 1902
22 *Evening Herald* 22 December 1906
23 *Irish Independent* 26 September 1904
24 *Hansard* 13 February 1891 p 598
25 T. M. Healy *Letters and Leaders of My Day* London: Butterworth 1928 p 339
26 P. Somerville–Large *Irish Voices: 50 years of Irish life 1916-1966* 1999 London: Chatto & Windus p 185
27 *Freeman's Journal* 18 December 1903
28 *Evening Telegraph* 17 December 1903
29 *Freeman's Journal* 23 January 1909
30 *The Irish Times* 18 March 1904
31 *Idem.* 19 December 1904
32 *RNLI Journal* February 1896, *Lifeboats Ireland* 1995 pp 40-3
33 *The Evening Mail* 26 December 1895
34 *The Irish Times* 4 April 1935
35 *Evening Telegraph* 18 January 1911
36 *The Irish Times* 24 January 1911

7. Our Dublin Theatre—the Star, later the Empire Palace

One of the more surprising ventures of the Findlater family was our 85-year old involvement in the raffish world of music halls and variety theatres. The involvement seems to have started with John, who in the late 1870s was bankrolling George West, the owner of the Grafton Theatre and Hotel in South Anne Street. The connection between the two in fact extended beyond the theatre. George West was involved in the building of several houses in Moyne Road, now Dublin 6, and in 1878/9 John advanced him £600 [over £40,000] towards their completion; later the number of houses grew to five with continuing advances; and in 1879 £100 [£7,000] plus interest at 5.75 per cent towards the erecting of seating, boxes and stage at the Earlsfort Skating Rink.

The music hall tradition in Ireland had begun in song-and-supper rooms and singing saloons where guests were entertained by travelling musicians while they ate. The next stage was the evolution of 'free-and-easies', as they were called, which were less pub-like, concentrating on entertainment—mostly quite risqué, such as in Henry Jude's in Grafton Street, where students from Trinity (including no doubt Adam, who graduated in 1876) and the medical schools beat the spoons flat in appreciation of the Fulton sisters' can-can dances.[1] The Grafton Theatre was more upmarket; and it also allowed smoking in the auditorium but separated the bar. Its bright interiors and colourful sets, with the top entertainers, attracted a mixture of working class and the more raffish gentry.[2]

The second half of the 19th century was a trough period in Irish and British theatre. In an age when an audience of 1,800 was described as 'small' producers had to appeal to popular taste.[3] This meant melodrama, spectacle and showmanship. As an historian of the Abbey Theatre put it 'burlesque, operetta, musical comedy, melodrama, frivolous comedy and farce occupied most of the London theatres', and Dublin was no different.[4] By the 1890s there were three legitimate, officially-patented theatres in Dublin—the Theatre Royal in Hawkins Street and the Gaiety in South King Street both subsisted on warmed-up versions of British hits presented by touring companies while the Queen's Theatre in Brunswick (now Pearse) Street took a slightly higher ground. It specialised in patriotic melodrama in which 'a mythical land of blarney and blather, [was] peopled by patriotic heroes of exclusively aristocratic descent, betrayed by villainous informers and mourned by impossibly innocent colleens'.[5] The Irish playwright Dion Boucicault (1820–90), who had been extremely popular in London, was the master of this genre. (It is not surprising that audiences who enjoyed this style found *The Playboy of the Western World* hard to take.)

Dan Lowrey 1879–92

The best known, and most popular of the Dublin music hall proprietor/managers were the two Dan Lowreys. Dan Lowrey the first was born in Roscrea in 1823. His parents then emigrated to England, By the time he was thirty he owned a tavern in Liverpool where he also entertained his patrons with songs and stories in addition to serving food and drink. Some time later Lowrey returned to Ireland and opened the Alhambra in Belfast before coming to Dublin in 1878 to purchase the site of an old military barracks in Crampton Court in Temple Bar. This had also been the site of a tavern, and the so-called Monster Saloon Music Hall. On Monday 22 December 1879 his Star of Erin opened to the public.[6] This was a genuine music hall, charging admission (as opposed to the 'free-and-easies' which provided entertainment free and made their money from the sale of drink). Licensing regulations prohibited Lowrey from putting on plays, or even sketches involving two people, but he could provide music. The entertainment provided was quite broad, and strictly for men only.

In 1881 Dan assigned the running of the Star of Erin to his son, also Daniel, who changed the name to Dan Lowrey's Music Hall. John Findlater funded the enterprise through a mortgage on the properties; the decorations etc cost £121 [£10,000], S. H. Bolton the builder received £414 [£27,500] and new 'sittings' were supplied by James S. Lyon of High Holborn, London. John kept Daniel in funds by various cash advances to meet specific bills. It seems to have been quite a job keeping both George West and Daniel solvent. In 1882 John was picking up the costs of George West's dishonoured cheques and paying the costs of the assignment of Daniel Lowrey's insurance policies.

In 1889 the theatre's name was changed again, to Dan Lowrey's Palace of Varieties. In July 1890 Dan senior died at the age of sixty-six in his cottage in Terenure and was buried in Glasnevin Cemetery.

Dan, or Daniel, the second continued to run the music hall, despite continuing sniping from the official patent-holders, notably Michael Gunn who made strenuous attempts in the late 1880s to have the Star closed down on the grounds that it was infringing his patent. The entertainment was cheerfully lowbrow: there was the male impersonator Vesta Tilley, the Christy Minstrels, and Mr and Mrs Johnson 'unclothing in the flickering limelight of La Studio', there was 'the daring young man on the flying trapeze' (or at least there was until one appalling night when John Lilly of Leeds leapt from rope to rope 25 feet above the stage and missed the bar of the trapeze. He crashed to the ground, cracking his skull. He died soon after being carried to Mercer's Hospital). Occasionally there were boxing matches, with the popular Jem Mace, ex-Champion Bareknuckle Fighter of the World.

A good deal of the comedy took off the upper classes, not always benignly: there was Champagne Charlie, of course, and 'Two Girls of Good Society, Too wise to wear a Ring' as the buxom Leamar sisters sang. More pointed was the ditty sung by the Great Macdermott about the Parnell divorce: 'You want Home Rule for Ireland, And you can't Home Rule yourself'. A great favourite was his sketch of the scene when Kitty O'Shea and Parnell were caught in a bedroom together, spoken in a finicking upper-class accent:[7]

> 'Heavens! Wot a situation! Hardly time to draw on one's gloves! No chance of avoiding detection, no way to save the lady's reputation–no way, no way-Oh yes, fthank Goodness there is one! A happy, happy, fthrice happy fthought!–The Fire-Escape! the Fire-Escape!
>
> *It was indeed a merry jape*
> *When Charlie Parnell's notty shape*
> *Went scorching down the Fire Escape!*

The 1892/3 reconstruction

In his new year address to the city in 1892 Daniel Lowrey announced plans for the reconstruction of the Star. He also declared his intention to update the acts by including sketches and dramatic items, and he resolved to secure the rights to produce opera and short musicals. Adam was on hand to help put the finances together in order to attract the kind of stars the theatre needed. The borrowings were again secured on the properties in Crampton Court.

The architect for this project was James Joseph Farrall, one of the top names in commercial building. Farrall acted as advisor to leading banks and business groups, including Findlaters for the design of some branch houses. According to Watters and Murtagh, Farrall was a wealthy man who took a keen interest in the investment opportunities in the Star. However, as we shall see, within two years there was to be a falling out between Adam and Farrall* due to the mess in the construction of the theatre in Belfast.

The board of directors of the new company, the Star Theatre of Varieties Company (Limited), was: Adam in the chair; John J. Farrall, architect; Thomas Ritchie, wine merchant; and Daniel Lowrey, managing director. For his interest, Lowrey received £19,000 [£1.4m]; of this £14,000 was in cash, and £5,000 in deferred shares. He further agreed to accept no interest on these until a dividend had been paid to the buyers of ordinary shares, although he did receive a salary as managing director. Out of the cash Lowrey received, he had to pay off all debts and mortgages on the premises (amounting to over £7,000). 'My father was a fool in business,' says Norah Lowrey. Her story is that the Lowrey family was against the sale to the syndicate, but that Daniel was blinded by the lure of the big money and sold his birthright for a seat on the syndicated board.[8]

The new-look Star, which now seated 1,600 people, was ready for the Dublin international season, Horse Show Week, and was opened to the public at a cost of £3,000 [£230,000]. On Saturday 20 August 1892, the invited guests who attended the grand re-opening admired the many changes that had been made.

* Farrall was a nephew of architect John McCurdy to whom he had been articled. McCurdy was Adam's father-in-law. Farrall, who died in September 1911, was described in the *Irish Builder* as 'friendly and genial. Socially a very popular personality, he was much sought after at all social functions as the possessor of a magnificent baritone voice, an accomplishment he used with delightful taste and cultured skill.'

Compliments slip from the 'Star'

The stalls, pits and galleries had all been extended and the partitions that separated the bars from the auditorium had been removed on all three floors. The whole interior was now more open and spacious. The 'Hebes' serving the drinks wore new high-necked gowns, while the doormen and attendants were dressed in dark gold-braided uniforms with brass buttons. The special souvenir programme, advertising the celebrated burlesque actress Kate Stanley as topping the bill, was printed on pink silk.[9]

Daniel was now a popular Dublin character. His name was a byword in Dublin, even inside Trinity. The goodwill of the College was one of his great assets. *Infinity Variety* records:

> On the night following a Rugby match, especially if the College won, team and followers would descend upon The Star to celebrate and Dan, on the lookout for mischief-makers, often prowled through the House disguised in an old coat and tweed cap. The students' favourite sport was 'prigging'–swiping mirrors, jugs, tankards, juggler's balls, wigs, greasepaint, notice boards, 'right under the nose of Dan'–trophies for their rooms. Norah relates 'we had a very comfortable lounge in the theatre, with nice armchairs, carpet, a fire in winter and a coal box. One night my father noticed five students leaving with a hunchback amongst them. He said: 'Just a moment, Gentlemen!' and found the coal box in the hump. This was going too far. He decided to call the Police. They pleaded, he gave in, gave them a severe telling off and let them go. Years later a clergyman appeared in his office. 'I was the hunchback' he said, 'you were kind to me that night, Mr Lowrey, and saved my career.'[10]

Cinématographe 1895[11]

One of Dan Lowrey's great talents was the ability to predict what novelties would prove attractive to his audiences, and so it was with the advent of cinema in Dublin. The motion picture finally became a reality when Auguste Lumière of Lyons, France, patented his first projection machine for the large public showing of celluloid film on 15 February 1895. He called the whole contraption *Le Cinématographe*. Thanks to Dan and Adam's efforts, the very next year the cinématographe arrived at the Star Theatre in Dublin less than two months after it was first seen in England. Unfortunately, the first night was not a success. The audience sat expectantly, but for a long time nothing happened. Then, periodic sparks of light lit up the screen, but nothing could be made out. For a brief moment, the image of two prize-fighters graced the screen, but then the machine broke down.

After consultation with the Lumière brothers, the cinématographe was booked again for the first week in October 1896, and this time everything ran smoothly. Seven thousand people thronged through the doors at Crampton Court and Sycamore Street for the first week of the pictures. The *Freeman's Journal* summed up this new wonder:

> This very wonderful instrument produces with absolute correctness in every detail animated representations of scenes and incidents, which are witnessed in everyday life. To those who witness the exhibition for the first time the effect is startling. The figures are thrown upon a screen erected in front of the audience—the effect is so realistic that for the moment one is almost apt to forget that the representation is artificial. When the train comes to a standstill the passengers are seen hurrying out of the carriages, bearing their luggage, the greetings between themselves and their friends are all represented perfectly true to life and the scene is an exact reproduction of the life and bustle and tumult to be witnessed at the great railway depots of the world. The representation of the sea-bathing was also wonderfully true to life. The audience witnessed the bathers jumping into the water and the spray caused by the plunge rose into the air and descended again in fleecy showers.

Reconstruction 1897

On 1 January 1897, from his office at Sycamore Street, Daniel Lowrey issued what was to be his last address to the public:

> Since the time when, seventeen years ago, I took possession of its site and year by year have striven—and succeeded too—in raising it from the slough in which it then in the eyes of the public stood to the proud position it now occupies–a financial colossus patronised by the elite standing in the very front rank of the foremost theatres and now it has been a matter of notoriety that the accommodation of the theatre is now inadequate for the enormous patronage. I intimated my intention of having it enlarged to double its present capacity and having a grand main entrance from Dame Street. Already the work of rebuilding is greatly advanced, and when the Star Theatre is re-opened, the eyes of the public will also be opened to the finest amusement palace inside or outside London. A structure of beauty worthy of the city of Dublin and of the generous support with which its citizens have always upheld my efforts in catering for their healthy enjoyment.
>
> I remain, Faithfully yours, Daniel Lowrey.[12]

Reconstruction began and was hoped to be completed by Horse Show week six months later. The new design was by R. H. Brunton, the noted theatre architect. The change was to be radical: not only was the capacity to be greatly

The Olympia by Pat Liddy,
Dublin Today (1984)

enlarged and the name changed from the Star to the Empire Palace, but the whole theatre was to be turned round. The new stage would now be situated at the Dame Street end instead of at the Sycamore Street end. This is the Olympia Theatre as we know it to-day.

However, financially Lowrey was in trouble, as he now had to finance the theatre in Cork, and his share of the Empire in Belfast and the Empire Palace in Dublin. He thus mortgaged all his leases and properties including his home, Roslyn Park in Sandymount. Everything rested on the success of the new theatre.

In September 1896 Adam announced that H. E. Moss of the Moss and Thornton Group* had joined the board of the Star Theatre Company Ltd, with a view to gaining early access to fresh artistes coming to London. For a charge of £100 [over £8,000] per annum Lowrey was to have the benefit of a London office. It was agreed that the Empire Theatre of Varieties in Belfast and the Cork Palace Theatre of Varieties would each subscribe one-third of the cost.

The new Dublin theatre re-opened as the Empire Palace on 13 November 1897 to great acclaim. At the gala opening in 1897 Charles Coburn was top of the bill. He had two hits which kept him going for years, the first 'Two Lovely Black Eyes', a political song, and the other, which he bought in 1891, became one of the most famous music hall songs of all time, 'The Man Who Broke the Bank at Monte Carlo':[13]

As I walk along the Bois de Boulong with an independent air,
You can hear the girls declare, He must be a millionaire.
You can hear them cry and wish to die
You see them wink the other eye,
At the Man who Broke the Bank at Monte Carlo.

Irish Society[14] spoke of the new theatre's 'brilliant interior' under electric chandeliers, and noted the auditorium 'opulent in curves of neo-baroque', the 'immense proscenium', and the mirrors, summing it up as 'a place of satin and gold'. Seating accommodation was provided for 1,664 persons, with large vacant spaces on each floor available for standing where room could be found for at

* Moss Empires Limited was founded in December 1899 and celebrated its jubilee in 1949. It was founded by Sir Edward Moss and the first board members were Richard Thornton, Oswald Stoll (later knighted) and Frank Allen. Stoll Moss Theatres are now London's leading theatre operators.

The Olympia in the 1970s

least 650 people, giving a total accommodation in the house for at least 2,300 people.

At the dinner for selected guests on the night prior to the opening Adam, as Chairman—whose more moderate unionist views were to evolve later—said that 'the first toast they would honour in that new theatre was the health of her Gracious Majesty the Queen (applause). Long might she reign over the Empire, and might all her palaces be gorgeous as that one (loud applause).' The Dublin *Daily Express* report continues:

> The Chairman said that at least Dublin had one theatre which was a credit to the city and one which marked a new era in theatrical Dublin (applause). It was not many years ago when the music hall to a large section of the respectable citizens was the name of a place where they should not go, where they could not bring their friends, and, in fact, the name of a place where, if they went at all, they ought to slip in by a side door (laughter). The Empire, however, now opened into Dame Street; it reared its head proudly with the large theatres that were opening in the city, and would rival that new and gorgeous theatre that was being erected on the site of the old Theatre Royal (applause).[15]

To handle the enormous audience, the management introduced the new 'queuing' system. On 14 November 1897, *The Irish Times* published the following letter from the acting manager of the theatre:

> Sir, The Police authorities have resolved to co-operate with the Directors of the Empire Palace Theatre in enforcing the queue system at this theatre. The directors trust that this system, which has proved most beneficial to the public elsewhere, will receive the support of the public of Dublin.

The system was enforced and on 16 November 1897, the Dublin *Daily Express* reported its success:

> Last night the Empire Palace Theatre in Dame Street was opened to the public and the first performance was received with the utmost enthusiasm by a crowded audience.

From the *Irish Figaro*, November 1987

What is known as the queue system of admission was adopted in Dublin for the first time, and not withstanding the great crowd of people who assembled in Dame street, desirous of gaining admission, there was no disorder or crushing, the admirable arrangements made by the police preventing any inconvenience. The people readily perceiving that the new system has been adopted to promote their comfort, fell in with the idea at once, and took up their places in double lines along the footpath, entering in rotation as the cue was given from the various entrances. In this way all were admitted more rapidly than would otherwise have been the case, and no confusion whatever arose.'

Despite this success, queuing did not become widespread until the last years of the First World War, when the German U-boat campaign provoked food and other shortages.

Playing 'God Save the Queen' 1897–8

Another innovation, the decision to play 'God Save the Queen' at the close of each performance, received considerably less support. We have seen how Adam and his board changed the name of the theatre from innocuous 'Star' to the more committed 'Empire Palace', and how in his speech at the opening dinner Adam had specifically connected Queen Victoria and the British Empire with the new theatre. With hindsight it seems clear he and his colleagues misread the mood of Dublin theatre-goers, who were by no means as royalist as their counterparts in Belfast or London. To nationalists 'God Save the Queen' was no more than a 'party tune', as they called it. The letters to the Editor in the *Daily Independent** (bought by William Martin Murphy in 1905 and changed into the *Irish Independent*) tell the story:

> Sir, I . . . must protest against this innovation which I can consider as little less than an insult to many Nationalists who wish to partake of a night's amusement at the Empire. Many of my friends who attended the Empire on the opening night have informed me of their resolve not again to enter the theatre until the practice of playing 'God Save the Queen' is discontinued. I am sir, yours faithfully. A Nationalist
>
> Sir, I refer to the playing of 'God Save the Queen' at the conclusion of the performance. The advertisements and posters on the dead walls say nothing about this item, but when a person is about to go home at the end of the programme this air is pro-

* The *Daily Independent* was founded by Parnell in 1891, merged with the anti-Parnellite *Daily Nation* (owned by William Martin Murphy) in 1900 and relaunched as the *Irish Independent* in 1905.

duced by the new orchestra. I do not know who is responsible for the innovation, but certainly Dublin got on well enough hitherto without it, and if the theatres in Liverpool and Manchester can do without it there is no reason for its introduction in Dublin. Yours faithfully, Gallery.[16]

The opposition continued into the new year, 1898, when on 1 February the *Herald* ran the heading: 'The Empire Theatre and the Introduction of Party Tunes':

> The playing of party tunes at the Empire Theatre has given rise to a great deal of resentment in the city and we have received several letters of protest in regard to the offensive innovation.

The management were not planning to step down, and nor were the nationalists going to.*

On the same day the *Independent* printed another letter on the subject:

> Sir, May I suggest a way out of the difficulty with the Empire? It is that on the first strains of 'God Save the Queen' or 'Rule Britannia', some Nationalist present lead on with 'God Save Ireland' or the 'Wearin' of the Green' or 'The Boys of Wexford' or 'Who Fears to Speak of '98' etc.—all present who sympathise to take up the strain, and so drown the obnoxious English party tune. The practice could be discontinued on the cessation of the cause, to be renewed if necessary. It would also give an opportunity of hearing National songs to those who have no other means of hearing them. TJR.

Daniel Lowrey dies, 1898

On 16 August 1898 Daniel Lowrey died from a brain tumour. Newspaper obituaries mourned the passing of Lowrey. As the *Irish Figaro* wrote: 'It is generally agreed that he was the father of the profession'.

Lowrey was buried on the very same day that the Duke and Duchess of York visited Kingstown. As chairman of Kingstown Commissioners, Adam had to present the royal couple with an address, which he did, in the pouring rain. As they left to drive into Dublin to meet the Lord Lieutenant, he had to race across to Sandymount to attend the funeral.

At the subsequent AGM of the theatre company, shareholders noted that the chairman surprisingly made no reference at all to the late managing director.

> 'I would not refer to this matter at all', wrote one, 'but for the extraordinary attitude of Mr Findlater who, in his opening speech, did not make a single reference to the departed dead, but calmly moved the adoption of the report and statement of accounts without saying anything concerning the personality of the individual who in the main provided the citizens of Dublin with such a splendid music hall. This silence on the part of the chairman did not, I am sure, please the majority of the shareholders

* The 'party tune' remained a source of contention. In 1915 Peadar Kearney, the composer of our National Anthem, turned a fire hose on the orchestra and, as Pat Liddy puts it, 'washed them out of the pit for playing the British anthem'. See *Dublin Today* Dublin: Irish Times 1984 p 145

who, bearing in mind what Mr Lowrey had done for the theatre, naturally expected to hear some words of eulogy respecting him and of the great loss the company had sustained by his untimely end.'

Adam had good reasons to be unhappy with Lowrey. He and Lowrey and Farrall had built the new theatre in Belfast at great expense, only to find that large numbers of the audience could not see the stage with the result that the theatre had to be pulled down and rebuilt. Lowrey's feeble declaration that 'he could never understand plans', was hardly adequate explanation for this expensive debacle.

Theatre patents 1898

As we have seen, music halls, where the commodious drinking and smoking areas were separated from the auditorium, had fully-equipped stages, and were in constant dispute with the licensed theatre holders (i.e. the Theatre Royal, the Gaiety and Queen's) as they introduced dramatic skits, sketches, opera items and so on into the fare.

But it was not only professional theatre that the legitimate patent-holders attacked for breaching their monopoly. In 1898 a determined effort was made to curtail amateur performances as well. Relying on an Act of 1786 the proprietors, led by the redoubtable Gunn family of the Gaiety, announced that they intended to proceed against any public theatrical performance other than in their theatres. There was of course a storm of protest, during which Adam made the shrewd point that a licence to do something was not the same as a licence to prevent others doing the same. It was a shield, not a sword.

Adam's friend and fellow Kingstown Commissioner, Alfred Manning, wrote to the *Irish Daily Independent* on 20 January 1898:

> Sir, Having seen an advertisement in your paper threatening legal proceedings against any persons giving theatrical performances, surely the time has come when the public of Dublin and suburbs should at once get such an absurd old-fashioned law changed. Are the commissioners and public of Rathmines, Kingstown, Pembroke, and Blackrock going to sit still and be bullied? The short-sighted selfish policy of endeavouring to stop amateur performances is not only unwise, but quite intolerable in 1898.

It appears that the licence holders did not stop at public advertisement, but actually wrote threatening letters to well-known amateur actors. At a meeting of the Town Commissioners of Kingstown, Adam informed them that

> some of the best known amateurs, who were in the habit of performing in the Town Hall, and giving the public so much amusement, had received certain letters calling upon them to desist from such performances, under pain of having to pay something like £300 [£23,000] for each performance. That action to his knowledge had resulted in one case in a great deal of injury to a very deserving charity. No town in England situated like Kingstown was hammered in this way. The Town Hall was a place dedicated to the amateurs of the township, who would in turn amuse the residents and the general public.

No doubt as a result of the general protest, the licensees drew in their horns, and the following year, Kingstown put on an amateur pantomime called *Julius Caesar* that received excellent reviews.

On 4 February 1899, the *Saturday Herald* sketched in the background to this new production:

> The worthy folk on 'the coast' look forward to the annual production of the amateur pantomime in Kingstown with the same certainty as they expect the east winds, the Horse Show, or Christmas itself. And when it comes it brings not only good cheer, but it ushers in a week of social gaiety and downright amusement. The Kingstown amateurs are unique in a way. They write their own plays, paint their own scenery, design their own dresses and arrange their dances. Few professional undertakings could accomplish more than this.
>
> Kingstown is perhaps the one town in Ireland that can boast an active dramatic association. Last year the amateurs there produced in the most creditable fashion a burlesque entitled 'Christopher Columbus', and now the same company of players announce an original pantomime to be presented on the 8th inst., which will be a skit on the life and times of no less a person than Julius Caesar. As noted, the most striking feature of the production is that all the work, from the designing of the dresses to the arrangement of the 'business' and the painting of the scenery, are by the amateurs concerned in the affair.

Julius Caesar opened a few days later and proved to be a very successful undertaking, as we can see from the *Saturday Herald's* review:

> This very attractive amateur pantomime is doing tremendous business in the Town Hall, Kingstown, since the opening night, and this is all the more satisfactory as the profits go to a deserving charity. For the last two or three nights the hall has been so densely crowded that over one hundred people were reluctantly refused admission each evening. Certainly nothing in the amateur line has been so well produced before. The scenery nightly receives rounds of applause, the dresses are superb, and the dialogue sparkles with wit; so that it is no wonder the Dublin and Kingstown public, who are always quick to recognise merit in a performance of the kind, are supporting it so enthusiastically. By special request, the management have agreed to give another matinée on Saturday next at 2.30.

As the *Irish Figaro* noted, it was not surprising that this play was a success as it had in it 'all the elements of popularity': 'The words are full of fun, and there is plenty of movement in the action of the piece. The music also is above the average."[17]

True to form, a member of the family was in the midst of the action. Adam's brother, Herbert, who was still an active twenty-five year-old sportsman, performed the part of the aged high priest of the Druids. The *Dublin Lantern* commented that Herbert 'should have scored better for his singing of "Gold, Gold" which, by the way, is the best song in the pantomime, but appears to be lost on the audience.' The recorder concentrated on his appearance: 'We are now intro duced to Mystorus, High Priest of the Druids, (Herbert S. Findlater) who reveals

Herbert as Mystorus in 'Julius Caesar'. The previous year (1898) he played Sir Marmaduke Pointdextre in the Gilbert and Sullivan operetta 'The Sorcerer'.

Herbert, solicitor and sportsman, in the late 1890s.

the future to the Royal family. He is very impressive in his snow white garb, and with his solemnity of expression.'[18] Although the amateurs seemed to have won that day, the struggle between the legitimate theatre and its boisterous rivals was to continue. (Indeed the patentees took their monopoly so seriously as to impede for some time the establishment of the tiny Abbey Theatre, whose recondite programme could hardly have been a serious threat to the commercial theatre.)

Arthur Griffith and the city of dreadful knights

Adam's stance on the 'God Save the Queen' question was not forgotten by the nationalists. In August 1903, Arthur Griffith, a constitutional nationalist, and later President of Dáil Éireann 1921-2, wrote in his *United Irishman:*

> Sir Thomas Brown, it will be recollected, is the little tobacconist in Dunleary who was rewarded with a Knighthood for deserting the principles he professed at his election time. The circular is printed on foreign paper. This evident design of Adam Findlater should meet with some recognition from the powers that be. For years past Mr Findlater has been begging for a knighthood and there is no reason on earth when Brown of Dunleary has received one that Mr Adam Findlater should be considered ineligible.[19]

And in September he continued on the same theme:

Mr Adam Findlater—he is still unknighted—cheerfully set out some years ago to ram his political opinions down the throats of the people who were wont to patronise the Star Theatre. He ordered the orchestra to play the British national anthem at the conclusion of each performance and he changed the 'Star' into the 'Empire', with the gratifying result that the shareholders' dividend dropped from 17 per cent. to just nothing at all.

Evelyn Thompson, who married Herbert in 1904, as Lady Olivia

Maybe Adam would have liked a title—it would have been natural for someone of his character and determination to strive to achieve such an honour. In what looks now like a deliberate attempt to attach the Irish great and the good to the Empire, so many had been honoured that wags now called Dublin the 'city of dreadful knights'. His cousin, Billy Findlater, now Sir William, twice president of the Incorporated Law Society, had been knighted in 1897; as had Adam's successor in the chair of the Kingstown Town Commissioners, manufacturing and pharmaceutical chemist Thomas Robinson (1900). Adam's cousin, Malcolm John Inglis (1900), chairman of Heitons and in the chair of the Dublin Chamber of Commerce on the occasion of the visit of Queen Victoria in 1900 had one; and Robert Gardner (1905), first president of the Institute of Chartered Accountants and married to Adam's aunt, had one; Horace Plunkett (1903), founder of the co-operative movement had one, as had numerous others.* Some, such as William Martin Murphy actually turned down the honour—an event which put King Edward VII's nose out of joint as he waited with the sword at the Irish International Exhibition in Ballsbridge in 1907[20]—and it is said that John Jameson considered that his name was greater than any knighthood.

Motor racing 1903

After the initial experiments in 1895 cinematograph shows became a regular part of the evening variety performances. In 1903 the world-famous Irish Gordon Bennett Race was filmed by the Mutoscope and Biograph Company. John

* For example: seed merchant Sir James Mackey, builders' provider Sir Maurice Dockrell and baker and confectioner Sir Joseph Downes. Baronetcies for Sir William Goulding, Sir John Arnott, Sir Henry Cochrane (who was on the board of Findlaters), Sir James J. Murphy, steam ship owner, Sir Richard Martin, timber importer, and senior of the lot distiller Sir John Power.

Motor–racing, 1903 style

Gordon Bennett was the millionaire owner of the *New York Herald* and the Commercial Cable Company. His great wealth had been amassed by his father, a Scottish immigrant who, in 1835, founded the newspaper. As Bob Montgomery records in his history of the Gordon Bennett Rally: 'This was an important first for motor sport, in that it was the first occasion on which an official film record was made of a motor race anywhere in the world.'[21] The film was processed in a tent near the course immediately after the race and shown that very evening in the Empire Palace Theatre, as the posters recorded: 'Edison operators have achieved the most marvellous success in the annals of animated photography; the operators only arrived from the course at 5 o'clock last night and . . . produced the intensely exciting race . . . to-night and until further notice Edison's Irish Pictures will show a complete reproduction of The International Motor Contest . . . from start to finish.' The speed trials were held in Phoenix Park. The race took place on 3rd July 1903 and was won by Michael Jenatzy, a Belgian driving a four cylinder Mercedes. His average speed was 42.9 mph. He held the world record as the first man to reach the staggering speed of a mile a minute, achieved in northern France in 1893.

So far so good, but two days later disaster struck. The Dublin *Daily Express*[22] reported the story:

> During the past week the management of the Empire Palace Theatre have been occasioned keen disappointment and considerable financial loss in consequence of being unable to exhibit the photographs taken in the Phoenix Park on Saturday last during the progress of the motor speed trials . . . The photographers were successful in obtaining three splendid series of pictures, showing the different races, and the competitors taking part therein at different intervals. The photos were in every detail graphic and correct illustrations of the cars at the starting point, running neck and neck at full speed at the most dangerous positions, and as they swept by the winning post. . . . The negatives of the photos were sent on Saturday evening last by letter post to London, in order to have them properly developed. They were carefully put up in a

tin box, and parcelled in strong wrappers, firmly secured with twine. Inside a note was enclosed stating that the films in the box were perishable, and were not to be opened except in a dark room. Every precaution was used to ensure that the films would be protected from the light, and that they should reach their destination safely.

In some unaccountable manner, however, the boxes containing the films and the wrapping in which they were placed parted company, and, after the lapse of three days, the label, twine, etc. were delivered at 68 High Holborn, London, and the negatives at Cope street, Dublin. As a result of the unwarrantable tampering which has been perpetrated by some officious individual the negatives have been rendered absolutely worthless. Through the destruction of these instantaneous records not only has the Empire Company been subjected to a large financial loss, but the general public has been deprived of the opportunity of witnessing the only reproduction possible of a series of races which attracted a large amount of interest at home and abroad.[23]

One of the young and intrepid reporters at the Gordon Bennett race was twenty-three year old James Joyce who recorded the cars' joyous return to Dublin in a story entitled 'After the Race'.* He had previously interviewed the French competitor in Paris on behalf of *The Irish Times*.[24]

The theatre AGM 1905

Despite Arthur Griffith's reservations, from 1900 to 1904 the theatre was recording commendable profits, according to the *Irish Investor's Guardian.* These averaged £3,300 [£250,000], and this despite some criticism of the quality of the fare. In May 1900, for instance there was a scathing attack in the *Irish Playgoer,* and in the following issue it concluded:

It is all very well to have the 'circus form of entertainment' on all the time at such halls as the Alhambra, or the Empire London, where they make a speciality of such turns, but what we want here is variety, and we have not been getting it. I would respectfully suggest that our principal 'hall' be renamed 'The Empire Theatre of Monotonies'—it would be more appropriate.'

In 1905 the annual report had to disclose a decrease in profits from £2,915 to £963 [£70,000]. The report stated that a sum of £884 [£65,000] had been appropriated by the late manager and that the defalcations occurred during the short period at the close of the present year. It continued, 'he was held in the highest esteem by everybody, and his default at the time was never considered as he had been connected with the Empire management for several years before being appointed manager.' The shareholders' meeting that ensued was a bumpy one for Adam.

On 20 September 1905 the twelfth ordinary general meeting of the shareholders of the Empire Palace Company was held at 36 College Green. The agenda

* In 1909 James Joyce returned from Trieste and spent some two and a half months setting up Dublin's first cinema, the Volta at 45 Mary Street, which was backed by a group of Trieste businessmen. However the diet of continental films was not to Dubliners' tastes and after a few months the Italians sold out.

was to receive the report of the directors and the statement of accounts for the year ended 31 May, and to declare dividends and the other ordinary business of a general meeting. Adam presided, and there was a large attendance of shareholders. As the following letter to *The Irish Times*[25] makes clear, this meeting caused quite a controversy which, by a few timely concessions, Adam quite adroitly kept below boiling point.

> Sir, For the first time since the inauguration of this company the directors met the shareholders yesterday behind closed doors. The Press was excluded, and the shareholders were informed the directors would send a statement for publication. The report, which appears in your issue of today was, I presume, received from the secretary, although it is not marked 'communicated.' That report, so far as it deals with the statements of the chairman, is correct, but the concluding paragraph viz., questions asked by shareholders as to the general business of the company and the deficiency in the accounts of the late manager—very inadequately represents what took place. For the benefit of shareholders who were not present, I think it well to state shortly what took place at the meeting.
>
> There were three questions dealt with (1) The deficiency of the late manager; (2) the purchase of wines, etc., for the bar; (3) the remuneration paid the directors. In reference to the first, the chairman very judiciously conciliated the meeting by admitting that the directors had omitted to obtain any security from the late manager, and while not admitting personal liability, stated he and his co-directors were considering how an arrangement could be made which would take the loss off the shoulders of the shareholders. Had he not done this the shareholders had arranged I should move an adjournment of the meeting to take the opinion of counsel on the subject, and I have little doubt it would have been carried.
>
> (2) The question of the management of the bars was very fully discussed, and the opinion expressed that while not objecting to the firm which at present supplies goods to the bars, the shareholders considered that some one of themselves, in whom they have confidence, should have a voice in those purchases, and that two directors of Findlaters should not be selling to the directors of the Star Theatre, represented by themselves and Mr Armour. Upon this question the chairman was also conciliatory, and offered if the shareholders selected one of themselves for a seat on the Board he would be co-opted. The third question, the remuneration of the directors, would never have been raised had the chairman at an earlier period made the statement he did yesterday, that his fees amounted only to £300, a sum which I, for one, do not consider excessive.
>
> For the first time in the history of the Star a number of shareholders came up from the country, attended the meeting, and expressed their opinions. The meeting of the Committee of the Shareholders will be held at once, the selection made as suggested by Mr Findlater, and the name adopted by them will be forwarded to him.
>
> Yours, etc
>
> Loftus Walshe, Chairman of Shareholders' Committee.

The elephant at court

After years of pursuing the music halls for infringement of their patent, the legitimate theatres, notably the 2,000-seater Theatre Royal, had decided that if you can't beat them, you'd better join them. Their shows became increasingly like music hall and variety. In 1906, for instance, among the attractions was a song and dance troop called 'Eight Lancashire Lads' whose main claim to subsequent fame was that one of the lads was Charlie Chaplin.[26]

In March 1906, Adam had the opportunity to turn the legal tables on the Theatre Royal. He sought an injunction to restrain it from presenting two particular entertainments advertised on the grounds that they infringed the patent. Mr Blood KC, acting on behalf of Adam and the Star (Empire) quoted a regulation which specified that no exhibition of wild beasts or dangerous performances were to be permitted on the stage. He submitted that two of the Royal's performances infringed this.

An elephant's day in court.
Evening Herald, 5 March 1906

The first was a new sensation called the 'Globe of Life' where a motor cycle was ridden at the speed of forty miles an hour inside a glass globe. The second was the introduction of an elephant on to the stage. According to counsel for the Theatre Royal, however, the 'Globe of Life' had been successfully paraded in many establishments and no accidents had ever ensued. Secondly, the elephant in question was not wild, but tame, and therefore not affected by the regulation. In fact, counsel credited this animal with more than the usual share of elephantine wisdom, and claimed for it a most distinguished past. The elephant had, apparently, been exhibited all over the United Kingdom, and had mixed in the highest society. Indeed, the elephant's counsel produced a photograph of him in Windsor Park, and another describing him as having been ridden by the Prince of Wales, his present majesty. The *Dublin Daily Mail* takes up the story:

> The enormous animal stood outside the court in evidence, followed by a huge retinue of adults and juveniles, which had grown in volume as he made his progress

The Empire Palace Theatre, Dublin, tug-of-war team who won the British Isles Tug-of-war competition outright in 1911. Adam in the centre.

> along the line of the Northern Quays. Entering the courtyard by the entrance from Chancery Place, the monster proceeded along quickly until he halted within earshot of the court where his character was subsequently to be attacked by counsel as that of a 'wild beast'.
>
> Taking his stand to one side of the passage leading from the main buildings to the coffee-room, the Lord of the Jungle did his best to dissipate prejudice by looking benignly on his surroundings and appearing the embodiment of all the virtue that a quadruped of his proportions should possess.
>
> Fortunately, or unfortunately, his avoirdupois prevented him from being treated as an ordinary 'exhibit', and handed in and marked in the usual way, but at all events, he was in personal attendance to see that judgement should not be given against him through default.
>
> For over an hour he submitted himself to an examination–not in the orthodox way of witness by one counsel at a time, but by hundreds of scrutinising eyes, all bearing at once upon his points. Apparently he came off with flying colours and proved himself a counter-attraction to the argumentative proceedings inside which were to determine whether he was to be respited from his stage labours for a while.
>
> Before the case had concluded he had established his popularity with the crowd, and when it became known that the injunction against him had failed, the elephant turned his head indifferently as if to say, 'I told you so,' and his trainer climbed into position on his back and galloped gaily off; the huge animal, as one might playfully imagine, feeling satisfied that he left court without a stain on his character. [27]

The patented theatres, having failed to stop the music hall, resolved instead to join in their success by increasingly promoting 'hippodrome' or circus seasons. Despite this hotting up of competition for audiences, a new manager turned things round at the Empire, and we read in the *Irish Investor's Guardian* on 19 September 1908 that financially, the company were doing well:

> There was a further improvement in the trading result of the past year's operations of this Company, which, considering the counter attractions of the Irish International Exhibition, and the competition offered by the Hippodrome seasons at the Theatre Royal and other places of amusement, must be considered satisfactory evidence of the success of the management during a trying year. The net profits for the year ended 31st May last amounted to £3,488 [over £250,000], an increase of £1,211 [£90,000].

According to the *Belfast News Letter* on 14 September 1908, Adam took the threat from the legitimate theatre coolly: 'There is,' he said, 'room in Dublin for any amount of light amusements. There is a craze for light opera simply because in the present-day rush people do not want anything that makes them think or worry. In the old days people went to the Theatre Royal to criticise the heavy plays in which Barry Sullivan appeared. They took notes of such pieces as "The Lady of Lyons" and "Hamlet", and they spent days afterwards discussing them. Since then there has been a change in popular taste.' In public, Adam declared that he saw no reason why the present desire for light entertainment would not continue. He had been told fifteen years ago in Belfast that vaudeville could not live, but at the present moment it seemed that most of the theatres were indulging in it and nothing else. The competition which would follow would make the theatres produce good material. They would see better turns in all the theatres as the result of this movement.

However, the minute book of the Empire in Belfast reveals that privately there was some concern: 'In view of the Theatre Royal running Hippodrome for the next eight weeks introducing Madame Albani, Harry Lauder and other eminent artists, followed by the re-opening of the Gaiety with variety performances on the 2nd August, immediate action must be taken on our behalf to secure strong attractive turns.'

On Adam's death at the age of fifty-six in 1911, his brother Willie took over as Chairman of the Empire Palace Theatre. In 1923 control of this theatre passed to Robert Morrison, impresario and theatrical agent whose family had various investments in the entertainment business and who owned the first film-making company in Ireland. At the same time the theatre name was changed to the more politically acceptable 'Olympia'. Willie remained an investor in order to retain the bar business for Findlaters, and between 1929 and 1937 received an excellent flow of dividends. In 1951 the company was taken over by a company controlled by Stanley Illsley and Leo McCabe whose slogan was 'World Theatre—at Your Doorstep'. Audiences were entertained by international ballet and dance companies, and to top class plays and drama, pantomime and revue. There were few international stars of the day that did not appear in front of the appreciative Irish audiences. The memory of Dan Lowrey has faded in Dublin but will forever remain part of Irish theatre folklore.

In the meantime, Findlaters retained their interest in theatre, with the ownership of the Empire in Belfast which stayed in the family until 1961, as you will read in Chapter 14.

Notes and references

1 Eugene Watters and Matthew Murtagh *Infinite Variety: Dan Lowrey's Music Hall 1879-97* Dublin: Gill and Macmillan 1975 p 34
2 *Ibid.* pp 35-6
3 F. R. Wolfe *Theatres in Ireland*, a booklet published under the auspices of the Amateur Dramatic Defence Association, Dublin: Humphries and Armour 1898 p 18
4 Hugh Hunt *The Abbey: Ireland's National Theatre 1904-1979* Dublin: Gill and Macmillan 1979 p 5
5 *Ibid.* p 5
6 Philip B. Ryan *The Lost Theatres of Dublin* Westbury: The Badger Press 1998 pp 199-201
7 Watters & Murtagh *op cit* pp 110–111
8 *Ibid.* p 139
9 *Ibid.* p 132
10 *Ibid.* p 131
11 *Ibid.* p 165
12 *Ibid.* p 168
13 Watters and Murtagh *op.cit.* p 156–7
14 *The Irish Society* 13 November 1897
15 *Dublin Daily Express* 13 November 1897
16 *Irish Independent* 18 November 1897
17 *Irish Figaro* 9 February 1899
18 *The Recorder and Suburban Visitor* 18 February 1899
19 *United Irishman* 29 August 29 1903
20 Thomas Morrissey SJ *William Martin Murphy* Historical Association Dundalgan Press 1997 p 37
21 Bob Montgomery *The Irish Gordon Bennett Race 1903*, Irish Transport Series, Dreoilin Specialist Publications 1999
22 *Dublin Daily Express* 11 July 1903
23 *Dublin Daily Express* 11 July 1903
24 Brendan Lynch *Green Dust* Dublin: Portobello Publishing 1988 pp 16, 26
25 *The Irish Times* 22 September 1905
26 Ryan *op. cit.* p 31
27 *The Mail* 5 March 1906

8. *Gallipoli 1915*

'There will be no retiring.
Every man will die at his post rather than retire.'[1]

This is the story of how seven Findlaters went to war and only three returned home, one with a limb missing. They were among the Irish heroes of the 7th Royal Munster Fusiliers, the 5th Inniskilling and the 6th Dublin regiments, from all strata of society, who served and suffered, so many of them fatally, in the First World War.

The declaration of war in August 1914, was the signal for an extraordinary outbreak of self-sacrificing patriotism, a great rallying of those who were loyal to the empire. For most Irish Protestants, the reaction was visceral and instinctive. F. H. Browning, the president of the Irish Rugby Football Union for 1914, issued a circular to the rugby football clubs in the Dublin district. This circular called upon the union to urge their members to place their services at the disposal of the country in carrying through the war which had just begun. As soon as Browning discovered that there would be a large and ready response, he inaugurated a volunteer corps, subsequently known as the Irish Rugby Football Union Volunteer Corps, which had its headquarters at the Lansdowne Road football grounds, Dublin. Browning perceived at once that the corps could be made a nucleus for recruiting for home defence, and he extended membership to men not only from rugby football but all other sporting clubs. He engaged several drill sergeants, and inside a few weeks had over three hundred recruits of business and professional men from the city, both young and old, learning the elements of military instruction and drill.

He then got in touch with his old friend Lieutenant-Colonel Geoffrey Dowling. Dowling had been given command of the newly formed 7th Battalion of the Royal Dublin Fusiliers and had been well known in the football world in earlier years (1883) as captain of the first fifteen of Monkstown Football Club. Colonel Dowling agreed to keep open a special company, 'D' Company as it was subsequently known, for 'Pals' from the Irish Rugby Football Union Volunteer Corps.

The men of the Findlater family were perfect fodder for this ill-fated escapade. Oldest to volunteer was my Great-Uncle Alex, aged fifty-four, who had qualified as a doctor at Trinity College and was practising in Edgware, Middlesex. He joined up with the Royal Army Medical Corps, 1st London Mount Brigade Field Ambulance, and was posted to Gallipoli. Grandfather Willie stayed at home to mind the business, but his next brother, Charles—a member of Monkstown

Rugby Club, a Trinity graduate, an engineer and a bachelor—decided to enlist despite the fact that he was forty-four years old, and that the upper age limit was supposedly thirty-five. Their younger brother, Herbert, enlisted—a Trinity graduate and practising solicitor—despite being forty-two, and married with two young sons. Elsewhere their cousin Victor, thirty-six, saw active service with the Royal Irish Rifles and his brother Percy, thirty-four, with the Royal Army Service Corps. More remote cousins, two sons of John Findlater who had emigrated to Texas in 1883, also signed up and suffered.

When war broke out in Europe in August 1914, Irish-born Lord Kitchener, Secretary of State for War in the British Government, had appealed for one hundred thousand men and John Redmond, notwithstanding the fact that home rule had again been deferred, offered the services of his Volunteers to the Empire. Thus on Wednesday 16 September 1914 those who had up to that date enlisted at Lansdowne Road—barristers, doctors, solicitors, stockbrokers, barbers, medical students, engineering students, art students, businessmen who had responsible positions, civil servants and insurance agents—marched off to Kingsbridge Station en route to the Curragh Camp for training, receiving a great ovation from the public and their friends as they went. From almost every window in Nassau Street, College Green and Dame Street, handkerchiefs and hands were waved to them.

The training at the Curragh Camp was arduous and involved drilling, musketry training, digging trenches and route marching. The most memorable route march took place on 7 and 8 December 1914 when, following a mid-training break as guests of Lieutenant Stanley Cochrane at Woodbrook, Bray, South County Dublin, 'D' Company undertook the march from Bray to the Curragh in full battle gear.[2] 'D' Company trained at the Curragh for seven months. During this time a correspondent from the *Dublin Evening Mail* visited them. He watched the recruits of the 7th Battalion of the Royal Dublin Fusiliers at 'the labour of love and loyalty' they had undertaken. Of particular interest to the reporter were the men of 'D' Company:

> I was particularly interested in 'D' Company, the 'Footballers', as they were known when they were first drafted to the Curragh. The title is steadily drifting into abeyance. They were footballers when they went to the Curragh. They are soldiers of the King now; and proud to be nothing else; and, above all, proud to be serving in the 'Old Toughs'.
>
> I watched them at their drill in Gough Square vicinity; and they went through their movements with splendid precision and confidence. It was difficult to believe that the majority of the men were civilians like the rest of us only a month ago. They marched and countermarched, and formed fours; and wheeled and counterwheeled, and deployed and performed all the other evolutions of the parade ground with, so far as I could judge, the smartness and certainty of veterans. The Prussian drill-sergeant is supposed to be the last word in efficiency production. No cursing, swearing, jack-booted, bullying Prussian non-commissioned officer could have his men in better shape or fit-

ness.

I am not going to say that in this case, as they say before the footlights, it is all done by kindness. It is all done by keenness. Men, non-commissioned officers and officers are all animated with the one desire: to do credit to the regiment; to get on with the business in hand; and then to get to the Front. They have to work very hard. They are at it before breakfast and again before dinner, and again before tea. They seemed to me to be gluttons for work, and more work, and harder work. The labour they delight in physics pain.

Charles

I saw them again, after dinner—and they have their dinner at one, and are at work again at two—marching out to the veldt of the Curragh, and practising the great war game. In half an hour you see them dotted in detachments across the plain. Over there to the left men are practising signalling. In front of you a platoon is marching away and gradually opening out their line, as you would stretch an elastic band. They are advancing in extended order. Others are scouting towards the wood on the horizon, dropping behind cover and progressing by short rushes. Others again are lying in a saucer-like hollow in the grass and practising rifle-drill for the future work in the trenches. They are getting hard as nails, busy as ants, and keen as mustard.

The report ended with a reference to the Findlater brothers:

The men are well fed, well led, and well housed, and as pleased as Punch with their new life. Private Findlater, one of the two well-known brothers who have joined the corps, and whom I met at the station, gave me a cheerful account of the cordial relations between the men, and of the respect and regard that are entertained for the officers. Under Colonel Dowling, who, I hear, may be induced to authorise an Irish terrier for the regimental mascot, the 7th Battalion of the Royal Dublin Fusiliers is becoming already a fine regiment. It will soon be a picked regiment. When it goes to the Front, as I believe it will do in a couple of months, it will carry the confidence as well as the good wishes of the class and territory it will worthily represent.[3]

Fate had earmarked 'D' Company for participation in one of the most ill-judged ventures of the war, the attempted invasion of Turkey through Gallipoli. The war on the Western Front, on a line from the English Channel in the north, running hundreds of miles to the Alps in the south east, was in stalemate. Neither side was able to dislodge the other. Winston Churchill, then thirty-nine years of age and First Lord of the Admiralty, entranced by what he called later the 'soft underbelly of Europe' proposed to attack the Germans from the east and to split their forces by moving up the Danube valley from the Black Sea. The plan was to land the British, French, Australian and New Zealand units on the Gallipoli Peninsula in Turkey and, with the assistance of the Royal Navy, to open up the Dardanelles Straits in order to gain access to Constantinople (now Istanbul) and the Black Sea. This would allow supplies of ammunition to the hard-pressed Russians and permit shipments of Ukrainian wheat to France and England. Seventy-four-year-old Admiral Sir John Fisher, First Sea Lord, was extremely sceptical of the plan and warned Prime Minister Asquith of his concerns.

Nevertheless the invasion went ahead and resulted in one of the greatest disasters in British naval and military history. Out of nearly half a million allied soldiers and sailors, who served at Gallipoli and the Dardanelles, nearly half became casualties. The campaign was a disaster mainly through sheer political irresponsibility—planning the campaign with no thought as to its value—as Robin Prior observed in his contribution to the *Oxford Companion of Australian Military History:* 'Gallipoli had no influence on the course of the war as a whole. More depressing still, even if the expedition had succeeded in its aims, it is doubtful if the war would have been shortened by a single day.'[4] Undoubtedly, the force sent to Gallipoli was not only comprehensively defeated by the Turks, but betrayed by the incompetence of their own leadership. As New Zealand general of Irish parentage, Alexander Godley, wrote to his cousin in Cavan, Lord Kilbracken, 'I do not suppose in history, that anything so utterly mismanaged by the British Government will ever be recorded.'[5]

Indeed, the British leadership of the Gallipoli campaign was nothing short of a disgrace. Captain Milward, one of the few GHQ staff officers present on the battlefield, described the expedition as 'badly-planned and ill-conceived'.[6] In fact, as Michael Hickey demonstrates in his excellent book *Gallipoli*, the whole military operation was inept and incompetent, from the War Council to the generals in the battle zone. He notes that in London 'the political and military interests were in collision' and that there was 'no firm line of policy' for the campaign.[7]

However, when the Irish troops eventually departed from the North Wall on 30 April 1915, their hearts were high. Their war was to be a glorious adventure. Thousands of Irish people thronged the streets to wave off the volunteers. *The Irish Times* reported the event:

> Headed by the band of the 12th Lancers, and the pipers of the Officers' Training Corps, Trinity College, the battalion moved out of Barracks. As they emerged through the main entrance they were cordially cheered, and the cheers were taken up all along the route. They looked exceedingly fit, and presented a fine military bearing. As they marched by in perfect order and in swinging, rhythmic step, every one felt that they were worthy of the city and of a country noted for its soldiers. The men were in great

Charles in uniform

> spirit, and laughed and joked along the way. The Union Jack and the Irish Flag were carried on the spikes of the bayonets, and wherever they were noticed cheers were raised. In addition to their heavy packs, some of the men carried melodeons strapped to their kit-bags. As they passed down the Quays, the crowd on the pavement and the occupants of windows lustily cheered, and the men, recognizing friends along the route, returned their farewell greetings with hearty cheers. In front of the Four Courts a large crowd of barrister, solicitors, and officials gave a cordial send-off to the men. Amongst the crowd were judges, whose sittings had concluded for the day, and they cheered as spontaneously as the others as the men passed. In the ranks were members of the Bar who had forsaken excellent prospects to keep the Old Flag flying and as they were recognised they were cordially cheered . . . Fashionably dressed ladies walked beside their brothers and relatives, and women in shawls kept step with their husbands, brothers, and sons. The contrast was marked, but it served to show the spirit that animates the people. Men going to the Front under such conditions, with their minds set on one purpose, could be depended upon to act up to the glorious records of their regiment.[8]

Just six months later only 79 of the original company of 239 would leave the war zone alive.

Having departed from Ireland on 30 April 1915, the battalion underwent a further ten weeks of tough training, this time at Basingstoke in the south of England. The voyage to the east on board the liner *Alaunia* was relaxed and agreeable. The battalion embarked on Friday 9 July at Devonport, reached Gibraltar on the 14th, Malta on the 17th, Alexandria on the 20th and Mudros Bay in the island of Lemnos on 24 July.

By this time the Gallipoli campaign was turning sour. The allied forces had failed to batter a direct entrance, and were defeated in an attack on the southern and western sides of the peninsula. (Having, as they thought, comprehensively reduced the Turkish defensive position from the sea, the generals sent detachments of Dublin and Munster Fusiliers to invade the beaches in open boats. This gave the Turks time to emerge from their shelters and set up machine gun posts. As the Irish regiments approached they were simply slaughtered in the boats, many of which sank, and some of which drifted out to sea, with a ghastly load of bloody corpses.)

Nothing daunted, the generals had decided on one last push, this time to the

Herbert

north of the Dardanelles peninsula, into Suvla Bay on the coast of Turkey. On 7 August 1916, as dawn broke just before five o'clock, the trained but unseasoned troops arrived in Suvla Bay. The morning of the landing was beautifully fine. 'A' Company went first, under Major Harrison, and 'D' Company landed later, the lighter which took them ashore bringing back some wounded. As the historian of the Dublin Pals described:

> The Bay was full of every kind of shipping. The naval guns were vigorously shelling the ridges round the Bay. The shells exploded with bright red flame edged with a black fringe of smoke, just like a tulip with the red leaves tipped with black. The noise was terrifying . . . as the light became stronger nothing was visible to the naked eye on the shore save the stretcher-bearers carrying wounded down the slopes of a hill. One could see a large number of men digging themselves in just behind the crest about half a mile from the shore . . .
>
> Here they had their first sight of the horrors of war, the stretchers passing them with many of their burdens soaked in blood. The effect of this and of first coming under shellfire when they landed was a severe trial, but they passed through it well.

The Pals were soon in the battle zone:

> The engineer officer had advised the lowering of the parapet of the trench occupied by 'D' Company, which was on the north-east and north-west corner of the hill, but when the attempt was made it was found that a good part of the parapet was composed of dead Turks, so the earth was only removed down to within a few inches of them—but the result was very unpleasant, and the smell became overpowering as the day became hotter.[9]

The Pals, like all the other troops, had little or no chance. There were no specialist landing crafts for the initial invasion, nor prefabricated piers and jetties and there was a lack of trench stores. There was a shortage of barbed wire and defective wire cutters and no corrugated iron to roof over the trenches against hand grenades. There was a lack of standardisation and uniformity of weapons and at times a shortage of ammunition and weapons, especially hand grenades so effectively used by the Turkish soldiers. One of the Pals reiterates the battle scene:

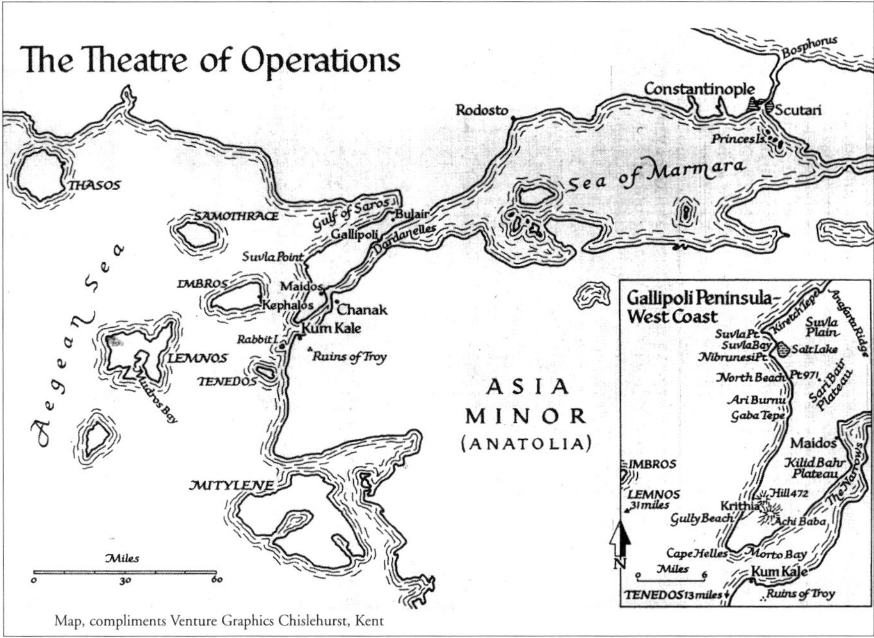

Map, compliments Venture Graphics Chislehurst, Kent

> The sights I saw going along that place I shall never forget. Some of our fellows throwing back the bombs which the Turks threw over and which had not exploded. One fellow caught them like catching a cricket ball. Wounded and dead lying everywhere. The sun streaming down and not a drop of water to be had. Neither had we bombs to reply to the Turks and drive them out.[10]

Maps, so vital in the alien terrain, were old and inaccurate and as a result advances became ill-directed shambles. Medical arrangements were hopelessly inadequate at the outset. As Brigade Major Captain Arthur Crookenden noted, 'The military situation at this juncture beggars description.'

Indeed, the allies had little idea of the true strength, or battle-worthiness, of the Turkish forces in the Dardanelles area, even on the eve of the landings. On the other hand there were many Turkish and German agents in Egypt who were able to deliver a complete allied order of battle to the head of intelligence in Constantinople by the middle of March 1915. Kitchener in London had only a vague idea of what was required and merely fervently hoped that his commander on the spot would come up with a workable plan.

It is clear that the battle was lost well before these men went ashore at Gallipoli. Even the generals were inexperienced and unprepared to cope with the horrors of the war front. Michael Hickey in *Gallipoli* cites a case of a Lieutenant Douglas Hallam, a Canadian in the Royal Navy Volunteer Reserve. 'He had been in uniform just five months and had no military experience whatsoever. Now he was on a strange shore, under fire and with no idea of what he was supposed to do with the thirty men and six machine guns under his command!' Leon Uris, in *Redemption*, deduces that the blame for this military disaster must be placed on Winston Churchill: 'When all the commissions of inquiry are done, the finger pointing and cover ups and the lying and the justifications are told and retold, I realise that one glaring fact shall remain, that is that the name of Winston Churchill will forever be synonymous with one of the greatest disasters in military history'.[11]

In the first five days allied casualties were heavy; a witness who saw the 30th Infantry Brigade described the scene:

> I witnessed these regiments drag their weary limbs over the ridge of Karakol Dagh. The drawn face and haggard look told of that dreadful week into which more privation and suffering had been compressed than fall to the lot of most men in a lifetime. Their faces were begrimed with smoke and sweat. The clay of the trenches showed on their hands and through the unshaven beard and close cropped head, for water was still too scarce for washing purposes.[12]

However, what lay ahead for these men was even more horrific. Let us now turn to read an account of the terrible battle of 15 and 16 August in which Herbert and many other Pals died:

> The Turks remained in their position under the shelter of the crest and 'lobbed' the bombs over the ridge among the Dublins, causing terrible casualties. The Dublins had no bombs and when they endeavoured to retaliate they had to creep, two or three men at a time, to the crest and, leaning over, fire downwards at the concealed Turks, or roll large boulders down on them, thus necessarily exposing themselves. It was enough to dishearten and try the bravest and most experienced troops to be in such a helpless plight. But they held on to the position for several hours, being practically unable to do anything by way of defence except 'sit tight' and trust to luck. Then shortly after six o'clock, in the bright early sunshine of the morning, came the incident which, to the 7th Dublins and especially 'D' Company, was the most fateful of the campaign. Somewhat earlier in the morning, before dawn, 'C' Company under Captain Palmer had been taken to reinforce the firing-line at the left, where it was being sorely pressed near the knoll. This was the hottest corner of all, and twice the line wavered and nearly broke, but with grim determination still held on.[13]

It was then that Major Harrison, who had until then been with 'A' Company on the right of the line, sent word that 'D' Company should be brought in to further reinforce the left. When they came they were told that the only chance they had of keeping the hill was to charge the bombers:

> To every one it was obviously a deadly undertaking, but no one flinched. Those who were first to get out, mostly from No. 14 Platoon, fixed their bayonets and, having had indicated to them the position of the bombers, with a terrific shout rushed off to the top of the crest, led by Captain Hickman . . . immediately on coming into the open a bullet struck Captain Hickman and mortally wounded him.
>
> The men never stopped, but Major Harrison, without a cap, and waving his cane, rushed forward, and calling out, 'I will lead you, men,' dashed out in front. He got as far as the edge of the Turkish trench, which was about ten yards in front, when he was struck in the body by a bomb and killed. Almost every one in the charge was killed or

> wounded by the machine-gun fire from the right flank; and only four, Sergeant Burrowes, Sergeant Drummond, and Privates Synnott and Verdon were able to crawl back over the ridge to the cover from which they had come.[14]

Among the men who followed the Major was Lieutenant-Colonel Herbert Findlater and his platoon. As one of his comrades wrote to Willie (Findlater), 'It was a mad-man's charge, but on the other side a very brave one–we were relieved at 6 that evening by the 5th Royal Irish Fusiliers. It was a hard job fighting and ducking from 5 in the morning until 6 in the evening and the only thing to keep our spirits up was an odd song and a smoke from a woodbine–that was how poor Findlater went.'[15]

By this stage the effort to dislodge the bombers by bayonet charge seemed hopeless. By the following Monday morning (16 August) Lieutenant Hamilton, (a Trinity medical student) was the only officer left in 'D' Company. And even though he was wounded in the foot, he was now in command. As Henry Hanna recorded in *The Pals at Suvla Bay:* 'It was a sad roll-call for the regiment. Their casualties during the night stood at 11 officers and 54 men, killed or wounded, and 13 missing; 'D' Company, which had landed 239 strong, being now reduced to 108 all told.' The official dispatch notes that 'reinforcements were promised, but before they could arrive the officer left in command decided to evacuate the front trenches. The strength of the Turks opposed to us was steadily rising and had now reached twenty thousand.' Hanna wrote that it was during this time that the 'company felt most the loss of so many gallant officers. From August 17 to the end of September 'D' Company had no officers (Lieutenant Hamilton having gone to hospital on account of his wound), and was under the command of Company Sergeant-Major Wm. Kee.'[16]

Charles and his remaining colleagues, although weary and saddened, had to press on. Hanna continues the story:

> The following morning (Saturday, August 21) broke clear and fine, and our artillery both on land and sea replied to the Turkish batteries which had opened the ball previously, and the shells fell very close to us but did not do much harm. We stopped in our cover for the morning, and at one o'clock in a blazing sun the Fleet and all our land batteries began a bombardment of the neighbouring hills, which were held in force by the enemy and which we were to attack later. The bombardment lasted for over an hour, and at the end the hills were on fire in many places and it seemed impossible that anyone could possibly be left alive there—the Turks had not once replied to our fire; they were too cute.
>
> About 3 p.m. on this blazing Saturday afternoon we got the order to prepare to advance, and as we got into our equipment and gave a last touch of oil to our best friend (the rifle), I can tell you that our hearts were going pit-a-pat, as we all knew well what awaited us as soon as we left our cover. However, not a soul hung back when the order came to advance—we defiled as smartly as on parade over the hill and took up our positions in the open in lines of companies. We advanced at a brisk pace across into the open plains which lay at the bottom of the hills, and until we had gone

> about a mile and a half there was no notice taken of us by the enemy, except the snipers, who were busy picking off the officers but without much success, as the range was too long. However, things were soon to hum. Just as we got nicely into the middle of a great field, which had been ploughed up by the Turks to render advancing more difficult, the enemy opened fire!
>
> Good Lord! They didn't half plop the shells into us—shrapnel, high-explosive and lyddite shells were bursting in absolute hundreds in front, above, and behind us, and now and then to add intensity to their fire numerous land mines blew up, throwing men and rocks into the air and blinding us with sand. Men fell all around, and the shouts and smell of the lyddite were awful. Soon the air was laden with pungent smoke which caused great smarting to the eyes, but those of us who were lucky enough to be still unhurt advanced. When we got out of the field the order to extend came, as we were now under rifle-fire, and we advanced at the double, throwing ourselves down as flat as possible every twenty-five yards to get our breath, then: 'Prepare to advance. Advance!'. Up and away in a rush forward for another twenty-five yards and down again. Our casualties were much more heavy now, as the range was suitable to rifle-fire and the Turks would wait until we were getting up, and at each halt we left many men to mark our rests.[17]

The Turks during the remainder of the campaign were never dislodged but some were taken prisoner and the only comments recorded were that they were all fine fellows physically and seemed quite contented and pleased with their fate when captured! As an opponent, the Turkish soldier was both feared and admired by most Irish soldiers.

For Herbert's family, the following few months would prove to be a difficult time. Herbert had not returned from the battlefield, but confirmation as to whether he was dead or alive eluded them. Doubts about Herbert's death were finally put to rest by an affidavit made by Ernest Hamilton, who had been the second lieutenant in command of Herbert's platoon on the fateful morning. Hamilton was bright and extremely handsome. However, the appalling horrors of the war turned him into a chronic alcoholic and he was subsequently court-martialled and 'dismissed the service'. He returned to Ireland but never continued his medical studies. Indeed, he never worked again and did nothing with his life, which to all intents and purposes had come to an end while he wore the uniform of the Dublin Fusiliers on the ridge in Gallipoli. Perhaps those who did not return were the lucky ones. The following affidavit gives a gruesome portrayal of Herbert's last moments:

> On the morning of the 16th day of August 1915 I was stationed with my Company behind a ridge somewhere in Gallipoli and at about 5 o'clock a.m., just shortly after dawn broke a charge was ordered over the ridge and down the hill towards the Turks who were in a very strong position about 80 to 100 yards away from us; my Company charged in two lots of about 80 men each, I (this Deponent) having charge of the second lot which included the said Herbert Snowdon Findlater. Immediately we went over the ridge a most severe machine gun fire was poured into us together with a fierce

shell fire. We had to go through a gap immediately over the ridge and then into the open towards the Turks. When I was crossing said ridge a shell burst close beside me and I was blown back again behind the ridge and wounded, but still possessed consciousness and, on looking up to see how the charge was progressing, I found that every man in both lots of my Company was either lying on the ground dead or wounded. I remained in the ridge and a second party came up to take the place that our Company had left and we held the ridge for about three hours and were then relieved by another Regiment. The ground in front of the ridge mentioned by me and where the casualties in the said charge took place was never re-taken by us, and for the three hours during which we held the ridge after the charge the entire ground was most heavily shelled and a constant machine gun-fire swept over it, making it impossible, as I verily believe, for anyone to survive who was on the ground during said shelling and fire . . . [18]

Hoping against hope, the family made strenuous efforts to establish whether Herbert was held prisoner by the Turks. They tapped contacts in the Mazawattee Tea Company in London. At last the final word came from Cairo: 'Findlater was in a bayonet charge made by two other platoons on August 16th. Only four men returned and they said that he and all the others had been killed. Signed for Sir Louis Mallet.'

Herbert died leaving two young sons, Maxwell (Max) who eventually graduated at Cambridge and spent a lifetime teaching at Pangbourne Nautical College, Reading, and Godfrey who settled in Canada.*

When the invading forces were finally removed by January 1916, the count showed that 30,000 men had been killed or had died of their wounds, 8,000 were missing or prisoners, and 74,000 were wounded. Of the original Dublin Pals 'D' Company of almost 239, only 79 remained to leave the peninsula.

As these survivors looked back from the transport at the scene of so much unavailing bloodshed, they were only human if they hoped that there might be some little recognition or word of praise for them. But it was not to be and little effort has been made to retrieve from oblivion the live human detail of their deeds. They with others may have failed in accomplishing all that was placed before them. Looking back it still seems to them to have been an impossible task that was set, but they faced it cheerfully and gave of their best to achieve the goal. *Spectamur agendo*—We judge them by their deeds. As they steamed away into the darkness every one's heart was saddest at the thought of leaving their courageous dead on the hill-sides and cliffs that they were abandoning, but to their comrades and their friends the memory of all they did and tried to do will never fade.[19]

* Herbert was born in Dublin in 1873. Educated at Strangeway's School and Trinity College Dublin, he qualified as a solicitor in Sir William Findlater's office. He attended Findlater and Empire Theatre board meetings as the family solicitor. He was a member of the Royal Irish Yacht Club and was an accomplished amateur actor. Like his brothers he was a keen sportsman and a founder member of the Monkstown Hockey Club in 1895. He married Evelyn Thompson in 1904.

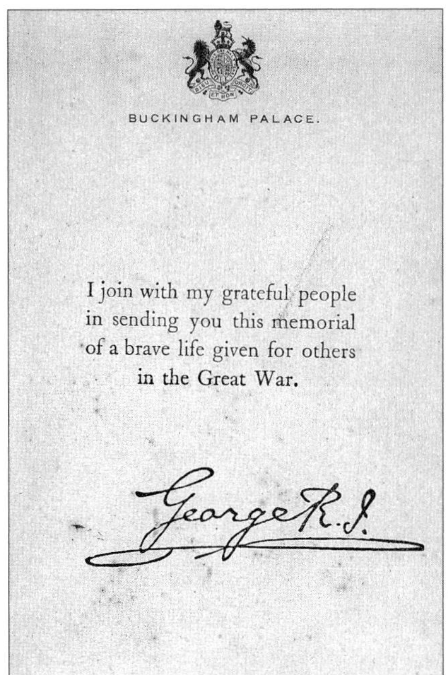
BUCKINGHAM PALACE.

I join with my grateful people
in sending you this memorial
of a brave life given for others
in the Great War.

George R.I.

G V R I

HE whom this scroll commemorates
was numbered among those who,
at the call of King and Country, left all
that was dear to them, endured hardness,
faced danger, and finally passed out of
the sight of men by the path of duty
and self-sacrifice, giving up their own
lives that others might live in freedom.
Let those who come after see to it
that his name be not forgotten.

L/Serjt. Charles Arthur Findlater—
Royal Dublin Fusiliers—

Royal acknowledgment of a life given for the Empire

Even those who did not fight, but who witnessed the carnage and tried to support those left behind, they too played a part. As one officer said:

> I really must say something about Father Murphy and Canon McClean, the Church of Ireland minister. These are our clergymen of the 6th and 7th Dublins and 6th and 7th Munsters, which four battalions form the 30th Brigade. The Canon, a dear old Irishman, from Limerick, holds his service side by side with Father Murphy. They put great spirit into the men, who love them both, in fact almost adore them. I personally think that nothing is good enough for these two noble gentlemen. Catholic and Protestant are hand-in-hand, all brought about by the gentleness and undaunted courage displayed by these two splendid soldiers of Christ. Never since the landing has the roar of battle, be it ever so ferocious (and God knows it is bad here at times), prevented these clergymen from forcing their way into the firing-line and attending to our gallant sons of Ireland.[20]

Herbert sadly was not to be the only member of the family to give up his life for the Empire during this long war. His brother Charles was also killed in action when, after a period of recuperation, he joined up with the 10th Dublin Fusiliers and went to France. It is easy to assign the war dead to a memorial stone in a far-off field. But each had his own personality, his achievements and his ambitions. Charles was no exception. Educated at High School, Dublin, and at Armagh Royal School, he subsequently entered Trinity College, Dublin. For a number of years he was associated with the family firm, after which he turned his attention to engineering. In 1902 he went to South Africa, and worked as an engineer in Johannesburg. Returning home, he became interested in the cycle trade and was later associated with the development of the motor car industry in Dublin. As a sportsman he was well known. He was on the gymnastic team of the Sackville Hall Club. He was a well known cyclist, and won a number of long-distance races in the Irish Road Club. He was also popular in Trinity College, was a member of the Monkstown Football Club, and he distinguished himself in the keenly competitive days of the Dublin Swimming Club.

The *Evening Mail* on 12 December 1916, tells the story of his death.

> Charlie, as he was so popularly known, was a son of the late John Findlater, Esquire, J.P., and Mrs Findlater, 'Melbeach', Monkstown, Co. Dublin. He was killed in action (in France) on 13th November, in the big battle on the Somme front, in which his regiment, the Dublin Fusiliers took so glorious a part. The attack took place in appalling conditions that foreshadowed the horrors of Ypres the next year. German snipers made it their business to shoot the Dublin's officers and many were hit. Nonetheless the Dubliners were able to take all their objectives. However, about one hundred Dublin Fusiliers died that day. Charlie who was in his forty-seventh year was not the kind of man to plead his years when his country needed his service. Those who served with him at the front describe him as a splendid soldier; anxious, above all, to come to grips with the enemy. In the ordinary course his official duty would have kept him behind. He asked permission to go 'over the lid,' as the parapet is called, with his comrades, and the service for which he volunteered cost him his life.[21]

Charles and Herbert's cousin Percy was thirty-six when he was killed in 1918. *The Irish Times* (Friday 5 April 1918) reported:

> Captain Percival St George Findlater, Army Service Corps, was killed instantaneously by a shell in France on the 28th March. Capt. Findlater, who was a graduate of Trinity College Dublin and held full diplomas of the Engineering School there, obtained a commission in the Army Service Corps on the outbreak of war. He was shortly afterwards attached to the French front, and had served there continuously since 1915, being mentioned in despatches in 1916. Captain Findlater was educated at St. Stephen's Green School, and subsequently at Elstree (Herts) and Harrow, and was the younger son of the late Sir William Findlater. He was a member of the University Club.

Percy's elder brother, Lieutenant Colonel Victor Findlater, served with the Royal Irish Rifles, survived the war and settled in Kent where he married and had two sons. He died in 1957 aged seventy-seven.

Two nephews of Herbert and Charles, sons of John Findlater who emigrated to Texas in 1883, also signed up. Frank, the eldest, enlisted with the Canadian field ambulance department of the Medical Corps as a stretcher bearer for fifteen months, then transferred to the Scottish Canadian 16th Battalion (known as the Caddies from Hell) in which service he was wounded losing the use of his arm. His brother James Ronald was not so lucky. He was a private in the 3rd Canadian Overseas Reinforcement Battalion and died, in Bradshot Military Hospital, of broncho-pneumonia following influenza on 26 October 1918 aged twenty-seven.

Herbert's brother Alex, known to all as 'Dr Alex', was the third brother in

Dr. Alex

Gallipoli. He was awarded the DSO 'For conspicuous gallantry and devotion to duty on several occasions, notably on 29th September 1915, at Chocolate Hill, Gallipoli Peninsula'. Here Alex crossed over two hundred yards of open ground under very heavy shellfire to render aid to two wounded men. He saved the life of one, but the other was beyond help.

In a letter home written on 27 August 1915, Alex delineates the traumatic and dangerous plight of the medical corps:

> We were under fire all the time (in fact we have been under fire for the last 10 days), 5 of our men were put out of action on Saturday dressing the wounded in the field, one shot thro' the chest when assisting one to dress a case and the others close by—we were sniped at and under fire all the time. We are really an advanced dressing station and are in the midst of the troops and suffer the shelling equally with them. So far I have not been touched, but out of 70 of our lot—8 are out of action and one dead. Am writing this in a dug-out, a hole in the ground on the side of a hill. Believe me, have left no stone unturned to find out all about Herbert and do not give up hope. All very fit and well, very very dirty and so far have not been touched, many narrow squeaks as everyone has had.
>
> The General came round this morning and complimented us and particularly the stretcher bearers on the good work they had done. He said it was the task of the entire camp, so after that nothing matters, and have done our job. They are shelling away at present—at night we get a rest from the shelling, as they don't want to give away the position of their guns, but we are constantly sniped at. Thank God have got over nerves.
>
> Felt a bit jumpy before the flag fell, but now feel as if I am in the middle of a good hunting run as I used to enjoy when having a hunt with poor Adam with the Ward Hounds. I must admit I will be very glad when it is all over as if one waits long enough one must be 'kilt'. Big naval guns firing from sea 2 miles off and practically shake the dug-out each time they fire.[22]

When Dr Alex returned to Edgware where he was in practice, in June 1916, there were scenes of great rejoicing, with processions and civic addresses. This was in sharp contrast to the lack of welcome accorded to his colleagues returning to Ireland. As recorded in the *Edgware Times:*

> A procession, led by the band of the 9th Middlesex Depot, Mill Hill, was formed and the hero (Dr Alex) was drawn in triumph through the streets in a brougham from

> which some of his most enthusiastic admirers had detached the horses. He was several times called upon to respond to eulogistic addresses. The town was gaily decorated with flags and bunting, and a banner inscribed 'Welcome to our Doctor and friend' was carried in the procession.[23]

But for those few Pals who returned to Ireland alive there was no hero's welcome. In 1916 the population was just digesting the shock caused by the executions of the leaders of the Sinn Féin Rebellion—as it was then called. The attitude of the new state was notably ungenerous to the men who had fought in the British Army in the trenches. Laymen and soldier volunteers alike had fought valiantly, most of them knowing they would not return home. But little was done by the Irish government to accord some respect to the many men who died, to offer some thanks to the few who survived. Some were more generous than others. Todd Andrews wrote in *Dublin Made Me*:

> Tom Reilly was to me a symbol of the 50,000 Irish men who lost their lives in the British Army in the Great War. He went to war with another 250,000 Irishmen at the behest of the leaders of the nation. I could never feel that they were less patriotic than we who took part later in the Volunteer Movement. It was, I think, a mistake on the part of the post-1916 leaders of the Volunteers to have repudiated the Irish survivors of the war; they should have publicly sought to recruit them into the Volunteer Organisation.
>
> At the time of the 1916 fiftieth anniversary celebrations in 1966, Harry Mundow, the Chairman of the Office of Public Works, suggested to me that, as a symbolic gesture of recognition that these ex-British soldiers were part of the historic tradition of the Irish nation, a bridge should be built across the Liffey linking the Phoenix Park with the very beautiful War Memorial Park designed by Lutyens on the other side of the river. I thought it was a highly imaginative and generous idea. I broached it to Seán Lemass. He was not prepared to go along with it, feeling it was too late to do anything. I regretted that Dev was no longer Taoiseach. It might have appealed to his expressed desire for a union of hearts. Dev believed with Pascal that the heart has its reasons of which reason knows nothing.[24]

Many families, like ours, lost men during this appalling war. It is up to us never to allow their bravery to be forgotten. It is sad that it took until the Robinson Presidency (1990-97) for families of the 35,000 Irishmen who died in the Great War to enjoy official Government presence at the Armistice Day remembrance services in St Patrick's Cathedral, and in the beautiful memorial gardens at Islandbridge.

The memorial gardens, designed by Sir Edwin Lutyens, are now fully restored and a credit to the Board of Works. The garden, on which work originally commenced in December 1933, was completed in 1939 at a cost of £56,000 [£2.2m] and was to have been officially opened by Éamon de Valera in that year. However, the event never took place due to the outbreak of war in Europe. By the 1970s, as a result of official neglect, the gardens had fallen into disrepair and decay, the pavilions were broken and the doors destroyed. A new restoration by

ALEX. FINDLATER & CO., LTD.

Roll of Honour

DECEMBER 1st, 1915

1. Captain Alex. Findlater, 4th (London) Mounted Brigade Field Ambulance, Mediterranean Expeditionary Force.
2. Lce.-Cpl. Herbert S. Findlater, "D" Co., 7th Battalion Royal Dublin Fusiliers.
3. Private Charles A. Findlater, "D" Co., 7th Battalion Royal Dublin Fusiliers.
4. Michael Doyle .. Royal Irish Rifles.
5. Patrick Mannion .. Connaught Rangers.
6. Reginald Red .. Royal Army Medical Corps.
7. John A. James .. Royal Army Medical Corps.
8. George Twamley .. Irish Guards.
9. Harry Johnston .. Royal Field Artillery.
10. John Kemsley .. Royal Dublin Fusiliers.
11. James Doran .. Motor Transport.
12. William Marshall .. Cycle Corps.
13. Tom Connor .. Royal Dublin Fusiliers.
14. Herbert Fallon .. 5th Dragoon Guards.
15. Ted M'Kenna .. East Yorkshire Regiment.
16. Joseph J. Kelly .. Royal Dublin Fusiliers.
17. Maurice Ardiff .. Irish Guards.
18. D. Goyer .. 7th Canadian Infantry.
19. John Farrell .. Inniskilling Fusiliers.
20. James Taylor .. Canadian Infantry.
21. Maurice Mack .. Royal Field Artillery.
22. Thomas O'Brien .. Royal Field Artillery.
23. Richard Kavanagh .. Irish Guards.
24. Simon Nevin .. Connaught Rangers.
25. William Magill .. South Irish Horse.
26. James Byrne .. Army Service Corps.
27. William Murphy .. Connaught Rangers.
28. — Cole .. Royal Dublin Fusiliers.
29. Robert Kent .. Royal Dublin Fusiliers.
30. Edward Byrne .. Royal Army Medical Corps.
31. Richard Tracy .. Army Service Corps.
32. Thomas Inglesby .. Motor Service—R.A.M.C.
33. Patrick Beggs .. Royal Dublin Fusiliers.
34. John Healy .. Irish Guards.
35. William Newman .. Royal Dublin Fusiliers.
36. William Kenny .. Royal Dublin Fusiliers.
37. John Hatchell .. Royal Dublin Fusiliers.
38. William Grant .. Rejoined Colours.
39. Edward Gormley .. D.C.L. Infantry.
40. Patrick M'Clean .. Royal Dublin Fusiliers.
41. T. Ryan .. Inniskilling Fusiliers.
42. T. Rourke .. Connaught Rangers (with 16th Irish Division).
43. Bernard Murphy .. Royal Army Medical Corps.
44. William Arnold .. Royal Dublin Fusiliers.
45. Richard Haughton .. South Irish Horse.
46. Patrick Tyre .. Royal Navy.
47. J. Treston .. Royal Naval Reserve.
48. James Gallagher .. Royal Dublin Fusiliers.
49. Chris. Whiston .. Royal Army Medical Corps.
50. J. Hynes .. Royal Dublin Fusiliers.
51. C. Byrne .. Army Service Corps.
52. John Baker .. Transport Ship.
53. William Bryan .. Royal Dublin Fusiliers.
54. William Tracy .. Royal Dublin Fusiliers.

The Lady of the House recorded the 54 Findlater staff who had enlisted by December 1915, out of about 350 men and women employed at that time. I estimate from a perusal of *Ireland's Memorial Records 1914–18* that as many as 20 of these lost their lives and no doubt others were scarred for life.

the Board of Works was completed in 1988. A service of dedication and blessing took place in the presence of the British and French Ambassadors and representatives of both the United States and Turkish Embassies—but there was no representative from the Irish government. Today, however, feelings have changed, and the government is officially represented at the Armistice Day remembrance services in the capital.

Notes and references

1 Commander of the 29th Division quoted in Michael Hickey *Gallipoli* London: John Murray 1995 p 143
2 Henry Hanna *The Pals at Suvla Bay* Dublin: E. Ponsonby 1916 pp 20-22
3 The *Evening Mail.* Quoted in Hanna *op. cit:* pp 24-27
4 Quoted in Myles Dungan *They Shall Grow Not Old, Irish Soldiers and the Great War,* Dublin: Four Courts Press 1997 p 106
5 *Ibid.* p 101
6 Quoted in Hickey op. cit. p 229
7 *Ibid.* pp 48, 61
8 *The Irish Times* 1 May 1915
9 Hanna *op. cit.* pp 60, 64, 90
10 *Ibid.* p 110
11 Leon Uris *Redemption* London: Harper Collins pb 1995 p 681
12 Hanna *op. cit.* pp 98-99
13 *Ibid.* 105-6
14 *Ibid.* p 106
15 Unpublished letter in the author's possession
16 Hanna *op. cit.* pp 113-118
17 *Ibid.* pp 120-121
18 Unpublished affidavit courtesy of A. J. M. Findlater, grandson of Herbert Findlater
19 Hanna *op. cit.* pp 129-130
20 *Ibid.* pp 132-3
21 *The Evening Mail,* 12 December 1916
22 Unpublished letter in the author's possession
23 *Edgware Times* 20 March 1931
24 C. S. Andrews *Dublin Made Me* Cork: Mercier Press 1979 p 78

9. Easter 1916

Only a short while after the defeat of the Pals in Gallipoli, an event occurred in Dublin that was to change the course of Irish history—and my maternal grandfather, Captain Harry de Courcy-Wheeler, was a close witness to some of its most poignant scenes, while grandfather Willie stoically defended his headquarters from vandals and looters.

At this time Sackville (O'Connell) Street was described as one of the four greatest streets in Europe. 'It was one of the chief gems of the beautiful classic city of Dublin. On Easter Monday the old street looked glorious, as it always did in sunlight. Its substantial lines appeared to be time-defying—a veritable thing of beauty and a joy forever.'[1] That bank holiday Monday morning people in Sackville Street were in a relaxed mood, strolling in the sunshine, enjoying the holiday.

Suddenly a troop of men swung out from in front of Liberty Hall and marched the few hundred yards to the GPO, which they entered and proceeded to take over, expelling the workers inside. Being well used to seeing bodies of men marching through the streets, Dubliners no doubt assumed this was another exercise. But this was serious. The Sinn Féin rebellion* began at noon on Easter Monday, 24 April 1916. A few minutes later a proclamation setting up a republic in Ireland was read in front of the GPO by Commandant Pearse. In other parts of Dublin bodies of Irish Volunteers, as they were called,† captured the magazine in Phoenix Park, the Four Courts, the College of Surgeons, Stephen's Green, Jacob's Biscuit Factory, Boland's Bakery and various other places of vantage. An attempt was also made to capture Dublin Castle, but it failed. Telegraphic communication was destroyed, and two of the local railway termini were seized.

The skeleton police and military force left on duty during the holiday was powerless to control the situation. The rebels barricaded themselves into a series of strongholds across the city, and also sent snipers into the rooftops (the 'hill tribes' as the British Tommies later called them). Eventually the British military machine recovered from its surprise and began to pour troops into the centre of the city. A gunboat started to shell Liberty Hall and the GPO. It soon became

* To use the contemporary term.

† The original Irish Volunteers were founded in 1913. On the outbreak of the First World War (fought, so the British argued, in defence of the rights of small nations) William Redmond called on the Volunteers to support the British effort. The Volunteer movement split, and the hard-liners (much in the minority) retained the name Irish Volunteers while Redmond's supporters became known as the National Volunteers. It was the Irish Volunteers who were 'out' in 1916.

clear that the position of the Volunteers was impossible. They had in effect locked themselves into a series of besieged positions, without the possibility of helping one another. Militarily their position was hopeless.

Meanwhile on the south side of the city in Northumberland Road and around Mount Street Bridge, there was about to be carnage. A large detachment of Sherwood Foresters had been sent via Holyhead to Kingstown. They were inexperienced troops and somewhat confused. Some even thought they were in France. Food was short because the kitchens and rations had not arrived, though the officers enjoyed the hospitality of the very unionist Royal St George Yacht Club, where members were able to pass on the latest rumours about the fighting, with no doubt generous doses of paranoid talk about Irish treachery. As a result the officers became extremely suspicious, and forbade the ordinary soldiers to accept the gifts of tea, chocolate, oranges, bananas, sandwiches and sweets that the loyal residents of Kingstown and Blackrock showered on them. Big Billy Vaughan, manager of the Blackrock Findlater's, solved the problem by rolling apples and oranges down the street for the young soldiers to pick up.

Another Findlater link with events was to prove more poignant. Among the officers was Frederick Christian Dietrichsen (probably of Danish stock), the barrister who had married the sister of my Aunt Marjorie's husband Edmund Mitchell.* Unknown to Christian, his two children had been sent from Nottingham to stay with his parents-in-law in Blackrock to escape the danger of Zeppelin raids. As he marched his squad through Blackrock, to his astonishment he saw his own children standing on the pavement waving flags. 'His fellow officers saw him drop out of the column and fling his arms around the children. It was a joyful scene, with no hint of the tragedy to come.'[2]

After a brief rest at the Ballsbridge show grounds, the Foresters passed up Northumberland Road towards Mount Street Bridge, where they received a terrible attacking fire from Clanwilliam House. By the end of the day twelve Volunteers, armed with a rifle each and some revolvers, had accounted for seventy British troops. Among them was the Nottingham barrister Frederick Christian Dietrichsen.

The disruption caused by the Rising meant that basic necessities such as bread, milk, fuel and groceries, which were typically delivered to shops and homes every day, could not get through. This caused real hardship. Totally indifferent to the historic events going on around them, Dublin's poorest people began looting the shops and department stores of Sackville Street. Clerys was a favourite target, as would Findlaters have been. But on our side of Sackville Street the Gresham Hotel and Findlaters remained intact. I recently asked my Aunt Sheila, who was fourteen at the time, whether there was any explanation for this. She confessed that the ladies in the household were not informed on business mat-

* Edmund, who in 1914 married my father's eldest sister Marjorie, was a second cousin of the Kildare Street wine merchants of that name. Quartermaster Captain RAMC in Ismalia, Egypt and mentioned in despatches. Assistant managing director of Findlaters 1919–45. His sister Bea, Beatrice Agnes, was married to Dietrichsen.

ters but added: 'Your grandfather sat on a chair outside his premises with a blunderbuss on his lap and threatened to shoot all looters!'

The looters horrified ordinary Dubliners—both inside and outside the GPO. Crawford Hartnell, in a lengthy article in *The Lady of the House* on the Rising, described the scene that he encountered on the Tuesday of Easter week:

> It was Sackville Street with the accent on the 'sack'! The street was crowded, and the worst of the slum population—the wretched folk who inhabit the tenements formed of the old mansions of the dead and gone, or emigrated aristocracy—were about in great and quite universal force. A filthy gutter-snipe with an old fowling piece was menacing an aged man, and a few steps further a dirty unwashed woman of the slums, ragged and unkempt, with her matted hair surmounted by a fashionable hat, shuffled past, her dirty naked feet thrust into fashionable patent-leather shoes. The pavement was ankle deep in finely broken plate glass, shattered by blows in order to place the shopkeeper's stock at the mercy of the itching fingers from the slums. The thieves and bad characters of Dublin had swarmed from their dens into Sackville Street. What a scene. Had I been a photographic plate, exposed in Sackville Street that Easter Tuesday morning, I could have presented one phase of the French Revolution in miniature.[3]

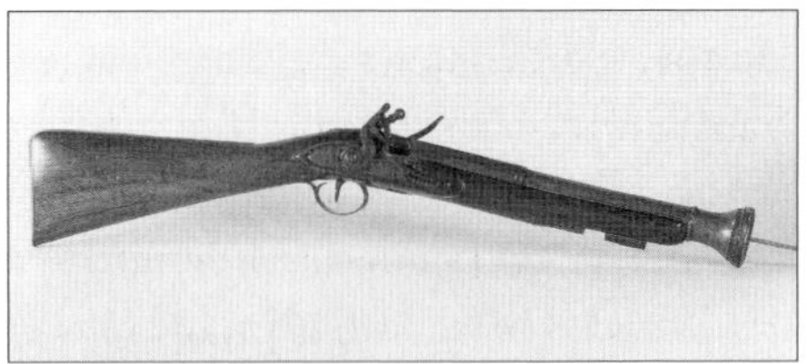

Maybe the blunderbuss used by Willie in 1916

Apart from the hardship caused to non-combatants, the Rising was a minority affair. In March 1916 there were about 2,000 Volunteers in Dublin involved in the Rising, as against 150,000 Irishmen serving in the British forces, and over 160,000 in the National Volunteers, who supported John Redmond. Nonetheless it was this small group who were to be the ultimate rulers of Ireland.

It is sad that no personal records survived of life in Findlater's Sackville Street for Easter week 1916. The shop was closed for the bank holiday and most of the resident employees from the country would have returned home to their families—and indeed the disruption of transport allowed them a few days, extra holiday. The few that remained might have seen the events from the vantage-point of the staff billiard room on the first floor or the bedrooms higher up, which would have given a prime view of the British front line massed by the Rotunda, though there was always the risk of being hit by a sniper or even a stray bullet. There would have been a small staff tending to the horses although these could have been enjoying a couple of days' grazing. It is certain that Grandfather Willie would have had to make a circuitous journey from his home, Melville in Blackrock, to his premises and, with senior managers, supervise the protection of the property.

A couple of weeks after the cessation of hostilities, Findlaters placed an ad in *The Irish Times* (12 May) to:

> apologise to their Customers and Public for the inconvenience caused them during

the last fortnight. Owing to the dislocation of business it was impossible to serve their many customers as they wished, and deliveries of goods were almost impossible. They have to thank their customers for their forbearance under very trying circumstances. The Directors also wish to thank the Managers and Staff at all their Houses for the hearty manner in which they tried to meet the requirements of the public and also the volunteers who kindly helped at the Branches, knowing the shortage of staff owing to some employees being unable to return from holidays. They especially wish to thank the Resident Staff at Head Office for their successful efforts to save the premises there.

Captain Harry's adventures

Captain Harry de Courcy-Wheeler was born on St Patrick's Day—17 March 1872. He took a degree at Trinity College, Dublin, graduating as a Greek and Latin scholar. He then qualified as a lawyer, but never practised at the Irish Bar. He married Selina Knox, the youngest daughter of Hercules Knox, of Rappa Castle, Co. Mayo, in 1904. They lived at Robertstown House, Co. Kildare.

As a reserve officer of the 8th King's Royal Rifle Corps, he was ordered to England in 1914. The local company of Volunteers—and the whole village—paraded at Robertstown to see him off. But when he reached Dublin a telegram from the War Office in London sent him back to the Curragh.

My mother, Harry's eldest daughter Dorothea, remembered those days:

> We transferred from Robertstown House to the Curragh Camp in 1914 where my father took up his duties as Officer in charge of the service side of the barracks. My father desperately wanted to go and fight in the Great War. He got called up twice and then called back to the Curragh. He wanted action. When an airfield was set up and the first planes arrived at the Curragh, he was crazy with enthusiasm and tried to transfer to the Royal Flying Corps. But his application was refused. I was only five at the time and I remember being in the back seat with nanny and my baby brother Annesley and with a big silver tray on our knee. We were in Daddy's Ford car with canvas roof and windows that we took down if it wasn't windy. The car had big kerosene lamps. It had to be wound up to start, often with a back kick, which nearly broke an arm. Mother and Father were in the front seats and the villagers stood at the gate waving goodbye. The silver tray belonged to the family and was used for tea in the afternoons. The house was locked up for the duration of our stay at the Curragh.
>
> We moved to a large square house on the edge of the Curragh plains, with a big garden around it. The airforce was stationed outside our back gate. My father had his horse in the stables and there was a man looking after the horse. I think he doubled as groom and houseman. We also had a cook, a parlourmaid and a nurse. My twin sisters, Joan and Nancy, were only just two and the youngest, Kathleen, in her cradle. My mother was an ex-hockey international so she immediately organised a hockey team with the army and officers. The officer's mess was next door to us. They used to play hockey down on the grass at the bottom of the garden and the officers would come back to our house afterwards. *[And the hockey sticks?]* Oh, we fashioned them out of the hedgerows!

Captain Harry

I remember going to church and my mother had a lovely sunshade, which I now have. And I had a parasol to match my mother's parasol, though mine was frilly! There was a Colonel Porter and he had six children and I used to play with them a lot. There was a lake or pond in his garden in the Curragh and they had a raft that they used to go out on, and I fell in when I was getting on to the raft. It was terribly cold in the winter on the Curragh and my mother used to stitch my father into newspapers under his tunic, his military jacket, to keep out the biting wind and the cold. I remember very distinctly standing in the study watching the sewing.

Presenting Arms

Harry was Staff Captain to General Lowe for the duration of the Rising and took the surrender from the various leaders, including from his wife's first cousin, Countess Markievicz. His subsequent friendship with Éamon de Valera and Seán T. O'Kelly may therefore seem a bit surprising. Harry kept the revolvers of the executed leaders in a locked drawer in his desk until 1949, when he presented them to Seán T. O'Kelly, then President of the country. They are now on display in the National Museum in Kildare Street. He concluded his presentation speech:

*Now, in conclusion, I wish to present to your Excellency the articles which came into my possession in Easter Week 1916. Before doing this I might point out to those present the appropriateness of his Excellency as the recipient of these memories of 1916. Thirty-three years ago I was Staff Captain to Brig. General Lowe, commanding the British Troops in Dublin at the very time when his Excellency had the privilege of occupying an identical position as Staff Captain to Commandant-General Pearse, Commanding the Irish Troops in Dublin.**

A 1915 Model-T Ford

* Wheeler speech made in Áras an Uachtaráin, Friday 29 April 1949.

Harry *(centre)* with President Seán T. O'Kelly *(right)* and *(left)* William Norton, Tánaiste & Minister for Social Welfare (*The Irish Times* 30 April 1949)

Arms presented to the President on Friday 29 April 1949

Countess Markievicz

German Mauser pistol 162742 Waffenfabrik Mauser, Obernorf A. Neckar

Repeating pistol .25 474251, Fabrique Nationale, Brownings Patent FN

General Pearse

Repeating pistol 7.65mm, 54541, Fabrique Nationale, Brownings Patent FN Pouch of ammunition and canteen or mess tin

College of Surgeons

Two repeating pistols, .25, Harrington & Richardson Arms Co., self-loading

Other

Revolver, six chambers 19916 Smith & Wesson

Why Harry, who was 30 miles away in the Curragh camp, was called on to act as General Lowe's Staff Captain is unclear. Perhaps it was no more than his being of the right rank, competent and available. He was known to be a good administrator and certainly performed his difficult task with integrity and fairness.

In 1966 Harry's eldest son, my uncle Wiggie (Wigstrom Hercules Beresford de Courcy-Wheeler), presented Harry's papers to the National Museum where they were received by the then Minister for Education George Colley.

As the Rising began, Harry was enjoying a peaceful bank holiday Monday, putting his papers in order prior to spending the day with his wife and six children in their house and garden on the camp. For him it would be a carefree day, far away from his office telephone and its incessant jangle. He was about to close the door behind him when the telephone shrilled. The voice of an officer from the orderly room crackled into his ear. 'The Sinn Féiners are out! They are trying to seize Dublin.' Shocked, Harry hung up the receiver. He flicked his cuff to look at his silver watch with its oversized winding button. It was 1.10 pm. Out came a well used notebook from his tunic pocket. He made an entry under 24 April in the diary that was to record the events of the next few days in great detail: 'Sinn Féin Rising reported in Dublin.'

For the next few days there was great bustle in the Curragh as the ponderous Army machine ground into action. His daughter remembers 'going up with my mother into the water tower on the Curragh, which was very high, to look at the flames in Dublin—you could see them from the top of the water tower. I was seven then.' Like all soldiers at the time of war Harry was anxious for the safety of his family. In his diary he wrote, as if to reassure himself, 'I was called up as a reserve officer for the war with Germany I was very friendly with the local Volunteers. They told me whatever happened in the future . . . my wife and children would come to no harm. They would see to this. Will they see to it now?' They did.*

On the Friday night, Harry came out of the wings and onto the stage of history. His diary of the momentous events he was about to witness was long afterwards serialised in the *Sunday Express*.[4]

> At 10.30pm the garrison adjutant rapped at the door of his quarters with a message from Room 13, the communications centre at British headquarters in Park Gate, Dublin.
>
> 'Report immediately to General Lowe's staff' he said. Brigadier-General William Lowe was the general officer commanding British forces in Dublin. . . . [Driving into

* On his departure from Robertstown the local Volunteers sent him a letter promising that his family and property would be kept safe, and they were, even while a detachment of British cavalry was billeted on his land. The letter, oddly addressed to *Colonel de* Courcy-Wheeler stated:
Robertstown 10th Aug. 1914.
To Col. H. E. de Courcy-Wheeler.
We the members of the Robertstown Company of Irish National volunteers beg to offer to Col. H. E. de Courcy-Wheeler our regret that he has been called away from his young wife and family to fight the cause of his country in Belgium, at the same time we would congratulate him on the fact that the Govmt has selected him, and promoted him to Rank Col., to take his place in such a sacred cause.
We wish him to convey to his Regiment that the cause for which they are about to fight has the entire sympathy of the Irish N. Volunteers and for which they also are willing to take up arms (if they had them) if necessary and required.
We assure Col. Wheeler that Mrs. Wheeler, his family and property will be safe in the hands of the Irish Volunteers until he returns.
Wishing Col. Wheeler God Speed and Success on behalf of the Volunteers.
James Dowling. Commdg.

Dublin] his was the only car about, and he began to wonder if what was happening had already come to an end. . . . He met the first signs of life at Islandbridge where houses were occupied by British soldiers.

'I was suddenly pulled up with the cry of "Halt or I fire," all along the line and when the car stopped a rifle with fixed bayonet was thrust through the window, the pass-word demanded and information as to my identity and destination. . . . I said "If you take that b------- bayonet away from my chest I will be able to give you the information you want." The sentry scrutinised the pencilled instructions that the Curragh adjutant had scrawled. I climbed out of the car and stood on the running board. From that point the whole city seemed to be ablaze. Rifle fire was going on in all directions and shells were bursting at intervals. . . .

The Mauser used by Countess Markievicz. The detachable butt turned it into a rifle.

'Inside the headquarters building, I found the general and his staff in their offices sleeping on the floor dressed in their uniforms. In Room 13 a staff officer was hunched over a telephone which was going continuously. "Thank the Lord for some help," he said wearily. "Take over on this telephone, will you? We've had no rest for three nights." With those words he lay down on the floor and went to sleep.

'All sorts of messages came through as to the direction of troops, asking for orders, reports of snipers located in various and distant parts of the city, houses blown up and fires here, there, and everywhere, especially in the neighbourhood of Sackville Street.

'The manager of a bank in Upper Sackville Street telephoned that the bank was on fire, that there was a caretaker with a large family in the house. "How can we escape?" he asked. Upper and Lower Sackville Street were being swept by the fire of snipers and the British military were replying. I asked the General what was to be done about the family trapped in the burning bank and he said "Tell them to march out with a white flag." I phoned these instructions to the manager. The telephone rang again. It was the manager to say that they had no white flag. He asked me: "Would a Union Jack do?" That put the lid on it! I advised him to be quick and to make a white flag or they would all be burned or shot.

'In the morning, one of the general's orderlies brought a cup of tea and bread and butter. A very limited supply. Rations were very uncertain and few and far between. We had to go to Kingsbridge Station to get something to eat and to Ross's Hotel near the bridge.

'At 12.30pm information came that a Sinn Féin nurse—Miss Elizabeth O'Farrell—was waiting at the Parnell monument. She had been sent by Commandant General Pearse to negotiate terms of surrender. General Lowe ordered me to accompany him.'

Nurse O'Farrell had been sent out to seek the British commander from No. 16 Moore Street, a grocery store [where the GPO garrison had retreated. Nurse O'Farrell had taken a makeshift flag and hurried along Moore Street making for Parnell Street.] She could hear the bullets whining ahead of her, but they ceased when the soldiers saw

O'Connell Street immediately after the Rising

her nursing red crosses and the flag which she was waving from side to side.

An officer motioned her over to the barricade. 'Commandant General Pearse wishes to treat with the British commander,' she said. . . . She repeated the message to the area commander when he came up. 'Will your leader be able to travel on a stretcher?' he asked. 'Commandant Pearse does not need a stretcher,' she said. 'I think he does,' insisted the officer who had heard that the GPO commander was wounded and was confusing Pearse with Connolly. . . .

The officer ordered the Red Cross badges to be removed from her tunic and apron and that a woman should search her as a possible spy. Nothing more dangerous was found than two pairs of scissors and some sweets and cake. Nurse O'Farrell was taken to the newsagent's shop of Tom Clarke, one of the signatories to the proclamation of the Rising. From there a message was rushed to Room 13.

General Lowe sprang to his feet when he heard the news and said: 'Come on, Wheeler we're on our way.' His son, Lieutenant Lowe, went with them in the army car. Wheeler's diary records a nightmare drive.

'In peacetime the journey from Park Gate Street to our destination, the shop at the Parnell monument, would have been a matter of mere minutes. We took a zig-zag course in and out of side streets, taking the intervening corners at high speed to dodge the sharpshooters who were posted at vantage points on the roofs of the houses.

'Two bullets did get the panel of the near door of the car which was an official saloon supplied for the use of staff. Owing to the skilful driver and the speed, I do not expect the snipers realised who were in it until it had skidded round the next corner. Eventually we arrived at a small newsagent's shop a few doors from the corner of Great Britain Street, where it joins Upper Sackville Street at the Parnell monument.

'The general communicated the terms to Nurse O'Farrell and she was allowed half an hour to return with the reply from Commandant General Pearse, who was in command at the rear of the GPO and controlled Moore Street and the adjoining thoroughfares. Upper Sackville was still swept by snipers and while waiting for the return of the nurse, General Lowe, who was in his staff uniform and a very conspicuous mark, strolled into Sackville Street to note the position.

'As the whole of Upper and Lower Sackville Street was held by the rebels at this time, and I felt responsible for the general's safety, I pointed out that he would draw the fire on himself if spotted. He made little of it, but in the end I persuaded him to return to the newsagent's shop, and wait there for the dispatches from Commandant General Pearse.

'Soon after the nurse returned with a reply imposing conditions. These were refused, and the general sent her back again to say that only unconditional surrender would be accepted. She was given half an hour to return with the reply.

'At 2.30 pm Commandant General Pearse surrendered to General Lowe accompanied by myself and Lieutenant Lowe at the junction of Moore Street and Great Britain Street. He handed over his arms and military equipment. His sword and automatic repeating pistol in holster with pouch of ammunition, and his canteen, which contained two large onions, were handed to me by Commandant General Pearse. Onions were carried by insurgent troops as iron rations. They were believed to be high in nutriment value.

'Two Army official cars were waiting. Commandant General Pearse, accompanied by Lieut. Lowe, was driven in the general's car, proceeded by the general and myself in the other car. We drove to headquarters, Irish Command, to interview General Sir John Maxwell, the British Commander-in-Chief. After the interview, Commandant Pearse signed several typed copies of a manifesto, which was dated by himself, Dublin, 29th April 1916 and read as follows:

'"In order to prevent the further slaughter of Dublin citizens, and in the hope of saving the lives of our followers, now surrounded and hopelessly outnumbered, the members of the Provisional Government present at headquarters have agreed to an unconditional surrender, and the commandants of the various districts in the city and country will order their commands to lay down arms."

'After signing these documents, Commandant General Pearse was conducted to a sitting room at headquarters.

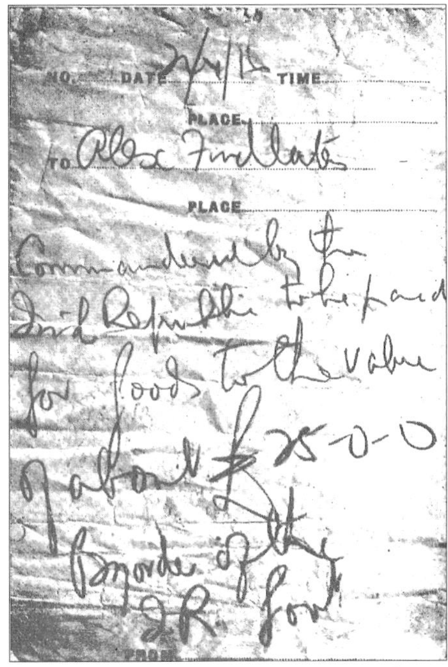
NO. DATE 29/4/16 TIME
PLACE
TO Alex Findlater
PLACE
Commandeered by the Irish Republic to be paid for goods to the value of £25-0-0
by order of the IR Govt
FROM

Receipt given for goods commandeered from Findlaters during the Rising (*Evening Mail* 12 May 1916)

Pearse *(right)* surrenders to General Lowe *(centre)*.*

I was ordered to keep guard over him, and was locked in the room alone with him.

'I was handed a loaded revolver with orders to keep it pointed at Commandant Pearse, and to shoot should he make an effort to escape. This was a very responsible and serious order to obey and to carry out should it have become necessary. Pearse did not seem in the least perturbed and greatly to my relief, I was on this duty for only 15 minutes when I was sent for by General Lowe and another officer was sent to relieve me.

'General Lowe ordered me to go at once to the castle, show the manifesto of Commandant General Pearse, the Commander-in-Chief, to Commandant Connolly, in command of the Irish Citizen Army, who had been brought in wounded and a prisoner, and get him to sign the document or a similar order to his own men. When I arrived at the castle, part of which had been turned into a Red Cross hospital, I was brought up to the ward where Commandant Connolly had been carried. He was in bed, and I waited beside him while his wounds were being dressed. I told him my orders and asked if he was well enough to comply.

'He said he was, and he read the manifesto signed by his Commander-in-Chief. Commandant Connolly then dictated the following—as he was unable to write himself—which I wrote down underneath Commandant Pearse's typed manifesto and it was signed, and dated, April 29, 1916 by Commandant Connolly: "I agree to these conditions for the men only under my own command in the Moore Street district, and for the men in Stephen's Green command."

'This document containing the orders of Commandant General Pearse and Commandant Connolly was presented on the following day by me to Commandant Thomas MacDonagh who added the following words and signed and dated it. 30.IV. 1916, 3.15p.m. "After consultation with Commandant Ceannt I have confirmed this order agreeing to unconditional surrender." . . .

'On the night of April 29, 1916, General Lowe, accompanied by myself and two other members of his staff, paraded at the Parnell Monument to receive the surrender of the rebels in accordance with their commander's instructions. Up to 10.30 pm about 450 surrendered there. I took down the names and addresses of 84 and delegated other

* Harry is almost concealed on Pearse's right; the man in the white breeches is Lt. Lowe (not Harry as is often supposed). Photo first published by *Daily Sketch* in London 10 May 1916.

officers to take the remainder.*

'The prisoners were drawn up in line and I walked down the ranks taking down each name and address as given to me. As it was physically impossible for me to write down all the names I sent word to the General that I required assistance and he then detailed 14 other officers to help me. The lists made by these officers were handed in to the Assistant Inspector General of the Royal Irish Constabulary at a later date. . . .

'That night I received orders from the general to be at the bank at the corner of Rutland Square and Upper Sackville Street at 8 am the following morning, Sunday, April 30, 1916, to meet Nurse Elizabeth O'Farrell—known to the British Army as the "Sinn Féin Nurse"—who had undertaken to conduct me to the headquarters of the various commands in and around the city for the purpose of communicating the surrender orders.

In order to prevent the further slaughter of Dublin citizens, and in the hope of saving the lives of our followers now surrounded and hopelessly outnumbered, the members of the Provisional Government present at Head-Quarters have agreed to an unconditional surrender, and the Commandants of the various districts in the City and Country will order their commands to lay down arms.

P. H. Pearse
29th April 1916
3.45 p.m.

I agree to these conditions for the men only under my own command in the Moore Street District and for the men in the Stephen's Green Command.

James Connolly
April 29/16

On consultation with Commandant Ceannt and other officers I have decided to agree to unconditional surrender also

Thomas MacDonagh

The Surrender of Headquarters.

The surrender note, with Harry's handwriting in the centre—signed by Pearse, Connolly and MacDonagh

'A military car–No. R1 4064–was waiting, driven by one of the Royal Army Service Corps drivers, with the sergeant major of the 5th Royal Irish Regiment as escort. I was unarmed, Nurse O'Farrell carried an old white apron on a stick as a flag of truce, and she and I sat behind.

'I decided to go first to the College of Surgeons, Stephen's Green, which was strongly held by the rebels and which was keeping up a continuous fusilade with the British garrison in the United Service Club and the Shelbourne Hotel. On the way I had, by the general's instructions, ordered an escort of military to be in readiness at Trinity College to take over the College of Surgeons if the rebels surrendered. At Lambert Brien's shop in Grafton Street my motor was brought to a standstill by the cross-firing, and I decided to allow the nurse to proceed alone and deliver the document at the college under cover of the white flag. Both she and it would be recognised and respected.

'She returned about 9.30 having delivered the message.

* Among the 84 names Harry recorded in his field notebook were: Harry Boland of 15 Marino Crescent, Clontarf; Michael Collins, 16 Rathdown Road, North Circular Road; John Lemass, 2 Capel Street (Lemass, the future Taoiseach, evidently announced himself as Seán, for Harry began the first name 'Ch . . .' before reverting to the English version); John Frances McEntee of Belfast (who as Seán MacEntee became Minister for Finance in successive Fianna Fáil governments); Lieut. John Plunkett, Larkfield, Kimmage; Wm Pearse, St Enda's College, Rathfarnham (executed 4 May). Most of the prisoners gave Dublin addresses, but there was also James Robinson, from Glasgow, Patrick Rankin from Co. Down, Peter Murphy from Dundalk, Fred Newsom from Wexford, James M. O'Brennan and Peter Bracken from Tullamore and Francis M. Kelly from London.

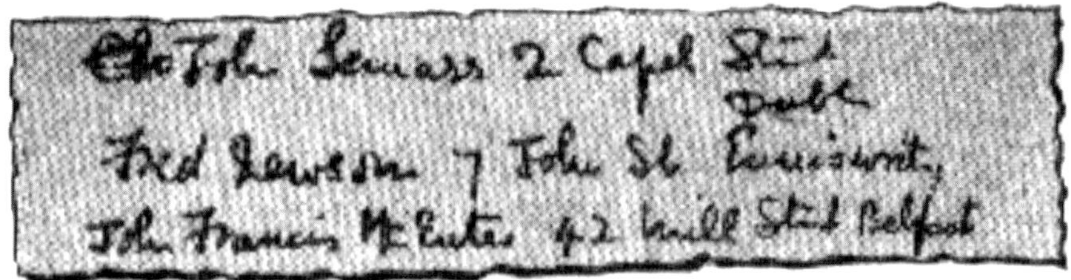

John Lemass 2 Capel St Dub
Fred Lewson 7 John St Enniscorthy
John Francis McEntee 42 Mill St Belfast

The entry in Harry's notebook recording the arrest of Seán Lemass and Seán McEntee.

'Thence I endeavoured to drive her to Boland's Mill, Ringsend. Owing to the barricades across Lower Mount Street, and having tried all the routes down by the river which were held by the rebels, and hearing reports of continuous firing further on, I had again to allow the nurse to proceed on foot to deliver the document under cover of the white flag.'

Boland's Mill, commanded by Éamon de Valera, was a seemingly impregnable fortress. De Valera had avoided shells from the naval reserve boat Helga, firing from the River Liffey, by the simple ruse of hoisting his flag on a building some distance from the mill. British soldiers encircling the mill shouted and waved their rifles at Nurse O'Farrell as she made her way towards it. She waved her white flag back at them and went on. Volunteers lifted her through a window into a small room. There she came face to face with Commandant de Valera, who was ghostlike with his uniform spattered with flour from the bakery. He said: 'My immediate superior officer is Commandant MacDonagh. I will take orders only from him.'

The nurse made her way back to the captain's car.

'I took her up again and drove her through the Castle, up Ship Street to St. Patrick's Park, being the nearest point that the motor could approach to Jacob's Factory as this and the surrounding neighbourhood was very strongly held by the rebels. I was to meet her again at 12 noon. These visits were for the purpose of handing in the orders to surrender to the various commandants, not to receive their surrenders.

'Nurse O'Farrell was very intimate with the situation of all these command posts and had no difficulty in directing the motor on the best route to take and where to go next, so that no time was lost.'

To reach Jacob's biscuit factory, now a high, embattled fortress, Miss O'Farrell had walked through a maze of streets which were a death trap to the troops. From its two towers vigilant Volunteers had a magnificent view of the whole city. Its lofty windows dominated even Dublin Castle—the city's administrative centre.

The strength of its garrison was 150 men, some boys of the Fianna Eireann, the Republican boy scout movement, and a party of Cumann na mBan, the women's wing of the freedom movement to which Miss O'Farrell belonged. The commander of this stronghold whom she now sought was Commandant Thomas MacDonagh.

Near the factory Miss O'Farrell, with her white flag resting on her shoulder, asked for him. There was a whispered conversation among the Volunteers and a large white bandage was produced. 'We will take you to him, but you will have to be blindfolded,' she was told.

She was led along streets for a few minutes and eventually she heard and recognised

Scenes of destruction of central Dublin immediately after the Rising

the commandant's voice. The bandage was removed from her eyes. She handed over the typewritten surrender manifesto, which Padraig Pearse and James Connolly had signed. Commandant MacDonagh, his face grave, declared first that he would not take orders from a prisoner.

'I will not surrender myself,' he said, 'until I have spoken with General Lowe, my brother officers who are already prisoners, and the officers under my command.'

Meantime, Captain Wheeler, who was waiting for Nurse O'Farrell in St Patrick's Park, went to Dublin Castle. He writes:

'I obtained information from the garrison adjutant that a telephone message had been received from O.C. Troops, Shelbourne Hotel, that the Republican flag over the College of Surgeons had been hauled down and that troops were required to take over the college and supervise the surrender of the garrison. I motored back at once to Trinity College and ordered the military escort which was in waiting to proceed up Grafton Street as far as possible and to keep the men out of view of St Stephen's Green as there was still sniping from various points.

'From there I went to the Kildare Street entrance of the Shelbourne Hotel and interviewed the OC Troops, who pointed out the position from the top window where he had his Maxim gun placed. Having informed him of my plans, and having telephoned to the OC Troops, United Service Club, not to "open fire" as I was about to receive the surrender of the rebels, I returned to Grafton Street, picked up the sergeant-major with the motor and drove to the front door of the College of Surgeons.

'I ordered the sergeant major to bang the door, and, having waited for a reasonable time without any response, a civilian signalled that there was some excitement going on down York Street. A white flag was hanging out of the door of the college. Two of the rebel leaders came out, advanced, and saluted. The commandant stated that he was

Michael Mallin [–he had once been a drummer boy in the British Army–] and that his companion was Countess Markievicz. That he and the garrison wished to surrender.

'The Countess [–a cousin of Captain Wheeler's wife–] was dressed in the uniform of an Irish Volunteer, green breeches, putties, tunic, and slouch hat with feathers and Sam Browne belt, with arms and ammunition. I asked her would she wish to be driven in my motor under escort to the Castle, knowing the excitement her appearance would create when marching through the streets. She said: 'No, I shall march at the head of my men as I am second in command, and shall share their fate.'

'Accordingly, I requested her to disarm, which she did. When handing over her arms she kissed her small revolver reverently. In addition to this small automatic pistol, Countess Markievicz was armed with a German Mauser pistol, which she also handed me. This latter was retained by General Lowe until leaving the Curragh, when he presented it to me.

'Commandant Mallin was not armed and I requested him to order his followers to lay down their arms in the college and march out and form up in front. While they were doing so I sent a message to the escort in Grafton Street to come up, as there were no British troops picketing this part of the city and I had only 25 men in Grafton Street. I then inspected the rebels in the college and ascertained that they had disarmed, and inspected the arms in a large room in the upper part of the building, a portion of which had been curtained off as a Red Cross hospital.

'Commandant Mallin and Countess Markievicz accompanied me during my inspection. The whole building was in an indescribable state of confusion and destruction, furniture, books, etc., being piled up as barricades and the large picture of the late Queen Victoria torn to pieces and destroyed. Food, clothes, arms, ammunition, mineral waters, surgical dressings were mixed up and lying about in all directions.

'On my inquiring about the wounded, the countess informed me that they had been removed. There was one prisoner, Mr Lawrence Kettle, who was handed over to me and whom I drove to the Castle and handed over to the authorities there. Having carried out the inspection, I ordered the Commandant to march out his followers, whom he informed me numbered 109 men, 10 women, the Countess Markievicz, and himself. I phoned from the nearest telephone instrument—the Mineral Water Direct Supply Co. at Stephen's Green—to headquarters to inform the general of this surrender.

'Immense crowds of civilians had, in the meantime, assembled in York Street and Stephen's Green, as there were no troops guarding this portion of the city, and it was with much difficulty that the officer commanding the escort, which was small, succeeded in getting the rebels away in safety.

'Tremendous cheers greeted the rebels as they surrendered. The crowds followed them and continued this down Grafton Street until I succeeded in getting a cordon across the street. The crowds were held back at the point of the bayonet to allow the escort and their prisoners through to safety to the Castle. In the meantime I had detailed one NCO and four men to take charge of the college until a stronger guard could be obtained. The escort and prisoners reached the Castle yard in safety at 1.45 p.m.

'I then proceeded to my rendezvous with Nurse O'Farrell at St Patrick's Park but

Henry Street immediately after the Rising

was informed that she had not returned from Jacob's factory although it was two o'clock. She was now two hours late.'

Nurse Elizabeth O'Farrell was three hours late returning from the beleaguered Jacob's factory where, under cover of a white flag, she had gone to deliver surrender documents to Commandant Thomas MacDonagh. Captain de Courcy Wheeler was waiting for her in St Patrick's Park sitting in the staff car, No. R.1 4064, which had already carried them on the same mission to other leaders. But now he had company. General William Lowe, Commander of the British troops in Dublin, had driven up with his staff officers to join him. He told Wheeler that there had been a new development: that two friars had offered to persuade the insurgents to surrender and he had agreed to let them try. They had gone to Jacob's factory.

Nurse O'Farrell came at last, with the friars—Fathers Aloysius and Augustine–and with Commandant MacDonagh. Wheeler, MacDonagh, and the two friars, accompanied by the general's son, who was his ADC, drove to insurgent outposts at the South Dublin Union and the Marrowbone Lane Distillery to arrange the surrender.

At the distillery, Captain writes in his diary:

'Dense crowds surrounded the motor car and we were warned that irrespective of the white flag and the friar who was carrying it, anyone wearing khaki would be fired upon. In spite of this, nothing unpleasant happened. However, although there seemed to be great relief in this district that hostilities had ceased, it was perfectly plain that all the admiration was for those who surrendered. I ordered the motor to go to Ship Street close to St. Patrick's Park and wait there until the garrison in Jacob's factory had surrendered.

'An unpleasant incident then occurred. Commandant MacDonagh arrived followed by crowds and accompanied by the friar with a white flag. He stated that although his men had laid down their arms in order to surrender, the soldiers had opened fire on them, were throwing bombs into the houses, and that the military had broken into the factory and were killing his men. He had seen one of our soldiers taking up a position in the factory and using his bayonet.

'I told MacDonagh that it was impossible, as there was no troops there, and that if it was an individual soldier I did not understand why he and his men could not deal with him. He replied that if they interfered with the soldier they were afraid it might be serious for them.

'Commandant MacDonagh was so positive about the occurrence that I reported it to the GOC, 176th Infantry Brigade, and brought MacDonagh before him. The general stated that none of his troops was there. He instructed me to ascertain at Dublin Castle whether any troops had been sent independently. Accompanied by General Lowe's ADC, I went with MacDonagh to the castle and brought him before the colonel in command, who also stated that there was no troops at Jacob's.

'I then drove MacDonagh back and he requested some officers to go and ascertain the fact. I took upon myself to advise strongly against this and refused to allow General Lowe's ADC to go, pointing out to the GOC, 176th Infantry Brigade and to the OC Troops in the Castle that it was an impossible story got up for some purpose.

'Accordingly, I told MacDonagh to return accompanied by Nurse O'Farrell, a secular priest and the friars and to order his men to surrender. The G.O.C. 176th Infantry Brigade and the O.C. troops in the castle pointed out that if there were soldiers firing at the rear of the factory it would not prevent his own men from coming out at the front.

'Shortly afterwards the two friars, the secular priest and Nurse Elizabeth O'Farrell returned and stated there had been no foundation for the accusation against the military, that none of the commands had been injured, and that it was looters who had broken into Jacob's and were doing mischief.

'I immediately reported this to the GOC, 176th Brigade and to the OC Troops in the Castle and asked them to hear the secular priest on the subject, which they did.

'Shortly afterwards the commander from Marrowbone Lane and from the South Dublin Union arrived and laid down their arms in St Patrick's Park along with the commander from Jacob's.

'I then set off again with Nurse Elizabeth O'Farrell to drive her to Boland's Mills at Ringsend, but as it was now getting dark and she said she would prefer to go in the morning, I drove to Trinity College with her and telephoned to General Lowe for instructions. He replied that the following morning would do, and that in any case it was reported that the Ringsend commands had surrendered to the OC Troops, Ballsbridge, and to place Nurse Elizabeth O'Farrell in the Red Cross Hospital at the Castle until the following morning leaving her in care of the matron, not as a prisoner. . . .

'After leaving Nurse O'Farrell at the Castle hospital I returned to headquarters and the following morning, May 1, 1916, was kept busy in Room 13 with various matters pending the handing over of the command of the troops in Dublin by General Lowe to General Sandbach, which was to take place at 12 noon.

'General Lowe introduced me to Captain Prince Alexander of Battenberg, ADC to

General Sir John Maxwell, and I accompanied them to the inspection held in Trinity College Park of the Irish regiments engaged in Dublin during the Rising.

'To each of the units General Maxwell made a speech, complimenting them on their behaviour and praising them for their skill and courage in the execution of the most distasteful form of warfare to a soldier—against his own countrymen and in house-to-house fighting.

'After luncheon in the college, I motored back to headquarters. From there I went to deliver a letter from General Lowe to Nurse O'Farrell and order her release from the Dublin Castle hospital.'

[The general wanted to ensure her safety and the letter that was hand-written and signed by him, stated: 'Miss Elizabeth O'Farrell was of great assistance by voluntarily accompanying a staff officer to various rebel commandants, and I trust that this may be taken into consideration at any future date.']

'When I arrived Nurse O'Farrell had been removed to Ship Street Barracks guard-room by Captain Stanley, RAMC, where she was handed over by the OC Troops to the military police as a prisoner. Captain Stanley had not been informed by the assistant matron that Nurse O'Farrell was not to be considered a prisoner, but only to be detained in the hospital until sent for by the G.O.C. Troops, Dublin, and had therefore discharged her as an ordinary prisoner when finding her fit. I considered this a very serious matter and a grave reflection on the honour of everyone concerned.

'I then went to the provost marshal and explained the position to him but he stated that he had sent Nurse O'Farrell to Richmond Barracks, and that he could give no assistance. I was determined to have the matter put right, and it was quite plain that the general would put all the blame on me and in the meantime I was considering what Nurse O'Farrell must be enduring, and thinking of the grave breach of faith on the part of the general and his staff. Captain Stanley then procured an ambulance, and with the assistant matron we went to Richmond Barracks.

'To my alarm, when we arrived I was informed that Nurse O'Farrell had been sent from there to Kilmainham. Every minute was then of consequence as the prisoners were to be embarked that night for England, and orders had been issued for a draft of 400 men to escort the prisoners to the North Wall, and a detachment of 80 men to form an overseas escort.

'At last, in great anxiety, which was shared by Captain Stanley and the assistant matron, we arrived at Kilmainham, where I peremptorily demanded the release of Nurse O'Farrell, and threatened court martial if the orders of the general officer commanding were not complied with forthwith.

'This had become necessary as the officer commanding at Kilmainham had already received orders from the provost marshal that Nurse O'Farrell was to be deported. I had no written order to the contrary, only what I knew were the general's intentions with regard to her. I said I could not leave without Nurse O'Farrell and that I would send for the general if there was any further delay.

'The assistant matron and Captain Stanley explained also that it was through a mistake that she had been allowed to be removed from the Castle and that they were to blame.

'The officer in charge then handed her over to me, and she was brought back to the Castle hospital in the ambulance with Captain Stanley and the assistant matron, where we arrived at 5.05 pm. I left her there with instructions, as before, that she was to be detained as a patient and not as a prisoner, until the general issued further orders.

'In the meantime, whether by telephone from myself or otherwise, General Lowe had heard of the grave mistake, and himself chased round in my tracks until he found her safe in the hospital where I had left her. He told me that he was not at headquarters when my telephone message arrived, but that when he heard of the position he went round in pursuit himself, and that he had seen Nurse O'Farrell and ordered her immediate release from the hospital. He then asked me, "Why could you not have done that?" My reply was, as I think it was a bit hard–"I had done it all before you!" The general and myself were fast friends and he always said he liked soldiering with me.

'It was on account of the general releasing Nurse O'Farrell that his letter was not delivered to her, as I never saw her again, and he said it was unnecessary.

'Hostilities had now ceased, the order for "cease fire" having been given. Of course I was in the thick of all the other happenings, but, as will be gathered from what I have recorded, I had no time to give any but superficial attention to what was going on all round me, except to my own special orders which followed and jostled each other in quick succession.

'My next duties were in reference to the courts martial, as having been present at the surrenders it was considered that my evidence would be indispensable.

'These courts martial were held in Richmond Barracks, and I was backwards and forwards continuously, during which time Mr Asquith, the Prime Minister, crossed from England, paid a visit there and recommended that the prisoners should be supplied with pillows. These were evidently not available (as they were not a barrack room issue), because of the unexpected addition to the numbers normally in occupation of those barrack rooms.

'Martial law had been proclaimed over the whole of Ireland and an order was issued prohibiting anyone leaving their houses between 7.30 pm and 5.30 am, and licensed premises were only allowed to remain open between 2 and 5 pm in the city and county of Dublin, so that the streets were absolutely empty and deserted. There was no traffic of any kind, and I seemed to be the only individual abroad after 7.30 p.m.

'Being detached from my own unit, I lived at one of the hotels—the Shelbourne or Hibernian—and after dismissing my official car for the night used to tramp the streets alone being challenged here and there by a sentry. There was not a sound, nothing stirring, no lights visible, and the streets took on quite a different shape and appearance, and the whole surroundings were weird.'

Captain Wheeler gave formal evidence at the courts martial of Commandant Padraig Pearse, Commandant Michael Mallin, Commandant James Connolly, Countess Markievicz and Commandant MacDonagh.

He records these incidents in court:

'Countess Markievicz was asked by the president of the court whether she wished to ask me any questions. She said, "No, this officer has spoken the truth. I have no wit-

Harry with the walking stick given to him by Commander Mallin (alas it was subsequently stolen). (National Library of Ireland)

nesses, what I did was for the freedom of Ireland and I thought we had a fighting chance."

'Before her marriage Countess Markievicz was Constance Gore-Booth, eldest daughter of Sir Henry William Gore-Booth, fifth baronet, and sister of the present baronet, Sir Joselyn Gore-Booth, of Lissadell, Co. Sligo.

'She was a relation of my wife (née Knox), both being descended from Sir Paul Gore, first baronet of Manor Gore, and to commemorate the event my daughter who was born on The Curragh a short time before the Rising, was christened Kathleen Constance Gore after Countess Markievicz. As Miss Constance Gore-Booth I had met her previously at castle and other social functions.

'On the same day—May 2, 1916—I was again ordered to be present to give evidence before another field general court martial of the surrender of Commandant Michael Mallin who was in command at the College of Surgeons. My evidence was as described previously:

'"Commandant Mallin came out of the side door of the college, advanced and saluted and stated that he was in command, and that he and his command wished to surrender."

'The president then asked Commandant Mallin whether he wished to ask me any questions. He said, "No, but" (turning to me) "I would wish it placed on record how grateful my comrades and myself are for the kindness and consideration which Captain Wheeler has shown to us during this time."

'The president of the court said that his wish would be carried out. The court then dismissed me.

'In the reproduction of the photograph taken by one of my brother officers of myself standing by the ambulance, it will be noticed that I am carrying a walking stick. This was given to me by Commandant Mallin, and was carried by him when he surrendered at the College of Surgeons. The ambulance is that in which Countess Markievicz was brought to and from her court martial.

Not mentioned in his diary was the Singer sewing machine which Harry found in Liberty Hall, which had been used for making uniforms and flags for the Volunteers. Presenting this and Harry's papers to the National Museum in

1966, Harry's son Wiggie* explained: 'My father observed a number of these sewing machines in Liberty Hall and thought one would make a good souvenir for his wife and family. In due course the Singer sewing machine arrived at the Royal Irish Automobile Club and has been in active service up to a year ago, sewing garments for the family. I believe the year of manufacture was 1896 which as well as being a good year for sewing machines, was an excellent year for port.'

It is said that a 20th century Chinese statesman, when asked what were the effects of the French Revolution, replied that it was too early to tell. In *The Lady of the House* of Christmas 1916, Crawford Hartnell, expressed early a view that many have also adopted about the events of Easter Week: 'The other day I heard a great man, a non-politician who knows this country most intimately, observe: "This rebellion has been the greatest mistake in Ireland's history and the method of its suppression the greatest error England has ever made in Ireland".

Notes and references

1 *The Lady of the House,* Christmas edition 1916
2 Max Caulfield, *The Easter Rebellion* London: A Four Square Book 1965 pp 221–2
3 *The Lady of the House,* May 1916
4 *Sunday Express* March 1966

* Wigstrom Hercules Beresford de Courcy-Wheeler, born at Robertstown 10 November 1908; educated Dover College, apprentice wine merchant in Mitchells of Kildare Street. Served in Second World War, Captain in the Irish Guards and Commandos. Wine merchant in Kidderminster and Worcester after the war.

10. The Wheeler Family

Up to now, this book has been mostly Findlater. However, when my father died in 1962 my mother quietly suggested that the Wheeler side of the family were not such a bad lot! And she was right. While the Findlaters were mainly merchants, the Wheelers, and one Knox, were predominantly medical people, eight to date, two of whom attained the Presidency of the College of Surgeons.

The Wheeler family in Ireland trace their roots back to the Rev. Jonas Wheeler DD, who was appointed Dean of Christ Church Cathedral, Dublin, in 1594 and was first Protestant Bishop of Ossory from 1613 to 1640. He was Chaplain to Queen Elizabeth I and King James I. He died in his ninety-seventh year on 19 April 1640 and is buried in St Canice's Cathedral. His direct line is now extinct. Our line is descended from the Bishop's nephew.

Great-Grandfather, Surgeon Wheeler

Harry Wheeler's father William Ireland de Courcy-Wheeler, known as Surgeon Wheeler, was the eldest son of George Nelson Wheeler and his wife, Williamza Florence Ireland, of Annesborough House, Robertstown, Co. Kildare.* George Nelson met a tragic end while shooting on the bog in Robertstown. He was shooting game with a muzzle-loading hammer. He fired once and the gunpowder failed to ignite. Then he did just what one is taught not to do. He looked down the barrel to see what was going on, and—boom—off went his head!†

Surgeon Wheeler was born in Co. Kildare and received his earlier education by private tuition and subsequently at Dr Fleury's well-known school in Leeson Street. He entered Trinity College in 1862 and studied medicine both there and in the Royal College of Surgeons, graduating in 1866. In 1867 he entered the Army Medical Service, and studied at Netley where he obtained the highest marks, winning honours in military science and other subjects. After a short term of duty at the Royal Hospital, Kilmainham, he set off with the expeditionary force to Abyssinia (now Ethiopia) in 1868, where he served with distinction, receiving the Abyssinian Medal for the meteorological reports compiled during the expedition. During his army career Surgeon Wheeler became well known for both his medical expertise and his physical prowess. He was one of

* She was the daughter of William Ireland of Low Park, Co. Roscommon. He in turn was descended from William Ireland, who married Hon. Margaret de Courcy, sister and heiress of 23rd Baron of Kingsale, by his wife Dorothea. William Ireland Wheeler assumed the name de Courcy-Wheeler in 1897.

† That was one of a pair of guns that were subsequently converted to breech-loaders and remained in the Wheeler family into the second half of the 20th century.

the strongest men in her Majesty's Service. One of his ordinary feats in the gymnasium at Canterbury was to take a 56lb weight in each hand, and then rise from a sitting posture on one leg, elevating the weights at arms' length. He was frequently seen to lift from the ground a 120lb dumb-bell, and elevate it with extended arm without a jerk, which was regarded as an extraordinary performance.

Surgeon Wheeler in the robes of the President of the Royal College of Surgeons

After leaving the Army he became Doctor of Medicine, Master of Surgery, and Member of the Royal College of Physicians of Ireland. He was appointed demonstrator of descriptive and surgical anatomy to the Royal College of Surgeons in Ireland and shortly afterwards surgeon and lecturer on clinical and operative surgery to the City of Dublin Hospital.

Surgeon Butcher

It was soon after this appointment that he was appointed assistant to the eminent surgeon and university lecturer on operative surgery, Richard Butcher.* Chosen by Butcher to assist him in all of his operations Wheeler became known as 'the Butcher's boy'. During this period he also achieved considerable success working with Dr Stoney, a successful medical teacher: their pupils obtained outstanding distinctions, three of them winning at the same examination first places for the British, Indian and Naval medical services.

In 1882 he was elected Vice-President of the Royal College of Surgeons of Ireland, and in the following year—the centenary of the College—he was elected President. An incident in his career brings us back to troubled times of the early 1880s. Surgeon Wheeler was sent by the government to attend a wounded

* Richard G. Butcher was President of the RCSI in 1866. In 1879 Surgeon Wheeler accompanied him to Fenit on Tralee Bay in County Kerry where he presented the community with a new lifeboat and lifeboat station in remembrance of his father Admiral Samuel Butcher RN and of his brother Samuel Butcher Bishop of Meath.

The launch of the 'Admiral Butcher' lifeboat, Tralee bay, 1879

landlord at his residence beyond Belmullet, the most westerly town in Co. Mayo. The landlord, a Mr Shaen Carter*, had been badly wounded by moonlighters—illicit distillers, who were probably also poachers. The journey to the north-west had to be undertaken under police protection, especially the forty mile drive from the station through the desolate countryside. On his arrival Surgeon Wheeler found his patient's knee joint badly shattered and promptly amputated the leg. The actual operation took only sixteen seconds but there were several return visits, and each journey to the west took a day and a half. He charged 125 guineas a visit and 50 guineas for the operation. The total bill came to £1,147.15.0. The government contested the fees, but after Butcher was called as an expert witness the court directed that the account be settled in full.

Surgeon Wheeler married Frances Victoria Shaw, daughter of Henry Shaw and grand-daughter of Bernard Shaw of Sandpitts, Co. Kilkenny (related to the Shaws of Bushy Park, Terenure and first cousin of the author George Bernard Shaw). They lived at 32 Merrion Square, which was integrated into Holles Street Hospital in 1932, many years after the Wheelers left.† Their country home was Annsborough‡ in Co. Kildare where they played an active part in local life, Surgeon Wheeler serving as JP and as High Sheriff of the county in 1892. They had nine children. Surgeon Wheeler died on 25 November 1899 of typhoid fever

* William Henry Carter, probably Shaen's father, was recorded in 1824 as being the sole proprietor of one third of Erris covering 47,500 Irish acres. It was also stated that he was the second of his family that ever visited their Mayo estates, 'though in their possession upwards of a century': *Erris in the Irish Highlands and the Atlantic Railway* P. Knight, Dublin: Martin Keane & Son 1836.

† In the intervening years No 32 was used as a book depository for Carnegie Libraries.

‡ Annesborough was the original house of the Robertstown estate. The Wheelers had rented it from the Irelands until Surgeon Wheeler's purchase of the estate, in which it was included.

aged fifty-five, two years after his wife. His eldest daughter Wuzzie (Williamza Florence) then managed the household. I gather that they had quite a wild time. Ho-Ho (Horatio) was eleven, Hillary thirteen, Diamond (Robert) fifteen, Frances seventeen, Billy twenty, Gerry twenty-two, Harry twenty-seven and George in exile twenty-eight. (Martha Kathleen died in infancy.)

The Shaw Family

My Shaw great-grandmother, Frances Victoria, was known as Coo in the family. Her father Henry (born 1819) was a wealthy Dublin merchant, who lived at Tullamaine, near Waterloo Road. He was descended from William Shaw, who was a captain in Sir Henry Ponsonby's regiment at the Battle of the Boyne (1690). During the battle Ponsonby led a charge over the Boyne, galloping before his men with sword uplifted, when a musket ball knocked him from his saddle. William was nearby and lifted his commanding officer on to his back and carried him to safety beyond the mêlée. He was rewarded with a grant of land in Kilkenny. According to Burke[1], Ponsonby had married, in 1674, Dorothy, daughter of a Captain Shaw of Drogheda, so the two men may have been related, or connected by marriage.

The Shaws had their share of financial misfortune. Henry's father Bernard, father of fifteen children, spent much of his time in the country in his function as High Sheriff of Kilkenny and neglected his Dublin legal practice. On hearing that his partner had absconded with his clients' money, he collapsed and died of shock.

His widow, Frances Carr Shaw, daughter of the Rev. Edward Carr, had to cope with the upbringing of the eleven surviving children. She was helped by her late husband's first cousin, Sir Robert Shaw, who was hopelessly in love with her, although to no avail. He provided her with an attractive place to live in Terenure called Harmony Cottage, near to his residence, Bushy Park.* Sir Robert was a partner in Shaw's Bank in Foster Place, which became the Royal Bank in 1831. His father, also Robert, had been a Director of the Bank of Ireland at the time of his death in 1796.

Despite losing £60,000 [almost £3m] on a coal-mining venture Henry was still able to leave his family reasonably well off. He contributed generously to the building of Christ Church in Leeson Park, Dublin. Not so fortunate was the playwright's father George. He had a partnership in a corn mill at Dolphin's Barn. It did not prosper and was almost put out of business by the bankruptcy of a debtor. The richer members of the family seem to have had little compassion for George who was thought of as a boozer and he was left to fend for himself. His wife's family were no more sympathetic. The playwright remained a teetotaller for all his ninety-four years.

* My Findlater aunts Doris and Sheila used to bicycle up to Lady Shaw for tea in the late 1940s and returned to their home, Glensavage in Blackrock, with their bicycles heavily laden with rare and interesting plants. Bushy Park is now a fine public park and leisure area.

The Wheelers of Robertstown

Some of the family thought that Harry had come into a fortune from his sponsor, Miss Wigstrom, but the reality was that any fortune he might have inherited had been dissipated before he got it and he was always selling pictures, glass and silver to make ends meet. He wanted to keep both Robertstown, which his father had purchased from William Ireland (his father's first cousin), and Annsborough, the other house nearby. He liked living in the country and participating in local activities,* but did little with the land. As it happened, he was perhaps as well off as those who did. Agricultural Ireland in the 1930s was in a most appalling state because of the economic war with Britain. It ruined the farmers. One of his friends had marvellous land, but always said that during the Economic War they would have gone bust but for the fact that they bred Prince Regent, one of the all-time National Hunt greats.

Harry was not a bit commercial in the running of the estate. He had a number of tenants on the land at Robertstown and every Friday he would receive the rent from them, 10d per week or whatever it was. He was well liked by them and fair handed in his dealings. When a tenant paid his rent, Harry would give him a bottle of beer. Of course there were occasions when the tenant came in and said: 'We haven't got the money this week, can we come back next week and pay?' To which Harry would reply: 'Of course you can, and here, have a bottle of beer!' The price of the rent was 10d and the value of the bottle of beer 6d!

Selina Knox, Harry Wheeler's wife, was the daughter of Hercules Knox of Rosslare in Co. Sligo and Rappa Castle in Co. Mayo and Harriet who was the daughter of Rev. John Fox of Fermanagh. She and her sisters were great hockey players. She won six caps for Ireland between 1899 and 1902 and her sisters Elise and Anita, seven each. When she married Harry and moved to Robertstown, she formed the Kilmeague hockey team and later the midland branch of the Irish Ladies Hockey Union. When she died, in 1928, reputedly as a result of a blow from a hockey ball while playing for Kilmeague, both these organisations were dissolved.

I have fond memories of her elder brother, my great-uncle Jack. When I called on him in retirement in Sefton, Liverpool, he liked to reminisce on his rugby playing days. He was capped ten times for Ireland. His father had been a keen rider to hounds and his brother was twenty-five-mile cycling champion of Ireland by the time he was eighteen. As he told me:

> I took up rugby at the age of twelve. We used to challenge anyone willing to play us. I contemplated retirement after breaking my leg in 1898 but changed my mind and went on to represent Trinity College Dublin, Lansdowne and Leinster in addition to playing international rugby against all the home countries and Gallaghers original All Blacks.
>
> When I was at the High School in Harcourt Street, Dublin, I played right wing three-quarter until my last year at the school. Feeling that I would not get anywhere in

* Like his father, he was a JP and served as High Sheriff of the county in 1906.

Harry and Selina

> senior rugger, I played in the forward ranks and front row of the scrum. Being a very fast mover, I became the hooker, a position that I enjoyed tremendously and proved successful, being awarded an international cap against Wales in 1904.
>
> I shall always remember the match against the All Blacks (New Zealand) at Lansdowne Road in 1906. Firstly, when the ball was burst, the scrum collapsed and the ball could not be found; the forwards of both sides were battling for a shapeless scrap of leather! Secondly, the speed with which the All Blacks ran and passed and re-passed the ball from one end of the three-quarter line to the other. The match was a very clean game—no sparring and no fisticuffs nor dirty work. One could only take objection when an All Black player was tackled with the ball and three or four of his team mates would fall down behind him and thus form a barrage to prevent the Irish forwards going through to the All Black goal line. New Zealand won three goals from the conversion of three tries.
>
> After graduating at the Trinity Medical School I moved to the Merseyside in 1907 where I took a post at Bootle General Hospital. The Irish weather didn't agree with my health. The sky always seemed to be sitting on my head so I moved here and joined the Liverpool Club. I may add I have never regretted it.

Neither did Merseyside. They gained a brilliant player who used to train by running up and down alongside the hoardings and catching the ball as it rebounded at speed. He was also an unofficial international scout for most of his lifetime and self appointed medical officer to the Liverpool Club for forty-five years. In this latter capacity he once revived the great H. C. Catcheside, later President of the English Rugby Union, by commandeering a bottle of champagne and tipping it down the victim's throat after the latter had seemed destined for the hospital: 'It certainly did the trick. The next minute he was back on the field and scoring the winning try!'[2]

Black and Tans and the Civil War

Between the arrival of the Black and Tans in 1920 and the end of the Civil War in 1923 at least 210 mansions and country houses were deliberately burned in the twenty-six counties, most of them belonging to the Protestant community. This represented only a very small proportion of the total number in the south of Ireland but the 'mania of house burning' vividly marked the end of a long era of ascendancy rule in Irish history.[3]

In 1922 Robertstown came under threat. My mother recalls:

> Dev's lot, the Irregulars, in order to wreck the Treaty, started a campaign of burning houses. It was initially directed against members of the new Irish Parliament and Senate, but quickly spread. The question was, of course, what to save. A few minutes grace was usually given. First the people in the house, then the dogs, horses, cattle and poultry. Pictures seldom survived.
>
> My father heard them coming up the drive and leaned out the dressing room window, which was over the hall door. Our governess, Miss Bradley, was there and so enraged was he that she held onto his legs for fear that he would fall out the window. He shouted: 'One step further and I'll blow your heads off.' He had his revolver in his hand. So they paused and retreated. On another occasion they came to the hall door which we covered in corrugated iron every night and also the windows. This particular night someone knocked on the door, father said 'Who's there?' and they said 'We have come to burn down your house—get everybody out' and he said 'Show your authority from Michael Collins under the door; and I will let you in.' There was no reply. Nothing happened. They retreated. In my father's eyes, Collins was a good man. *[Collins was amongst those from the GPO whose surrender he had recorded in 1916.]* And my mother admired Collins and she was sorry when he was killed and I was also rather upset, even at that age.
>
> On another occasion I can remember rushing into my father in his study and shouting that his friend Lord Mayo's house had been burnt down. He remained totally unmoved and did not look up from his papers having thought that I said: 'The Lord Mayor's house had been burnt down.' When mother entered with the same news he reacted as if electrified and shot off in the direction of Naas in his model T Ford to see what assistance he could be to his friend.

As a Senator, Lord Mayo was a prime target to have his house burnt. An order had gone forth from republican headquarters that, in a desperate attempt to bring the government to its knees, the houses of senators were to be destroyed. Because it was a cold night they came wearing the woollen jerseys which Lady Mayo had recently given them. She was given time either to retrieve her jewellery from her bedroom or her fowl in the yard; she chose the latter.[4] Their house was Palmerston House near Johnstown outside Naas in Co. Kildare.

> During the troubles when my father was out and about in the Ford he brought with him a spade and two planks, to get across trenches dug across the road and a saw to cut through the branches where trees had been felled. We sometimes had to climb over two or three trees getting from our house in Robertstown to the church in Kilmeague,

'Liberated' by Harry from the ruins of Liberty Hall, this sewing machine served the family well for many years (National Library).

two miles away, on Sundays. It may have upset our parents but it didn't upset us. That was life—it was fun!

And one night we heard a terrific gun battle going on and in the morning we went down with our nanny to our other house called Annsborough, which was at the bottom of the hill. It was empty at the time and one military had occupied it overnight, I don't know which, and the other party had attacked it. There was a terrific gun battle and we went down in the morning to see where the bullets had gone into the wall.

On yet another occasion, when the family were having breakfast in Robertstown House, a platoon of British soldiers suddenly rushed into the house, tore around the house and tore out again. They were looking for a fugitive and a few minutes later a little officer came panting in and asked had we seen his platoon. He had lost it. Maybe that was during the Black and Tans.

I had a wonderful childhood. I remember walking through the woods beside Robertstown and thinking there is nothing I want—I have wonderful parents, a horse, hockey, and tennis. I couldn't think of anything I wanted. I must have been thirteen or fourteen then. I had no friends but I didn't miss that because I didn't know anything about friends. There were six of us and we did everything—I didn't know what to do when I met a girl my age.

There was a loft in Robertstown about 100 feet long with a beautiful polished floor and we used to have hockey matches and roller skate there when we were teenagers. Father was a classical scholar, a Greek and Latin gold medallist. He didn't have anything on his fields except a cow that gave us milk and retired horses. He had won the high stone wall championship in the RDS in 1904 on a horse called Sportsman. He stood 14-2. Sportsman lived out his retirement in great comfort at Robertstown. I used to ask father why we did not farm our land like our neighbours but to no avail.

I kept hens and I used to give Mr Greening, the Rector, a couple of dozen eggs to take up to town to his friend who liked fresh eggs. That way I earned pocket money with which I could buy more hens or something I needed. I got my father to buy me a hen house and I paid him back dutifully. My egg money! Then the foxes came one night and took all my hens. That was the end of that! And at another time I had a beautiful white cock that I kept in a cage. I washed his legs and gave him a bath and polished him up. I trained him and I had lots of people looking at him and talking to him. Then I sent him to the RDS with my father and he was shown. My father sent me a telegram to say that he had been very highly commended. I was thrilled. It was the simple things that gave pleasure compared to now.

I never went to school. I had a governess until I was about twelve and then I went to the Rector who taught me along with students who were preparing for Trinity entrance. He taught me Latin, maths but not much English, French or history. I learned history with my governess—the kings of England and some Irish geography. The Rector's son came to teach me Irish but that wasn't very successful. I was then sent up to the French School in Bray to sit for the junior Cambridge. I was staying with Aunt Mabel, uncle Diamond's wife, at Monkstown Castle. He was the local GP and attached to Monkstown hospital. I was late for the exam because the bus was late! I passed the exam into Trinity because I had done quite a lot of Latin, a bit of Greek and was quite good at writing English. I played a lot of hockey at Trinity and later with Maids of the Mountain and we won all before us. I got my International cap for Ireland on tour in America in 1936.

After I graduated in 1932 I married Dermot. My brother Annesley qualified in the Trinity Medical School and Wiggie did his apprenticeship in Mitchells of Kildare Street, Wine Merchants. At the outbreak of war Wiggie signed up with the Irish Guards and trained as a Commando in Scotland. After the war he reverted to the wine trade, in Wolverhampton and Kidderminister. My sister Joan married Oliver Lloyd who, late in his career, was appointed head brewer in Guinness.

The Irish Grand Prix

Harry had a model T Ford. It was beautifully kept and he had his crest on the front driver's door. He was a conscientious committee member at the Royal Irish Automobile Club and played a prominent role in the organisation of the Irish International Grand Prix motor races in Phoenix Park in 1929, 1930 and 1931. He was assistant race Secretary to Walter Sexton.[*] 150,000 spectators watched the event in 1929 and there was great excitement on account of the presence of Malcolm Campbell. The previous year at Daytona he had broken the world land speed record averaging 207 mph. However he failed to finish in the Irish Grand Prix.[†] The government of President Cosgrave was very enthusiastic and saw the Grand Prix as a wonderful shop window in the world press. The loss in 1929 was £3,256 [£130,000] in addition to which £7,000 [£280,000] was spent on the roads in the park. However de Valera's government, which came into power in 1932, baulked at having to subsidise the event, and it ceased.

---

* Walter Sexton was an original member of the club in 1901; Honorary Secretary from 1913 to 1933 and active until his death in 1941. He was a goldsmith, jeweller, silversmith and watchmaker at 118 Grafton Sreet.

† A Russian, Boris Ivanovsky, driving an Italian Alfa-Romeo at an average of 75.02 mph won the 1929 race. He drove daringly and skidded here and there because he knew he was being pressed and had to take risks at the corners.

Turf cutting

The new government turned up trumps when Harry conceived the idea of the first National Turf Cutting Competition. The object was 'to bring the Turf Industry to the position which rightly belongs to it as one of the country's greatest assets'. The turf producing communities were organised into co-ops by the Irish Agricultural Organisation Society in conjunction with the Turf Development Board.

As part of this campaign he initiated the competition, and persuaded members of the Fianna Fáil government (some of whom he had first met accepting their surrender in 1916) to honour the event by their presence.

The programme of the competition included seven contests. Of these, the first two, devoted to the 'breast slane' and the 'wing slane,' were the most prestigious. 'Breast slane' involved the cutting of sods, eleven by four and a half inches, from the face of the bog with the special type of spade used by turf-cutters. 'Wing slane' involved cutting from a lower level and placing the sods to dry in a different part of the bog. There was also a 'footing' competition—the building of sods in small piles of twelve or so for drying; a 'camping' contest—the erection of sods in 'camp' formation, so that the rain would run off the rounded roof, and wind get in beneath to hasten the drying process, and a bog-clearing competition—the clearing of the bog surface of the upper layers of earth and heather preliminary to the actual cutting operation.

Each team entering for the various competitions consisted of three persons—a 'cutter,' a 'catcher' and a 'wheeler'. The major award was a silver perpetual cup, presented by Alex Findlater & Co. for the 'wing slane' competition. A cup for the 'breast slane' contest was offered by Odlums the flour millers of Naas and Sallins.

In April 1934 President de Valera cut the first sod and inaugurated the first turf-cutting competition which was held at Allenwood, Robertstown, Co. Kildare. All the members of the Free State Executive Council, as well as deputies of all political parties, were present. The competition, which was the first of its kind in Ireland, and probably in the world, was organised by a representative committee, under the chairmanship of Harry de Courcy-Wheeler, 'on non-political lines, as a purely industrial and social event.' Its object was to popularise the use of turf.

The President and members of the Executive Council were entertained to lunch in one of the marquees erected in the bog for the occasion and the No. 1 Army Band played musical selections during the afternoon. The day ended with a ceilidhe and an aireadheact. Seán Lemass, Minister for Industry and Commerce, spoke at the festival, and addressed the question of grates designed to maximise the benefits of coal being less effective with turf:

> As a fuel peat is very suitable for a sitting room. In this connection it is worthy of note that fireplaces in most of the Georgian houses seem to have been constructed more for the use of turf than coal. They are certainly roomy enough to burn turf satis-

Éamon de Valera with Harry (above competitor 97) at the first turf-cutting competition in 1934.

> factorily. Modern fireplaces, except those of the basket type, are not quite suitable for peat fuel. On basket fireplaces the turf burns as easily as it does on the hearth. The best type of turf grate or fireplace has yet to be discovered, but we understand that the Industrial Research Council is investigating the matter.

The festival was held again in 1935; this time Lemass said that he had been reliably informed that there was on exhibition in one of the Baltic countries a house and furniture completely made from peat, including even the carpets. He was pleased that such things could be done but he wanted to know if they could be done at a price that would permit of commercial exploitation. Rather oddly, given the rural setting, Eamon de Valera in his speech chose to give a lecture on commercial morality:

> We have not had much experience as a people of widespread commercial activity—we have not had any long industrial tradition. Those people who have those traditions know that there is no such thing as getting rich quickly. If they try to do that they are going to kill the goose that lays the golden egg. It is only by strict honesty, keeping to bargains, scrupulously fulfilling contracts and being in time with orders that we really can succeed in business. If we are going to be self-sufficient we must have a very high standard of commercial morality. If I were asked what is the greatest benefit that can be given to our people by our schools I would say that it is by teaching the simple virtues of truth, honesty and fair dealing, one with another.

On one of these occasions de Valera confided in Harry that he, Dev, was extremely fortunate in 1916 not to have been arrested by him. On being queried why, Dev reminded Harry that all the leaders that he arrested had been executed!

In 1938 *The Irish Independent* opened its lengthy coverage by recording that 'Four hundred men carrying sleans, which glinted in the fitful sky—the march past of competitors—providing a striking scene at the National Turf-cutting Competitions at Allenwood, Robertstown, Co. Kildare yesterday.' It noted that thousands of people were present in the morning at the opening ceremony by the Minister for Local Government, Seán T. O'Kelly, who said that

> in the last five years the term bog-trotter had become one of patriotism and honour. This change of opinion was chiefly due to the great work of turf development undertaken by Major de Courcy-Wheeler and his committee. He understood that an effort was being made to make these competitions international. He also said that five years ago they were made aware that in the bogs of Ireland they had a treasure, and thousands were successfully put to work in co-operative societies. There is no limit to the good that work will do. Good clean work will be made available for thousands of men and the public will have a cheaper and cleaner fuel than coal and when the bogs are exhausted there will be a lot of new land on which crops can be grown.

During the Emergency (1939–45) shipments of coal to Ireland were restricted, as Britain needed all that they could produce for the manufacture of munitions. The Bog of Allen, and the skills honed by the Turf-Cutting Competitions, provided the solution. An army of turf cutters housed in temporary accommodation along a twenty mile stretch between Newbridge and Edenderry cut turf for Dublin's half million inhabitants. Twenty-nine new wooden canal barges were ordered and the stock conveyed to Phoenix Park and built into enormous ricks on both sides of the main thoroughfare—now named the New Bog Road.

However, there was a cloud on a far off horizon that would take some sixty years to cast its shadow. In 1938 the new Turf Development Board had learned from their visits to Russia and other countries that better and cheaper turf could be obtained by machine cutting. Over the next thirty years Bord na Mona became an increasingly efficient lifter of turf, and was a major employee in the midlands. But there was a price to pay.

Half a century later (August 1998) a circular from the Chairman of the Irish Peatland Conservation Council landed on my desk:

> As I write to you the great Bog of Allen is no more. In front of me stretches the vast brown expanse of a dead bog—consumed by our modern need for energy. This brown desert was once a magnificent wilderness area that stretched from the outskirts of Dublin to the Shannon River. Here was an Irish Eden for plants, insects, birds and mammals. We will never explore this lost landscape or learn about the wealth of animal and plant life that was found in it, nor the secrets it contained.

Alas, we were warned. In an edition of the *Lady of the House* in 1903, the year 2003 was predicted: 'The bogs of Ireland during the next century will be completely used up for fuel and manufacturing purposes, and a wealth of gold ornaments and antiquarian remains, drawn therefrom, added to our local museum collections'.

Great-Uncle George

Little was spoken about Surgeon Wheeler's eldest son, George. He had a degree from Trinity, but he was disinherited and banished to Australia, or so the story goes. History does not record his misdemeanour. Perhaps he had an affair with one of the domestic servants, a common reason for banishment. Family tradition has it that he never actually left No. 32 Merrion Square, which was a large house with plenty of people milling around. On Sundays at least a dozen people would sit around the dining room table. Surgeon Wheeler carved the baron of beef while the maids brought the vegetables up from the kitchens. Unobserved by the carver, one of the plates, well-laden, would leave the room and be brought upstairs to the servants' quarters in the attic. Here George had been secreted away by his mother. Years later, in 1900, he married Christina Oliversson of Southport which suggests he finally went away to England. He died in 1924 aged fifty-three. His funeral was well attended by the family.

Great-Uncle Gerry

Great-uncle Gerry was born on 8 July 1877 and educated in Trinity College Dublin (BA 1897). He became a regular soldier, and rose to become Lt.-Col in the 2nd Royal Dublin Fusiliers and the Welsh Regiment. He served in South Africa 1899-1902 and in the First World War, and was mentioned in dispatches. He married Margaret, younger daughter of Colonel Edward L'Estrange of Sligo. He lived happily in retirement in Foxrock and was an expert bee-keeper.

Great-Uncle Billy

Great-Uncle Billy, Surgeon Wheeler's fourth son, was a quite different matter. He was a colourful character whose full title was Surgeon Rear Admiral Sir William Ireland de Courcy-Wheeler.* Billy was born on 8 May 1879 at 32 Merrion Square. He was destined to achieve the same high honour as his father, being elected President of the Royal College of Surgeons in Ireland for 1922-4. He studied medicine at Trinity College where he gained honours and prizes as well as fully participating in university life. At a meeting of a debating society, he presented a bear's skull excavated in Connaught. 'The Bear to which the scull belonged', he said in a modish comment aimed at the Land League, 'lived contemporaneously with primitive politicians in the West of Ireland and, if we believe in Darwin, it is hard to see why the politicians survived and the bears became extinct.'

If Billy was guilty of the complacency engendered by good fortune, fate supplied a drastic corrective, an accident in St Stephen's Green in which a spiked railing damaged an eye beyond recovery. The sight of the other eye was threatened temporarily by sympathetic ophthalmia. His medical studies were interrupted by the necessary treatment and by protracted litigation in the action

* Many of his escapades are recorded for posterity in J.B. Lyons's *History of Mercer's Hospital* and in *An Assembly of Irish Surgeons, Lives of Presidents of the Royal College of Surgeons in Ireland in the 20th century* on which this account of his life is largely based.

against the Board of Works, which was eventually settled in his favour. Then, greatly to his credit, he resumed his studies still determined to follow a career in surgery. Graduating in 1902, he became FRCSI in 1905, having meanwhile visited Doyen's Clinic in Paris and spent three months with Kocher in Berne.

Billy was just twenty-five and relatively inexperienced when appointed honorary surgeon to Mercer's Hospital in 1904, one of a group of young appointments, so that Mercer's became known as 'The children's hospital'. But the Governors' decision to appoint such a youthful staff was justified by their appointees' performance. Billy's reputation as an operator and teacher was soon established. He published many surgical papers including the book *Operative Surgery* which went to four editions.* He gained international renown in the surgical world. Sir John Lumsden† spoke of him as 'The man who made Mercer's'.

He married Elsie Shaw, the eldest daughter of Lord Shaw the first Lord Craigmyle‡ in 1909 (no connection with his mother's family of Shaw). They lived in 23 Fitzwilliam Square and had two children, Tom and Desirée. Billy was surgeon-in-ordinary to the household of the Lord Lieutenant.

Despite his personal charm, some of those in close professional contact found him demanding, irascible and overbearing. He was, for instance, not always polite about the professional skills of his colleagues: indeed it is said that he always wore a small crucifix around his neck, so that if he was knocked down in the street he would not be taken for surgery to the Adelaide Hospital. Nor did his own mishap make him sympathetic to the misfortunes of others. The anaesthetists who worked with him included a Dr Morrison, known to his colleagues as 'Sticks Morrison', because disablement by poliomyelitis made him dependent on two sticks. During the course of a difficult operation, Wheeler noticed his hampered movements. 'I'm afraid, Morrison, you are not up to this kind of case.' 'Well, Sir William, it's a case of the blind leading the halt.'

During the First World War Billy was consulting surgeon to the War Office. He was surgeon to the Duke of Connacht's Hospital for limbless soldiers and placed his private nursing home, 33 Upper Fitzwilliam Street, at the disposal of the St John's Ambulance Brigade and the British Red Cross as a hospital for wounded officers.

He was mentioned in dispatches for courage in treating wounded soldiers under fire during the Easter Rising. On Easter Monday, ignoring snipers he made his way across St Stephen's Green to Mercer's Hospital to attend an officer with a chest injury. Two days later he attended a soldier at the corner of Dawson

* The Wheeler-Butcher collection of medical books is housed in the Mercer Library of the RCSI. He also provided for the annual award of the Sir William Wheeler silver Memorial Medal in surgery.

† Sir John Lumsden KBE, MD, visiting physician to Mercers 1897-1939, Board member 1939; chief medical officer to Guinness brewery.

‡ Lord Craigmyle was formerly Lord Shaw of Dumfermline. He was a law lord and formerly a Liberal MP who, when he retired from the bench in 1929, became Lord Craigmyle. He was in Dublin recuperating from major surgery (performed by his son-in-law) when he got caught up in the 1916 Rising.

Street in the early morning hours. He also administered to two officers of the Sherwood Foresters who were wounded in Fitzwilliam Street.

Surgeon Rear-Admiral Sir William Ireland de Courcy-Wheeler

While Billy, now Major Wheeler, surgeon to the forces in Ireland, was moving around the city attending to the wounded, his wife Elsie and baby daughter Desirée were in Greystones, desperately worried about her father (Lord Shaw) and she had also heard a rumour that Billy had been killed. She became so anxious that her faithful Scotch nurse was determined to get into Dublin and get news or die in the attempt. It is an extraordinary story of endurance and devotion. The girl started from Greystones at 2.30 pm on the Thursday carrying for the officers' home 14 lbs of beef and 4 lbs of butter, as Mrs Wheeler feared supplies would have run short, since nothing could be got in Dublin except at exorbitant prices.

She walked to Bray (five miles) and took a train to Kingstown; here she had to take to the road, as the line beyond Kingstown was wrecked. She walked to Merrion Gates about four miles along the tram line, when she was stopped by sentries. She retraced her steps as far as Merrion Avenue (one mile), went up Merrion Avenue, and tried the Stillorgan-Donnybrook route. Here she got as far as Leeson Street Bridge (six miles), when she was within 800 yards of her destination. Here again she was stopped by sentries and turned back. She walked back to Blackrock (seven miles), when she was again stopped by sentries. She then returned up Merrion Avenue and, seeing that all routes were impossible to Dublin, took the road to Killiney (five miles), where she arrived about 11.30 pm, having walked thirty miles. Here she got hospitality at a cottage and stayed the remainder of the night there, paying for her accommodation with the 4 lbs of butter.

Next day she walked five miles to Shankill, when she met a cart going to Bray via Killiney, so she rode back to Killiney on it and thence to Bray. She then walked the five miles from Bray to Greystones, her starting point. She reached home absolutely exhausted, having walked forty miles, and dropped down saying, 'There's your beef, and I never got there or heard anything'. Elsie Wheeler was greatly distressed at her having carried the meat back when so exhausted and asked her why she had not given it away. 'And what for should I give it away when we'll be wanting it ourselves maybe?' Next day Billy managed to get a telephone message through to Elsie and relieve her anxiety.[5]

No 23, Fitzwilliam Square, where Billy Wheeler lived in the early 20th century was coincidentally next door to Billy Findlater's residence in the latter half of the nineteenth century, No 22.

In 1931 Billy had a serious accident to his hand, which he described in what Professor Lyons refers to as 'a most interesting paper.' 'Bennett's fracture of the thumb: a personal experience' describes how Wheeler was knocked down by a lorry outside Victoria Station in July 1931.

> He lost consciousness briefly and, on coming too realised that his left hand, the dominant one, was injured. 'Only those who have experienced the injury', he wrote, 'can appreciate the helplessness which follows, nor is it generally realised how much the function of one hand depends on the co-operation of the other. The pain at the time was of the sickening kind suggestive of fracture but not intense'. The injury had broken the proximal end of the first metacarpal bone, causing the fracture described in 1881 by Edward Hallaran Bennett, Professor of Surgery in TCD. An attempted reduction under local anesthesia was unsuccessful but next day it was reduced under a general anesthesia by Mr W. R. Bristow.[6]

A short fishing holiday in the West of Ireland followed. Using a miniature Hardy rod, which could be held against the plaster in the palm by the four free fingers, Billy was able to cast effectively. Desmond, his nephew,* takes up the story:

* Dr Desmond de Courcy-Wheeler MB TCD (1945) Anaesthetist and general medical practitioner in south county Dublin and attached to Adelaide and Monkstown hospitals. He and his wife Doushka and family lived for many years in Cooldrinagh in Foxrock, the birthplace of Samuel Beckett. Billy Wheeler, earlier in the century, lived in Carrickbyrne, close by on Brighton Road. Peter Pearson, in *Between the Mountains and the Sea,* says that Carrickbyrne is perhaps the most outstanding Edwardian house in Carrickmines.

The ghillie gaffing a fine salmon for Desmond some years ago on the Slaney. (Gaffing is no longer legal.)

It was at Lagduff, a fishing lodge on the Owenduff River in Co. Mayo. My father, (Diamond), took Lagduff from Sir George and Frances Murphy each August. I would have been about 10 when Billy came down. He stayed in Mulrany, in the old Railway Hotel twelve miles back the road. On this particular day the river was in flood and Billy was fishing at George's pool half a mile above Srahnamanragh Bridge. Because of his bandaged left hand he was fishing light-heartedly with the miniature Hardy rod. Conditions were right and Norman, the Ghillie, suggested that they substitute a larger fly—immediately he was into a substantial fish. Although Norman was a big strong fellow and the best weight-thrower in Co. Mayo, the chances of landing the fish seemed slim. In addition to the light rod the silkworm gut could break at any moment. There was no controlling the salmon, it played for two good hours. It ran for a half mile with the flood down river towards and under the bridge. I was watching all this. Norman stripped off and waded half way under the bridge with the rod but could not get through. He was up to his waist in the dangerously fast-flowing river and the fish was mighty big. Even he had difficulty in taking the force of the river. Someone on the lower side of the bridge managed to get hold of the eye of the rod and pull the line off the reel altogether. Amazingly the salmon was still attached but had virtually drowned itself swimming downstream. Because of the high river it ended up in soft water and only needed to be scooped out, all of 20 lbs. Billy asked everyone back to the hotel the following night where we celebrated and ate the salmon. It was an extraordinary event. I have very vivid memories of it.

However, after the fishing feat Billy's hand felt different inside the plaster and before long it was evident that the metacarpal had slipped. The surgeon began to fear that his thumb would never control a scissors again or tie a ligature.

Diamond, in dark jacket, with a group of shooting friends. *(Left to right)* Desmond Collins, Billy Boydell, Tommy Murphy, Diamond and Claud Odlum.

Sir Robert Jones was consulted. He was within easy reach of Dublin. His method of approach to an injury of this kind was interesting and instructive. He was full of optimism, he refused to recognize defeat, he cared nothing for text-book platitudes; his experience was greater than any other living authority, he could tell the past, present and future of a case of this kind with equal accuracy.

Sir Robert examined the joint under a fluorescent screen and, to Wheeler's relief, the movements were not impeded. Occupational therapy was commenced. Several times daily he immersed the hand in a basin of hot water with soapsuds added. He practised using scissors and artery forceps and tying ligatures in the easeful heat. He regained his dexterity gradually and after seven weeks was able to operate again, supporting the joint with Elastoplast over which he drew on two rubber gloves.

Billy came through a troubled epoch and in an address he expressed thoughts many would have shared:

> There have been times in the recent history of this country when some of us tired of the turmoil, bewildered at the outlook, anxious for the safety of our families, felt inclined and were offered temptations to seek peace elsewhere. The impulse was fleeting for in the whole wide world whether in peace or in war there is no place like the city in which we live.

However, problems with his marriage tempted him to accept an offer of a job in London by his friend Lord Iveagh, with whom he often stayed in Ashford Castle, Co. Mayo. His professional success did not falter in London, where he held posts at All Saints Hospital for Genito-Urinary Diseases and the Metropolitan Ear, Nose and Throat Hospital, but it was suspected that he missed his friends back in Dublin.

At the outbreak of the Second World War, Billy became consulting surgeon to the Admiralty with the rank of Surgeon Rear Admiral and was posted to Aberdeen in charge of the Northern Command. His duties necessitated much travelling. Though by then in his early sixties, he was active enough to enjoy flights in fighter aircraft and to climb up a ship's side by the pilot ladder. His death in Aberdeen when dressing for dinner on 11 September 1943 was sudden and unexpected.

Great-Uncle Diamond

Surgeon Wheeler's fifth son was my great-uncle Robert, 'Diamond' to his family, friends and patients. Another of the sporting Wheelers, he showed great prowess on the playing field and was a first class game shot and an international clay pigeon shot. He was also a top class club tennis player. He was an international rugby substitute for three years and unlucky not to win a cap. Later he achieved fame as a referee. In 1922-24 he was President of the Association of Referees and in 1925 he referred the Scotland v. France match in Inverleith.*

Diamond graduated through the Trinity Medical School and Mercer's Hospital. He joined the RAMC in 1915 and was posted to Malta and France. On his return in 1919 he set up a general practice in Monkstown in south County Dublin and followed Dr Beatty as a doctor in charge of Monkstown Hospital. He developed it into a small acute general hospital.

Diamond lived at 7 Clifton Terrace until 1925/26 when he moved to Monkstown Castle which he rented from the Longford and de Vesci Estate. He married Elsie's best friend, Mabel Hunter-Craig the daughter of Robert Hunter-Craig, MP for Lanarkshire. She founded the Jersey Society of Ireland and was the second woman to hold a driving licence in Ireland. He also inherited Drummin, near Carbury, Co. Kildare, from a Miss Anne Grattan in 1915, which he passed on to his son Cecil in 1939.

In contrast to Diamond, who was very careful in the handling of a gun, other Wheelers had a rather casual approach, leading to some near misses. I have already told how George Nelson Wheeler lost his life. Harry's son Annesley† had his own near mishap. He had been shooting on the bog and came back into

* The family had it that the match was in Paris and that he gave so many free kicks against the French that he had to be escorted off the pitch by the gendarmes to avoid a lynching. The French, the story went, were cut out of the championship and that was the last time they played until after the Second World War. In reality France dropped out of the Championship in 1931 but Diamond was not the referee. The moral is to treat family pass-me-down stories with caution. I hope that I have not made too many errors.

† Dr Annesley Eliardo Beresford de Courcy-Wheeler, born in Robertstown 1912, educated at Mountjoy School and Trinity College Dublin. BA 1934, MD 1946. Served in the Indian Medical Service of the Army stationed in the North West Frontier. He became a proficient polo player. In 1949 he joined a medical practice outside London. In 1964 he transferred to Mullingar and took over the main general practice in the town. An active council member of the Irish Medical Union and national Honorary Treasurer. President of the Irish College of General Practioners for one year.

Robertstown through the front door with his gun fully loaded. At that very moment his sister Dorothea, my mother to be, was walking down the corridor directly in front of him and his father was fast asleep in the room above. Annesley tripped over the first step, fell flat along the corridor, the butt of the gun slammed against the floor and both barrels went off, blasting a big hole in the ceiling and rocketing his father out of bed. My mother was directly in the line of fire and might well have received two barrels on her backside had not the butt hit the floor.

I had my own near mishap when Grandfather Harry was showing off the 1916 pistols prior to the presentation to President O'Kelly in 1949. I was playing about with one of the pistols like any twelve-year-old would, when my mother grabbed it, and, to the horror of those present, demonstrated to her father that they were still loaded!

Notes and references

1 Burke's *Peerage* 1934
2 *Liverpool Daily Post* 15 February 1956
3 R. B. McDowell *Crisis and Decline The fate of the Southern Unionists* Dublin: Lilliput Press 1997 p 98
4 Elizabeth Fingall, *Seventy Years Young, memories of Elizabeth Countess of Fingall told to Pamela Hinkson*, Dublin: Lilliput Press 1991 p 415
5 Mary Louisa Hamilton Norway *The Sinn Féin Rebellion as I Saw It* London: Smith Elder & Co. 1916 and reproduced and edited by Keith Jeffery as *The Sinn Féin Rebellion as They Saw It*, Dublin: Irish Academic Press 1999 pp 70–1
6 Prof. J. B. Lyons *An Assembly of Irish Surgeons* Dublin: Glendale Press 1983 p 64

11. *Grandfather Willie and the New State*

❧

Willie

An old saying has it that commercial dynasties rarely survive the third generation. The first establishes the business, the second builds it up, and the third, educated and moneyed, lets it all slip away. The Findlaters were an exception to this rule. John took over from his uncle, the founder Alexander, and saw that all his sons had a first class education, two graduating with honours in Logic and Ethics from Trinity, others gaining degrees in law, medicine and engineering.

Of John's six sons, only two—Adam and Willie—joined the business. Adam, as was the destiny of the first-born, assumed the business mantle from his father, but given a free choice might well have followed a career in politics. Of the others, we have seen that Herbert became a solicitor, and was killed at Gallipoli in 1915; Charles, who became an engineer, also joined up, and was killed on the Somme in 1916. Alex became a medical doctor, was also at Gallipoli and settled to a practice in Edgware, then a village outside London.

American John

The second son, John, born in 1858, went to the United States, like so many Irishmen—Protestant and Catholic—to earn a living. In fact contrary to the received wisdom, the 'bulk of the Irish ethnic group in the United States at present is, and probably always has been, Protestant.'* John was born in Dublin in 1858, educated at High School like his brothers and attended a school in North Wales. He then studied for some years on the Continent, in Germany, Holland and France. He must have acquired good knowledge of the wine trade although he

* Donald Harman Akenson 'Irish Migration to North America 1800-1920' pp 111-112 in Andy Bielenberg *The Irish Diaspora* London: Longman 2000: 'The Protestant proportion of Irish persons in the United States was 58.6 per cent of those professing Christianity'.

John who emigrated to Texas in 1883

never practised as such. In 1883, he set off for Texas. In 1884, no doubt with family money, he went into the cattle business at South Mulberry Creek in Tom Green County near Sterling City. His ranch comprised some 15,000 acres, on which he had a large herd of cattle. In addition he transported windmills, pipefittings and towers, largely for the benefit of neighbours, and was instrumental in the installation of water supply systems on a number of ranches.

In 1887 John returned to Dublin, and became engaged to Helen Corscaden, daughter of James and Frances Corscaden, a shipbroker in Londonderry. The marriage took place at All Souls, Langham Place, London on 10 December 1888, a month after the birth of Frank, the first of their four sons. This was the third Findlater/Corscaden marriage. John's finances evidently did not prosper for Adam wrote to him in 1891 about some money invested in the Texas property: 'The whole object in having the amount in AF & Co's name was that if at any time if you were not making money it preserved the property against any of your creditors—think over this point, and put it into your own name if you think it advisable or advantageous to yourself to do so. My Dear John, Your affectionate brother, A. S. Findlater.' (Endearingly, a scribbled postscript notes: 'Confound the above formal business—I will try tomorrow Sunday to write to you—yours in an infernal hurry.') John and Helen's son James was also born in London in 1890, and their next two children, Mart 1892 and Jack 1894, were born in San Angelo. Sadly, Helen died after the birth of Jack. Shortly afterwards John returned to Dublin with the four children, including Jack in arms, to see the family and, well perhaps, find a new wife. And so he did, by luck or possibly by family arrangement. His brother's wife's sister, Edith, said 'Yes' and, in 1895, with husband John and his four sons, returned to a new life in San Angelo.

Selling the ranch, John established the Findlater Hardware Company in San Angelo, Texas in 1895, which was at one time reputed to be the largest hardware business mid-point between Fort Worth and El Paso, towns 600 miles apart. It was sole agent for Samson windmills, Buckeye Mowers, New Casaday Sulky plows and cultivators, Studebaker wagons, Crescent bicycles, St Louis well-drilling machinery and a variety of other ancillary equipment. It sounds tremendous but profitability was slow to materialise.

The newly established business did not diminish his interest in oil exploration, always with the hope of big riches. In 1900 he took a drilling lease on 100,000 acres but was short on success and he looked for more funds from Dublin; his father replied sternly: 'I must ask you in future not to draw on me under any circumstances, as it places me in a very unpleasant position, since they [Findlaters] have become a public body. With very kind regards to all, my Dear John, Your affectionate Father, signed J.Findlater.'

And so the letters back to Dublin continued, success being always just around the corner. In 1934 he was still trying: 'drilled a new well Jan. & Feb. hoping for a big return, 5 or 600 Brls. But only realised 100, however that will help us out considerably, as we have been paying off all the debts of the company and will soon be receiving a monthly dividend, i.e. if I can continue meeting the quarterly interest payments on $14,000 I borrowed to pay on my stock a few years ago.'

Sometimes there is a nice little touch, such as the postscript to a letter of 18 May 1921: 'Would it be asking you too much to purchase for me a dozen really first class large tooth brushes out of the funds I have over there? It is impossible to get any here that the bristles do not come out of.'*

John had a daughter Mary (1895) and a son Stevenson (1899) with his second wife Edith. It is said that John was one of the most outstanding men of his day in San Angelo; certainly the hardware business flourished for over seventy years. After John died in 1935, at the age of seventy-seven, the business was continued until 1968 by his sons Frank and Mart. Descendants of John, Helen and Edith still live happily in San Angelo and in various parts of the States.

Dr Alex

John and Mary's third son, Alex, was born in Dublin in 1860. He was also educated at the High School and afterwards Trinity College Dublin where he read medicine. He was appointed Medical Officer and Public Vaccinator for the Edgware district in 1890, and was also Medical Officer to the Redhill Institution and Children's Home, and honorary consulting physician to Redhill Hospital.

As we have seen, he was with 1st London Mounted Brigade Field Ambulance, Royal Army Medical Corps, from its formation and served with them from August 1914 to February 1917 in Egypt, Gallipoli and Salonika in east Greece which was occupied by French and British troops in November 1915.

His obituary records that he was frank and outspoken, but none the less ready with a kindly word and was a friend of those in need. A man of very generous nature, he was never deaf to a deserving appeal and he did a lot of good work of which few people knew.

He was a huntsman and a steeplechaser of some renown, A hard rider, he was always happy with a horse of spirit and it was common to see him astride a horse

* Readers will remember John's father's regular purchase of toothbrushes in the 1850s, two for himself and one for his wife.

Lucie, who married Willie in 1891

Willie in Nice in 1890

rearing up on its hind legs in the High Street. At one time he drove an Irish jaunting car, and in the winter he drove a one-horse sleigh when the roads were at all suitable. For some years he captained Kingsbury Polo Club, being well mounted on Roulette and on Pride of Kildare. He died in 1931. His daughter Helen was my godmother.

Grandfather Willie

The next of John's sons to go into the business was my grandfather Willie, born in 1867, twelve years after his brother Adam. He was the fourth of John and Mary's six sons. Like his brothers he went to the High School and then to Trinity College where he graduated in Logic and Ethics with a Gold Medal. In his youth he was dashing and debonair but soon knuckled down to the business where his brother Adam was Managing Director and his father Chairman.

Willie married Lucie Heinekey on 4 May 1891. She was the daughter of G. M. Heinekey, a wine merchant with branches in London and Sackville Street, Dublin. It was her sister Edith who, in 1895, became the second wife of Willie's elder brother John and settled in America. Yet another Heinekey sister, Dolly, married English wine merchant, W. Chartres Cock thus forging a lasting relationship with the family in Dublin. Four generations of the Cock family traded as Cock Russell & Co. in London.

Willie and Lucie had five children. The eldest, Marjorie, born in 1892, married Edmund Mitchell, second cousin of the Dublin wine merchant family. He joined Findlaters and was assistant Managing Director from 1919. The younger daughters, Doris, born 1895 and Sheila, born 1902, are the subject of Chapter 12. The elder boy Desmond was born in 1898 and died in 1900, and Dermot, the youngest in the family (my father), was born in 1905 and is the subject of Chapters 13, 14 and 15.

Many years later, on the Silver Jubilee of his becoming Managing Director, Willie reminisced about his earliest days in the firm, the late 1880s:

> It is nearly fifty years ago since I first appeared in the Cash Desk in Sackville Street, as it was then called. I cannot have been much of a success there as I was put into the cellar for some time, and after was promoted to the whiskey bottling department. Things were different in those days; everything was done by hand—whiskey corking with a stick, labelling by hand, capsuling with a bit of string (which made your hands very sore). Head Office had only one shop, no goods were displayed in the windows. We were wine merchants and so had screens in all our windows. Later on we showed a cask of whiskey, then jars of whiskey and eventually groceries. Then we became ordinary grocers with shop windows, goods displayed, prices marked and actually went into the sale of provisions which seemed to be quite a come-down to the old firm of Findlater, Wine Merchants. However, it is a great mercy we did so as the Wine Trade now would not have kept us alive, and the Grocery Trade, on account of its increase, has enabled us to employ a great number more hands.

An old style employee—Mr T. Mooney (Rathmines branch 1859-1913)

The key to Findlaters' success was an absolute commitment to quality in all product areas of our business, and a very high level of service. The knowledge and dedication of the staff made an enormous contribution. In May 1913, one of the oldest employees, Mr T. Mooney, completed 54 years' service with the firm. Based in Rathmines, he was respected for his extreme punctuality and regularity—claiming never to have missed a single day's work, or failed to turn up on time. Questioned on his retirement by the *Freeman's Journal,* he attributed this to his habit of attending early Mass in Rathmines Church, close by. This finished just in time to allow him to arrive at the store at eight o'clock. 'And did you never miss a day in the whole 54 years?' Mr Mooney was asked. 'Never,' he replied. 'I have always enjoyed perfect health, and was not ill even for a day since I began business life.' In the press picture he looks a fine man: three piece suit, long frock coat, high collared shirt and waistcoat, polished leather shoes, watch chain, neat trim beard and white moustache.

> 'I suppose, Mr Mooney, Rathmines has changed greatly within your memory?' 'It has, indeed; it is a different town now altogether. In 1859 there were only a couple of shops in Rathmines besides ours. There was a wide space opposite Findlaters, and a semi-circular range of cottages stood where the Belfast Bank is now; the pump that supplied Rathmines with water stood there too; that was before the Waterworks system was working. Along Rathgar road was green fields and open country, and Rathgar Chapel was not built then; the district was in Rathmines Parish.'

ALEX. FINDLATER & CO., Ltd.—XMAS, 1902.

CHRISTMAS CRACKERS.

TOM SMITH'S, CALEY'S, BATGER'S, & OTHER MAKERS.

IT is impossible to list all the various Crackers we have in hands. We have a most extensive and varied stock, and are constantly receiving new designs. We append a few descriptions of some of these goods, chiefly for the benefit of our country customers, who may not be able to inspect our stock. It may happen that some of the numbers quoted may be sold out before the orders come in. As it may be impossible to replace them, and inconvenient to delay the order till the exact numbers arrive, we will, in such cases, send the nearest kind to that required.

Tom Smith's 6d. Box Jewel Crackers.

No. 1130.

Containing Rings, Pins, Brooches, Pendants, with Children's Mottoes. The Crackers are made in two shades of fancy Blue papers, decorated with heads of Eastern Children, and the box is mounted with a beautifully executed Chromo Picture of Children. Per box, **5d.**

Tom Smith's Box Toys and Jewels.

No. 200.

The Crackers contain miniature Toys and pretty Jewels, with Children's Mottoes, and are printed in assorted colours of tasteful design.

Per box, **5½d.**

Noah's Ark Crackers.

No 201.

Containing a variety of Toy Animals, with Children's Mottoes. The Crackers are of Azure Blue Bronze, and represent the various Animals entering the Ark. Per box, **5½d.**

Funny Japanese Box.

No. 14.

With clever design in bold colours on lid, filled with bright attractive Crackers, containing a variety of Japanese Novelties. A Conundrum is enclosed in each Cracker. Per box, **5½d.**

Mother Goose Box.

No. 16.

With bright label in colours on lid, filled with Crackers of appropriate design, containing an assortment of Toys, such as Paper Trumpets, Punch and Judy Talkers, Button-hooks, Caps, Necklets, Wooden Spinning Tops, Steel Puzzles, etc., etc.; also a Novel Conundrum with detachable answer in each. Per box, **5½d.**

Oriental Jewel Box.

No. 17.

With clever original design on lid, filled with appropriate Crackers of Oriental design, containing a selection of Jewels. A Conundrum is enclosed in each Cracker. Per box, **5½d.**

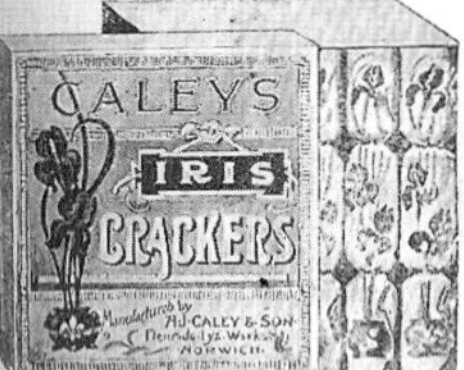

Iris Box.

No. 35.

With floral design on lid, filled with Crackers printed in Gold and rich tints of Blue, containing an assortment of Hats in various shapes, sizes, and colours, together with a Novel Conundrum with detachable answer in each.

Per box, **9½d.**

Forget-Me-Not Box.

No. 36.

With pretty floral design on lid, filled with Crackers printed in rich Gold Bronze and delicate colours, representing growing Forget-Me-Nots, containing a variety of Luggage in different designs, sizes, and colours; also a Novel Conundrum with detachable answer in each. Per box, **9½d.**

Tom Smith's Surprise Toy Crackers.

No. 205.

Containing the latest Novelties in miniature Toys and Children's Mottoes. Of exceptionally brilliant design, printed in Gold and Crimson, and Decorated with French Clowns, performing Dogs, &c. Per box, **10d.**

Tom Smith's 1/- Box Hats and Caps.

No. 835.

Richly designed in Gold, Dark Blue, Azure Blue, decorated with children wearing Head-dresses as contained in the Crackers. Per box, **10d.**

Little Red Riding Hood Box.

No. 51.

A most attractive box with artistic label on lid, filled Crackers packed one layer in a box, containing a variety of Caps and Costumes in many new styles. A Novel Conundrum is enclosed in each Cracker. Per box, **10½d.**

Tom Smith's Terrier Jack Crackers.

No. 206.

Containing Dog Masks, Hats, Caps, and Bonnets, and are printed in Pale Blue, Crimson, and Gold, decorated with Dogs.

Per box, **11d.**

Santa Claus' Motor Car Crackers.

No. 208.

Designed in brilliant Green bronze, decorated with Father Christmas Figures, and containing Toys, Jewels, Puzzles, Hats and Caps, with new and original Love mottoes. Per box, **1/0½.**

Musical Toy Crackers.

No. 866.

Of marvellous value. The Crackers contain all the latest Novelties in Musical Toys, and are appropriately designed in Gold Printed Papers, covered in Gelatine.

Per Box, **1/0½.**

Larks ! ! ! Crackers for Boys.—No. 768.

Designed and arranged for creating the greatest fun among the boys. The Crackers contain Fools' Caps, Musical Toys, harmless Fireworks, and many other juvenile novelties, and are decorated with a series of subjects representing School Boys in their night attire, while the box is mounted with a picture illustrating Larks in a College Dormitory.

Per box, **1/4½.**

73

1902: Crackers were a large and important part of Findlater's Christmas business. Orders were placed with the manufacturers in January and delivered in November.

The bus tragedy:

> There was a service of buses running between Rathmines and the city. In 61 a dreadful tragedy happened at Portobello Bridge. There was only a light wooden hoarding where the stone parapet of the bridge is now. The horses attached to a bus got restive on the bridge, and backed the conveyance against the hoarding, which gave way at once, and horses, bus-driver, conductor, and passengers went over into the canal basin. They might have been rescued, but in the confusion the sluice gates were opened, and an avalanche of water poured in on the unfortunate men; six passengers were drowned like rats in a trap, but the driver and conductor escaped. The accident happened at night, and next morning thousands of people came out from the city to view the scene.

The first twenty years of Willie's business career, from 1890 to 1910, were prosperous and exciting for the Dublin business and professional class, a significant part of Findlaters' clientele. (Though by no means the whole—to sell all cuts of bacon for example needs all classes of people, and teas and other products covered the full price range.) Census returns showed that this group represented about a quarter of the population of the Dublin area, living mainly in the self-governing townships of Rathmines, Pembroke, Monkstown, Kingstown and, on the northside, Clontarf and Drumcondra. In 1900, just eight months before her death, Queen Victoria paid her last visit to Ireland where it was estimated that one million people were in Dublin on that day. And the following year the last of the thousand horses that pulled the Dublin horse-trams gave way to electric trams. In 1907, on the eve of King Edward's visit, the Irish Crown Jewels were suddenly found to be missing, a still unsolved theft.

By the beginning of the new century, Findlaters was a strong and profitable business, with sales of £133,949 [over £10m] a year, and profits of £10,400 [over £800,000]. It was diversified, with interests in groceries, beer, whiskey, wine and hotels; it also owned the leading social and fashion magazine of the day *The Lady of the House.* The magazine's promotional material described it as:

> Written by Gentlewomen for Gentlewomen, exquisitely illustrated, and published on the 15th of each month. Sold everywhere. One penny. Post free for one year, two shillings. Each issue contains the current fashions, finely illustrated by leading French artists; Portraits of Leaders of Society; Interviews; an instalment of a novel by a popular writer; Articles on various charities, household matters, health and the toilet; Delineations and Portraits of our Readers' faces; gossip, valuable prizes, etc. Non-sectarian and non-political.

The Lady of the House was first published in 1890, just at the time Willie was entering the business. The renewed agreement between Wilson Hartnell, the publishers, and Findlaters in 1909 stated that Findlaters would have ten pages of advertisements in four of the monthly issues and eight pages of advertisements in the eight monthly issues, and also two pages in the special Horse Show issue and eight pages in the special Christmas season issue. Findlaters were to purchase three thousand copies monthly at sixpence per dozen copies, probably for dis-

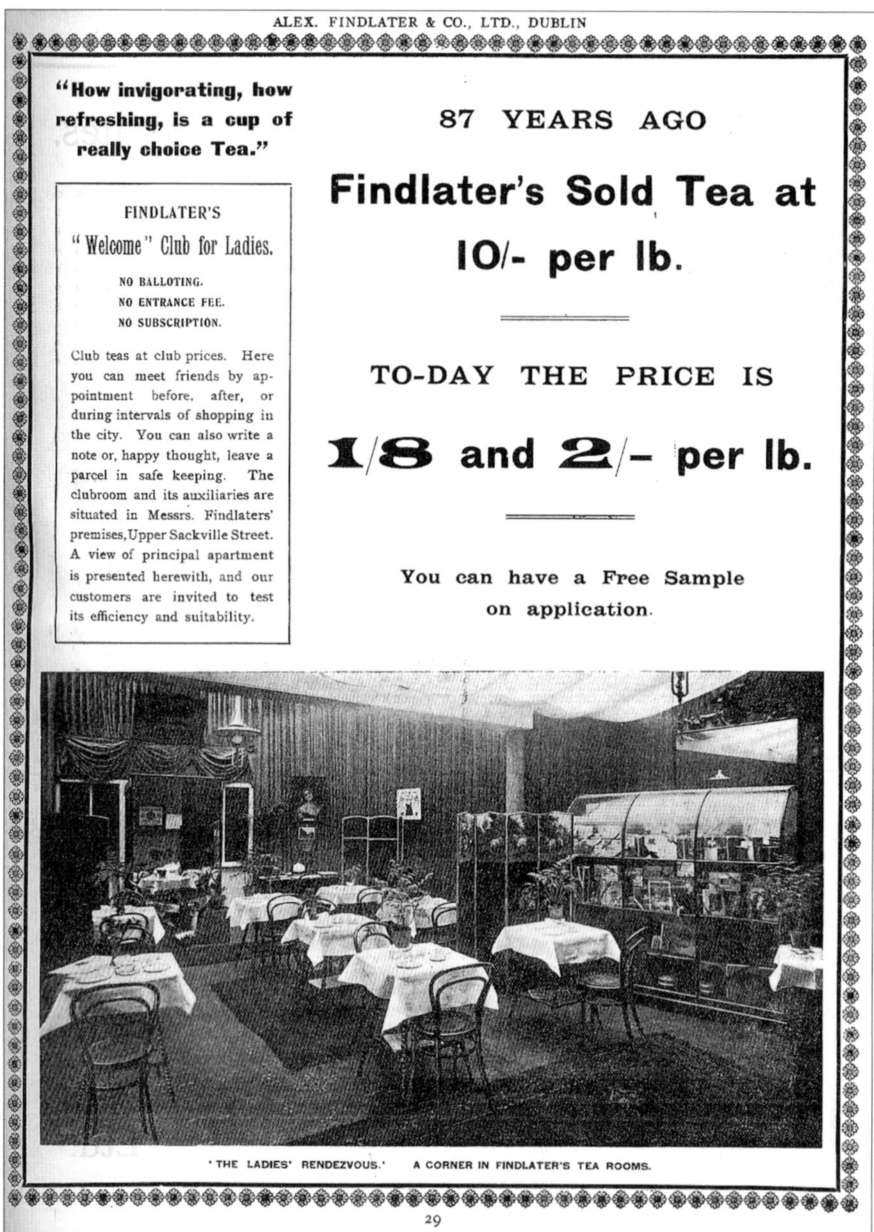

'THE LADIES' RENDEZVOUS.' A CORNER IN FINDLATER'S TEA ROOMS.

The 10s per lb in 1823 was a slight exaggeration, 8s was more or less the top price. That is the equivalent to paying £20 lb today. However there was tea available by 1830 at 3s lb equivalent to £17.80 per kilo. In the year 2000 a kilo of Lyons Tea would cost just £6.60.

tribution to our account customers. Hartnell, who referred to himself in the journal as the 'Conductor', undertook that the literary tone and character of the periodical and the printing paper and illustrations would be of a style and character not inferior to that of the issues of the twelve months preceding the agreement. It had a sister publication in Findlater's *Ladies' Housekeeping Diary*, from which I have already quoted.

A vivid idea of the style and scale of Findlater's business at this time can be gleaned from the numerous catalogues of prices we produced (many of which were included in *The Lady of the House*). These were extensive and thorough—a typical offering, dated April 1909, runs to 56 pages. The various branches of the business are listed on the first page. The head office was at No. 29-32 Upper Sackville Street (now O'Connell Street), with a bonded stores to the rear, cellars extending out under O'Connell Street and a beer bottling hall and in Thomas Street there was a cake factory. There were twelve branches, three in central Dublin, and one each in Rathmines, Sandymount, Kingstown, Blackrock, Dalkey, Bray, Howth and Foxrock. Telephone numbers often indicate early adoption—1 Blackrock, 5 Howth, 9 Foxrock, 13 Dalkey, 19 Bray, 23 Kingstown, 32 Ballsbridge for Sandymount and 50 Rathmines.

Pride of place in the catalogue is taken by the wine department. However, noting that 'whiskey is, to a great extent, taking the place of wine on the tables of the upper classes', wines are introduced somewhat tentatively. The section is headed by the reassuring words of the famous food scientist Baron Liebig: 'as a gentle corrective and tonic compensation to restore the equilibrium of the constitution; as a safeguard against organic disturbance; as a soothing refreshment where vitality is feeling exhausted; and as a means of giving energy and strength when man has to struggle against the various ills that flesh is heir to—wine cannot be surpassed by any product of Nature or Art.'

Many of the pages of the catalogue devoted to wine set out to establish that wine is good for you. Port, we are told, was once thought of as the cause of gout, but doctors now 'recommend it as antidote to that distressing remedy', and of course 'thousands who are reduced in vitality and resort to drugs will find renewed strength and life' in Findlater's Invalid Port (36s per dozen). 'Burgundy', says one Dr Druitt, is 'a most powerful agent in diseases of the nervous system', and he adds 'what Bordeaux is to the blood, Burgundy is to the nerves.' Moselles 'are recommended by the medical profession as preventatives against gout and stone'.

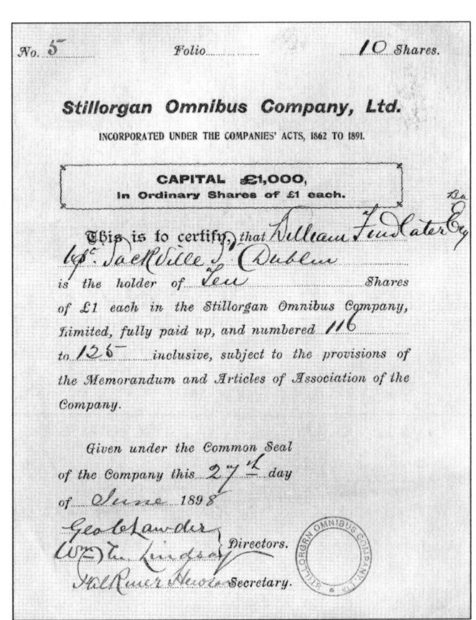

No. 5 Folio .... 10 Shares.

Stillorgan Omnibus Company, Ltd.

INCORPORATED UNDER THE COMPANIES' ACTS, 1862 TO 1891.

CAPITAL £1,000,
In Ordinary Shares of £1 each.

This is to certify, that William Findlater Esq
29 Sackville St Dublin
is the holder of Ten Shares of £1 each in the Stillorgan Omnibus Company, Limited, fully paid up, and numbered 116 to 125 inclusive, subject to the provisions of the Memorandum and Articles of Association of the Company.

Given under the Common Seal of the Company this 27th day of June 1898

Geo Lawder
Wm Lindsay } Directors.
[illegible] Secretary.

History does not relate what happened to the Stillorgan Omnibus Company

10 THE LADY OF THE HOUSE. [15TH MAY, 1891.

OUR PRIZES.

THE PRETTY CHILD PRIZE.

"THAT land of lovely children—Ireland," has well proved the justice of Thackeray's description. Our offer of TWO PRIZES, one of Five Guineas for the portraits of the prettiest child between the ages of two and seven years, and one of Three Guineas for the portrait of the prettiest baby under two years of age, has met with a response which the hapless judges little anticipated when they undertook the task of adjudication. Up to the first day of this month, when the competition closed, every post brought us a steady and daily increasing stream of photographs widening, to pursue the metaphor further, into a broad river indeed, as May-day approached and forming in the aggregate a huge accumulation of youthful loveliness such as we believe has never before been got together at one time. So great and varied is the display that we considered the advisability of holding a public exhibition of the photographs in one of the large halls in Dublin, but were obliged to abandon this idea as difficulties stood in the way of framing so tremendous a quantity of portraits suitably for exhibition in the short period at our disposal.

The photographs represent children of every age within our defined limits, and every cast of countenance, arrayed in a marvellous variety of attire, and "caught" in almost every pose; they come from all quarters of Ireland, and there is hardly a photographer of any note in the country who is not represented. The quantity of children's photographs specially produced for these competitions at the Dublin studios far exceeds anything ever known since the first Daguerreotype Portraitist opened that quaint little gallery of his upon the roof of the Dublin Rotunda; indeed, one of our chief photographers states that the number of children's photographs taken in the month of April alone far exceeded the quantity "sat for" during any previous six months of his experience.

The judges are now actively engaged in framing their awards, which will appear in our next (June) issue, with the portraits of the winners, and a selection from the portraits of the prettiest competitors, who, despite their many charms of face and figure were, unfortunately, what so many of us must always be in this world, unsuccessful.

CHILDREN'S OUTDOOR FASHIONS.

Fig. I.

Fig. I.—Boy's Costume of navy blue serge, and of white serge with stripes across. A plain white under-vest buttoned slantwise, with small knob pearl buttons. Blouse sleeves and plain wristbands. Fancy straw hat with blue pompons, striped socks, same colour as hat.

Fig. II.

Fig. II.—Garden Frock, for young child, of streaked white and rose woollen with rose satinette frill round the neck, and a stripe of same down the left side. Full sleeves with close wristbands. A bolero hat with rose feather pompons. Rose socks.

Fig. III.

Fig. III.—Child's Costume.—Gathered skirt of plaid woollen or poplin with barege body of ivory white. It is fastened down the back, and ornamented with a frill. A plain rounded yoke of the plaid will be found lighter for a young child than a chemisette bodice underneath. Plaid gauntlet cuffs and waistband. Straw hat with open work border and fancy lilies of the valley and bows the shade of the colours in the plaid.

FASHIONABLE FABRICS.

Mr. John Henry's Dress House, 6 Lower Sackville Street, is full of tempting novelties at present, the light embroidered silk muslins being quite perfect of their kind. One of the finest creamy muslins, looking like silk gauze, had the material for the skirt completely covered with graduated sprays of natural-looking heliotrope and leaves, embroidered in silk by hand; the well-known chickweed was utilised to adorn another, and various small and distinctive blossoms were shown, all reproduced in the correct colours. Tussores with quaint Turkish and Eastern designs, worked in silk, were novel and stylish, and the embroidered zephyrs afforded infinite variety. The new "silk effects in cotton," were very pretty, and will doubtless be much run upon this summer; those in pale blues and pinks with silvery white discs being perhaps the most elegant.

Amongst the woollen materials for summer wear I greatly admired some vicunas with artistic filagree embroidery, in deeper tones than the cloth; another pleasing variety was French vicuna, figured in silk arabesques, or linked rings; those in the new greys will be very fashionable. To ladies who are constant in their patronage of check goods, some of the new designs will be most acceptable, notably the large squares, which are composed of an arrangement of small checks, with a bright-coloured line crossing them at intervals. Some of the *mousselines de laine* are very attractive, and the black silks and velvets will sustain the reputation of the house. For mourning and half-mourning a number of new fabrics are displayed, and will not fail to find many admirers.

A speciality of Mr. Henry's establishment is that buttons, linings, and foundations to match any and all of the dress materials are supplied, and thus an immense saving of trouble and expense is effected, this to country customers is a veritable boon. Patterns can always be obtained, and Mr. Henry tells me that his business with the provinces is assuming large dimensions. With such *fetes* as the Lawn Tennis Tournament and College Races coming on, ladies ought to make a point of seeing Mr. Henry's materials before deciding on new toilettes.

To Darken Gray Hairs.—Lockyer's Sulphur Hair Restorer is the quickest, but safest; [illegible] Lockyer's [illegible] is the only English Hair Restorer universally sold.

[T]o obtain the LADY OF THE HOUSE regularly send 12 stamps to defray cost of year's postage to WILSON, HARTNELL & Co., Commercial Buildings, Dub[lin]

15TH MAY, 1891.] THE LADY OF THE HOUSE. 9

FRENCH OUTDOOR TOILETTES.

Fig. 1.

Fig. 2.

FIG. 1.—A TRAVELLING COSTUME of streaked woollen, in a shade of yellow, called banana fruit, and a greyish blue. The front is a panel of light cloth, either white or one of the costume shades. A cashmere vest, double-breasted, with skirt front underneath and stiff collar. The woollen bodice is entirely coat-made and machine stitched. The buttons on the white vest are mother-of-pearl. A coloured straw hat with lace butterfly, and flowers above the crown.

FIG. 2.—WALKING TOILETTE, a grey pongee figured with dahlias. The opening down the skirt forms a slight panier below the hip. The narrow panel between is of plain silk in one of the dahlia colours. The bodice is made without basques, and fastens with four buttons. The chemisette is a streaked, fine, woollen-like veiling. The sleeves are coat-made and of the plain silk. A small *capote* with dahlia buds and bows.

"The Lady of the House" Series of Cut Paper Patterns.

We have made arrangements for supplying paper pattern models, specially cut by Parisian dressmakers, of all Paris costumes illustrated in our pages. In each issue, for the future, we shall append a list of prices for the cut pattern models illustrated in that month's number, and on receipt of postal order or stamps for the amount specified, the pattern models will be forwarded to any address. *Eight days*, however, must elapse from receipt of application, and remittance before pattern models can be supplied.

Prices of models appearing in May issue:—

THREE-QUARTER-COAT, MANTLES, &c. (Figs I, II, III.)	Page 7	1/- each,	post free.
SUMMER MANTLE (Fig. I.)	" 8	1/- "	"
WALKING COSTUME (Fig. II.)	" 8	1/- "	"
FULL DRESS BODICE JACKET (Fig. III.)	" 8	1/- "	"
TRAVELLING COSTUME (Fig. I.)	" 9	1/3 "	"
WALKING TOILETTE (Fig. II.)	" 9	1/3 "	"
CHILDREN'S FASHIONS (Figs. I, II, & III.)	" 10	1/- "	"

To obtain the LADY OF THE HOUSE regularly send 12 stamps to defray cost of year's postage to WILSON, HARTNELL & Co., Commercial Buildings, Dubli[n]

Fashion from *The Lady of the House* May 1891

8 THE LADY OF THE HOUSE. [15TH MAY 1891.

FRENCH OUTDOOR TOILETTES.

FIG. 1.

FIG. 2.

FIG. 3.

Fig. 1.—SUMMER MANTLE or for the Drive, of nut-coloured cloth and stout silk of the same shade. The body part is cut like an ordinary jacket, and braided over with mohair or silk cord in arabesque design. The full sleeves are taken from the shoulder and back pieces towards the front, then laid in folds which are brought to the jacket plastron slit into which they are draped. Plain coat sleeves underneath, with silk wristlets over the hand. A capôte of flowers, black lace, and a bird. Curled hair.

Fig. 2.—WALKING COSTUME. Cigar coloured velveteen and fine woollen in the lighter havannah shade, or ribbed silk instead of velveteen. A cut-away jacket front with round scallops, which are braided with silk and beaded with steel. The back width is laid with box pleats. A scarf piece of the woollen is laid crosswise to simulate a scarf. Light suède gloves. A band of steel beaded passementerie above the flounced foot-border.

Fig. 3.—FULL DRESS BODICE JACKET of pale blue silk poplin and white silk poplin, embroidered with blue and gold. The bodice is laid in wide folds into the shoulder seams, and are close to the figure down to the waist line, whence the draping forms a panier set in all round with a border, of the white embroidered goods. Full poplin sleeves and open wristlet cuffs at the elbows. Embroidered front bodice pieces and plastron, a plain collar, a white foulard skirt with blue ring design, a white rice straw hat, with fancy straw open-worked brim, hazy blue tulle, on which tinsel dots; white marguerites.

If we can deduce something of our ancestors' drinking habits by the number of lines stocked, by far the most popular tipples were whiskey (14 Irish, 9 Scotch) and champagne, the staple of the dining table. Twenty-eight vintage and 9 non-vintage brands are offered, including such famous names as Clicquot, Ayala, Heidsieck, Moët et Chandon, Mumm, Roederer and Pol Roger. Prices of the vintage wines vary from 53s per dozen (Viardot Freres) to the seven-year-old Mumm Cordon Rouge at 125s per dozen.

Some Wine prices from the 1909 List	**Price per dozen***
Clarets	
Château Lafite 1896	42s
Léoville Barton	30s
Montrose	30s
Duhart-Milon	20s
Burgundy	
Clos de Vougeot	48s
Aloxe-Corton	42s
Beaune	30s
Fleurie	18s
White wines	
Very Superior Sauternes	30s
Chablis	24s
White Hocks	
Johannesberg	72s
Marcobrunn	48s
Oppenheim	15s
Moselles	
Bocksteiner	42s
Berncastler	36s

* 20s (£1) is equal to £76 in 2000, so the Château Lâfite cost the equivalent of £160 a case, or £13.30 a bottle. In 1908 we listed Ch. Langoa Barton at 24s, Leoville Lascases at 30s, Gruard-Larose at 36s and Mouton Rothschild at 36s (vintages not stated).

MARCH, 1891. SPRING ISSUE.

The Lady of the House

CIRCULATION.

TWENTY THOUSAND COPIES *OF THIS NUMBER OF THE "LADY OF THE HOUSE" HAVE BEEN PUBLISHED. THIS CIRCULATION, WHICH IS MORE THAN DOUBLE THAT OF ANY IRISH PERIODICAL, IS ATTESTED BY SWORN CERTIFICATE.*

20,000 copies is a good circulation even today

The catalogue boasts that 'few merchants in Ireland hold as large a stock of whiskey as we do, all of which has been stored by ourselves since it was distilled.' The merchant's practice was to buy overproof whiskey in casks from the distillers, and store it in bond (i.e. before excise duty was paid) for the requisite number of years. Pure water was then added to bring the strength down to 25 per cent under proof. It was then despatched in five or ten gallon earthenware jars to the trade or bottled for the consumer. A typical price was that of our famous A1 brand at 21s per gallon, or in bottles (43s per dozen—about £12 a bottle in current terms).

Wine types were much less varied than today, though fortified wines were more in evidence. There were 11 different ports, 20 sherries, 15 Marsalas and 7 Madeiras. By contrast there were only 9 Burgundies—including a sparkling red at 59s per dozen—eight clarets and three Sauternes. Some of the text suggests that the firm felt that an educative role was appropriate: claret, we said (in contrast to fortified wines) 'is by nature and vinofacture, a wine totally different from all others and is as much a child of nature as they are children of art; their process of production is long and arduous while that of claret is so simple that it really make itself.' Another page of the catalogue says that this applies to Burgundy as well. Noting a trend towards increased consumption of 'white wine', six still and two sparkling hocks are offered, and four still and four sparkling Moselles. Hogsheads could be bottled and laid down in Findlater's own bins and drawn off as required.

Tea was always an important part of the tea, wine and spirit merchants' business and had been a core activity of the firm since the 1830s. We offered Indian, Ceylonese and China tea ('as recommended by physicians'). Since the 1880s we packed Findlater's Pure Indian teas in silver foil bags with coloured wrappings to identify the different blends. In 1909 Pink was the most expensive, at 3s 4d per pound, followed by Green at 3s, Salmon at 2s 8d, Blue at 2s 4d, Yellow at 2s, and a variety of other blends down to the daunting 'Strong Tea' at 1s 2d. Other blends were described as 'useful blend', 'strong flavouring and wonderful value', 'the best value that can be bought in tea at the price', 'wonderfully fine tea at a moderate price', 'The Tea our reputation has been built on', 'our special five o'clock tea', 'the tea of luxury' and finally 'connoisseur's tea'.

It is often said that Irish cooking was quite limited in those days (and perhaps the popularity of ready-made sauces such as 'Dargai Dash' is corroborative evidence), yet our 1909 list shows a surprising range of quality foods available: for instance, almonds (seven lines), anchovies, bottled apricots, 66 named brands of biscuit (including three brands of Bath Oliver), caviar, eight types of chutney, two full pages of cakes, sweets and chocolates, crystallised fruits, curried lobster, choice dessert figs, Heinz Specialities (including stuffed olives, evaporated horseradish, and tomato ketchup at 7½d per 8 oz bottle), a wide range of tinned or bottled fruits, fish and vegetables, hominy grits, macaroni (and, as it happens, no other pasta), olive oil (specially imported by Findlater's from Leghorn), paté de foie gras, soups at 9½ or 10½d per tin (grouse, game, mock turtle, hare,

1907

1908

1910

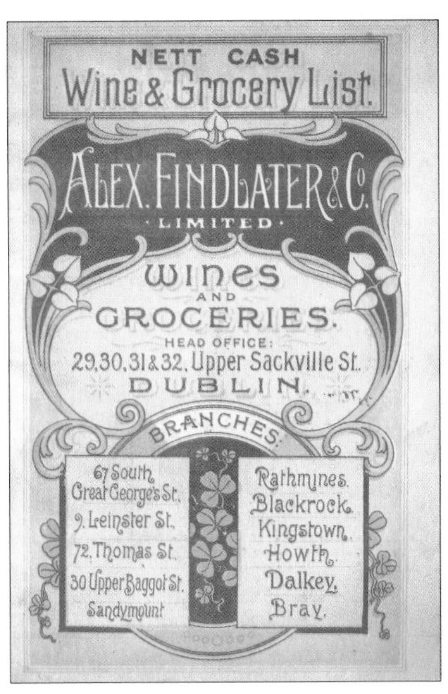

Wine and grocery list

Wine List covers

julienne, and, at 1s per tin, the expensive Heinz tomato), spices, sardines (nine varieties), tinned shrimps and bottled truffles—the choice is wider than in many modern supermarkets.

The list also includes a comprehensive range of purely domestic purchases such as boot polish, candles, dog biscuits (6 brands), eau de cologne, furniture polish, ink, lavender water, patent sardine knives and (an unexpected touch) special housemaids' gloves.

As well as these goods, there was the provision counter, which sold ham, bacon, butter, eggs, sausages, black and white puddings, brawn beef and cheese—varieties named included cream, Cheddar, Gloucester, stilton, gruyère, parmesan, camembert and Dutch.*

Not all of these goods would have been available at every branch, though horsedrawn deliveries were available (three times a day from each branch, or so the list says) with a weekly schedule of deliveries from head office covering the city and outlying areas as far as Leixlip, Oldtown, Saggart, Celbridge, Dunboyne, Tara and Dunshaughlin. After the First World War, the Trojan vans started to replace horse-drawn deliveries. Ned Kelly, an engineer who in the 1920s worked with Ashenhurst & Williams, the Leyland agents, who supplied and serviced the Findlater vans, remembers the vans well:

> The Trojan was ahead of its time. You had to be a bit of an engineer to drive it. The engine was under the driver's seat. The fly wheel was literally under where you sat. It was connected to the engine by a series of springs. And, God bless, if ever a spring broke it would tear the backside off the driver. The front of the Trojan was empty. The engine was transverse. Epicycle gearbox. The chain went down to the back axle. No differential on the back axle.
>
> If you wanted to turn in the roadway you were advised to go around the block. The

* The tradition of abundance of stock was celebrated by P.O.P. in *Dublin Ditties* Dublin: Cahills 1930

FINDLATERS
Would you buy a Turkey?
Would you buy a Ham?
A Goose, a Leg of Mutton,
Or, perchance a Pot of Jam?
Go you to Findlaters, for Findlater's everywhere,
For Groceries there's no one with Findlater to compare.
Would you buy sweet Raisins,
Sultanas, Candied Peel?
Fruits both fresh and crystallised,
To grace a Christmas meal?
Go you to Findlaters, for Findlaters you can't beat,
For anything you'd like to drink and everything you'd eat.
Would you stock your cellar
With choicest wines of France?
Buy your Christmas Crackers
For dinner or for dance?
Go you to Findlaters, where you're sure of what you get,
Go you to Findlaters–and you'll go again I bet.

ALEX. FINDLATER & CO., LTD., DUBLIN.

COFFEE-BREWING A FINE ART.

Exhibition Brewing of Coffee at the Royal Dublin Society's Winter Show, Ball's Bridge, Dublin.

FACTS ABOUT COFFEE.

COFFEE is grown in a wide range of countries, being practically indigenous to most places lying within twenty-five degrees north and south of the Equator.

India, Ceylon, the West Indian Islands, Sumatra, Java, the Phillipines, Australia, and the various States of Central and South America all contribute in supplying us with the stimulating beverage. Mocha, in Arabia, is popularly supposed to be the finest coffee exporting district in the world; but the glory has departed from it in recent times, due no doubt to the lack of commercial spirit and ignorance in up-to-date cultivation on the part of the native races.

Costa Rica is keeping up its good name, and some of the finest samples come from this little central American State.

Coffee is an evergreen plant, in its wild state growing to a height of from 18 to 20 feet, but under cultivation it is a shrub of close growth, its height being kept down to an average of from 4 to 6 feet. It is remarkably productive, inasmuch as at all seasons of the year leaves, blossoms, and ripe fruit are to be seen at the same time on the same tree. Indeed fruit may be gathered at any period, although there are usually but two regular harvests in the course of the year. Each cherry or pod contains two seeds which constitute the raw coffee. These seeds pass through the processes of washing, drying, etc., before being shipped to British or other markets.

The roasting of coffee is a matter of the greatest importance. By means of the intense heat applied to the roasting cylinder, the fragrant oil is driven out, thereby producing the aroma peculiar to roasted coffee, and possessed by no other known substance.

When the coffee has been roasted—which is a delicate operation requiring much judgment and experience—comes the grinding—another important process calling for great care and exactitude—for if the coffee be ground too coarse it will not be sufficiently susceptible to the action of boiling water, while if ground two fine the opposite effect is produced. It is difficult to assign a reason for the small amount of coffee consumed by the British as compared with our Dutch, French, and German neighbours. It cannot be on account of any inferiority in the quality of the coffee imported into the country, for as a matter of fact the best coffee that is grown finds its way into our home markets.

One of the reasons is, perhaps, that we do not as a rule take as much pains to make a cup of coffee as we do to make one of tea, and it may be we do not use enough at a making. There are many methods of preparing coffee. Simple infusion is, however, the easiest, and, on the whole, most satisfactory method of preparation. If good coffee be used and the following directions carried out the result will give a delicious cup of the "intellectual" beverage:—First boil the water, and then inserting the ground coffee—one ounce to a pint of water—allow the vessel to stand from seven to ten minutes, as with tea, the coffee being ready for use when the powder swimming on the surface sinks to the bottom on slightly stirring. Hot milk should be used for mixing with coffee, but not heated to boiling point. .

It will repay a little trouble and study to attain the art of preparing coffee to perfection, but the art once learned is easy to follow, and the difference between a well-prepared and a badly-prepared cup is very great indeed.

Findlater's Pure Coffee ... ... per lb. 1/10
(A combination of the best mountain growths—the perfection of high-class coffees)
Findlater's Cafe Francais ... ... ,, 1/8
(Roasted on French principles—a delicious beverage)
Findlater's Breakfast Coffee ... ... ,, 1/6
Findlater's Breafast Coffee with Chicory ... ... ,, 1/4

ALEX. FINDLATER & CO., LTD.

30

1903: Coffee, like tea, was an integral part of the tea, wine and spirit merchant's business. In 1830 good Jamaica coffee retailed from 1s 2d to 1s 8d lb (equivalent to £2.82 per 250g). Unusually this commodity is actually dearer today than in 1830. Instant coffee first appeared on our list in 1934. Maxwell House at 3s 9d lb is equivalent to £4.84 per 200g—not much different from today's price of £4.49. Nescafé was first listed in 1953 at 4s 6d, size not stated.

Joe McAuley, who worked in the company for 54 years, driving a Trojan van (July 1924)

two wheels would travel at the same speed—solid tyres. One day one of your drivers was late returning from his delivery run. When he finally got back he was questioned on what delayed him. His excuse was that the solid tyres of the Trojan van got caught in the tram lines and he had to stay that way until he arrived at the tram sheds in Phibsboro before he could free himself! The extension system and the ignition was on the running board. They were very good. Did not have to carry a spare wheel but we were often called out to repair the rubber on the solid tyre–quite a job.

A large proportion of business was done on account. On entering a typical store, such as that at Bray, the customer stepped between the arms of a long U-shaped counter stretching to the back of the shop. Immediately to the left was the confectionery counter with fresh cakes, sweets and Jacobs biscuits under glass lids, then came the provisions areas—eggs, butter, cheese, chickens and bacon, in that order. At the very bottom of the U would be the fruit and vegetables, behind which was the cash desk, manager's office and storage areas. Then came the wines, spirits and beer counter, and finally, immediately on the right inside the entrance, the general grocery department. In the 1960s, to increase trade, I tried to reverse the grocery and wines departments, and moved the wines next to the window in the Bray shop. The power of the Church, in the form of the Protestant vicar, Rev. Billy Rooke, caused the decision to be rescinded.

Most of the assistants were male, though women typically looked after confectionery, cheese and butter and eggs. On the grocery side were a couple of light chairs, so that the shopper could sit while giving her order, resting her handbag on the special shelf provided.

First World War shortages

Although the firm employed almost four hundred people at this time, all the buying, price setting, employment of staff, rates of pay, promotion and property matters were dealt with by the Boss, Mr Willie. By the time the First World War broke out in 1914 Ireland had become surprisingly dependent on overseas sources for food, and the German submarine blockade, which started early in 1917, demonstrated how far this process had evolved. An interview with Willie appeared in *The Lady of the House* of October 1917. As 'the largest distributors of food products in Ireland' Findlater's was very conscious of the 'food difficulties which confront the Irish housekeeper under present conditions' and in particular the difficulty in obtaining good quality butter. He explained:

> Danish butter at the port of arrival in England is fifteen pounds per hundred weight, or two shillings and eightpence farthing per lb. This very day the Food Controller has lessened what was practically a protective duty on Danish butter by advancing the controlled price of Irish creamery butter to eleven pounds, four shillings per hundredweight, and this has raised the price twopence per pound. The Irish creameries are still dissatisfied, and not without reason, for they consider that the controlled price should be raised to twelve pounds sixteen shillings per hundredweight, thus putting Irish butter on something like a fair basis with Danish butter in the British market. The controlled prices have left the creameries with a distinct grievance, and they have not been putting butter on the market with any freedom during the past few weeks. Hence the extreme shortage and the price. In the London market there has been nothing except a small supply of Irish and a little English for the past few weeks.

The interviewer then inquired whether the shortage would continue, especially during the winter.

> 'I don't wish to take too gloomy a view,' replied WF, 'but for the next three months the butter supply will, no doubt, be scanty enough and the price a rising one. Later on, things may improve. Colonial supplies—cold storage butter from New Zealand, Australia and Canada will begin coming in at the close of this month—October. New Zealand butter is a really fine well-flavoured article, a good second to Irish creamery butter, which, to my mind, has a delightfully fresh taste, not equalled by the product of any other country. Then there are Australian and Canadian butters about equal in merit, but a second to the product of New Zealand. This will shortly be available.'

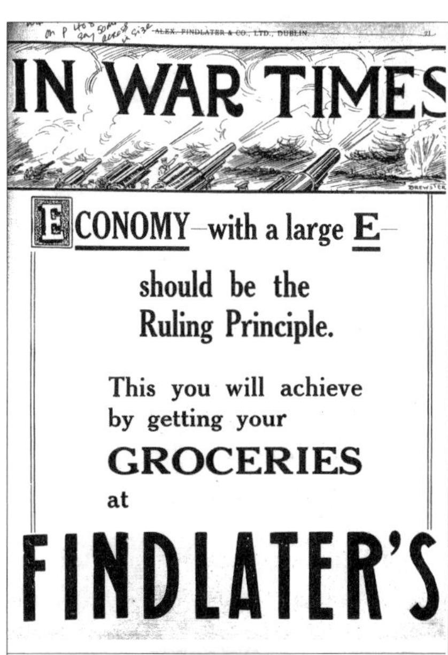

Sandymount branch (on the Green) dressed to impress, before the First World War

The interviewer then inquired what was the general attitude of the public towards butter substitutes observing that the price of butter was 2s 6d per lb, and that of margarine 1s 3d, or just one-half to which WF replied

> Ireland now is going straight ahead in the production of fine brands of margarine. Messrs Dowdall, O'Mahoney & Co. of Cork, are producing two really splendid qualities and other Cork and Waterford firms, are sending out fine qualities, which are being well received. These brands are amongst the finest butter substitutes in the market, and are of excellent flavour, and made from pure, clean, wholesome ingredients.

The interviewer proceeded to inquire about the prospects for 'the other furnishings of our breakfast tables—bacon and eggs?' Willie gave graphic examples of the price inflation that occurred in the last two years of the war.

> 'Black enough', replied WF. 'Bacon has reached unheard-of figures. As with butter, which, in the 1870s, was one shilling a pound, is now two shillings and sixpence, so the ninepenny bacon of the seventies now costs two shillings and fourpence for the best cuts. All Irish meats are very scarce, and the would-be buyer of twenty-four middles of bacon in a week is oftentimes lucky to secure four.'

And Irish hams for Christmas?

> Irish ham will, I fear, be both scarce and high-priced next Christmas, but the Canadian imports may bring us some comfort by relieving the shortage and placing ham on our tables at something approaching reasonable price. A specially appointed Purchasing Executive is working in Canada on behalf of all the Allied Countries purchasing meats and fats—bacon, ham, butter, lard and cheese—so that control will start in the Colonies where the meats and fats are raised.

The discussion then moved on to eggs, and WF explained that

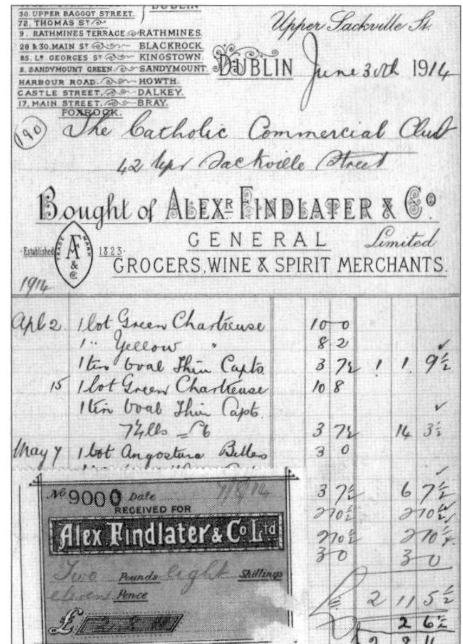

30. UPPER BAGGOT STREET.
72. THOMAS ST
9. RATHMINES TERRACE RATHMINES.
28 & 30. MAIN ST BLACKROCK.
85. Lr GEORGES St KINGSTOWN.
8. SANDYMOUNT GREEN. SANDYMOUNT.
HARBOUR ROAD. HOWTH.
CASTLE STREET. DALKEY.
17. MAIN STREET. BRAY.
FOXROCK.

Upper Sackville St.
DUBLIN June 30th 1914

(190) The Catholic Commercial Club
42 Upr Sackville Street

Bought of ALEXr FINDLATER & Co.
Established 1823 · GENERAL Limited
GROCERS, WINE & SPIRIT MERCHANTS.

1914

Apl 2. 1 bot Green Chartreuse 10 0
1 " Yellow " 8 2
1 tin Oval Thin Capts 3 7½ 1 1 9½
15 1 bot Green Chartreuse 10 8
1 tin Oval Thin Capts
7¼ lbs = 6 3 7½ 14 3½
May 7 1 bot Angostura Bitters 3 0

No 9000 Date 7/8/14
RECEIVED FOR
Alex Findlater & Co Ltd
Two Pounds eight Shillings
eleven Pence
£ 2.8.11

3 7½ 6 7½
2 10½ 2 10½
2 10½ 2 10½
3 0 3 0
2 11 5½
2 6½
£2-8-11

Clubs of all sorts were a good source of business

the supply is altogether inadequate. Poultry-breeders, cottagers and people who 'keep fowl' are killing their hens for table use, and so the egg-producing capacity is growing less and less. The high prices of poultry and chicken feed are the cause of this. Long ago we grew great quantities of wheat in Ireland, and Ireland was a large exporter of wheat and flour. There were a multitude of mills scattered up and down throughout Ireland, the residuals from these mills gave the cheapest and best of feeding stuffs for pigs and poultry. Those were the days 'when every rood of earth maintained its man'. Since then we have become accustomed to depend on foreign countries for the bulk of our food, and now we see the result. Now the first demand upon the meagre supply is, of course, the needs of our vast army of wounded men and the enormous number of sick. There are no Danish eggs, and the foreign lands which helped out the demand of Great Britain either cannot or will not send us supplies.

He continued:

In Ireland we are ultra fastidious about butter, bacon, eggs, and much else that is eatable. Ireland is a great producing country, the quality of our production is first class, and we have all got so accustomed to really first-rate food that we have become hypercritical and will consider no other. Hence, the very cheap eggs, such as Siberian eggs, used to come into Great Britain in quantities, but nobody in Ireland wanted these 'ancient lays of the East', and they never reached these shores. Nearly every source of British supply is now closed, and the Irish egg, always highly popular in Great Britain, has now a hundred hands held out to grasp it, and the price is increasing alarmingly.

The reporter then inquired about egg substitutes:

'There is no replacement for the boiled egg or the poached or fried eggs,' explained WF, 'but for puddings, custards and cakes, and indeed for a dish of scrambled eggs, excellent dried eggs are to be had in cartons the equivalent of 12 eggs for 1s 6d or of 24 eggs for 3s 0d. These newly laid eggs, taken from the shell and dried, are free from preservatives, of excellent colour and flavour, and are guaranteed pure. Then there are the liquid eggs in tins with screw tops, each tin containing one dozen eggs, price eighteen pence. These have for years been well known in the confectionery trade, but are now being introduced for domestic use. They are fresh eggs canned during the plentiful periods of the year.

British soldiers in suspicious mood searching for arms amongst the cabbages. (Hogan)

And cheese?

In Ireland, cheese has never been anything like so popular as it is in Great Britain. Why this should be so I confess I do not understand. It is equal in food value to nearly thrice its weight of prime beef. The price of cheese has not been so much affected, for the controlled price of sound Colonial cheese is now one shilling and fourpence, and fourpence more buys prime English Cheddar. One little hint—a scrap of good cheese makes war bread easily assimilated, and that is a point worth remembering.

ALEX. FINDLATER & CO., LTD.,
DUBLIN AND BRANCHES.

PRE-WAR WINES AT PRE-WAR PRICES.

CLARET.

As a Christmas speciality for those who have still a taste for Fine Clarets, we offer the balance of our Stocks of these Wines during the month of December at prices quoted.

The Wines cannot be replaced, and we would strongly advise our Customers and the Public to avail themselves of this final opportunity of obtaining Clarets of a type which made Ireland famous for its Clarets during the last century.

These Wines can be sold on the London Market at much higher prices, but as it would be necessary to pay Duty and other charges sending them over, we think it better to give the benefit to our Customers on this side.

The Wines are Listed at about 15/- per Bottle in the High-class Restaurants in London—they are scarcely dearer than the poor quality War Wines which have flooded the Market of late, and have almost killed the Claret Trade.

We have only a limited quantity—we can offer cheaper Clarets, such as MEDOC at 24/- per Dozen, St. Estephe at 30/- per Dozen, but there is no comparison between these and our PRE-WAR CLARET AT PRE-WAR PRICES.

	VINTAGE.	PER DOZ. BOTTS.	PER DOZ. ½ BOTTS.
Chateau Leoville Barton,	1905.	54/-	—
Chateau Larose, - -	1905.	54/-	29/-
Le Monteil Segur. - -	1909.	50/-	27/-
Chateau des Andiottes, -	1909.	48/-	26/-
Chateau Beycheville St. Julien - - -	1909.	—	26/-

Pre-war claret at pre-war prices for Christmas 1924 (*The Irish Times*, 24 December 1924)

The final question touched on a recent Findlater's innovation—closing for lunch. 'How has closing for the dinner hour worked? It is quite an innovation. The staff will like it famously, I know, but what does the public say?'

WF concluded:

The dinner hour closing is an assured success. The staff do like it, for it considers their comfort and well-being, and the public have been so good as to acquiesce, and are receiving in return even better and prompter service than ever before. I have had dozens of letters and opinions from valued customers expressing high approval of the new departure. You know what the good lubricant does for intricate machinery, makes it run smoothly and sweetly; well, I find this closing down for the staff dinner hour the

1903: A 1 lb jar of strawberry jam was 7d in 1903, equivalent to £2.09 for the standard modern 340g jar which today would cost around £1.50. From 1904 to 1968 Findlater's jams were supplied by Lamb Bros, who had fruit farms in Rathfarnham, Churchtown, Donabate and in County Kildare.

> best lubricant I ever tried. I may say that many other Dublin business houses have recognised the merit of this dinner hour closing operation, and have adopted the system.

Willie was fully aware that the staff were vital to the success of the firm: in 1919 he announced a system of adding profit bonuses to the wages and salaries throughout the year rather than as a lump sum at the end of the year. In announcing this change he was conscious that 'the successes of the last two years' were going to be hard to repeat in the troubled post-war conditions: 'It will need a strenuous effort on the part of each of us. Everyone of us can do something to help—by a little bit of extra enthusiasm, a bit more care in getting up orders and a little extra attention to customers and their wants—some saving of waste and a kindly working together of the staff amongst themselves.'

A month or two later he was able to announce that the Board had agreed to pay the staff a 'Peace Bonus', from the good profits generated in the last years of the war.

From 1909 to 1917 the average profits dropped to £7,700, but lifted again to just over £11,000 [around £350,000] from 1918 to 1920.

The *Irish Investors' Guardian* in July 1911 commented: 'The accounts reflect an improvement in both earnings and financial position after all the outgoings (interest, depreciation, reserves, bad debt provisions). Net profits were £ 5,781 [just over £400,000], an increase of £2,614 [£185,000].' And the following year profits were reported at £6,393 [£438,000]. In 1914 the Board announced a further reduction in the share capital by reducing the 11,000 preference shares of £5 each to the same number of £3 shares and further scaling down the existing £2 ordinary shares to £1 each. In other words, since the flotation of the company fifteen years previously, the preference capital had been reduced by £22,000 and the ordinary, in the hands of the vendors, by £44,000. The net profit for 1913/4 was reported at £6,557 [£445,000], which after debenture interest, left a carry forward of £3,097 [£144,000].

To conclude this section on a good note the *Investors' Guardian* in 1918 said that there was reason to be pleased. The actual profits of £12,465 [£450,000] showed an increase of £3,855 [£100,000] subject to income tax of £1,669 [£60,000] and commented 'the financial position of the company was never stronger and the increased balance forward will help the Board to face the future difficulties of successful trading with at least equanimity.'

National troubles

When Willie succeeded his brother Adam as Managing Director in 1911, he was dealt a tough hand. He had to navigate the company through a great deal of change, both political and social. Head office in Sackville Street often had a front seat in events between the Easter Rising in 1916 and the Civil War which only came to an end in May 1923. The most spectacular incidents were the Rising itself, during which, as we have seen, Willie personally protected the stock against looters with his blunderbuss, and the troubles of 1920, which spread across the country. Elizabeth Fingall sets the scene well:

> All through 1920 things in Ireland were getting steadily worse. There had been shootings of policemen, village bonfires night after night as the police barracks were burnt, tragic fires, involving sometimes loss of life. Presently the British Government made one of the worst mistakes they had ever made. Unable to combat the campaign of assassination with their ordinary forces, they decided to fight their opponents with their own weapons. If they could not find an assassin and get a jury to convict and execute him, they would employ men who would take the law into their own hands, without trial. They increased the numbers of the Royal Irish Constabulary with new recruits, many ex-soldiers fresh from the battlefields—and some ex-convicts fresh from gaol. The supply of green cloth being limited, these appeared half in their old khaki and half in RIC uniform, and were christened after a famous old pack of hounds, the Black and Tans.
>
> In addition, a new force was formed, called the Auxiliaries. These were mostly ex-officers, many of them shell-shocked. They had little or no discipline, being all of equal rank. Some were Irishmen, wanting any job after the War, and little knowing what they were going to be asked to do. They were assigned to barracks through-out the country. Their barracks were fortified with steel shutters and barbed-wire entanglements. No social life was possible and they drank a lot. They spent their days in the barracks with occasional lorry drives at break-neck speed through the country, leaving terror and destruction behind them.
>
> If a policeman had been shot, it was the signal for a reprisal, and a reprisal could mean the burning of a village. Very often the inhabitants had very little to do with the first outrage. Then, as reprisal, the neighbouring big house would be burnt down and so it went on.[1]

Nevertheless, the city was taken by surprise when the Assistant Under-Secretary in Dublin Castle ordered the military to carry out an armed raid starting at 1.30 in the morning on Findlater's, for reasons which were never made clear. The *Freeman's Journal* of Tuesday 16 March 1920 takes up the story:

> The military left Messrs Findlater's stores at 3.20 last evening, after being on the premises since 1.30 on that morning. The premises searched included bonded warehouses, stores, and residential dwellings on which some of the employees live. The soldiers first entered the main building and detained Mr J. Byrne, a traveller for the firm, and the following assistants:–Messrs J. Broderick, John Kennedy, J. Kelly, J. Murray . . . The bonded stores extend underneath the premises for a considerable distance. The military, who were armed with pick-axes and crowbars, paid special attention to the stores, where packing cases, crates, barrels, floors, etc., were minutely examined. The flooring, it is stated, was dug up.
>
> While the operations proceeded no persons but police or military were allowed to enter the premises. Large crowds congregated in the vicinity during the day waiting on the chance that the soldiers might come on so that they might observe what, if any, was the result of the prolonged visit.

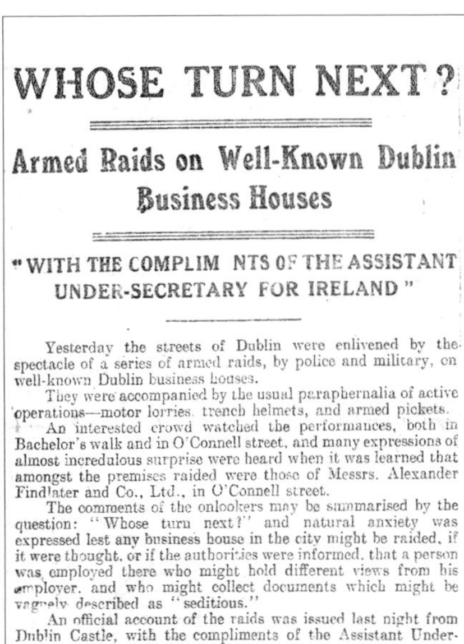

WHOSE TURN NEXT?

Armed Raids on Well-Known Dublin Business Houses

"WITH THE COMPLIM NTS OF THE ASSISTANT UNDER-SECRETARY FOR IRELAND"

Yesterday the streets of Dublin were enlivened by the spectacle of a series of armed raids, by police and military, on well-known Dublin business houses.

They were accompanied by the usual paraphernalia of active operations—motor lorries, trench helmets, and armed pickets.

An interested crowd watched the performances, both in Bachelor's walk and in O'Connell street, and many expressions of almost incredulous surprise were heard when it was learned that amongst the premises raided were those of Messrs. Alexander Findlater and Co., Ltd., in O'Connell street.

The comments of the onlookers may be summarised by the question: "Whose turn next?" and natural anxiety was expressed lest any business house in the city might be raided, if it were thought, or if the authorities were informed, that a person was employed there who might hold different views from his employer, and who might collect documents which might be vaguely described as "seditious."

An official account of the raids was issued last night from Dublin Castle, with the compliments of the Assistant Under-Secretary.

Freeman's Journal, 16 March 1920

A rumour that the military were about to leave the premises caused a flutter of excitement amongst the crowds that had assembled in the lane, and the police began to push them back. An altercation between the constables and some members of the crowd resulted in two women being arrested and conveyed to Store street Police Station.

Both women are of the respectable working class and the action of the police was unfavourably commented on. The crowd made a hostile demonstration, and the police drew their revolvers to prevent any attempt being made to rescue the prisoners. The military motor lorry shortly before 3.20 pm left Findlater place and were then driven off amidst a storm of groans and hisses.

Mr William Findlater, managing director of the firm, declined to make any statement when approached by a *Freeman's Journal* representative. He apparently knew nothing of the cause of the raid. Mr Findlater is well known in Dublin business circles. He is a Conservative with broadly tolerant views, but takes no active part in politics.

The *Freeman's Journal* was baffled as to why Findlaters should have been raided in this way, and certainly did not approve. WHOSE TURN NEXT? ARMED RAIDS OF WELL-KNOWN DUBLIN BUSINESS HOUSES, ran its headlines, and the paper declared that ' the latest stunt is not only a mystery, but is rapidly becoming to every citizen the gravest of menaces . . . the result is that when the rattle of a military lorry is heard after midnight, no man, however clear his conscience may be of offence against the Executive, can be sure that the next minute his door may not be smashed in by rifle butts and he himself dragged off to swell the list of victims'.[2]

The Dublin Chamber and the Treaty

Like many of his fellow businessmen, Willie took an active part at that time in the Dublin Chamber of Commerce. In the heated political atmosphere of the time, it was difficult for the Protestant voice to be raised in any but a few constituencies, so the Chamber of Commerce made a convenient arena. These were important times for the Chamber which national politicians used as a sounding board for moderate unionist opinion. In fact in 1921, Éamon de Valera, having been invited to meet Prime Minister Lloyd George, sought 'the views of a certain section of our people of whom you are the representatives' and on 4 July, in the Mansion House, met with Sir Robert Woods, Sir Maurice Dockrell, Andrew Jameson, Lord Midleton and Sir James Craig.

During the Treaty negotiations in 1921 Willie was a member of the Council of the Dublin Chamber of Commerce that urged Éamon de Valera and Arthur Griffith to accept the Treaty in December 1921. He served on various committees, including Trade and Commerce, Law, Parliamentary, Municipal, House and Finance and Education. The secretary of the Irish Industrial Development Association summed up the views of the businessmen in the Chamber in the final paragraph of his excellent analysis of Irish trade and industry published in 1920:

> We have in Ireland all the resources necessary to build up a thriving community: endless proof is available of the ability of Irishmen to cope successfully with economic problems; our workpeople are comparable with those of any other nation, both in regard to skill and intelligence; all that we lack to enable us to take our proper place among the prosperous nations of the world is the power to determine our own economic policy. Until that right is granted us it is unfair to place the blame for her present industrial condition at Ireland's door.[3]

On 25 January 1922 it is recorded in their minutes that the Chamber had approved the following statement of its views on Condition 5 of the Treaty:

> Briefly stated, this condition offers Ireland complete control of finance and taxation, modified by the provision that free trade without any restrictions should be maintained in perpetuity between Great Britain and Ireland. There is no reason to doubt that Irish businessmen engaged in established industries or business, being able to hold their own, would depreciate any discrimination in their favour against British competition, or any measures calculated to interfere with the flow of trade between the two countries, but it is apparent that there are weighty reasons why Condition No 5 should not be accepted on behalf of Ireland.
>
> An Irish Parliament, under this condition, would find it impossible to follow the example of the Parliament at Westminster in passing an act for safeguarding of new or struggling industries which might become a great national asset. Ireland would also be bound, in advance, to a British trade policy without regard to its adaptability to the circumstances or conditions of the country. This Council would urge that in view of the need for exhaustive and patient inquiry before the vast interests involved can be wisely dealt with, the framing of the commercial treaty between the two countries

should be postponed until a political settlement is reached, and that Condition No 5 should be eliminated from the conditions which it sought to impose as preliminary to the settlement.

Condition 5 was omitted from the agreement subsequently reached by the conference in December.[4] The Treaty that established the Irish Free State was signed by the British and Irish representatives on 6 December 1921, and ratified by Dáil Éireann a month later. The majority of Irish people ultimately confirmed it at the ballot box. However, the anti-Treaty faction, those that did not agree to the exclusion of six northern counties from Dublin jurisdiction, led by Éamon de Valera, walked out on 10 January 1922.

The Dublin Chamber of Commerce had met on 30 December 1921, those present being Andrew Jameson (distilling)[5], in the Chair; William Hewat (Heitons coal and steel); James Shanks (sanitary engineering); E. H. Andrews (tea, wine, spirit and provision merchants): Richard Booth (engineering works); Sir Maurice Dockrell (builders' providers and timber merchants); William Findlater; John Good (master builder); John Hollwey (ship broker); George Jacob (biscuit manufacturing); Patrick Leonard (sales master and auctioneer); S. W. Maddock (secretary Mount Jerome cemetery); Harry Millar* (wholesale tea, wine and spirit merchants) Laurence Martin (timber importers); Sir James Percy (publisher); William Wallace (coal distributors); John Wallis (carrier and steam packet agent) and Alderman J. Hubbard Clarke, High Sheriff for the City of Dublin. Apologies were received from David Barry (British & Irish Steam Packet Co.); William Crowe (timber, slate and tiles merchants); Sir W. J. Goulding Bart (fertilisers); W. Lombard Murphy MD, Sir Horace Plunkett and L. C. Cuffe (cattle salesmen and auctioneers).

The meeting was called to consider what action the Chamber should take in the present crisis. After a very full discussion it was decided that a resolution in favour of the ratification of the Peace Treaty should be passed by the Council, and published in the press on the following day. The Secretary was instructed to send copies to the press, de Valera, Arthur Griffith, and the Speaker of Dáil Éireann:

> The Council of the Dublin Chamber of Commerce, realising the extreme gravity of the issues now awaiting decisions by the responsible representatives of the Irish People and the acute anxiety prevailing in the Country lest a conflict of opinion amongst the representatives may defeat the hopes of peace, cannot maintain silence in a situation so pregnant with danger to the vast interests of the whole community.
>
> The Council also recognises its obligation to the great business community which looks to it for a frank and emphatic declaration to all concerned that a recurrence of the disastrous conditions which threatened to overturn the whole structure of the

* Harry Millar was a director of the Bank of Ireland from 1923 and Governor 1930-1932; and first chairman of the Wine & Spirit Association. He played rugby for Ireland 1904-1905. Adam Millar & Co was founded by his grandfather Adam. Harry's grandson David is a director of Findlater Wine Merchants.

> Country's industry and trade would bring ruin to its prospect of National progress.
>
> The Council therefore declares that rejection of the Peace Treaty, and a return to chaos and civil war with its untold miseries, as an alternative to acceptance is unthinkable.
>
> The Council further records its opinion that the reconstruction of Ireland by her own people is made possible by the terms of the treaty, and most earnestly hopes that the body of Irishmen entrusted with its fate will secure its final ratification.[6]

Disturbed times provide troubled waters for all sorts of predators. In January 1922, the Metropolitan Police Office handed a memo to the firm stating that: 'there are at present gangs of armed robbers operating in Dublin. They are well informed as to the habits and movements of their victims and are no doubt assisted in some cases by confederates in the employment of such victims'. The memo was particularly concerned with the transit of large sums of money. It advised that a certain number of employees should be armed and that the arms should be carried 'on person' ready for instant use; that an armed guard should be placed in position covering the interior of the building where he would not be observed by raiders and from where he could shoot in security; and that 'a powerful electric alarm be fitted to sound outside the building which can be set in motion to ring continuously by the pressure of hand or foot, such as is now fitted to the Bank of Ireland and the Belfast Bank in College Green'.[7] I very much doubt that Willie took the advice to arm any of his staff, either in head office or any of the branches.

The Civil War

On 13/14 April the anti-Treaty forces, the Irregulars, took over the Four Courts as their headquarters and refused to recognise the authority of the Provisional Government, headed by Michael Collins who held the legitimate seat of power. During the subsequent months the Irregulars raided private premises and the plundering of property became a frequent occurrence throughout the city. Oliver St J. Gogarty, surgeon, wit, writer and senator (1922-1936) wrote: 'I could never countenance this euphemism, Irregulars. They were mostly town riffraff misled, or country dupes and discontents whom de Valera aroused when he found that his methods had landed him in a minority.'[8]

On 29 April 1922, a fortnight after anti-Treaty forces had seized the Four Courts, a meeting was called at short notice

> to consider the present dangerous condition of the country as it affects Trade and Commerce. It was resolved that the Chamber:
>
> representing a large portion of the manufacturing and trading interests of Ireland, views with deep concern, the present want of security for life and property in our city and country. It calls upon all who are responsible for good government in Ireland to provide at the earliest possible moment such conditions of security and tranquillity as will permit of Irishmen living their lives in peace and quietness, and developing to the utmost the resources of their native land'. The secretary was instructed to send copies

Éamon de Valera addressing a crowd outside Findlaters at the top of O'Connell Street, a customary place for political rallies (EMI-Pathé)

to the Peace Conference at the Mansion House, the Provisional Government and Dáil Éireann.

The kidnapping of Michael Collins' assistant chief of staff, Lieutenant-General O'Connell, by anti-Treaty forces was the signal for the civil war to hot up. On Tuesday 27 June 1922 the Provisional Government under Michael Collins issued the following public statement, which with its support for normal business and economic activity must have been welcome to the businessmen of the Chamber:

> Since the close of the General Election, at which the will of the people of Ireland was ascertained, further grave acts against the security of person and property have been committed in Dublin and in some other parts of Ireland by persons pretending to act with authority.
>
> It is the duty of the Government, to which the people have entrusted their defence and the conduct of their affairs, to protect and secure all law-respecting citizens without distinction, and that duty the Government will resolutely perform.
>
> Yesterday one of the principal garages in the metropolis was raided and plundered under the pretext of a Belfast boycott. No such boycott has any legal existence, and, if it had, it could not authorise or condone the action of irresponsible persons in seizing private property.
>
> Later in the same evening Lieutenant-General O'Connell, Assistant Chief of Staff, was seized by some of the persons responsible for the plundering of the garage, and is still held in their hands. Outrages such as these against the nation and the Government must cease at once, and cease forever.
>
> For some months past all classes of business in Ireland have suffered severely through the feeling of insecurity engendered by reckless and wicked acts, which have tarnished the reputation of Ireland abroad.

Upper O'Connell Street after the Civil War (1922). Findlaters is behind the left hand lamp post. (Hogan)

> As one disastrous consequence, unemployment and distress are prevalent in the country, at a time when, but for such acts, Ireland would be humming with prosperity.
>
> The Government is determined that the country shall no longer be held up from the pursuit of its normal life and the re-establishment of its free national institutions. It calls, therefore, on the citizens to co-operate actively with it in the measures it is taking to ensure the public safety and to secure Ireland for the Irish people.[9]

Actions quickly followed words. Early on Wednesday morning, 28 June, parties of National (Government) troops were on the streets, stopping vehicles and pedestrians and searching them for arms. Snipers were also active in many parts of the city and several business premises and hotels were reported to have been seized and barricaded by the Irregulars. The business life of the city came to a standstill, shops and offices closed up, and, except for the bravely curious, the citizens beat a hasty retreat to their homes. Barricades were also erected across the main thoroughfares and strongly guarded by National troops, and pedestrians as they passed were subject to a careful search.

The Four Courts were shelled, and eventually blown up by the Irregulars inside. The fall of their headquarters, did not, however, mean that the final defeat of the Irregulars had come, for desperate fighting was at this time being waged in other parts of the city, principally in a wide area just north of Nelson's Pillar in O'Connell street.

The fighting continued on and off all day on Sunday 2 July. The official report issued on this evening stated: 'National forces are now carrying out a big concerted movement round the O'Connell Street area, which is the stronghold of the Irregulars. From early evening they are closing in and drawing a cordon round O'Connell Street, Marlborough Street, and Gardiner Street.'[10]

A fresh attack on the occupied premises in O'Connell Street was launched on Monday afternoon, the heavy guns again being brought into play here. Further successes quickly followed for the National arms, several of the remaining positions held by the Irregulars being captured, including the Gresham Hotel and the YMCA premises opposite, and it was officially reported that a large number of prisoners were secured, many of whom were trying to get away with their arms and ammunition.

Some time about noon on Wednesday 5 July a fire broke out in the neighbourhood of the Hammam Hotel and another building. The firing continued with increased force, and amid the din the Fire Brigade, in charge of Captain Myers,* dashed up to subdue the outbreak, which by this time seemed to have involved the entire buildings. Soon after the arrival of the firemen the front walls of the Hammam collapsed with a loud crash, accompanied by blinding volumes of dense black smoke. Undaunted by the magnitude of its task, the Fire Brigade got to work strenuously, and its efforts were mainly directed to preventing the fire from spreading in a northern direction towards Findlaters where large quantities of over proof whiskey were stored in bond underground. A terrific explosion was next heard near the Gresham Hotel, and was followed by a deafening roar of machine guns. The Gresham Hotel was still standing, but later on it, too, became involved and was quickly a mass of flames. The white flag was displayed at 7.30 p.m. from the Granville Hotel and some twenty Irregulars marched out and surrendered.

Thus ended a week of terror and destruction that was equalled only by the Rising of Easter, 1916. The loss of lives in the case of the military totalled 19 dead and 122 wounded, and of civilians over 50 dead and 200 wounded.† The value of the destroyed property, which included some twenty of the finest buildings in the city, is estimated at £3m-£4m, while, besides the many ruined homes, the damage resulted in the disemployment of several hundred men and women.[11] My father told me that the Pro-Cathedral and Findlater's bonded warehouse were the nearest buildings to Nelson Pillar that remained standing, thanks to the efficiency of the Dublin Fire Brigade. Willie Findlater on that occasion, it was reported, made a presentation to the Captain of the Fire Brigade as a tribute to the valour and the efficiency of his staff. However I was told that Grandfather swore under his breath that all the other traders got a new building and he did not!

The Findlater Minute Book entry of 28 June 1922 records: 'Owing to the Disturbances, our premises in Sackville Street were closed from 30th June to 9th July and were partially burned. The opposing forces were in turn in occupation of the premises. Considerable looting was done at a number of our premises.' Findlaters put in a claim for compensation for losses occasioned by commandeering, looting, fire, loss of rents and trade to the Corporation amounting to £14,800 or more than £½m in modern terms,

The claim was of course long, and immensely detailed, and included:

* Great-uncle of the celebrated *Irish Times* journalist.

† Among those killed was Cathal Brugha who was shot by Free State soldiers based in Findlaters buildings. (*see* John Pinkman *In the Legion of the Vanguard* Cork: Mercier 2001 pp 127–142)

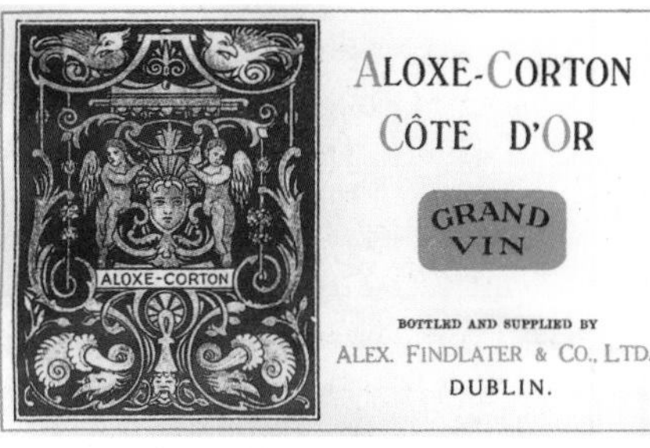

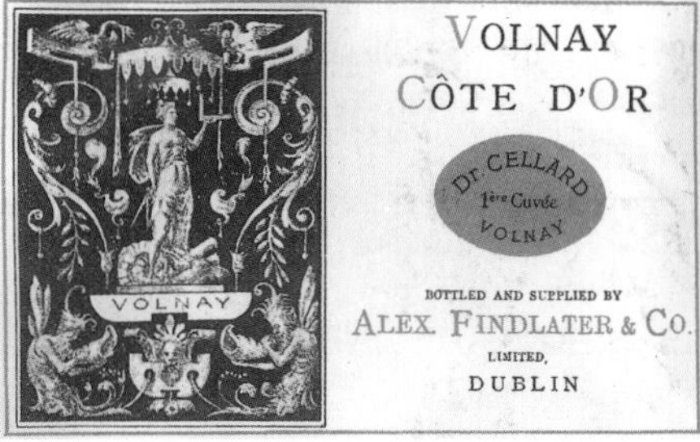

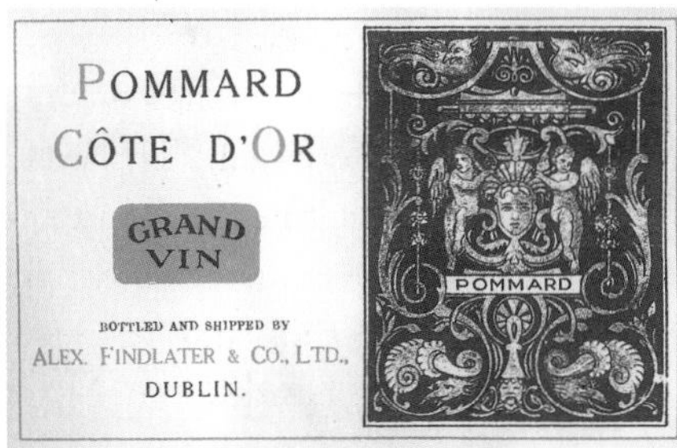

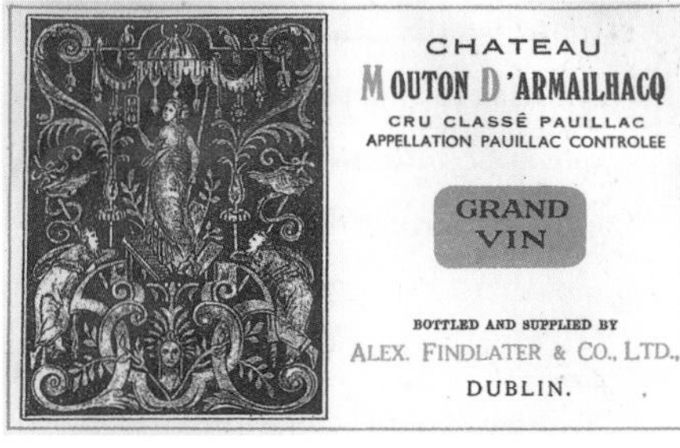

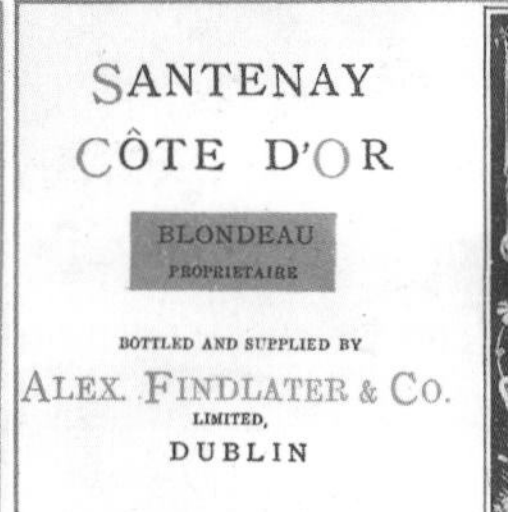

Every drop of wine was imported in cask and bottled and labelled by Findlaters. Label design was worked out between the Boss and the printer and this continued right up to the end of my father's custodianship of the company.

Claim	Amount £	Yr 2000 equivalent
Sackville Street: Damage to Motor Cars and Horse Vans by reckless use of–and, subsequently by being put into Street Barricades, or employed at unlawful work by Irregulars–as per Statement attached	£276	[£10,000]
Looted by Irregulars–Contents of Postal Clerk's Desk	£19 16s	[£740]
To large shell lock on Stable entrance gates destroyed by Irregulars during occupation of premises	£10.15s 6d	[£400]
Dorset Street: Goods lost–stolen–or destroyed by Irregulars' Raid	£349.16.3	[£13,000]
Consequential loss of trading profits estimated for the period the premises were in occupation by Irregulars 30.6.22 to 6.7.22 and for the two weeks immediately ensuing a shortage in output £5,611 and Gross Profit on this @ 18 per cent	£1009 19s 7d	[over £20,000]
Claims for Goods commandeered, or looted, by Irregular Forces, on and after April 20th 1922, for which the signature of the raiders was obtained at our branches at: 67 South Great George's Street; 9 Leinster Street; 30 Upper Baggot Street, 35 Castle Street Dalkey; 84/85 Lower George's Street Kingstown; Harbour Road Howth; Station Road Foxrock; 72 Thomas Street; Main Street, Malahide.	£302 10s 8d	[£11,000]

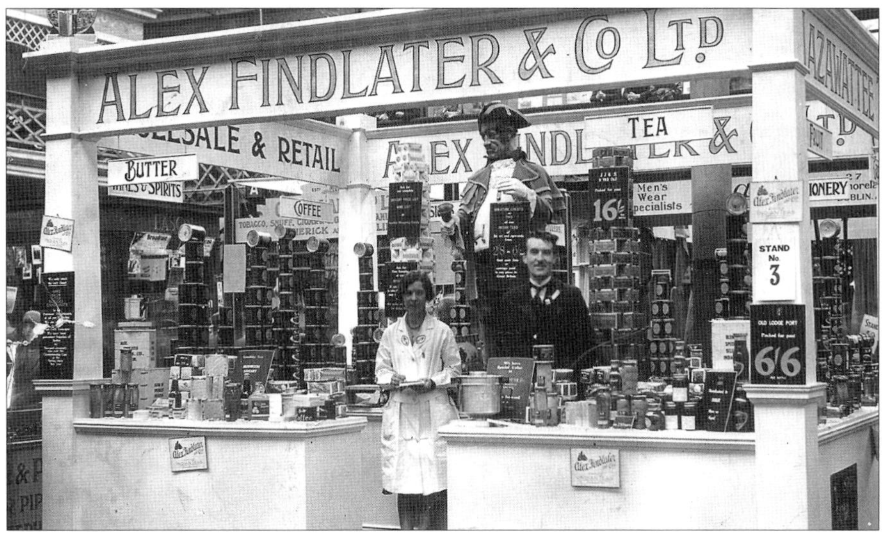

Findlater's stand at the RDS, 1910

There was also a claim relating to the Free State Army's occupation of the Royal Hotel, Bray. They took possession of the entire hotel on 4 July 1922 and kept it till 27 October 1922.* Then the new Civic Guards (later called the Garda Siochána) took over part of the premises and handed back the remainder. They remained in possession until 24 March 1923. During these occupations considerable damage was done to the premises and to the furniture. Our claim amounted to £1,235 4s 9d [£45,000]. The Board of Works said that they would only allow £487 0s 1d [£18,000]. There were seven pages of counsel's opinion. As to the main claim, Findlater's eventually settled for a mix of compensation, including the purchase by the corporation of various premises in Findlater Place to permit the creation of Cathal Brugha Street.

No doubt there was a certain amount of gamesmanship in putting in these claims—for instance, though it is true that gross profit reached 17.6 per cent in 1918, that figure was never repeated before or since. On the other hand there were incidents that could hardly be claimed for, as Johnny McDermott in Baggot Street branch remembered:

> In the winter of 1923 there was a civil war on here—the Irregulars and the Free Staters. The Manager was up in an office and he was dead drunk. 'Go down and see what all that commotion is about.' I ran down to the window and there were six guards outside with bicycles and they were after putting a brick through the Christmas window and they were loading turkeys and hams and everything into sacks—it was nothing but lootin' and robbin'. And I ran after this guard and I said: 'The Manager up here wants to know what all this thing is about.' He put his hand in his trench coat pocket, his green trench coat pocket and brought out a gun, held it up to my head.

* Marie Lock told me her mother, Ellen Phelan, was housekeeper in the hotel for twelve years around this time. 'When the Black and Tans used to force their way into the hotel she used to take their guns. She held strict morals in the hotel and placed a Sacred Heart picture on the stairway which was there for years after she left to get married.'

ALEX. FINDLATER & CO., LTD., DUBLIN.

PRICE LIST OF FINDLATER'S TEAS.

Findlater's Pure Indian Teas.

The Brands which we sell under our own name have stood the test of the keenest competition, and they are recognised in Ireland as Standard Brands. Their never-varying quality and their constant uniformity are the reasons for their well-deserved reputation.

PRICES:

		s.	d.	
DELICATE AROMA.	Pink Wrapper	3	4	per lb:
	Green Wrapper	3	0	„
	Salmon Wrapper	2	8	„
	Blue Wrapper	2	4	„
	Yellow Wrapper	2	0	„
	Good and Strong	1	8	„

We make Specialities of the 2/- AND 2/8 Teas.

China Tea.

As Recommended by Physicians.

	PER LB. s.	d.
Finest Kintuck—This is the Finest China Tea sold this season. It is a revelation to the modern Tea Drinker of the cup of tea our grandfathers enjoyed when tea was retailed at 7/- and 8/- per lb	3	6
The Fashionable "At Home" Tea	3	0
Really Fine China Tea	2	6
Good Sound China Tea	2	0

There is a greatly increased demand now for really Fine China Tea, as it has more bouquet than the stronger Teas of India and Ceylon, and can be drunk with impunity by those with whom these Teas are apt to disagree. Fine China Tea is free from astringency and contains but little tannin. The finer qualities have a larger proportion of theine, in which is the great value of this tea as a dietetic. The lower priced Teas are of no use whatsoever—our lowest price which we can recommend is, therefore, 2s. per lb. China Teas also contain a large quantity of volatile oil, an ingredient which makes these teas so agreeable in flavour. The demand for these Teas is daily increasing, many of the public finding them more agreeable.

30

1903: Note the wide spread of prices between 'Good and Strong' at the equivalent of £5.99 per lb and 'Pink Wrapper' at £13.20 per lb.

'Go back, or I'll blow your head off'. I was only a kid in short trousers and worn rubber shoes. I remember the Manager got fluthered that evening and he says at five to six: 'Go and get me Silver, the cab man.' He stood up at Baggot Street Bridge, and Silver would be waiting—a white horse, a hard hat and a cab. When he seen me appearing and he'd be arising and he'd be down quick, quick, quick into the cellar to get his tumbler of whiskey. 'And that's the God's truth.'

The civil war rumbled on for the whole of 1922, and into 1923. As late as 29 January 1923 Horace Plunkett's house in Foxrock was burned by irregulars, in pursuit of a policy of harassing those appointed as Senators. On 31 January 1923 the Chamber's report read:

> The formidable attack on the Provisional Government, initiated earlier in the year, is maintained with unabated virulence, and its authors, to serve their manifest purpose, are leaving untried no device likely to embarrass commercial effort and enterprise. The effect of the frequent robberies under arms and illegal seizures of goods has been that, in many districts, trade is restricted within the narrowest limits . . . The Free State Government and Parliament established under a Constitution of their own framing have accepted a heavy obligation in the task of restoring order to a country sorely harassed. Their successful discharge of the task, in which they are now effecting progress, will nowhere be applauded more heartily than in the Chamber.

Luckily for the country, the Civil War was now in its last stages, and on 24 May 1923 de Valera ordered his supporters to lay down their arms.

Managing the bank manager

During the troubled years 1921-1923 the average profit fell to £5,200 [under £200,000]. This trend was identical to that of Arnotts, the department store in Henry Street. From 1924 to 1939 Findlater's profits seesawed along, providing a good service, giving sound employment and keeping the shareholders modestly rewarded. The graph of Arnott's sales for the period showed the same flat performance.

This moderate financial performance, admittedly in difficult circumstances, alerted the banks. On 4 January 1924 the Royal Bank wrote pointing out that the overdraft, which had been £5,000 in 1914, was now upwards of £50,000. The account had been in credit during 1917/18. (The consumer price index, having shot up from 100 in 1914 to over 200 in 1919, fell between 1925 and 1933 from 190 to 151 and only rose modestly to 178 by 1939.) It was noted that this large overdraft had been a temporary accommodation, and had not been repaid as agreed. Willie replied slightly evasively, aware that outside forces were pushing his requirements up rather than down. He pointed out that his sales in 1914 had been less than a quarter of his present turnover, and in fact his overdraft had been as high as £70,000 and had come down. He described trade credit as very tight, and duty payments as heavy; another factor he cited was the loss of trade caused by the destruction of part of the Sackville Street premises during the Troubles, for which he expected a 'fair compensation' within the month. Turning on the charm, he thanked the directors and the bank officials for their consideration and courtesy, and sought an extension until the end of his financial year.

The bank replied ten days later, asking that the overdraft be reduced by £2,500 [£100,000] before I April, and by a further £2,500 a month thereafter. Willie agreed to abide by this schedule as far as possible, but noted that such a curtailment of the firm's credit would seriously hinder the financing of the business and perhaps injure the firm's earning power. In the event he did manage to hold the overdraft below £50,000, but it was not until 1942, in the middle of another war, that the account was in credit again.

The imposter

In 1919 the firm was alerted to the fact that a very well-presented gentleman was calling on various suppliers in London, claiming to be from 'Findlater, of Dublin'. He called for instance on Tom Smith & Co. Ltd., the world renowned Christmas cracker manufacturers, as they wrote:

> A tall, well-dressed gentleman, grey hairdo, with a grey moustache, called to our office at 9.20 a.m. this morning, giving the name of 'Findlater, of Dublin', without presenting a card, and asked to look at our London Directory, which was readily handed over; he then asked if we had any Toffee to sell, and on seeing a sample in the Showroom, requested to take it away, but it was explained this would be no credit to us or him, as probably it was very stale, and not intended for tasting purposes, which seemed to upset the gentleman, who made out that we were very discourteous.

More understandably, at Benedictine he tried to get a free sample:

> He requested that he might take away with him a bottle of Benedictine. This, owing to our Wholesale Licence, could not be supplied, and he accordingly went away without the bottle.

At Cinzano Ltd. he had more luck:

> He certainly conveyed to us by his conversation and bearing, also his knowledge of the trade, that he was the senior of your firm. He said he had seen our wine advertised considerably and as he happened to be in London that day (the following day going to the Waddon Chase Hunt meeting) asked to taste our wine. He expressed his appreciation of the wine and we informed him that up to the present and as 'Cinzano, Brut' Sparkling Wine had only been placed on the market such a short time, we had confined our sphere of activities to London and the big hotel concerns, but that we were anxious to send a traveller to Ireland or to make some arrangements by which we could be represented in that country. We must admit that he did not appear to have called in solely for a drink as by his method of tasting it was evident that he knew something about wine.

Perhaps he just enjoyed the imposture, for he also called on Oxo, Heinz and Escoffier who sold a range of fine sauces.

Findlater's of course issued a disclaimer, on 20 December 1919, which alerted our suppliers:

> Having just received letters from two London Firms reporting the call on them within the past few days of a gentleman giving the name 'Findlater of Dublin' (without presenting a card), we think common courtesy on our part—not to say common sense—demands that we should write you a line of warning on the subject.
>
> The individual in question is not known to us, and there certainly is no one in England at present authorised by us to use our name or obtain favours or personal attentions of any kind.

Eleven years later the mysterious imposter reappeared at Campbell Soups in London:

> This man was in his late sixties or early seventies. His height was about five feet eight. He guessed my riding weight at eleven stone and said that he rode at ten stone, which would seem correct to me because he was the slender, athletic type. He was neatly dressed and wore a small but valuable fox headscarf pin, painted, under glass, which only a man thoroughly interested in hunting would affect. He mentioned by name, and I could see must have personally met, a number of Americans of my acquaintance who have hunted in Ireland. He also talked interestingly about the Masters and Packs in both England and Ireland when he found that I was interested. There was very little discussion about Campbell's Soups except with the young man in the office of our Sales Agents, but he did say that his son expected to visit London shortly and he would give him the facts. There was no indication then or later of an ulterior object in his visit. He did not ask for money.

We never found out who the imposter was—and the mystery remains unsolved.

Memories of old Findlaters

Despite his somewhat authoritarian appearance in later years, Willie was fondly remembered by Linda Browne, who was Dermot's secretary for many years.* During the late 1930s Willie

> used to visit the O'Connell Street premises on a regular basis. He appeared to be a very strict and severe man on the surface, but when I got to know him better I found him kind and human. An example of this occurred one day when I was taking dictation from him. He asked me if I smoked. In trepidation I admitted that I did. Instead of telling me off, he turned around to his desk behind him and took a fistful of cigarettes from a box and gave them to me! [She added] In the basement of the shop was a staff cafe which was very good value. It needed to be with the very low wages paid!

The tradition of personal service was Findlater's hallmark, as Mary Kane of Blackrock recalled in the 1960s:

> My mother-in-law arrived from Kerry, a widow with her three sons, one Saturday afternoon in 1922. She came down to the village to go to the bank beside Findlaters. It was closed of course after 3 pm. Mr Vaughan, Manager of Findlaters, was standing at

* Linda Browne (née Canning) wrote this on 23 September 1986.

FINDLATERS,

Confectioners,

UPPER SACKVILLE STREET, DUBLIN

AND BRANCHES,

HOLD THE CHOICEST STOCKS OF

British, American and French Confectionery

IN IRELAND.

FINDLATER'S CAKES (ANY QUANTITY CUT)

The materials used in this Department are of the highest quality. We therefore can, with every confidence, recommend them to our customers. All Cakes are made fresh daily in our own factory by experienced workmen, and the strictest regard is paid to hygienic principles. **NOTE.—We use no Substitutes for Eggs or Butter.**

		s.	d.
Carlton Sultana, almonds on top	per lb.	1	2
Banquet, rich fruit, almond paste on top	"	1	2
Kingstown Sultana, almonds on top	"	0	10
" " " round about 3 lbs.	"	0	10
French Cherry	"	0	10
Oxford Lunch—Sultana, almonds on top	"	0	8
" " " " oblong about 3 lbs.	"	0	8
Grafton Fruit	"	0	8
Grafton Madeira	"	0	8
School Fruit Cake	"	0	6
Cherry, Fruit, Seed, or Madeira Cake, round about 1 lb.	each	0	6
" " " " ... 2 lbs.	"	1	0
Sponge Cakes, rich in eggs	"	0	2

SPECIAL QUOTATIONS FOR LARGE QUANTITIES, SCHOOLS, INSTITUTIONS, &c.

26

1910: Cakes were made fresh daily in our bakery in Thomas Street and this continued until the early 1950s.

the door of the shop, saw her distress and asked if he could help. She told him her predicament and he said: 'Come in, order what you want and I will have them sent right away.' She said: 'But you don't even know my name!' Mr Vaughan said: 'I know that when the bank opens on Monday you will get your cheque book and money and will come in to me and open your account.' He had a very big smile on a very red face—a big, kindly man.

When I got married I also dealt there. When children arrived he could hardly wait till they sat up in the pram so that he could give them those bright pink biscuits. In those days tins were outside the mahogany counter. He was a very fair and just man, good humoured, but woe betide when orders went wrong or were late. Those responsible got the roar of his booming voice. There was such a day when I happened to be in the shop. You know, there was such a silence after he spoke. There was a large packet of matches on the counter, part of an order, and as it was the nearest thing to him he picked it up and slammed it down with such force it burst into flames. There was not a sound except the crackling of the matches as each box burst into flames. My small daughter thought she was at a party and gurgled away in her pram. That was the only human voice. Suddenly the door opened. In came a lady who sniffed and said in a high pitched voice: 'Something burning?' The shop came alive then. Everyone tried to look the other way!

Those were very happy days. We thought that the big clock that was such a part of Blackrock would be left there, but no, it was taken away with every sign of the shop. I remember the overhead money rail that so delighted my children. Even to this day they tell their children about the man that used to give them biscuits.

There was tall Mr Long at the bacon counter and short Mr Long at the provisions. Those are the only names that I recall just now, but I must say that all the staff were always polite and courteous at all times—no matter what size of order given. I am going back to June 1938 when I got married. Going down to Findlaters as a married woman twenty-one years of age, feeling so very important.

My family dealt with Mr Galloway in your Dalkey branch many years ago. I remember being sent down at the age of ten with a small basket on my arm and with a note for some butter or sugar which was weighed into brown paper bags.

The atmosphere and style of the shops remained much the same from the late 19th century to the 1950s. Rosalind Matthews of Killiney has happy memories of the Kingstown (Dún Laoghaire) shop in the 1930s and 1940s.

We were a big family and money was always scarce. Every week I walked up to the central confectionery counter on my own, feeling very important, whilst my mother was elsewhere in the shop, and with my precious one penny pocket money I would buy a cream bun. That memory still gives me joy.

Mabel Hanlon, a dark haired beauty, worked at the fruit and veg. behind the confectionery counter, and every week she would slip me a banana, then an apple, when war made the former scarce. I loved Mabel but used to worry lest she would get the sack for stealing on my behalf. Bacon and dairy produce were all sold on the counter at the left hand side of the shop as you went in its central doors. I always felt very irritated with my mother as she never gave me enough time to get my fill of the slicer at work. I can still hear the 'whrr whrr' noise it made, going forwards and backwards at every cut.

But best by far was the butter lady. I used to wish she would run out of supplies and have to open a new box for my maximum pleasure! The butter rested on cold marble. Then with her ridged wooden pats taken from the water jug she would lop off lumps and cleverly carry each between the pats and place them on the scales until the required weight was reached–or exceeded. This on/off job was fascinating. When the desired poundage was reached, she would slap-bang it repeatedly into a respectable shape. There was no doubt in my mind: I was going to be a butter lady when I grew up!

The counter that I least liked was the groceries (tea, sugar etc.) on the right. This was very dull and seemed without action, apart from weighing. Here was where my mother spent the most time every Thursday, placing her order. She would sit on the high stool provided for customers and the assistant seemed just too grovelly–'Yes Mrs Hanaghan', 'Certainly Mrs Hanaghan', 'Whichever you like, Mrs Hanaghan'. He had no time for me! But once the boring order was written in his book and the carbon paper moved under the next free page—then came the climax. Always I told her to give more money than was needed so the assistant would both load and unload the cash, and I would watch the coin-box zoom overhead twice on its wire, up to and back from the raised cash desk at the back of the shop. Never once did your man offer me the chance to pull the leather starter strap! So what if food was a bit dearer in Findlaters? Wasn't it worth it, to see this wonderful contraption work? Good as the train set I never had.

The big Findlater clock was the heart of the town, as the Pillar was to the city. Kingstown then seemed full of deeply shrouded black-clad nuns, women in black shawls and barefoot children running on the cold, wet, wintry pavements. I still regard myself privileged to be fortunate enough to have always had shoes on my feet! My mother was a great manager of money. She would separate her cash each week into little piles and place them on the mantelpiece: so much for the bread man, milkman, cobbler and so on.

But the story doesn't quite end there. For next day came the horse drawn delivery. Far more exciting than a motorised van. Mind you, Findlaters didn't keep the horse and bridle etc. in such good nick as the coalmen did. But I can still see the writing on the cart. Part of the fun was watching the horse to see would his bodily functions take place. These both disgusted and fascinated me at one and the same time. But the driver was no fun, unlike the bread man, he never gave us a ride. Anyway, his cart seat wasn't half as high as J. M. & O'B![*]

Of course the view from the inside was different, as Johnny McDermott, who started as a delivery boy, told my sister Suzanne:

I used to collect a few orders from Northumberland Road, in between even as a messenger boy … The German Consulate, 58 Northumberland Road, the Argentine

* Johnston Mooney and O'Brien's bread-vans.

Consulate at 54 Northumberland Road and an alcoholic lady in No. 50—tragic about her. A Miss Nugent in No. 62, a magnificent house—two or three maids and all that. But the alcoholic lady—a quart of whiskey every second day (a broken romance, I believe). She had a separate wine account. Her father used to be at the window watching. I used to have to go down and to try and sneak the quart to the cook—the cook was 'in the know' too—and 50 Gold Flake every day. Then maybe for a few weeks she would change onto bottles of sherry—two or three bottles a day–Alfino.

This particular morning I had the basket full, that height, and I struggled out. Mr Edmund Mitchell came up the floor, a big tall man—he was in the First World War, he was a major, he was a director. Anyway, I was nearly killed lifting the basket. 'Put down that basket', he says. 'Take out all that stuff'. He had seen the quart of whiskey in it for a start—it was on the top. 'Take all them parcels out,' he says. 'Take everything out on the floor.' I remember he put on glasses, looked at everything, seen everything invoiced. 'Put them back now,' he says. So, I put them back—I had to. The basket was very, very heavy. 'That's a bit heavy for you,' he says. Your dad walked over to the counter. 'Somebody up there give this lad a help with the basket.' Your dad was only just coming into the firm then.

Williams, the Manager, was a slave driver. He was there to make the branch pay and, by God, he did. But he says to me, 'You're going out on the road now', and he brings down an old bicycle from where he lived with double handlebars and all, an old antique, and he gives it to me. I was too small to ride it, it was too high, and I used to have to stand on the pedals, but he sent me out. And I thought, that's handy, there were only about a dozen accounts to call on. My mother (we were very poor) got a provident cheque from Sloan's of Parliament Street and got me a suit of long trousers and a pair of shoes to make me look respectable calling on houses. I was out for about four months and Williams comes down to me—I was afraid of my life of him—and he says 'Do you ever look for new custom?' Oh, he was a slave driver, but he trained me well. I looked at him in amazement because I'd no experience, you see. 'I want you to get new business. Get it around.' I was desperate for business. I called at a Dr Jackson at 8 Upper Fitzwilliam Street and the receptionist there says to me, 'Yes, I can get you a couple of orders if you give me a kiss.' I was so innocent. I didn't know what she was talking about–that's the God's truth. So, to cut a long story short, she got me Pringle and O'Grady and Fegan. I never looked back. I started canvassing like nobody's business. Whenever I seen furniture arriving I went into the house.

As a matter of fact, I got so much money that I got married on my Christmas boxes. I canvassed the Holy Faith Convent who used to buy cases of oranges, a couple of hams, cases of apples, 1/2 dozen milk fed chickens, maybe a couple of hens—all at retail price. The nuns used to have a cook, Molly was her name, and wanted a nice box of chocolates. The nuns didn't look for anything. A van load of stuff used to go down. I'd a job getting a big box of chocolates out of Williams. It should have been a wholesale order instead of retail. I canvassed St Andrew's College—retail. It should have been a wholesale order, 30 lbs of sausages at a time. Then Gateaux Swiss Rolls—we became the agents for that. Two dozen Swiss Rolls at the weekend, a cwt of sugar.

Then a fellah on the provision counter after the war couldn't sell all the rough ends of bacon. He was on to me about the bacon. At that time it was only nice pieces of bacon and ham people were looking for—not the rough ends, the collar, the jowls and all that. He had me pestered so much that I got cracking. I seen the matron of the Molyneux Home for the Blind first. That was a retail order that should have been a wholesale one. There was only one wholesale order that I canvassed and that was Baggot Street Hospital. But that was not the only wholesale order we had. Now, St Andrew's College, St Conleth's College, Church House, Holy Faith, Molyneux Home for the Blind. I used to call there once a week for a van load of stuff and I got an order for the rough bacon that they used to buy. St Andrew's College was the same, 1/2 cwt rough bacon. At times the stock was enormous. One of the clerks of the office came to me and said 'there is a letter of congratulations about the business on the provisions counter—marvellous percentage on the stock.' I was getting retail prices which should have been wholesale.

Then Williams went back on the ledgers over the years, bad accounts. And he'd have a list every evening. 'I want you to go out and get some of that money back.' Some of the accounts were due in from the early 20s. I cleared a heck of a lot. You see, I was afraid of him. 'Now, what money did you get in this evening?' I'd have my receipt book with me you see. We kept expanding, expanding, expanding and I got out to Stillorgan Road then. Hume Dudgeon of Merville, Walsh's of Belfield, O'Toole of Oldtown House, Stephenson of Cranford, University College, Cranford where all the luxury offices are now. I got them all. We had three horse vans. That was the secret of it you see—the deliveries.

I'd be out at half eight or quarter past eight in the morning, over across Baggot Street Bridge. The cook, there'd be a cook and maybe two maids and maybe a receptionist and all where the doctors had their waiting rooms, and they'd be delighted when I'd get over their lists 'cos they'd have their orders over for lunch. At that time I'd be back at the shop at maybe half past nine in the morning with a book of orders and Micky McDonald would be waiting in the back. Orders that I collected the day before were delivered to Stillorgan that morning. A big box of potatoes, cabbage, cauliflower, carrots—the whole lot.

Although the atmosphere of the business was much the same as it had been when he started so many years before, there were of course changes, some of which Willie remembered during the speech he gave while celebrating his silver jubilee as Managing Director.

During my time with the Firm eight more branches were opened. Personally I trust that we won't open too many more for some time as I would never like the Firm to get into the position of what is called 'Chain Stores'. We ought to be satisfied with what we are doing and to improve on this. But, of course, nobody can tell what is for us in the future.

Of course a great number of changes have taken place in my time. Perhaps the chief one is the employment of girls. It was quite an event when, many years ago, two girls were employed by my brother, Mr Adam as he was called, to attend behind the confectionery counter. Now I think we have more girls than boys, and they have bright-

Menu

Irish Amateur Swimming Association.

(Founded November, 1893.)

International Water Polo,

IRELAND v. ENGLAND.

DINNER

In honour of the Visit of the English Team to Ireland,

GROSVENOR HOTEL,

WESTLAND ROW,

SATURDAY, AUGUST 6th, 1898.

Chairman:

WM. FINDLATER, Ex-President I.A.S.A.

Always a winner!

ened up our establishments very suitably.

In the old time all our young men lived in; the hours of work were much longer. All our Staff were expected to be good boys and go to church regularly, and not to smoke. Also, the old partners did not encourage them to get married. We were, to a great extent, a happy family and knew each one of our staff personally, and their family history. When boys went away to the States or the Colonies, my father used to keep in touch with them and write to them and send them papers regularly. I trust we are still a happy family. I can assure you your Directors have constant thought for your welfare.

Willie's clubs, associations and directorships

In his young days Willie was an active and successful rugby football player and was President of Monkstown Football Club (founded 1883) in 1888/92 and again in 1898/1900 and one of his brothers was Captain four times. Willie was also a founder member of Dublin Swimming Club, the first and oldest swimming club in Leinster. In 1897 he was President of the Irish Amateur Swimming Association, the second Leinster man to be so honoured. His term of office was perpetuated by the Findlater Cup which he donated for the Men's 440 Yards (now 400 metres) Freestyle Championship of Ireland, and the third oldest of the trophies competed for annually.

One of Willie's main social achievements was the founding of the Dublin Rotary Club in 1911.* He was credited with being the first man in Europe to join the movement, which had its origins in the United States. The Dublin branch's

* Rotary is a world-wide, non-sectarian charitable society of businessmen and women and professional people. Its main business is to meet for a monthly lunch where there is usually a guest speaker.

first Hon. Secretary was William A. McConnell and J. H. Fleming was first President. In 1913 Willie helped in the formation of the British Association of Rotary Clubs, and for 1913/14 he became the first Rotary International Director representing Great Britain and Ireland, when he was at the same time the third President of the Dublin Club. In 1914/15 he was Vice-President of the British Association of Rotary Clubs.

Willie was proud of his very early membership status, and was not pleased when one rather too enthusiastic Rotary Secretary renumbered all members alphabetically and he was thus no longer Rotarian No.3! However he was fondly remembered for his term in office in Dublin as T. A. Grehan recalled:

> The helm of our affairs was taken over by the breeziest of skippers, William Findlater . . . during his reign we revelled in a beanfeast of Findlater philosophy, unorthodox a good deal of it, but alluring all of it. Among Findlater's distinction—he has quite a number about which he does not speak—was that of almost stunning Sir Harry Lauder* in a five minute speech full of cunning humour and delightfully itching sarcasm when seconding a vote of thanks to the great Scotsman, who happened to be our guest here some years ago. Before he took the chair we knew that Findlater would be worthwhile, he certainly was.[12]

His bonhomie and social skills were appreciated by his colleagues, and at the early age of thirty he became President of the Dublin Family Grocers' and Purveyors' Association. The trade magazine *The Grocer* wrote:

> The business of the eminent Dublin firm of Alex. Findlater & Co. is one of the most extensive in the city, and the subject of our portrait, though one of the youngest members of the firm, is regarded as one of the best experts in all matters relating to the grocery and wine trades. In the latter respect he is facile princeps, and the extensive cellars of the firm, which are entirely under his management, are one of the features of Dublin commercial life. Mr Findlater is only thirty years of age, and as he is possessed of great business capacity, as well as with a desire to promote the interests of the Association of which he is now president, the best results may be expected to follow his election.

The paper went on to report that Willie had made an excellent impression at the conference in Cardiff the previous year, exhibiting an intimate knowledge of matters connected with the combined trades. The (British Isles wide) Federation was invited to Dublin for the meeting in 1898, so it was a special compliment that he should have been chosen to be President in such a responsible year.

Although Willie did not follow his brother Adam on to the political stage, he had numerous interests and commitments outside the business. He was Chairman of Jury's Hotel, a director of Bolands, Thomas Hanlon and Co., the Blackrock Promenade Pier and Bath Co., the Trawling and Pure Ice Co., Central Meat Products; he was the second Chairman of the Empire Theatre Belfast and

* Sir Harry Lauder was a well-known Scottish comic singer; he appeared regularly in the Findlater theatres (see Chapter 14).

a partner in the Olympia Theatre. He was on the Council of the Industrial Development Association and 'he showed a deep and practical interest in the encouragement of Irish manufactured goods, indeed it may be said that his company was a permanent exhibition of goods of home production'. In 1933 Findlaters published an Irish price list, with eighteen pages devoted entirely to goods of Irish manufacture—until two pages of wines and spirits were slipped in at the end. He was actively interested in the Royal Hospital for Incurables, a member of the managing committee for many years, and Chairman of the Board of the Incorporated Skin and Cancer Hospital.

Protestant businessmen in Irish politics in the 1920s

It has been said (by my cousin Brian Inglis for example) that after 1922 the Protestant community tried to ignore the new state and remained, in his words, West Britons.* This was certainly not true for the majority of the Protestant business community. In the 1923 general election the Dublin Chamber of Commerce put forward five candidates to represent the Dublin business interests.[13] Among these was William Hewat, chairman of Heitons, who was President of the Chamber of Commerce in 1922, and was elected to the Dáil for North Dublin. He was treated in the Dáil as the spokesman for business, finance and commerce interests.[14]

Another was John Good who was returned to the Dáil for South County Dublin in 1923. He was President of the Dublin Chamber of Commerce in 1920, a unionist candidate pre-Treaty (1918) who now described himself as 'a businessman and not in any sense a politician'. He was instrumental in getting Trinity to introduce a degree in Commerce (1925) and in 1930 headed a deputation to the Department of Education to discuss the provision of the Vocational Education Bill. In his will in 1941 he left £5,000 [£150,000] to the Trinity College School of Commerce.[15]

James Douglas (1887-1954), a Dublin businessman and a Quaker, played a unique, behind the scenes, part in the early days of the new state. During the Civil War he and Senator Andrew Jameson were asked by de Valera to act as an intermediaries to try and find an agreed settlement. After the Treaty Collins asked him to become secretary of the committee established to draft the first Irish Constitution in 1922. He declined but agreed to serve on the committee which came up with three possible drafts within a mat-

* The thrust of Brian Inglis's *West Briton* was that the Protestant community remained at heart part of the British Empire. 'They read *The Times* at breakfast, revered the Royal family, detested the Sinn Féin rebels as murderers and gunmen, and regarded the 1921 Treaty as the great betrayal.' This may have been the way for ladies at home, the retired and the widowed, but not for the business community.

ter of three months. Douglas was elected to the first Senate of the Free State and served in that body with distinction for thirty years 1922-36, 1938-43 and 1944-54. His son Harold Douglas succeeded him in the senate. Their business was a large drapery company in Wexford Street, Dublin and an electrical business in Dawson Street.[16]

Andrew Jameson, head of the distillery (1905-41) and President of the Dublin Chamber of Commerce for 1921-22, was much involved in the Home Rule negotiations to achieve a better deal for the Southern unionists.[17] He was one of a handful of prominent Protestant leaders, like Adam in the previous decade, who were keen on bridging the gap between nationalists and unionists and enthusiastic that unionists should play a part in the public life of the new state.[18] After independence he continued to play a prominent role in the Chamber and was a member of the Senate from 1922 to 1936, and was one time Governor of the Bank of Ireland.

Bryan Cooper, a friend of Willie's in Rotary, was another important voice, though not from the business community. He was head of the Sligo landed family and had served with distinction in the First World War. He was elected Unionist MP for South County Dublin in 1910, the constituency in which Adam had caused Walter Long so much stress in the 1906 election. In 1919 he was Press Censor in Ireland. After independence Bryan was again returned to the Dáil and held his seat from 1923 to 1930, representing South County Dublin, first as an Independent to 1927 and then for Cumann na nGaedheal.

Sir Maurice Dockrell (1850-1929) head of the builders providers and timber merchants' firm bearing his name, and a noted unionist, was prominent in the affairs of the city in Adam's time, and sat on various committees with him. This family, more than any other in public affairs, bridged the unionist/nationalist changeover. In 1902 the Hibernian Bank, on whose board William Martin Murphy sat, had a representative of the Dockrell family. Louis Cullen comments: 'The Dockrell link with the nationalist circle around the Hibernian Bank may explain how the family came to play such an active role in the public life of the state after 1922.'[19] Henry Dockrell (1880-1955), his son, was President of the Dublin Chamber of Commerce in 1933 and Maurice Dockrell (1908-86), his grandson, was prominent in business and politics in the post-1945 era and Lord Mayor of Dublin in 1960-61.

Findlater's only strike

Jim Larkin is best remembered as the charismatic leader of the workers in the 1913 confrontation with the employers, arising from the Lock-out that had such a devastating effect on the less-well off citizens of the city. Little is known of the stress he caused in Findlaters in 1924. He was in America during the 1916 Rising and the Civil War, and only returned to Dublin in April 1923 having spent some time with Stalin as a Secretary to the Third International in Moscow. On his return to Ireland he led his followers into a split with the ITGWU and on 15 June 1924, with his brother Peter, formed the Workers' Union of Ireland (WUI). By July the following year Peter Larkin was corresponding with Findlaters on pay issues for the porters and vanmen.

It would appear that Findlaters had established a working relationship with the ITGWU and grievances were dealt with in a business-like manner. However, the clerical and selling staff were represented by the Irish National Union of Vintners, Grocers and Allied Trades, and it was that union that in 1925 initially called a strike in pursuit of a wage claim, which Findlaters had rejected. Among the union's demands was an insistence that Findlater's only employ union members. 'We could not even take on an apprentice—not even the son of one of our own men—unless he enrolled as a member of the union', Willie protested.

The following week Larkin brought out the WUI members, mostly motormen and porters, in sympathy, informing Willie that 'The Union has instructed its members to withdraw their labour, until such times as the dispute with the Purveyors' Assistants is settled and the Police Protection is withdrawn. Yours faithfully, Executive Committee, (Signed) Jim Larkin'.

As usual with any strike Larkin was involved in, feelings quickly ran high. The strike was not solid, for many of the staff decided to stay working. The branches were picketed, and the familiar cat-call of 'scab' was heard. On 18 April Jim Larkin wrote in *The Irish Worker:*

> In the Howth branch of Messrs Findlaters, the motor driver, a W.U.I. man, was withdrawn. On Sunday one of the Civic Guards out of the local barracks went into Findlaters and drove the motorvan around the village, delivering the provisions, excusing himself on the grounds that he could not see the people starving. We would suggest that this act of scabbery might merit the attention of the responsible authorities. There should be a limit, even to police scabbery.

The *Evening Herald* then reported:

> Messrs Bewley, wine merchants, Middle Abbey street, lent the services of their lorry and driver, Matthew Murphy, to Messrs Findlaters to take or deliver goods to or from them.
>
> Murphy was on his way home when two men approached him from the opposite side of the street and fell upon him. He was struck a violent blow to the face, followed by another which split the man's nose and from the injury it could not have been caused by the naked hand.
>
> Murphy fell to the ground, and the other man deliberately kicked him on the head.

Group of Alex. Findlater & Co.'s Clerical and Shop Staffs,
Taken at St. Lawrence Hotel, Howth, on the occasion of their Annual Picnic, July, 1913.

Group of Alex. Findlater & Co.'s Delivery and Bottling Stores Staffs,
Taken at St. Lawrence Hotel, Howth, on the occasion of their Annual Picnic, July, 1913.

Photographs published in *The Lady of the House*, August 1913—carefully showing a happy and united staff at the height of the 1913 Lock-out

> Such was the horror caused by this abominable and shocking outrage that everyone in the neighbourhood set upon the two dastards who ran away.[20]

The above report in the *Evening Herald*, and the conditions of the strike generally, stimulated many letters to the Editor–with the authors hiding behind more or less fanciful pseudonyms, as was the custom of the day–where those involved described the issues involved.

> Sir—I welcome the letter from 'Pax' and hope that some one will come forward to settle the dispute without further delay. I am not breaking a secret when I say that the greater number of us assistants that are out on strike, are absolutely sick of the whole affair. Most of us unfortunately realise that the men in control of our Union who are

running this strike are a small body of extremists whose political friends did their utmost to ruin the country and are now engaged in a forlorn attempt to destroy the business of some of the most considerate and best employers in this city.

Many of us had no grievance in any shape or form, and it was only in loyalty to our Union that we came out at the word of command, but now realise our mistake. Some of our best men have gone back to work and forsaken the Union.

'Footsore'

Sir—'Footsore' states that he had no grievance. He had every opportunity at all the general meetings prior to the strike of expressing his opinion and protesting against extreme action. This he did not do. Only one member voted against a strike. His employer settled with his employees, and that member is working.

The writer refers to those people who are fighting us as 'considerate and good employers'. Some of those good and considerate employers were, prior to the strike, paying girls the princely sum of 10s. per week. I personally know of a girl who, after ten years' service with the one firm, receives 23s. per week.

S. MacEidnain.

Sir—I would like to ask 'Footsore' if he is an assistant, what was his attitude at the general meeting, when a clear and unmistakable ballot vote gave a mandate for the strike. Where, then, does the 'small band of extremists' come in? The responsibility for the strike rests on the general consent of the body of assistants.

I doubt if 'Footsore' is so blind, granting he is an assistant, as not to know that amongst the assistants comprising the Grocers' Union there are men of every political shade of opinion and of different religious creeds. The organisation is not an extremist political machine: it is for the safeguard of workers in our trade.

'Footsore' is apparently not a follower of his convictions or he would not show such base ingratitude to those 'most considerate and best employers' by going on strike. He is free to prove he is one of the 'best men' and go back to them.

Banba.

When I entered the company thirty years later, in 1956, the staff spoke in hushed tones of 'The Strike'. I was put to work with Bryan, the loftsman who, I was told, was the only person re-employed in Findlater's O'Connell Street after the strike. Actually, records show that Joe McAuley, driver, was also re-employed. Bryan said very little, but busied himself handling the sacks and always had a needle and bodkin to hand to sew up holes made by small vermin overnight!

I learnt of the harrowing story of a family who, not having been re-employed were left destitute as a result of the strike, and had to make their way out of Kingstown (Dún Laoghaire), towards Dublin, with their few possessions on a cart. I was therefore interested to find that Willie had consulted with all the branch managers, who in turn consulted the non-striking staff, on the question of re-employing the strikers. It appears that the non-strikers had been given a hard time by the picketers, and they were in no mood to forgive and forget. Their responses were as follows:

From the Kingstown branch:

In reply to yours of 18th inst., the general feeling here is not favourable to the strikers being taken back, except where an application was made a couple of days after going out. The fact is this staff don't want to come in contact with them in any way, saying they had no cause to go out. Personally I would not let one striker work again in the firm. They well knew what they were doing and thought they would succeed. Had they done so, no consideration would have been shown to the firm.
Yours faithfully,

A. Browne.

From Dalkey:

In reply to yours received this morning. The staff are all of the opinion that under no circumstances should any of them be taken back for two reasons:

First, that they had no real grievance, only an unfair demand

Secondly, at the eve of a holiday to ruin our trade, and which might have resulted in putting them all out of employment.
I remain, Sir, Most respectfully,

Geo. Galloway.

From Thomas Street:

In reply to your letter of 18th inst., my staff are very anxious to return to their work but are too frightened of the Union to apply for re-instatement. I am very anxious in the interest of trade to have them re-engaged as they were a very suitable staff. Yours faithfully,

Denis Daly.

From Rathmines:

As far as I can find out, the Rathmines staff do not like the idea that any of the 'strikers' should be taken back, as for two or three days after going out they had every chance of returning to work if they wished, after they knew the position in which they stood. In our Branch the manager went to several of his staff to appeal to them to return but without success. Now when defeat is in sight they want to get back. Your obedient servant,

J Flynn.

From 65 Upper Dorset Street:

I am sorry I cannot let you have the views of my staff regarding those on strike, as they are all on strike.

Two of the girls called in here several times and asked to be taken back. They are not so much to blame as the male members, who went a bit too far, and for whom I have no sympathy. Yours faithfully,

WB.

And from 28-32 Upper Sackville Street:

The feeling seems to be general that no one will work with any of those who went out on Strike on April 6th last., as not only had they no reason to join the 'Outsiders' but went further to stimulate a very hostile feeling amongst those 'Outsiders' against the Staff who remained on at their work—this I can personally vouch for—Only in a few cases did I hear any sympathetic reference—viz. to Joe and Lewis McAuleys (motor drivers), Bryan Farrelly (loftsman), William Shields (packer). They remember the concentration of Strikers that took place on the 6th and 7th April outside these premises, and many other days at Opening and Closing time, and that former employees, both from here and Branches, were very active at such times in leading and inciting hostile demonstrations, particularly against our respectable Girl workers.

A few days after the strike, Willie addressed a large assembly of the remaining staff in Clerys Restaurant to 'discuss matters concerning the business of the firm'. He started with a wry reference to recent events:

It is a gratification to me that we have as large a staff as are present tonight, because within the last ten days, if you had behaved differently to what you have, the number of staff that would be here to meet us would be very small indeed. I must first thank you all for sticking by the old firm and sticking to your work!

This reminds me of the last meeting that we had at Howth some years ago. We talked about the question of Trade Unionism and I told you that it was perfectly at your own option whether you would join or not. I had no objection in any shape or form but on the other hand I told you that I would not join any Trade Federation against you that might dictate to me what I should do under any circumstances, nor would I be bound to any forced lock-out of my staff. *(This was being proposed by Maypoles, Liptons, Home and Colonial and Sheppards, prominent retailers of the day).*

Most of you have joined the Union which is intimately connected with the licensed trade. For years, you know, the licensed trade has been doing wonderfully well and are able to pay better wages than the average grocer, because of all our expensive deliveries and everything else, we get far less money for what we sell than the licensed trade who hand the goods over the counter.

I would like to remark here that you girls ought to feel a little bit annoyed because you had been considered as 15 per cent or 20 per cent less value than men. My point is that you girls ought to be compensated equally with men, provided you do the same work . . . and you must also consider supply and demand, if there are too many girls and not enough of them get married and taken off the market (laughter) . . .'*

Not many years ago I tried to get my son, now eighteen or nineteen years of age, to make up his mind what he intended to do. His mother naturally thought it would be a good thing to make a gentleman of him (laughter), that it was a good thing to have one gentleman in the family; whether he would go to Oxford or Cambridge, and so on. I thought I would have to put up out of this £400 somehow or other. The boy said that he did not intend to go to a University—first of all because he had no pretence to brains, and he was not going to waste four years at Trinity College or elsewhere.

The real fact is that he has no special desire or taste to go in for any profession. However, he said he would like to come into the business. At that time he was at school, and I wrote him pointing out the difficulties of business. That is to say, with

* Up to the mid-1950s or even later, female employment ceased on marriage.

The presentation of an illuminated address to Willie by the staff congratulating him on his Silver Jubilee as managing director of the company. It stated that 'the past 23 years have been very trying and difficult for the commercial community, and it is gratifying that the company under your leadership, has been enabled to overcome all obstacles'. In a similar address to John and Adam in 1883 the purpose was to show appreciation of the many acts of kindness which they had lavished on the staff especially those living-in: 'Our domestic comforts, recreations and amusements have ever had your prompt attention' and went on to thank them for the billiard table 'which has given unqualified pleasure'. The picture shows Ruby McConnell who illustrated the Address, Willie, and Leo Whelan RHA who painted the portrait. The staff who contributed to the address were:

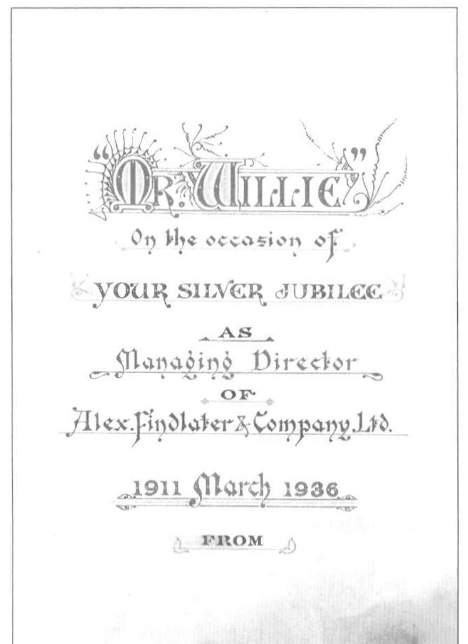

"Mr. Willie"

On the occasion of

YOUR SILVER JUBILEE

AS

Managing Director

OF

Alex. Findlater & Company Ltd.

1911 March 1936

FROM

Findlater's Corner

T. Reynolds.
J. J. Colgan.
R. Red.
A. J. Gibney.
W. R. Hall.
J. Bowen.
J. Scullion.
P. McCormick.
P. J. Kelly.
A. Malley.
P. Dunne.
T. Roche.
S. Robinson.
J. Kearney.
T. Walker.
E. Moulhall.
L. Lennon.
J. Parkinson.
W. O'Keeffe.
J. Tuck.
P. McCormick.
S. O'Toole.
K. Walsh.
J. Mannion.
A. Kelly.
T. Nolan.
J. Corrigan.
B. Corrigan.
T. O'Connor.
D. O'Connor.
W. Collins.
W. O'Donohoe.

F. O'Flynn.
G. Ryan.
P. Murphy.
M. McElroy.
M. P. Kelly.
J. Johnston.
H. Johnston.
J. O'Toole.
G. Bowe.
B. Farrelly.
N. Kelly.
J. Kane.
T. Dunne.
T. Jones.
G. Bowerbank.
M. Hobson.
H. Powell.
J. Marshall.
T. Dunne.
J. McAuley.
J. Biggs.
J. Hunt.
B. McDermott.
W. Elson.
T. Murphy.
M. Dunne.
J. Farrell.
T. Johnson.
W. O'Keeffe.
D. Donegan.
C. St. Ledger.
F. Hegarty.
J. A. Kinnear.

M. Fitzgerald.
J. Dunne.
F. Jackson.
R. Spittle.
P. Walsh.
A. Donovan.
L. Keenan.
C. Ryan.
B. McDermot.
J. McDermot.
Miss J. E. Roch.
Miss H. Coyle.
Miss K. Tiegan.
Miss L. Tanner.
Miss K. Maguinness.
Miss E. McElroy.
Miss V. Simpson.
Miss B. Walton.
Miss E. Nolan.
Miss M. Fowler.
Miss J. Doherty.
Miss F. Cherry.
Miss L. Whelan.
Miss G. Nolan.
Miss A. Dunne.
Miss M. Hannigan.
Miss D. Gumley.
Miss C. Payne.
Miss U. Fagan.
Miss K. Frazer.
Miss L. Coleclough.
Miss E. Coleclough.

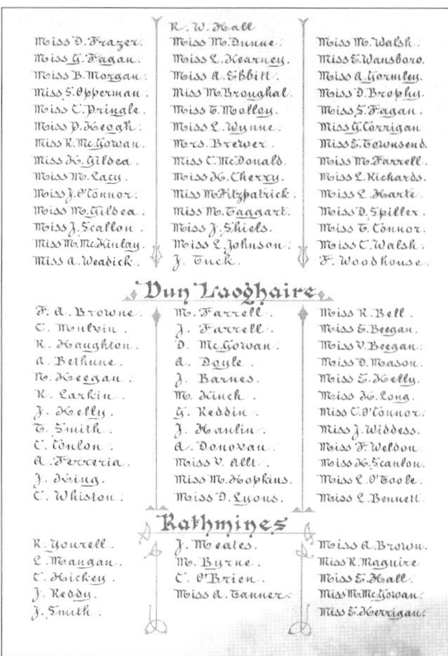

	R. W. Hall	
Miss D. Frazer	Miss M. Dunne	Miss M. Walsh
Miss G. Fagan	Miss L. Kearney	Miss E. Wansboro
Miss B. Morgan	Miss A. Ebbitt	Miss A. Gormley
Miss S. Opperman	Miss M. Broughal	Miss D. Brophy
Miss C. Pringle	Miss E. Molloy	Miss S. Fagan
Miss P. Keogh	Miss L. Wynne	Miss G. Corrigan
Miss K. McGowan	Mrs. Brewer	Miss E. Townsend
Miss K. Gildea	Miss C. McDonald	Miss M. Farrell
Miss M. Lacy	Miss K. Cherry	Miss L. Richards
Miss J. O'Connor	Miss M. Fitzpatrick	Miss L. Harte
Miss M. Gildea	Miss M. Taggart	Miss D. Spiller
Miss J. Scallon	Miss J. Shiels	Miss E. Connor
Miss M. McKinlay	Miss L. Johnson	Miss C. Walsh
Miss A. Weadick	J. Tuck	F. Woodhouse

Dun Laoghaire

F. A. Browne	M. Farrell	Miss R. Bell
C. Moulvin	J. Farrell	Miss E. Beegan
R. Haughton	D. McGowan	Miss V. Beegan
A. Bethune	A. Doyle	Miss D. Mason
M. Keegan	J. Barnes	Miss E. Kelly
R. Larkin	M. Kinch	Miss K. Long
J. Kelly	G. Reddin	Miss C. O'Connor
T. Smith	J. Hanlin	Miss J. Widdess
C. Conlon	A. Donovan	Miss F. Weldon
A. Ferreria	Miss V. Allt	Miss K. Scanlon
J. King	Miss M. Hopkins	Miss E. O'Toole
C. Whiston	Miss D. Lyons	Miss L. Bennett

Rathmines

R. Yourell	J. Meates	Miss A. Brown
L. Mangan	M. Byrne	Miss K. Maguire
C. Hickey	C. O'Brien	Miss E. Hall
J. Reddy	Miss A. Tanner	Miss M. McGowan
J. Smith		Miss E. Kerrigan

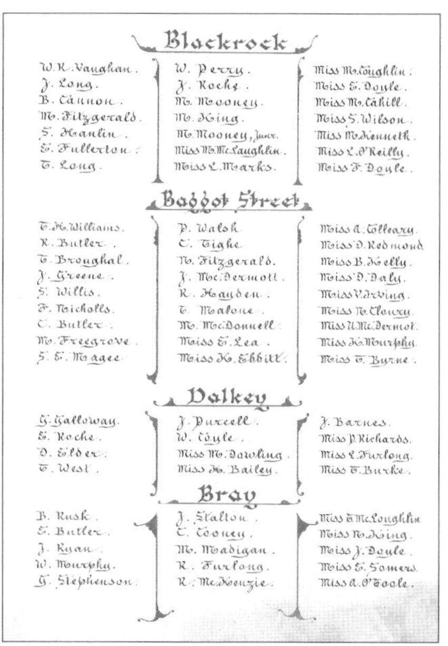

Blackrock

W. R. Vaughan	W. Perry	Miss M. Coughlin
J. Long	J. Roche	Miss E. Doyle
B. Cannon	M. Mooney	Miss M. Cahill
M. Fitzgerald	M. King	Miss S. Wilson
S. Hanlin	M. Mooney, Junr.	Miss M. Kenneth
E. Fullerton	Miss M. McLaughlin	Miss L. O'Reilly
T. Long	Miss L. Marks	Miss F. Doyle

Baggot Street

T. H. Williams	P. Walsh	Miss A. Cleary
R. Butler	C. Tighe	Miss D. Redmond
T. Broughal	M. Fitzgerald	Miss B. Kelly
J. Greene	J. McDermott	Miss D. Daly
S. Willis	R. Hayden	Miss V. Irving
F. Nicholls	T. Malone	Miss M. Cleary
C. Butler	M. McDonnell	Miss U. McDermot
M. Freegrove	Miss E. Lea	Miss K. Murphy
S. E. Magee	Miss K. Ebbitt	Miss T. Byrne

Dalkey

G. Galloway	J. Purcell	J. Barnes
E. Roche	W. Coyle	Miss P. Richards
D. Elder	Miss M. Dowling	Miss L. Furlong
T. West	Miss K. Bailey	Miss T. Burke

Bray

B. Rusk	J. Scallon	Miss T. McLoughlin
E. Butler	C. Cooney	Miss M. King
J. Ryan	M. Madigan	Miss J. Doyle
W. Murphy	R. Furlong	Miss E. Somers
G. Stephenson	R. McKenzie	Miss A. O'Toole

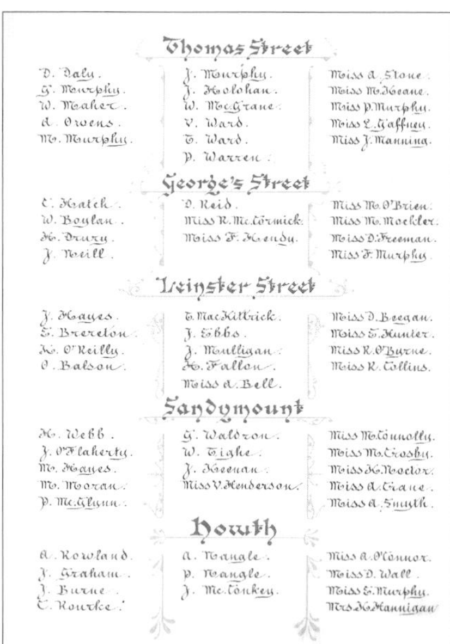

Thomas Street

D. Daly	J. Murphy	Miss A. Stone
G. Murphy	J. Holohan	Miss M. Keane
W. Maher	W. McGrane	Miss P. Murphy
A. Owens	V. Ward	Miss L. Gaffney
M. Murphy	T. Ward	Miss J. Manning
	P. Warren	

George's Street

C. Hatch	D. Reid	Miss M. O'Brien
W. Boylan	Miss R. McCormick	Miss M. Moekler
K. Drury	Miss F. Hendy	Miss D. Freeman
J. Neill		Miss F. Murphy

Leinster Street

J. Hayes	T. MacKittrick	Miss D. Beegan
E. Brereton	J. Ebbs	Miss E. Hunter
K. O'Reilly	J. Mulligan	Miss R. O'Byrne
O. Balson	K. Fallon	Miss R. Collins
	Miss A. Bell	

Sandymount

K. Webb	G. Waldron	Miss M. Connolly
J. O'Flaherty	W. Tighe	Miss M. Crosby
M. Hayes	J. Keenan	Miss K. Noctor
M. Moran	Miss V. Henderson	Miss A. Crane
P. McGlynn		Miss A. Smyth

Howth

A. Rowland	A. Mangle	Miss A. O'Connor
J. Graham	P. Mangle	Miss D. Wall
J. Byrne	J. McConkey	Miss E. Murphy
C. Rourke		Mrs. K. Hannigan

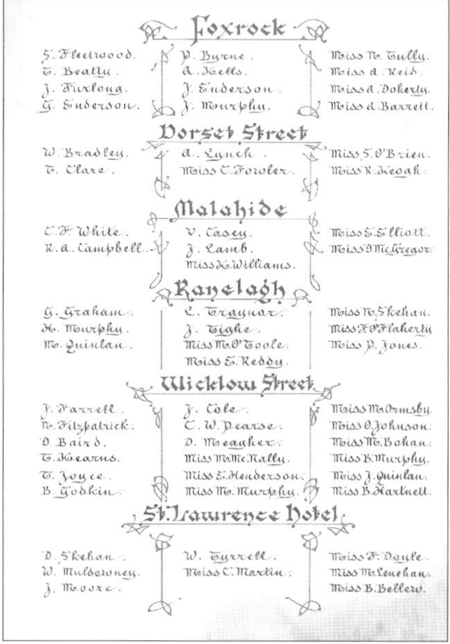

Foxrock

S. Fleetwood	P. Byrne	Miss M. Tully
T. Beatty	A. Kells	Miss A. Reid
J. Furlong	J. Sunderson	Miss A. Doherty
G. Sunderson	J. Murphy	Miss A. Barrett

Dorset Street

W. Bradley	A. Lynch	Miss S. O'Brien
T. Clare	Miss C. Fowler	Miss R. Keogh

Malahide

C. F. White	V. Casey	Miss E. Elliott
R. A. Campbell	J. Lamb	Miss D. McGregor
	Miss K. Williams	

Ranelagh

G. Graham	L. Traynor	Miss M. Skehan
K. Murphy	J. Tighe	Miss F. O'Flaherty
M. Quinlan	Miss M. O'Toole	Miss P. Jones
	Miss E. Reddy	

Wicklow Street

F. Farrell	J. Cole	Miss M. Ormsby
M. Fitzpatrick	C. W. Pearse	Miss O. Johnson
D. Baird	D. Meagher	Miss M. Bohan
T. Kearns	Miss M. McNally	Miss B. Murphy
T. Joyce	Miss E. Henderson	Miss J. Quinlan
B. Godkin	Miss M. Murphy	Miss B. Hartnell

St. Laurence Hotel

D. Skehan	W. Tyrrell	Miss F. Doyle
W. Mulcroney	Miss C. Martin	Miss M. Lenehan
J. Moore		Miss B. Bellew

labour and the employment of men or girls or anything else; I also said that Ireland was in a very dangerous condition; that nobody knew how things were going to go; that all our best customers were leaving the country, and that I didn't see any future in business. I got a letter back from him in which he stated: 'After all, that Findlater's did fairly well out of it; that they got a good living, that I had a fair house and not only that, but that it was curious with all my thoughts running that way that I would let my son-in-law, Mr Mitchell, join the business.' But now, if we have to submit to the rules of the Union, I suppose I cannot bring him into the business without asking permission. I am not, however, worrying about that. I want to get him into the business

> and he will come in a year or two because I want to show you that we intend to keep up the continuing of the business . . . this shows that I have no intention of closing it down (applause).

This was the last strike in Findlaters. The son was, of course, Dermot, my father, who joined the company in 1927.

Willie died aged seventy-three on 31 July 1941 at his home, Glensavage in Blackrock, and is buried in Dean's Grange with his wife Lucie and their elder son Desmond, who had died many years before aged two. My grandmother Lucie died a few months later, on 11 November 1941.

Notes and references

1 Elizabeth Fingall *Seventy Years Young* Dublin: Lilliput 1991 pp 393-4
2 *Freeman's Journal* 16 March 1920
3 E. J. Riordan *Modern Irish Trade and Industry* London: Methuen 1920 pp 290-1
4 Dublin Chamber of Commerce Records, National Archive Dublin
5 J. Anthony Gaughan (Ed.) *Memoirs of Senator James G. Douglas Concerned Citizen* Dublin: University College Dublin Press 1998 Chapter 3
6 Minutes of Special Meeting, Dublin Chamber, 30 December 1921, Findlater archive
7 Findlater archive
8 Oliver St J. Gogarty *As I was Going Down Sackville Street* London: Rich and Cowan 1937 p 186
9 *Souvenir Album of the Dublin Fighting 1922* Dublin: Brunswick Press 1922
10 *Ibid.*
11 *Ibid.*
12 T. A. Grehan *Mellowed Memories: A Review of Dublin's Rotary Club Presidents.* An address delivered at the Dublin Rotary Club luncheon meeting on Monday 1 January 1934 and printed by wish of all those present
13 Tony Farmar *Heiton's–A Managed Transition* Dublin: A. & A. Farmar 1996 p 78
14 *Ibid.* pp 80-81
15 L. M. Cullen, *Pirates and Princes, The Dublin Chamber of Commerce 1783-1983* Dublin: Dublin Chamber of Commerce p 102
16 J. Anthony Gaughan *op. cit.*
17 R. B. McDowell *Crisis and Decline, The Fate of the Southern Unionist,* Dublin: Lilliput Press 1997 pp 60, 67
18 L.M. Cullen *op. cit.* p 92
19 *Ibid.* p. 75. The Dockrell story is well documented and waiting to be written
20 *Evening Herald*

12. My Aunts Doris and Sheila

My grandparents Lucie and Willie had five children (including Desmond who died aged two). The eldest, Marjorie, married Edmund Mitchell in 1914 and the youngest, Dermot, entered the business in 1927. This chapter is about my Aunts Doris and Sheila, known as Auntie Do and Auntie She, whose lives covered almost the entire 20th century, and it shows the quiet contribution made by these two wonderful ladies.

My story starts in Glenageary in the spring of 2000. As we relaxed over a glass of sherry, reflecting on another pleasant hour of taped conversation, my ninety-seven-year-old Aunt Sheila said that she had had a wonderful life. We had spoken of her thirty-two years as secretary to Lady Meath in Kilruddery, her years in the Irish Girl Guides, from its inception to Commissionership; of the carrying of the tricolour around Wembley Stadium in the First World Girl Guide Conference and a visit to Buckingham Palace; of her days travelling Ireland for the Irish Countrywomen's Association and the teaching of handcrafts, judging at country shows and staying in the most humble of abodes; of her love of the Church and her term as Chairman of the Friends of St Patrick's Cathedral; of her shared loved of the garden with her sister Doris and above all the happiness of seeing all her nephews and nieces and their offspring turning out so well.

> I remember I wanted a bicycle, I suppose it was about 1910 or so, and in those days the family didn't give you a bicycle, you either tried to earn a few pence weeding the garden or doing odd jobs, or you collected your pocket money and Christmas presents. We did everything on bicycles—we went to church, to our friends, to shopping and on picnics in the countryside. It was wonderful in those days.
>
> My grandmother came to dinner with us on Christmas night. She always gave us a five shilling coin. You felt you were a millionaire with that. Then the day came when you got a little half sovereign. I think of nowadays when I hear the young saying: Oh yes, they have this, that and the other thing—they don't know what it is to save. I had saved up towards the bicycle and Uncle

Marjorie, Sheila and Doris in 1904
(Photo: William Lawrence)

Charlie [the engineer, who died on the Somme] was asked to see what he could do—he may still have owned the bicycle shop in Dawson Street. Anyway, I was thrilled. It was a Raleigh bicycle, it was a real bicycle! I had it until the last war, the Second World War, and eventually the gardener got it for his family.

Once in a blue moon, Uncle Adam would come around in his car—or was it Uncle Charlie?—and take us out for a gander up the road. It was one of those original cars, say 1910 style. He wore a soft cap back to front. If you live long enough you live history! But life has changed so much since then.

Aunt Sheila remembered that the business was never far from the family's thoughts:

Findlater's in those days gave a dinner for the staff in the middle of the day in O'Connell Street, not the branches—there was a big staff dining room for the staff. I remember when I was little you'd be left in there while mother went out to do a bit of shopping and one of the staff would look after us. And then there was the director's dining room. I vaguely remember the staff billiard room—they would have their dinner and then there would be a quarter of an hour or half an hour, and we would hear the billiards balls clacking.

I remember how one time the Howth peninsula was more or less cut off and my father went in a boat from Ringsend with sacks of flour for Howth—perhaps that was 1922.

I used to go with my father on Saturday and we'd go either out to Howth to visit the St Lawrence Hotel and the shop or alternatively we'd go to Bray. I'm sure I visited the Royal Hotel in either Bray or Howth, I think we used to own both. We'd get one of the cabs that waited outside Findlater's in those days, a horse-drawn cab. And my father would say: 'Westland Row, and take your time'—it always puzzled me. He surely knew the cabs weren't going to go at fifty miles an hour! And so we trotted down to Westland Row and we'd get the train down to Bray, or we'd go to Amiens Street to go to Howth. But it struck me one day that he needn't have said: 'And take your time!'

Transferring to the Church of Ireland

My father had been brought up a Presbyterian, but mother was the stronger Christian and a member of the Church of Ireland. Thus the next generation were brought up Church of Ireland. My father was a twice a year Christian —he went to church on Christmas Day and Easter Sunday——he was a renegade! Originally we went to Booterstown—that's the church on Merrion Avenue. We were then living in Melville, Avoca Avenue, and in those days we hadn't cars. You just walked to church. And then I think it was when my sister Marjorie got engaged to Edmund Mitchell that she persuaded mother to go to All Saints in Carysfort Avenue, Blackrock where Edmund sang in the choir and could play the organ if the organist was away. Doris and myself sang in the choir and we held the church féte in Glensavage for some twenty-five years. We were very good friends with Harry Dobbs, the vicar, and his wife Katie.

Edmund Mitchell, who died in 1945, was fondly remembered in the parish, as Canon Dobbs wrote in the Anglican newspaper the *Church Gazette:*

From the time he was a choir boy, fifty years or more ago, until the day he lay down to die, Edmund Mitchell served our Church with an almost unparalleled fidelity. Others of its friends might come and go, might serve it for a while and then fall away and walk no more with us, but Edmund Mitchell never failed in his allegiance and, true as steel, stayed true until God touched him and he died. The quietest, most modest, most self-effacing of men, he brought a pure and peaceful wisdom to our Councils, which soothed acerbities, and a quaint humour all his own which dispelled in smiles and laughter what might have been the beginnings of one of those petty storms which rage from time to time in every Parish and so made everyone happy and friends again. In return the Parish gave him everything it had to give and heaped its little honours on him until it had given all.

He was a vigilant guardian of our Church traditions, such as they are and in many ways helped to create them. Attempts to lower its standards, to change its distinctive note, its gentle but effective traditions, moved him at once to protest and found him standing foursquare for the simple dignities that have marked its ceremonial from its Foundation. A sensitive musician, an artist to his fingertips, he was the most faithful of choristers and was seldom absent from his place. Many of our older folk have told us that one of their chiefest pleasures on Christmas Day was his singing of 'Nazareth' before the Eucharist, but his singing at all times was a delight. And now, this good, kind, greatly loved man, this loyal Churchman, this steadfast Christian gentleman is gone from us and another loneliness, another deep sadness has fallen upon a Church that has lost many friends in recent years. But he will be remembered always with affection and gratitude, and with thankfulness that we had with us for so many years, so good and true and wise a man. May light perpetual shine upon him.[1]

This tribute was written by Canon Dobbs[*], himself a great local character who later in life propelled himself about his parish in his motorised wheelchair, even to the top of Newtownpark Avenue where we lived. His comment on the parish fête in Doris and Sheila's garden in the summer of 1944 gives a flavour of the Anglican religious spirit of the day:

We cannot but think they could have pleased God. We think our Fêtes must please Him. He liked Parties Himself, and a Parish Party that brings people together in friendly social intercourse and mixes them all up and makes them rub shoulders with each other and play and talk and laugh together, must delight Him. Anyway, He has always blessed it, and never more than this year. What can we say to these things except to thank Him for having put into so many hearts such good desires, and for giving them grace in such generous measure to bring their desires to such marvellous effect, and not least for having put it into the hearts of the Misses Findlater to give us the use of their glorious garden.

* Rector of All Saints, Carysfort Avenue, Blackrock, 1914 to 1949; Treasurer St Patrick's Cathedral 1942 to 1949 and Precentor of the Cathedral 1949 to 1952. Born in 1876 in Castlecomer, the youngest of 10; died 1961. Married to Kate (Kathleen), a grand-daughter of the Earl of Rosse. He used to say: 'Kate has the blue blood and I have the brains.'

He returned to the theme after the 1946 fête, which was not blessed with such good weather, and yet—

> it was a huge success. It rained of course, the skies wept copiously, but in spite of the rain, in spite of Moiseiwitsch, Leopardstown, and another Fête not far away, Glensavage was so filled with friends that we laughed and sang as cheerfully as if it had been the loveliest day of the year. For could there be anything lovelier than the loyalty, kindness and goodwill which brought as many, if not more, people than ever on such a miserable day to help us along and to spend so gaily that the receipts were actually twenty-five to thirty pounds above the average. And not a grumble, nor a melancholy face to be heard or seen anywhere. The gardens were sopping, of course, but so enchanting that one stranger was overheard to say to another that it wouldn't have been a bit surprising to meet Adam and Eve there. They might have added 'or a more August Person than either' for where kindness and goodness and love are, there God is also. No one likes to be thanked on these occasions, many people dislike thanks intensely but we must acknowledge gratefully all that so many people did to avert disaster and to secure success—to the helpers who worked without fuss or plaint; to Mr. Vere-Westrops, who did everything and forgot nothing; to the Miss Findlaters, who took the spoiling of their house by muddy boots and dripping clothes as if they liked it; to the people who spent their precious petrol as though it were water bringing invalids and others to and from their trams or homes; to the friends who lent and transported chairs, and to the kind people who unable to come remembered us; to them all, whether they like it or want it or not, our most grateful thanks.

After Canon Dobbs retired Doris and Sheila transferred their allegiance to St Patrick's Cathedral. Sheila continues her story:

> I worked with five Deans in St Patrick's Cathedral. I was nominated by the Cathedral Chapter to the newly formed Council of the Friends of St Patrick's Cathedral in 1948 and served continuously until 1978 when I was appointed Chairman. I remained Chairman until 1982. My sister Doris also served on the Council, from 1959 to 1966. She was very active in the Cathedral Flower Guild, doing large floral arrangements for important services. I enjoyed needlework and repairing the embroidery on the clerical stoles and making up new stoles. I also made cloaks for the choirboys.

Naturally Canon Dobbs would get his grocery requirements in Findlater's in Blackrock, though on one occasion the ebullient manager Billy Vaughan (whom we have last seen rolling oranges and apples to the Sherwood Foresters in 1916) let him down. The Canon discreetly whispered his order over the mahogany liquor counter at the back of the shop, and was embarrassed to hear Billy repeating the order in his deep booming voice: 'A bottle of best Jameson for the Canon.'

Alexandra College

My aunts went to Alexandra College, then in Earlsfort Terrace. Founded in 1866, it had strong Church of Ireland links but was open to all religions. It took girls up to university entrance and provided them with a good broad education. In

1897 the Head Mistress, Miss White, proposed the formation of a bond of union between the College and her past students and the Alexandra College Guild was formed.[2] It was suggested that the Guild should have some definite objective to justify its existence and thus was born the Alexandra Guild Tenements Company Limited. It was started with a capital of £1,000 [£80,000] consisting of 200 shares of £5 each. It claimed to be the first public company in Great Britain and Ireland started by and managed entirely by women.

The object was to buy rundown tenement buildings, do the necessary repairs, charge rents in the range of 1s to 3s 6d a week and give the investors a return of 2½ per cent. The rent was strictly enforced. It gave the girls a great insight into the social deprivation in certain areas of the city and taught them to be caring.

Doris and Sheila were too young to be in at the inception of the Guild. Nevertheless Sheila recalls that it was the senior class in the College who collected the rents on Monday mornings and that Doris would always bring a bunch of flowers. Later, they were joint Treasurers of the Alexandra Guild for several years and held various fundraising events in their garden in Blackrock. When gas was rationed they used to bring cooked meals to some of the needy families, quite tasty meals. The tenants were suspicious of strange food and on one famous occasion one asked: 'What's this?' and the woman next to her replied: 'Don't be silly, this is educated food!' and that became the aunts' stock phrase for a good dish.

The houses chosen were well built, but they were in an almost indescribable state of dirt and neglect. The sanitary accommodation was of the very worst description, and quite inadequate; a large outlay was therefore necessary to put them into proper sanitary condition. The roofs were also dilapidated, and had to be mended. Ashpits were removed and corporation bins provided. The yards, basements and passages had to be concreted and the staircases and passages whitewashed, and all rooms by degrees papered and painted.

The object of the Tenements Company was not to provide cheap dwellings, but to make available comfortable rooms in fairly well-kept houses. It also strove to teach the rudiments of home-making to the average residents of tenement houses in Dublin. That this was needed, said *The Lady of the House,* was an undisputed fact: 'The Irishwoman is the most faithful wife, the best and most unselfish mother and the worst home-maker in Europe.'

First World War

Sheila continued:

> In 1992 my eldest sister Marjorie celebrated her hundredth birthday. She received messages from both the lady President of Ireland and the Queen of England. The latter because she had emigrated [to England] when she was ninety to be nearer her daughters Jill and June, Ann lives in Scotland. Marjorie was married on 1 September 1914 and widowed in 1945. During the First World War, like a great many girls from Alexandra College, she and Doris joined the Voluntary Aid Detachment and served as

Doris

nurses, cooks and ambulance drivers, Marjorie and myself in Monkstown House and Doris in the Linden Convalescent Home in Stillorgan. Mother and some friends ran whist drives for the wounded soldiers and held craft classes for them so that they had some occupation.

During the First World War my Aunt Doris, who was twenty-one in 1916, got work at the Royal College of Science in Upper Merrion Street, now Government Buildings. Her reference on leaving shows how she coped with the strange environment of the munitions factory:

> I have pleasure in stating that Miss Doris Findlater has been engaged in the manufacture of War Munitions in this College for the last three and a quarter years (January 1916 to March 1919). During this time she has had considerable experience in the operation of capstan lathes, drilling machines, milling machines, and other appliances all engaged on the manufacture of Graze Fuse Caps and Adapters and Aeroplane Turnbuckles. She has also had much experience in the use of limit gauges. For some time she was in charge of shift workers, and ultimately for some months she was lady superintendent of our work until our contracts terminated.
>
> In addition to the work she did in the shops she was also exceedingly helpful in the drawing office, where for some time she made all requisite drawings, tracings and prints of designs for jigs, fixings, chucks and special tools etc., and also of the capstan lathes which we designed and manufactured.
>
> Miss Findlater was a most satisfactory worker in every way, capable and energetic and thoroughly reliable. She was a keen and rapid worker, and her services throughout were of the very greatest help to us. I would like to add my appreciation of the spirit with which she came forward to help us at a time of great national need, and which animated her work throughout.

Signed by the Professor of Engineering and dated 27 March 1919.

The tiger shoot, Nepal 1920*

Some time after retiring from the munitions factory, Doris had the chance to visit India, and during that visit had the once-in-a-lifetime experience of a tiger shoot in Nepal, complete with 36 elephants. She wrote home describing the experience:

* Compiled from Doris' letters home by my sister Grania Judge.

Muzaffarpur

My dearest Family,

I had a marvellous time at the shoot, we got three tigers and I saw one out in the open, wasn't it great. Altogether we got 3 tigers, 1 leopard, 2 sambhur (deer), 2 ceetal (spotted deer), 3 Nilgai (antelope), 2 pig, 30 peafowl, 2 jungle cocks, 5 black partridge, 2 ducks. I enjoyed every minute of it. I was extraordinarily lucky to have been asked as it is a shoot that anyone would give their all to be asked to. It was done on an enormous scale, like a Rajah's shoot.

There was Mr & Mrs Wilde. He is under-manager of the estate. Mr & Mrs Hill & Mr and Mrs Murins, both planters and Judy and Irene. Major Davis, an ex Major in the 16th Lancers, who is first out for the cold weather like me. He is mad on photography, he took cinema photos of the shoot! He also has 2000 roses and buys all the new ones. He lives in Scotland and has a shoot there. He has just been left £5,000 [just £140,000] a year by his mother. They all thought him most suitable for me but after a day in the howdah with him I decided it couldn't be done!! However we hope to meet in London to compare photos if we arrive about the same time!! There was Mr. Cameron—the Forest Officer of the District, another Scot, with piercing blue eyes and sandy hair and red moustache. A bit old but I wouldn't have guessed it!! I went two days with him in his howdah as he was awfully interesting and directed all the shoot but I was afraid the day would be fatal so I didn't risk it—aren't men fools?? I am also to meet him in London as he gets home in April too!! And there was a Wattie Ross, a middle aged planter and Mr Collins who was here for the meet. I made it 15. As I was the only unattached female I was unmercifully teased. I never met such matchmaking people in my life!!

The camp was a topping one. The tents were pitched in a mango grove. They seem to have grown small groves of mango trees for camping grounds years ago as they give very dense shade.

Thursday morning, 10th, we were up early and had breakfast at 8 o'clock and set off on elephants at about 9 o'clock. This was quite a different sort of shoot to the Christmas one. Here it was tall grassy jungle and we had 36 elephants!!! The idea was to make an enormous ring round where you think the tiger is and gradually close in. Then when the elephants are shoulder to shoulder you will probably be able to shoot him! Naturally very few people can raise enough elephants to do this, so very few get the opportunity of seeing it.

We all went off in howdahs, 2 in most of them. I think Wattie Ross and Major Davis went in single howdahs and the rest of the elephants had pads on their backs and are called guddi-wallahs. I went the first day with Mr Cameron. It was awfully interesting being with him and he directed all the operations. We first of all made a big ring all round a dense bit of forest and gradually closed in to the centre, the elephants tearing down the branches and trees to get through the forest. We worked by degrees into the centre which was an open space with a big shallow pool in it surrounded by 10 ft rushy grass. About 5 wild pig rushed across the pool bounding through the water in an amusing way, but we didn't shoot them, as we hoped for panther. From there we went on into tall grassy jungle stuff like pampas grass only it does not grow in dense clumps as it does at home but just like a field of oats spread out for miles and about 15 ft high. Mr Cameron shot a Nilgai or antelope and we got lots of peafowl.

We had lunch out under the trees and it was really sumptuous to eat. We had cold ham, spiced beef and meat or game pies and sometimes cold peafowl and partridge, lovely lettuce and two large bowls of salad (tomato, beetroot, potato, peas and dressing), fruit salad, a stilton cheese and a mild one, an enormous plain plum cake, celery, cream crackers, lemon squash, soda beer, whisky and plain water, cigarettes and cigars!

It really was marvellous fun—After lunch we beat back to camp getting there about 4.30 to find tea laid out on tables under the trees—after tea the men went out to shoot again on foot, quite close to the camp but didn't get anything. I had my bath and lay down on my bed and went sound asleep until nearly dinnertime 8.30. After dinner there were two tables of bridge and the rest of us played some game.

Doris' hunting expedition in Nepal in 1920. She is in the centre of the lower picture.

Friday 11th we packed all our clothes etc. up before breakfast as we were moving camp that day. We moved about 6 miles further north. We just went off shooting after breakfast and went to the new camping ground at teatime and there were all the tents up, beds made, furniture arrived and tea laid and made 5 minutes after we arrived. It certainly is a wonderful country. We had 50 bullock carts, 2 bullocks to each, to move our luggage, tents, furniture etc. from one camp to the other. I don't wonder as we had proper beds not canvas camp ones and dressing tables with ordinary swing looking glasses and big tin baths and real washstands and chains in our tents and durries on all the floors. We also had 6 cars with us and a sort of matting garage, which they moved from place to place. I don't know how many servants we had, it must have been about 130 as each bullock cart had a man and each elephant had one or sometimes two and there were dozens for our camp.

On Saturday 13th I went with Mr Cameron. We beat for about 300 yards gradually closing in the circle all the time. When we were about 30 yards from the stops some of the elephants began to scream and trumpet. Mr Cameron shouted orders and a few of the elephants tried to refuse to go on. Suddenly there was a wild rush in the grass from near Mr Wilde (No. 1 Gun) right round past us within 5 yards of our elephant and on to Judy, next gun to us (No. 8), where it tried to break through the ring. He fired and it turned back to Mr Wilde who fired twice and hit it. It then rushed back roaring horribly and Guns 4, 3 & 2 each fired and it broke through the ring between Guns 2 & 3 and jumped across the drive and fell dead just beyond. It was wildly thrilling. It was shot through the lungs, leg and side. It was great as everyone had a chance of hitting it. Mr Wilde got in the first shot, so it was his tigress.

Mr Cameron & I went back to shoot the buffalo which the tigress had eaten some of but hadn't killed. We came across it suddenly in the grass. Our elephant was so worked up, it got frightened and stampeded wildly. However, the mahout forced it back and Mr Cameron put an end to the buffalo.

The Shoot continued for some days but I had to leave. The motor run through the Jungle providing one last thrill. In the pitch dark we saw two bright green eyes shimmering in the middle of the road a little distance ahead. Of course we all gasped 'Tiger'! But—praise be! It was only a harmless deer and we reached our journey's end safe and sound.

Home from the excitement of tiger shooting, Doris got herself a job as manageress of the catering department in the Bank of Ireland. That was from 1928 to 1930. Her duties comprised arranging dinners or optional luncheons for a staff of about 270 and also a four-course luncheon for the directors. She had a staff of twenty-three to supervise in the kitchens and lunchrooms. She received an excellent reference.

A full life

Sheila continued:

I was of the generation whose young men that might have been looking for a wife, like brothers of school-friends and so on, all joined up in the First World War and an awful lot of them didn't come back. There just weren't so many eligible bachelors around looking for young women. I make that my excuse, as I never got asked!

I realised after a bit that I had no means of support for my future. Daddy had a couple of old friends that he looked after and saw that they were all right and would help them with their accounts and so on. I thought, 'I am not going to be one of those awkward creatures with no means of support'. So I decided that I would take a secretarial course so that I had something to offer. There was a family crisis, and that's what happened.

I went to Alexandra College as a mature student in 1928. I had previously been there as a girl, after which I went to Switzerland to learn French. I got beautiful looking certificates from the Secretarial Training College.

The certificates attest that Sheila holds a Pitman's Certificate in Shorthand for a speed of 90 words a minute, and the Certificate of the Royal College of Arts for Stage 2 in Typewriting, Book-keeping, Arithmetic (1st class) and Precise Writing, and for Stage 3 in French. She also obtained the London Chamber of Commerce Junior Certificate for Book-keeping (with Distinction).

Miss White, who was the head of the College, wrote a lovely reference:

I think very highly of Miss Findlater in every way, she is a gentlewoman, and she gave me satisfaction in all respects. She has many personal qualities which, in addition to her educational and secretarial attainments, will make her a valuable and efficient Secretary. She has wide interests, and is cultured and well-read. She has good organising ability, she is artistic and she has helped greatly with all the various functions in connection with the College.

Very quickly, she got a job that began as temporary, but was in the end to last thirty-two years.

Lady Meath required a secretary for about six weeks or so to deal with all the letters of condolences from abroad on the death of old Lord Meath, that was Reginald, the 12th Earl, who died in 1929 at the age of eighty-eight. Miss White thought I would be suitable. I was older than the seventeen-year old girls. I remember Lady Meath, Aileen, wife of the 13th Earl, came into Alexandra to interview me and she evidently thought I was a suitable person and there I was! She said she thought it was short-term, and that they were planning to go away. However Lady Maureen, the elder daughter, fell and hurt herself while hunting. They went away for a short time, not as long as they had planned. When they returned she rang up and said 'Will you come back?' and I was there for thirty-two years until she died!

The Lord Meath who died last year [1999] at the age of eighty-seven was the 14th Earl and the son of the one I worked for. He and his wife have visited me here and she came in at Christmas (1997) with a box of chocolates–so I'm not forgotten!

I became goods friend with Sheila Powerscourt. She only died about five years ago. Her daughter is Grania and she married Sir Hercules Langrishe who sadly died last year. They were a very nice pair. We did the flowers in the house for her wedding. I remember all the Powerscourt weddings. Sheila would ask whether we would do the flowers in the Cathedral or the house. We usually chose the house. We also did the

Christmas cards sent to Doris and Sheila in the 1930s

flowers for the Guinness family christenings and weddings at Farmleigh.

When I went to Kilruddery first there were 14 indoor staff. When I left there was only the butler. It was real 'Upstairs Downstairs' but it was fun. We had a great experience. Lady Meath had a little sitting room and I would work there. She loved doing crosswords and when we had done the letters we would get down to the English *Times* crossword. Lord Meath would probably look in before he went to do whatever he had to do.

It must have been for Punchestown that they held a house party in the grand style and were having caviar. The next morning he came into the study and said: 'What happened last night, there were no lemons with the caviar. Any little servant girl would know how to serve caviar.' I thought, yes, your lordship has very little clue what a little servant girl knows.

From our home, Glensavage in Avoca Avenue, Blackrock, I'd walk up to Stillorgan where the bus went past. It was the Greystones bus, and I'd get the bus to the gate at Kilruddery. They had a pony and trap when there wasn't a car, and it would take Lord Meath down to Bray Station to get into town for his meetings. He was on the Boards of the Bank of Ireland and the Irish Lights and high up in the Boy Scouts. Then they'd come back and it would wait at the gate until I got out of my bus to take me up the drive. I remember the same trap taking the present Knight of Glin to his first day's school at Aravon.

When George V and Queen Mary were celebrating his Silver Jubilee in 1935, people in England were making presentations and somebody here suggested that we, at Kilruddery, ought to do the same. But it wasn't a very good moment politically [in the middle of the Economic War]. However, people said to Lady Powerscourt, that's Sybil: 'can't you do something about it?' She started in a quiet way, just between her friends

The dish rings

The presentation scroll

and acquaintances, and small amounts were contributed, five bob here and there. The Meaths were going away for a spring holiday and she said to Syb, as we used to call her: 'You can use my Miss Findlater while we are away', and our friend Eileen Beatty was in it too. We got going at it. Where we knew somebody of their own ilk in a county we got them to organise it. We collected quite a bit of money from those who would normally not be stingy.

Three Irish silver dish rings were purchased and West's made a shamrock shaped case to hold the three, as they were from different periods. Eileen Beatty and I typed a book with the names of all the people who had participated and had them nicely bound. I brought it over to London for the Powerscourts. One of the papers covered the event:

'At Buckingham Palace to-day Viscount and Viscountess Powerscourt and the Earl of Fingall presented to King George three Irish dish rings which were acquired with part of the sum of £3,300 [almost £150,000 in 2000] subscribed by over 36,700 people in the Saorstát as a Silver Jubilee gift, together with an illuminated list of subscribers of Celtic design and bound in Irish poplin.

'The King, in accepting the dish rings, asked that an expression of his sincere thanks might be conveyed to the subscribers, and expressed the wish that the balance of the money subscribed should be given to the Queen's Institute of District Nursing in the Irish Free State and to the Lady Dudley Scheme for Nurses.'

The Irish Girl Guide movement

The scouting movement was initiated by Sir Robert Baden-Powell in England in 1909, and quickly spread to other countries. Initially Sir Robert resisted the idea of guides, but the demand was irresistible and he persuaded his sister Agnes to adapt his idea for girls. Later his wife Olave devoted her life to the movement.

The Girl Guide movement in Ireland began in 1911. Companies were started mostly in the Protestant parishes around Dublin and later in Cork. Later there were companies for the Roman Catholic girls and for girls in the Jewish community, each run by guides of their own faith.

My friends and I started as Girl Scouts about 1913. We got our mother to make us khaki shirts and we bought scouts' hats for 2s 6d each. At that time we considered ourselves to be very much a part of the British Empire and we used to tie the Union Jack onto our bicycles. We considered ourselves to be Girl Scouts. However as soon as the Girl Guides heard about us they gathered us into their movement. This was the beginning of a 40-year association with the Guide Movement. It was a terrific character-building organisation.

In the early days we learnt skills like bed making, no duvets in those days, and First Aid. We used to help out in Linden Convalescent Home in Stillorgan where wounded soldiers were recovering. We were used as patients for First Aid and Home Nursing classes given by doctors when war was declared.

With the outbreak of the First World War in 1914 and then the Easter Rising in 1916 there was neither enthusiasm nor expansion in the Scout movements which had their origins in GB and whose leaders were probably not available.

Later, my sister Doris was Captain of a Guide Company in Alexandra School and also Captain of a Ranger Company in Dublin, Rangers were aged 17 upwards. I was Captain of Guides in Blackrock and later in a school in Dublin and also a Ranger Company.

Hearing that Guide Companies were being organised in hospitals and children's homes in England I got in touch with the Orthopaedic Hospital in Merrion Street in Dublin, where there is now a prestigious hotel, and I ran a group there of Guides and Brownies for about eight years. Nowadays this would probably be called occupational therapy. We did simple handicrafts as many of the children were in hospital for long-term stays. Handicrafts became my speciality and I set up a lot of different tests for the Girl Guides to take all over the country.

Later Doris and I took on organisational responsibilities in Guiding. We were commissioners for various areas in Dublin, Doris ending up as County Commissioner for Dublin and I was a Division Commissioner. We were also on various committees. Doris was Head of Camping and I became Commissioner for the Training of Guides and I was also International Commissioner. The latter was very interesting as it entailed a certain amount of travelling and attending conferences.

The most interesting was the first world conference to be held after the Second World War in 1950 in England at Oxford. There were many interesting outings. The Guides of London had a party in the Moat of the Tower of London. The Lord Mayor invited us to coffee in the Mansion House and Lady Baden-Powell who was living in a grace and favour residence in Hampton Court invited us to tea. The most exciting was an invitation to tea in Buckingham Palace where we were greeted by the Queen Mother and Princess Margaret. Another day there was a Rally of Guides in Wembley

Ethel Warbrook, Olave Baden-Powell and Sheila, 1951

> Stadium. The delegates were invited to join in by carrying their native flags, and I had the honour of carrying the Tricolour around the stadium.
>
> During our time the Guide Cottage at Enniskerry was built on a site at Powerscourt given by Lord Powerscourt. Later there were other cottages which were used for Guides going for a week or weekends in the country and for guides from England and elsewhere.

What Sheila did not recall was the role that she and Doris played in the development of this cottage, now known as The Irish Girl Guides' Baden-Powell National Memorial Cottage.

In a thank-you letter to Doris in July 1950 Olave Baden-Powell wrote:

> I don't know how to begin to express to you and your sister my gratitude and my appreciation of all that I have seen, and heard, and felt this week end. . . .I just can't get over the charm of that cottage and the fact that you have raised the funds, and built and equipped it, and made it so utterly delightful. I think I realise how hard you and your committee must have worked, not only raising the funds, but in making the plans for the building itself, and gathering together all those attractive 'bits and pieces' which make it so homely and delightful.

The letter ends with a little thank-you for staying at Glensavage and

> 'I do so enjoy going to see your house and garden again, and altogether, though it was so very short, my visit has been a very happy one to me'.

Doris was the cottage's first warden (1950–58).[3]

> In 1932, the year of the Eucharistic Congress, the IGG held a large camp at Powerscourt, so that guides from the country could attend the Congress in Phoenix Park and there were also guides from the USA and European countries. I think that the American Guides found camping in the wilds of Powerscourt a bit rough!

In 1939 Doris and Eileen Beatty led a contingent of guides to a world camp in Paxting in Hungary just before the outbreak of war.

Sheila thinks that the whole face of the movement has changed enormously over the years—in many respects for the better.

> In the early days when we joined the Girl Guides, it wasn't a very popular movement, because it was still considered to be very Protestant. Lady Baden-Powell was always anxious that we should increase our membership here and when she came over, she would ask me: 'Have you got the Catholics yet?' It is good to see that the movement doesn't have those divisions any more.

In 1928 a new organisation for Catholic Guides only was inaugurated. This later spread round the country as a separate movement but it was not recognised by the World Association of Girl Guides and Girl Scouts, as, in Sheila's words, 'it was too exclusive'. Not until 1993 was the Catholic organisation recognised by world associations and they now have a joint committee relating to World Conference and Camps.

One change which Sheila does regret is the demise of the uniform and although she accepts it as a necessity in many respects she comments:

> 'In recent years, I was invited to a Girl Guides event in Christchurch Cathedral. I was horrified—in my day we would have had our shoes polished and everything matching perfectly, but that's all gone now.
>
> As time went by we realised that it was time to let younger women take over, as this was a youth movement so we faded out of our responsibilities by degrees, that was around 1955. After that I became actively involved in the ICA.'

As Sheila Powerscourt said in a personal letter to Sheila when she retired as International Commissioner: 'Again all my personal thanks to you for your superlative work as International Commissioner. You and Doris and Eileen (Beatty) are *The* Irish Guides.' And of her sister Doris another guide wrote:

> When we remember Doris we think of one who was always cheerful and a delightful person to work with. Her sense of humour was one of the things that endeared her to her friends and it is quite impossible to describe. She was involved in so many aspects of Guiding that she had friends all through the Movement, and there is no part of Guiding that does not owe her a deep sense of gratitude. Others will remember her as she organised the refreshments at sales and exhibitions in the Mansion House. Helping

her was always fun and if it looked as though things would not be ready in time she would laugh and suggest we should stop and make a pot of tea! Those of us who knew her and loved her will always have happy memories of Doris and Sheila and be thankful for their friendship.

The Irish Countrywomen's Association

When Sheila was young 'handcrafts was one of my strong subjects, that is: embroidery, needlework, weaving, wickerwork and so on. After it was time to hand over our Guiding activities to the next generation I got involved with the Irish Country Women's Association (ICA).'

Muriel Gahan was the moving force behind the ICA and many other initiatives.[4] She was a unique woman. Her passions were the traditional Irish crafts and making Ireland a better place for rural women. She and her friends established the Country Shop, at number 23 St Stephen's Green, in 1930. She also provided a home there for the ICA (from 1937 until 1964) and the Country Markets (from 1946 until 1975). The Crafts Council of Ireland was set up by Muriel Gahan in 1971. The ICA roots lay in the United Irishwomen founded by Horace Plunkett and prominent ladies in 1910 to 'help Irish women take up their rightful part in building up a rural civilisation in Ireland'.[5] Muriel was inextricably involved in all these bodies. No. 23 became the centre of operations for the women and crafts of rural Ireland as well as a cosy, friendly restaurant serving traditional, homely fare.

Sheila was one of the group who organised the Craft end of the ICA and judged at local shows and taught crafts at the local ICA Guilds. The object was 'to encourage crafts of good standards and help outstanding craftworkers'. 'I travelled up and down the country judging and advising at shows. At that time education in handcrafts was in its infancy in Ireland. Muriel, who was born in 1897 and also an old girl of Alexandra College, was impulsive and would land new ideas on myself and my sister Doris, and others in the small coterie, without having thought them through.'

Sheila tells of a day in the country:

> Muriel would insist on filling the car up with a load of good work to display. On arrival you had to put up the exhibition. Then you had to do a long day's judging and advising. You escaped for a bit of lunch if you were lucky and when you got back you had to deal with complaints, such as: 'My Granny didn't get a prize for her socks, why not?' By the time it was all over and packed back into the car, it was late into the night. Judges travelled in pairs and had to bear all their own costs. If far from Dublin they would be put up locally, sometimes in a warm hospitable house or cottage and sometimes shown to a cold bedroom with not so much as a cup of tea! However, it was a lot of fun and a job well done.

Sheila became President of the Dublin Town Association of the ICA in 1952. At that time the need for a residential college was top of the ICA agenda. The Findlater firm were the original Irish importers of the Kellogg breakfast cereals in the 1920s and had close personal relationships with the head of their UK operation, Harry McEvoy. Sheila's brother Dermot thought of the Kellogg Foundation, which had been established for charitable purposes in 1930. The Foundation was interested in the development of co-operative programmes in the field of agriculture and in adult education. Dermot made the connection between Muriel Gahan and their Director, Dr Emory Morris. He was impressed by her experience, her enthusiasm and the ideas that she expounded. They provided the funding that had been turned down by James Dillon, Minister of Agriculture. The result was that An Grianán in Termonfeckin became a reality and the ICA have had a good friend in the Kellogg Foundation over the years. Sheila continued her love of craft work into old age, and when the pleasure went out of travelling, she became a member of a small self-help group in Dún Laoghaire.

No chapter on Doris and Sheila would be complete without reference to Tessie Dunne, who looked after my aunts for just over fifty years, becoming part of the family in the process. Tessie was in their service from shortly after the death of their mother in 1941 until she passed away in her early eighties in January 1992. There was no compulsion in this stay well beyond normal retirement but she had a strong sense of duty and loyalty. Furthermore the aunts had bought her a house in Dalkey where she went every Saturday to join her sister and then back to the aunts on Sunday evenings. She kept the house in pristine condition and knew each of our favourite dishes. 'Master Alex,' she would say, 'likes good plain food and the sponge cake for tea.' Formalities were maintained even after Doris and Sheila moved from Glensavage to a more modest house in Glenageary. Tessie preferred the big house and the visiting Guides, horticulturists, ICA members, tea and wine merchants and the family spending a few days holiday. The grandchildren, uncomprehending of the 'upstairs downstairs' manners of former times, could never understand why 'Auntie' Tessie did not take her place in the drawing-room or at the dining-room table.

Gardening at Glensavage

In 1937 Doris was co-opted on to the Board of Findlaters and was a very regular and conscientious member for the next thirty-two years. The Board met every Wednesday at 2.30 pm in Findlaters in O'Connell Street, which to her always remained Sackville Street, as it did to many of the older generation.

In Glensavage, the fine old house in Blackrock where the family lived from 1932 to 1968, Doris's passion for gardening developed and she created several new cultivars, and in 1966 became Chairman of the Royal Horticultural Society of Ireland.

Sheila starts the story:

> We have always lived with gardens, for my mother was a keen gardener with real 'green fingers', and she encouraged all the family to take an interest in plants and how they grew. At Alexandra School there used to be a voluntary holiday task which took

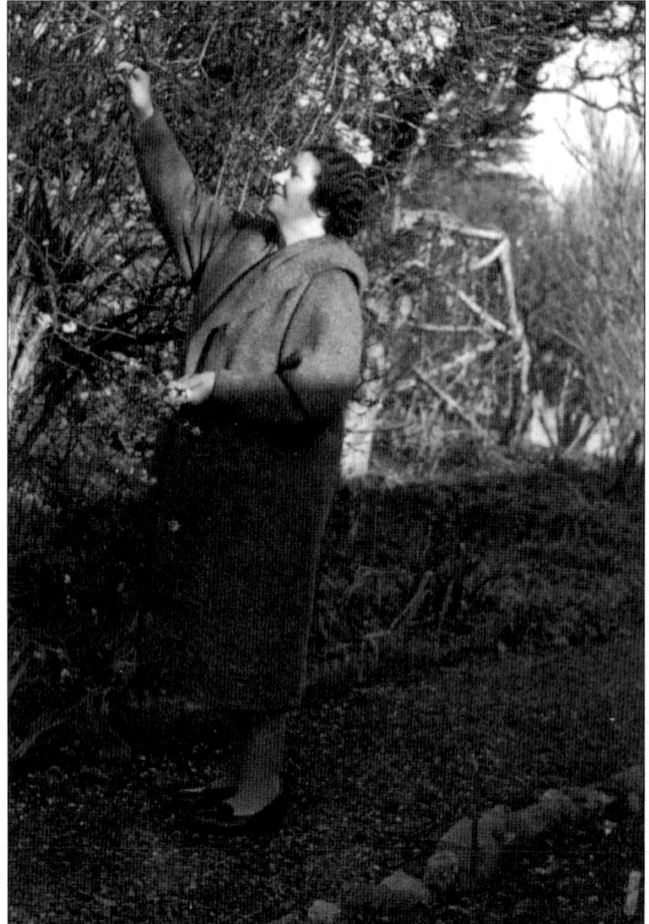

Doris in the garden at Glensavage

the form of a collection of wild flowers each year, consisting of plants of three or four different families. As everyone getting 80 per cent got a prize, it was an easy way to get a nice book! This made one very observant in looking for the different flowers and one pored over the Revd. John's *Flowers of the Field* to help in identification. A holiday away where the soil was different could be very exciting. The result was that one noticed the different flowers and soon learned the families to which they belonged. During Doris's last year in Alexandra College in 1914, she took classes in botany and horticulture given by Canon F. C. Hayes, and at the end of the year she was awarded scholarships in both.

There was always plenty to be done in the garden at home, first, at Melville in Blackrock, then at The Beeches in Glenageary (where there was a large rose garden and a long herbaceous border) and then at Glensavage in Blackrock. During the early years, Doris was interested in roses, and George Dickson of Hawlmark Nurseries in Newtownards, named a rose for her, but unfortunately, it soon dropped out of circulation. From the classes with Canon Hayes grew an interest in propagation, and it was probably from his lectures that Doris became keen on hybridisation.

I cannot remember when she started to hybridise daffodils—possibly some of the

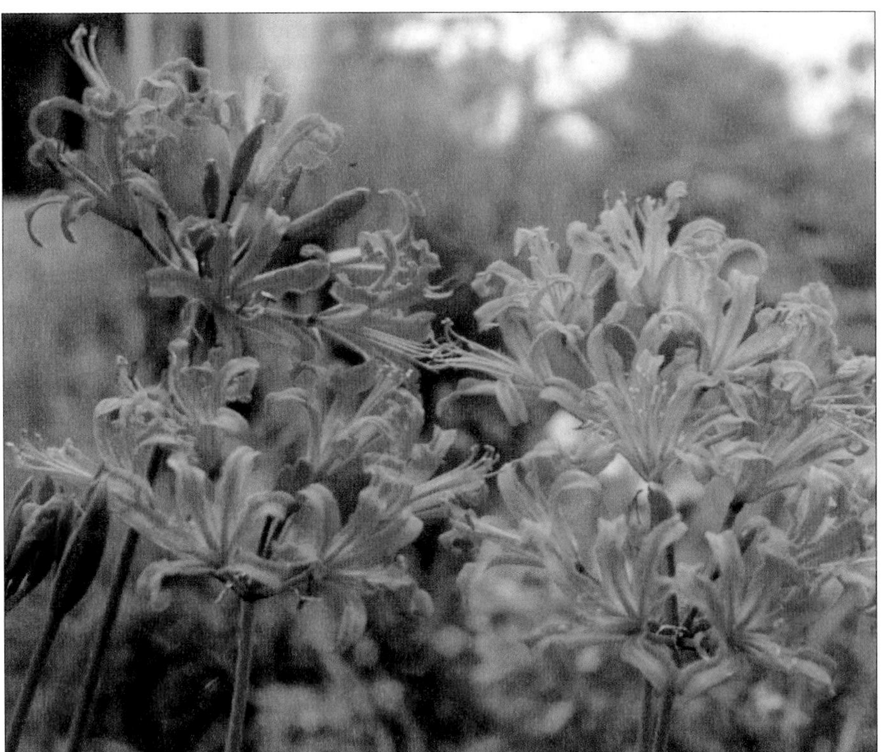

One of the Glensavage nerines (*The Irish Garden* October 1999)

flowers set seed one year and she sowed them. This was the time when Mr Richardson and Mr Guy Wilson were producing many fine narcissi, and the latter encouraged Doris to hybridise. She showed for many years at the Royal Horticultural Society of Ireland and the South County Dublin Horticultural Society shows, and won many prizes, including some for her seedlings. In 1961 she took some seedlings to the Royal Horticultural Society show in London and won some prizes. Later, she often judged daffodils at various shows.

Doris and Sheila's garden at Glensavage was the magical setting where I spent many happy weeks in my youth. I remember the flowers and borders and butterflies and bees, and frogspawn and little sailing boats in a great big pond sheltered by overhanging trees and plants and the sun dappling through; all memories fast fading into the nether regions of the memory. The big attraction was the large natural frog pond ideal for sailing little boats and yachts amongst the tadpoles.

How it appeared to an outsider was recorded in *The Irish Times* in 1964 by Nora Reddin:

The Misses Findlaters' garden at Glensavage, Blackrock, Co. Dublin, has all the mellowness of a Dutch flower painting and the feeling of having matured and ripened in the sun for many years. It is in fact an old garden. It was established about fifty years ago and their house is much older. It was built in the 18th century. But unlike other old gardens around Dublin there is nothing forlorn or sad about it, as it is still flourishing and being added to every year.

A tree-shaded avenue leads to the house, which faces east. In June the house wall on this side is garlanded with roses: the deep red Allen Chandler, the creamy Alberic Barbier and the warm Shot Silk. Here too is the charming bunch-flowered yellow Banksian rose which climbs into a slender tree, grown from a cutting by Miss Doris Findlater.This tree is Azara Microphylla which has dark foliage something like Box, but of more graceful habit, and small flowers growing behind the leaves and smelling of vanilla. Opposite the hall door is a very well grown Eleagnus with its beautiful deep-green and golden foliage. It is beloved by flower arrangers and as it is an evergreen is excellent value all the year round. To the right is a lawn with two very beautiful old cedars making a background for the winter-flowering cherry, Subhirtella Autumnalis, and the later white-blossomed cherry Yedoensis.

On the south wall of the house, a wisteria has climbed to the roof and through it grows Clematis Tangutica, one of the most attractive of all the family with its yellow flowers rather like Shirley poppy buds and silky greenish-silver seedheads. Further along this wall is a peach and in a sheltered corner a grey-leaved Teucrium Fruiticans and two kinds of Abelia—Grandiflora which has rosy trumpet-shaped flowers and the most graceful shiny foliage and Schumannii with mauve flowers. . . .

This year she and her sister decided to make a new annual border and it is still gay and colourful. 'We like to grow them in boxes first and then plant them out. Otherwise the slugs get in first.' Amongst the annuals they have a delightful daisy-like flower, Arctotis Grandis, a glistening silver-white with dark blue central zone. Another rather prim daisy-like flower they grow is Layia Elegans, yellow with a neat white border to the petals. Its familiar name is 'Tidy-tips'. They have a new petunia too, the true red 'Fire Chief'.

Nasturtiums are enchanting but a great nuisance because of their persistent roving habits. Here they have a non-rampant dwarf variety which is deep rose-madder in colour. Something quite new to me anyhow.

Beyond a low wall of pink brick there is another lawn that narrows between two wide herbaceous borders still full of colour from clumps of Michaelmas daisies, phlox and golden helianthus. I noticed too a fine plant with elegant flowers the colour of good country butter! It is Kirengoshima and would be a lovely flower for arrangement.

Like all really appealing gardens, this one has not too formal an atmosphere. The kitchen garden is alongside the flower garden—the apple trees laden with fruit. Scarlet and white-striped dahlias grow here, and a pretty rose like those one sees on old china tea-cups. It is called Perle d'Or. There are also many fragrant shrubs, including a large Viburnum Burkwoodii, which has fresh pink heavily scented flowers in spring. They have a Chimonanthus Fragrans too—a mass of blossoms in spring, with an elusive sweet scent. White lavender grows along with the commoner purple type.

This is a garden that is of interest all the year round and where many unusual things have been grown from cuttings. Its owners, as well as being greenfingered are devoted gardeners. It has a sense of leisure but I feel that it is only visitors who relax here as so much thought and hard work must have gone into its making.

Doris was a member of the RHSI and she served on the council for a number of years and was Chairman in 1966. She was elected an Honorary Life Member in 1975. She was a member of the South County Dublin Horticultural Society, and served as President for two years. In 1980 she was elected an honorary life member of the Society. She was also a member of the RHS for many years and attended some of the shows when she was in England.

A serious plantswoman, Doris began to hybridise daffodils, but found it difficult to produce good results on a relatively small scale. After daffodils, Doris turned her attention to hybridising nerines and named one 'Glensavage Gem'. This was technically more difficult, as at that time there were few different bulbs available, especially in Ireland. Most people growing or showing nerines in Britain at that time were owners of large gardens with a staff of gardeners. Finally the Nerine Society was formed, Tony Norris being the secretary. Doris and he began a correspondence which lasted until her death.

During the 1960s he came to Dublin for a business conference and asked if he could come to see her nerines. He was so thrilled with 'Glensavage Gem', that he asked her to give him an offset of the bulb when one was available. This she did, and a year or two later, he showed the flower at an RHS show, where it was awarded a Preliminary Certificate. One year she took specimen blooms to the London show, but unfortunately that year there were no competitions, the Nerine Society putting up a combined stand of blooms instead. Some of the Dutch growers took an interest in her bulbs having seen them at this show.

There is an article about Doris and her nerines in *An Irish Florilegium II,* with paintings by Wendy Walsh,* of two of her cultivars: 'Glensavage Gem' and 'John Fanning'.†

When Charles Nelson came to see the nerines one day he noticed an uncommon Daboecia growing in the garden. As Sheila remembered:‡

> Being very interested in heaths he asked me about it. I confessed that we had found it in Connemara while eating our lunch near a wild mountainy road. It was a young plant, and though we knew we should not dig up native wild plants, we felt it might be lost in such a situation, so we brought it home. A year or two later, when driving along the same road, we found a cartload of rubbish had been emptied at the spot where we discovered it. Dr Nelson realised that it was a new variety, and later had it registered with the International Heather Registration Authority under the name 'Doris Findlater'.

* *An Irish Florilegium II, Wild and Garden Plants of Ireland with 48 Watercolour paintings* by Wendy Walsh and notes by Charles Nelson. London: Thames and Hudson 1987. Wendy Walsh has illustrated several books including *An Irish Flower Garden* (1984), *The Native Dogs of Ireland* (1984), and a book on the flora of the Burren. She was awarded the Gold Medal of the Royal Horticultural Society in 1981.

† John Fanning, one-time Assistant Keeper of the National Botanic Gardens, Glasnevin and a well-loved figure in Irish gardening circles. He died in 1971.

‡ Dr Charles Nelson, one time taxonomist at the National Botanic Gardens, Glasnevin, Chairman of the Heritage Gardens Committees, foundation chairman of Irish Garden Plant Society and author of several academic papers on botanical and historical subjects.

Each of our gardens were very different but all of them were full of colour and interesting plants—perhaps not planted in a well-planned design—often plants were popped in wherever there was an empty space. Many of these came from cuttings or 'bits' from the gardens of friends. If you were uncertain of the proper name of the gift you would call it after the giver—John Fanning, Ralph Walker* and so on, and Doris also loved to share her treasures with her friends.

Our gardens were always full of flowers but they were also full of memories of friends and their gardens. What a lot of happiness can be found in a garden.

Doris and I also belonged to the South County Dublin Horticultural Society and she was President of the Society for two years. Later when I was eighty-nine, I was elected President and held office for two years. I had suggested that they should find someone younger but the Council insisted!

Doris described her experiences with hybrid nerines in an article written in 1974:

I had been growing Nerine bowdenii in the garden from about 1950 and I found it produced seed very easily. There seemed to be quite a lot of variation in the seedlings produced, but not much variation in the colour—I was not very fond of the rather hard pink. In 1957 I got some bulbs of Nerine 'Corusca Major' from Guernsey; it is a good hybrid from the original Guernsey lily (Nerine sarniensis), scarlet, with a lovely gold sheen when the light falls directly on it. The grower sent full instructions about how to pot them, only covering the bulbs halfway up and not watering them until growth had started.

I must say this species is inclined to be shy about flowering and one must not be disheartened if all the bulbs do not flower every year. The flowers appear before the leaves in September or October. When the buds appear, you give the pots a good soak by standing them in a bucket of water for an hour or so when they start into growth. The leaves go on growing until about May, when they turn yellow and dry off. Leave the pot in a sunny place in the greenhouse to bake during the summer until the bulbs start into growth again in September. In a very hot year such as this [1974], you could water them about once a month to keep them from shrinking. Nerine sarniensis bulbs are not hardy and must be kept in a frost-free greenhouse in the winter.

Now I had material for hybridising; it is quite a simple operation. Take the pollen from the stamen of one flower and put it on the stigma of another flower of a different variety or colour. Some breeders cut the blooms and let them mature in water, but I find they ripen better on the plant. They are inclined to damp off in water, but once they are ripe, they stand quite a lot of hardship. When the seed has developed and is ripe (ready to fall), sow it. I have found it best to sow the seeds on the surface of a pan of John Innes No. l compost and anchor them with coarse sand or vermiculite, but not bury the seeds. Cover with glass or cellophane and stand the pan where it is warm (the experts say 70 degrees F, but I found the sitting room or kitchen quite satisfactory). The seeds germinate in a few weeks; they send out a little stem and the bulb forms

* The late Ralph Walker was the owner of Fernhill, Sandyford, one of the finest gardens in south county Dublin. It is open to the public in the spring, summer and autumn.

at the end of it. The seeds of different varieties vary considerably in shape; those of Nerine bowdenii are round and quite big and may be green or dark red. In many other varieties, the seeds are green and pear-shaped. I have occasionally forgotten to sow seed, and when I found them months later, they had already formed their little bulbs and all I had to do was plant them in pans.

For the first year you may only have one leaf on the little bulb—the second year, two or perhaps three. I leave them in the pan for two years without disturbing them. Don't let these small seedlings dry off in the summer. The third year I pot up the bigger seedlings singly in small pots or sometimes three in one pot, or well spaced out in a larger pan for another year (still in John Innes No. 1), always covering the bulb only halfway up. Some grow quickly and make great big bulbs, and a few flower in the fourth year, but they do not generally flower until they have formed six leaves and that may be in the fifth or sixth year.

It was in 1965 that I had my first thrill when two of the seedling bulbs flowered and each produced a new type of flower. One was crimson-rose in colour and the other rose-opal. . . .

I went on crossing some every year with varying success; the Glensavage strain does not bear seeds so it was mostly the scarlet Guernsey lily seeds that I used. About 1969 I got a pot of Nerine flexuosa 'Alba' from Mr Ralph Walker, and crossed it with the scarlet Guernsey lily. A new crop of seedlings resulted, the first flowering in 1973. I hoped for a startling red and white striped blossom but so far they have produced rose-flame-coloured flowers, the colour of the rose called 'Super Star'. However the petals are more curled and narrower than my other seedlings.

The outdoor species Nerine bowdenii which flowered so marvellously this year [1974] and grows freely here is, according to scientists, parthenogenetic—that is, it forms seed without fertilisation of the ovules. In fact you often notice the seed swelling before the flower opens. This means you are unlikely to get a new variety from its seed, but if you use its pollen on another variety, the progeny is likely to have its size and vigour. It was by putting the pollen of the pink Nerine bowdenii on the stigma of the scarlet Guernsey lily, that I got the Glensavage hybrids.[6]

Sheila presented Doris's collection of nerines to the National Botanical Gardens in Glasnevin, replacing their own collection, which was destroyed by frost in about 1930. They are on view to the public as they come into bloom in the late summer.

Appendix 1: Mid-winter flowers at Glensavage

November, at the latest, for most Irish gardeners, heralds the end of the season but not so for Doris and Sheila as *The Irish Times* of 28 January 1955 explains:

> Two lists of mid-winter flowers have been published recently. The list from Miss Findlater contains the names of the flowers she could pick in her garden in Glensavage, Blackrock, on January 5th. It is a very interesting and comprehensive list of 87 items, and is remarkable for the number of flowers that have lingered on from the summer or autumn. Summer seems to die slowly in Blackrock. It is characteristic of our winters that severe frost rarely occurs before Christmas, and provided that our gardens are well-stocked we should be able to pick an interesting mixed bunch of flowers up to that season. Doris' list of mid-winter flowers:
>
> Anthemis tinctoria; Achilleca Gold Plate; Achillea argentea; Dimorphotheca Nerine Bowdenii; Forget-me-not; Tagetes pumila; Cornflower; Campanula; Schizostylis Mrs Hegarty and Schizostylis Viscountess Byng; Gentiana acaulis; Cxalis; Brompton Stock; Potentilla; Candytuft annual and perennial; annual variegated Thistle; Aconite; Crocus; Snowdrop; Onosna; Lupin; Nigella; Primrose; Polyanthus (various); Viola; Pansy; Valerian; Erica carnea (various); Bergenia Pink; Saxifrage apiculata; Eripsinun mauve and brown; Scabiosa annual and caucasica; Helleborus niger and Lenten; Vinca alba; Calendula; Aubretia; Hollyhock; Welsh Poppy; Violet; Parma Violet; Dianthus (various); Azara microphylla; Cydonia japonica; Escallonia macrantha and Donard Seedling; Prunus subhirtella autumnalis; Pulmonaria; Fuchsia dwarf; Mahonia Bealei; Olearia; Buddleia auriculata; Garrya Elliptica; Rosemarinus prostratus and Miss Jessop; Iris stylosa; Gumcistus; Viburnus fragrans; Burkwoodii; Grandiflorum and tinus nirtum; Hammelis mollis; Ceanothus Gloire de Versailles; Chimonanthus fragrans; Lonicera Standishil; Salvia Grahamii; Hypericum various; Jasminum nudiflorum and revolutum; Roses various; Lithospermum rosemarinifolus; Spartium junceum; Genista (species); Forsythia; Chrysanthemum maximum; Teucrium fruticans azereum; Veronica hulkeana; Hepatica; Camomile; Antirrhinum and Prunus Davidii.

Appendix 2: Miss Doris Findlater's Nerine Cultivars[7]

[This is an abbreviated version of the technical notes by E. Charles Nelson to my aunt's article.]

In her work with nerines some 30 hybrid seedlings were produced of which the best known are:

1. 'Glensavage Gem'–flowers claret-rose [021 or geranium lake 20/1]. The stems are tall, to 26 in. and the perianth is 21¼ x ⅜ in.

'Glensavage Gem' is the only *Nerine* cultivar raised by Miss Findlater to receive an award, when shown by A. Norris of the Nerine Nurseries, Welland, in October 1968, it received a Preliminary Certificate of Commendation. Miss Findlater sent Norris the bulbs in May 1967. The cultivar has been officially named in the Nerine Society Bulletin 2 (1967: p. 11). In *Bulletin 3* (1968: p. 3), Norris remarked that he had high hopes for this cultivar. In a letter to Miss Findlater dated 23 October 1969, he stated, 'I really think that ['Glensavage Gem'] has a better head than anything else I have got.' Earlier, on 10 October 1968, he had congratulated Miss Findlater on producing a completely new strain of '*Nerine*'. In January 1976, Mr Norris remarked that 'Your "Glensavage Gem" continues to produce one of the best flowers in [my] collection and I like it very much'. The praise continued in a letter dated 22 February 1977–'I think "Glensavage Gem" is quite one of the best'. In August 1982, after Doris Findlater's death, Tony Norris paid this tribute to her–'[She] will always be remembered by many who grow *Nerine* for her hybrids–especially "Glensavage Gem" which is now growing in many lands. I have sent bulbs of this variety to America, Japan, Australia and New Zealand . . . I rate it amongst the best. However it is a pity that there is no *Nerine* that carries her name . . .' It is still in cultivation and is depicted in Walsh and Nelson, *An Irish Florilegium 2* (1988).

2. 'Glensavage Glory'–flowers rose opal [622/1]; stem to 30 in., leaves c. 13 in. long and 2 in. broad, mid-green; perianth segments 2¼ x 7/16 ins. Name not published.
3. 'Silchester Rose'–flowers in late September, leaves mid-green about 7½ in. long, ¾ in. across; stem to 20 in., perianth segments 1½ x ⅜ in.
4. 'John Fanning'–flowers in late October, leaves dark green, bluish on the back, 12 in. long, to ¾ in. across. Flowers full claret-rose [HCC 021 to 21/1], segments 2 x ⅜ in . . .

Nerine John Fanning' is depicted (with 'Glensavage Gem') in *An Irish Florilegium* 2 (1988).

5. 'Sheila'–leaves 6 in. long, dark-green, stem to 20 in. Flowers rose-opal with a slightly, deeper stripe which is crimson [HCC 22/1 fading 22/2]. Perianth segments 2 x ⅜ in., early September.

Miss Findlater took this to the Royal Horticultural Society in London in 1971, where it was greatly admired. In particular it impressed H. J. Paul Wülfinghoff of Rijswijk in

Holland, who asked to purchase bulbs of it; Miss Findlater sold bulbs to Wülfinghoff Freesia BV in January 1974. She also supplied Wülfinghoff with the Glensavage Nerine cultivars No. 1 ('Glensavage Gem') and No. 10 ('Alfino'). It is not known if 'Sheila' is still in cultivation in Holland.

Notes and references

1 *Church Gazette,* February 1942
2 *The Lady of the House,* November and December 1913 and January 1914, 'Woman's Life in the Dublin Slums'
3 *History of The Irish Girl Guides'* Baden-Powell National Memorial Cottage, Enniskerry, Co Wicklow, booklet compiled by Doreen Bradbury, 1999
4 Geraldine Mitchell *Deeds not words, The life and works of Muriel Gahan* Dublin: Town House 1997 pp 153, 173, 177
5 IAOS Annual Report 1910 quoted in Trevor West *Horace Plunkett–Co-operation and Politics-* Gerards Cross: Colin Smythe 1986 pp 102-103
6 *Moorea—the Journal of the Irish Garden Plant Society* Vol 7 Sept. 1988 pp 27–32
7 *Ibid.*

13. My father Dermot from 1905 to the end of the Emergency

Dermot, who was to see the firm through the grim years of 'the Emergency' and the 1950s, was born in October 1905, the youngest of his family. He had three sisters, Marjorie, Doris and Sheila, and a brother Desmond, who died aged two in 1900. Dermot's early schooling was at Avoca in Blackrock. A little essay has survived from his kindergarten days in which he surveys his eventual inheritance:

> There are 13 Findlaters, the biggest is Sackville Street, and I think the second biggest is Howth and Dalkey and I think all the rest are about the same. Sackville Street is very big; it has four big offices and a terribly big cellar and rooms full of pepper and tea. One day when I went in one of the people brought me in to see the pepper room and she said that I would sneeze but I didn't and she did.
>
> There is a big room full of salt and a place where you clean bottles, that is a thing with little brushes on it which you put through the bottles, and then you turn it round, when the bottles are clean you take them off and put wine into them and then you put the corks on and they are ready to sell and they have a great number of weighing machines and a great many stables.
>
> As well as cleaning bottles they make bags to put tea into, the way they make them, they have some silver coloured paper and a square piece of wood, they first get the paper and shape it into a rough square and then they put the wood into it and that shapes it, then you put the tea in and close it up, and they clean currants and weigh them and put them into bags.
>
> Dalkey shop is fairly big and it has a little garden and some stables in the back, and they sell ham and biscuits and flowers etc.
>
> All the shops have lots of horses and stables and carts and motor vans.
>
> The End G. D. Findlater

At the age of twelve, in 1917, Dermot went to Portora Royal School in Enniskillen and in 1920 to St Bee's School in Cumberland, now Cumbria. I imagine this schooling reflects the uncertainties of the period and the desire to get him educated and equipped to face whatever the future threw up. Though safely in England, St Bee's was only a rail journey away from the Liverpool boat home. He enjoyed St Bee's, was on the 2nd rugby XV, a sergeant in the Officers Training Corps (compulsory at the time) and a school prefect.

A few days before his Confirmation he received a letter from his local Church of Ireland Rector, Canon Dobbs of All Saints, Blackrock, whom we have already met as a friend of my aunts. The characteristic mixture of piety, a breezy public school bluffness, a sense of historic certainties being abandoned, combined with

This postcard, sent to Dermot while at school in England, must have been a little unnerving.

a confident sense of what God likes and does not like, could never have come from the pen of an Irish Catholic priest. It provides an insight into the moral atmosphere in which the young Dermot was raised, at least by his mother, a favourite of the Canon's. The fact that he kept the letter suggests that it was taken seriously by its recipient.

> My dear Dermot . . . I wonder is there any use my giving you a bit of advice about things in general? I'm an ancient antiquated greybeard, thousands of years old, and you are one of the young bloods and it is not easy for a Methusalah like me to see things from your point of view. But I'll tell you this. I heard one of the three very greatest English Statesmen of our time, a man head and shoulders above everyone in intellect and character and position—Lord Robert Cecil*—speaking to a huge meeting of English men and the whole burden of his speech was this: that the whole Western world is on the edge of an abyss and European civilisation in the most imminent danger of being utterly destroyed, and that the only thing that can possibly save it is Christianity . . .
>
> So on Monday, you just say to yourself that you've just got to be a genuine out and out Christian at any price, not merely for your own sake, but for the world's sake. So that you may do your part in the saving of it and help to save it. For to make Europe Christian means to make every man and woman in it who has anything to do with the directing of its public life Christian. And some day you have to play your part and take a share in the life of your particular bit of Europe and if you are an out and out Christian you'll always act from the highest motives and inspire other men to do the same. You'll be straight and square and honourable, upright and fair minded, and

* Lord Robert Cecil, English politician who helped draft the Charter of the League of Nations, was awarded the Nobel Prize for Peace 1937.

you'll hate humbug and crookedness like the Devil, and you'll infect other people with your own straightness and so help to shape the destiny of Europe and to save it. . . . You won't become a first-class Christian all at once. It takes time. One dinner doesn't seem to make any difference to the growth of your body. One prayer or one Communion won't make much difference to the growth of the higher part of you either. It is a slow process in either case. You've got to stick to it and the results will come in due time.

After some comments on the importance of controlling one's animal instincts 'until the time comes for their lawful gratification', Canon Dobbs continues:

You ought to make a first-class Christian. You've good stuff in you. Your mother is a grand woman. You are a lucky fellow to be her son. And there is good stuff on your father's side too. The Findlaters are a fine race and go back in long succession through a great line of good, stout, honourable Scotchmen. And all that ought to stand to you. It's a good clear, wholesome strain. It's the strain God likes immensely—straight and strong. I'm sure God hates weak, namby pamby sort of people. Strength—the strength which is very gentle and true and kind—is what God likes because it is what he can best use for the big job of cleaning up the world. And you ought to be strong like that because of the stock you spring from.

Well, God bless you and give you the strength you most need, and make a man of you, a true, straight, brave, honourable, gentleman. You can't be anything better than that, for that, after all, is just what our Lord wants. I'll pray some sort of a prayer like that for you on Monday.

Ever yours affectionately, Harry B. Dobbs

If ever I can be of use to you, mind you write–or come and see me!

After St Bee's Dermot spent a year at Dijon University, where he acquired a knowledge of, and made friends in, the wine industry. It would have been expected that he would have then gone to Dublin University (Trinity College) where his father and four of his uncles had graduated, one in medicine, one each in law and engineering and two in philosophy. But Dermot had taken a strong dislike to Trinity, so much so that when it came to my turn, it was only after the intervention of my godfather, surgeon Nigel Kinnear, that agreement was grudgingly given, providing that I did an apprenticeship in the firm at the same time, and the reason may be found in Terence Brown's analysis:

In the 1920s and 1930s Trinity suffers one of its bleakest periods. The buildings and grounds became dilapidated and a little unkempt. A sense of isolation and economic insecurity was not alleviated by much intellectual or imaginative enterprise. Many of the graduates sought their careers abroad and the college was unable to play its part in the developing life of the Free State in the way the National University did. Indeed the college in the centre of Dublin bore in its isolation and decline a striking resemblance in social terms to the Big House of the countryside—each symbolising a ruling caste in the aftermath of its power.[1]

Dermot chose the grocery trade and served his apprenticeship at Coopers, the

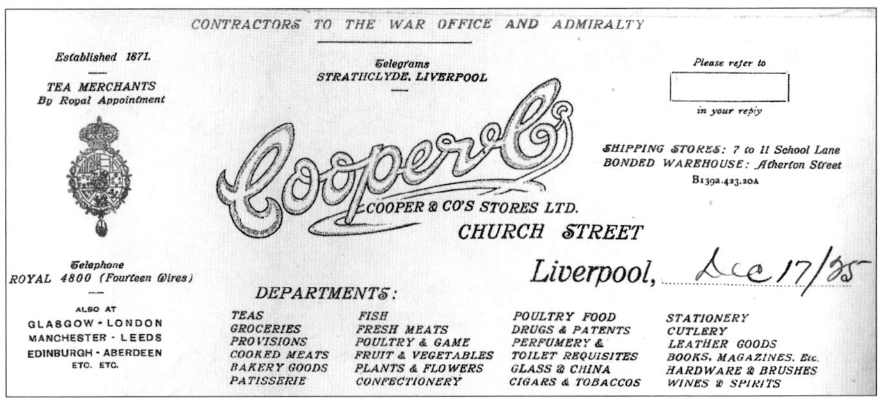
CONTRACTORS TO THE WAR OFFICE AND ADMIRALTY

Established 1871.

TEA MERCHANTS
By Royal Appointment

Telegrams
STRATHCLYDE, LIVERPOOL

Please refer to
in your reply

Cooper & Co

SHIPPING STORES: 7 to 11 School Lane
BONDED WAREHOUSE: Atherton Street

B139a.423.20A

COOPER & CO'S STORES LTD.
CHURCH STREET

Telephone
ROYAL 4800 (Fourteen Wires)

Liverpool, Dec 17/25

ALSO AT
GLASGOW · LONDON
MANCHESTER · LEEDS
EDINBURGH · ABERDEEN
ETC. ETC.

DEPARTMENTS:

TEAS	FISH	POULTRY FOOD	STATIONERY
GROCERIES	FRESH MEATS	DRUGS & PATENTS	CUTLERY
PROVISIONS	POULTRY & GAME	PERFUMERY &	LEATHER GOODS
COOKED MEATS	FRUIT & VEGETABLES	TOILET REQUISITES	BOOKS, MAGAZINES, Etc.
BAKERY GOODS	PLANTS & FLOWERS	GLASS & CHINA	HARDWARE & BRUSHES
PATISSERIE	CONFECTIONERY	CIGARS & TOBACCOS	WINES & SPIRITS

Coopers, where Dermot served his apprenticeship, was a magnificent emporium of foods and associated products.

once great Liverpool grocery and provision emporium. He remained there from 1925 until the beginning of 1927. During this time he applied himself to all the duties of an apprentice, from sweeping the floors and washing down the shop fronts to the finer points of salesmanship and store management. Work began promptly each morning at 8 am, and the store closed at 6 pm. Two nights in the week, the staff worked until 10 pm. In a letter to Willie, the manager of Coopers thought Dermot had coped well with the challenge. 'He has "mucked in" and done his job in a most practical fashion. From my own observation I consider him extremely steady in his work, taking everything most seriously and if early promise goes for anything he has all the makings of a real sound businessman in him.'[2]

While Dermot's mind was firmly made up to enter Findlaters the ladies in the family were showing concern at the turn of political events, for the Civil War was entering its last and most desperate stage. In January 1923, Dr Alex's wife Emily in Edgeware wrote to Dermot's mother in Dublin: 'I am sure it must be awful in Ireland now, you really ought to leave it and start something over here. There is no chance of making good for anyone, when there is no law or protection of property.' A few days later Horace Plunkett's house in Foxrock was burnt to the ground. As it happened, the Civil War was not to last beyond May of that year.

In 1927, Dermot finished his training and joined the company. The directors were keen to benefit from the knowledge that he had acquired in Liverpool and after a little over a year he was invited to join the board. He wasted no time in making changes in O'Connell Street and by August 1929 was able to advise customers: 'We have enlarged our Butter and Provision department, and fitted them with up-to-date and hygienic fittings. We have opened a Delicatessen and also a Cooked Meat department. We have enlarged our Cake and Confectionery department, also have added the following departments a) Poultry and Dog Foods b) Patent Medicines, Toilet Requisites and Infants and Invalids Foods c) Chandlery which will contain a few items of hardware.' A few years later the *Irish Grocer* (August 1933) described how this appointment worked out, espe-

HORSE SHOW NUMBER See our Stand No. 3 CENTRAL HALL

ALEX. FINDLATER & CO., LTD.

Head Office—UPPER SACKVILLE ST., DUBLIN.

MONTHLY SHOPPING GUIDE.

Try FINDLATER'S OXFORD LUNCH CAKES

No. 29 AUGUST 1929

This Month's AFCOGRAM

A Fruit which many of us have never tasted as it rarely appears in the fresh fruit markets.

SUPREME QUALITY

LOGANBERRIES

in Sweet Syrup.

No. 2 Tins 1/2 each. Per doz. Tins 13/6

The first arrival of new Season's Dessert Loganberries. Choice grade fruit possessing the distinctive flavour allied to both the Raspberry and Brambleberry.

A New Department

Owing to a quickly increasing demand for **delicacies** of various kinds, both English and Foreign, we have just opened a new department in our Head Office for all varieties of **delicatessen** goods. This department is fitted with all the latest hygienic fittings. A full list of goods stocked will be found on the two centre pages of this issue. They are well worth looking over. These goods are not stocked by our branch houses, so if your account is with a branch house send your order to our Head Office on a postcard and we will deliver the goods to you through the branch at which you usually deal.

ALFA PEACHES, per large Tin 1/6

ALEX. FINDLATER & CO., LTD.

(FINDLATERS LIMITED)

HEAD OFFICE—FINDLATER'S CORNER, DUBLIN

Monthly Shopping Guide

PÂTÉ DE FOIS GRAS, 2/6, 3/9, 5/6, 10/6, 21/-

No. 38 MAY 1930

AFCOGRAM

This month's Speciality or AFCOGRAM is a new product from our model bakery—

ALMOND GINGER BREADS

1/6 each

These are made from a Yorkshire Parkin recipe, decorated with burnt Valencia almonds and flavoured with finest ginger preserve. Each Cake is wrapped in cellophane transparent paper in the interests of hygiene.

WINE DEPARTMENT

In the last two issues of this Shopping Guide we have called the attention of our customers to our choice old bottled Clarets in ½ bottles. Several customers are now ordering these regularly, evidently having a small bottle for dinner each evening. For those who buy in dozen lots we make the following offers:—

HALF BOTTLES

Medoc	16/- doz.	Chateau des Andiottes	26/- doz.
St. Julien	20/- „	Chateau Le Monteil Segur	29/- „
St. Emilion	23/- „	Chateau Leoville Barton	32/- „

Chateau Palmer Margaux .. 35/- doz.

August 1929 — May 1930

Little 12 page shopping guides were issued monthly in the 1920s and 1930s. The system of monthly special promotions, called 'Afcograms', continued into the 50s. I remember once naively looking for the word in the dictionary!

cially in the early days of the Economic War:

> It may be safely assumed that the fine record which Messrs Findlaters have maintained during the past few years is due, in no small measure, to the progressive outlook and capacity of Mr Dermot Findlater. He takes not only a great interest in his business, he practically lives for it. Such an attitude in a young man of 28, is indeed remarkable . . . his business day is very full. He attends to the buying of all the firm's commodities, in addition to advertising, inspection of branches, tea tasting, and the interviewing of the many members of the staff. Lately, buying has become the most difficult duty to perform. In addition to watching the markets, it is now necessary to watch the exchanges as well. It is almost impossible to know at what price goods purchased on contract from abroad may be delivered, owing to the extraordinary fluctuations in the money markets of the world.

In 1932 Dermot married Dorothea, eldest daughter of Harry and Selina (née Knox) de Courcy-Wheeler of Robertstown, Co. Kildare. They had five children: Jeanette, born in 1934, myself, born in 1937, followed by Grania 1939, Suzanne 1942 and John 1948. Dermot settled down to life as a family man, a businessman, and (as was common among the Findlaters and Wheelers) a man devoted to his sport. He first appeared on the hockey field in 1927 where he played on the left wing for Three Rock Rovers and gained junior interprovincial honours for Leinster. Somewhat later his club was short a goalkeeper, Dermot volunteered for the hazardous position, acquired the gear, practiced assiduously and became the regular and reliable custodian of the position on the 1st XI.

Dermot and Dorothea on their wedding day (Lafeyette)

He was captain of the club first XI in 1935/36 and also captained the all-victorious Irish touring team, the Buccaneers, at the 1939 English Folkestone Easter Festival. The Buccaneers were drawn from Three Rock Rovers, Trinity College and players of international standard. It was an honour to be invited to join them. On this occasion Dermot refused a fixture with the German touring side whose practice it was to give the Nazi salute before the start of each match, when lined up in front of their opposition. One of the local papers reported: 'The Germans "Heiled!" in approved style with right arm uplifted at the beginning of each of their matches, and they played grim, relentless hockey, as if their very lives depended on it. Each player wore a black swastika on his shirt.' The article also added that the spectators 'were a trifle surprised to find that most of the German players were shorter in stature than their English confrères'!

This was the period during which Ireland won the Triple Crown—in 1937, 1938 and 1939, and also in 1947 and 1949. While Dermot never achieved international honours, his wife Dorothea, her mother and two of her aunts all represented Ireland and the subsequent two generations have all turned a good hand at the game. Signal honours go to Dermot's son-in-law, my sister Grania's husband, David Judge, gaining 124 caps for Ireland and 15 for Great Britain (when the four home countries played as one in the Olympic Games), a total that earned him a place in the *Guinness Book of Records*. My mother Dorothea, playing consistently to her 13 handicap, surprised herself and her golf club, Carrickmines, by winning, with her partner Dorothy Beattie, the Irish section of the *Daily Mail* Ladies Foursomes and qualified for the 1981 finals in Hoylake, North Wales. She was applauded by the chairman of the *Daily Mail* for being the most senior participant in this highly competitive tournament.

But it was as an administrator that Dermot excelled. He first came into prominence in 1938 when the debt on the Leinster Branch hockey grounds at Templeogue was causing a serious strain on their minimal resources. To wipe out the debt he formed a club called the Sporting Stiffs; and so that no difference of opinion would ever take place between club officials, he occupied all three positions, that of President, Treasurer and Club Secretary. Only one match was played, on Boxing Day 1938, and the result was a 6-1 victory for the Stiffs. The Stiffs fielded a team of ten Irish Internationals plus Dermot, against a strengthened Three Rock Rovers XI. Membership of the Stiffs was through a little white dice engraved with the letters and figures: H1, O2, C3, K4, E5 and Y6. Everybody desired to have one, enabling the debt to be paid off and the club was disbanded. In the 1940s and 1950s Dermot, with his firm grasp of financial realities, was a dominant figure in Irish hockey as an administrator and organiser of home tournaments and foreign tours.

Dermot in Buccaneers H.C. blazer as 'Mr. Hockey' in the 'Famous Irish Sportsmen', cartoon series by Pike.

Even at school I was aware of my father's ability to organize the most unusual events. I was on the Repton hockey first XI and had suggested to him that it would be nice if he could organise an exhibition match at the school during my final term. Incredibly it came to pass that the full Dutch team, after an international match in Dublin, were diverted on the homebound flight to an airport in England and played an exhibition match against us on Repton's beautifully manicured grass pitch.

Dermot's interests were not confined to hockey. He was a member of the Royal Irish Yacht Club and during the 1930s raced the Water Wag *Alfa* (the brand name used by Findlaters for many of its products). His uncle Herbert had been a member of the Water Wags in 1899, though probably as crew rather than skipper, as he did not have his own boat. *Alfa* was built in 1932, after the original one-design plans had been lost, and models had to be re-created from scratch. Several other Wags were subsequently built from these moulds. The boat was a good one, and under other owners appeared regularly in the prize lists. Dermot was also patron of the Dublin Swimming Club, vice-president of the Howth Swimming Club, patron of the Sub-Aqua Club of Ireland and a vice-president of the Boy Scouts' Association of Ireland.

Canned fruit labels introduced in 1927. Prices ranged from 1s 4d to 1s 6d tin with three for 4s. (1s 6d for a 2lb tin is equivalent to £3 today).

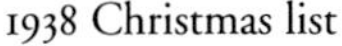

1938 Christmas list

1940 Calendar

1943 Calendar

1944 Calendar

1823—SAW THE BIRTH OF IRELAND'S GREATEST GROCERS

FINDLATER'S

LIMITED

ONE-HUNDRED-AND-TEN YEARS LATER WE ARE AT YOUR SERVICE—1933

WE HAVE *ALWAYS* SPECIALISED IN IRISH GOODS

Hockey in Ireland

Hockey is usually identified as an English game. However T. S. C. Dagg wrote in 1921 that hockey might be described as a scientific development of the ancient Irish *baire*, or game of hurling, which is probably the oldest field game of which any authentic records exists. He goes on to describe a match between the Tuatha De Danann and the Firbolgs in BC 1272. In *The Irish Sportsman* of 11 January 1879 under 'Hurley notes' stated that amongst those members of the Dublin University Hurling Club who had retired from the field were Palmer, Blood, Findlater, Ross and Caulfield, 'who have all done much towards the progress of hurling in this, its native country'. The Findlater is most likely nineteen-year-old Alex, studying medicine. The previous year High School first XII beat the University second XII by 4 goals and 1 disputed goal to 1 goal. In a report on another match there is mention of a missed 'puck' at goal and 'dribbling', and of the goalkeeper deliberately taking the ball in his hand and throwing it away. On another occasion both teams played splendidly, or rather 'savagely'. A bit of hockey and a bit of hurling perhaps.

In October 1878 there were six clubs in Dublin and they were 'forming their rules to coincide with the English rules' so that a team could go on tour there. In the following year the first meeting of an Irish Hurling Union was held in Trinity College. At this stage the games of hurling and hockey seemed to diverge. Laws were introduced in hockey denying players the freedom to 'push, hold or trip an adversary, or to strike out or crook his hurl or throw his own'. No one was allowed to play with his stick on his left side and kicking the ball forward was abolished. Over the ensuing decade a dispute broke out. Thus the Gaelic Athletic Association was formed in 1884 and espoused the ancient, southern, wilder and more airborne form of hurling often played with one whole parish against another with the parish boundaries as goals or from ditch to ditch in a large field, the number of players being between fifteen and twenty-one. Wrestling was permitted up to the end of

1886. When two players came into collision they at once got into handigrips. Only one fall was allowed. Trinity College adopted the new rules of the game drawn up by the Hockey Association in England using a heavier, harder ball which led to the ball more often being played along the ground and requiring flatter playing fields. Sticks were still made of ash, oak or gorse but the width was restricted. The umbilical cord was finally cut in 1893. Dublin University Hockey Club was founded followed by six others including Three Rock Rovers, Corinthians and Monkstown, Herbert Findlater being the initiator of this latter club. In the same year the Irish Hockey Union came into being. [3]

Although these were good contributions, it was in running the business that Dermot was to gain national recognition. The 1930s were a time of much change in Ireland. In 1932 Fianna Fáil, under Éamon de Valera, gained power, and inherited serious economic problems. As Tony Farmar wrote in the *History of Craig Gardner*, 'The yield on key taxes had fallen alarmingly. Consumption of alcoholic drinks had been slipping since 1924, exports were in serious decline, agricultural prices were down and unemployment up.'[4] De Valera immediately set about trying to implement the Sinn Féin vision of Ireland as an independent, rural republic detached certainly from Britain and to a degree from the world at large. He sought to abolish the offensive aspects of the Treaty of 1921 such as the Oath of Allegiance to the Crown, he downgraded the role of the Governor-General and, crucially, withheld certain annuities due to Britain under terms of agreements entered into by the previous administration. In response, the British government established tariffs on Irish agricultural produce, which provoked in return further Irish tariffs on British goods and the two countries entered on a state of economic warfare:[5] At this time the Free State imported £32m worth of goods annually from Britain which represented 8 per cent of the country's total trade. For the Free State, on the other hand, Britain represented 95 per cent of all exports.[6] As a leading banker once said to me, 'It was not very clever of Dev to cut off his best customer, but to cut off his only customer was an act of complete folly.'

De Valera's Minister for Industry and Commerce was Seán Lemass, a wholehearted believer in the Sinn Féin approach, but lacking a good grasp of the way the food economy operated. One of his first presentations to the new cabinet, just after the Economic War was set in train, took a melodramatically gloomy view of the Irish economy: 'The situation is black,' he said, 'we have reached a point where collapse of our economic system is at hand. By collapse I mean famine conditions for a large number of our people. You will ask how there can be famine in a country which produces more food than it can consume. Famine can come not because our farmers cannot but because they will not continue to produce food.' (Given the aggressive economic policies he was planning to pur-

1937 Calendar

1942 Calendar

1941 Calendar and 1940 Christmas list

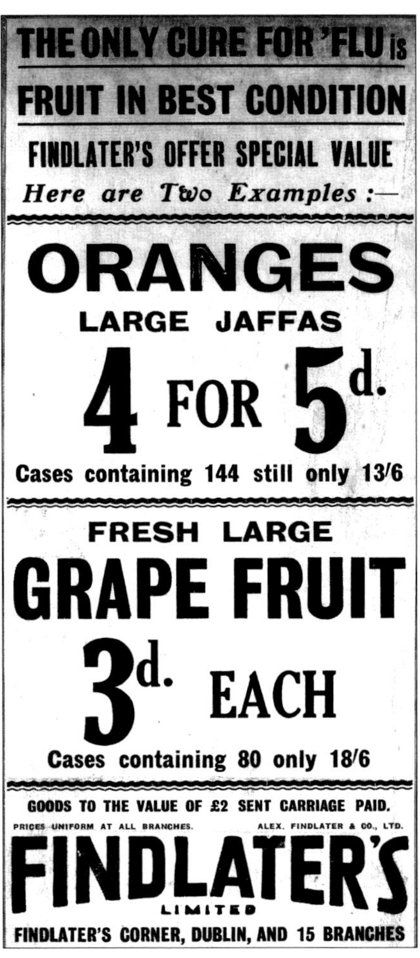

THE ONLY CURE FOR 'FLU is
FRUIT IN BEST CONDITION
FINDLATER'S OFFER SPECIAL VALUE
Here are Two Examples :—
ORANGES
LARGE JAFFAS
4 FOR 5d.
Cases containing 144 still only 13/6
FRESH LARGE
GRAPE FRUIT
3d. EACH
Cases containing 80 only 18/6
GOODS TO THE VALUE OF £2 SENT CARRIAGE PAID.
PRICES UNIFORM AT ALL BRANCHES.
ALEX. FINDLATER & CO., LTD.
FINDLATER'S
LIMITED
FINDLATER'S CORNER, DUBLIN, AND 15 BRANCHES

This hardhitting advertising of the early 1930s was typical of Dermot's approach to promotion

sue, it is not impossible that Lemass decided to soften up potential opposition with this kind of analysis.) Among his new policies were the establishment of the Industrial Credit Corporation, restriction of foreign ownership of Irish manufacturing concerns, and wholesale tariff protection. Within a few months the Free State passed from being a predominantly free-trading country to one of the most heavily protected economies in the world. At the end of 1931 there were tariffs on 68 articles; by 1936 281 items were covered, and by the end of 1937 it was calculated that 1,947 articles were subject to restriction or control.[7] However, on the other side of the balance sheet, employment in industry rose from 110,588 in 1931 to 166,513 in 1938 and industrial output rose by 40 per cent between 1931 and 1936.[8]

Dermot identified with the new Ireland and its institutions. His promotion and advertising were forceful and forward-looking and a number of his initiatives were the first of the era. Large display advertisements in the press were the norm. In 1934 he took a four page supplement in the *Irish Press* (the first four page food supplement printed in an Irish newspaper), undeterred by what has been described as the paper's 'partisan, bitter and uncompromising' treatment of opponents of Fianna Fáil.[9] Price lists were issued every month. Consignments of special value were sought out and promoted with vigour. He was young, clear-headed, energetic and totally immersed in his work. He knew his market and he knew his sources of supply.

At this time the trade magazine *The Irish Grocer* produced a recommended price list for various products, and by comparison with Findlaters' monthly lists we can see that we were usually able to maintain a slight edge in quality and pricing. For instance, in September 1936, where the Grocery Trades Association suggests 3d per lb for cocoa shells, Findlaters have them at 4d; first quality strawberry jam, GTA 11d, Findlaters 1s; tea, best quality Indian, GTA 3s 6d, Findlaters 4s; on the other hand, sugar (presumably as a result of adroit bulk buying) is cheaper at Findlaters—3¼d per lb to the GTA 3½ per lb.

This was still a world where the large grocers such as Dermot did their own international purchasing in bulk (through Dublin-based commercial agents such as Wilfie Weir and his son trading as W. F. Weir Ltd who were also the agents for the highly successful Mazawattee tea at the time). The trade journal has two pages of lists of prices from London and Liverpool of all sorts of goods which read like the obscurer pages of today's *Financial Times*–for instance, rice ('Rangoon Two Star, ex-warehouse on spot 9s'), tapioca, sago (quiet, spot sellers 13s 6d), macaroni, various types of tea (Indian, Ceylon, Java and China), sugar, coffee ('a few sales of Mysore and East Indian at 48s per cwt; Jamaican grades are offered at 70s and Kenyan at 49s to 56s 6d'), currants, sultanas ('Australians are in good demand . . . Smyrnas and Greeks are in extremely limited supply. Stocks of Cretans are practically exhausted'), fresh and dried fruit, and of course spices—pepper ('Lampong black spot 2¼d per lb, forward Aug/Oct 2d cif'), ginger ('demand quiet, Cochin fair washed unbleached 85s, African bleached 75s to 85s'), cloves, mace, cinnamon, and nutmeg.[10] Another two pages in the same paper gave the prices of such wares in Dublin for the benefit of those buying smaller quantities.

It was perhaps inevitable that Lemass and Dermot, who were so different in background, beliefs and experience, should fail to see eye to eye. Lemass himself over-estimated the degree to which Ireland could cut itself off from the rest of the world, as the Fine Gael leader James Dillon pointed out:[11] 'The country seems to think it can cut itself off from the rest of the world, and by doing that save itself from the consequences of its own economic folly.'

FINDLATER'S
WEEK-END OFFERS

GROCERIES

I Large No. 2 Tin Pine Apple Slices
I Tin Cleeves Irish Cream
PARCEL COMPLETE
10½d.

Finest Dessert PRUNES Per 6d. lb.

Findlater's CREAMY CUSTARD Per 9d. tin

TEA

Finest Indian Blends - 1/4, 1/6, 2/- to 3/4 lb.
Pure China Tea - - 3/6 and 3/10 ,,
Fine Ceylon - - 3/- and 3/4 ,,

FRUIT

MELONS from 6d. each

EGG PLUMS 12 lbs. for 3/6, or 4/6 CARRIAGE PAID

PURPLE PLUMS 12 lbs. for 5/6, or 6/6 CARRIAGE PAID

BUTTER

CORK BUTTER ... ... 1/1 lb.
CREAMERY BUTTER ... ... 1/4 lb.
PRIMROSE HILL (1lb. Packets) ... ... 1/5 lb.
EVERY POUND Guaranteed 16 ozs. NET.

CREAM

FINDLATER'S FRESH RICH CREAM - 3d. 6d. 11d.

EGGS

1/-, 1/2, 1/4 doz.

BACON

	Limerick Smoked and Dry Salt Cured.	Limerick Pale and Dry Salt Cured.	Kehoe's Irish. Smoked	Pale
Back	1/6	1/5	1/4	1/3
,, Wide ...	1/5	1/4	1/3	1/2
Streaky	1/4	1/3	1/1	1/-
,, (Narrow)	1/2	1/-	11D.	10D.
Hock	6½D.	6½D.	6D.	6D.
Flank	5D.	4D.	5D.	4D.
Collar	11D.	10D.	10D.	9D.
,, (Whole)	10½D.	9½D.	9D.	8½D.
Gammon (Whole)	1/2	1/1	1/1	1/-
,, (Corner)	1/4	1/3	1/3	1/2
,, (Centre)	1/5	1/4	1/4	1/3
,, (Shanks)	1/1	1/-	1/-	11D.
Sides	1/1	1/-	11D.	10D.

CARRIAGE PAID ON GOODS TO VALUE OF £2 AND UPWARDS TO ANY PART OF IRELAND.
PRICES UNIFORM AT ALL BRANCHES.

FINDLATER'S
LIMITED
ALEX. FINDLATER & Co., Ltd., Findlater's Corner, Dublin.
AND FIFTEEN BRANCHES.

Week-end offer August 1933—1s in 1933 is about £2.50 today.

Over the next few years, particularly when Lemass became Minister for Supply, this relationship was to deteriorate; Dermot felt it his duty to point out in public how, in his opinion, the government was mismanaging the supply of crucial grocery items such as tea and bacon. In the 1950s my father conceded that as Taoiseach, Lemass had done a good job, but it had taken him a long time to learn. He declared that no man in Ireland had had as expensive an education as Seán Lemass, for which the nation had paid dearly—as James Dillon put it, the end of the trade war was a return to political and economic sanity, but it had 'cost the country £50m to educate Fianna Fáil'.[12]

On the whole, however, Dermot was happy with the high tariff policy. On 3 December 1936 he reviewed the relations existing between consumers, retailers and manufacturers in a speech to a meeting of the National Agricultural and Industrial Development Association at the Mansion House, which was reported by *The Irish Times* on the following day:

> He reminded those present that their association had been in existence since 1905 and was the central rallying point for the defence and promotion of Irish Industry. Its influence, he asserted, counted for much in preparing the way for the new policy in 1932. Mr Findlater concluded that, on the whole, the policy was being worked out well. One good feature, as he noted, is that the new industries have not been crowded together in a few selected spots, but have been spaced as widely as possible throughout the country, so that nearly every county in the Free State has benefited from the employment which they give. He maintained also that, on the whole, the factories are well-run, that they pay good wages to their workmen, and that the quality and variety of their goods are satisfactory. On the latter point it was inevitable that there should have been some grumbling on the part of consumers, but comparatively small factories, working for a comparatively small internal market, cannot be expected to supply the varied range of goods that can be obtained from the great mass-producing firms in England. The same consideration applies to price. A higher cost of living is one of the penalties which the Free State has to pay for turning out manufactures at home instead of importing them, and the factories themselves cannot be justly blamed for it.[13]

Findlater Mackie Todd's business under the Todd family proprietorship was expanding up and down England and in the words of Roy Jenkins to me 'I well remember the firm . . . they seemed to produce most of the sherry consumed in England around the war years.' Dry Fly, a medium amontillado, was their standard bearer.

The protection policy created the opportunity to establish a local cider industry and in 1936 Dermot, with Willie Magner of Clonmel (who already made a cider, as well as tomato sauces, table waters, and fruit squashes) and Bertrand Bulmer of Hereford, established Bulmer Magner Ltd to produce cider in Clonmel. Dermot was a very hands-on chairman of Bulmers and paid frequent visits to Clonmel. On one occasion there was a large discrepancy in the stocks. It took a lot of ground work to establish that the foreman in production on one side of the road was not on speaking terms with his opposite number in kegging and bottling on the other side and that there had never been any reconciliation of quantities. Elementary, my dear Watson!

Although Dermot was now becoming a publicly recognised leader of the industry, he was not yet boss in Findlaters. My grandfather Willie, now with a convivial preference for Leopardstown, Cheltenham and a few glasses of best Jameson with his cronies in the club, after the Chamber of Commerce meeting or at Rotary, friendly chats with the cabbies and an easy pace of life, was still very much in charge. Dermot, on the other hand was near teetotal and completely and energetically immersed in his work. In these circumstances, father-son conflict is almost inevitable. The father has usually completed most of his lifetime's work by the time the son joins and is happy that everything is running smoothly. The son sees the need for change and is keen to get ahead and implement it, the father has wisdom and conservatism and is averse to excessive risk. The explosions are usually big and of short duration.

The conflict surfaced at a board meeting in 1937 when Willie (seventy) decided to hand over managing directorship to his son-in-law Edmund Mitchell (fifty-eight). Edmund had been on the board since 1920 and assistant managing director since 1922. Dermot, then thirty-two, was surprised and very annoyed, and left the meeting before the vote. The non-executive directors, Lewis Whyte, board member since 1911, James A. Denning, board member since 1917, and James A. Kinnear* (seventy), Company Secretary and with the company since 1889, voted, and the appointment stood. Dermot remained assistant managing director supposedly reporting to Edmund, but was additionally made deputy chairman. An interim board meeting was called during the row to appoint Dermot's unmarried elder sister Doris (forty-two) to the board. She would have been well capable of managing the company. Was this possibly what the old men had in mind if Dermot had not toed the line?

Dermot was dealing with the cut and thrust of everyday trading and the nitty-gritty of management. He had ideas and plans. Edmund, on the other hand, was conservative, strong on the fiduciary aspects of management but with few innovative ideas for the development and modernisation of the company. Theirs was not an easy partnership. But from this point onwards Dermot was *de facto* managing director.

* I met JAK when he was a very old man. He ceremoniously presented me with a signed copy of my great-great-grand-uncle's will (December 1873). He claimed to have known five generations of the family and this was recently confirmed when I found his date of birth, 5 June 1867; he would have been six when Alexander died and twelve on Adam senior's passing.

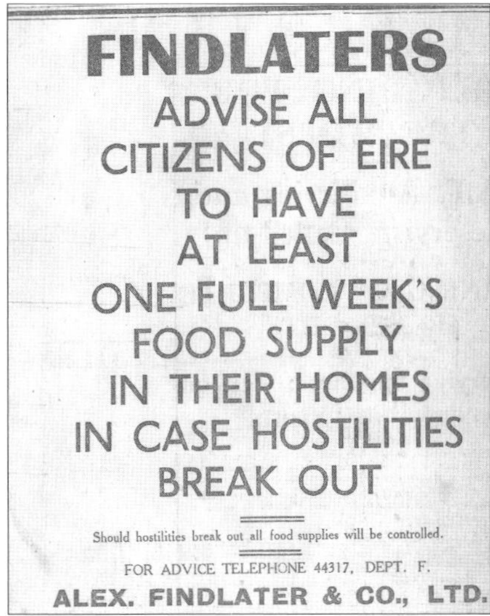
FINDLATERS
ADVISE ALL
CITIZENS OF EIRE
TO HAVE
AT LEAST
ONE FULL WEEK'S
FOOD SUPPLY
IN THEIR HOMES
IN CASE HOSTILITIES
BREAK OUT

Should hostilities break out all food supplies will be controlled.

FOR ADVICE TELEPHONE 44317, DEPT. F.

ALEX. FINDLATER & CO., LTD.

Dermot's advertisement, published a week before the outbreak of war in Europe, caused quite a stir and unfavourable comment in the Dáil.

By the late 1930s it was obvious to most people that a major war was coming. Hitler's Germany was becoming increasingly aggressive and it was unlikely that France, the Soviet Union or Britain would tolerate the threat to the balance of power for long. In 1938 the Munich Crisis provided a relief, but many feared it would only be temporary, as it proved. For Ireland, and for Findlaters in particular, war would expose the dependency of the economy, despite the brave words of the previous decade. Many of the most basic goods were imported through Britain, including tea, coffee, sugar, wheat for white bread and petrol, as were more luxurious goods such as wine, chocolate, soap and silk stockings. De Valera had long since declared that in the event of a European war, Ireland would remain neutral. However, the experience of the last years of the First World War had showed how easy it was for Germany to blockade Ireland, and how quickly shortages would be experienced. There was virtually no Irish mercantile fleet and it was unlikely that Britain would be inclined to allow too many of its sailors to die in the process of shipping tea and wheat to Dublin.

In this context, a week before the war broke out, on 24 August 1939, Findlaters took large advertisements in the newspapers announcing that: FINDLATERS ADVISES ALL CITIZENS OF EIRE TO HAVE AT LEAST ONE FULL WEEK'S FOOD SUPPLY IN THEIR HOMES IN CASE HOSTILITIES BREAK OUT. This advertisement was severely criticised in the Dáil by government ministers. One minister went so far as to say that we were creating a panic, and that no matter how long the war went on no rationing would be necessary in this country. The advertisement may not have been tactful, but Dermot was one of the country's largest distributors of food and his particular expertise was in sourcing commodities both nationally and internationally. To hear government ministers spouting such nonsense must have infuriated him. His real aim in fact was not to earn a quick profit by creating a scare, but to free up warehouse space. Lemass was new to the food industry and had a tough job keeping the country fed. Dermot offered his help, and, the day before war broke out, was politely refused, in the best civil service manner.

'The roads being impassable as a result of the recent snow-storm, Messrs Alex. Findlater & Co., Dublin, availed of the Iona National Airways service to send food supplies to isolated areas in Co. Meath. Photo shows the plane being loaded at Kildonan Aerodrome, Finglas'.
Irish Independent, 1 March 1933

The van, Leyland IF 2507, was based in the Egyptian desert during World War 1

2nd September 1939.

Dear Mr. Findlater,

I have to acknowledge your letter of the 1st instant and on behalf of the Government to thank you for your offer of assistance in the present emergency which will be very gladly availed of should the need arise.

With best wishes.
Yours sincerely, Seán Lemass
Department of Industry and Commerce

On the day after Lemass wrote to Dermot, Neville Chamberlain announced on the BBC that Britain was now at war with Germany, and Éamon de Valera confirmed Ireland's neutrality. A week later, on 11 September, de Valera announced the setting up of a Department of Supplies under Seán Lemass. This was immediately followed by the Emergency Powers Control of Prices (No. 1) Order fixing prices at those ruling on 26 August previous. This was coupled with a severe warning against hoarding.

The first months of the war were a time of frequent government warnings about the unfairness of hoarding food, petrol and other supplies, and hints that petrol would soon have to be rationed. The Government announced a new form of compulsory tillage: at least 12½ per cent of all holdings of over ten acres would have to be made available for tillage, and whole page government advertisements extolled the virtues of potatoes, the perfect diet, full of vitamins and easy to grow anywhere.[14] Agreement was reached between Dublin and London that Britain would take 2000 tons of Irish butter and the whole of Ireland's exportable surplus of bacon.[15]

The plain people of Ireland faced the conflict with mixed feelings. The October issue of *The Irish Tatler & Sketch* in 1939 was headed by an editorial which addressed one point of view: 'The third of September changed the whole face of the world. . . . we are fortunate in being one of the neutral states yet even in our neutrality we must suffer the effects of the terrible upheaval. The one idea for the time being is to try and keep Ireland as sane as possible. There is the need for entertainment and social activities . . . our theatres here are evidence of public opinion and next month dances are to take place.' Brave words, and so it worked out—and the new legend of Ireland as a haven of welcomes—'away from it all'—took root! Our neutrality was qualified—anyone who wanted to go and fight the Nazi menace could do so—and thousands did, if only in the certain prospect of finding work. Once more Irish generals found fame in foreign battles, whether as staff-planners or actively leading armies to victory. Meanwhile *The Irish Tatler,* in common with others, faced drastic paper rationing and suspicious censors, while the urban citizenry coped with extreme restrictions in fuel, services and supplies.

Dermot took his position as one of the largest food suppliers in the country extremely seriously. As news came month after month of shortages of this commodity or that, he was regularly asked for his comment by the press. In the *Irish Press* on 31 January 1941, he observed that 'two ounces of tea per week is quite a reasonable ration, except in the west, where tea drinking is considerable. It will mean a little cutting down.' But within a year the ration would be down to half an ounce and all levels of society resorted to recycling tea leaves. Dandelion tea was another alternative. Tea registration cards were introduced.

Tea had traditionally been bought through the London market where Dermot had good contacts. Wartime conditions made this unsatisfactory. These included a resentment in London official circles against Irish neutrality, which manifested itself in a petty tendency to demonstrate to the Irish just how dependent they were on British goodwill. In June 1941 Seán Lemass announced the setting up of Tea Importers Ltd to purchase direct from India, the main source of supply in those days. In February 1942 the *Irish Independent* announced that 'Assigning delays in the shipment of teas to this country as the reason for being unable to increase the ration, Mr Lemass, Minister for Supplies, has announced that consumers must each be still content with one half ounce per week . . . This tea was, as stated by the Minister early last month, to be first shipped to the United States of America and thence conveyed in Irish ships to this country.'[16]

Coffee drinkers didn't fare much better. On 18 July 1941 *The Irish Times* reported that supplies of coffee in England consigned to Éire had been held by the British authorities. It was also stated that no further export licences were to be issued in England: 'The coffee situation looks very serious. Mr Dermot Findlater said that "present stocks of coffee will certainly be exhausted by December or February next at the latest."'

In May 1941 Dermot took out a press advertisement to give his local suppliers a well deserved pat on the back:

> During a period of Emergency such as this, the Manufacturer must change his method of production and the variety of lines which he manufactures; the Wholesaler gets less to distribute to shops; the Shopkeeper gets less to serve from his counters, and the Customer must buy less. When the pebble is dropped in the pool the effects are felt to the very edge. When a lifetime has been spent building up trade, it is hard to believe that some of that hard-won trade must be sacrificed for the common good. For accepting the necessity without complaining, for playing the game fairly, for explaining and easing the situation for their customers: Manufacturers, Wholesalers, Representatives, Staffs in retail shops and Customers of those shops may well feel

See Bacon Prices, page 4

ALEX. FINDLATER & CO., LTD.

(FINDLATERS LTD.)

HEAD OFFICE—FINDLATER'S CORNER, DUBLIN

MONTHLY SHOPPING GUIDE

Try "PAGODA" Oranges, 1/6 doz.

No. 37 APRIL 1930

A New Size

The Heinz Company lately introduced a new size Tomato Sauce to retail at 9½d. After being on the market for a short time however they discovered that it was such good value that people confused it with the 1/- size. They have, therefore, introduced a new pack—a small bottle to sell at 8½d., but have sent all their remaining stock of the 9½d. size to ALEX. FINDLATER & CO., LTD., and authorised them to sell it at the price of the new smaller bottle, namely, 8½d.

HEINZ TOMATO KETCHUP OR SAUCE

Per 8½d. 6-oz. bottle

HOT ✚ BUNS

FINDLATER'S famous Hot Cross Buns are made of the choicest ingredients, well fruited, spiced, and beautifully baked. Please place your orders early for delivery on Thursday, April 17th (Good Friday is on April 18th).

Hot Cross Buns, per 1/- doz.

April 1930

FINDLATER'S SHOPPING GUIDE.

HEINZ
—58th—
VARIETY

New size, **6½d.** per bottle.

New size, **6½d.** per bottle.

CREAM OF ASPARAGUS SOUP is a new addition to the large number of Heinz lines which we stock.

This soup is made from finest green asparagus tips with a garden freshness of flavour hitherto unknown. Most popular on cold days. Medium size only.

CREAM OF ASPARAGUS SOUP,
Per **1/2** tin.

If you are ordering Asparagus Soup for the first time and you mention this month's *Shopping Guide* when ordering, you will only be charged **1/-** per tin.

CREAM OF CORN SOUP.—Something out of the ordinary—and delicious. And wholesome too, for it is made from the hearts of sweet corn—and cream. A soup you'll enjoy. Medium size only.

CREAM OF CORN SOUP.
Per **1/2** tin.

Trial tin **1/-**

To prepare both—Place tin unpierced in boiling water for 15 minutes, then open, placing a cloth around can opener to prevent steam spurting, and place in soup tureen.

TWO LINES in favour during the festive season—

MINCEMEAT .. .. .. per bottle **1/2** & **2/-**

PRESERVED GINGER .. .. per bottle **1/8** & **2/6**

Alex. Thom & Co. Ltd. Dublin.

November 1930

In 1930 Heinz passed their 57th variety with Piccalilli, mixed pickles, cream of asparagus soup and cream of corn soup.

proud of the part they are playing to help this country through this difficult period.

Such was Findlaters' position that Dermot's opinion was not resented—quite to the contrary. As a Dublin newspaper commented:

> That firm is among the largest food retailers in the country and handles an enormous variety of products. That firm gave a magnificent testimonial to our Irish manufacturers. These manufacturers had enabled that firm to maintain its huge turnover because as soon as one article had to be erased from stock owing to impossibility of production the Irish manufacturers had immediately made available an appropriate alternative. These manufacturers had stood loyally behind the firm and the quality and finish of the commodities produced were such that Messrs Findlater with their long experience, expert knowledge and opportunities for comparison were satisfied. A word of praise from a firm of such standing is worth recording.

Johnny McDermott, who then worked for Findlaters as an errand boy remembered ration coupons:

> It originally started great, 2 ounces of tea and a pound of sugar per week—then things got rough and Hitler over ran things and it was reduced to 1 ounce of tea and half a pound of sugar and butter, plus the soap coupons. Half the shops in Dublin had no tea or sugar. They couldn't get supplies. But Findlaters being in such a big way had supplies always, and used to give two weeks' rations instead of one week. Then there were permits. Now, all the diplomats got permits, maybe for a stone of sugar, a month extra plus their rationing of 5 pounds of tea, so much butter and all that, so much soap and all that. The American chargé d'affaires, the American Air Attaché, the American Public Relations, the Belgian Legation, the Swiss Legation—but they never drew rations. All that stuff was sent in direct by their countries. The only one that drew their ration permits and everything was Herr Hempel, the German at 45 Dartmouth Square. Everything was in it there, and there used to be a crowd going into that house, a gangster. Must have been a spy at 45 Dartmouth Square—he was the only one drew them.
>
> I don't know what Williams done with the tea and sugar. I suppose he had clients too, and was able to give them extra tea and sugar and all, some friends and all that. I had a Belgian in Shrewsbury Road—they never drew their permits. Sometimes they would send for what their staff needed, and maybe got 10 pounds of tea and 2 pounds of sugar as England got a grip of the war.

For customers accustomed to Findlaters' delivery service, the years of the Emergency were difficult, as Mary Gunning recalls:

> Findlaters had to stop delivering groceries during the War, on account of the petrol shortage, so my job was to fetch the groceries once a week, riding from Clontarf to Howth with a basketfull in front and a large box on the carrier. I had to wait for a dry day! One day on my way home, I was cycling along the narrow path beside the tram tracks at Raheny when a man who was behind me most of the way came up beside and ran his cycle into mine, knocking me off. He tried to attack me so I struggled and quite accidentally knocked off his glasses. They got broken in the scuffle and he appar-

ently could not see well without them, so I picked up some of the messages and rode like mad, against the wind. I was exhausted when I got home, and very upset. My father went to report the incident to the police. From then on we started dealing in Findlaters of O'Connell Street. My job was to weigh out six ounces of butter for each family member and put it in a glass dish, each portion labelled with a piece of paper on a cocktail stick. They looked like small yachts on the table.

By 1942 bread supplies were being affected. In February the government cut down supplies of flour to bakers to four-fifths of the normal deliveries. In addition, the country was to have darker bread, and it was announced that the Irish mills in future would produce 100 per cent extraction flour. According to the Minister for Supplies, there was now no possibility of making up for 100,000 tons deficit in the wheat harvest, and Irish households would have to be satisfied with four loaves where formerly five were eaten. 'I ask', said the Minister, 'that all those who can afford other foods, and who have the facilities for cooking them, should try to cut out flour and bread almost entirely, and they certainly should not buy more than a quarter of what they formerly bought. New responsibilities are being placed on bread and flour retailers, and on hotels, to ensure that there will be a fair distribution of bread and a drastic restriction in the supply of anything containing wheat to their customers.'[17] As Bernard Share writes in *The Emergency*, bread was part of the nation's staple diet: 'The ending of wheat imports heralded the introduction of the brown or 90 per cent wheat extraction loaf, undoubtedly nourishing but anathema to many Irish palates. The consumer hankered after the white loaf which eventually returned at the end of the

HALLOWEEN PRICE LIST.

ALEX. FINDLATER & CO., LTD.

(FINDLATERS LIMITED)

HEAD OFFICE—FINDLATER'S CORNER, DUBLIN

Monthly Shopping Guide

PRICE LIST OF NUTS—see page 6

No. 43 OCTOBER 1930

This month's AFCOGRAM

This Halloween we ask you to

HELP THE HOSPITALS

by buying one of our

WRAPPED HALLOWEEN

BARM BRACKS

Containing rings at

1/- 1/6, and 2/- each.

Each barm brack contains a ring, but as well as that a minimum of one barm brack in each district in which a branch shop is situated will contain a free ticket in the Hospitals Sweep value 10/- making a guaranteed minimum of 16 tickets. The lucky recipient of each ticket stands a chance of securing part of the sum offered in prizes.

As we were sold out of barm bracks last year, place your order early this year.

HALLOWEEN—OCTOBER 31st

is generally known to us as the kiddies' festival. In the afternoon the children are given a sumptuous tea with "Barm Bracks" containing rings, and after tea we sit round the fire cracking nuts and telling ghost stories. The other customs of bobbing the apple, pouring lead, etc., are well known to all.

Full list of Halloween items, see page 6.

USE PELICAN PINE CUBES, 11½d. tin.

October 1930

Christmas List, 1930

ALEX. FINDLATER & CO., LTD.

Head Office—FINDLATER'S CORNER, Dublin

Established 1823

No. 45 DECEMBER 1930

FINDLATER'S Specialise in

Irish Turkeys and Geese

and will have huge supplies on display during the fortnight prior to Christmas.

Plump hen turkeys, 12-14 lbs. average, are recommended for the average sized family, but birds can be obtained up to 20 lbs. weight.

Turkeys and geese are sold by weight, plucked but not dressed. Customers when placing their orders should state whether the birds are required dressed or not. 1/- per bird is charged for dressing.

We have a special department for packing

IRISH

Turkeys * Hams * Geese

and Spiced Rounds

for despatch to Great Britain and abroad. An Irish Turkey or Ham is a gift which will be really appreciated by your friends not resident in Ireland.

Price of Turkeys and Geese will be advertised in the *Irish Times* and *Evening Herald* during the fortnight prior to Christmas.

December 1930

Free tickets for the very first Hospital Sweepstakes on the November Handicap (10s=£16 today).

war, leaving in its wake an ingrained prejudice against brown bread.'[18]

Indeed, by 3 March 1942, a journalist for *The Northern Whig* wrote, 'I have seen my first bread queue. It was in a mean Dublin street; tired women and pale-faced children stood clutching shopping baskets, looking up at intervals to make sure that the magic notice was still there—"Bread Now Ready, 3¼d. a Loaf". That was for a 1lb loaf.' And by May of that year, to sell or serve bread or wheaten food at dances, races, sports, whist or bridge drives, bazaars, carnivals or work sales became illegal under an order by the Flour and Bread Supplies Controller.[19]

Other foodstuffs affected were bacon, sugar, eggs and oatmeal, the latter virtually unobtainable in Dublin by wintertime 1942 when a substantial cargo of oats had to be purchased for the Irish market in Canada. In April a reduction of 25 per cent in the sugar ration of householders, catering establishments and institutions was made by Order of the Minister for Supplies. The weekly ration of a registered householder became ¼lb for each person specified in the householder's tea or sugar registration forms.

Two months later it was announced that a shortage of bacon would be acute for the following three months, and a few weeks later 'Macon' went on sale: 'Macon,' wrote the *Irish Press,* 'the name applied to the new "bacon" made from mutton—is now on sale in Dublin. Some time after the outbreak of war, the idea of salting and drying mutton was tried out in Britain, in order to relieve the shortage of bacon. It is now being tried here. Lambs have been used for the purpose, and the finished product looks the same as lean bacon rashers when cut, but is darker in colour.'[20]

Indeed, such innovation became commonplace during the war, as can be seen from the following report in *The Waterford News:* 'We learn that, near Bellevue, not far from the city, a factory is established for the making of carrot tea. It seems to be doing well at it as they are employing ten girls and are able to make five shillings per lb charge on their product.'[21]

And as for soap, *The Irish Times* of 19 October 1942 reported:

> The use of fat from the shark and dog fish obtainable off the Irish coasts for the manufacture of a soap substitute is at present being examined, an *Irish Times* reporter learned on Saturday. The fats, as well as a wax obtained from holly leaves, could be used as 'soap fillers' to supplement the soap ration. Both, however, require factory processes, impossible to imitate in the home. The wax from holly leaves can be extracted and milled up along with soap, and, although the result is not '100 per cent', the cleansing properties are only slightly impaired and by lessening the lathering value the soap lasts longer.

By October 1942, the butter rations in Dublin and Bray were reduced from ¾lb to ½lb, a move which angered Dermot:

> The company, during the winter of 1941, realising that, due to the fact that margarine had gone off the market, there would be a greater demand for butter, applied for permission to store 1,000 boxes, (each 56lbs), in addition to the quantity we then held a permit for. The Department concerned refused the necessary permit, but in the

following Spring, when the shortage became apparent, the Minister concerned announced the shortage was due to the fact that traders had not stored sufficient butter.[22]

CHAMPIONSHIP CREAMERY BUTTER 1/4 lb.

ALEX. FINDLATER & CO., LTD.

(FINDLATERS LIMITED)

Head Office: FINDLATER'S CORNER, Dublin.

Monthly Shopping Guide.

HAFNERS SAUSAGES per 1/3 lb.

No. 60. MAY 1933.

This Month's AFCOGRAM

A new department has been opened in all branches except our Sandymount Branch.

ALFA ICE CREAM BRICKS

6d. each.

Our Ices are a dairy product and are made with fresh cream. Doctors recommend them.

OTHER VARIETIES AVAILABLE ARE

Wafers, each	1½d.
Tubs, each	2d.
Fruit Kups, each	3d.
Bricks, each	6d.
Pint Blocks, each	1/6.

The new Ice Cream Department is worked on a special cash basis and no credit whatever may be given.

S. & W. CANNED FRUITS ARE DELICIOUS WITH ALFA CREAM ICES.

May 1933 – ALFA ice creams, but only for cash.

In November 1942, Findlaters were fined £5 on each of two prosecutions for having on 27 March sold ¼lb lard at 3d, the correct price being 2¾ and for having, on 7 February sold ½lb of lard at 6d, an overcharge of ½d. In his defence Dermot stunned the jury with figures. He said the firm had been trading for 120 years. Since the Emergency began they had made 5,773,206 cash sales, and executed 3,579,396 orders, and the only complaint made was in respect of ¼d and ½d. The sales complained of were obviously due to an error on the part of an assistant. Since the emergency began he had issued nearly 400 circulars to his assistants to help them maintain correct prices.[23]

One of the few commodities not yet affected by shortages was wine (which reflected its relatively low popularity at the time). Acccording to the *Irish Independent:*

> While the light table wines of France and Germany are virtually unobtainable in Britain or Northern Ireland, stocks in Éire are by no means exhausted, and bottles are still being retailed at relatively moderate prices. Stocks of French and German wines cannot, of course, be replaced during the war; but Éire, on the whole, is not a wine-drinking country, and a number of still Portuguese white wines are coming into favour. Sherry and port are the two wines in most demand in Éire. There has been a phenomenal increase in the demand for sherry in recent years and this has led to serious inconvenience in the wine trade because sherry is scarce and cargoes from Spain are irregular. The demand for port has remained steady and normal supplies are obtainable. There is a considerable quantity of wine under bond in Éire.[24]

At least there was no danger of drink driving, as in April 1942, private motoring was banned due to a shortage of fuel.

The 'frugal comfort' that de Valera spoke about in his St Patrick's Day broadcast of that year was coming nearer, although there were still few takers for his idea, expressed some years before, that the Irish people would be better off if they drank light beer for breakfast instead of tea.[25]

In the ensuing years relations between Dermot and Seán Lemass became strained. Dermot saw food supply as a technical issue, and he was much better qualified than Lemass in that area. During the Emergency and after, Dermot began to air his increasingly pointed criticisms in public, such as the one reported in *Irish Industry* in 1942: 'We have a half-planned economy in our agriculture, something less in our industry and practically none at all in our distribution, hence nothing but complaints.' And the journal concluded 'businesses, such as Mr Findlater's, run on such a system, would be a catastrophic ruin in six months.'[26]

By 1942 Dermot was reported at the AGM as criticising the government's policies concerning foodstuffs:

> Your directors have had the experience and results of at least four major wars passed down to them and were in a position to judge what would be the results of the present emergency. The Government made no capital available in the early years of the war for firms dealing in essential foodstuffs except in so far as the firms would themselves provide security for loans or overdraft. This was their first great mistake, and, in my opinion, they made another major error—that is, that too often they try to control imports of goods or consumption of goods after a shortage has taken place instead of before it occurs.[27]

Dermot regularly used the firm's AGMs, and occasionally other events, to comment not only on the performance of the company, but also to address government on a wide range of topics. These reports were eagerly reported in the daily papers. In 1944 he spoke on the question of farthings: 'The Government . . . have fixed the price of many items at a price which includes a farthing. This may be satisfactory from the point of view of the cash shop, but it is extremely difficult in the case of credit transactions, and it is hoped that farthings will be eliminated from all price orders in the future.'*

New fruit department at our Dún Laoghaire Branch, 1934

* The farthing was finally withdrawn in 1961.

Directors' pay was an on-going sore: 'The control order concerning remuneration of directors has reacted very unfavourably in the case of this company, for, by a peculiar set of circumstances, your directors now may only receive approximately 75 per cent of the sum paid to the then directors in the pre-emergency period. There are perfectly legal but not desirable ways of overcoming this situation but your directors would not consider acting in a manner contrary to the intention of the order. They hope that this Emergency Powers Order will be revised in the near future.'

The background to this remark was that Dermot had succeeded to the position of chairman and managing director within three months of the passing of the Emergency Powers (No. 83) Order 1941, which had limited firms' ability to raise salaries. So Dermot was precluded from receiving any extra remuneration above the £1,500 he was receiving before his father's death, despite his very considerable added responsibilities. To put this in perspective, his salary was the equivalent of £36,000 a year in current terms, and was at or below that paid to previous managing directors since the incorporation of the company in 1899. Even before that, almost fifty years earlier, in 1894 for example, the managing directors each received £2,442 plus their share in partnership profits. Counsel's opinion was taken on Dermot's unusual position but to no avail until the end of the war.

By the end of 1942, Lemass announced that the worst of the war was still to come:

> During 1941 and 1942 we felt that the war was becoming more remote, moving away from us. Now it is moving westward again, and it seems certain that it is in the west that the decisive battles will be fought. Our dangers are growing, not lessening. Until the last shot has been fired, and perhaps not even then, can we hope for an improvement in our national circumstances or a lessening of the dangers that threaten us. Danger of physical attack is not the only one we have to face. If economic collapse came the workers would suffer most.[28]

In February 1943 the maximum weekly tea ration of a domestic consumer became just one ounce. The other problem with tea making was the fear of the glimmerman. The country was operating on 16 per cent of its gas coal requirement and if the glimmerman called when use of gas was restricted and found the gas jets still warm you could expect no mercy and the bleak prospect of cold dinners.[29]

By March the headlines read NO SUGAR FOR JAM THIS YEAR when Lemass announced that owing to the limited supplies, it would not be possible to make any special allocation that year to enable householders to make jam in the home. That same month it became clear that the shortage of tobacco ranked with that of tea and bread as one of the most serious afflictions of the time.[30] However, smokers' pangs were eased when a shipment of 20 million pure Virginian cigarettes arrived from the United States, to be sold at 2s 4d (6d less than the normal price).

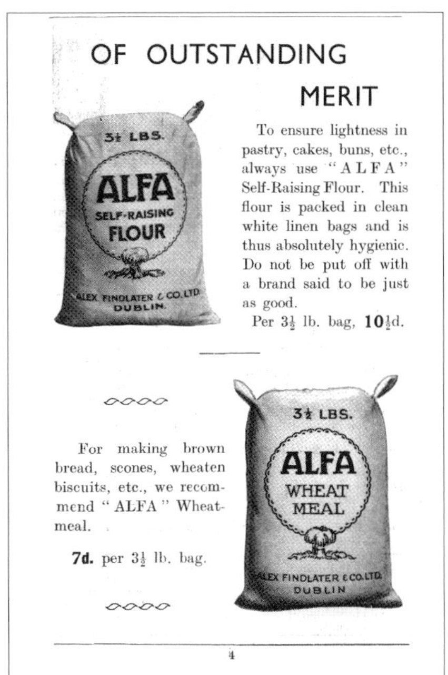

March 1934 ALFA Rolled oats. The 3½lb bag at 1s is the equivalent of £2.30 in the year 2000 against a current price of £1.68. The ALFA brand is growing in strength.

After eight years of very unsatisfactory control it was announced that there would be virtually a free market for pigs in Éire. The only difficulty was that there were very few pigs to market. Indeed, bacon was still in very short supply, and a black market in illegally cured bacon had risen, as *The Irish Times* reported in November 1943: 'Officials of the Pigs and Bacon Commission yesterday raided a number of Dublin hotels and restaurants and seized large quantities of illegally cured bacon. The bacon found in these hotels was unbranded, and all bacon handled by the licensed curers is branded. It is understood that the Commission's objection to illegally cured bacon is based on health grounds, since it is not subjected to veterinary inspection, and the pigs might be diseased.'[31]

If there was any good news on the food market that year it was that, notwithstanding the drop in wheat acreage, the white loaf would be returning to Irish tables the following year. And on 11 November 1943 Lemass announced that white flour would be on sale before Christmas: the flour would be around 85 per cent extraction, made from nine parts wheat and one part barley, and there would be no restrictions on its sale. At the same time he revealed that the government had received advice 'from high medical opinion' that the continuance of the 100 per cent flour was having ill-effects on the health of the people, particularly the young'.[32] So much for the popularity and health giving qualities of wholemeal bread today!

In March 1944 Dermot seized an opportunity to attack Seán Lemass again. Licences had been issued for the export of prune wine (an essence, used as an additive to rum and whiskey) to Britain. Unfortunately for Lemass, the only manufacturer of prune wine in the South was a company that had been inherited by the Secretary of the Department of Supplies, the redoubtable John Leydon. There was of course a political question as to why scarce shipping capacity had been taken up for such a product. At the following AGM Dermot could not resist a comment (which was of course widely reported in the press): 'I still feel that is definitely undesirable that any government official should have any connection with any public or private company. It is high time that legislation was introduced to make it compulsory for such officials to choose whether they wish to give their full time service as a paid official of the State or whether they would prefer to vacate their State appointment and take part in industry or commerce on their own behalf.'[33]

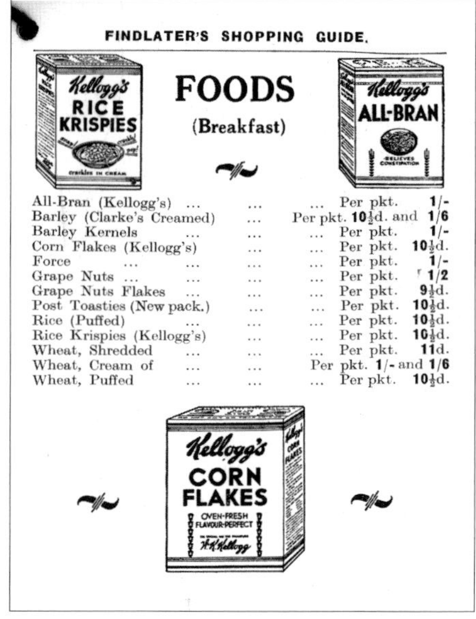

FINDLATER'S SHOPPING GUIDE.

FOODS

(Breakfast)

All-Bran (Kellogg's)	Per pkt. 1/-
Barley (Clarke's Creamed)	Per pkt. 10½d. and 1/6
Barley Kernels	Per pkt. 1/-
Corn Flakes (Kellogg's)	Per pkt. 10½d.
Force	Per pkt. 1/-
Grape Nuts	Per pkt. 1/2
Grape Nuts Flakes	Per pkt. 9½d.
Post Toasties (New pack.)	Per pkt. 10½d.
Rice (Puffed)	Per pkt. 10½d.
Rice Krispies (Kellogg's)	Per pkt. 10½d.
Wheat, Shredded	Per pkt. 11d.
Wheat, Cream of	Per pkt. 1/- and 1/6
Wheat, Puffed	Per pkt. 10½d.

Breakfast cereal prices June 1934. Cornflakes were first listed in 1922 and Kelloggs from 1927. All Bran also dated from 1927. Shredded Wheat was on the market in 1903. 10½d is the equivalent of £2.00 in 2000, somewhat more expensive than a 250 gram packet at around £1.20 today.

A year later Dermot was back on the attack on Leydon's business interests: 'I still feel that it is undesirable that any government official with access to trade returns, or with any say in any capacity to allocate shipping space, should be allowed to have any connection whatsoever with any public or private firm.' These attacks got to Lemass. In one Dáil debate on the subject he retorted: 'It is true that the Secretary of my Department has some interest in that firm, but that firm has been in existence for over seventy-five years, and for that period its trade has extended all over the world. It receives no facilities not afforded to any other firm.'[34] In principal, we can feel that Dermot was right. In practice, Leydon was one of the great Irish civil servants since 1922; as T. K. Whitaker wrote: 'For most of his time in ministerial office, in Industry and Commerce and Supplies, Seán Lemass had the good fortune to be assisted, and at times creatively inspired, by a Permanent Secretary of outstanding quality, John Leydon.'[35] It was not until 1975 (long after his retirement) that Leydon divested himself of his interest in W. & P. Thompson to Maurice Kelly of Kelly & Co.(Dublin).

After four years of war the constant shortages of basic foodstuffs and fuel, the movements of population and the general stress of wartime conditions began to manifest themselves in a steadily worsening tuberculosis epidemic. More and more vulnerable young people died, and influential citizens, including Dermot, became increasingly concerned.

At the time there were 24,000 people with tuberculosis in the twenty-six counties. Between 1942 and 1945 16,186 had died of the disease. In 1943 there were 4,220 deaths. Because of the dread of the social implications—tuberculosis was widely believed to be hereditary—it was not even a notifiable disease (to preserve family sensibilities doctors often concealed the disease on death certificates). The Department of Health at this time was a sub-office of the Department of Local Government. Although the new wonder-drug BCG had been used before the war, it was scarce, and dedicated beds were insufficient. Furthermore, the inadequate social security system encouraged afflicted wage-earners to conceal their illness, especially since everyone knew that a stay in a sanatorium could last as much as a year during which they could earn little or nothing. Until people with TB sought help they only increased their chances of infecting their fellow-workers; delay also meant that when they were forced to present their symptoms to the doctor, they were too far gone for anything to be done.

It took me by complete surprise in 1994 to receive a copy of a book by a former TB sufferer which detailed my father's part in the campaign to eradicate tuberculosis, a story completely unknown to the family. The author Charles O'Connor highlighted the plight of sufferers in a letter to the *Evening Mail* on 17 July 1944. In his book, *The Fight against TB in Ireland in the 1940s*, he takes up the story:

> On the following day the Dublin *Evening Mail* published this letter from Mr Dermot Findlater,
>
> T.B.–MUST THEY DIE?
>
> Sir–Having visited several hospitals in the last fortnight and consulted with some of the staffs, medical and secretarial, and members of the Board, I have reached the following conclusions:
>
> 1. It should be compulsory to notify T.B.
> 2. Bed accommodation in sanatoria should be sufficient
>   a) to enable patients to obtain immediate admission
>   b) to enable patients to remain in the sanatorium as long as considered necessary by the medical staff
> 3. Dependants of persons receiving treatment in sanatoria should receive equal pay equivalent to their usual weekly earnings up to, say, the sum of five pounds per week.
> 4. In all general hospitals there should be a special isolation hut or building.
> 5. In general hospitals only specially trained nurses on special diet, should handle T.B. patients, and such nurses should undergo frequent medical examination.
> 6. Old country houses should be converted into temporary sanitoria without delay.
> 7. Existing sanatoria buildings should be added to to provide extra beds–Government grants should be made to enable this to be done.
> 8. Nurses in sanatoria should live in buildings apart from the main hospital when off duty.
>
> The above suggestions might have the effect of stopping the incidence of the disease until the main Government scheme is produced. The Government must make an immediate move to prevent the spread of this dreaded disease. Sufferers are being daily

condemned to death because treatment is not available NOW.

What can we do? If you know a T.D., a Senator, a member of the Anti-T.B. Section of the Irish Red Cross or a member of the Hospital Commission, we should ask him to do something NOW. If we personally do not know one of the above officials, then we must write and keep on writing to our local T.D. until something is done.

The ever-growing weight of letters and enquiries will enlighten our public representatives to the fact that we, the citizens of Éire, want immediate action and not a scheme in a year, three years' or ten years' time when the position will be far worse. If you do nothing, you too are blameworthy.

Dermot Findlater.*

This letter was followed by a spate of others, together with editorials and reports, over a protracted period, in the Dublin morning and evening newspapers, particularly in the Dublin *Evening Mail*, which devoted two columns on its editorial page to letters from readers. Most of them dealt with the plight and the grievances of persons suffering from tuberculosis, the alarming spread of the disease or epidemic, and the failure of the Government and local authorities to introduce the obvious reforms so urgently needed.

On 26 July 1944 the Post-Sanitoria League was established with the object of securing an immediate improvement in the conditions of those suffering from tuberculosis. At the meeting Dermot said it was his sincere wish that the League would achieve its objects. He commented on the large number of stamps an employed person was required to obtain before he became eligible for any benefits under the National Health Insurance Scheme. He finally commented on the discharge of half-cured patients and their subsequent return to conditions worse than those they had experienced prior to their illness. He then gave the League use of spacious offices and secretarial services, all free of charge, in the Findlater headquarter premises at 28 Upper O'Connell Street.

Large meetings were held in the Mansion House and public authorities canvassed, but progress was slow. Dermot used his company's AGM to highlight injustices in the State and published the text of his speech in full in *The Irish Times*. Charles O'Connor continues: 'Mr Dermot Findlater's interest in the campaign never diminished. While I was in my office in the building adjoining his, he sent for me one morning and told me he was preparing his Report for the following day's annual meeting of his company in which he wished to refer to the allowances and benefits granted to tuberculosis patients. I returned to my office, consulted my files and gave him the figures.'

Here is an extract from the Report Dermot presented to the meeting on 5 June 1945:

My board are aware that I am very interested in the problem of Tuberculosis. It is

* Dermot's interest in the Anti-TB Campaign may have arisen as a result of the failure of the similarly named Anti-Tuberculosis Campaign to get established, after an intervention by the Catholic Archbishop of Dublin, John Charles McQuaid, in an area somewhat outside his remit. As Ruth Barrington put it: 'The Archbishop clearly thought that such a crusade would be safer in the predominantly Catholic hands of the Red Cross.'

. . . . Yes !—It does make things so much easier when one can order all the household supplies by 'phone. Of course with Findlater's it can be done with the utmost ease—they're so reliable, deliveries up to the minute, and all the assistants are so polite and painstaking. Why don't you try it ?

By 1934 Foxrock branch was taking so many orders over the telephone that a new line was installed. The numbers were changed from Foxrock 9 to Foxrock 208 and 209. The following month Baggot Street and Rathmines branches also installed new lines.

necessary that we, handling foodstuffs, should be very careful not to employ anyone suffering from this disease, and we do take that precaution. It is possible, however, for an employee to contract this disease by contact with an active TB sufferer. What then is his position? His full weekly sickness benefit is payable only if he is insured and has 104 contributions to his credit and payable for 26 weeks after the fourth day of incapacity.

A recipient of benefit, who is in necessitous circumstances, is eligible to receive a food voucher entitling him to 3½ pints of milk and ¼lb creamery butter per week and 6lbs of bread per fortnight. In an area where the Food Voucher Scheme is not in operation, a recipient in necessitous circumstances receives an additional allowance from the Public Assistance Authorities at a rate not exceeding 2/6 per week and at a rate not exceeding 1/6 to cover all his dependent children. These rates are lower than those received by able-bodied unemployed. There are somewhat similar allowances for what is termed necessitous cases, but time does not permit me to go into these in detail. The futile little allowances encourage TB sufferers in employment to hide the fact that

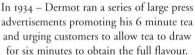

In 1934 – Dermot ran a series of large press advertisements promoting his 6 minute tea and urging customers to allow tea to draw for six minutes to obtain the full flavour.

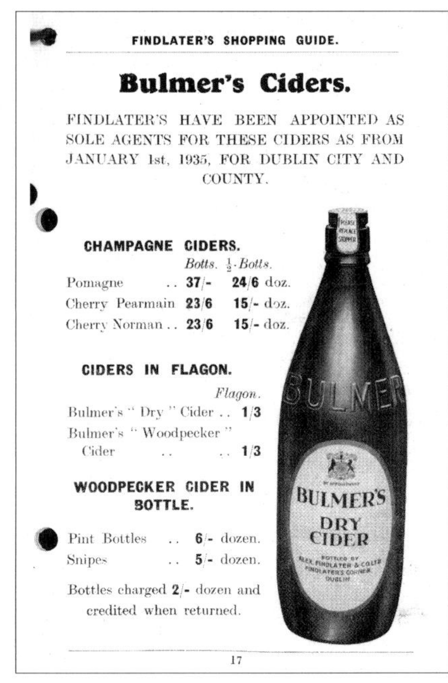

1935: Findlater's sole agency for Bulmer's Cider ahead of the opening of the cider plant in Clonmel.

they have contracted the disease and thus they spread it.

The problem is a Government problem and should be dealt with at once, and all employers should join together and press for a revision of allowances. Dependants of TB sufferers undergoing sanatorium treatment should be paid the employee's full wages less a sum equivalent to the cost of his upkeep at home, and when he is discharged from the sanatorium suitable employment must be found by the Government for him, so that he may maintain himself, or if married, maintain his wife and family. I hope that the responsible Minister will not contradict me and suggest that this is unreasonable.'

'A year later', *writes Charles O'Connor*, 'Mr Findlater returned to the topic. In proposing the adoption of the Report and the Statement of Account at his company's annual meeting on the 12th June, 1946, he said that a single man unable to work due to ill-health or accident got a sum ranging from 15s to 27s 6d per week. These small allowances forced many a man to return to work in an unfit state, his only alternative being to run up debts which would take years to work off. These rates were quite inadequate, and it was time that the whole position of State insurance was revised.

He added that he would like to mention the new Public Health Bill and the onus it appeared to put on shopkeepers and individuals suffering from certain specified diseases. It would seem to be more satisfactory to make certain diseases notifiable and then to let the authorities concerned deal with cases individually.[36]

The sterling work of Charles O'Connor and his committee is fully told in his book, and culminated in the election of Noel Browne to the Dáil, and his

A well-known Foxrock resident in LDF uniform. (Lafeyette)

appointment as Minister of Health on 18 February 1948 with the declared intention of tackling the lack of sanatoriums. Charles O'Connor concludes his book as follows:

> A man had at last emerged with enough drive and determination to implement the reforms advocated for so many years by Dermot Findlater, the Post-Sanatoria League, the Press, newspaper correspondents, eminent chest specialists, Medical Officers of Health, Trade Unions, TDs and Senators of all parties and others. Under his direction the number of beds for tuberculosis patients was increased from approximately 3,000 in 1944 to 5,500 in 1950, and the death rate dropped from 123 per 100,000 in 1947 to 73 per 100,000 in 1950.

Local Defence Force

During the Emergency Dermot undertook another public responsibility. He was in charge of the Local Defence Force. The LDF and the LSF—Local Security Force—performed similar functions, and personnel were often interchangeable. The LDF came under the Army, the LSF under the Gardai. Dermot was ably assisted by good friends and relations, in South County Dublin. Involvement in the LDF had done Jimmy Brohan a good turn, as he remembers:

> It all happened for me the last week of August 1941. Mr Dermot Findlater arrived with his Local Defence Force fire fighting company at Shiels Institution, Leopardstown, for a fire fighting demonstration. It was an old ladies' Home and after the exercise people were invited to re-roll the fire water hose properly. I volunteered and was successful, and Mr Dermot Findlater was so much impressed that he told me to report to him at his office in O'Connell Street Head Office on the following Wednesday. He offered me the position as apprentice and I joyfully accepted, and started in O'Connell Street on the following Monday in September 1941 at a wage of 15 shillings per week. Two weeks later I was transferred to Foxrock branch.
>
> In those days [1941-1950], especially at Foxrock branch, passing trade was very limited, which necessitated that the staff there had to go out from house to house to sell and collect orders—in other words, we were called canvassers. I enjoyed this and I created a company record by opening 120 new accounts in 6 weeks and received great praise from my directors, manager and seniors.
>
> I remember a little boy who used to come with his mother to place an order and on

two occasions he brought me a little bunch of flowers from his garden—his name was Alex Findlater. I spent 24 years with the firm and when I look back I have to say they were happy years.

My mother Dorothea remembers other excitements:

When war broke out in 1939 men joined the LDF and women the St John's Ambulance. Lectures on First Aid were given and it was necessary to do 90 hours in a hospital. I attended Monkstown Hospital, made beds, fed patients and attended operations in the theatre and applied dressings to out-patients.

A First Aid station was established in Foxrock village. After the bombing of Birmingham a number of people fled to Ireland—we would meet them at Westland Row and transport them to Foxrock for bed, bath and dinner. They usually had only what they stood up in. Many had relations or friends in Ireland so it was usually an overnight stay. Alternatively after the initial shock others returned home to England to stick it out.

Our men patrolled at night, watching out for invaders and parachutes—they spent quite a time warning young courting couples to go home or else. We were very moral in those days! One night two men spotted a parachute waving about on Three Rock. They cautiously crept up, dodging from rock to rock until they bravely apprehended the backside of a gray mare!

One time a British plane came down on the Leopardstown race course. It was important to get the plane away in a certain number of hours or the crew would be interned. The military were called in to blow up some trees to allow the plane to take off—unfortunately the blast shattered half the windows on Torquay Road. Alex visited the plane with us and received some lovely sweets. Another time a plane came down, some secret papers found their way to the British Ambassador's wife in a box of chocolates delivered by Findlaters!

At Rush where we were holidaying, a Wing Commander from Belfast appeared for breakfast—later we heard that a number of soldiers had escaped from the Curragh—British frequently escaped but never Germans—they had nowhere to go. Towards the end of the war householders were invited to take officers fighting in the war for a rest. We had two very glamorous Australian pilots—they were with us for quite a while. We fed them steaks and entertained them lavishly. They were with us when Hiroshima happened and they were absolutely stunned to hear that the war was over. They returned to their unit in the South of England to be returned to Australia and we did not hear from them again. One Christmas we had two Canadian airmen—one tall and thin, the other short and square—the very genuine pair—we called them Mutt & Jeff!! They wrote frequently after returning to Canada and sent us presents.

In October 1944, with the war moving away from the western front, and with no lessening of responsibilities in the firm, Dermot felt it was the opportune time to step down from the LDF. Chief Superintendent W. P. Quinn sent a very positive letter to Dermot regretting his departure: 'My sincere thanks and appreciation for the great service you rendered as Group Leader of Cabinteely Group of the LSF. It is a matter for regret that business reasons compel you to sever your

Special half bottle sale for Christmas 1937, probably to correct an over-stocked position as the vintages suggest.

connection with the LSF, but I feel sure that should any emergency arise we can count on your good services.'

What Dermot had not said was that he had been devastated by the death, on 12 February 1944, of his ten-year-old daughter Jeanette, a blow that was perhaps the catalyst for his health problems with the consequential effect on his management of the company.

As the Allied Armies approached Berlin, and hundreds of thousands of refugees straggled across Europe, there was worrying, if parochial, news for the drinking man:

> Ireland's cork supply position has never been more acute than at present. Unless a substantial cargo of cork arrives in this country very soon, draught stout and porter will have to take the place of bottled stout. Already one large firm of cork traders has had to resort to cutting long wine corks in half and supplying the half-corks to its clients for use in stout bottles, but the wine cork supply is far from inexhaustible and this trader feels that it must reserve a stock for the wine bottlers for whom the corks originally were ordered.[37]

For most consumers, shortages of butter, sugar and tobacco still presented the biggest problems. In January 1945 the butter ration was once again reduced although from February a weekly ration of 2 ounces of margarine was introduced. By May it was learned that Ireland's offer of 20,000 cwts of sugar for the relief of Europe could not be taken up at an early date, and sugar rationing was not reduced as was previously predicted.

In the summer of 1945 Findlaters were prosecuted for overcharging on eggs. The Ministry of Supplies had issued a summons against the company following

FINDLATER'S
ALEX FINDLATER & CO. LTD
FROM 1823—
For the past one hundred and ten years Findlater's have supplied pure food to the Irish Public. During this period they have gained a reputation which is second to none for the excellence and quality of their supplies.
Illness and convalescence are times when more than ever it is necessary to eat only the best; that is why the leading hospitals and nursing homes purchase their requirements from Findlater's.
The following Hospitals are Supplied by FINDLATER'S :—
MEATH HOSPITAL, DUBLIN.
CORK STREET FEVER HOSPITAL, DUBLIN.
ROTUNDA HOSPITAL, DUBLIN.
COOMBE HOSPITAL, DUBLIN.
ADELAIDE HOSPITAL, DUBLIN.
ROYAL VICTORIA EYE AND EAR HOSPITAL, DUBLIN.
GRANGEGORMAN MENTAL HOSPITAL, DUBLIN.
RATHMINES & PEMBROKE HOSPITAL, VERGEMOUNT, CLONSKEAGH.
ROYAL CITY OF DUBLIN HOSPITAL, BAGGOT STREET, DUBLIN.
SIR PATRICK DUN'S HOSPITAL, DUBLIN.
MERCER'S HOSPITAL, DUBLIN.
PIGEON HOUSE HOSPITAL, DUBLIN.
BENEAVIN CONVALESCENT HOME, GLASNEVIN.
DUBLIN UNION HOSPITAL, DUBLIN.
SIMPSON'S HOSPITAL, DUNDRUM.
PORTRANE MENTAL HOSPITAL, PORTRANE.
CROOKSLING SANATORIUM, BRITTAS.
CHEEVERSTOWN CONVALESCENT HOME, CLONDALKIN, etc., etc.
FINDLATER'S
LIMITED

Our enormous buying power enabled us to wholesale as competitively as retail.

a complaint by a customer relevant to an overcharge on the purchase of three eggs at our Leinster Street branch. No wonder there was no love lost between Dermot and Lemass.

There were, of course, lighter moments, and the *Irish Press* recorded one such in October 1945:

> Three thousand people, thinking they had a ringside seat for a 'crime does not pay' episode, blocked Upper O'Connell Street, Dublin, last night, and stopped all traffic for half an hour. Cause of the excitement was the violent and prolonged clanging of a burglary alarm in Findlater's shop at 11 o'clock. Spectators gathered in dozens and scores. Carloads of Gardaí raced up the street, and there was a blaze of light from the shop. With the alarm still sounding, hundreds of people, going home from the pictures and the dances, milled around the shop, and waited for the apprehension of the burglars. People climbed drainpipes at the back and peered into windows, expecting to see tussles between the gardaí and the criminals. The crowd swelled into thousands who blocked the traffic, and there was much difficulty in having them dispersed. It was then discovered that the alarm was due to a defect in the bell.[38]

By this time (late 1945) the war was over. The Germans had surrendered in May and the Japanese in August. The world of trade struggled to get back to normal. By October, things began to look up, especially for brandy lovers:

> Trading between Éire and France has started off briskly—150,000 bottles of finest Hennessy brandy will be taking their places soon on the now empty shelves of Éire's hotels and public houses. The Brandy is already in the country. It came in casks because France, recovering from her war wounds, had not enough bottles to carry it. Some people may be puzzled to know why Éire should have received such a large cargo of brandy. The Hennessy family has many roots in Éire, and the present head of the family always has kept in close touch with affairs here. When he was taking up again the reins of his business, badly shattered by the war, he recollected Éire, and ordered that she should be amongst the first countries to receive a share of his product.

> During the war Éire kept going fairly well on Portuguese brandy but the public did not take to it. Still, they took it when there was nothing else.[39]

There was also good news for car owners with the resumption of private motoring in November after three and a half years, as the result of an expected early substantial improvement in the petrol supply position. However, Dermot had a request for government: 'I feel that a petrol subsidy should be issued for commercial goods vehicles that ran on coal gas or producer gas throughout the Emergency period. Our company still has to use producer gas propelled vehicles in order to give an adequate service.'

Then, in December the *Argentina,* a Swedish-owned ship, arrived from Brazil, her hold packed with 1,177 tons of oranges. The cargo represented nearly a pound of oranges for everybody in Éire.[40] Christmas was suddenly looking good, with the first sultanas to arrive since 1940. Commenting on the prospects for Christmas 1945 Dermot declared that turkeys and poultry would be fairly plentiful. Plum puddings in the shops, however, were likely to be scarcer than expected, owing to the shortage of earthenware bowls in which they were sold. While port and sherry were plentiful, white wines, Burgundy and claret were scarce. The remaining stocks of Champagne and gin were gone. Whiskey was no more plentiful than the previous year. However, there was likely to be a good supply of bacon and hams, as the allocations to traders that month were nearly double those of November.[41]

FINDLATER'S
SHOPPING SERVICE
10 REASONS WHY IT PAYS TO USE IT

The following facilities are offered to housewives by Findlaters:—

(1) Weekly or Monthly Credit Accounts may be opened at any of our seventeen branches. Two solvent references and a banker's reference only are required. Application Forms are available at all branches.

(2) Each Findlater Branch has the following departments:—Wines, etc. (Licensed Branches only); Tobacco and Cigarettes, Groceries, Fruit and Vegetables, Confectionery, Bacon, Butter, etc.; Poultry and Dog Foods, Chandlery and Soap, Toilet Requisites, etc., etc.

(3) All our Goods are sold at Manufacturers' advertised prices.

(4) Our prices are not laid down; our vast buying permits us to sell at very keen, fair prices. (We do not cut prices to catch trade.)

(5) Our Goods are unquestionably the finest offered to the public, fresh, spotlessly clean, and of the finest standard obtainable.

(6) Our Customers in outlying residential districts are called upon every morning, and goods ordered are delivered within an hour or two of the order being placed.

(7) Our free order collection and delivery service saves you more money on 'bus fares, time, and avoidance of wettings than you will save by purchasing goods at cut prices.

(8) Goods purchased at Findlater's will readily be exchanged if they are not required, or if they do not suit for any reason.

(9) Our credit system is especially convenient to salaried officials.

(10) Our Shopping Service is ever growing, and after over 14 years' trading our public is bigger and our friends more numerous than ever before.

NO DISCOUNTS GIVEN

FINDLATER'S
LIMITED
FINDLATER'S CORNER, DUBLIN

'We do not cut price to catch trade', and 'no discount given' yet we remained a leader in the trade for very many years.
The Irish Times 20 September 1937

However, on 19 December 1945, the *Irish Independent* reported that 'a shortage of stout and porter, described in some areas in the country as the most serious since the outbreak of the war, threatens a somewhat dry Christmas. No imports of the special type of wood for the manufacture of casks have been made since before the war so that casks worn out or damaged could not be replaced.'[42]

At the AGM immediately after the end of the war, Dermot took the opportunity to address the question of Ireland's contribution to the destruction of

Nazism.

> I must, on behalf of our Staff, Shareholders and Customers, take this opportunity of thanking our British and American friends for the magnificent way in which they continued to send us supplies of fuel, foodstuffs, and goods for the licensed portion of our business, throughout the war in Europe—notwithstanding the fact that they themselves were in short supply. We will never forget their help. We in Éire did much to help them during the past five years, not alone with manpower but also with food supplies. And I feel that if the true facts were set out better relations would be established between our Governments and our peoples, and it would be clear that we in Éire did more than our part to free Europe from the tyranny which has beset it for so many years.

In thanking the staff he could not resist giving the Department a nudge.

> I would [also] like to take this opportunity of thanking our Staff for their inestimable help during the Emergency. They have been sorely tried by the hundreds of emergency orders, altered, revised, cancelled, and renewed often at a moment's notice. They have dealt with thousands of problems, they have suffered uncalled-for abuse, and they have even been put in the dock for the matter of a farthing. All I can say is, I thank them 100% and I believe they trust your board and myself, and because of their loyalty I look forward to a further year of trading as good as this one.
>
> Before closing, I must thank all the manufacturers, wholesalers, distributors, and consumers for their help and initiative during a trying five years. I must also thank all the departmental officials, junior and senior, for their courtesy and their tact and their understanding of our many difficulties.

Thanking departmental officials obviously went against the grain, for he then launched an attack on government policy in respect of wholesalers (of which of course Findlaters was one).

> It is difficult to ascertain the government policy with regard to the distribution of foodstuffs, but we believe that a firm with multiple shops, such as ours, is the most economic method of distribution, provided of course the shareholders and directors are all Irish nationals. It is felt that the government considers wholesalers unnecessary, creating an extra cost between the producer, manufacturer or importing broker and the consumer. This is definitely not the case. The wholesaler in normal times acts as banker or financier to the smaller shops, and divides up the imports in quantities suitable to their needs and to their ability to pay for them, and very often the wholesaler gets very little in return for doing so.

But he had criticism for the one-man shop:

> To my mind the only uneconomic cog in the wheel of distribution is the one-man shop, which has such unlimited opportunities of defrauding the revenue authorities, trading for cash and giving no employment, and often keeping no proper account books.

With money in the bank, business was on the move:

> During the year under review we have opened new branch shops in Cabinteely and Dundrum. These shops were opened at the request of former customers unable to avail of the Findlater Service by reason of the restrictions of the use of private motor cars and motor vans for delivery purposes, which restrictions, we hope, will be unnecessary in the near future. We have completely modernised our Baggot Street and our Blackrock branches. We have obtained a new lease of our Malahide branch, which is to be rebuilt and fitted on modern lines. These three shops will be in advance of any retail shop in any part of the world. They are completely vermin proof and absolutely hygienic, and as soon as equipment is available special arrangements will be installed for the comfort of our staff and customers.

The new world order slowly became clear as the smoke of war cleared. It became obvious that it was in more than Marshall Aid that the Americans were going to dominate. For the next twenty-five years, the lessons that Dermot had learned in Coopers of Liverpool, and in Sackville Street (as some still liked to called our headquarters), were to be less and less important.

Notes and references

1 Terence Brown *Ireland, A Social & Cultural History 1922-1985* London: Fontana 1981 pp 115-16
2 Findlater archives
3 See Marcus Webb (Ed.) *Hockey in Trinity, The story of Dublin University Hockey Club, 1893-1993* Dublin: DUHC in association with the Trinity Trust and CUCAC 1993 p 6; and T. S. C. Dagg *Hockey in Ireland* Tralee: The Kerryman 1944 Chap. 1
4 Tony Farmar *A History of Craig Gardner & Co* Dublin: Gill & Macmillan 1985 p 142
5 Brown *op. cit.* pp 142-3
6 Maurice Manning *James Dillon* Dublin: Wolfhound Press 1999 p 57–8
7 Farmar *op. cit.* p 143
8 Brown *op. cit.* p 144
9 Manning *op. cit.* p 117
10 *Irish Grocer* September 1936
11 Manning *op. cit.* pp 72, 113
12 *Ibid.* pp 72, 138
13 *The Irish Times* 4 December 1936
14 Tony Gray *The Lost Years, The Emergency in Ireland 1939-1945,* London: Warner Books p 47
15 *Ibid.* pp. 48
16 *Irish Independent* 3 February 1942
17 *The Irish Times* 20 February 1942
18 Bernard Share *The Emergency* Dublin: Gill and Macmillan 1978 p 38
19 The Irish Press 4 May 1942
20 *Ibid.* 8 July 1942
21 *Waterford News* 21 November 1942
22 *The Irish Times* 17 June 1943, Chairman's AGM speech
23 *Irish Independent* 19 November 1942
24 *Irish Independent* 28 August 1942
25 See *The Irish Times* 30 April 1942
26 *Irish Industry* 1942
27 *The Irish Times* 17 June 1943
28 *Irish Press*, 16 November 1942
29 Share *op. cit.* p. 13
30 Ibid., p 37

31 *The Irish Times* 15 October 1943
32 *Ibid.* 11 November 1943
33 *Ibid.* 17 June 1943 Chairman's AGM speech
34 *Irish Press* 16 March 1944
35 T. K. Whitaker *Interests* Dublin: Institute of Public Administration p 78 footnote
36 Charles O'Connor *The Fight Against T.B. in Ireland in the 1940s* Cape Town: Oz Print 1994 pp 39-40
37 *The Irish Times* 22 January 1945
38 *Irish Press* 27 October 1945
39 *The Irish Times* 5 September 1945
40 *Irish Independent* 5 December 1945
41 *Idem.* 7 December 1945
42 *Idem.* 19 December 1945

14. The Empire Theatre of Varieties, Belfast

Shortly after putting the Star of Erin in Dublin back on its feet in 1892, Adam turned his attention to the rapidly growing city of Belfast, and made an investment there that was to remain in the family until 1961.

Belfast was the great Irish growth story of the 19th century. Driven by linen, shipbuilding and engineering, it had been half the size of Dublin in 1861 when George Wallace built a small hall on the site which he called 'The Imperial Colosseum'. By 1879, the population of Belfast had soared to 200,000, and the management of this enterprise was taken over by Lindon Travers, who made the most strenuous efforts to raise the status of the hall. These efforts resulted in the name of the hall being changed, first to 'Travers Musical Lounge' then to 'The New Colosseum, the Select Musical Lounge'. But it was apparent that it was not the name that was at fault, but rather the size of the building. Travers gave up the unequal struggle, and in 1879 the building was remodelled and opened as 'The Buffalo'. It enjoyed mixed success before a radical new plan, entailing a new ownership structure led by Adam, and the complete rebuilding of the theatre was embarked on.

By the 1890s the population of Belfast was as great if not greater than that of Dublin. In 1894 Adam established a new company, the Belfast Empire Theatre of Varieties Ltd, for the purpose of acquiring, as a going concern, the 'Belfast Empire', a theatre in construction, and conducting it as a variety theatre in concert with the well-known and highly successful Star Theatre of Varieties, Dublin. This required resources beyond the pockets of the then proprietors, and it was Adam and his associates in Dublin who arranged a public flotation. The Northern Bank and the Royal Bank sought public subscription for 25,000 ordinary shares of £1 each [£80] and 500 five per cent debentures of £10 each. For the theatre as a going concern the company paid £20,700 in cash [£1.65m] and £8,300 in shares. The balance of £1,000 [£80,000] was to be available as working capital. The vendors were Daniel Lowrey and the architect James J. Farrall, who, as we have seen, was a director and the architect of the old Star of Erin.

Adam was appointed chairman, and he was doubtless the largest shareholder. Daniel Lowrey Junior (No. 3) became managing director of the company for a period of five years at a yearly salary of £300 but should the shareholders not receive a dividend at the rate of 10 per cent per annum, he agreed that he would accept only half of this amount for his services. By comparison with the Dublin theatre, which made a net profit of £3,296 in 1893 [over £ 250,000], the Empire Belfast in 1894/95 was forecast to make £5,724 [£450,000] exclusive of directors' fees, management expenses and depreciation.

However, there was to be considerable trouble ahead before such profits could be attained. The Empire opened its doors for the first time on Monday 3 December 1894 and as the packed house waited for the first item on a star-studded bill, they expressed great admiration for the finish, comfort and general appointment of the whole theatre. Outside, an even vaster crowd had assembled, at first with high hopes of securing a vacant seat for the performance, and afterwards as these hopes dwindled, of seeing the apparently endless procession of theatregoers, and watching while the hansoms and stately carriages deposited their occupants at the doors of this new palace of entertainment.

A special excursion train, first class only, with three hundred invited guests, was run from Dublin for the occasion and the opening show received rave reviews from all the publications of the day in Belfast and Dublin. The *Northern Whig* reported: 'A brilliant opening was the unanimous verdict of the overflowing crowd', while the *Belfast Evening Telegraph* described the house itself as 'a marvel of Moorish magnificence'. *The Irish Times* compared the decoration of the theatre with that of 'The Palace in London', and approvingly noted that the opening performance was 'a brilliant success, every part of the beautiful building being crowded by a fashionable assemblage'.

But it quickly became apparent that there was a serious problem with the new theatre. Unbelievably, the stage could not be seen from many parts of the house because of the old-fashioned arrangement of the galleries in straight lines. As the *Belfast Evening Telegraph* facetiously observed:

> Now it may be prejudice, but it is nevertheless a fact that when people go to a place of entertainment they seem to think they have a right to see the performance. And having paid (as he argues) to see a dance or a tumble, it is not surprising that the Belfast 'young man' should insist on value, and refuse to be put off with a glimpse of an angel in stucco or of a section of decorations in cream and gold. Therefore it was that the 'old-new' Empire fell into disrepute. People did not care to go to a place where they had no certainty of witnessing the performance, preferring less elegant houses where, however, they could reckon on getting reasonable value for their shillings and sixpences.
>
> Owing to the peculiar arrangement of the boxes, the view of the stage was obtained through a species of lane. The result was that the wings of the circular portion of the house—notably of the balcony and gallery—were cut off from a view of the stage. It was not so bad in the pit, but if standing were allowed at the sides (where under the circumstances many persons might have witnessed the performance with perfect satisfaction), an enormous number of seats would have been deprived of a view of the stage. But perhaps the worst defect of all was in the balcony (one of the best parts of the house), where the back portion was wasted, through the floor of the gallery coming down below the level of sight.[1]

Adam had been landed with a problem of enormous proportions. He had raised capital for a sound business venture promoted by men with a proven track record—Lowrey in the theatre, Farrall as an architect, Stokes Bros and Pim as

The Empire Theatre of Varieties, Victoria Square, Belfast

financial advisers (they were auditors to one-third of the Dublin stock exchange companies) and Battersbys as valuers. A lesser man would have thrown his hat at the problem and walked away. Adam called in a London specialist in theatre architecture, and they advised that there was no alternative but to pull the theatre down and rebuild. The *Belfast Evening Telegraph* of 26 October 1895 continued the story:

> Mr Lowrey naively confesses that he 'never could understand plans', but he knows a house when he gets it. Alarmed and chagrined at the results, which he witnessed, he determined to exercise the powers of his position as co-vendor of the property and Managing Director of the company to have things put right. With this object, he laid his doubts and determination before Mr Adam Findlater, the chairman of the company, with whom he had been associated for years in connection with the Star Theatre of Varieties, Dublin. From this gentleman he received hearty support, and between them they resolved Mr Lowrey to be no party to selling, and Mr Findlater to be no party to buying a house which did not give absolute satisfaction to the public. What proved to be a fatal omission in regard to the building of the old house was now remedied—viz. the services of Theatrical Architects in London were employed. Mr C. J. Phipps, F.R.I.B.A., and Mr T. H. Watson, F.R.I.B.A., both reported that no adequate improvement could be obtained without dismantling. There was nothing left, therefore, if the requirements of the public were to be adequately supplied, but to make a clean sweep of the dainty, but defective, theatre which charmed us for a few brief weeks at the close of last year. After a careful consideration of suggestions and plans, Messrs Lowrey and

Findlater resolved to adopt this courageous course; and it is due to the firmness of these two gentlemen that the company now possesses a building which skilled opinion declares to be relatively perfect without the expenditure of an extra penny of the shareholders' money. It is certainly hard on Mr Lowrey that he should, under the circumstances such as these, lose his justly-earned profit on an enterprise which was essentially his own, but he has submitted to his fate with customary courage and good humour, feeling only too glad that he has been able to protect the interests of the public who have stood by him for so many years. We trust he will be recompensed by a long run of success, and that, when big dividends arrive, his self-sacrifice will not be forgotten by grateful shareholders.

The new building has been carried out from plans prepared by Mr R. Henry Brunton, M.Inst, C.E., F.R.G.S., of London, which were submitted to, and approved by Mr T. Watson, F.R.I.B.A., also of London. Mr Brunton is a gentleman who has for many years been connected with the construction of theatres and music halls, and has also carried out large structural works in different parts of the world. In designing the new house Mr Brunton had two requisites to keep steadily in view—to afford the audience a full view of the stage, and second, to provide accommodation for larger audiences.

The company needed and had a strong and resourceful chairman to see them through this extremely difficult episode. By March 1895 litigation had been instigated against James Farrall, the architect who was a board member and one of the vendors to Adam's Empire Theatre company. In September the leading architect, Henry Brunton, indicated that the theatre would be ready by 21 October. Six days later, on 26 October the Empire re-opened. As the *Belfast Telegraph* put it: 'It is the merest figure of speech to describe the "function" fixed for Monday evening in Victoria Square as a "reopening". The theatre we were invited to view last evening is literally an entirely new building, bearing little or no resemblance to the structure, which rose up rapidly some twelve months ago, and as rapidly disappeared.'

The legal ramifications took longer to work out. On 4 November 1895 Battersbys received a letter from the company's solicitors (William Findlater and Co., of course) seeking 'an explanation of the statements which were in their valuation dated 27 November 1894'. Apparently Battersbys had approved a valuation claiming that the theatre was capable of accommodating about 2,000 persons; whereas, in truth, it could not accommodate more than 1,100. There were also false and fraudulent representations that the theatre was adequately designed and constructed, whereas there were grave and radical defects in its design and construction. And that the floors, staircases, vestibules and bars were fireproofed, whereas they were not. The document also stated that Daniel Lowrey (presumably junior, the manager in Belfast), 'has throughout admitted that, though personally innocent in the matter, he is liable for the frauds, acts and defaults of the plaintiff, his co-vendor'.[2]

January 1896 seemed to presage a year of even more trouble. It started with a fire in the newly restored theatre that destroyed the engine room and dressing rooms. Adam was in Dublin at this time and had to communicate with his board by telephone. It was decided that Henry Brunton should be again instructed on the re-building. In the meanwhile, Dan Lowrey devoted the proceeds of the matinée for the benefit of those artists who had lost their wardrobe by the fire. A total of £60 was raised [£5000].

In March the balance of account due to Henry Brunton was submitted. Despite a letter written by Dan Lowrey that he was 'thoroughly satisfied that the excessive re-modelling effected will prove most profitable to the company', the company were less than satisfied with the amount charged by Brunton. Lowrey accepted responsibility for the delay, and offered to let the new company deduct from the moneys owed to him sufficient to pay a 5 per cent dividend to the shareholders. Even this did not satisfy the board and on 24 March 1896 the secretary was instructed to write to Henry Brunton stating that the board considered the fees charged excessive, especially in relation to the rebuilding of the dressing rooms. They later queried his per diem charge of £5 5s [£435] which he was receiving in addition to a commission of 7½ per cent on the building cost.

Lowrey's letter, accepting financial responsibility for the closing of the theatre, may seem odd to the modern businessman. However, the minute books of the Star Theatre show that this practice was not an unusual one. For example, in 1916, the directors of the theatre are recorded as having unanimously agreed to renounce their claims to 'any fees and remuneration' to which they were entitled.[3] And the exact same decision was made in 1931 when it was recorded that: 'No provision having been made in the accounts in respect of Directors' Fees and remuneration it was unanimously decided by those present to waive any claim for remuneration for that year.'[4] Indeed, a year previously, when it was impressed on the manager of the Star the necessity for cutting down expenditure, he 'expressed his willingness to cut his own salary by 30s per week, and undertook to curtail expenditure under all headings.'[5] Not only managers were financially liable—a note from the minute book of 1912 confirms that artists were also expected to pay a non-performance fee: 'Under the terms of release Mr George Formby would pay to the company an equivalent sum to that which he would have received for salary in respect of each date he would have to perform.'

Farewell benefit for Dan Lowrey the third

In July 1895 Farrall resigned, having been formally asked to by Lowrey, and on 29 October 1895 Thomas Richie resigned and was indemnified from the various actions pending. Then in February 1896 formal notice was served on Messrs Farrall, Lowrey, Richie and Twamley regarding forfeiting shares on which calls had not been paid up. And in March Charles Reynolds, the last of the original non-executive directors, resigned his seat on the board.

1897 saw the departure of Dan Lowrey the third from the theatre. It was not a happy event. Lowrey had had to accept responsibility for the fiasco of the rebuilding of the Empire, Belfast, and must have resigned with bad memories of his endeavours to improve the theatre. However, according to the *Belfast Newsletter* his farewell benefit was

> a fitting tribute to that gentleman's excellent services over a long period of time on behalf of the music-hall going section—a very considerable one—of the Belfast public . . . The name of Lowrey is inseparably identified with the Empire in Belfast, and Mr Lowrey's departure is a distinct loss—a fact which was evident from the many expressions of regret last night that the occasion was one of a farewell nature. Not only with the public has Mr Lowrey been a favourite, but among the members of the profession he is held in the highest esteem, as a token of which it is only necessary to point to the lengthy and excellent programme that was last night presented to an overflow house. During an interval Mr Lowrey came forward and made a brief speech. His appearance was the signal for a loud and prolonged outburst of cheering. He said—Ladies and gentlemen, I am not going to try to make a great speech, because I have not the language at my command on the present occasion to do so. I can only convey in a few words that I thank you from the bottom of my heart for the great send-off you are giving me tonight (applause). It shows me that I have not been too bad in your estimation, and as long as I live I shall never forget it. I thank you once more heartily, and wish you good-bye' (loud applause), following which the audience, rising, sang 'For he's a Jolly Good Fellow'.[6]

Director resident in Belfast

Three years later, in 1900, Adam invited Alfred Edwards on to the board of directors of the Empire. Edwards was the proprietor of Maguire and Edwards, furniture manufacturers and wholesalers who had supplied much of the furnishings to the Empire. He was a gentleman of undoubted integrity and business acumen and attended to all the business issues that arose on a daily basis in Belfast. The board meetings were held in Dublin and the minutes record their appreciation of 'the excellent services rendered by Mr Edwards' over a period of seventeen years. He died in 1921. Joseph Connolly, later a Senator, was a friend of Edwards, and recorded his attempts to keep the music hall respectable.

> In the early nineteen-hundreds the music halls were at the peak of their popularity, but were still frowned on as being not quite respectable by a great many people who were by no means ultra-Puritanical or Calvinistic. There was considerable justification for their hostility for there was much on the stage and around the bars that was objectionable. Old Alfred [Edwards] and I often discussed this, and it is to his credit that he set his face against anything that would be unseemly. I remember him summing it up to me briefly when he said: 'A lady doing her show at the Empire can come in, go to her room, go on and do her stuff, go back to her room, dress, turn the key in the door and go to her hotel or lodgings just as your typist in the office does.' Maybe it did not all work out so smoothly as that, but that was how Alfred wanted it and how the manager was directed to run the house. Similarly on the stage it was his policy to have anything objectionable cut out.[7]

However, as Louis Gilbert wrote in 1961, not everyone believed in his policy:

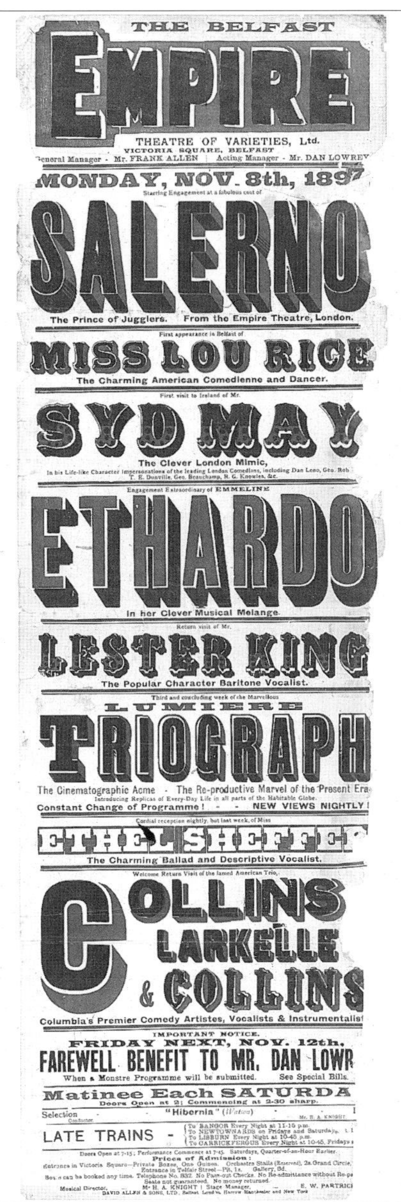

1897 Empire Theatre bill

Many people will regard the passing of the Empire as a calamity, but I remember a time when it was not held in such high esteem by the citizens of Belfast. Thirty years ago, my Aunt Louisa—who regarded herself as respectable, broadminded and artistic—considered it a den of iniquity. Yet she was a woman who liked the theatre.

She went to the Opera House regularly and had no objection to queuing for an hour or more at the pit early door. And there were occasions when she would go to the first house of the Hippodrome when Sir Harry Lauder, Will Fyffe or Dorothy Ward topped the bill. But the Empire–it was completely out of the question!

When I was at school she always took me to Fred Warden's pantomime in the Opera House as a Christmas treat, but once when I suggested that she might take me to the Empire instead she was horrified.

She was so shocked at my suggestion that she told my parents and the Rector about it. The Rector was very grave and concerned and he spoke to me seriously. I was to keep away from the Empire on the peril of my life. It was no place for me. I would imperil my future watching sparsely-clad dancers, hearing bold women singing questionable songs and listening to broken down humourists telling jokes of bad taste.

The Rector's words impressed me so much that I kept away from the Empire for a number of years. I visited it in the early thirties for the first time when I was 16. The Will H. Glaze Stock Company was playing a summer season there and the prices of admission were reduced. Stalls 2s. and 1s 6d., Circle 1s. and Gallery 6d.

The play that aroused my curiosity was described as an emotional drama called 'The Sins of the Rich.' The advertisements stated that it was 'For adults only' and that 'No person under 16 would be admitted'.

I could always afford 1s on a Saturday night, so I loitered in front of the theatre long enough to ensure that there was nobody in Victoria Square who would recognise me, then I darted quickly to the circle entrance.

The interior of the Belfast Empire in the 1950s

The Empire was drab and a bit threadbare in those days. The paintwork was dark and heavy, the upholstery well worn, torn and musty—the air reeked of oranges and strong drink. The girl attendant wore a black dress with a maid's white cap and apron.

The audience was small, but the thought of the theatre closing had not been conceived. While I waited for the play to start I listened to the seven-piece orchestra under the direction of a little bearded violinist, Mr J. C. Evans, rattling its way through the William Tell Overture.

I was not disappointed. I did not feel that my precious shilling had been spent foolishly because I was fascinated by the highly-strung story presented on the stage. I was seeing a play for the first time. I was watching human beings—not pictures!

Their actions gripped me as no film had ever done. I was one with the hero. I was almost moved to tears by the plight of the wronged working-class girl, and I sincerely expressed my hatred when I hissed the rich villain.

I do not know who wrote 'The Sins of the Rich', but as I watched this melodrama which must have been dated even in the early thirties—there was born in me a love of drama which has never faded, and on looking back it seems strange that such a thing should have happened in a music hall like the Belfast Empire.

I went back to see other productions by the Will H. Glaze Stock Company—'A Royal Divorce', 'Temptation', 'Con the Shaughran', 'Murder in the Red Barn'. Each of these helped my appreciation of plays to grow.

I saw my first Ulster play in the Empire about this time too. The Limavady players presented George Sheil's 'Professor Tim.' And after seeing this I realised for the first time that the life of my own people was material for stage and very entertaining.[8]

Undoubtedly, the Empire was a theatre that survived on tradition. The first show was topped by the 'World-renowned London Star, Little Titch.' Also in the programme was 'La Belle Rose' billed as the latest Parisian terpsichorean novelty, 'The Great Karno Troupe', 'Minnie Parker the Dashing Soubrette' and the 'World-renowned White-eyed Kaffir Chirgwin.'

Dublin Comedian Jimmy O'Dea using Sir Harry Lauder's famous walking stick for a show at the Empire (*Belfast Telegraph*)

The two Empires, Dublin and Belfast, were linked up in what was known as the Moss-Thornton tour. The artists normally came to Belfast from Glasgow or Liverpool; they played for a week and then proceeded to Dublin for another week before resuming their tour of the English and Scottish cities and towns.

Tommy Davy, who worked backstage at the Empire from 1904 for more than fifty years, remembers his early days:

> In those days a big star would come here year after year singing the same songs, doing the same dance, going through the same patter; and the audience came because they knew what to expect and they loved it, no matter how often it was repeated. Each star then had his or her own songs and routines that no one else dared use. I remember seeing Charlie [Chaplin] in 'Casey's Court'—a sort of Cockney forerunner of the 'Our Gang' type of fun. But that was when I was a youngster and was able to sneak in when the manager wasn't looking! In 'The Mumming Birds', Charlie played a toff seated in a box at the theatre. Hostilities opened when a boy produced a peashooter. Charlie was at the receiving end of a few custard pies, but emerged victorious, and walked off escorting a soubrette, who meanwhile had been doing her act in midstage. Charlie stayed in a house in Joy Street which was used regularly by theatrical people.[9]

In 1955 at the theatre's diamond jubilee celebrations the thrill of the evening came when the chairman read a telegram from Charlie Chaplin sent from Switzerland: 'My best wishes to the Friends of the Belfast Empire Theatre of Varieties on its Diamond Jubilee. May you enjoy long years of peace, prosperity and happiness.'

Other artists Davy remembers were Marie Lloyd, whom he describes as 'the most friendly of all'. Then there was Harry Lauder, the Scottish comic singer and first artist of his kind to be knighted. He got £8 a week for doing the same Scottish song-and-patter, 'Roamin' in the Gloamin'' that later brought him thousands. George Formby senior also played at the Empire. According to Davy, 'he kept on appearing even when he was nearly dying, but he was too good an artist to let the audience notice that there anything was wrong.' The list contains all the great music-hall stars: Eugene Stratton, Marie Kendall, Marie Loftus, Vesta Tilley, Lillie Langtry, Chas Coburn—they all came to the Empire. And as the decades rolled on, new stars began to emerge. Bud Flanagan and Chas Allen started in the Empire in 1927 with a Florrie Ford revue. Initially they had separate parts in the revue, but backstage they decided to make a comedy team.

And then there was the RUC constable who, according to Davy, stepped straight off his beat outside the Empire; out of the blue he called in for an audition, mounted the stage, unhooked the collar of his uniform, and sang. No sooner had the notes of 'The Holy City' faded into silence than the singer found himself hired to sing twice nightly at £3 10s during the Jimmy O'Dea variety programme. In that incident is crystallised something of the romance and excitement of the triumphs and trials of show business, for the singing constable was Joseph McLaughlin, later the great star of stage, radio and recordings—Joseph Locke.

The theatre managers and staff

The theatre managers and workers played a key part in the success of the theatre. Frank Reynolds, a Dubliner who gave up a job as a bank cashier to become manager of the Empire in 1950, kept up the tradition set by famous managers in the past: Gerry Morrison, who reigned for about twenty-five years until 1945; Norman Crayton from 1948 to 1950; and Barney Armstrong, whose tenure ended in the early 1920s. Indeed, a former manager was believed to have haunted the Empire Theatre. The manager, the story went, had been seen walking the corridor at the back of the stalls where he used to make his nightly rounds. Two painters were the first to report seeing the figure; when a secretary employed by Mr Reynolds, the then manager, saw the figure too, she described it to old-time members of the staff who recognised the former manager from her description. The ghost story hence became part of the theatre's legend.

Reynolds recalls one particularly unhappy incident during a revue. The orchestra had just had a break and was returning to its place for the next song. One of the members stood up, collapsed and died from heart failure. The audience was rocking with laughter at what was going on on the stage, and true to the tradition of the theatre the show went on without anybody being aware of what had happened. 'There was the contrast of the stark tragedy on one side of the curtain and the fun on the other.' Reynolds had the unpleasant task of breaking the sad news to the man's wife.

One famous act was Dr 'Dickie' Hunter's annual circus. Dr Richard Hunter, former secretary of Queen's University and a lifelong animal lover, came out of retirement for six weeks each spring to tour Europe looking for the best international acts over the Christmas season. In scarlet frock coat and white waistcoat, he was ringmaster on the Empire stage, presenting a wonderful collection of circus acts from Britain and Europe The doctor brought his 'turns' from all parts of Europe. One day he told Mr Reynolds that the snake woman had arrived and asked him would he like to see her. 'I knocked at her door and the first thing to greet me was a boa constrictor,' he recalled. 'I nearly dropped dead with fright but she said "don't worry". We were formally introduced and she had Peter draped round my shoulders.' The 'snake woman' was married while the circus was in the theatre and the bride and groom returned to the Empire on the backs of elephants.

Dr 'Dickie' Hunter

Reynolds was no doubt as enthralled as the Belfast circus audience in January 1958 as they watched an eighteen-year-old artist swing from a trapeze high over the stage: seconds later they screamed as Michele Carlo lost her grip and fell 15 feet onto the stage of the Empire Theatre, as her mother and sister Annette (sixteen), watched from the wings. She was carried unconscious to the wings as the curtain was rung down. Michele, daughter of an Italian father and a Welsh mother, was given first aid and recovered. She insisted on performing again for the second house audience, who watched the act unaware of the earlier accident. Said Michele later: 'It was nothing; it happens.'[10]

Low staff turnover is a a sure sign of good working conditions, and the Empire could certainly boast that. As Reynolds noted, 'We were like one big family.' Tommy Davy had been stage manager for fifty years when he retired in 1955. Herbie Stilling was the electrician for thirty-four years, Leslie Beresford, musical director for twenty-six years, and Margaret Cunningham ran the box office for twenty-one years, alongside Maureen McGovern for fourteen years. Then there was Nan Stirling, who hailed from Dundee. She was with the theatre for nearly forty years. Nan ran the grand circle bar and her judgement of a show was eagerly awaited—if she gave a show thumbs up, it was all right. So devoted was she that during her forty years, a week was as much as she could bear to stay away. And she was late on only one occasion and that was when, indulging her fondness for 'the sport of kings', she was delayed getting back from the Maze racecourse.

Herbert Stilling, theatre electrician and later stage manager, first came to the theatre in 1927. His recollection was that the record 'house' for the Empire was achieved during a two-week run by a stock drama company playing *Maria Marten,* or *Murder in the Red Barn* back in 1932. This spine-chilling thriller was challenged about two years later by a show with a completely different appeal—Jimmy O'Dea in *Blarney.*

Gertie and Kathleen McDowell were sisters who found happiness in working for the Empire. Gertie began as an usherette in 1922 and she and her sister, who joined about the same time, were devoted to the theatre, getting to know everybody who attended it. Then there was May Hall, secretary to Frank Reynolds, who said she would work at the Empire for two years, and ended up staying for nine.

The Findlater company in Dublin employed James A. Kinnear & Co., a firm of professional accountants and secretaries to record the minutes of the board meetings. James A. Kinnear had joined Findlaters as a clerk before 1900, became company secretary and later set up on his own, while continuing to supply secretarial services to Findlaters. He was father to Nigel Kinnear, surgeon, who was instrumental in my attending Trinity. As the years passed different partners in Kinnears acted as secretary to the theatre. In 1919 Tom Bell took over from W. A. Davy, who left Kinnears. He held the post for fifteen years and was succeeded by Robert Cashell. He, in turn, was succeeded by Mervyn Bell. All these men were, in their time, senior partners in Kinnears, and were also board members of the Empire and contributed to its success. They provided similar secretarial services to Findlaters and many a young trainee can recall stock-taking in the Empire in Belfast, in the St Lawrence Hotel, Howth or in a troublesome Findlater branch. Kinnears were also auditors of high standing but the Findlater audits were undertaken, since incorporation at the end of the last century, by Stokes Brothers & Pim.

Gerry Morrison's *Come to the Show*

The great wars of the 20th century each brought their quota of familiar songs for the Empire's artists to sing. At the beginning of the century there were the songs of the South African War, then the World War of 1914-18, then of the Second World War, 1939–45. In this last war, battle was brought nearer to the people, when the first enemy bombs descended on Belfast in 1941, just as the last of the audiences was leaving the theatre. That night the entire cast was accommodated in the theatre.

Soon afterwards, an even heavier air raid on Belfast resulted in the theatre being closed for one night because of damage to the municipal electricity supply. That was the only occasion on which the theatre closed its doors during the war. When the doors were re-opened, at first the artists performed to tiny audiences. Slowly, however, perseverance on the part of the artists brought full houses again, and the theatre settled back into its important role of keeping the people happy and helping them forget, for the time being, the tension of the times.

One of the most dedicated employees of the Empire was Gerry Morrison who worked as manager between 1920 and 1945 (not to be confused with Robert Morrison who was a director). Gerry was employed at £10 per week plus a commission of 5 per cent on all profits over £500. It was primarily thanks to Gerry Morrison that entertainment was kept running at the Empire throughout the war. When a ban prevented artists from travelling to Northern Ireland, Morrison trained his own chorus of pretty local girls.

At the beginning of the war the governor of Northern Ireland, the Duke of

Abercorn, ordered all theatres in the province to close as part of a general UK-wide ruling. With some chutzpah, Morrison rang No. 10 Downing Street, where the war cabinet was in session. He contacted a secretary there, and after some delay was advised, and it was later confirmed in writing, that the Belfast Empire could remain open. It was the only Belfast theatre to do so and even the famous Windmill Theatre in London, which boasted 'we never close', respected the closure.

The show running at that time was a London bill being put on by Mr Victor O'Mara with a revolving stage which was inadvertently recorded in the press as Victor Mara's 'Revolting Stage'. This stage was made to revolve by backstage staff pulling a large rope attached underneath it and the story goes that the rope was so long they had to pull the end out into Telfair Street—at the end of the performance Tommy Davy and the backstage staff arrived at the door of the kitchen bar still pulling hard on the rope!

Come to the Show ran for seven years between 1939 and 1947. The 100th performance took place on 8 July 1943 and was broadcast to the Irish forces overseas and the 250th on 28 November 1945, the proceeds of which were donated to two charities. The 1,500th performance was celebrated on 28 November 1946, a performance attended by the governor of Northern Ireland and numerous other dignatories.

Many of the Empire's anniversaries were celebrated by live broadcasts from its stage. The first theatre broadcast from Ireland took place from the Empire in December 1927, when a portion of Richard Hayward's revue *Hip Hip Hoo-Radio* was relayed through Belfast to Cork and Dublin. In 1936, the Empire celebrated its 50th broadcast, which was made in two parts. The first portion was broadcast on Tuesday 10 November from 7.30 pm to 8 pm and was relayed through the Empire transmitter at Daventry to the British Empire overseas, as well as through the Northern Ireland station. The second part of the broadcast took place on 12 November at 7.30 pm and was also relayed through the London regional transmitter. Two years later, in 1938, the Empire had the distinction of providing No. 6 in the BBC series of famous music halls, the commentator on that occasion being the then comparatively unknown Raymond Glendenning who was subsequently a distinguished BBC sports commentator.

Dermot chairman of the theatre

Dermot succeeded his father Willie as chairman of the Belfast Empire in 1941. In those days the board met monthly in the chairman's office above Findlaters in O'Connell Street. The meeting at 2.30 pm was preceded by lunch in the directors' dining room overlooking the Parnell monument. The manager travelled down on the Enterprise from Belfast, occasionally smuggling banned publications in a great brown envelope pompously labelled 'Theatre Plans'.

Belfast being Belfast, questions of religion were bound to arise, but the Findlater policy was clear, as the only reference to religion in the board's minutes states. In December 1934, in reply to a letter in the *Ulster Protestant:* 'The services of the late musical director were not dispensed with owing to his being a Protestant; as a matter of fact, the musical director who succeeded him was of the same denomination. The question of religion does not enter into the constitution of the staff in any way.'

The Catholic priest was as welcome inside the theatre as his Protestant counterpart. This was at first queried by some of the stage staff, but the chairman firmly insisted. The first night of a new show was always a Monday, and Dermot invited a representative of each Church and the trade unions, to see the show and to tell him if they found any aspects of it offensive.

On one occasion a well-known London revue bar had sent over its chorus of scantily clad young ladies. There were of course requests for a little bit more clothing, but the chairman handled these with diplomatic deftness and chose not to pass it down to the stage. On the other hand occasionally the public could provide a surprise, as in this letter from a lady: 'As I have written several times to you advocating nude shows I feel I must write now to congratulate you on the super-excellence of the show you have there this week. I thought that no superlatives are good enough for it. However, do you think it is absolutely necessary that the nudes should wear loin-clothes or flesh-coloured tights, I don't . . . or in the Ballet scene where you show the two almost complete nudes would it not be much more attractive if they were not wearing those very ugly skin coloured tights.' Not everyone was so liberally-minded. John McGrail, a director of the Theatre, was less comfortable with some of the more smutty acts, as he explained to Tom Bell, a fellow director and secretary to the theatre:

> The show was very good apart from Angus Watson, who was pretty blue, and after the show on Monday night I wanted Graham and McKay to take out one sketch of Watson's which I thought was beyond the pale; but this could not be done apparently, and it was agreed to tone it down.
>
> I had quite a long session with Graham and the producers about objectionable stuff going over, and made it very clear to them that we simply would not stand for the Theatre getting a bad name for smut. Frankly, I was rather disgusted with the comedy last Monday night.

Dermot was not averse to a practical joke on his Dublin friends, whom he liked to have as companions on his visits to the North. One night his friend, the insurance broker Blayney Hamilton, was accompanying him. Dermot invited Blayney behind the scenes. A colourful tram backstage, hidden from the performance by a large curtain, seemed a reasonable place to stop and chat. Dermot left his guest seated and talking to a stage assistant while he went to the artists' bar, just off the stage, to replenish their glasses. A nod and a wink to the stage manager and the orchestra struck up immediately, the curtain rose and Jimmy O'Dea, as Biddie Mulligan, the Pride of the Coombe, delivered the re-charged glass to the startled Blayney, who was now centre stage and in full view of the audience. All he could do was sit fast in his tram seat, and hope that nothing further was required of him.

More seriously, Dermot had a unique position in Irish life, as managing director of a major food and drink distribution company in the South, and as chairman of the Empire Theatre. In Belfast he played host to all sorts of celebrities and public representatives, and from time to time was invited to Hillsborough, the governor's residence. In Dublin he was the occasional guest of the president, Seán T. O'Kelly and his wife at Áras an Uachtaráin. But relations between North and South at this time were so frosty that there was no question of this connection being turned to advantage.*

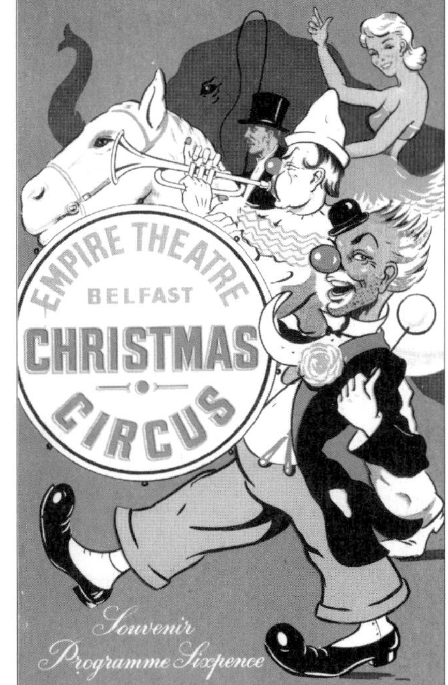

Charities

The Empire hosted many charity gala performances; colourful dress events under the patronage of the dignitary or celebrity of the day. The full box office takings were presented, often capped by the directors, and nothing was held back for production costs. The earliest charity performance that I can trace is a special matinée in connection with the linen stall in aid of the Ulster Hospital for Women and Children on Wednesday 9 December 1903.

Other notable occasions were the visit of the Princess Royal in June 1945 to receive a cheque for £1,000 [£24,000] for the YMCA War Fund. In November 1946 there was another gala night for charity 'Melody, Magic, Mirth' attended by the Governor and Countess Granville and the Prime Minister and Lady Brooke. The event earned a goodly sum for the Variety Artists Benevolent Fund and the Newspaper Press Fund.

In December 1953 six hundred youngsters, including two hundred orthopoedic patients from the Royal Belfast Hospital for Sick Children, the Ulster, City and Musgrave Park Hospitals were entertained by Dr Dickie Hunter's famous circus of trained animals. The bill in 1954 included, as well as eight clowns, performing sea lions, dogs and horses and many 'serious' acts as well as a wire-walking act in which comedy was heavily underlined.

On 14 February 1955 the National Playing Field Association, Northern Ireland branch, benefited by £5,000 [£82,000] which was the entire proceeds of a gala performance celebration of the diamond jubilee of the theatre under the patronage of the Governor of Northern Ireland, Lord Wakehurst. Amongst the sport-

* The historic meeting between Seán Lemass and Terence O'Neill took place on 14 January 1965, four years after the Empire closed. Dermot died in 1962.

A full house for a gala performance at the Empire. October 1953

ing celebrities present and introduced to the audience were Thelma Hopkins (athletics), Dr Jack Kyle (rugby), Dr Kevin McGarry (soccer), Denis Coulson (hockey) and Fred Daly (golf). And in October in the same year the theatre was honoured by the attendance of the Countess Mountbatten of Burma at a gala performance in aid of the Royal College of Nursing. No doubt Mother's influence was at work: 'the Theatre was magnificently decorated with many shades of chrysanthemums, dahlias and gladioli. The Royal box was particularly effective garlanded with flowers, and the beautiful dresses added dignity and charm to the already outstanding occasion.'[11]

Difficult times

Apart from these gala occasions, most weeks during the 1930s the audiences at the Empire were pitifully small, although the theatre never abandoned its twice-nightly programme. Unemployment hit Belfast hard during this time, and this, juxtaposed with the rapid increase of wireless sets, heralded a bleak future for the Empire. Big names in variety like Lucan and McShane, Dave Morris and the Five Sherry Brothers did little to increase the takings. As Louis Gilbert noted, 'more and more theatregoers stayed at home and by twisting a knob brought to their kitchens music, drama, and variety from London, Paris, Berlin, and even as far away as America.'

Another great menace was the growing popularity of 'talkies', and suddenly Holbin and Martin had to compete with Laurel and Hardy, Sheila Daly with Ginger Rogers. Many theatres, such as the Hippodrome, became cinemas, but the Empire carried on being a theatre despite dwindling audiences. Indeed, the

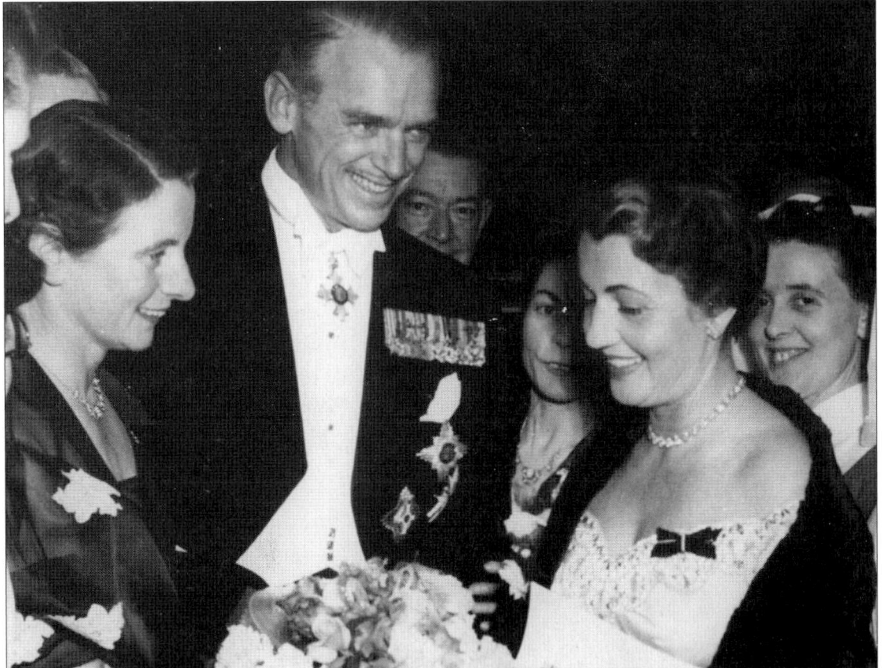

My mother *(left)*, a Director of the Theatre, presenting a bouquet to Douglas Fairbanks Junior's wife at a Gala charity performance. October 1953 (Studio Seven)

Empire only ever showed one short film billed as 'The Bioscope' which was shown every evening as the last item on the programme. Senator Connolly cynically remarked that the reason for this was probably that it 'afforded an equal opportunity to those who wanted to get "one for the road" and to those who did not want to be present when "God save the King" was being rushed through by the orchestra.'[12]

The audiences stayed on for many years after the war, but then a challenge bigger than wireless or talking-picture came to compete with the Empire: the television set. Suddenly the Empire was facing financial ruin. Something radical had to be done to pull the audiences back in.

Over the Bridge

At the end of the 1950s there was a brief new opportunity for the Empire as a serious theatre, when Dermot, reading of a row about a new and controversial play called *Over the Bridge,* decided to offer the resources of the Empire to allow it to be staged. 1959 was a difficult year for Ulster theatre. There were palpable differences of opinion between the councils of CEMA*, the Group Theatre and the Arts Council, and it was felt by many that the future of Northern Ireland theatre was at risk.

Dermot saw the need for a municipal theatre that would serve as a national theatre for Northern Ireland, and the directors of the Empire agreed with this view realising that the era of variety and the old music hall was passing.

* Council for the Encouragement of Music and the Arts, the Northern Ireland equivalent of the British Arts Council.

Ireland's Saturday Night - 23 Jan 1960

I tell you it has nothin' whatsoever
to do with traffic problems!
Belfast Telegraph 23 Jan 1960

Accordingly, they entered into negotiations with various influential groups interested in the Northern theatre. But according to an unpublished article written by Dermot and John McGrail, his co-director, negotiations were not as productive as they would have wished them to be:

> Although the Belfast Empire Theatre by virtue of its size, design and intimate atmosphere is eminently suitable for adoption as a National Theatre, the negotiations failed. The Directors then conceived the idea of a National Theatre Group associated with the Empire Theatre and as a result they arranged with Ulster Bridge Productions for the presentation in the Empire of Sam Thompson's highly controversial play 'Over the Bridge.'
>
> This now famous play, although rejected elsewhere, was considered by the Empire Directors not only to be a play of great merit but also to be a play of considerable importance particularly to Belfast and Northern Ireland. Its main theme, the evolution of Trade Unionism in the shipyards, reflected one of the most important social developments of these times whilst the sectarian issues represented the variable factors that in other environments would be expressed in other forms. The language of the play was certainly strong, but it was the authentic language of the characters it sought to depict. At the same time it was a highly moral play, wholesome, honest, sincere and it had the great attribute of simplicity—simplicity in the classical sense of being uncomplicated. Considered against the background of most modern plays it was refreshing to find a play that had neither the need nor the time to indulge in the all too familiar sex motif. All in all the directors felt strongly that to deny the play a platform would be a tragedy whilst on the other hand its well staged presentation in a suitable theatre might well mark the beginning of a renaissance in the Ulster Theatre.[13]

Over the Bridge, written by a forty-two-year-old shipyard worker, Sam Thompson, was originally intended for the state-aided Group Theatre and had been scheduled to be staged. However, the play was thought to be too explosive and liable to stir up religious strife in the country and shipyard. The board of the Group Theatre wanted a mob scene removed, but Sam Thompson refused to take out one word, contending that it was unbiased: 'It mixes sectarian feeling

(Left to right) On the set: J. G. Devlin, Sam Thompson, Cecil Reynolds, Dermot, Joseph Tomelty, Harry Towb and Jimmy Ellis (Photo: *Studio Seven*)

with trade unionism after a time bomb blows up a transformer in the shipyard. Belfast is the one place where the play should go on. I am holding up a mirror. It took me two years to write in the attic of my home every Sunday.'

Jimmy Ellis must take the credit for seeing that this important play was staged. He was at the time the producer director at the Group Theatre. He felt very strongly that it should be staged, and without cuts. He resigned over this issue and formed a new company to make certain that Belfast would see it. 'We are not afraid of this play. It is honest and should be judged from that standard.'[14] The *Evening Herald* said of it 'it is not so much a play as a typhoon, sweeping trivialities brusquely aside and exposing to view the hard core of intolerance and hatred that can exist in the name of religion.'[15]

When Dermot heard about this furore he read the play, phoned his co-director John McGrail and the Empire manager in Belfast, Frank Reynolds, and suggested they stage it. Reynolds and McGrail agreed with Dermot. As McGrail said in an interview with the *Irish Independent*: 'Sam Thompson, a Belfast man and former shipyard worker, has important things to say about the lives of men spent building ships in the great Queen's Island shipyard that lies just across the Lagan beyond Belfast's Queen's Bridge. While Thompson believes that what he has to say is of universal interest; he has the unshakeable conviction that it has to be said first in Belfast!'[16]

The play went ahead and received much coverage in the local newspapers. The headlines tell the story: BANNED PLAY GOES ON; CONTROVERSIAL PLAY WILL BE STAGED; PLAY IS PLEA FOR TOLERANCE; THE SS-S-SH SHIPYARD PLAY GETS AN AIRING.

On opening night, 26 January 1960, the tension was immense. The RUC were thick in Victoria Square and the streets around the Empire. There was an expectation that there could be trouble but none materialised. The theatre was packed to capacity and the audience responded to the powerful plot and outstanding performances. Dermot, his wife Dorothea, John McGrail, Frank Reynolds and Jimmy Ellis, all directors, must have shared a great sense of elation as the evening concluded successfully and without incident. And to top it all, the reviews were excellent. The following morning, playwright and Empire management met at the theatre early to discuss the possibility of Dublin and London runs, and to consider rearranging the Belfast schedule to accommodate an extended run. As Dermot commented at the time: 'All wildly exciting and giving us renewed hope for the future of the Theatre.'

Indeed, the play was such a success that the Empire Theatre had to extend its run for a fifth week, a fact that the *Belfast Newsletter* picked up on, noting that 40,000 people were likely to see the play on its opening run, a record for the city. Indeed, previous to its extended run 14,000 had seen the play and queues for bookings were commonplace.

Newspaper reviews of the play were highly favourable. Michael Mills, of the *Irish Press*, described it as 'a moving and exciting work', and 'one of the finest tragi-comedies that theatre has thrown up in many years. As O'Casey knew his Dublin, Thompson knows his Belfast and especially her shipyards; he knows the moods of her people; their weaknesses and their strengths; their love and their bigotry. Above all he is aware of the smouldering bitterness which lies behind religious bigotry. Mr Thompson adopts here the role of impartial observer, flaying the people responsible for victimisation, whether the victim is Catholic or Protestant. He takes no sides, but uses his play as an eloquent and most effective theme for toleration, not only of the Catholics by Protestants but of Protestants by Catholics.'[17]

Similarly, the *Presbyterian Herald* noted that the play was 'strikingly fair to both sides' and that it had 'a quality of inhibitedness which gives it great force.'[18] Both newspapers hinted that the play needed a more contemporary background, but neither felt that this detracted in any way from the drama. The *Presbyterian Herald* continued, 'In its presentation of these social and industrial problems, in both characterisation and argumentation, the play is intelligent, penetrating and worthy of serious study.' The *Irish Press* agreed: 'This is theatre in its most entertaining and exciting form.'

According to the *Irish Press* the characters were all 'real and teeming with life' and 'excellently portrayed'. 'Outstanding is J. G. Devlin as the union branch secretary, a glib witty character whose Bible is his union rulebook. Harry Towb also gave a strong performance as the younger union member, selfish and generous by turns. Joseph Tomelty, after a shaky start, found his feet in the second part. Charles Witherspoon, Sam Thompson himself, James Ellis, John McBride and Ray Alcorn all gave a delightful performance. In fact there was no weakness in the very large cast.'[19]

FINAL WEEK OF THE

EMPIRE THEATRE

NIGHTLY AT 8 SATURDAY 6.15 and 8.45

Commencing Monday, 29th May, 1961

ADIEU-FAREWELL!

A CAVALCADE OF VARIETY OF ARTISTS PAST AND PRESENT WITH

BRIDIE GALLAGHER

BILLY DANVERS ALEXANDER BROS.

FRANK CARSON BALLET MONTMARTRE

★ ***and full supporting company*** ★

* * * * * ***FINALS*** * * * * *

"MISS EMPIRE" CONTEST

ALL PROCEEDS OF WEEK TO LOCAL CHARITIES

BOOK NOW TO AVOID DISAPPOINTMENT

BOX OFFICE 11 a.m. to 8 p.m. Phone: 24833

PRINTED BY TRADEPRESS, 19 ADELAIDE STREET BELFAST

The bill that signalled the ending of the family's 80-year involvement in the theatre business.

Following the success of *Over the Bridge* a new policy was inaugurated at the Empire to bring much more 'straight' theatre to Belfast. Cyril Cusack's company of players presented Shaw's *Arms and the Man.* Samuel Beckett's *Krapp's Last Tape* acted as a curtain raiser to inaugurate this change of policy.

The sun sets on the Empire

However, despite these and other excellent productions, such as Milo O'Shea, Rosaleen Linehan, Frank Kelly and others in *Glory Be!,* a ballet season with the Western Theatre Ballet, Siobhan McKenna in *The Playboy of the Western World* and Danny Cummins in his review *Funzapoppin,* costs continued to exceed revenues and an attractive offer from Littlewoods, whose department store fronted the block, ended the family's sixty-seven-year theatrical involvement with the city. Just a month earlier the Opera House (opened in 1895) and the Royal Hippodrome (1907) had been acquired by the Rank Organisation.

In true Findlater style, the final week in 1961 was memorable and nostalgic and in the words of Frank Reynolds, the manager, the theatre 'went out with all flags flying'. The seats were booked out weeks in advance. The Governor of Northern Ireland, Lord Wakehurst, a regular at the Empire, and his party, paid his farewells to the cast and the staff on the Friday night. Donegal's own Bridie Gallagher, the great Irish ballad singer of the era, sang down the final curtain. The entire proceeds of the week went to charity, except for the last night which went to the staff.

The closing of the Empire was heartbreaking for those who had been part of this theatrical family for so long. As Louis Gilbert lamented: 'It was hard to visualise what Victoria Square will look like without the Empire. When the little theatre is demolished serious faced businessmen and efficient shop girls will take the place of comedians and glamorettes. In the modern 20th century store that is to replace it, we will be able to buy many things–but not the happiness the Empire sold to so many.'[20]

But perhaps the last words should go to Jimmy Devlin who, only eighteen months earlier had performed in *Over the Bridge:* 'The Irish have been noted for going to a wake; there used to be a lot of fun about a wake but this is tragic, the last of the Empire.'

Notes and references

1 *Belfast Evening Telegraph* 26 October 1895
2 Farrall *v* Reynolds and others (High Court), Findlater archive
3 Board Minutes 6 December 1916
4 *Idem.* 3 March 1931
5 *Idem.* 16 July 1930
5 *Idem.* 25 September 1912
6 *Evening Herald* 13 November 1897
7 J. Anthony Gaughan (Ed.) *Memoirs of Senator Joseph Connelly* Dublin: Irish Academic Press 1996 pp 55-9
8 *Belfast Telegraph* 20 January 1961
9 *Sunday Independent* 13 February 1955

10 *Irish Press* 21 January 1958
11 *Belfast Newsletter* 5 October 1955
12 Gaughan *op. cit.* p 56
13 D. Findlater and J. McGrail 'The theatre in Ulster–the Empire Theatre of Varieties' unpublished. Findlater archive
14 *Daily Express* 19 January 1960
15 *Evening Herald* 15 March 1960
16 *Irish Independent* 19 January 1960
17 *Irish Press* 27 January 1960
18 *Presbyterian Herald* August 1960
19 *Irish Press* 27 January 1960
20 *Belfast Telegraph* 20 January 1961

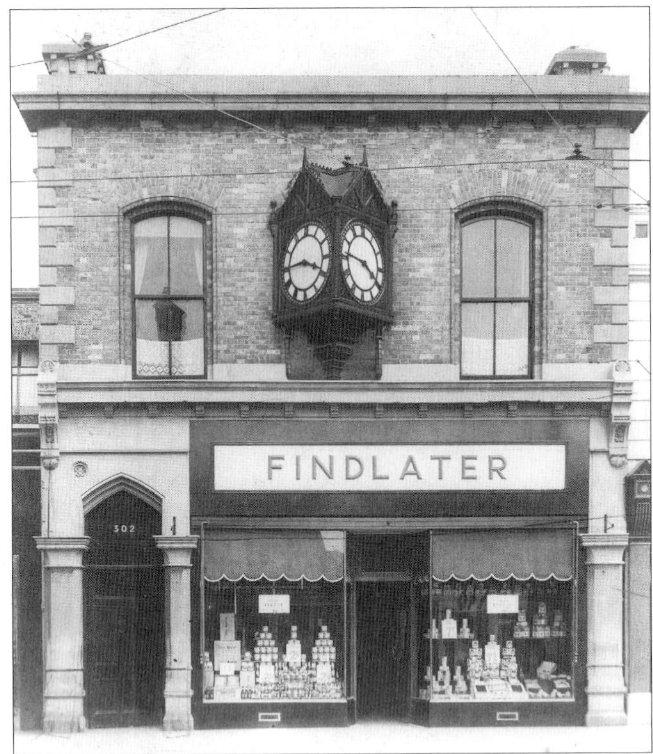

Top; Rathmines 1830-1969 *and bottom;* 72 Thomas Street 1896-1969. The new style shop fronts of red lettering on white and black, introduced in the mid-thirties and in use until the early sixties.

15. Dermot 1945–62

Once the war was over, people wanted to return as quickly as possible to pre-war normality. In 1946 it seemed for a moment as if this was going to happen, with trade routes reopening and luxuries such as bananas and nylons reappearing in the shops. But the following year, 1947, showed that this was an illusion. The world could not rebuild in a few months what had been destroyed over the previous six years.

In August 1948 the Labour government in Britain announced a return to wartime restrictions, some of which had been loosened—petrol rationing, a ban on foreign travel, continuation of rationing of basic commodities, combined with an increase in purchase tax, and a drastic curtailing of imports. Ireland, which was very closely tied economically to Britain, followed suit. A supplementary budget in October increased taxation on beer, spirits, tobacco, entertainment and petrol. Labour disputes and disturbances followed the increased cost of living. And to exacerbate problems, an extremely severe winter in 1946/7 with continual gales and heavy snowstorms hit farmers badly. Fuel supplies dwindled and coal rationing was re-introduced. Gas and electricity were limited to two hours a day. Passenger rail traffic ceased again.

In 1946 and again in 1947 Dermot went on record to praise the officials of the Department of Supplies: 'I would like to pay tribute to all those officials of that Department who were so polite and so helpful when we businessmen went to them with our problems. Mr Lemass, the Minister in charge of this Department, carried this country successfully through the Emergency due to his own unfailing hard work backed by the loyalty of the officials working under him who were always ready to listen to and often accept expert advice when tendered to them'.[1] This public thank-you by Dermot was acknowledged by John Leydon: 'I read with pleasure the remarks which you were good enough to make about the officials of this Department on the occasion of the Annual General Meeting of your Company yesterday. We all appreciate very much indeed your courtesy in giving public expression to these sentiments and thank you for them.'

Despite this exchange of courtesies, relations with Seán Lemass remained strained. It was not until 1968, six years after Dermot's death, that Lemass was our guest for lunch in the board room in O'Connell Street. He had then retired as taoiseach and was chairman of the property developers, Ronald Lyon, who were to take over our premises for redevelopment. Len Jackson, their managing director, confided that on the morning of the event his chairman needed a lot of persuasion before consenting to attend. The lunch, attended by the board and senior shareholders, went off well and the events of the past were put to rest.

Left to right; Len Jackson, Seán Lemass and the author.

To English visitors immediately after the war Ireland was the land of plenty, but it took time for the supply position to return to normal; indeed, temporarily, things got worse. The *Irish Press* recorded in December 1946: 'The weekly butter ration in Éire of six ounces a head may soon be reduced to four ounces. The reduced ration will probably be supplemented by two ounces of margarine'.[2] And

> The Government's decision to ration bread and flour in the 26 counties, from January 18th, was announced by Mr Seán Lemass, Minister for Industry and Commerce, over the radio last night. This new measure, forced upon them by the impossibility of obtaining supplies of foreign wheat for several months, brings Éire finally into the long list of European countries where the staple food already is under control. Under the Government's scheme, in which the simplest possible procedure has been adopted, every person in the country will be entitled to a weekly ration of 4½lb of flour, or alternatively 6lb of bread, including confectionery. The ration may be divided between flour, bread and confectionery, but the total may not exceed the equivalent of 4½ lb of flour.[3]

Actually these quantities sound quite large to us today!

At the 1946 AGM Dermot told the shareholders how the ending of the war had encouraged a programme of refurbishment:

> Many necessary repairs, replacements and improvements have been carried out at our Branches in Ranelagh, Rathmines and Dún Laoghaire and our head shop at O'Connell Street. Instructions have been given for the complete modernisation of our Branch in Bray, Co. Wicklow and it is hoped that the work will be completed before the end of the present year. Our Hotel, the St Lawrence Hotel in Howth, has been

> maintained in good order; the kitchens have been completely reconstructed in a modern manner in the interests of hygiene and a new café or dining-room has been constructed in place of one of the bars. There is much necessary work that should be done to many of our shops if they are to approach the standard set by America, Britain and other countries. Many require new fronts, tiled floors and walls, new plant and equipment and many other items too numerous to mention. It is not possible for us to do this necessary work because of high taxation, revaluation of property when modernised and high rates.

At the same meeting he touched on a significant change in trading conditions that had occurred during the Emergency: 'One of the items revealed the remarkable change in business methods that the war brought—the disappearance of credit. Mr Findlater said that in a turnover that amounted to £900,000 [£21.6m], bad debts were less than £5. When one recalls that the habit of credit was almost chronic in this country, not only in farming districts, but even in the towns, the change is startling.' (Unfortunately, this was not to last.)

However, the payment of excise duties was a heavy burden on cash flows: 'The duty on spirits is ever increasing and the time has almost come when distributors will ask the Revenue Authorities to give us a month's credit—a month to collect the duties from our customers before we pay it over to the Government.* At the moment a considerable amount of capital is tied up in duty paid on goods pending sale of them. The duty on one bottle of whiskey at 24 under proof is now 12½d.'† At this time wine was imported in cask and had to be duty paid before bottling and then cellared for a number of years to mature. Dermot observed: 'Supplies of French red and white wines, held since before the war, are almost exhausted. Plentiful supplies of these goods are freely offered to us by wine merchants in England on a re-export basis payable in sterling but unfortunately present finance regulations prohibit us from accepting these offers. It is hoped that these regulations will shortly be relaxed. The prices at which the goods are being offered would allow a ready sale in this country.'

April 1946 saw the arrival of 1,950,000 bananas in Dublin, and a few weeks later the papers reported: 'As with the oranges, there have been numerous instances of flagrant profiteering in the disposal of the first consignment of bananas to reach this country for many years. Some dealers have extorted sixpence to eightpence each for bananas, a price equivalent to anything between two shillings and four shillings per pound, while the fixed maximum charge amounts to one shilling and three-pence.'[4]

As well as buying tea, spices and sugar in bulk, Dermot was himself also responsible for buying the Christmas turkeys. In December 1946, with a team of buyers, secretarial staff and two lorries, he visited Mullingar, and bought prize-winning turkeys in competition with local butchers at prices up to 3s 6d per lb. In all he bought 3¾ tons of poultry, including chickens, ducks and geese.[5] He

* This was finally granted in 1985.

† 12½d = £3 in 2000 money against a present duty rate of £6.09 plus VAT for a lower strength and smaller bottle.

Jimmy Graham serving happy customers. A French journalist wrote: *Chez Findlater—grand magasin de O'Connell Street (les Champs-Elysees de Dublin)—les clients jouent joyeusement au 'jeu de Massacre' avec les dindes qui iront garnir leur table; 2000 dindes et 1000 jambons de Limerick par jour!'* I think the last two words might be a bit of an exaggeration. Source: *Sciences et voyages, la vie des hommes (Dec. 1967)*

had also been buying at the shows in Athlone and Ballinacargy. This was an annual event that spanned most of Dermot's commercial career and much fun for those invited to accompany him. The highlight was always tea with Father Kilmartin in Ballinacargy and a drop of the hard stuff in the cup.

The very bad winter of 1946/7 gave rise to considerable difficulties in feeding isolated farms, and Findlaters sponsored a much publicised relief party in attempts to get supplies to farms in the Wicklow mountains. In February the butter ration was further reduced from four ounces to two, which the *Irish Independent* (admittedly, never a fervent supporter of the Fianna Fáil party, which was then in power) described as 'a staggering blow to the households of the country.' 'It is astounding,' it fulminated, 'that an agricultural country which at one time was able to spare for export dairy products to the value of millions of pounds annually, should be able to do no better than to supply what can only be regarded as a starvation allowance of butter for home consumption.' (An ounce of butter is approximately the size of a walnut.) Other goods still affected included eggs, sugar and tea.

A few days later the United States authorities made 8,000 tons of flour available to this country. It was expected to arrive by the end of March or early in April.[6] In March 1947, three 8,000-ton American Liberty ships were chartered to bring 20,000 tons of Peruvian sugar to Ireland.[7] Direct importation of tea from India, which since 1942 had to be channelled through the British Ministry of Food, was resumed in the twenty-six counties early in June, giving rise to hopes that tea rationing might be discontinued in due course. However, problems with meat now took over. Prices, it was reported, had shot up, so that the family joint now cost 50 per cent more than a year before; as one paper put it, there were more steaks than customers in Dublin butchers' shops. To combat the shortage, the government put a stop to the postal traffic in meat to England. According to the Scottish Sunday paper, the *Sunday Post,* something like 55,000 parcels of meat were being sent weekly from Irish to English and Scottish recipients.[8]

Food controls were rigorous and tightly policed. In October 1947, Findlaters were taken to court, and were 'fined 10s, conditional on their adding £5 to the Poor Box in the Dublin District Court, for selling a jam roll without receipt of a coupon. For the defence, it was stated that there were two kinds of jam roll, one made from corn flour, which was unrationed, and the other which contained wheaten flour and was on the ration, requiring a coupon. In some unexplained way this roll sold to the Department's Inspector got into a consignment of unrationed rolls.'[9]

The following month Findlaters were granted a licence to import 25,000 cases containing 32 12oz packets of Kellogg's Corn Flakes[10]—800,000 packets of cornflakes! Findlaters also airlifted to Kellogg's Manchester each Christmas a large hamper containing a turkey, a ham, a plum pudding and one or two other delights, for each of their three hundred or more employees. This lucrative business came to an end in 1960.

1947 ended with wine tax being eased; merchants would now be able to supplement their nearly-exhausted stocks. Dermot, discussing the importation of wines with an *Irish Independent* representative, said their stocks were very low. 'If the Government permitted a big enough quota the merchants could buy some for immediate sale and put away some for maturing. They wanted to get wines

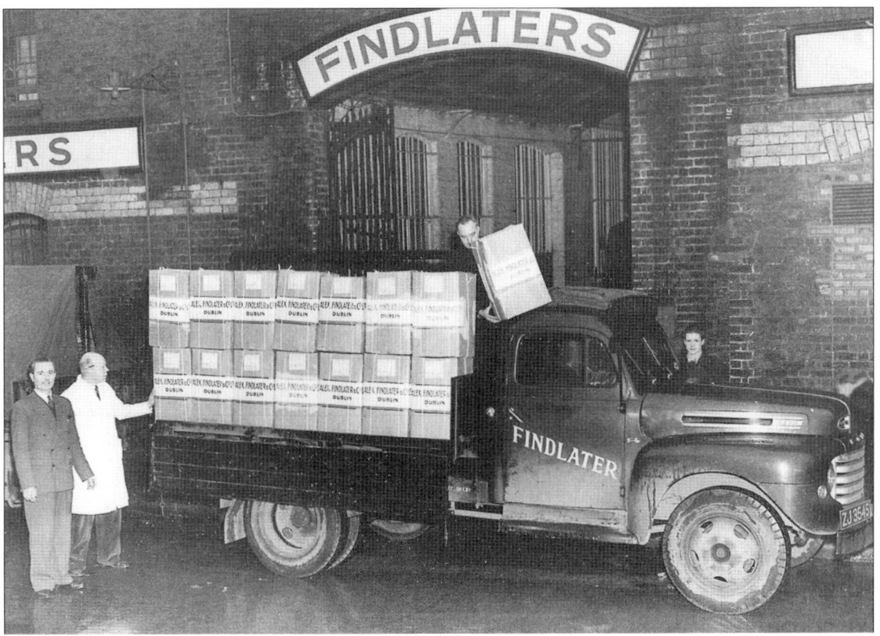

Loading the Kellogg gift hampers, Dan Skehan and Peter Dunne supervising.

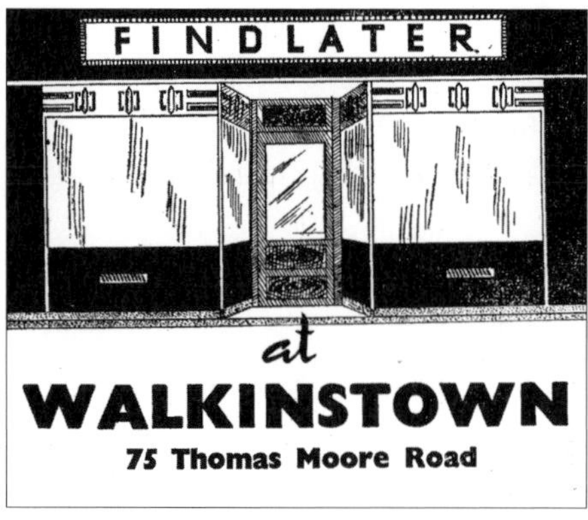

Walkinstown 1950–68
The following year a branch was opened at Crumlin Cross (1951–69)

which would mature and improve in bottle. Claret and Burgundy and white wines from France were all in short supply as was sherry.'[11]

The years of the Economic War and the Emergency kept shareholders' expectations subdued, and Dermot was not one to change that, as he told the 1947 AGM: 'We have made much the same profit as in previous years for we deem it our duty to spend any available money on amenities to the staff and amenities to the public. It is not our intention to increase dividends to our Shareholders, who are now receiving the same dividend as they received during the pre-war years.' Dermot made it clear that Findlater shares were not for quick-buck merchants: 'Speculative investors hoping for a quick return on their outlay need not consider the purchase of shares of this company, for although the cash sum involved in paying an increased dividend is small, your directors feel that the dividend now paid is an adequate return on the money originally invested, and anything available must be used to stop the constantly rising cost of living figure.' The great and the good agreed. His attitude, commented *The Irish Times*, was not merely sound from his own business point of view, but 'is one which must be regarded as essential on a national scale.' However, repeated over very many companies, this practice eventually led to the loss of shareholders' loyalty that made the aggressive takeover boom of the 1960s and 1970s possible.

The style of the firm in those days is well expressed by J. P. Donleavy in *The Ginger Man*[12] when his character Dangerfield was living in Howth:

> 'If we had something to eat we'd be able to use it. They've got one of those big shops down there in the town, why don't you pop down with that English accent of yours and get some credit. As much as I like your company, Dangerfield, I'd prefer it on a full stomach.' . . .
>
> The counter was covered with rich sides of bacon and wicker baskets of bright eggs. Assistants, white aproned, behind the long counter. Bananas, green from the Canary Isles, blooming from the ceiling. Dangerfield stopping in front of a gray-haired assistant who leans forward eagerly.
>
> 'Good day, sir. Can I be of any help?'
>
> Dangerfield hesitating with pursed lips.
>
> 'Good day, yes. I would like to open up an account with you.'
>
> 'Very good, sir. Will you please come this way.'
>
> The assistant opening a large ledger across the counter. Asking Dangerfield's name and address.

'Shall I bill you monthly or quarterly, sir?'

'I think quarterly.'

'Would you like to take anything with you today, sir?'

Dangerfield caressing his teeth together, his eyes darting among the shelves.

'Do you have any Cork Gin?'

'Certainly, sir. Large or small size?'

'I think the large.'

'And anything else, sir?'

'Do you have any Haig and Haig?'

Assistant calling to the end of the shop. A small boy goes behind the scenes and comes out with a bottle. Dangerfield points to a ham.

'And how many pounds, sir?'

'I'll take it all. And two pounds of cheese and a chicken.'

Assistant, all smiles and remarks. O, it's the weather. Shocking fog. No day for them ones at sea or the others either. And clapping his hands to the little boy.

'Come here and carry the parcels for the gentleman. And a very good day to you, sir.'*

Dermot regularly took the opportunity presented by his chairman's speech at the AGM to give his views on national and international political matters. He clearly enjoyed his role as a gadfly. The annual reports show an impressive range of interests, revealing a lively, inquisitive and not easily daunted mind. One year he recommends that the government build up poteen as a national drink equivalent to schnapps or vodka; then he proposes that the government abolish altogether the duty on good wine, on the grounds that it is good for the digestion. Addressing the Commercial Travellers Association, he notes that putting cats' eyes in the middle of the road encourages motorists to drive dangerously in the middle; he complains about the nationalisation of the railways, the flight of country workers to the towns (especially Dublin) and the cost of the civil service.

His interventions were popular with the press, who were no doubt delighted to have something more substantial to report than the normal bland chairman's remarks. Sir Basil Goulding, chairman of Goulding Fertilisers and a director of the Bank of Ireland, achieved the same popularity with his idiosyncratic speeches in later decades.[13] In 1948, Dermot signalled that he had moved from being a supporter of protectionism to free trade. 'I am glad to see that they [the government] believe in freer trading between this country and others, for until free trade comes back there will be people starving in one country and food being destroyed in another.' This was not the common view and he came under a stinging attack from Kevin McCourt, then Secretary of the Federation of Irish

* Bad debts, of which we can assume this is one, were recorded in a special black book in head office. On reading *The Ginger Man* in the mid-1960s I was unable to trace a record of this particular debt. Mr Donleavy confirmed to my brother John that the event had taken place and that the person concerned was Gaynor Stephen Crist. In all probability the manager, Mr Rowland, would have borne the debt, it not having been authorised by head office.

Michael O'Flanagan explaining the finer points of a hen turkey to me at a Poultry Show in 1956. Michael was one of Findlater's characters. He fought in the Four Courts area in 1916 and was imprisoned in England. He later joined the civil service. Every Christmas he took a week off to pluck and dress up to 1,000 turkeys. The only time I met Dev was at Michael's funeral in Cabra, in 1965 (Picture: *Independent Newspapers*).

Manufacturers Ltd: 'In the face of the flood of manufactured goods which has swamped this market in the last twelve months . . . Mr Findlater has arrogated to himself the function of declaiming against a policy . . . without study of the facts.' McCourt declared that the total bans on imported goods in Argentina, Denmark, Dutch East Indies, Egypt, France, Holland, Iceland, Norway and Palestine; the rigid import restrictions in British East Africa, Burma, Cyprus, Hong Kong, India, Iraq, Malta, Mexico, New Zealand and Sweden, and the tariff walls on an average much higher than those in Ireland rendered it impossible to compete with home-manufactured goods in the United States, Australia, Belgium, Canada, Newfoundland and South Africa.[14] In the long run of course, Dermot was right, for the tariff walls behind which Irish manufacturers worked did nothing for their long-term efficiency, as the national performance during the 1950s amply demonstrated.

Dermot's views on the development of the business were clear: 'We have had applications from residents in various districts asking us to open shops in their districts and we feel that we must give the Findlater Service to such areas as Glasnevin, Crumlin, Donnycarney, Inchicore, Mount Merrion, Clontarf, and Donnybrook.' At the same meeting he reported some of the problems stemming from the firm's long presence in its older branches:

> It is to be expected that after 125 years of trading floors will get dry rot, etc.; joists which were adequate to hold up floors when trams passed by our premises four times each hour are now of inadequate depth to withstand the strain when heavy C.I.E.

> buses dash past our premises at the rate of from five to ten every five minutes. When we have to replace these joists, which necessitates taking down the floors and ceilings, the Valuation Office steps in and increases the valuation of our property, thereby increasing the annual fixed payment made in respect of rates by our company. If we, as others do, continued to trade in dangerous buildings, in infected premises, in unhygienic conditions, we would not have our rates adjusted.

Conditions in some of the shops were far from what would be required today. A small entry in the board minutes of 1951 conveys this: 'A discussion took place regarding the installation of a wash-hand basin in the gents' cloak-room in Ranelagh branch as recommended in the new Shops Hygiene Act. Estimates for a hand-basin in Ranelagh considered high due to the fact that there is no water supply in this branch, but only in the yard common to three premises at the rear of same.'[15]

Three new branches were open in the following five years. We were still thinking counter service—self-service had not entered our vocabulary. We chose Walkinstown (1950), Crumlin Cross (1951) and Mount Merrion (1953). This brought the total number of branch shops to 21. Thereafter we always used this figure, just as Heinz used 57 for their produce count. In the former two areas money was very tight—sausages and rashers were a daily purchase sold by the count, rather than by weight, leaving nothing in the purse even for the simple luxuries that were Findlaters' speciality.

On taxation Dermot appealed to the Minister for Finance 'not to re-impose the Excess Profits Tax for with it in force we are left virtually nothing out of our earnings to put back into our business'; in true Dermot style he proffered a solution—tax the inefficient! 'Surely it would be more fair to raise the rates of those companies or shops which have not been brought up to date and leave those which have been brought up to date alone. I never can understand why those companies who try to improve the amenities of their city should be so heavily penalised and those who do nothing, in comparison, be so heavily subsidised.'[16]

There are early signs that staff costs, the bane of the 1950s and 60s, were beginning to concern him:

> Wages for our head office and branches in existence in 1939 have increased from approximately £52,000 to approximately £90,000, an increase of about 73 p.c. But I admit this figure does not necessarily show the true position, as, due to rationing, we most likely do employ more personnel than we did pre-1939.* It does, however, show that we are playing our part to see that Irish workers can obtain good employment in Ireland and need not have recourse to emigration. Indirectly we employ many other persons, for in 1948 we spent—out of revenue—on repairs and renewals over £29,500 [£650,000] and on upkeep of motors, we paid out £6,900 [£150,000].

* In reality it does not take the substantial wartime inflation into account. In 'real' terms, £50,000 in 1939 was equivalent to £92,000 in 1948. The shifting value of money was more or less ignored by businessmen until the 1970s.

1948 was an Olympic year, the first since the war, and Dr Alf Delaney was selected to represent Ireland in the sailing events which took place in Torbay, England. Dr Delaney recalled to me:

> Myself and my crew were in a Swallow class, chartered to the Irish Yachting Federation by the late George O'Brien Kennedy, a distinguished Irish yacht designer. We were advised to bring 'Our Welcome' as there was still food rationing in England. We sought advice from your branch in Wicklow street, where we were customers. We lived in Clontarf and they delivered all our household requirements, what a wonderful service we got in those days. I was a good hockey playing friend of your father's, playing together in Three Rock Rovers. Anyhow I am sure that he was consulted on what we should bring with us to England. We were foot passengers on the 'Munster' to Liverpool and made the rest of our journey by rail, laden down with the following: 2lbs Butter; 2lbs Sugar; 3 dozen Eggs; 1 Tin Marmalade; 5lb Caerphilly Cheese; 2 Boxes Three County Cheese; 1 Tin Jam; 1lb Gold Grain Biscuits; 1 Tin Oval Thin Captain; 500 Cigarettes; 5lbs Chocolates; 3 Bottles Spirits; 5 Tins Meat and 5 Tins Milk. And the total cost came to £10 13s 0d. In addition to all this we set off with 2 dozen bottles Whiskey, compliments of 'Jem' Sullivan who was a reserve crew. 'Jem' was a wine merchant with Turbett's, better known in that trade as Desmond. Alas the British customs would have none of it, they considered one case sufficient, and consigned the other back to Dublin! Remember whiskey in those days was packed in heavy wooden crates, none of your easy to carry six bottle cardboard boxes of to-day. As for the sailing, well, let's say: 'we have sailed better, having had no previous experience of the type of yacht sailed!'

As we have seen Dermot was very much a skilled grocer, responsible in the old way for buying goods in bulk and in season, perhaps from distant parts, storing them and making them available to the local purchasers. Dermot's brother-in-law Edmund Mitchell was responsible for the wine buying pre-war, and there was none to be purchased during the Emergency. The skills of understanding and relating year after year to many different commodity markets, from eggs and turkeys to exotic spices and sugar had by now largely been taken over by producers and manufacturers. There was very little understanding of the skills and complexities of the grocers' craft, and a considerable amount of prejudice, as cousin Brian Inglis noted in his book *Downstart*, which was published after my father's death: 'I did not realise it until after the war, but the reason I had not met my cousin Dermot Findlater was that he owned and ran the chain of grocery shops which spread out of Dublin in the 1930s. Grandmother was proud of her husband's Findlater connection [Findlater's Mountjoy Brewery], and the branch of the family in the wine business was socially acceptable, as part of The Trade. Besides, theirs was basically a wholesale business. Retail was a different matter—and as for groceries!'[17] Brian was obviously unaware that the same branch of the family managed the two businesses and that his parents were great friends with Dermot's two sisters. This snobbery ran through various strata of mid-20th-century society; for example, solicitors were not popular with the land-owning classes; they were generally seen as those who had aided and profited from their ruin. Elizabeth Bowen's grandmother noted: 'She would receive barristers, not solicitors . . . she would countenance wine merchants . . . but not brewers. The Church, the Army . . . the Navy were the only professions she regarded as normal'.[18]

In another publication, *West Briton*, Inglis expanded on this attitude: 'Grandfather had been a brewer; but a man in The Trade [brewing] was not regarded as being in trade. Nor was a distiller. A wholesaler too might be acceptable.'[19] Of his maternal grandfather, John Redmond Blood, he wrote: 'His father had taken him from school at the age of sixteen to put him into the family business. But there was a significant difference: the business was the Findlater's Mountjoy Brewery, owned by Jack's mother's family. "I do not know why it should be a crack thing to be a brewer,' 'Herbert Pocket remarked to Pip in *Great Expectations,'* 'but it is indisputable that while you cannot possibly be genteel and bake, you can be as genteel as never was and brew."'[20]

The stigma of being in trade was not confined to grocers. Beatrice, Lady Glenavy, who was born an Elvery of Spanish stock, owners of the sports goods shop in Dublin, recalled that

> when her parents moved to Carrickmines, in the heart of Dublin's equivalent of a stockbroker belt, she could not make friends there. 'We are not allowed to play with you,' a girl at Sunday School told her, 'because your father has a shop.' . . . when young Gordon Campbell, [later Lord Glenavy] proposed to her . . . 'When his family heard of our plans that bogy of my father's shop made one faint effort to put in an appearance, but quickly faded away.'[21]

Distant cousin George Bernard Shaw had his own line on the matter:

> It was simply the rule in Dublin that though business had to be admitted as gentlemanly, it must be wholesale business. Keeping a shop was unpardonable. Lucy was troubled all her life by the guilty secret that our father's mill at Dolphin's Barn had a little village shop attached to it. I rebelled contemptuously against this convention: it amazed me to see my father's tailor, who was rich, deferring to my father, who, as the opulent tailor had the best reason to know, was poor. All this has died of its own absurdity; but it was the laws of the Medes and Persians in my father's time. Such exclusiveness could have hardly been possible, or even intelligible, in Australia, except among the aboriginal blacks.[22]

It was even worse in Brian's version of events when, in 1917, Findlaters opened a branch shop in his beloved Malahide: 'This was another embarrassment to grandmother. She felt bound to patronise it, as the owners were cousins. This was not something to be proud of, certainly not something to boast about; but grandfather, she felt, would like her to shop there, because his mother had been a Findlater. On the other hand, he would not have wanted her to leave Hogan's. She compromised by dividing her shopping between them . . .'[23]

Of course there was a solution and it was this that made his Inglis grandfather socially acceptable. ' . . . Malcolm had been 'in trade'. Worse, it was the coal trade, which had an unenviable reputation. Everybody assumed that the coal merchants lavishly watered the "slack" that accompanied the coal, and was used in households to keep the fires in overnight.'[24] Malcolm had been a partner in the coal importers Thomas Heiton and Co., which had become very profitable on the surging increase of coal usage in the late 19th century. When the company incorporated in 1896 he became Chairman, as well as holding several directorships and being President of the Dublin Chamber of Commerce.

The social distinction between retail and wholesale had a long history. In *Princes and Pirates,* the history of the Dublin Chamber of Commerce, Louis Cullen describes an attempt by the Chamber to segregate the activities (note that the wine trade is treated as an exception):

> Only those manufacturers who engaged in foreign trade by importing on their own account were the social equal of merchants, and they achieved this by being accepted as merchants in their own right rather than by their importance as manufacturers.[25]
>
> The Council represented wholesale merchants, and it was anxious that it should not be infiltrated by less prestigious trades. At a meeting on 13 January 1784 a resolution from a committee on membership included the proposal that 'every person who sells or disposes of any goods or merchandise save and except wines in any other than the package said goods or merchandise is imported in ought to be deemed and considered a retailer'. However, at the meeting the clause 'save and except wines' was deleted. The original proposal from the Committee avoided discrimination against the specialist wine merchants who did a retail trade as well as import wines. The resolution as amended in the course of the meeting was itself rejected.[26] . . .
>
> The wine trade was the most conservative of the major branches of the city's trade. Customers then were mainly among the landed classes.[27]

Eventually however, the distinction was lost, as wholesalers and retailers were overtaken by manufacturers:

> The essence of the mid-19th century changes was the eclipse of the merchant. As communications improved, both wholesalers and manufacturers could dispense with the services of the merchant as an intermediary. Typically he had handled both exports and imports. . . . If merchant houses survived, it was by conversion into a wholesale house in a single commodity. Moreover, both wholesaler and merchant were now frequently overshadowed by manufacturers in wealth and prestige. The Guinness's progressed to the peerage and to London social life in conservative political circles. No wholesaler rivalled the Jamesons, the distillers, in prestige by the end of the century. As trade and wealth grew, retailers too emerged from obscurity often to play a prominent role in local business life. Retail trade thus lost its stigma among businessmen; wholesalers like the Findlaters through their wholesale interest in tea and spirits eventually opened a chain of retail shops . . . .[28]

The Meath Hospital saga

According to Tony Farmar, the author of the history of Craig Gardner and Co., the 1950s were not a comfortable time for those who were not part of the mainstream:

> The most vigorous entity in Ireland was the Catholic Church, led by the redoubtable Archbishop John Charles McQuaid . . . In 1951 the government accepted the views of the bishops on the Mother-and-Child Scheme, and throughout the decade the faithful generally were made vigorously aware of the hierarchy's views on various other matters. The number of books banned by the Censorship Board soared to an average of 600 a year between 1950 and 1955. Dance-halls were forbidden to stay open after midnight, it was declared to be a mortal sin to marry a Protestant or attend Trinity without the Archbishop's permission, and plans for an agricultural university (or indeed almost any other state initiative) were denounced as creeping Socialism.[29]

But as R. B. McDowell points out in *Crisis & Decline:* 'the success of Protestants in professional and business life—a number of well-known Protestant firms continued to flourish—demonstrates that the majority in the Irish Free State set a high value on tolerance or refused to allow denominationalism to affect to their own detriment their behaviour in practical life.'[30]

But let's look at the statistics. Protestants (Church of Ireland, Presbyterians, Methodists and a tiny number of Baptists) represented 10 per cent of the population of the twenty-six counties in 1911. Of the 1.1 million in Ireland, 311,000 were in the twenty-six counties. By 1926 the number had fallen to just over 7 per cent and by 1981 the members of the three major denominations—Church of Ireland, Presbyterian and Methodist—numbered only 115,000, forming 3.47 per cent of the population (Roman Catholics amounting to 95 per cent). Dean Griffin, in *Mark of Protest*, writes: 'Mixed marriage has been the scourge of the Protestant community, particularly in the Republic. In spite of certain amendments to the *Ne Temere* decree, Roman Catholic teaching still insists that the Roman Catholic partner shall do all in his power to have any children of the mixed marriage brought up in the Roman Catholic faith.'[31]

During the 1940s and 1950s the Knights of Columbanus* ran a series of vigorous assaults on Protestant institutions in the state, as described by Emily O'Reilly in her book *Masterminds of the Right:* 'They moved to tighten their grip in every area of Irish public life, gaining representation on various state boards and committees, including the Irish Red Cross, the Royal Hospital for Incurables and the Meath Hospital.'[32]

Dermot was one of the nineteen members of the Joint Committee of the Meath Hospital during the Knights' attack on the institution in 1950. The hospital had a staunch Protestant reputation, and there was a widespread belief that

* An order founded in Belfast in 1915 with the aims: 'to fight discrimination against Catholics in all walks of life; to create "leaders of opinion" and to organise Catholic gentlemen with a view to such leadership.' Evelyn Bolster *The Knights of Columbanus* Dublin: Gill and Macmillan 1979.

The 1957 AGM. Back row: Frank A. Lowe and Harry Thompson. Front row: Mervyn Bell representing the secretaries J.A. Kinnear & Co., my mother Dorothea, Dermot, my aunt Doris and John A. McGrail. (Picture: Lensmen)

it was impossible for graduates of the National University of Ireland to get appointments to the medical staff. This was in fact true, because the enabling Act of 1810 which detailed the institutions from which medical staff could be recruited had not been amended to include the NUI, which was only founded in the early 20th century.

After careful examination of the procedural rules of the hospital, a small group of the Knights organised a coup, with the object of changing the hospital's orientation. The hospital was run by a committee that was elected annually by the votes of life and annual governors. To become an annual governor you simply had to subscribe two guineas a year. A few days before the 1950 AGM thirty-nine would-be governors had paid their subscriptions in cash, which was handed to the secretary-manager by a Roman Catholic chaplain to the hospital. The committee was completely taken by surprise. Instead of the few regular, mainly female, attenders at the hospital AGM, the room was packed with middle-aged men who voted out the Protestant members of the committee, seven lay and three medical, and voted in their own representatives.

Public opinion was stunned at the audacity and success of the plan. De Valera, then leader of the opposition, described it in the Dáil as a 'coup' and Dr Noel Browne as an 'ambush'. Five of the old committee initiated legal proceedings but the President of the High Court dismissed the action, while heavily criticising the coup, and expressed sympathy with the plaintiffs. Dermot had to share the substantial cost of the proceedings, totalling £3,000 [£65,000] with Major Kirkwood (Jameson's distillery), Henry Guinness (Guinness and Mahon bankers), W. Boydell, A. F. Buckley and the Medical Board of the hospital. It hurt. He requested the board of Findlaters of which he was chairman, to help him meet the cost. They declined. However, I think Dermot was subsequently granted a bonus that went some way to redressing the issue! The hospital issue was finally resolved when, on the instigation of W. T. Cosgrave, a former member of the joint committee and an ex-taoiseach, the Meath Hospital Bill was enacted and regulated the method of appointing members of the medical staff.

Under the new Act the committee was reconstituted with representatives of Dublin Corporation, Dublin County Council, the medical board, the governors and two co-opted members. The restriction on the appointment of medical staff was removed. Dermot declined to let his name go forward for re-election.[33]

Some argue that the Knights were simply a mirror image of the Masonic order, seeking similar advantage for their 'own kind'. I cannot answer that as I am not a Mason, but I have no evidence to suggest that they exercised any serious influence in the commercial and social affairs of the city. I was only once approached on the question of the Masons. Shortly after I joined the firm in 1956 and while doing manual work in the grocery lofts, the house phone buzzed and 'Master Alex' was instructed to report to the chairman's office. 'Alex, you know Mr Lowe?' Frank Lowe was a director of Findlaters, chairman of the Irish Times and Hely's of Dame Street and deputy grand master of the Masonic Order (and incidentally a member of the board that refused to help with Dermot's costs for the legal case). Distinguished-looking, with white hair, he was always impeccably dressed, with a gold watch chain to his waistcoat and a white handkerchief in his top-pocket. He was not excessively tall, probably five foot five or six. I dutifully greeted Mr Lowe. 'Alex, Frank would like to know whether you would like your name go forward for the Masons?' (or whatever words were appropriate for such a question).

My reply was immediate and spontaneous: 'No, thank you, Daddy.' To which he concluded my audience: 'That's all, Alex, you may now return to your work.' The subject was never raised again, not at home that night, nor at any time during my life. My father was a Mason (although I can never recall him attending) as were his father and grandfather.

Royal Hospital for Incurables, Donnybrook

The Hospital first opened its doors in 1743 when Jonathan Swift was still Dean of St Patrick's Cathedral, Dublin. The hospital pre-dated its London namesake by more than one hundred years. It took in patients from all parts of Ireland without any payment whatsoever, an incurable malady coupled with poverty being the only test, and it was absolutely unsectarian.[34]

The Findlater involvement started in 1860 when, as we have seen, Alexander (the founder of the firm) became a governor. Alexander's nephew Billy, later Sir William, followed his uncle and served on the board for thirty-one years. He, in turn, was followed by his cousin Willie, my grandfather. In 1937 Willie resigned and Dermot was co-opted as the fourth, or maybe fifth, member of the family to serve on the board. There are other families that have contributed in a similar manner to the hospital, most notably the Fry family, three of whom have chaired the board of management in the past hundred years.

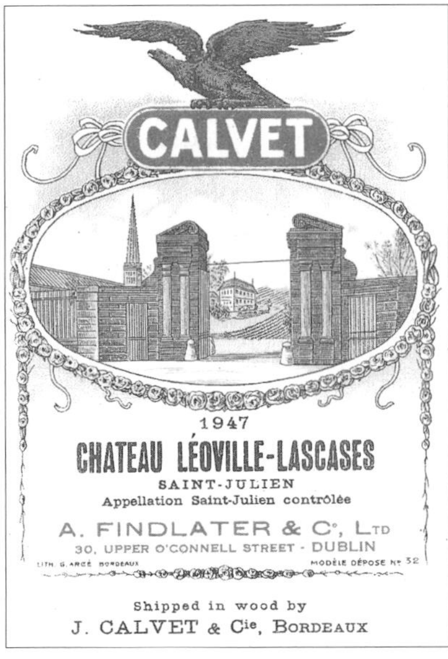

Léoville–Lascases label 1947

In 1939-45 war-time conditions once again forced up the hospital's costs and the managing committee grew increasingly worried about the financial situation. In August 1941 a special sub-committee consisting of the honorary officers, David Mitchell, Dermot, Frank Lowe, Joseph Walker and J. Lyons Jones, was set up 'to consider what steps should be taken in view of the annual excess of expenditure over income, viz. could our expenditure be reduced and by what means could we increase our income?' They made a number of proposals, accepted by the managing committee, which were to guide the hospital's policy in the years ahead. In 1949 Dermot set about doing himself what the special committee had recommended in 1941: he approached the leading business houses in the country for support for the hospital. This drive brought in over £2,960 [£65,000], one of the largest sums ever collected by an individual for the hospital. Unfortunately, this sum gave only temporary respite to the perilous financial position of the hospital and David Mitchell took over the difficult task.

Before departing the subject of hospitals and medical people I must tell a little story of Dermot's kindness to a friend in distress and his use of influence. It is recorded by Eric Fenelon, consultant surgeon to the Adelaide Hospital.

> I did quite a considerable amount of general surgery and quite a lot of Orthopaedic surgery with my old friend and colleague, the late Col Somerville-Large. In 1950 Col became ill, developing unfortunately lymphoma. As this involved a mediastinal problem which at first looked like a mediastinal abscess, and as chest surgery was in its infancy in Dublin, we decided to seek the best available advice in London and got him admitted to the King Edward VII Hospital for Officers and arranged urgently to transfer him there. The weather was appalling and Aer Lingus decided that there would be no planes flying to London. However, due to the good offices of an old friend, Dermot Findlater, we managed to arrange this urgently. Dermot contacted a pilot and Aer Lingus agreed that the plane would be allowed to fly if the pilot agreed to do so, which he willingly did, and Col was transferred for further investigation and treatment in London. Unfortunately, the condition on his return became progressive and he died in 1951 at the early age of 48 years. Indeed a sad loss of a magnificent Orthopaedic surgeon, perfect gentleman, and a very good friend. Col had a holiday home upon an Island in Sneem Bay in Kerry and was most generous with his hospitality in inviting many of his friends to join him on the island.[35]

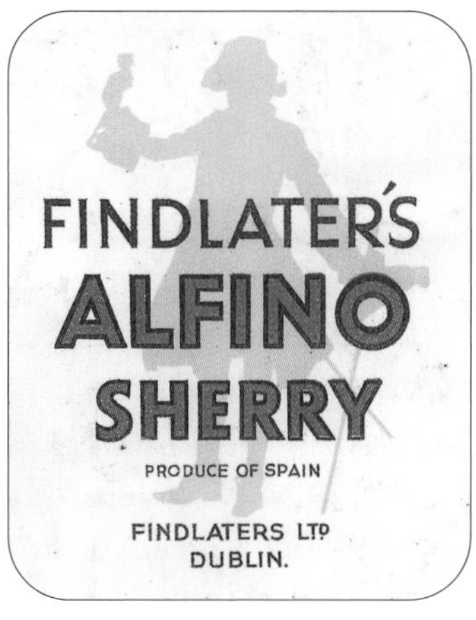

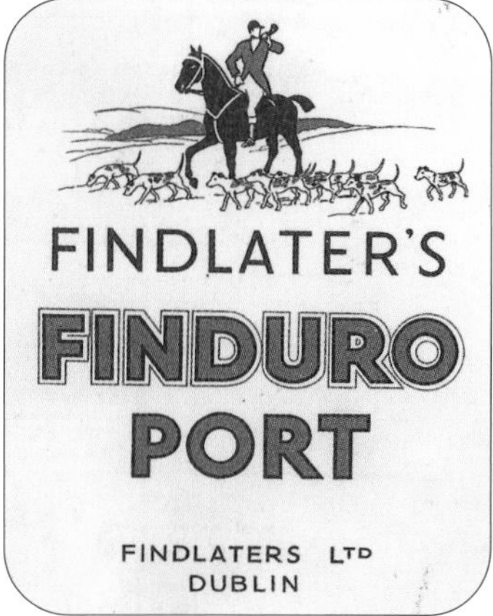

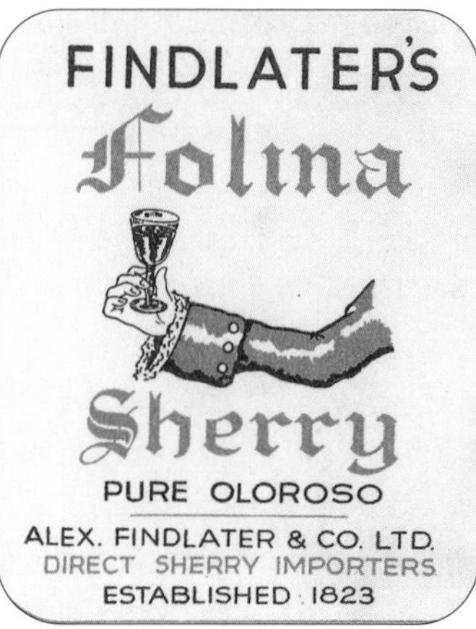

Findlater brand Sherries and Ports 1930s to the early 1960s, when fortified wines were in the ascendancy.

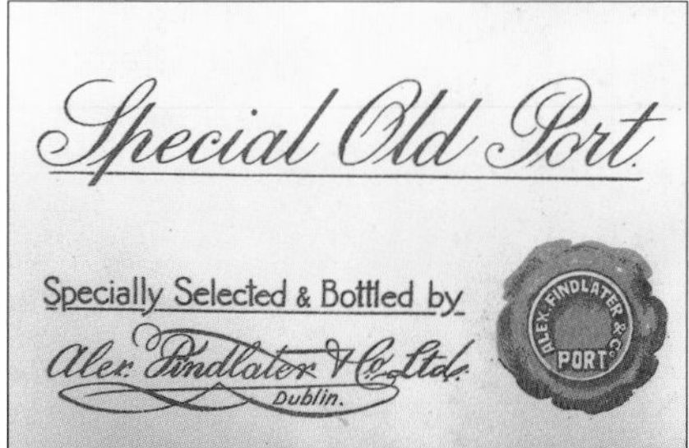

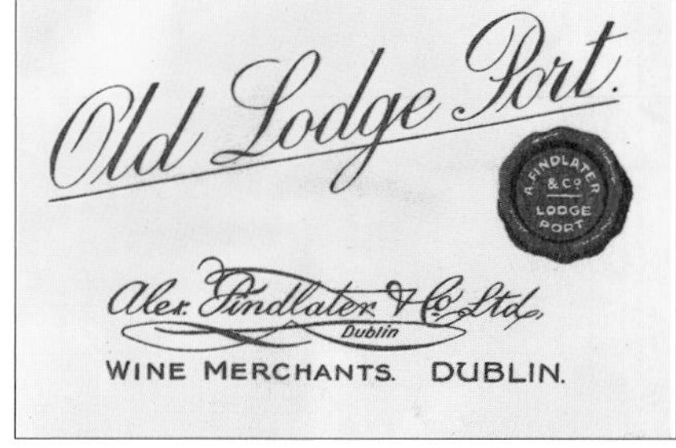

Wars are good for business

It is an uncomfortable fact that wars are good for business. When I joined the firm, I was told that profits had been good during and after the Emergency—up to 1952. In fact net profits were a mere 1.5 per cent of turnover in those years—and were to go down over the next decade to the impossibly slim 0.5 per cent. As we have seen, Dermot embarked on an extensive programme of investment in shop renovations. These costs were offset against revenue in the accounts. Normally 'repairs & renewals' would have amounted to between ½ and 1 per cent of turnover, but in two of the years in question they rose to over 4 per cent. Adjusting for these figures the profits were very respectable from 1940 to 1952, peaking at £50,000 in 1950[over £1m in 2000 values].

The low level of net profitability, combined with heavy investment in refurbishments and the build-up of new stocks began to put serious pressure on the company's bank account. It was in credit during the Emergency and remained more or less debt free until the end of 1949 (the credit balance having peaked at around £50,000 at the beginning of 1946). Now funds were need to restock and develop the company; there was some discussion about asking the Irish Assurance Company for extra capital in order to open new shops and generally develop the business. However, at a meeting of the directors on 28 September 1949, it was agreed to finance the proposed new branches at Mount Merrion and Walkinstown with the assistance of our bankers.

I have no doubt that there would have been a conversation between Dermot and Frank Klinger. Frank Klinger, who was senior partner in Stokes Bros and Pim, now KPMG, the firm's auditors, was on the board of the Royal Bank (chairman from 1952) and was a trustee to the Findlater debenture holders. Overdraft was the normal means of bank advances. The bank asked in a gentlemanly manner how much we would like, little anticipating that they would be tied in for the next twenty years. Once committed there was no looking back. At first it was unsecured at £25,000 [£550,000]. Then £50,000 [£1m] in 1951. At £100,000 [£1.7m] (at 5½ per cent) in 1955 it was secured with a second debenture.

Overdraft facilities were also needed to fund stocks and debtors as our wholesale wine and spirit business regained national distribution, on a bigger scale than pre-Emergency. As soon as wines became available after the war in Europe, Dermot set about replenishing the extensive cellars under our O'Connell Street premises. It took time. From Bordeaux and Burgundy we had to wait two years for the outstanding 1945 vintage to be ready for shipment and the relaxation of import controls. Wine imports then were almost entirely in cask. On arrival the wine had to be rested, bottled and matured before being offered for sale. The great 1945s were first listed in 1949. We also obtained a few Bordeaux wines which had been bottled in the Châteaux during the war, but the volumes were insignificant: Haut Brion 1944, Gruaud Larose 1944, Talbot 1943, Lagrange 1943, Lafite 1940 and d'Armailhac 1943. Champagne seems to have been available in all wartime vintages.

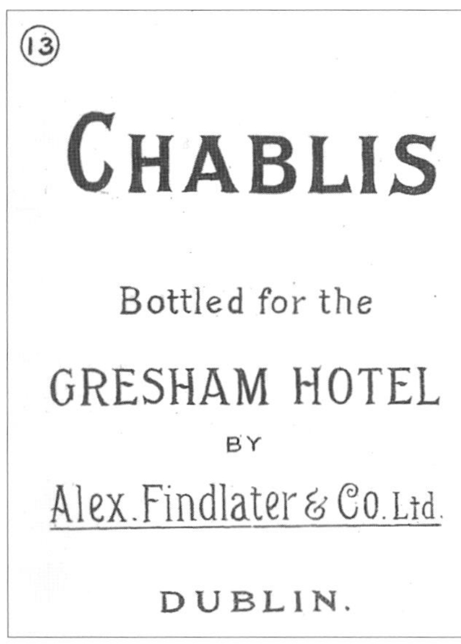

Chablis label for the Gresham Hotel.

Leoville–Barton label for the City of Dublin Steam Packet Co.

In a letter to me Dr Garret FitzGerald recalls purchasing the wines from this epoch:

> I remember doing a tour of all the Dublin wine merchants in 1953—there was only about half-a-dozen of them then—with a view to comparing prices. I recall that the second best value was Findlaters. They were about one shilling dearer than Thompson D'Olier—since unhappily defunct—but cheaper than Mitchells and significantly cheaper than Morgans who advertised quite a lot, which pushed up their prices. The dearest wine in Dublin at that time was a 1950 Château Yquem which was two guineas and the most expensive clarets—1945 and 1947 Château Lafite and Latour—were twenty-eight shillings. Some of the finer German wines were up to thirty-seven shillings each. The cost of living has risen sixteen-fold since then which means that in present day terms the finest clarets were available for £22.50. That was really good value!

In 1949 we again began to publish wine lists (there were none from 1940 to 1948), and the number of lines listed reflected Dermot's keen interest in growing that sector of the business; the count rose from 187 in the late 1930s to 240 in 1950 and 518 in 1960. It is difficult to justify this in the economic and social climate. The stock valuation rose from £103,000 in 1940 to £144,000 in 1950 and to £280,000 in 1960. This latter figure is equivalent to over £4m in 2000 values. To put these figures in perspective, modern day Findlaters operate a very successful wholesale wine business in a much expanded market on a stock level of £1.8m (September 2000 figure).

In those days the wine merchant shipped his Bordeaux, Burgundy and port in cask, bottled them in his cellars, laid them carefully on their sides into bins or racks holding up to 240 bottles and marked the topside of the punt of the bottle with whitewash to denote that the sediment would settle on the lower side.

This was important when the bottles were handled for sale or in a restaurant. In the case of vintage port the neck of the bottle was dipped in wax to form a wax seal over the cork. The shipper or producer of the port, and the vintage year, were marked on the corks as labels would not survive for a number of years in cellar conditions.* When all this was done and the wine matured, it was sold on credit to the hotel, gentleman's club or consumer.

The important wine customers at that time were the four leading hotels—the Russell, Hibernian, Shelbourne and Gresham, Jammets restaurant, the Dún Laoghaire yacht clubs, the Common Room in Trinity College Dublin and the city's gentlemen's clubs. Most notable for us was the Royal Irish Yacht Club. Reserves were agreed at a gentlemanly meeting over a glass of sherry in our chairman's office and bins marked accordingly. Findlaters only requested payment after the matured stock had been transferred to the club. In the cellars, in my early days in the firm, were large stocks of Léoville Barton 1955 and 1957 marked forbiddingly: 'Reserve RIYC, don't touch' and woe and betide a cellarman or apprentice who did. It was a great deal for the club.

In June 1950 the board decided that the time was now right to capitalise on the goodwill that had accrued to the firm by keeping many a country publican in supplies of spirits during the Emergency. Mattie McElroy, then manager of the Sandymount branch and formerly in the O'Connell Street wine department, was charged with the responsibility and appointed senior traveller. We were to be major players again in the wine and spirit business.

Spirits, whiskey in particular, and fortified wines (sherry and port), were the bedrock of the wholesaler's business in those days. The distilleries distilled the spirit and sold it in casks, perhaps 20 per cent over proof, to the merchant, who matured, blended, bottled and marketed it, often under his individual label such as Findlaters' Jameson Eight-year-old, Mitchell's Green Spot and Gilbey's Red Breast. Unlike a modern supermarket, what the customer saw on the shelves of a Findlater branch was only a fraction of the activity. However, from a financial point of view the commitment was considerable, tying money up for seven years or more in stock.

Dermot's judgement was to lay in healthy stocks. It was as good a home for Findlaters' capital as any, so it was said. The retailing revolution was not yet a speck on the horizon and the importance of fast stock turns a thing of the future. He was of the generation for whom cash management was not such a priority; they were bulk buyers, in sacks, boxes and barrels, a few months' supply bought in season at the right price. However the ratio of stock to sales was not too bad at 6½ weeks. The explanation may be that spirits were matured under bond and thus the valuation excluded duty and the company had a big turnover in per-

* In those days we fined (clarified) ruby and tawny ports and heavy red wines with fresh blood from the abattoir and light red wines with whites of fresh eggs thoroughly beaten. The blood albumen acted as a collagen taking all solids and impurities to the base of the cask. White wines were fined with isinglass, a kind of gelatin obtained from fish, especially sturgeon. It was also used to make jellies and for fining real ale. Today bentonite is used for the same purposes.

ishable foodstuffs bought weekly.*

When it came to bottlings of all commodities, we had the edge. Every wholesaler and most publicans and grocers bottled beer, sherry, port and spirits and the resulting quality variation around the country was enormous. Even today tastings suggest that as much as one bottle of wine in twenty is rejected because of faults caused by bad bottling. From the 1880s we exhorted customers to ask for 'Findlater's Bottlings' and featured the exhortation in our advertising and embossed the bottles 'Findlater's Bottling.' Good bottling and a reputation for a fine claret, Burgundy and port went hand in hand. The merchant's name on the label and capsule were signs to the purchaser of the quality that he might expect. Show a merchant 'Old Bottled Vintage Port' and he would readily pay a premium for the bottle from a good house and discount the less reputable.

That was the cream of the trade. At the other end competition was intense. Decisions were usually based entirely on price. Beaujolais, Chablis, Liebfraumilch, Powers Gold Label and Guinness were all price-sensitive. There was not a chance of any wholesaler becoming rich. And we in Findlaters fought it out with the other wholesalers for our share of the pub market. The wholesalers from time to time tried to curtail their price-cutting of spirits, but the very next day were again at each other's throats. The total wine market in those days, 1950, was only 248,000 cases in comparison to 4 million in 2000. Fortified wines (ports and sherries) represented something like a third of all wine imports at this time, as against less than 2.5 per cent today.

While I make much of Dermot's prowess in buying wine there were intermediaries between himself and the negoçiant. These were men of stature in the trade. They proferred samples and quotations and travelled the country once or twice a year with the principal whose name was on the label, calling on the merchants and booking orders. The merchant then shipped, bottled, matured, listed and sold. Good lunches and dinners were part of the ritual. This suited Findlaters fine with the directors' dining-room on the top floor. Eddie Doyle, who was a pure agent, carrying no stock, represented Jean Lawton of Lalande & Cie in Bordeaux, Patriache in Burgundy and Charles Heidsieck in Champagne. The characters were undoubtedly the duo in Lett brothers, Brian Hood and Tommy Hamilton. They represented Williams & Humbert sherries (big in those days), Calvet Bordeaux, Taylor's port and Deinhard Rhine and Moselle wines. Doyen of the agents was Turbetts, in business since 1770 and with an enviable porfolio of agencies including Barton in Bordeaux and Bouchard Père et Fils in Burgundy. Alex Turbett and Desmond Sullivan were very helpful to young men like myself entering the trade. They would organise prolonged visits to the vineyards and cellars abroad and educate us in the finer points of the product. This was also true of Paddy Keown of Begges of Bachelors Walk and John de M.

* The balance-sheet figures for 1950 were stocks £144,031, sales £1,166,251. The business methods in 1900 were fascinatingly different with stock at £69,603 supporting sales of £133,949, suggesting that over six months' stock was on hand at any one time. In 2000 values the 1900 stock is worth over £5m as against the 1950 figure at £3m.

Turton of Jas McCullagh Son and Co. Finally, we had a very close working relationship with David Hunter who doubled as a wine agent with several agencies that we supported, and also looked after all our tea tasting and our blending and packing factory in Rathmines.

Matthew McElroy of Raheny who joined the company in 1928. O'Connell Street Wine Manager 1932–1942; Manager Sandymount branch 1942–1950; Senior Wine representative 1950–1962; Co–opted to the Board of Directors 1960; Director in charge of wines and spirits 1962–69.

A good agency, then as now, is worth its weight in gold. In the 1950s the most sought after was that of Harveys of Bristol. Harveys were developing Bristol Cream into the biggest selling premium sherry brand in the world when sherry was a universally popular drink. In early days it was on quota due to the shortage of mature sherry stocks. Harveys were traditional wine merchants with ancient cellars in Denmark Street, Bristol, and a wine list more extensive than the best elsewhere. But they were at the forefront of modern management and were employing young Oxbridge graduates, using advanced warehousing techniques in a purpose-built facility, and marketing skills which were totally new to the traditional wine trade. They were then the biggest independent wine shipper in the UK and quoted on the stock exchange. Dermot got on very well with their managing director, George McWatters.

Dermot won the Harvey agency by a short head. He had been warned that their chairman, Jack Harvey, was a devil for blind tastings during the boardroom lunch. A call of nature mid-morning brought Dermot past the laboratory-cum-tasting-room, a room then new to the trade and a gem for the inquisitive. A friendly chat ensued. A *coup d'oeil* memorised the decanted bottles in the corner! The accuracy and fluency of his assessments of the test wines would have left the present day Masters of Wine* speechless! The chairman marvelled. The managing director had the agent he desired. Father summed up the lesson to me later–'Always do your homework'. The association with Harveys flourished for twelve years. Their sherries were in every worthwhile outlet in the country. It was a happy partnership, and there were even discussions of a closer association.

By the mid-1950s Dermot had cellars overflowing with good wine, a bond with an excess of maturing whiskey and the best sherry agency in town. This had required considerable capital, both in stocks and debtors. Margins were tight

* Master of Wine is the highest qualification in the wine industry. There are at present 231 certified Masters of Wine in the world. Out of 58 international candidates who took the four days of exams in 2000, only four passed. We are an industry of high standards!

and competition tough. There were at least a dozen wholesalers all fighting for a share of the market and price was the biggest weapon. Strategic positioning of premium brands was way in the future. However, Dermot had a good sales team. Mattie McElroy had been joined by Aidan Kelly, fresh out of Blackrock College, son of C. E. K., cartoonist and proprietor of *Dublin Opinion*. Aidan developed into a first class wineman. He had a fine nose, good palate, excellent judgment and expressed himself well. There were six in that sales team and they fulfilled their task with distinction.

Aidan Kelly recalls his early days in Findlaters:

> Jokes, practical or otherwise, were de rigueur—if unobserved by the manager or charge-hand. John's enemy number one was up on this bridge that linked the two grocery lofts where the dry groceries and sacks were stored. He called to John below: 'Hey, John, what are you doing for Christmas?' John looked up and said he didn't know, whereupon he was asked: 'Would you like to be a snowman?' Forthwith a bag of white flour was emptied over the rail. John stood in the yard, immaculate in white, with only a pair of eyes looking out under dusty lashes. Not for the first time John presented himself at the General Manager's office to give voice to what he thought of this world and some of its occupants, while his colleagues and adversaries fell about themselves in laughter.

As all this investment was being laid down, Findlaters continued the expensive tradition of service. The Findlater branch shops were giving a daily service to a large clientèle in and around Dublin, as (the late) Pauline Russell wrote:

> Findlaters of Howth was a friendly store. Spacious, clean, and the atmosphere of the old grocery emporium. The bacon counter, the smell of coffee beans and the friendly assistants. Also the feeling that the customer was always important. The service from Findlaters was 'different'. Most of the orders came from 'the knights of the road'. Three times a week a representative called to the house.
>
> A friendly face on a Monday, Wednesday and Friday with all the good offers from the store. Over the years they not only knew my order, but my growing family, and should I forget an essential item from my order they diplomatically reminded me of my omission! Then the delivery arrived that afternoon and any complaints were received kindly and immediately rectified.
>
> Of course, it all came back to the staff. Mr Rowland, the man at the helm. Jackie Graham and Christy O'Rourke on the road. Every house on the Peninsula was glad when they called. Not only did they take my grocery order—they fixed the fuse or mended the child's toy and, over a cup of coffee, gave the offers of the week. I even got Waterford cut glasses when I bought enough Findlater's Alfino Sherry!
>
> And, who could forget the van driver, Dick Bennett. He took the flak when something had been forgotten and returned with the missing item with a smile. Also, in an emergency he would pick up the prescription from the Chemist, move a motor mower or hoover from house to home, or give a message to a friend or relation on the delivery route.

At home we learnt at an early age the meaning of the Findlater service. It was

Collect these beautiful Waterford Sherry glasses
24 OF THESE SLIPS CAN BE EXCHANGED FOR ONE OF THESE GLASSES
ALEX FINDLATER & Co Ltd
Upr O'Connell Street
and Branches

A sucessful and long-running promotion for Alfino sherry.

not unusual for Dermot to be called out on Christmas Day. The usual complaint was 'my turkey has gone off'. Not unexpected if December had been a particularly humid month. Dermot often took an extra turkey home on Christmas Eve to cover this eventuality. We would drive to the customer's house—near or far, it did not matter. He presented a lovely new turkey and retrieved the offending bird. He then showed me the cause of the offence, the giblets which we had left neatly wrapped for the customer, just inside the bird. Once removed the bird was fit for the next in distress. We took a poor view of our competitors who did not automatically give the giblets to the customer. On another occasion he got a call from the nuns in Bray who had not received their 'standing order' for 6lbs of rashers, notwithstanding that it was Christmas Day! No trouble, we opened up head office, sliced the bacon and made the delivery.

And on yet another occasion he drove all the way to Kylemore Abbey in Connemara. As Feargal Quinn would say: 'That was the Findlater standard of service involving enthusiasm, dedication, commitment and energy'.

Of course old-fashioned ways occasionally had their drawbacks. Irene Lawless of Kilsallaghan, Co. Dublin, remembers an incident from Findlaters of Malahide in the 1950s:

> I remember on one occasion a few of us housewives were standing at the counter awaiting our turn when this 'retired Army type' man strode in the door. Ignoring the fact that several women were ahead of him he shouted to the Assistant: 'Send up a small jar of Bovril, will you?' and the Assistant answered: 'Certainly, sir.' At that time I was getting £2 a week housekeeping money and could manage all right, so a jar of Bovril must have been only a few pence. It speaks well for the firm that they would deliver so small an item. It also depicts the attitude of men of the time. Not only was it beneath his dignity to carry a small jar home in his pocket, but the fact that several women were ahead of him in the shop was completely ignored—a man should not be kept waiting and, sad to say, shop assistants always served the men first in those days, even when they gave the order across the heads of women already there.
>
> As a postscript I can say that when I got my messages and went out the door that same man was standing outside talking to a friend and I heard him say that a terrible thing had happened to him that morning. He had put on his plus fours and a bee was trapped inside and he got stung somewhere unspecified. I could have said 'Good for you, bee!'

And of course as we have seen, Findlaters did charge just a little more, as Anne Cronin remembers:

> I was a customer from about 1940 in Dorset Street branch to the time it closed. I telephoned in my order and it was delivered on Friday: meal for the chickens and my meat from Hearn's next door was brought as well as anything I wanted. I could always leave it to the staff to send the best, even at Christmas time. Ham or turkey and all the other things. Mind you, people said they were always 2d dearer than everyone else, but when you got all your goods delivered on your kitchen table what could one say? It was the usual thing to have the kettle boiling for Findlater's man about 1 o'clock every Friday and they sat out in the van and had their tea. Would that we had a service like that today!

Dermot continued to invest to improve quality. At the 1952 AGM he told shareholders: 'We have secured the services of a very efficient and qualified man to act as head baker of our model bakery in Thomas Street. This man won more than one prize in the recent International baker congress held in the Mansion House'. And on packaging: 'We have just received delivery of one of the most modern machines for weighing and packing flour untouched by hand, and very shortly will receive a similar machine for weighing and packing sugar. We have had similar machines for packing tea for many years. We are also in the course of installing a fully automatic unit for the bottling of beer, stout and lager and it is our belief that this unit, when in operation, will be the finest and most modern in this country.'

Operational systems were not neglected: 'We have completely mechanised our accountancy system at Head Office, by the installation of Burroughes accounting machines and electric invoicing machines. It enables us to get out our statement of accounts and invoices more quickly, more accurately and more efficiently.' (The famous old system of carrying cash by wires or tubes from the point of sale to a central cash desk was finally removed in 1960.)

And on kindly gestures to staff: 'At our Dún Laoghaire Branch we now have a member of our staff who some few years ago was completely incapacitated by blindness [from the bombing of the North Strand] and is now, as a result of training given to him by the National Council for the Blind of Ireland, in charge of our tobacco and cigarette department.'

1952 was perhaps the nadir of the post-war economy. With the public finances in serious difficulties, Finance Minister Seán MacEntee was obliged to withdraw the food subsidies that had been established during the Emergency, which as *The Irish Times* put it 'toughened the struggle for tens of thousands of citizens'. At the same time traders and the Revenue Commissioners found it increasingly difficult to collect debts, so credit was cut back, and garnishee orders became common. The budget of 1952 outraged Dermot, and many others besides: The headlines read: PUBLIC STAGGERED BY INCREASES; PENAL! CRAZY! THE FINAL BLOW! While higher taxes and duties had been expected, nobody seemed to have anticipated that they would have been so harsh. 'A crazy budget,' commented

Dermot when an *Irish Independent* representative discussed with him the increased prices of tea, sugar, butter, bread and flour. 'Customers having only the same amount of money to spend on these commodities would be able to buy less under the new prices, he said. The Minister had said that competitive selling of tea might mean increased sales. This was not so. What was wanted was competitive buying: they wanted to get back the experts to buy tea and not have semi-Government officials doing it.'[36]

Dermot in the fifties

At the next AGM Dermot continued his remarks:

> The budget of 1952 descended upon us and meted out tremendously harsh treatment, especially to the licensed portion of our business. The Minister concerned appeared to revel in the fact that he had reimposed the taxation mitigated by his predecessor in office. The trade in whiskey and beer dropped away, but the amount of capital needed to finance the reduced turnover actually increased. Cider was the only alcoholic beverage the duty on which remained unchanged in the Budget. The sales of it were almost doubled, showing that had whiskey and beer been left alone, a steady improvement in sales could have been expected, which would most likely have produced more revenue than the higher rates of duty did, and would have assisted the distilleries to increase their home trade and thus to encourage them to enlarge their production for export trade. A further result of the re-introduction of the penal taxation, as one might call it, was that more capital was required by wholesalers, because the banks were, at the same time, restricting credit.
>
> The Government's financial policy is resulting in the Minister for Finance taking more and more of a smaller cake. The conditions for prosperity require that more money be left to fructify in the pockets of the tax payers with the Government taking less and less of a larger cake. It has been urged by Ministers that plant and machinery should be maintained at the very highest level of efficiency and premises comply with certain set standards of hygiene. The Minister for Finance has again failed to concede to industry any concession by way of tax-free depreciation for plant and building. It should be possible to create out of profits, reserves sufficient to enable the replacement of plant and machinery by new or more efficient units.

This is the time the Mountjoy Brewery ceased operations and we can only assume they, and many others who fell by the wayside, had not the reserves to reinvest in plant and machinery. The Dublin distilleries and Cork breweries were surely also in this category.

The St Lawrence Hotel, Howth and public house with the shop (the tall building on the right in the background) and the filling station beyond.

Despite conditions that might have suggested a drawing-in of horns, Dermot continued to invest heavily in the company's properties, among which was the St Lawrence Hotel, Howth. In January 1949 the board discussed the possibility of selling the hotel to raise money for retail expansion. We had owned the hotel since the turn of the century. It was on Bord Fáilte's Grade A listing and the board had made a commitment in August 1950 to maintain it at that standard. Grade A then required the complete central heating of the hotel and a number of bedrooms with bathrooms attached. Between 1943 and 1950 £36,000 [almost £800,000] was invested in maintenance and improvements, a sizeable sum in those days. In 1954/55 another £8,000 [over £135,000] was spent on a modern lounge bar, one of the first of its kind—named the Alfino Rooms—which produced excellent returns immediately. An *Irish Licensing World* reporter noted that 'furnishings, equipment and decor reflect unerring good taste and combine to create an atmosphere that is at once luxurious and intimate. Small wonders that the Alfino Room is already a favourite rendezvous of a large and discriminating clientèle'.[37]

In 1961 a banqueting room was added to cater for dinners and wedding breakfasts. The hotel was overall profitable if read in conjunction with the investment in maintenance and improvements (£61,000 was expended between 1943 and 1968). The most profitable period was during the management of Una and Michael Lee, 1958 to 1963, and Oswell Johnson in the period before them.

In 1955 a profound change in trading conditions started a chain of events that eventually led to the demise of the old Findlater chain. This was the ending of retail price maintenance. RPM was the very commendable principle of selling goods at the prices recommended by the manufacturer. This meant that retailers competed on service and stock-holding rather than price. The ending heralded the start of price cutting. A commission was set up to explore the issue, but Dermot had gathered in advance that the government (including his old adver-

Staff party at Abilene in the 1950s

sary Seán Lemass) had made up its mind. In his evidence to the commission Dermot was expected to support the Retail Grocers Dairy and Allied Trades Association (RGDATA) line, in favour of the maintenance of RPM, which was in Findlaters' own best interests. Instead, to the shock of all those present (including myself, then aged seventeen) he played for maximum effect and sided with the commission and the ending of RPM. The eventual change in pricing was gradual, a trickle rather than a tidal wave. RGDATA, on behalf of its members, protested vigorously whenever possible. But competition by price was gaining momentum and self-service aided the process. Dermot, at the time, was quoted: 'Price cutting is merely a technique of selling and is suitable to certain classes of people. As long as only a few traders engaged in it, it will be profitable to them, but if everybody goes in for it they will wipe each other out.'

Bulmers and Tuborg

Following the establishment of Bulmers in Clonmel in 1936, Findlaters were their largest wholesale distributors and made good money. Cider was a cheap substitute for porter, and so very price sensitive. Two pence under the price of porter in the pubs and cider would sell coming up to pay day when pennies were scarce. If Findlaters added a penny the publicans would do likewise and sales would tumble. A falling-out between the cider company directors led to Findlaters ceasing to distribute for Bulmers.

The need to replace the cider volume was urgent and this led Dermot to Tuborg. He had anticipated the demand for a top class lager beer on the market and had initiated talks with the Danish Tuborg breweries while in Denmark on a hockey tour in 1947.

Continuous pasteurisation was the difficulty. Importation in bottles was out. Irish glass bottles were obligatory, on account of the weights and measure stamp embossed on the bottle, and had to be sent abroad for filling. Patz and ZHB

Micheál MacLiammóir, Cyril Cusack and young Master Alex, in 1956. Ivor Williams, bar manager, behind.

lagers were early on the market in the post-1945 era.* In July 1950 the board agreed to invest £15,000 [over £300,000 in 2000] in bottling equipment in order to overcome the difficulties of importing in bottle and to centralise all branch

Pre–war promotion of Bulmers Cider

* Lager beer has been around for longer than one realises. We have in our memorabilia an old Findlater Pilsener lager beer label belonging to the Findlaters Mountjoy Brewery and also a letter of 1908 concerning our bottling of Allsopp's Lager from Burton on Trent. In addition we were agents for Tuborg and Whitbread in the first decade of the 20th century. In 1937 Findlaters distributed Regal Lager, brewed in Enniscorthy.

Willie Elsen, Robbie Cowep and John Bowles.
Matador ZJ 187 loaded and ready to depart with a full load of Tuborg lager, 1955.

bottling into Findlater Place. In 1956 the new plant was said to have a capacity of 24,000 bottles a day and employment for 30 workers. Columnist Terry O'Sullivan reported on the lavish launch in his 'Dubliner's Diary' of 15 June 1956:

> Nothing in our experience prepared us for the gilt-edged opening by Findlaters of a new lager beer plant, a joint venture in which the brewers are the Tuborg Breweries in Copenhagen. In the first place, in the morning, the dispatch yard of Findlaters had been converted into a kind of open-air beer cellar, the kind of place you take for granted in Bavaria, with snow-white tables against white-washed walls, flowers all over the place, and of course, lots of ice-cold Tuborg Lager. Having tasted the lager, looked at a film, and tasted some more lager, everybody went off out to the St Lawrence in Howth, there to nibble a bit of lunch. It was the best lunch I ever read, and out of the twenty-six different items, here is the overture and prologue. Real Turtle Soup, Iced Volga Caviar, Corners of Smoked Salmon, Dublin Bay Prawns, Slane Salmon Mayonnaise, Medallions of Ireland's Eye Lobster, Boyne Trout in Aspic, Fillet Sole St Lawrence, Roll Mop Herrings and Silver Onions.

Our unique Guinness label. Note, that we, not the brewery, guarantee the excellence of the product.

The expansive style was typical of the Dermot of the 1950s. He was a sound businessman and enthusiastic supporter of his

John McGrail

products. He believed in his agencies and in the firm's brands: Alfino Sherry, Finduro Port, Guinness with the XX (not the Harp) on the label, our eight-year-old Jameson—and many others. Out and about, he untiringly called for his brands, Harveys, Tuborg or his favourite, little known Unna, the golden Danish liqueur from Elsinore, the home of Hamlet. He was a natural at public relations before it became a profession. He drew together his two worlds—the theatre and the drinks business. He threw receptions for visiting artists, sometimes in the cellars, sometimes at the St Lawrence and sometimes at Abilene, our home in Blackrock: José Greco and his Spanish dancers, the Royal Danish Ballet, the D'Oyly Carte Opera Company, the Carnival on Ice troupe, Leslie Henson the comedian, Cyril Cusack and Micheál MacLiammóir when they performed in *Hamlet,* Jimmy Ellis and Sam Thompson during the run of *Over the Bridge,* the Danish soccer team, the English hockey team, and Everton Football Club. He loved a party. If there was no party he made one: a staff party, a student party, or just entertaining company at an extended lunch in the directors' dining room; and, not surprisingly, he loved his role as chairman of the judges of Miss Ireland which was arranged annually by Lorcan and Billy Bourke in the Four Provinces ballroom at the top of Harcourt Street.

An assessment of Dermot's character by a handwriting expert is shrewd, and quite accurate.

> A strong will enabled him to make and carry out plans without wavering and led to a courageous, even bold, attitude. His mind worked quickly. He was a forceful individual, primarily interested in obtaining results. The strong effort could hurt others, not deliberately, if he was not careful. The desire for results came first. Listening skills were reasonable but he would not always hear what was being said. He had the facility for presenting ideas well and this led to an influential and persuasive approach. There was a tendency to rationalise his actions; and he would disregard any difficulties in the way. This was fine if there was somebody to look after the problems.

That's where his partner, John McGrail came in, for Dermot was essentially a pragmatist and a doer rather than a theoretician.

Dermot was obviously overworked during the war and was under a lot of board and family pressure to find a business partner. They realised that he could be extremely difficult to work with and were delighted that in John McGrail (or

Lorries loading outside the despatch in Findlater Place. The livery was maroon with gold lettering. Most of the 21 branches had a van.

Jack, as he was called in the business) he had found a partner with whom he was compatible. McGrail had been manager of H. J.Heinz in Northern Ireland prewar, and then with the Ministry of Supplies during the war. His friendship with Dermot had grown through the theatre in Belfast and was to develop further when he joined the company in Dublin in 1948. On his part Dermot had tremendous regard for McGrail and decisions in relation to the firm and theatre were taken jointly. They were a good team. John McGrail took particular responsibility for the hotel in Howth, the beer bottling and much of the theatre work. He shared the personnel work with Dermot and was able to throw a new critical eye over the trading in the branches. I think it was also important to Dermot that he was a Catholic. Firms in those days were typecast by the religion of the founding family. This Dermot did not like. He would not tolerate anyone using his or her religion to gain employment or a supply contract. In fact he was paranoid about it. Findlaters as an employer with its large staff naturally reflected the nation's religious ratios but Dermot wanted this to show through to the top. However, John McGrail was there on ability not as a token. The partnership worked well, but alas in the end it failed to meet the severe strategic challenges of the retail revolution.

Courtesy and helpfulness were imbued into the staff, as is illustrated by Ann Gaskins of Ballinasoe Farm, Roundwood, in Co. Wicklow:

> I live here in the Wicklow mountains and my husband died at an early age, leaving me with farm and young son. This, at that time (1958), was a formidable job to try and do. I sowed about 10 acres of potatoes in those years and, not knowing where to turn, a thought struck me. Try Mr MacKenzie the Manager in Findlaters! So in I go and, true to form, not alone would he take one ton of potatoes per week, but he would send out his van with Mr Michael Traynor driving to collect the potatoes. He

Traditional counter service. Dan Skehan attends to a celebrity at the dairy counter in O'Connell Street.

was a Bray man and an old family. These were the days of kindness in the full meaning of the word, and the Manager's response to me helped me to keep the farm that I still own.

In 1959 Dermot showed a consciousness that the traditional Findlater service was under threat: 'Whilst recognising that a large proportion of our customers require a credit and delivery service, the changing pattern of food distribution in other countries has compelled us to consider the desirability of converting one or two selected Branches to the Self Service or Supermarket method of trading.' The cost of credit and delivery was also beginning to concern him: 'The costly credit and delivery service we provide for our customers is becoming more and more difficult to maintain out of the relatively small profit yield on groceries and provisions.' In 1960 he returned to the subject:

> Last year I referred to the difficulty of maintaining our costly Credit and Delivery Service out of the relatively small profit yield on groceries and our efforts to continue this service without resorting to the practice that obtains elsewhere of making a specific charge for delivery. The wage increase mentioned above has aggravated this position and made the traditional Findlater standard of service well nigh uneconomic. Rising costs in every direction with the inevitable concomitant 'dear money' is another adverse factor in the economics of credit and delivery.

And on self-service he added:

> The trend towards self-service in retail food distribution continues and plans for the conversion to self-service of some of our shops is under active consideration. The conversion of a large retail food shop from counter service to up-to-date self-service involves careful planning, specialised training of staff and substantial capital outlay if the best results are to be obtained. By the end of the present year, we hope to accom-

Clear unambigious advertising of the fifties. Our name was then a household word. It was not until the mid–seventies, long after we had closed, that my mother was taken by surprise when asked to spell her name by a shop assistant.
(This CIE bus was lovingly restored by Gary Manahan of Churchtown)

plish the conversion of one of our large shops, which will then serve as the prototype for further development.

Of course, we had been receiving advice about getting into supermarkets, especially from our American friends such as Harry McEvoy, American chief of Kelloggs in Manchester. Henry Haserot from Ohio, our Hawaiian pineapple supplier, raved about the out-of-town supermarkets with liberal car parking and John McGrail's ex-colleagues in H. J. Heinz & Co. urged us to have a look. In America self-service had become widespread during the Depression in the 1930s, when vacant warehouses had been converted into supermarkets selling packaged groceries with the minimum of customer service. Since then they had grown in sophistication to become a highly efficient method of retailing. Supermarkets were cheap to develop in America because land prices were much lower than in Britain. The higher wages in America also meant that the less labour-intensive nature of self-service trading was attractive to food retailers in the United States. America's affluence contrasted sharply with the straitened economy of post-war Britain. In 1950, 59 per cent of American households had one or more cars compared with 12 per cent in Britain.

The board minutes on 24 June 1959 record that two visiting consultants from the UK met the board and gave their views on the possibilities of converting our Dún Laoghaire branch, which was over 5,000 square feet, into a supermarket, with a separate wine shop. This would have been considered very large in those days. A sketch was submitted and it was explained that they would submit detailed recommendations, plans and specifications to us in writing.

Dún Laoghaire would have been a wonderful flagship and would have put our stamp at the head of the fledgling industry. We would have been ahead of our competitors. Alas, it was not to be. Dermot's lack of enthusiasm for the new departure killed the project in 1960. He had already supervised the modernisation of the entire branch network in the previous two decades. Finances were tight. The overdraft in March 1960 was at £170,000 [£2.5m]. The beer bottling, hotel and wines and spirits had used up the capital. On the retail side price cutting was eating into margins. The retail revolution was at hand, but the company had committed all its available resources to the other sections of the business.

Feargal Quinn opened his first Superquinn in Dundalk in 1960, and in Finglas in 1965; Ben Dunne opened Dunnes Stores in Cornelscourt in 1966, and the Stillorgan Shopping Centre also opened in 1966. Ahead of these were individual traders who generated a lot of publicity but were not long-term players. H. Williams were the exception with self-service in their Henry Street branch in the late 1940s, not successful, and in the 1950s and 1960s with success, followed by a branch in Killester.

So great were the differences between the American situation and the British, that J. Edward Hammond, a leading retail commentator, stated in 1951 that it was 'improbable that this class of emporium will ever be introduced into Great Britain.'[38] The revolution in England got under way in the early 1950s.

The self-service technique of selling was sweeping the world of retailing when it arrived in Ireland. Its main attraction to the customers was the freedom to make decisions without embarrassment and at a greatly reduced cost. Thus the customers could decide to buy the lower priced item or the unknown brand without disclosing this to a possibly 'superior' sales assistant—and thereby save a great deal of money at the same time. A number of factors came together. As Feargal Quinn put it:

> The main factors influencing the growth of the supermarket idea have been the same in Ireland as elsewhere—growing affluence, the disappearance of domestic help, the rising costs of distribution through traditional wholesale and retail channels, the more widespread use of cars, the housewife's anxiety to cut down the time spent on shopping for ordinary household requirements, widespread use of refrigerators permitting storage of perishable foods and so on.[39]

However, self-service was more than just a change in selling technique. It was a wonderful new cash-producing business. It generated cash as never before: no more credit sales, no more counter service, no more deliveries. Simply put, the self-service proprietor bought and sold weekly on the old trade norm of two months' supplier credit. A shop with weekly sales of £10,000 had £80,000 in the bank before the first week had to be paid for. Development costs could be funded out of cash flow. Suppliers were squeezed for longer credit, 90 days if the shop could get away with it. Suppliers were then asked to stack their own goods on to the supermarket shelves, which was fine in a big store, but not practical in counter service shops.

Another benefit to the supermarket proprietor was much lower wages costs and therefore the ability to undersell his competitors even further. As volumes rose suppliers were pushed for extra discounts. They needed their goods on display. They had to agree. Then one proprietor learnt that banks would pay heavily for overnight money, often double the normal rate. Soon banks were competing for the large deposits. Eventually profitability was earned in the money markets and not on the groceries. Dunnes Stores had another trump card. They had draperies, traditionally with better margins than groceries. With their own-brand (St Bernard) and bulk buys, they could easily undersell their competitors and still make a fair margin. (These new retailing techniques were of course miles from the kind of skills that Dermot had learnt in Liverpool and while running the business for the last thirty years. As celebrity restaurateur Peter Langan, who had served his apprenticeship in Findlaters in the 1950s put it: 'It was a dying firm, living in yesterday's world. Dermot Findlater was too old and his son Alex was too young. Theirs was a firm of great style, but also an endangered species. The days of the gentleman businessman catering to a class that no longer existed had gone forever.'[40])

In the meantime wine and spirit sales seemed to justify the big investment programme of the early 1950s, as Dermot told the 1959 AGM.

> Our sales of both Jameson and Powers whiskey showed satisfactory increases over last year, whilst our sales of French, German, Spanish and Italian wines showed very large increases. This is undoubtedly due to the fact that we purchase only the finest qualities available and from companies whose integrity is well known to us since the turn of the century. The increase in our wine and spirit trade naturally results in greater activity in our bonded warehouse and makes increasing demands on space. Although it is, I think, the largest privately owned bond of any trader in Ireland, we must shortly introduce more efficient methods in the movement of goods and the use of space.

At the same AGM Dermot announced the introduction (relatively late, even for the conservative Dublin businesses of the day) of a non-contributory pension scheme for all managers and representatives under the age of fifty.

Between 1956 and 1964 £47,000 [over £700,000] was ploughed into plant and machinery in beer bottling. Tuborg was launched in June 1956 and local agents appointed around the country. Volumes built up to a peak of 106,000 dozen in 1960 out of a total bottling of stout, ales and lager of 311,000 dozen. These included Smithwick's Time Ale, Double Diamond, Phoenix Ale and Mackeson Stout. However, we had been beaten to the marketplace by Pat Loughrey of Bannow Bottlers, a subsidiary of Batchelors. They got on to the market first and with a lower strength Carlsberg at a more competitive price and distributed direct to the trader rather than through the traditional wholesaler. They took the lion's share of the market. The Danish successes had not gone unnoticed in St James's Gate. In 1960 Guinness launched Harp which quickly stunted Tuborg's growth. Carlsberg were happy enjoying a smaller percentage share of a much larger market.

Our Guinness bottlings peaked at 145,000 dozen in 1961. We prided ourselves in the quality of our bottling and were proud of our unique Guinness label with the XX. We could not use their standard label which stated 'who bottle no other

Managers' Conference 1962

stout or porter' in view of our bottling of Mountjoy stout and later Mackeson. In July 1959 Guinness reported that our bottlings of their product were 'second to none'. We liked to believe that this was because we had the advice of technicians from a variety of breweries.

In those days there were five competing contract bottlers. Amongst the large accounts worth chasing and capable of taking drops of 100 dozen or more were Dublin Airport (Johnny Oppermann), the Gresham Hotel (Toddy O'Sullivan), Butlin's Holiday Camp in Mosney and the ballrooms such as the Metropole and the Shelbourne. But quoting could be perilous—as low as 5d to 1s 9d per dozen delivered on credit and, another hazard, there were always losses on the empties account-returnable bottles and cases. More went out than came back and resulted in unwelcome write-offs.

When the bottling was put under scrutiny by a firm of consultants in 1967 it was evident that a volume of 500,000 dozen was needed to produce the required profitability. As our volume was in decline it was decided to withdraw from the trade. It was a fight to realise the cost in our books of the remaining £19,644 valuation of plant and machinery and the £10,000 [£100,000] in bottles and cases, but we succeeded.

In 1960, for the first time in the company's 136-year history, it was decided to employ the services of a chartered accountant. By today's standards that may seem amazing, yet the company's books were in pristine shape. Ledgers were beautifully and accurately written up, percentages calculated to two decimal places and branch weekly returns were on the boardroom table every Wednesday afternoon. The year-end accounts were audited, distributed and the AGM held within twelve weeks of the year-end. However, Alan Kirk, the new accountant, was not pleased with the high level of debt and the low level of profitability, notwithstanding the Royal Bank having pronounced themselves satisfied with the year's results. Kirk identified that the major internal problems in the company were the costs associated with our O'Connell Street head office (Findlater's Corner). What was needed was a detailed profit and loss for each department. In addition to the six retail departments, the company included extensive wine cellars, whiskey bonding and bottling, beer bottling, grocery warehousing and distribution to the branches and to institutions in the city and nation-wide. Stocks in September 1960 were £295,000 on sales of £1.55m giving a stock turn of 5.25 or a 10-week holding. As groceries and perishables turn relatively fast it was apparent that the cellar and bond were grossly overstocked. However, this was difficult to tackle as it was the chairman's preserve! Debtor levels on the other hand were not as severe as the outside world would believe for a company wholesaling wines and spirits nation-wide, wholesaling beers in Dublin, selling groceries both wholesale and retail, and retailing for both cash and credit.

Year	**1940**	**1945**	**1950**	**1955**	**1960**	**1965**
Debtors (£)	32,770	26,647	56,341	89,201	114,231	105,218
% Turnover	6.5%	4.3%	4.8%	6.6%	7.5%	5.7%

In May 1960 Findlaters began grappling with the problem, as a letter to all county district retail customers conveys:[41]

> Dear Madam, As from Monday next June 5th, our traveller will no longer call for your order which we would ask you to kindly send in to us by post or telephone. You can be assured that these orders will receive our most careful attention and they will of course be delivered to you weekly as heretofore. Yours very truly, Alex Findlater & Co. Ltd.

As is usual in such an old company, there was a reluctance to change from old familiar and tested ways. Board members argued that the problem was poor branch management. In August 1961 John McGrail, managing director, wrote to the chairman and directors on the subject of branches' profitability.[42]

> From time to time views have been expressed at Board level that the inadequate net profits earned in our Retail business are largely due to the increased cost associated with Credit and Delivery. It has been suggested that the remedy is to stop Retail Credit and Delivery and impose a service charge in respect of each order. It has also been suggested that to get rid of our Retail Credit and Delivery Trade and to concentrate on Retail Cash Trade only would be the proper and progressive policy for this Company.
>
> The attached exhibit showing the profitability of all our Branches, related to Capital Employed, for the year ended 28th February 1961, shows that Branches doing up to 80% Credit and Delivery Trade are producing net profits in excess of those expected on the Capital Employed. It can be concluded from the attached exhibit that our traditional type of Trade combining Credit and Delivery with Cash, can be extremely profitable if well directed and well managed.

> The knowledge, experience and background of this Company suggests that our main efforts at the present time should be directed to the promotion and improvement of our traditional type of Trade. The essential factor in the success of our Retail business is the level of sales and these seem to be more easily maintained in our traditional type of trade. In the few Branches where we have gone over to Cash only, we failed to produce the necessary profits due to not reaching the required level of sales. This would seem to indicate that much keener prices are necessary in shops that offer no service apart altogether from the attractiveness of the shop and the goods offered.

Findlaters' business was based on a high level of service and the senior generation believed that it would endure. They were right, but in a different form. Ireland of the 1960s was not wildly buoyant and pennies counted. A new retail concept had arrived where wages and salaries as a percentage of turnover could be over 6 per cent lower than traditional methods. Findlaters, with counter service and deliveries, operated at around 10 per cent. The difference was a sizeable competitive advantage to the newcomers. The shopper was benefiting enough to harm Findlaters' wafer-thin operating margin.

A few months after McGrail's note to the board, he had the serious task of announcing Dermot's death to the AGM.

> The Company has suffered a grievous blow in the irreparable loss of Mr Dermot Findlater, who as Chairman and Managing Director controlled the Company's affairs from 1941 until his death in April of this year. During those 21 years and indeed from the time that Mr Dermot joined the firm in 1927 the contribution he made to the progress and the development of the Company must surely be unparalleled in the field of individual endeavour. Most certainly his life long devotion to the interest of the Company cannot be computed mathematically or reduced to statistical form. It can best be appreciated perhaps by those who worked with him over the years sharing his efforts and profiting by his leadership and friendship.

Dermot died at the age of fifty-six in 1962. He was old beyond his age. He had packed a lot into life and had no outstanding ambitions. Undoubtedly the three decades managing Findlaters had taken a great toll on his health. He never got his personal finances in order following the war-time salary strictures and at the end the cupboard was pretty bare. John McGrail, who was a tremendous help to my mother at the time, wrote an appreciation of his colleague in *The Irish Times*. He summed up:

> [Dermot's] personal desires and aspirations were extremely simple, fashionable Continental holidays had little attraction for him—he was much more at home in the cottage in Connemara with his family and his boat. Mixing with the local people was one of his greatest delights. His sunny nature, the ready laugh and above all, his great kindliness endeared him to them all.
>
> Abilene was for him the star attraction for he was a great home-loving family man, but even in the contentment of his home his boundless energy kept him ever active. An early morning swim at Seapoint, or Killiney—a little ploughing in the vegetable garden before his day's work in the city, then home again and into the peace of his gar-

O'Connell Street head office (Findlater's Corner) in the late 1950s; note the cobble stones on the bottom left hand corner.

> den. His passionate love of flowers was apparent to all who visited Abilene and he delighted in giving to his many friends the fruits of his labour. And so it was fitting on Tuesday last when he was laid to rest that All Saints Church was filled to capacity with hundreds of bouquets of the most exquisite flowers, a last tribute from his bereaved friends.*

John McGrail (then fifty-seven) took over as chairman and managing director. Doris Findlater (sixty-seven), Dermot's elder sister, remained deputy chairman and Harry Thompson (seventy), managing director of Mineral Water Distributors (C&C) and on the board since 1945, was the main non-executive director. Executive directors were Paddy Murphy, general manager, Mattie McElroy (in charge of wines) and myself (aged twenty-five), assistant managing director. The team was augmented by Alan Kirk, the accountant, and John Clancy, sales and marketing. There was a tough job ahead for the remainder of the decade.

* Dermot particularly requested that Tennyson's 'Sunset and the evening star', played at his father's funeral, be played at his. He identified it to me by the lines 'And may there be no moaning of the bar, When I put out to sea' but substituting 'at' for 'of' in the third line! The most beautiful rendering of this hymn I ever heard was at the funeral of President Childers, sung by the choir of St Patrick's Cathedral.

Notes and references

1 *Irish Press* 14 June 1946
2 *The Irish Times* 28 December 1946
3 *Idem.* 3 January 1947
4 *Irish Independent* 22 April 1946
5 *Irish Press* 14 December 1946
6 *Idem.* 25 February 1947
7 *The Irish Times* 19 March 1947
8 *Irish Independent* 10 May 1947
9 *Evening Telegraph* 28 October 1947
10 Board minutes 3 November 1947
11 *The Irish Times* 31 December 1947
12 J. P. Donleavy *The Ginger Man* pb London: Corgi pp 11, 12-13
13 Basil Goulding *Alpha Basil* 1976. An entertaining business alphabet.
14 See Kevin McCourt's letter in the *Irish Independent* 8 January 1948
15 Board minutes 18 August 1951, 5 September 1951
16 *The Irish Times* 9 June 1949
17 Brian Inglis *Downstart* London: Chatto & Windus 1990 p 69
18 Peter Somerville-Large *The Irish Country House* London: Sinclair-Stevens 1995 p 3[43]
19 Inglis *West Briton* London: Faber and Faber 1962 p 19
20 Inglis *Downstart* p 4
21 *Ibid.* p 68
22 Charles Macmahon Shaw, *Bernard's Brethren,* with comments by author and playright GBS, London: Constable p 135. The reference to aborigines relates to an Australian cousin who had caused him to comment on the matter
23 Inglis, *Downstart* p 21
24 *Ibid.* p 4
25 L. M. Cullen *Princes & Pirates, The Dublin Chamber of Commerce 1783-1983* Dublin: Dublin Chamber of Commerce 1983 p 24
26 *Ibid.* pp 49-50
27 *Ibid.* pp 23-4
28 *Ibid.* pp 73-4
29 Tony Farmar *A History of Craig Gardner* Dublin: Gill & Macmillan 1988 pp 183-4
30 R. B. McDowell *Crisis & Decline, The Fate of the Southern Unionists* Dublin: Lilliput 1997 p 166
31 Victor Griffin *Mark of Protest* Dublin: Gill & Macmillan 1993 pp 207-8
32 Emily O'Reilly *Masterminds of the Right* Dublin: Attic Press 1992 p 23
33 Peter Gatenby *Dublin's Meath Hospital,* Dublin: Town House Chapter 13; Findlater family records.
34 The hospital's story is told in great detail by Dr Helen Burke in *The Royal Hospital Donnybrook–A Heritage of Caring 1943-1993* Dublin: The Royal Hospital and the Social Science Research Centre, University College Dublin 1993
35 Eric Fenelon 'Some random musings over nearly half a century' in *The Newsletter of the Association of Old Adelaide Students* 1987 p 22
36 *Irish Independent* 3 April 1952
37 *Irish Licensing World* December 1954
38 Bridget Williams, *The Best Butter in the World, A History of Sainsbury's* London: Ebury Press pp 125-6
39 Submission by Feargal Quinn of Superquinn Ltd to The Fair Trade Commission *Report of Inquiry into Grocery Goods for Human Consumption* 1972 p 158
40 Peter Langan *A Life with Food* London: Bloomsbury 1990 p 47
41 Minute book 31 May 1961
42 Minute book 9 August 1961

1960s Shop Designs

Main Street, Malahide 1917–69

2 The Green, Sandymount 1897–1969

65 Upper Dorset Street 1906–69

14 Main Street, Dundrum 1945–69

28 Main Street, Blackrock 1879–1969

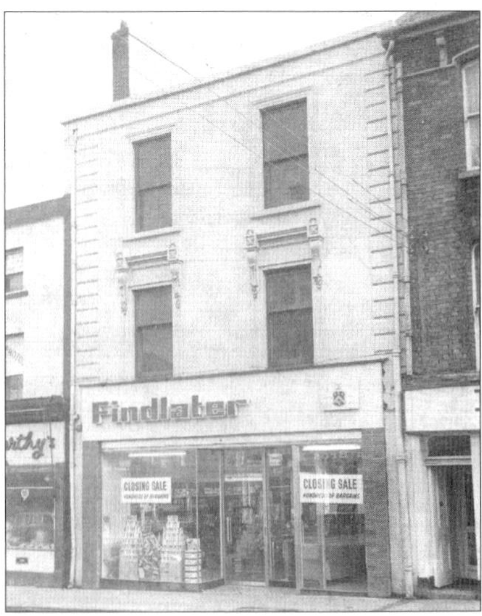

8 Main Street, Bray 1901–69

The branch shops not pictured
in the book are
47 Ranelagh 1922–60
4–5 Wicklow Street 1934–68
Main Street Cabinteely 1944–68
3+4 Mount Merrion Gardens 1950–68
Stillorgan Shopping Centre 1966–68

16. From old Findlaters to new

In our family business, as in so many others at the time and since, the eldest son went into the firm, and this had been my destiny since birth. My brother was only eight at the time of my father's death and in the fullness of time was to earn an excellent degree at Trinity. While reading for his PhD, he was invited for interview with Guinness, for the privileged position of junior brewer, which had traditionally been filled exclusively by Oxford and Cambridge graduates.

I was born in a Hatch Street nursing home (known appropriately as the Hatch), in the street in which I now work, on 25 September 1937. We then lived in a house called Glann in Gordon Avenue, Foxrock. I have distant memories of playing in the river that flowed through the bottom of the garden. In 1941 we moved a couple of miles to Abilene, a dilapidated farmhouse on the Blackrock side of the Bray road. The house was then in a very run down state, almost uninhabitable, and my grandfather Harry Wheeler is reputed to have commented that he would not have his daughter live in such conditions.

Abilene stands on three acres. To the west there's a large walled vegetable garden which in those days had every type of fruit and vegetable in between a great network of pathways. Daddy had a mechanical cultivator and could be heard at work early in the mornings while we lay on in bed. We also had a full-time gardener. Surplus produce and masses of flowers from the herbaceous borders would go into Daddy's car and I am sure were given away when he visited 'the Incurables', now the Royal Hospital in Donnybrook, or to the secretaries and staff in O'Connell Street. Other mornings he used the dogs, Bingo and Popeye, to herd us out of bed to the strains, played at full blast on the record player of 'Oh What a Beautiful Morning' and into the Bentley, for a shivery early morning cold plunge at Seapoint or Killiney, telling us that the iodine in the seaweed was very good for our health.

Later he hired Jock and Joe, whom he saw excavating a filling station site in Blackrock, to dig a great big hole in the middle of the 'Little Garden' to the south of the house and turned it into a perfect and ever-popular swimming pool amongst the flowers and roses.

From an early age I was instructed on the workings of the Atco mower and it was my job during the holidays to keep the tennis court in front of the house mown, rolled and marked in readiness for the frequent games. The ponies and a donkey in the fields between the house and the road were the responsibility of my sisters and had their stable in the 'hen-yard'. The hens provided us with all the eggs we needed and some were set aside in waterglass for winter baking.

Most large households had their own hens in those days and Findlaters supplied a full range of feedstuffs for all types of farmyard animals.

In the basement, which was only slightly below ground level, was a magnificent Hornby 00 electric railway covering the area of two rooms. Over our sixty years' tenure of Abilene this set-up has given hours of pleasure. Friends and relations would cycle over from all over the southside and parents knew that their young ones were having great fun (totally unsupervised) in these lovely surroundings. Mother always had an abundance of cakes and scones laid on for us at teatime. The mere mention of Abilene conjures up very happy memories in so many of our friends.

At the age of six I started at Greencroft School in Carrickmines. The school was run by Marjorie and Olive Creary and was a lot of fun. One of my first palgirls at the school was Jennifer Hollwey who later married the banker John Guinness and survived a harrowing kidnap. The school struggled with my reading problem, as one report records: 'Reading is his great difficulty and he does not seem to have any great desire to be able to read, though he enjoys reading the stories he knows by heart.' In contrast writing was 'very good' notwithstanding that I had been changed from left-hand to right-hand under Father's instructions, who was heard to comment 'I will not have a left-handed hockey player in the family.'* It did, of course, give me the benefit of being ambidextrous, useful when casting a fly, playing a tennis ball or doing a bit of carpentry. In September 1946 I started as a boarder at Castle Park School in Dalkey which I thoroughly enjoyed, in spite of my first letter home 'I don't like this school'. But a month later 'I am getting to like the school better'! Some of my letters had a request for more tuck. I was in an advantageous position. The Findlater van was frequently in the school yard where we played between classes, making deliveries to the school kitchen, and a quiet word with the co-operative van driver usually brought the necessary response. Otherwise my letters spoke about the matches against Aravon, St Gerard's and the new school in County Meath, Headford, whom we walloped in the first cricket encounter. We made 164 runs for 9 wickets and they made 7 runs all out in the first innings and about 10 for 6 in the second. But what impressed me was that they served ice-cream after the match. My school reports recorded that arithmetic was my strong subject and Latin very satisfactory. However, reading was still a problem.

Castle Park in those days was considered by some to be the last outpost of the British Empire. When John A. Costello declared us a Republic in 1947 we are reputed to have played 'Oh God our help in ages past'! The coronation of Queen Elizabeth II was a day of celebration. The headmaster, Donald Pringle, made a quick visit across the border to acquire the appropriate coronation shields and emblems, and badges showing the Queen's head and pencils with the dates of the kings and queens of England were distributed at breakfast. The old boys' magazine reported that 'the school now possesses a first-class wireless set and

* This was impossible, for unlike hurling, hockey is only played on the right-hand side of the body with the stick held left hand above the right hand.

Abilene enriched by the spring display of crocuses and snowdrops

loudspeakers in the classrooms relayed the BBC programme to which the whole school listened most of the morning.' After a special lunch, the afternoon was spent on Killiney beach after which prizes were given for the best floral design in the house gardens and the best coronation paintings. However, not everyone felt so euphoric about the event and when the schoolrooms were opened up the next morning it was discovered that all the Union Jacks had been torn up and the picture of the Queen was missing, later found burnt in the woods of the school grounds. The boys were exonerated when footmarks of the intruders, called vandals, were detected outside!

In the autumn of 1951 Mother took me on a voyage across the water to a village plumb in the middle of England called Repton. I was very homesick and burst into tears in Manchester when I could not understand their dialect. Repton is an old English public school founded in 1557 and included much of a 12th-century Augustinian priory set in the village of Repton in Derbyshire, once the capital of the Anglo-Saxon kingdom of Mercia. In the 20th century three of the school's headmasters went on to be Archbishop of Canterbury: William Temple 1942–4, Geoffrey Fisher 1945–61 and Michael Ramsey 1961–74. Fisher had also been a pupil from 1918 to 1923, and his son Frank, later headmaster of Wellington, taught me hockey and elementary soldiering (in the Combined Cadet Force) at Repton. The school did not have a noticeable religious bias but attendance at morning chapel and evening prayers was obligatory. Repton was chosen for me on two counts: first Donald Pringle was an old boy and recommended the school to my parents, second, one of my Aunt Sheila's best friends was married to a house-master there, Henry Davidson. We likened him to the character of the ageing old school-master, played by Robert Donat, in the 1938 film shot in Repton, *Goodbye, Mr Chips,* such was his loveable and caring character.*

I enjoyed my time there. The object of sending me away was to try and make a man out of me. I had too many privileges living and schooling around Dublin. The public school adventure started at the beginning of each term when our parents delivered us into the charge of the purser at the B&I gangway in the North Wall for the 7.45 pm sailing. On one occasion we were late leaving home and my father phoned the ship and requested the captain to delay the sailing until I was safely deposited on board. We travelled to our various schools across England by rail having much fun and mischief on the way. For example, sitting in the opulence of the Grand Central Hotel, Manchester waiting for our connection, we got up to such pranks as asking the callboy to page, in his high-pitched voice, for 'Mr I. P. Freely' and other such characters, putting us into stitches of laughter.

Repton excels at cricket and association football producing many of England's great amateur players. My life centred around the playing field, and a wide variety of sports: hockey, cricket, football, squash, tennis and cross-country running. My father had occasion to dictate a letter to remind me that a certain amount of academic study was necessary, but he never followed up the subject. His questioning focused on the playing field. I did just enough study to gain entrance to Trinity, which my father very reluctantly allowed, but anything in excess of a pass was considered a waste of good sporting time!

I could not find a course that interested me and again settled for the playing field and remained on the college books for four years, seldom taking an exam and never failing! In those days there was no business school, a commerce degree was taboo to my father, as was the wearing of the Trinity tie, and language courses were a continuation of text book study experienced at school and with no oral facilities. Trinity to me was hockey in College Park, wonderful tours to English and Scottish universities, attendance at the occasional debate at the Hist, and pints in the Lincoln Inn (the pub outside the back gates) or Jammet's back bar, and with fellow Knights of the Campanile. There was a bit of the Ginger Man style still in College in those days. Part of the deal with my father was that I undertake a full apprenticeship in Findlaters at the same time. So from the first of May 1956 my apprenticeship started and Daniel Skehan, manager of O'Connell Street, acknowledged that first week:

> My dear Master† Alex,
>
> I have great pleasure in presenting you with your first ever Time Card from 1st to 4th May 1956, inclusive, together with your first complete Time Card for week ending May 11th 1956.
>
> May I take this opportunity of offering you my heartiest congratulations on your entry into the Firm of Messrs. Alex. Findlater & Co. Ltd. and I wish to lay special

* A view of Repton through the eyes of a celebrated Irishman, Terry Trench, founder of An Óige (Irish Youth Hostel Association) is given in *Nearly Ninety*, Meath: Hannon Press 1966.

† On my 21st birthday I became 'Mr Alex' and it was considered insubordination for all but the most senior managers to use the term 'Master'!

Discussing post graduation plans at head office following their successful completion of the three month Dale Carnegie Sales course are Findlater Wholesale Representatives: (Left to Right) Mr. Walter J. Donnelly, Mr. Henry Carroll, Mr. Jim Grimes, Mr. Edward G. Robinson and Mr. Aidan C. Kelly, Field Sales Manager.

Findlater Herald. November 1967

emphasis on the fact that you carry the Firm's famous name. I now wish you many happy, successful years in the Firm which you are, I hope, destined to control some day,

Finally, I would like to have it placed on record that I am honoured to be your first Manager. Yours faithfully,

Daniel Skehan.[1]

Feargal Quinn tells a story of my apprenticeship. 'I learnt recently of a little story about Alex when he was serving his apprenticeship in their tea and coffee blending factory in Rathmines. Alex was given a task at the coffee roaster. Something went wrong. He took his eye off the ball, pulled the wrong lever, and mixed a ton of unroasted with a ton of roasted beans. Now, that presented a bit of a problem—but not so for Mr Findlater Senior. He just said to Alex: 'Your problem'—and Alex spent the next week sorting the roasted from the unroasted beans!'*

One of my first jobs in Findlaters was a week spent in a lock-up store, some 8 feet by 4 feet, breaking up Early Mist and Royal Tan chocolate bars. Joe Griffin, the celebrated owner of the Grand National winners Early Mist (1953) and Royal

* This incident was to repeat itself some years later when my brother John, fresh out of Trinity with a doctorate in biochemistry, was on his first shift alone in the Guinness brew-house. In true Findlater style he inadvertently blended 2000 barrels of single stout with 400 barrels of ale. The early morning call from the brewer-in-charge was decidedly frosty! The fact that his Uncle Oliver Lloyd was Head Brewer provided no solace. The new blend of stout and ale was facetiously known as st-ale, and years later was said to be the basis for the short-lived new brand Guinness Light. Notwithstanding this early setback John had a successful career in Guinness culminating in the position of Personnel Development Manager from 1994 to 2000 when he took voluntary early retirement to explore pastures new.

Tan (1954) had fallen from grace and the only outlet for the bars was as broken or cooking chocolate without the wrappers!

After six months it was thought that I would benefit from a trip to Donegal with senior traveller Mattie McElroy to experience at first hand the techniques of selling spirits, wines and on this occasion introducing Irish-bottled Tuborg lager beer to the pubs and hotels. I have always suspected that the object of the trip was to introduce young Master Alex to drink, so worried was father at my seeming lack of interest in all shades of the product (as it happened this attitude quickly changed when I had been in Trinity for a term or two). And so it happened on the first night in Jackson's Hotel, Ballybofey.

My brother, John at his farewell party in the Guinness' Storehouse. December 2000
Photo: Kenny Studios

The various company representatives met there at the bar. 'And who is this fine young man you have with you, Mattie?' Then to the barman 'Another Tuborg for Young Master Alex'. And after three he escorted me upstairs: 'are you sure you are all right Master Alex?' as I marvelled at the total normality of my state. I never looked back and I am sure he phoned my father that very night and reported mission accomplished! More seriously I was several years in the grocery buying office, learning first from Cecil Reynolds who had a lifetime of experience in the company and then with Paul Barnes whose father, and I think grandfather, had been attached to the Dún Laoghaire branch. Another stalwart who had worked his way up from messenger-boy to board room was general manager Paddy Murphy.

Findlaters had very able managers throughout the branches and head office and I hesitate to mention them here for fear of offending those whom I miss out. However, a few who may not have been mentioned elsewhere are Cecil White of Malahide who was in charge of all the fruit and vegetable departments, John McCormack, Peter Dunne, Jimmy Graham in the provisions and Jarlath Lynch and Des Holden, manager and wine manager respectively, all in O'Connell Street, and the Miss Tanners (as they were called), Ruth Bell, Polly Richardson, Violet Simpson, Anne Fahy, Helen Tracey and Rosamund Dempsey in the administration on the upper floors. In transport there were so many wonderful characters such as Joey Baker, Paddy Reddin and Jimmy Farrell and some families like the Dunnes and Christy St Leger, who lived on the premises in Findlater buildings. In charge of the whiskey house was John Parkinson, beer bottling Paddy Treacy, grocery lofts Christy O'Brien. On the road were Walter Donnelly,

Stanley Fleetwood, Manager of the Year 1960–61 (Photo Lensmen)

Eddie Robinson, and Jimmy Grimes of the old school, and also Noel Jordan and Henry Carroll; in the St Lawrence hotel was Ivor Williams, and managing a branch or large department were Willie Boylan (Crumlin Cross), Pat Byrne (Mount Merrion), Robert Campbell (Dundrum), Willie Delaney (Dún Laoghaire), Gerry Enderson (Dún Laoghaire), James Farrell (Dún Laoghaire), Pat Graves (Bray), Jimmy Greene (Baggot Street), Sam Hanlon (Foxrock), Tom Long (Blackrock), Dan Meagher (Wicklow Street), Johnny Murray (Georges Street), Reg Quinlan (Cabinteely), Tom Roche (where the need called!) and Joe Whelan of Ringsend, the best provision salesman in the business.

For me familiarisation with the business had begun early. It took the form of accompanying my father on branch visits and being well-informed on most aspects of the business by school-leaving age.* Dermot was anxious to get me installed and equipped as quickly as possible. To this end I was appointed a director at the age of twenty-one—far too young. Although this was well intentioned, I could add little to the board's collective wisdom. On the other hand, it was the finest training ground that I could have aspired to and was to give me a great breadth of experience that would stand to me in the difficult years ahead. Discussions ranged from union negotiations, personnel matters, bank relations, property maintenance and the purchasing of everything from eggs in Ballyhaunis to whiskey fillings from Jameson and Powers. Since the preference shares were publicly quoted, the company was subject to stock exchange regulations and board matters were handled in an exemplary manner.

Not only did Dermot want me to know everything about the business, he also wanted me to meet the characters of the city, from the top down to the street car-park man, an institution in those days. They would always have a good spot for his Bentley, but then he was a regular client and a good tipper. In fact Father advised me that these men were a great source of information on the welfare of other businesses in the city and who was a poor credit risk. On one of these occasions around town Father marched me in to the Dolphin Hotel to have the honour of meeting old Jack Nugent, the proprietor, in his sick bed, just before Jack shuffled off to the next world. On another he greeted Alfie Byrne, ten times Lord Mayor of Dublin, outside the National Stadium, and dictated to him what he

* Passed-down wisdom has certainly been a key to our on-going success over the ages.

should write in my autograph book—dare I accompany him without that book! He got his friend Lorcan Bourke, proprietor of the Four Provinces Ballroom, where I learnt my bar trade, to arrange a lunch at the Gresham for me to meet his son-in-law Eamonn Andrews; on another occasion he plucked me out of the grocery lofts in working garb to have lunch in the smart Russell Hotel in Stephen's Green as the guests of the directors of the all-powerful Scottish Distillers Group. He announced the setting of an extra place with the wave of his arm and all went well until I learnt of the existence of cold soup for the first time!

He orchestrated me on to the managing committee of the Royal Hospital for Incurables at the age of nineteen where I was the only member under the age of fifty—daunting! This was to keep up the family tradition that had run through five generations. At my first meeting the aged acting chairman asked the meeting to rise in silent prayer in remembrance of the hospital's great benefactor, Alexander Findlater; a quick nudge and a whisper from Connie Smith, the hospital's diminutive secretary, 'No! We are welcoming young Alex here for the first time today.'

Dermot had brought the company through from the 1930s to the 1950s and had strengthened its fabric. He had invested profits in the modernisation of the branches, the hotel in Howth, the beer bottling and in the head office in O'Connell Street (Findlater's Corner). He left a fully stocked drinks company with prime agencies in Harveys and Tuborg. But all this, especially the heavy post-war investment programme, had cost money and earnings remained pitifully low. Borrowings peaked at £199,000 [£2.8m] the quarter he died. That was the legacy that my father left John McGrail and myself, then twenty-five years of age.

The popular belief is simply that Findlaters missed the boat in respect of self-service. The true story is as usual more complicated. Dermot had not been in the best of health since the Emergency and had lost the incisiveness he enjoyed in the 1930s and 1940s. Many of his investments were not well thought through. Large tranches of wine were ordered with gay abandon at lunches in the directors' dining-room. In the next two decades many good English wine merchants got into serious financial trouble as a result of being hopelessly overstocked in maturing Grands Crus Bordeaux wines. Happily the vintages Dermot purchased were good and the quality excellent. Add to this the considerable investment in bonded whiskey stocks and the credit extended to hoteliers and publicans throughout the country, the money being ploughed into the beer bottling plant and the hotel in Howth, and the company's approaching problems become apparent. He was investing on too many fronts. There was a rationale for each, but collectively they were not sustainable. So when funds were needed for the self-service revolution the cupboard was bare.

The self-service revolution in England got under way in the early 1950s. Of course, like all such revolutions they are nothing like as inevitable at the time as they appear in retrospect. By 1960, when I was privileged to spend a month in

Sainsburys observing their systems, only 10 per cent of their shops had been converted to self-service. By the end of the decade the figure had risen to almost 50 per cent. In Dublin Findlaters were still strong and there seemed to be a continuing demand for the firm's traditional services. The pending supermarket invasion was only a small cloud on the horizon. The newspapers treated them as an amusing conversation point. 'Why we do or do not shop at supermarkets', wrote the *Sunday Independent;* 'Supermarket is not for me', reported the *Sunday Press*. On the other hand there was an army of competitors poised to invade our patch with new retailing techniques. Notable among these were Galen Weston,* the son of a Canadian grocer and biscuit maker, Ben Dunne, a Cork drapery retailer† and Feargal Quinn, the son of a holiday camp proprietor. Local competitor H. Williams was already well advanced.

John McGrail wasted no time in identifying the task ahead at the 1962 AGM:

> The immediate and primary purpose of the Directors [is] to raise the Company's profitability to a substantially higher level. The achievement of this purpose is no easy task. Trading conditions have rarely, if ever, been more difficult—on the one hand profit margins are reduced by the intensity of present day competition, whilst at the same time working expenses are continually growing as a result of higher wage rates and reduced working hours. The only solution to this problem is an increase in the productivity of the staff, because of course the real wealth of the company, like the wealth of a nation, is determined by the aggregate daily effort of each individual.

He repeated much of this in 1963:

> This Company has taken the lead in the Retail Food Trade by introducing a Staff Bonus Incentive Scheme. Staff participation in surplus profits conforms to the most enlightened and progressive social thinking and it will undoubtedly help to engender and maintain that spirit of co-operation that is so necessary in the Retail Food Trade with its extremely high ratio of labour content. I think I may say that at the present time the state of our relations with our Employees Association and with the three Unions to which the other sections of our staff belong leaves little to be desired.

Grappling with the need for increased productivity is one thing, but retrospective taxation is another: 'The provision in this year's Finance Act for an increase of 50 per cent in the rate of Corporation Profits Tax is discouraging and aggravates the already difficult problem that confronts all business concerns of endeavouring to finance development and expansion from their own resources. But however disturbing this measure might be, it is less disturbing than the further provision that seeks to make this increase retrospective to 1962.' And on top of that the introduction of a turnover tax: 'The other innovation in this year's

* It started as Powers Supermarkets, then became Quinnsworth on the purchase of Pat Quinn's stores, and now, as Tesco, vies for No. 1 position with Dunnes Stores. Its pre-eminent position in recent years is much to the credit of its retired chief executive Don Tidey. It has 76 stores.

† A great Irish success story. His first drapery outlet was opened in Patrick Street Cork in 1944. There are now 60 Dunnes Stores in the Republic of Ireland and 18 in Northern Ireland. Ben Dunne (senior) used to say to me at the Curragh races, with a twinkle in his eye: 'Dunne's Stores better value beats them all—you, too, Alex!'

Finance Act—the provision of a turnover tax—is one that, if ratified, will impose a heavy and inequitable burden on the Retail Food Trade, and we must register our strongest protest against its implementation'. At the same time the use of trading stamps was prevalent: 'The ultimate and inevitable consequences of the widespread development of stamp trading in this country would be an increase in the cost of living of something in the region of 2¾ per cent.' And finally a rap on the knuckles for the suppliers: 'Manufacturers of nationally advertised branded consumer goods might be well advised to devote more thought and attention to the quality and value of the goods they produce and sell, and less attention to the gimmicks their advertising experts produce and sell.'

McGrail's comments on the turnover tax were a signal that it was not a well thought out tax. This was confirmed a decade later in the 1972 Fair Trade Commission Report of Inquiry. On the tax it said 'The present Turnover tax system operates to the disadvantage of the independent retailer, due to the fact that there is no legislation governing the way in which the tax is collected.' This made the tax virtually optional. It provided the opportunity for taxes collected from customers not to reach the Revenue Commissioners. Some no doubt grew rich on it.

The full Findlater service involved canvassing for the order at each individual house or farm, assembling it, delivering it and getting paid a month later. Maureen Haughey remembered how the service operated:

> When we lived in Grangemore, Findlaters' agent called once a week. This took place on Thursday afternoon and was a major event of the week and I had to be on hand for it. He would sit down, carefully write out the order, advising me on the best things available that particular week and reminding me if he thought I was forgetting something.
>
> When the van arrived the next day, Friday, with the order, there was great excitement. The children would rush out to see what 'goodies' had arrived. The driver was very pleasant and would permit them to clamber all over the van and give them a lift down as far as the gate.
>
> On one occasion when the van was stationery they accidentally pressed the starter button—but luckily the driver was close by to keep the situation under control.
>
> Findlaters' old-fashioned, courteous service was very much part of our family life at that time and the weekly arrivals a pleasant domestic event.

Feargal Quinn, chief executive of Superquinn, foremost amongst supermarket proprietors in the country today and head of a group with eighteen supermarkets, put it clearly in a speech in 1993:

> When I was growing up the Findlater way of doing business was a byword in Dublin. It stood for personal service to the customer, but it was different—it was an individual service to each customer backed up by such good ethos as telephone ordering, home delivery and extended credit. And it was an example, I think, of what I would call nowadays the boomerang principle—running your business in such a way

> as to make it your prime aim to get your customers to come back to you again and again and again . . . it wasn't the Findlater approach to customer service that had reached its 'sell-by-date'. It was the Findlater way of delivering it and the whole cost structures that went along with that.

Oh how we would enjoy such a service today! But, as our accountant Alan Kirk rightly observed, 'On our present earnings and our financial position we cannot afford our present standard of workings, which is higher than many companies with which I have been associated where earnings are considerably higher.'

The conditions of trade turned gradually against us—first there was the abolition of retail price maintenance in 1955 and then the advent of self-service. The effect was a drop in the percentage net profit before tax from an average of 1.5 per cent to under 0.5 per cent, a very delicate margin on which to work.

Net profit per cent of turnover

1939-45	1946-55	1955-60	1961-66
1.5 per cent	1.25 per cent	0.5 per cent	0.45 per cent

A government report on the industry showed that the aggregate net profits before tax for seven major supermarket multiples for the years 1968, 1969 and 1970 were 1.5 per cent, 1.5 per cent and 0 per cent. Clearly trading conditions were tough, at their worst the year after we closed our retail outlets—good timing! Just as competitiveness was hotting up in 1966 the board instructed the firm's buyers to raise profit margins by 3¾ per cent or ½d in the shilling. This was the price of survival. It was calculated that the 10th round national wage increase would cost Findlaters something in the region of £15,000 [£180,000]—more than the previous year's profit.

The national wage increases in the 1960s were fast and furious. No sooner had management come to grips with one than the next was being negotiated. However, the one redeeming feature was that the extra spending power came straight back into the grocers' tills. Our 1962/63 accounts reflected the cost of the 8th round wage increase. 1963/64 reflected the increased purchasing power created by the 8th round up to 1 November 1964 when the 2½ per cent turnover tax was introduced. This was a severe setback to the trade and was reflected in the 1964/65 sales. At a board meeting on 24 June 1964 it was estimated that the round under negotiation would add £20,000 in the current year and £15,000 in the following year. All in all, a rough ride when the self-service operators needed fewer and less skilled staff.

Wages as a per cent of turnover

1945	1950	1955	1958	1960	1963	1964	1965	1966	1967
10	10	10.3	11.1	10.8	10.9	11.2	12.1	12.0	12.8

Expenditure on stables, motors and cycles as per cent of turnover (an index of the cost of service) rose steadily throughout the 1950s, peaking at 1 per cent in 1963, or twice the value of net profits; thereafter it dropped back to less than 0.8 percent of turnover.

When Dermot finally said 'No' to the plans for the conversion of Dún Laoghaire into a large supermarket in 1960, that was it. After Dermot died in 1962 aged fifty-six, I turned to Mother and said: 'Well, there may be one good thing out of this. Jack can now go ahead with the supermarket plans.' It was not to be. Probably for financial reasons, McGrail adopted my father's stance and vetoed the Dún Laoghaire development. Supermarketing was a young man's trade; for once there was no inherited wisdom, all the experience was gained from observing another man's successes in another country, usually the US or UK. I was twenty-five years old and impatient to be given the green light. I inevitably became a thorn in John McGrail's side.

After Dermot's death we all knuckled down to the task of managing the company. Findlaters' sales began to respond to initiatives and were increasing modestly. There was plenty of emphasis on training and trips to London to learn more about self-service. The overdraft was reduced by about £25,000 from its peak. There was an encouraging profit climb from 1961 to 1964 which gave hope. Everyone was kept busy with meetings and reports. A new second layer of managers was created.

Analysis showed that (as John McGrail had pointed out in 1960) our best returns were still coming from our traditional high service branches. However, this proved misleading, in that as other service competitors closed down we received a boost in trade. It looked as if we were doing well; in fact we were simply mopping up the remnants of a fast fading trade system. Of course, plenty of analyses of sales and expenses were produced. It was quite a complex business with up to eighty retail and wholesale departments to be supervised, many with overlapping costs, so it was usually hard to see the wood for the trees. Despite short term boosts to morale, the going was tough. In the three years 1965, 1966 and 1967 Findlaters made an aggregate pre-tax loss of £25,000 while our nearest rivals H. Williams chalked up profits of £350,000.*

Control of the company was presumed to be in the hands of the managing director, my father and his father before him. This was far from the reality. Considerable dilution of the shareholding had taken place as generation followed generation. When I entered the business in 1956 our branch of the family, descendants of Willie, held just 39 per cent of the 11,000 ordinary shares. The descendants of his elder brother Adam, who were now living in England, held 37 per cent. We had little contact with that branch of the family. Maxwell, son of Herbert who died in Gallipoli, held 9.4 per cent and was a housemaster in Pangbourne Nautical College; my godmother Helen, the only daughter of Dr

* H. Williams collapsed in the early 1980s as a result of severe price competition. Its managing director, John Quinn, claimed to be the only other 'certificated grocer' in Ireland apart from Dermot.

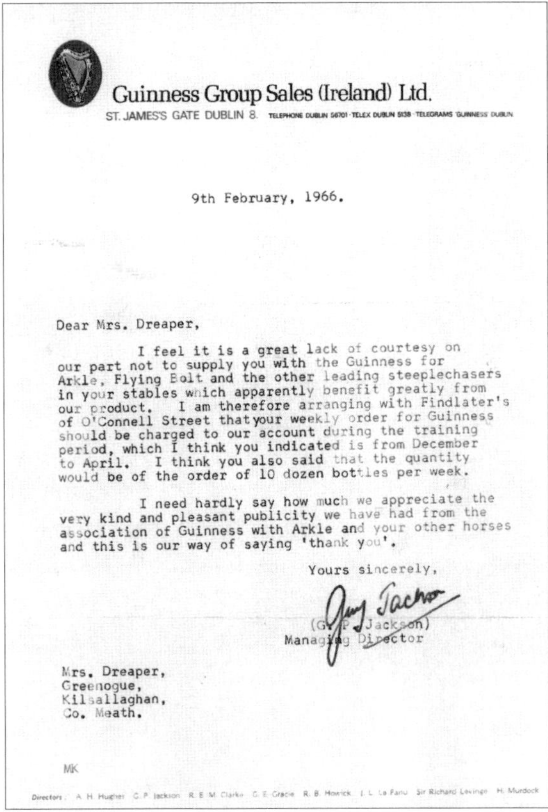

Guinness Group Sales (Ireland) Ltd.
ST. JAMES'S GATE DUBLIN 8. TELEPHONE DUBLIN 56701 · TELEX DUBLIN 5138 · TELEGRAMS 'GUINNESS' DUBLIN

9th February, 1966.

Dear Mrs. Dreaper,

I feel it is a great lack of courtesy on our part not to supply you with the Guinness for Arkle, Flying Bolt and the other leading steeplechasers in your stables which apparently benefit greatly from our product. I am therefore arranging with Findlater's of O'Connell Street that your weekly order for Guinness should be charged to our account during the training period, which I think you indicated is from December to April. I think you also said that the quantity would be of the order of 10 dozen bottles per week.

I need hardly say how much we appreciate the very kind and pleasant publicity we have had from the association of Guinness with Arkle and your other horses and this is our way of saying 'thank you'.

Yours sincerely,

(G. P. Jackson)
Managing Director

Mrs. Dreaper,
Greenogue,
Kilsallaghan,
Co. Meath.

MK

Directors: A. H. Hughes G. P. Jackson R. E. M. Clarke G. E. Gracie R. B. Howick J. L. Le Fanu Sir Richard Levinge H. Murdock

Arkle's success was based on a daily dose of Findlater's Guinness! Letter on display in *An Poitín Stil*, Rathcoole. Humans were also often prescribed stout, a snipe a day (⅓rd pint bottle) as a pick-me-up.

Alex, held 5.5 per cent. The problem of control was compounded in that the 66,000 preference shares had one vote for every ten shares held. Thus 8,800 votes were required for 50 per cent control. Calculations in 1958 showed that our branch had 8,518 votes before enlisting the support of Max and Helen.

On his death my father left everything, including his Findlater shares, to my mother. That's as it should have been. His father had acted similarly in 1941 when he left almost all his shares to his daughters, my maiden aunts, Doris and Sheila. At the time Dermot was a bit put out by this—having as he saw it all the responsibility as managing director but not the shares to support the position—but there was wisdom in Willie's ways. In fact the first time control became an issue was in the aftermath of my father's death. One of my first tasks was to secure control of the company for the Dublin branch of the family, Mother, Doris, Sheila and myself, with my godmother's shares and a few small purchases. With 51 per cent pooled we were then in a position to deal with predators on our own terms.

Findlaters Corner, at the top of O'Connell Street, covered 26,000 square feet. The complex was our albatross. It was one of very few buildings in Upper O'Connell Street that had been largely undamaged between 1916 and 1922; it was old and needed rebuilding. It was producing good revenues but the costs were excessive. Discussions on its redevelopment were continuous from 1964. Management consultants were taken on in the autumn of 1966. Early in 1967 they presented detailed reports covering every aspect of the business. They endorsed the sale of Findlaters Corner, recommended the cessation of the beer bottling and whiskey bonding and, most radically, recommended the creation of a new kind of home delivery service in the form of a closed-door supermarket in south county Dublin. The plan was to transfer the delivery business from ten of our southside branches into one central location, paying an industrial rather than a high-street rent, and operating a streamlined telesales and picking system.

The board gave the plan the green light. This was our last chance. There was no room for error. It had to be a success. We were transferring some £400,000 [£4.6m] worth of sales from the shops to the new operation. It would break even at half that level. Prices could be as competitive as the supermarkets. The customer was to receive a super service and the branches would be free for conversion to self service. The firm became a hive of activity. The plans were innovative and exciting. The ball had to bounce in our favour. The phased conversion of ten branches to self service, using the experienced Sainsburys' shop fitters, was approved.*

Savings needed to be effective in every corner of the business, and if the survival plan was to work, we needed the staff to be behind it, despite the fact that jobs were going to be lost. I called the staff to a meeting in Liberty Hall, gave them the facts on the conversion of our shops to self-service and the details of the rationalisation plans. The consequences of success and failure were clear. The meeting was receptive, and the general attitude positive, despite a natural fear of change. Staff numbers were reduced by one-third, from 341 to 227, with £70,000 being knocked off the wages bill [over £800,000]. Transport costs were cut by £10,000 [£115,000]. Stock levels were scrutinised and surplus sold off to free up capital, mainly whiskey and claret. The beer bottling unit was closed down and the plant sold off in an effort to recoup book value.

The fact that Findlaters was faltering was not a secret, and predators were circling the camp. Inquiries for the company came fast and furious: in August 1961 from Louis Elliman for the properties, in November 1961 from Urney's Chocolates, presumably to diversify, and in February 1962 from our long term competitors, Liptons.†

Dermot sent back a last spirited reply: 'Dear Sir, We thank you for your letter of 26th February 1962. We did give, to my recollection, consideration to an offer for our firm from Messrs. Lipton's in the year 1927, but on that occasion Messrs. Lipton's had not the necessary cash which we wanted, namely, one million pounds. If Messrs. Lipton's were to make us a stupendous offer, same would be considered by my Board, but I would state now that I personally do not think it is worthwhile pursuing the matter.'

Enquiries continued for the rest of the decade: in September 1962 from a law firm in Birmingham; May 1963 from a London broker; June 1964 from a London property company proposing sale and leaseback; May 1965 from D. E. Williams of Tullamore; July 1965 on behalf of Ben Dunne; November 1965 on behalf of Tesco. In 1966 Feargal Quinn called:

* Ronnie Nesbitt, MD of Arnotts, at that time urged me to be aware of the wisdom of gradualism.

† Liptons were founded by Thomas Lipton, who had Scottish parents and Irish grandparents. Born in 1850 he was knighted in 1898, and died in 1931. With over eight hundred stores in England, Scotland and Ireland they were one of the largest grocery chains in the early to mid twentieth century. Sir Thomas was a great sailor and philanthropist. In his enormous 'Shamrock' yachts he made five unsuccessful attempts to win the Americas Cup for Britain.

Labels from the 1960s

The 1960s range of wine labels which won an award of merit from the Irish Packaging Institute. Designed by Thalmadge Drummond and Partners of London who also created the Odlum owl design flour packs and redesigned the Jacob's Cream Cracker packets.

> I remember plucking up the courage to call and see Alex with the suggestion that maybe there was a future for us to work together. It was 1966 and I was in Finglas at the time and could see we had a profitable business formula but no money for new sites. It appeared to me at the time that the Findlater sites were underused. I had no fixed idea how we could work together but I remember going down and into those lovely hallowed wood panelled walls of O'Connell Street. I was shown to the fine office that Alex had. It was there that Alex broke the news to me that Findlaters were going into the supermarket business. 'We've sat back long enough,' he explained and told me of the decision to change from the traditional grocery methods to the new self-service concept. Those were very exciting years when change was sweeping through the trade. It was only then that we all began to realise that it was far easier to start from scratch than to create change in an existing business, with its established habits of management, employees and customers.

Feargal's last sentence was so true. Liptons, Pay-and-Take, Monument Creamery, Bacon Shops, Maypoles, Leverett & Frye and most of the traditional retailers worldwide failed to make the transition.

In parallel to these straightforward approaches there was another more circuitous approach. In December 1964 Garfield Weston, owner of Associated British Foods and Fine Fare Supermarkets in the UK and over 150 companies in Canada and North America, had tumbled to the fact that there were living in England ordinary Findlater shareholders who had lost contact with the present generation in Dublin. He was an old and experienced hand at the game. He offered £10 per share, increased it to £20 and probably settled a little higher after a Dutch auction. This gave him 19.5 per cent of the voting stock, a shareholding that hung over our heads. Rumours of Weston's holdings were published in *The Irish Times.* Three other shareholders were attracted by the new price but agreed to sell to us in Dublin. These shares were sold to our friends in Jacobs who saw Weston, with his biscuits and stores, as a potential threat, and so were glad to be on our side. They now had an 18.4 per cent holding, an investment which more than doubled in value as events unfolded. The family holdings were immediately rearranged into one controlling unit so that we were in the driving seat. Jeffrey Jenkins, chairman of Irish Biscuits (Jacobs), joined the board of directors.

At this delicate stage, we needed setbacks like a hole in the head. But they came, hard and fast. Harveys' profits faltered, weighed down by an import surcharge and tax increases in the UK, and they were taken-over by unpretentious UK cider and Babycham giant, Showerings, whose performance on the stock exchange had been impeccable. Apologetically, and full of praise at our performance, Showerings moved the Harveys agency to their own under-performing company in Clonmel (Bulmers). This was a big blow. The compensation did nothing for the long term.

We had invested time and money in the home delivery service, which was located in Carysfort Avenue, Blackrock. Unfortunately, it did not work. We muffed it. We launched the service on 4 December 1967. The goodwill was

New livery for the home delivery service 1967

there, and orders came pouring in: more than we could handle even with a smart new fleet of vans, with special wheel-in racks for the orders. We were perhaps foolish to open so close to Christmas. We made lots of mistakes. We fell short on performance measurements at all levels—telephone response, picking and deliveries. The weather was foul, and the service got off to a terrible start. The vans were too wide to fit through the average household gate—and those lovely clip-in delivery racks would not wheel on gravel! Elementary. Common sense is sometimes a scarce and valuable resource. I sadly ended the service after three months. There was, however, a consolation prize: by closing the home delivery service, the branches had been cleared of a lot of costs.

While all this was going on, the usual company routine of people joining and people retiring provided a reassuring atmosphere of normality and continuity. The men and women who had been the backbone of Findlater's service were given appropriate send-offs.

In August 1967 a reception was held in honour of Richard Haughton (seventy-one), grocery manager in Dún Laoghaire, and Francis P. O'Flynn (seventy-five), general grocery traveller who both retired from the company in that year. Frank was born in Collon, Co. Limerick. He worked with the Home and Colonial Stores from 1914 until he joined Findlaters in 1931, with the exception of two years spent in Flanders with the British Army Medical Corps during the First World War. He represented Findlaters to hospitals, hotels, restaurants and institutions. Richard Haughton retired with 56 years' service; he joined the Kingstown branch in 1911. In 1915 he was given leave of absence to join the British Army fighting in France; he rejoined the firm in 1919, and refused promotion to stay in the Dún Laoghaire branch until his retirement.

In November 1967 the house journal, the *Findlater Herald* announced to its readers that

> More than 300 years—that is the almost unbelievable total of service which seven Findlater employees who retired recently gave to the firm, bringing to almost 2,000 the number of years of cumulative service to Dublin shoppers by our 52 pensioners. And it is a measure of their own spirit as well as the company's regard for them that these seven have contributed over 40 years to the success story of Findlaters. Among the more recent retirements is that of Mr Joseph Hayes, much-respected manager of our Blackrock branch, who spent in all 48 years with Findlaters. Mr Ignatius Butler, who has retired as manager of the Sandymount branch, gave the company 41 years of service. Known to his colleagues as an extremely hard worker, he held in all three managerships, the others being at George's Street and at Baggot Street. His service has been

1960s shop posters

The proposed shop front for the planned supermarket in Dun Laoghaire

Miss Bridie Reddington, Butter Dept.; Miss Helen Tracey, Retail Office; Miss Mary Grimes, Comp. Dept.; Miss Kay Curtin, Secretary to Mr. Alex Findlater and Miss Rosamund Dempsey, Secretary to Mr. J. A. McGrail.

Findlater Herald. November 1967

much appreciated by staff and customers alike.

By way of contrast, Miss Mary McLoughlin, who leaves as office chargehand in Blackrock after 48 years, has been at that branch during her entire career. She was very popular with many local shoppers, having known many of them since they were toddlers.

Also well known was Miss Lilian Furlong, who leaves the fruit and vegetable department in Dalkey after more than 40 years of excellent work. Her counterpart in Rathmines, Miss Mary O'Toole, was renowned for her great enthusiasm for work, and has been described by at least one of her fellow-workers as one who was 'always rushing about the place'. Miss M. Dowling leaves the Dalkey branch, where she was employed as office chargehand, after 44 years at Findlaters. Miss Ethel Lea, who devoted so much work to the confectionery department in Sandymount, has been with us for 42 years, some of which she spent at Baggot Street.

Early in 1968, notwithstanding the improving ratios and an upward sales graph, all the exceptional and unexpected items outweighed the good work, and I decided to consult with the fledgling and thrusting Investment Bank of Ireland before we haemorrhaged further. There were only two merchant banks in Dublin at the time, the other being the venerable and long established Guinness & Mahon, then managed by the founding families. We were now looking for someone to buy us, but during the course of the next six months all the recognised suitors fell by the wayside. These included Le Riches stores in Jersey and H. Williams. Jack Cohen of Tesco was most courteous and tried to persuade me to take up a job with them. I protested that I was in his office to give him an opportunity to enter the Irish market. We even called on Jack Musgrave* in Cork but were ahead of our time. Garfield Weston's son Galen initially said 'No, thank you'. So I bought back his shares. Then finally he said Yes, he would do a deal. He would take over Findlaters with its tax losses, ex gratia pensioners, six of our branches and as many licences as would transfer. The assets that he did not want were to be moved into a parallel company. These included the O'Connell Street property, the St Lawrence Hotel and public house in Howth with the filling station attached, the wine division, and some fourteen branch shops.

In December 1968 I called staff and management together again, this time to announce that the retail operation had to close. Terry O'Sullivan, columnist in the *Evening Press,* happened upon the meeting in the Gresham on 30 December 1968 when I stood alone on the stage to announce the closure.

> I shall never again see the sight of a slim lone thirty-one-year-old man of impeccable presence carry so gallantly such a burden, no more than I shall ever again see a handsome, twenty-eight-year-old [Galen Weston] accept and lift that burden, in the Gresham yesterday afternoon, behind the closed doors of the ballroom. The young Alex Findlater spoke with grey haired gravity to the combined staffs of all his branches, to tell them that it was all over and that Findlaters, as Dublin knew it, was finished.
>
> In a silence so loud that I could hear it through the closed door, he announced the various degrees of taking care. Every one of the Findlaters' staff are being taken care of financially. There is a redundancy of some 175 people, but each and every one of the one-time Findlater staff have provision made for them. As befits a family business with a great and honourable tradition.
>
> The Findlater name survives as a wine and spirit merchants. It would seem that as far as possible everyone has been taken care of . . . the Findlater staffs, the Shareholders (a small, modest and undemanding group), and in the heel of the hunt there emerges the Findlater honour.

Eventually we sold our premises in O'Connell Street and Cathal Brugha Street to Ronald Lyon for property redevelopment; the St Lawrence Hotel to wine merchant, Bill Campbell. The branch shops not taken over by Galen Weston were sold individually, mainly at auction through Lisneys. With some difficulty plant and machinery, fixtures and fittings were sold for at least book value by a phased and diligent disposal within the trade over the course of a year. Wine stocks surplus to the requirements of the continuing wine division were snapped up by the trade and wine enthusiasts. The shareholders fared well. The whole wind-down and asset disposal was handled by myself and John McGrail, assisted by the able team in solicitors A. & L. Goodbody, and by the company secretaries Kinnear & Co.

Having sold the headquarters, the question was—what next? I told Louis O'Sullivan, editor of *Checkout,* in an interview published in February 1969:

* The Musgrave Group, which incorporates 165 family-owned Super Valu outlets and 270 Centras, now controls an amazing 22 per cent of the country's grocery market.

The author and Galen Weston in the Gresham Hotel. 30 December 1968.
(Photo: *Independent Newspapers*)

> When we sold the O'Connell Street premises for £353,000 [2000 = £3.9 million for 26,000 square feet] we had to make the decision whether the money should be reinvested in retailing (we had plans ready to develop our major shops in Dún Laoghaire, Foxrock and Rathmines) or in other fields. Naturally our first preference was the field we knew—retailing. However we took the best financial advice available and found it impossible to recommend that this money should be put back into the grocery trade. The ten shops we had converted were only on average breaking even. We had to look at the environment of the whole market and the future funds that would be needed to remain one of the horses in the race. Maybe we didn't move far enough, fast enough, but we did get to a point where we felt the temperature of the market and decided that it was too hot!

In such an enormous old place as the O'Connell Street head office, with many activities up and down stairs, in cellars and lofts, and an incredible variety of goods flowing continually through, it was perhaps inevitable that 'leakage' should occur. After we closed in 1969, ex-staff used to say sympathetically: 'I'm sorry Master Alex, you'se was robbed!' implying that there was more slipping out of the place undocumented than we detected, and we did have some big detections. The archive has many sad records, such as the letter from the Sandymount branch manager to Adam explaining how provision man O'Rourke had been caught stealing a ham just before Christmas 1899; or the barmaid sacked

DECEMBER 5, 1968

£1 million redevelopment:

Findlaters sells Dublin HQ site for £353,000 to development company

Selfservice and Supermarket December 1968

Ronald Lyon's proposed redevelopment of Findlater's Corner

from the theatre in 1900 for irregularities in the stock, and in 1930 the husband and wife team working scams in the gallery and pits bar, and in 1934 when 25½ bottles of spirits and 49 bottles of wine were found filled with water in the cellar, and the cellarman had to go.

On one occasion I saw a man loading a large amount of drink outside the O'Connell Street warehouse. Full of enthusiasm, I dashed up to give the customer a helping hand—later learning that I had contributed to a heist, which was being carefully watched by management! On another occasion there were inexplicable shortages in the provision department in Thomas Street. This store did a good trade in baby Powers and snipes of stout, but also in bacon. Eventually a plant was put in, in the form of a private investigator in Findlater shop attire, supposedly transferred from another branch. After the announcement of a surprise stock-take the investigator decided that he would not go out for lunch when the shop closed for the hour. To his surprise several sides of bacon walked into the closed shop from Liptons up the road. The stock-takers duly arrived back and confirmed that the stock count was correct, and the bacon then returned to Liptons after they had gone. Unfortunately, the management plant had seen all, and the secret was uncovered. Such are the vagaries of trade!

Long after we closed I was still receiving conscience money, when perhaps the priest or clergy counselled that restitution should be made. It usually arrived by registered post, anonymously, a money order or pound notes. It gave me a shiver down the spine. There was someone out there that 'knew'. Was it him—or perhaps her? Their conscience was now clear, the burden was transferred to me. It was customary to acknowledge receipt in the *Evening Herald* or *Mail.* The last one that I received was in 1987 (eighteen years after the firm closed!) and had this typed note—handwriting could be a giveaway. 'Last year I sent you per regis-

My sister Suzanne and Frode Dahl who married in Findlater's Church 17 May 1969 seen outside the church on the way to a friend's wedding.

tered post £200 in part settlement of goods received from your shop while in O'Connell Street. I now enclose the balance of £300 to fully settle the account. Once again I apologise for my slowness in paying account; better late than never. It has been worrying me for some time.' (In current terms, this writer was owning up to stealing some £5,500 worth of goods from the company.)

It had been our intention to set up our wine division independently. However, without premises, a merger with FitzGeralds, the wholesale tea, wine and spirit merchants, which had extensive premises in Westmoreland Street, was a more attractive option. This highly respected company had been established in 1861 by Martin FitzGerald (1864-1927), born in County Mayo, who was the proprietor of the *Freeman's Journal* (1919-24) and an intermediary between Michael Collins and Sir Alfred Cope, the British assistant under-secretary for Ireland 1920-2, in the negotiations leading to the Anglo-Irish truce in July 1921. Martin was a keen follower of horse-racing as was the celebrated Nora FitzGerald who passed the company on to her nephew and niece, Jim and Catherine FitzGerald. They were the agents for Haig Scotch whisky, then one of the biggest selling brands, Bisquit cognac, another good seller, and other important brands of wines and spirits. I was a non-executive director of the new company which traded as FitzGerald Findlater & Co. Ltd.

After a year selling stock and equipment in our O'Connell Street premises, I departed on a peregrination around the language schools of Germany, Switzerland and Spain, culminating in Insead, the international business school in Fontainebleu. While on this peregrination FitzGerald Findlater were taken over by Edward Dillon & Co. Ltd, distributors for Hennessy, Gordons, Sandeman, Lanson and other leading brands. My first move when back in

Dublin was to buy back the rights over the Findlater name in the wine trade by purchasing Findlater (Wine Merchants) from Nigel Beamish, managing director of Edward Dillon & Co. Ltd.* This set the scene for a return to the trade. One of the conditions of the sale of Alex. Findlater & Co. Ltd. to Galen Weston had been that I was forbidden from re-entering the grocery trade under my own name, but the restriction in the wine trade lasted for only three years.

After the Insead course I was still in my thirties, but quite unsure where my future lay. I attended a vocational guidance clinic in Harley Street, London in order to find out what my true vocation was. I was convinced that I should be leading safaris across the Sahara and in Latin America. I was fit, sporting and had a good command of languages. Rather disappointingly they pointed me back to my home base and the trades I had been brought up in and assessed that I was better at selling a service than a product. On reflection, that is much of what my role in Findlaters was all about.

But I had found a new confidence after Insead and, setting aside the advice gained in Harley Street, was receptive when the idea of theatrical promotion came up. With two much more resourceful friends the plan was to promote Sammy Davis Junior for a week in the Grosvenor House, London. The success of this was followed by a week of Marlene Dietrich in the same venue. Unfortunately, this time we learnt that the downside of theatrical promotion can be pretty painful. However, there's always a next time and some years later, in 1986, with some of the same friends, I was involved in the first full staging of the Bolshoi Ballet in Dublin. For the four performances a 4,000 seat theatre had been constructed within the Simmonscourt extension of the RDS. Such was the 'occasion' that many of the guests attended the opening performance in full evening dress. The reception was pulsating. The press headlines read: A BOLSHOI BALLET EXTRAVAGANZA!, FROM RUSSIA WITH GRACE, IVAN THE ATHLETE AND A PORTRAIT OF BOLSHOI BEAUTY. This was one of the first events at which 'corporate hospitality' had been offered with champagne before the show and dinner afterwards, in a purpose-built dining room on location. A truly memorable occasion.

New Findlaters

Our next step was to relaunch Findlaters as a wine merchant in its own right. Having examined a variety of options and locations we acquired a retail premises in Upper Rathmines, a suburb of Dublin. This time we clearly identified that we were to be wine merchants exclusively, the financial resources required to support spirit agencies being beyond us.† We re-entered at the tail-end of a slump in wine prices and could offer great value to our private clients. And so

* Dillons were, in turn, taken over and have had a variety of industry shareholders and remain to this day, a force in the Irish wine and spirit trade.

† Just as Alexander Findlater the founder moved into whiskey in the 1820 ahead of a boom in spirits, and then built a brewery in 1852 to benefit from the switch from spirit drinking to beer, history shows that we chose correctly. The Irish wine market has risen from some 800 cases a year in 1974 to over 4 million a year in 2000, and is still growing.

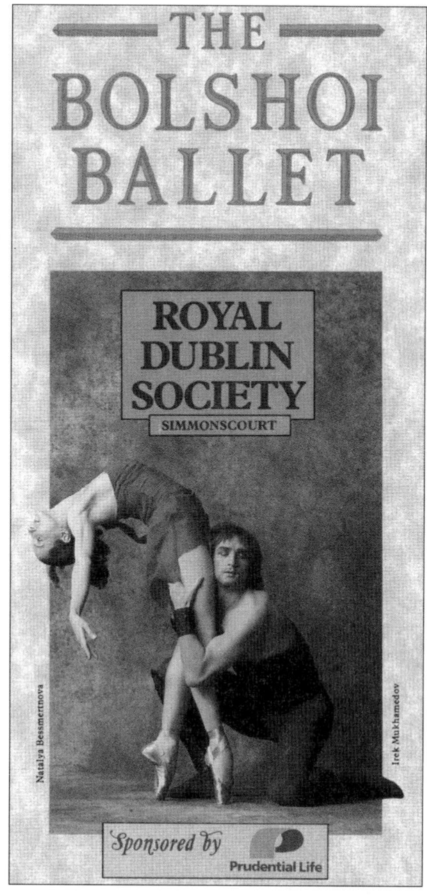

the business grew, offering good value and a lot of service. We bought freely on the market and one by one restaurants came to us for supplies. This was the encouragement we needed. Trade expanded and old suppliers reappeared, some who had had a lean time in Ireland since the changes to old Findlaters.

Shortly after we opened in Upper Rathmines in 1974 and were tight for money, a large car drew up at the door. The gentleman tendered a £100 note for a small purchase, an enormous sum at the time. We apologised profusely that we did not have sufficient change. He was not at all perturbed and left it in our safe hands. This was Joe Murphy, founder of Tayto Crisps. He was reciprocating a good turn. In the early days of Tayto, when he was in dire financial straits, he called on Dermot and offered him half of his company or more, then based in a small premises off Moore Street. He was on his knees. 'No', said Dermot, 'keep your company'—and he came up with a plan. He would promote Tayto in all Findlater outlets, get his commercial travellers to promote them to the trade, pay the account in seven days and more importantly, Joe's wife could buy her groceries on 'tick' in Findlaters' Malahide branch until the position was under control; six months or more, whatever was necessary, and then repay little by little as the cash flows permitted. It was a lifeline to Joe. He was relieved, Tayto became brand leader and Joe's thank-you was in turn much appreciated by us. Eventually Tayto was taken over by the American multinational, T. C. L. Beatrice Foods, in 1964 and, then in 1999, bought by Irish based international drinks group Cantrell & Cochrane, for £68 million.

Trade in the 1970s and 1980s was not an easy ride. We were constantly short of funds and seeking family support. Personal guarantees ensured that we paid ourselves modestly and put off the funding of pensions. Profits were ploughed back and by degrees the business strengthened. This was the time I did my service behind the counter, an activity denied me when I entered old Findlaters many years earlier. Slowly, we created an atmosphere in Rathmines which our customers liked. We were competing for much of our trade with Mitchells of Kildare Street, a fine old wine merchant with excellent agencies in Krug, Remy Martin, Famous Grouse, Deinhard, and other good brands. Thoughts of a

Selling with humour—From Christmas Wine Lists 1985-87.

Illustrations by Martyn Turner

Christmas Wine Lists

1988–Terry Willers

1989–Uto Hogerzeil

1990–Bob Fannin

1994–Tony Colley

Our lists in this period were designed to entertain and give knowledge. Other excellent lists were illustrated by Harry McConville (1977 & 1988), Veronica Haywood (1979), and John Donohue (1980). Martyn Turner also illustrated 1981, Tony Colley 1982 and Uto Hogerzeil 1983 & 1984.

merger were explored from time to time, but to no avail.

Nick Robinson speaking at the opening of the Vaults. (Photo: Photostyle)

By the early 1980s trade was going ahead in leaps and bounds but space was our major concern. We began to expand, buying the property to our right and behind us in Rathmines, but by the mid-1980s were again short of space. As an associated activity we had developed part of the area into the Wine Épergne Restaurant, created and managed first by my former partner Seong and then by Kevin and Muriel Thornton, who are now enjoying considerable success in Portobello with two Michelin stars.

One cold February day, at 10.30 in the morning, on the wet pavement in Lower Mount Street, after swearing under my breath at an unimaginative banker whose office we had just left, I was led to suggest to my colleague Frode Dahl that we return to the office via Harcourt Street. I pointed out the derelict looking property to the left of the old station with wild sycamores, elders and a host of weeds growing in the entrance yard. I said that there must be something inside those rusty steel gates under the old Harcourt Street railway station, so close to the heart of the city.

Mark Kavanagh of Hardwicke, whose father, with great foresight, had bought the whole property block from CIE when the railway closed in 1953, let us inspect the property. It was derelict. The walls and ceilings were grimy from years of seepage from the station above. The area had been used previously by Gilbeys as a bonded warehouse for maturing casked whiskey but they had surrendered their lease when the bonding of whiskey was taken over by Irish Distillers. The floors were, on the whole, of good sterile soil. The lighting was non-existent and the headroom between many vaults only four feet high. With heavy hearts we were about to walk away from the idea when Morrough Kavanagh suggested we consult an engineer. Christopher Pringle from Monaghan looked, paced, measured, shook his torch for more light, stubbed out yet another cheroot and said, 'Well, it could be done—at a price.'

The plan was simple—let's not call it a 'business plan' as taught at Insead—it was to press ahead with the development when we got title, and sell our Rathmines premises to fund the refurbishment, any shortfall to be covered by increased borrowings or by recourse to an investor. We opened in 1991 with six of the twenty-one vaults floored. We invited professional and business friends. Nick Robinson, Chairman of the Irish Architectural Archive performed the opening ceremony. Few gave us much chance of survival but they were polite and did not say it! We had not bargained on a depression and sky-high interest

Senior citizens at the opening of the Vaults. *(left to right)* My mother Dorothea, Stanley Fleetwood (retired manager), my aunt Sheila and Ned Kelly, who used to service the Trojan vans. (Ned passed away on 16 July 2001) (Picture: Photostyle)

rates in our first year. However, we only recorded one small trading loss and thereafter the graph climbed upwards. We were under pressure to bring in investors to reduce borrowings and fund the renovations to the other fourteen vaults. A detailed plan was written and three most suitable investors found.

Some credited us as with 'lateral thinking', moving into the city centre when others in the trade were moving out. Certainly, the location brought us into close proximity with the many city eating establishments which enabled us to give them a top class service. The splendour of the vaults and the presence of the museum, recording pictorially the story of our activities as merchants in Dublin over the past 175 years, coupled with a top class selection of wines, helped us to restore the company's public profile. As Philip Smith and Peter Leach in *The Family Business in Ireland* put it when discussing entrepreneurial characteristics: 'The need to achieve personal goals is central to their characters, and personal satisfaction (i.e. building a successful business) is usually a stronger motivating force than financial reward'. Times were tough but we doggedly won through.

Now the company is in outstandingly good health and a leader in its industry. Since the move to the vaults we are selling over seven times more wine and our market share has increased fourfold. Unusually for a private company of our size we have a strong board with two non-executive directors, Lochlann Quinn, chairman of Allied Irish Banks and deputy-chairman of Glen Dimplex, the world leader in electrical consumer products, and Brian Smith, until his recent retirement, a director of Beck Smith and Batchelors Ltd, part of Northern Foods, one of the UK's leading plcs.

It is recorded in Chapter 2 that my great ancestor 'exhibited a wonderful ability—indeed almost an intuitive power–in the selection of his employees,

The Excise office outside the vaults prior to our restoration.

The back vaults beyond the museum.

The main area, one of 8 vaults this size (c.360 sq metres each)

Museum, one of 10 vaults this size
(c.110 sq.metres.each, the others being used for document storage)

The Vaults are numbered 1 to 22 (but there is no number 12)
and cover the area of some 48,000 square feet

147-149 Upper Rathmines Road (Watercolour by Pat Liddy)

many of whom, as time passed on, became his partners.' And so it has been in modern Findlaters. Most business teaching advises against joint managing directors. It has worked well for us with Frode Dahl, my brother-in-law, in control of finance, warehousing and administration and Keith MacCarthy-Morrogh in charge of sales and marketing. Frode navigated the company through the choppy waters after our move to the vaults, found alternative sources of income when funds were needed, saw to improving performance ratios and, most importantly, protected margins against competitive pressures. It's a busy fool who builds volume at the expense of margin and reports profits unchanged.

Keith, who was invited to join us in 1993, had spent the previous twenty years with David Dand and Tom Keaveney building up Gilbeys of Ireland to the No. 1 position in the Irish wine and spirit trade and establishing Baileys as the largest selling cream liqueur world-wide. He came to us with a wealth of experience and enviable contacts. He repositioned the company as distributor of quality wines from renowned independent producers, giving us some of the world's best loved wine names, a policy that has proved an outstanding success.

Frode Dahl, Knight 1st Class, Royal Norwegian Order of Merit, being presented with the honour by H.E. the Norwegian Ambassador, Kirsten Ohn, 30th November 1990.

Quality has been the bedrock of the Findlater business since its inception. Nigel Werner, who joined Frode and myself from the start in 1974, is the present custodian of our enviable reputation for quality. He maintains a close working relationship with our specialist producers the world over. It is a job that requires an acutely sensitive nose and palate, a good memory of tastes, flavours and aromas and a recall of the characteristics of grape varieties, vineyards and vintages that make up the galaxy of wines available on the world market. All this must be coupled with a thorough knowledge of our market so that our lists have a good balance for all palates and pockets. Nigel also champions another important area where the buying of wine has changed since Dermot's days. Then we bought, cellared and matured on our own account. The carrying cost and uncertainty of this caused the downfall of many reputable English wine merchants. Now we market the top Bordeaux and Burgundy growths under a system known as 'en primeur' where the client is given the opportunity to invest in the maturing stock for his or her future pleasure, or perhaps for speculative gain.

'Wine-speak', the use of elaborate and flowery metaphors to describe the aromas and palates, has often left the aspiring purchaser no wiser as to what the choice should be. There is no better champion of easy to understand advice on the merits of all our wonderful wines than David Millar, whose joy it is to impart his knowledge to as wide an audience as possible. He, Barry Geoghegan, recently appointed sales director and Richard Verling, associate director (restaurants) are in the forefront of the sales team. All came to the company with a bundle of experience in the industry and have excellent wine knowledge and exceptional talents in their chosen areas of responsibility. They are part of the management team that has refocused us in the past and will do so again in the future. Findlaters is a happy company with a strong collegiate spirit.

This is the firm that I have led since 1974. Its success has been beyond all our expectations. In the last decade we consistently out-performed our annual business plan. There is no doubt the booming Irish economy has helped us along. But it needed, and we had, an exceptional team to capitalise on the opportunities. We also had our strokes of luck. We were rewarded for restoring the vaults as an historic building. This gave us an important tax break when we most needed it. By 1996 our finances were in good order, borrowings were almost eliminated, personal guarantees were removed, profitability was rising and dividends were beginning to flow.

The time was now right to relinquish some of my executive responsibilities. As Smith and Leach put it: 'Most entrepreneurs love the excitement and the challenge of this pioneering phase. . . ' Thus in January 1997 Frode and Keith took over as joint managing directors. For the first nine months I remained as executive chairman and started the research into this book. Smith and Leach continue: 'Succession should not be an event. Ideally, the owner's transition from MD to chairman is so gradual as to be imperceptible. Successors grow into their roles, earning the respect and confidence of the owner, and the owner gradually becomes accustomed to a new role.' In late 1997 I changed my role to non-executive chairman and full time researcher and scribe.

As we leave the year 2000 a new chapter in the history of the company is about

The Findlater Team at the company's annual trade Wine Odyssey February 2001.
Back row: Anthony Tindal, Werner Hillebrand, Dan Gregory, David Millar, Michael Williams, Tom Mullet, Barry Geoghegan, Matt Tindal.
Middle row: Karl O'Flanagan, Nigel Werner, David Geary, Richard Verling.
Front row: Keith MacCarthy-Morrogh, Maureen O'Hara, Aisling Norton and Alex.
Absent: Managing the vaults and keeping the show on the road: Frode Dahl, John McCormack, Brian McCollum, Damien Archer, Frank Donohoe, Marc Meehan, Sarah Malone, Anne Gahan, Juliet Brennan, Sarah Grubb, Genevieve McCarthy, Nicola Healy, Richard Nash and his merry team from Munster, and the hardworking bond and dispatch team. (Photo: John Geary)

to unfold. The industry is changing. Demand for wine is growing across the world. New vineyards are being planted, knowledgeable winemakers teamed with marketing people are replacing the gentlemenly winemen of yesteryear. The physical quality of the wine is now much less variable than it was in the past. They say that globalisation is taking over but there are still an enormous number of really good producers in private hands, who run excellent businesses and need distributors such as ours. We ourselves are on the threshold of a move from the Harcourt Street Vaults to a new purpose-built bonded warehouse and distribution centre in the west of the city, a project that will enable us to double the size of the company within the next five years.

Over its long and wonderful life the story of Findlaters has been about the family that owns the company, the producers who supply the goods, the executives who manage the business, the staff who serve the customers, and, not least, the loyal customers who support the whole. Smith and Leach put our advantage in perspective:

Culinary entrepreneur Darina Allen, Winner of the 2001 Veuve Clicquot Business Woman of the Year award, with Keith MacCarthy-Morrogh, joint managing director of Findlaters. Alexander, the founder, no doubt knew Madame Clicquot, advertising Champagne bought from her in her lifetime in *The Irish Times* on 26 December 1861, priced at 78s a dozen. (Photo: Kierán Hartnett).

Commitment and a stable culture lie behind the fact that family businesses are generally very solid and reliable structures—and are perceived as such in the market place. Many customers prefer doing business with a firm which has been established for a long time, and they will have tended to build up relationships with a management and staff. Also, the commitment within the family business . . . reveals itself to customers all the time in the form of a friendlier, more knowledgeable, more skilful and generally much higher standard of service and customer care.

Coat of Arms granted to Alexander the Founder

Sit mihi libertas.

Notes and references

1 Both papers March 1962

2 Philip Smith and Peter Leach *The Family Business in Ireland* Dublin: Blackwater Press and BDO Simpson Xavier 1993 p 38

Sir John Harvey-Jones in the foreword to Philip Smith and Peter Leach's excellent book *The Family Business in Ireland* said 'Family businesses comprise over 90 per cent of all the businesses in Ireland and it has been estimated that over 50 per cent of people employed are employed in family businesses'. Findlaters are proud to be amongst their ranks

17. *Bicycles, Blood, Bloom and Burgundy*

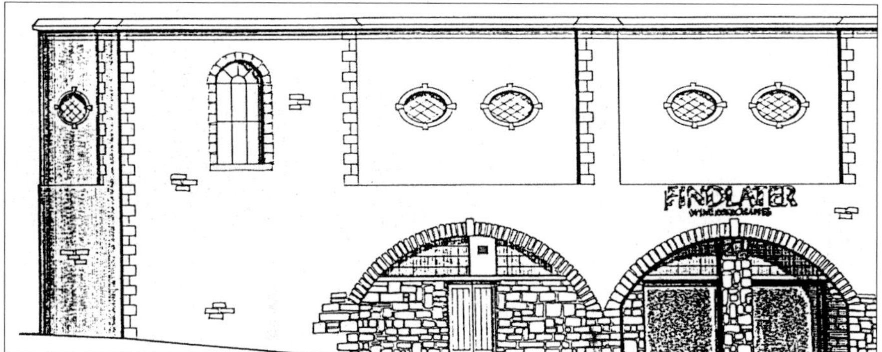

The entrance to the Harcourt Street vaults under the former railway station which was opened in 1859 and closed almost 100 years later. The entrance to Findlaters is on the right and the POD night club on the left (Sketch by Tony Colley)

In recent years, Findlaters have been identified with a fun item on the city's calendar of events, the Bloomsday Messenger Bike Rally. The idea, which was first floated to the guests of the Junior Chamber of Commerce during my acceptance speech for the Business Heritage Award 1993, was to add colour and pageant to Bloomsday, which then had no visuals and was confined to readings in Joycean pubs and wanderings along Leopold Bloom's route.[•] Bill Cullen, chairman of Renault Ireland, a guest that evening, caught the idea, and the Rally was born, in aid of the Irish Youth Foundation–after all to be a messenger boy at the age of say, fourteen, was the first rung on the ladder, as Bill had proven. David Norris,[†] Ken Monaghan and Bob Joyce[‡] were entertaining parallel thoughts about the development of a Joyce centre in North Great George's Street in the north inner city. In 1994 the Rally became a reality on a bright sunny 16 June and celebrity readings took off at the Joyce Centre.

Gay Byrne, who had once aspired to be a Findlater messenger boy,[1] gave the Rally a dream launch on the *Late Late Show*—riding onto the set were Feargal Quinn, Patrick Campbell, Bill Cullen and yours truly.[§] Pete St John, composer of 'Dublin in the Rare Ould Times' and 'The Fields of Athenry', launched a cassette, in word and in song, with the four bassoons above, merchant-bicyclists,

• Leopold Bloom is the main character in *Ulysses.* The first celebration of Bloomsday was in 1954 when John Ryan, Patrick Kavanagh, Flann O'Brien, Anthony Cronin and Tom Joyce toured the sites of Joycean interest on the 50th anniversary of Bloom's odyssey. They started at the Martello tower in Sandycove and reached the Bailey later in the day, failing to make their intended destination, Glasnevin Cemetery

† David Norris, Senator, TV personality and Joycean scholar

‡ Nephew and grand-nephew respectively of James Joyce

§ All chairmen or managing directors of public-spirited Irish companies

Feargal Quinn *left* and Dorothy Gray, President of the Junior Chamber of Commerce presenting the author with the Business Heritage Award 1993.

articulating with an amazing degree of professionalism!

When we started the Bike Rally, it was often suggested that there is little of bicycles in *Ulysses,* but they are there nevertheless: *College sports today I see. He eyed the horseshoe poster over the gate of College Park: cyclists doubled up like a cod in a pot. Damn bad ad. Now if they had made it round like a wheel. Then the spokes: sports, sports, sports: and the hub big: college. Something to catch the eye.*[2]

On 16 June 1904 there was a sports meeting in College Park, run by the Bicycle and Harriers Club. It was a 'pleasant sequel' to the College Races held one week previously. They consisted of four cycle races, three foot races and a composite race, and the events described by Joyce were the half-mile handicap cycle race and the quarter-mile foot race.[3] *As per usual somebody's nose was out of joint about the boy that had the bicycle always riding up and down in front of her window. Only now his father kept him in the evenings studying hard to get an exhibition in the intermediate that was on and he was going to Trinity college to study for a doctor when he left the high school like his brother W. E. Wylie** *who was racing in the bicycle races in Trinity college university.*[4]

George Russell, known as Æ, was a dominant figure in the Irish literary renaissance of the period. The bicycle was one of Æ's trade marks as he travelled all over Ireland organising farmers' co-operative societies. *His eyes followed the high figure in homespun, beard and bicycle, a listening woman at his side. Coming from the vegetarian. Only weggebobbles and fruit. Don't eat a beefsteak. If you do the eyes of that cow will pursue you through all eternity. They say its healthier.*[5]

In 1881 we find an ancestor of the Bloomsday Bike Rally sponsors, Guinness,

* W. E. Wylie was later a barrrister (1905), served with Trinity College officer corps during the Rising, became a High Court judge in 1920 and was chairman of the Royal Dublin Society for many years (See also Leon Ó Broin's *W. E. Wylie and the Irish Revolution 1916–1921*).

breaking the most unusual world record: 'On solid tyres and on a high bicycle Harry Guinness won the world record for slow bicycling at Crystal Palace cheered on by a large crowd of supporters'. The high bicycle, then in fashion, was almost impossible to ride at any other than top speed. To travel slowly was an art form.[6]

We are all proud that, in 1888, an Irishman invented and commercialised the pneumatic tyre.[*] *'Greatwheel Dunlop was the name was on him: behung, all we are his bisaacles'.*[7] Belfast vet, John Boyd Dunlop was experimenting with his son Johnny's tricycle tyres and developed the pneumatic tyre.[8] His veterinary practices were the largest in Northern Ireland and later he had considerable business interests in Dublin.[†]

But few know that in 1876 an Irishman, William Bindon Blood of Clare and Dublin, patented and produced the first new lightweight tricycle.[‡] These had been preceded by boneshakers with solid wooden wheels. The new tricycle was the alternative mount for those who were of the wrong age, temperament, physique or sex to ride the ordinary. Between 1876 and 1892 tricycling attracted thousands of adherents who saw themselves as somewhat superior to the common run of bicyclists.

The patent for the Blood tricycle

My said Invention relates to improvements in tricycles consisting in a novel method of mounting and operating the two front wheels so as to cause the tricycle to run in a curved direction to the right or left, as may be desired; also in an improved system of bracing in order to secure perfect rigidity in the frame; and, thirdly, in a new arrangement for carrying the treadles of a tricycle or other similar machine. My improved tricycle may also be made available for use by ladies.

To carry out my invention I construct a tricycle with one driving wheel which runs behind the seat, and two guiding wheels in front, which are carried in vertical forks.

---

* Unknown to Dunlop at the time, a William Thompson of Westminster had taken out a patent for an air tyre 43 years earlier, but did not develop his idea commercially.

† Among these was Todd, Burns & Co., the department store in Mary Street originally founded by Alexander and his partners Todd and Burns (see Chapter 2) where he was chairman.

‡ The Bloods were cousins of the Findlaters and were partners in Findlater's Mountjoy Brewery and in William Findlater & Co., solicitors. (See Burke's *Irish Family Records* 1976 edition for details of the Blood family.)

Bloomsday in Dublin

Photo: Peter Thursfield, *The Irish Times* 15 June 1996

Dawson Street

Joyce Centre

Singing the Rally Anthem—'Molly Malone' on the steps of the Mansion House

Photographs: Andy Murray & Paul Oatway

In 1893 in picturesque College Park, in Dublin's Trinity College, Charles Findlater won the one-mile bicycle novices' race and received a magnificent portico clock which one hundred years on sits proudly on my mantelpiece.* Some prize for a novices' race, it weighs all of three pounds! He also won a number of long distance races with the Irish Road Club. In 1899, again in College Park, surgeon, writer and wit, Oliver St John Gogarty, the basis for the character Buck Mulligan in *Ulysses,* won virtually all the cycling events in the College races; he was first in the mile, the mile handicap, and the three-mile and would have won the five-mile had his tyre not burst at the beginning of the race. He competed with the Dublin University Cycling Club and was the last of the great Trinity cyclists. Alas he never won an Irish title.[9] Those were the days when sport paved the way to student fame in Trinity. The College Races were the most important outdoor social event of the year in Dublin. The Viceroy and his court attended, while it was the occasion of the first showing of summer fashions. Thousands of people attended for the two days and the gathering was enlivened by bookies shouting odds from the back of the crowds. Here is how one spectator described the College Races as early as 1850: 'Taking my position on an elevation near the Park wall, the coup d'oeil was truly magnificent. Twenty thousand spectators, three-fourths of them the gentler sex, were circled round the scene of operations, and certainly the galaxy of beauties, adorned with all the grace of fashion suited for so brilliant a day, shed a lustre which must have astonished and delighted Phoebus, as it did the writer and all who witnessed it.'[10]

Bicycles were the trendy purchase of the day, and it is no surprise to find that the Findlaters were in the business, with Martin and Findlaters' bicycle shop at the lower end of Dawson Street where Waterstones now stands. The wife of Charles's partner Martin was a twin sister of Alfie Byrne's mother. Alfie served his apprenticeship in the bicycle shop and was a lifelong friend of the Findlater organisation. 'Alfie Byrne, the Perennial Lord Mayor of Dublin (ten times), with his neatly waxed moustache, his chain of office, his hand ever outstretched to shake and be shaken, and his wallet always at the service of the destitute. Elected simply on the strength of his personal popularity.'[11]

It was inconceivable that Joyce would overlook Alfie and so we find him in Joyce's fairy tale, *The Cat and the Devil,* published in 1936, where a Monsieur Alfred Byrne was Lord Mayor of Beaugency.

In 1897 while all this was going on in Dublin, two Irishmen, already mentioned in this book, had a most unusual encounter in Edgeware, then a village on the outskirts of London as George Bernard Shaw describes in his account 'On Pleasure Bent':

> It occurred to me that if I went into the country, selected a dangerous hill and rode down it on a bicycle at full speed in the darkest part of the night, some novel and convincing piece of realism might result . . . [and it did]. Probably no man has ever mis-

* Charles, an engineering graduate of Trinity, survived Gallipoli but died on the Somme, aged forty-six.

Interior of Martin and Findlater's bicycle shop in Dawson Street

understood another so completely as the doctor misunderstood me when he apologised for the sensation produced by the point of his needle as he corrected the excessive openness of my countenance after the adventure. To him who has endured points made by actors for nearly three years, the point of a surgeon's darning needle comes as a delicious relief. I did not like to ask him to put in a few more stitches merely to amuse me, as I had already, through pure self-indulgence, cut into his Sunday rest to an extent of which his kindness made me ashamed; but I doubt if I shall ever see a play again without longing for the comparative luxury of that quiet country surgery, with the stillness without broken only by the distant song and throbbing drum-beat of some remote Salvation Army corps, and the needle, with its delicate realism, touching my sensibilities, stitch, stitch, stitch, with absolute sincerity in the hands of an artist who had actually learned his business and knew how to do it.

It so happened that my voice, which is an Irish voice, won for me the sympathy of the doctor. This circumstance must appear amazing almost beyond credibility in the light of the fact that he was himself an Irishman; but so it was. He rightly felt that sympathy is beyond price, and declined to make it the subject of a commercial transaction. Thereby he made it impossible for me to mention his name without black ingratitude; for I know no more effectual way of ruining a man in this country than by making public the smallest propensity on his part to adopt a benevolent attitude towards necessitous strangers. I was no more to him than an untimely stranger with an unheard-of black eye, for this doctor actually did not know who I was.

With a cynicism for which his charity afterwards made me blush, I sought to reassure him as to the pecuniary competence of his muddy, torn, ensanguined and facially spoiled visitor by saying 'My name is G.B.S.', as who should say 'My name is Cecil Rhodes, or Henry Irving, or William of Germany.' Without turning a hair, he sweetly humoured my egotistic garrulity by replying, in perfect lightness of heart, 'Mine's F.; what are you?' Breathing at last an atmosphere in which it mattered so little who and

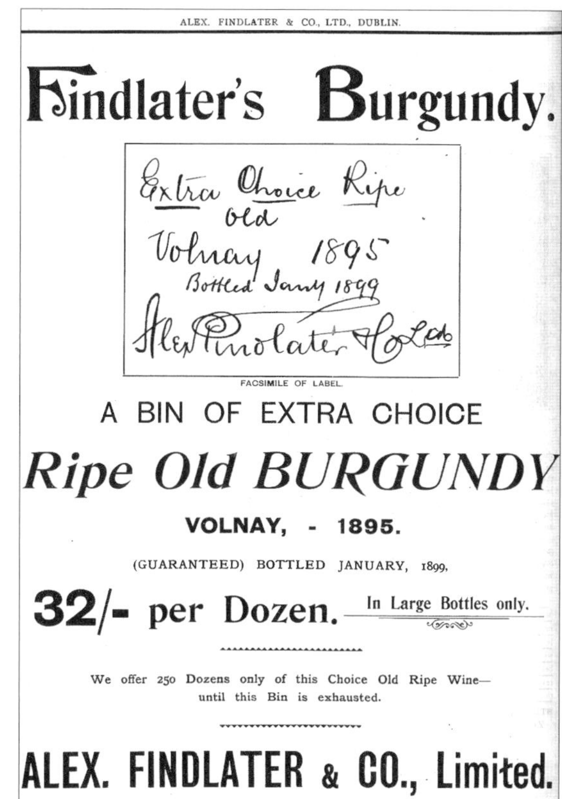

The still unopened Volnay bottle as advertised in *The Irish Times* on 16 June 1904 and another advertisement for the same wine.

> what G.B.S. was, that nobody knew either one or the other, I almost sobbed with relief whilst he threaded his needle with a nice white horsehair, tactfully pretending to listen to my evasive murmur that I was a 'sort of writer', an explanation meant to convey to him that I earned a blameless living by inscribing names in letters of gold over shop windows and on perforated wire blinds. To have brought the taint of my factitious little vogue into the unperverted consciousness of his benevolent and sensible life would have been the act of a serpent.[12]

The 'F' in this account was of course Dublin-born and Trinity-educated Dr Alex F., brother of Adam and Charles.

Joyce is well known to have used the Dublin street directory and papers of the day when writing his masterpiece, so it is no surprise to find that on the original 16 June 1904 Findlaters were advertising Burgundy in *The Irish Times* and that Burgundy finds its way into the text as Bloom lunches in Davy Byrnes 'Tiptop . . . Let me see. I'll take a glass of burgundy and . . . let me see', and 'Good glass of burgundy, take away that. Lubricate.'[13] and 'Sips of his wine soothed his palate. Not logwood that. Tastes fuller this weather with the chill off.'[14] Extraordinarily one unopened bottle of the wine that we advertised on that day has survived to this very day.

Most characters, merchants and traders of the day find their way into *Ulysses* and *Finnegans Wake*, and Adam Findlater Jnr (Chapter 6) is no exception:

> *Where do they get the money? Coming up redheaded curates from the county Leitrim, rinsing empties and old man in the cellar. Then, lo and behold, they blossom out as Adam Findlaters or Dan Tallons.*[*] *Then think of the competition. General thirst. Good puzzle would be cross Dublin without passing a pub. Save it they can't. Off the drunks perhaps. Put down three and carry five. What is that? A bob here and there, dribs and drabs. On the wholesale orders perhaps. Doing a double shuffle with the town travellers. Square it with the boss and we'll split the job, see'*.[15]

As well as in *Ulysses,* Adam also appears a few times in *Finnegans Wake*. Without a knowledge of our history the reader would be hard pressed to interpret: 'While for whoever likes that urogynal pan of cakes one apiece it is thanks, beloved, to Adam, our former first Finnlatter and our grocerest churcher, as per Grippiths' varuations,[†] for his beautiful crossmess parzel.'[16] Or a further play on the church: 'The Reverest Adam Foundlitter.'[‡] Or yet another 'By whom as my Kerk Findlater's, ye little chuch rond ye corner'.[17] Or 'Findlater and Gladstone's, Corner House, Englend'.[§] Or 'Is that the great Finnleader himself in his joakimono on his statue riding the high horse there forehengist?[18]

And again, more obscurely,

> Yes, we've conned thon print in its gloss so gay how it came from Finndlader's Yule to the day and it's Hey Tallaght Hoe on the king's highway with his hounds on the home at a turning'[¶]

Which however works better when read to the rhythm of:

> Do ye ken John Peel with his coat so grey,
> Do ye ken John Peel at the break of day,
> Do ye ken John Peel when he's far far away,
> With his hounds & his horn in the morning.

* Dan Tallon was a significant publican who became Lord Mayor of Dublin in 1899 and 1900; Adam was also a substantial licence-holder.

† Adam campaigned against a higher rateable valuation on licensed premises and succeeded. Urogynal = original; crossmess = Christmas; former: Adam died in 1911, 28 years before *Finnegans Wake* was published. Griffith's Valuation was published in the 1850s.

‡ *Finnegans Wake* p 420. The Abbey Presbyterian Church in Parnell Square, known as Findlater's Church, was paid for by Adam's great-uncle Alexander in 1864.

§ *Finnegans Wake* p 170. In the 19th century Alexander Findlater of Dublin and Thomas and Robert Gladstone of Liverpool were partners in various wine firms in England. The one Joyce refers to is probably that at Findlater's Corner under London Bridge. Thomas was related to the prime minister.

¶ *Finnegans Wake* p 334. I learnt that Adam hunted with the Ward Union from a letter written by his brother Dr Alex from 'a dug-out, a hole in the ground on the side of a hill' while engaged in the Gallipoli campaign in 1915: 'Felt a bit jumpy before the flag fell [fighting started], but now feel as if I am in the middle of a good hunting run as I used to enjoy when having a hunt with poor Adam with the Ward Hounds.'

The Rally is a jolly affair. Bikes come out of hiding in butchers' back stores and off pub walls. The bicycle trade comes up trumps with repairs and servicing. Sponsors love the event, there's a day of fun in and around Dublin's fair city in return for the modest contribution to the worthy cause. There's a great buzz of anticipation as the riders robe out in their Joycean garb and sign on in the Harcourt Street Vaults. It's then wobble, wobble down to St Stephen's Green and two circuits for the most agile to equalise the veterans and newcomers. The Lord Mayor awaits us outside the Mansion House. The rally anthem, 'Molly Malone', is sung with gusto by the participants from the Mansion House steps, conducted by a composer of note. It's 11 am and the Mayor must signal 'off.' Down Dawson Street, into College Green and on to O'Connell Street, up around Parnell Square and to the Joyce Centre for a courtesy call. TV cameras whirl, journalists jockey for position and microphones beg, 'speak to me'. Edwardian ladies and gentlemen swish and preen as the occasion requires and the old cob horse looks on as if he had seen it all before.

Moore Street, or an appropriate inner city street, calls. Free Guinness and oysters for the riders and stall-holders for twenty minutes. It's fun, it's bedlam, it's organised chaos, above all it's craic. Everyone gets sustenance, the residents of the street receive a few souvenirs, and the riders leave with their baskets lighter and a few choice words added to their vocabulary, the best to an elegantly dressed solicitor in black topper, 'You're a posh shite!' It's all in the fun of the day. We push on for pit-stop No. 2, one year it was in Temple Bar, another in the yard of

Grandparents Willie & Lucie's 'tandem' tricycle on which they used to go on picnics.

Dublin Castle, another amongst the antique shops of Francis Street, and yet another on the cobblestones of Custom House Dock. Tourists stand back in amazement as we crocodile along Henry Street or up Grafton Street, the penny-farthing man towering over the crowd. Bicycle bells ring-a-ling, hooters honk, and horns hooting achieve a narrow passage through the lunchtime throngs. We need to reach our destination by 1 o'clock, this year and last in the splendour of the newly restored Mansion House Round Room, previously the Shelbourne Hotel ballroom and Trinity College. Here we arrive to a rapturous welcome of some three hundred colourful lunchers who are entering into the spirit of Bloomsday, listening to the brilliance of the writings of James Joyce, enjoying Dublin coddle and contributing to the betterment of the young of the country and true to the motto of the Irish Youth Foundation: 'Achievement starts with opportunity'.

Notes and references

1 Gay Byrne *The Time of My Life* Dublin: Gill & Macmillan 1989 p 62
2 James Joyce *Ulysses* Harmsworth: Penguin 1968 p 87-8
3 Trevor West *The Bold Collegians—the development of sport in Trinity College Dublin* Dublin: Lilliput Press p 60
4 James Joyce *Ulysses* Harmsworth: Penguin 1968 p 347
5 *Ibid.* p 165
6 Michèle Guinness *The Guinness Spirit* London: Hodder & Stoughton 1999 p 204
7 James Joyce *Finnegans Wake* London: Faber 1950 p 58
8 Old Dublin Society *Dublin Historical Record* Spring 1996
9 Trevor West *The Bold Collegians–the development of sport in Trinity College Dublin* Dublin: Lilliput Press p 47 and Ulick O'Connor *The Times I've Seen—Oliver St John Gogarty* New York; Ivan Obolensky 1963 pp 16, 17
10 W. T. Meyler *St Catherine's Bells* Dublin: McGee 1868 preamble to the second edition
11 Brian Inglis *West Briton* London: Faber 1962 p 116
12 *Saturday Review* 20 November 1897
13 James Joyce *Ulysses* Harmsworth: Penguin 1968 p 171
14 *Ibid.* p 173
15 *Ibid.* p 60
16 James Joyce *Finnegans Wake* London: Faber 1950 p 619
17 *Ibid.* p 533
18 *Ibid.* p 214

Appendixes

GROCERY LIST.

		s.	d.
Allspice—Finest Pimento, Ground	per lb.	0	8
" " Whole	per lb.	0	8
Almonds—			
Extra Choice Selected	per lb.	3	0
Finest Jordan	per lb.	2	3
Finest Sweet Valencia	per lb.	1	6
Fine	per lb.	1	2
Fine Bitter	per lb.	1	6
Finest Ground, Sweet ...	in ½ lb. and 1 lb. tins, 9d. and	1	6
Salted, in bottles	each	1	8
Ammonia—			
A. F. & Co.'s	per bottle	0	6
Scrubb's Cloudy	per bottle	0	10
Anchovies—			
Findlater's and **Lazenby's** Finest Gorgona Fish	per ½ lb. bottle 10½d., 1 lb.	1	7
Fish in Oil	per bottle	0	11
Lazenby's Essence of Anchovies } **Findlater's** " "	per quarter bottle 5½d., half-bottle 9½d., bottle	1	4½
Lazenby's Anchovy Paste	per tin or jar 5d., per tin or jar	0	10
Anchovies in Barrels, Norwegian	per small barrel	1	4
Apples—			
Whole cored	per gallon tin	1	1
Normandy Pippins—Dried	per lb.	0	11
Apple Rings—Finest (Loose or in 1 lb. cartons)	per lb.	0	8
Apricots—Dessert A. F. & Co.)	per large tin	1	6
Extra Quality, A. F. & Co.'s	per large tin	1	0
First Standard Quality	per large tin	0	9
Extra Quality in bottle	per bottle 1s. 2d. and	1	9
Dried—Finest	per lb.	0	11
Crystallised and Glace	per lb.	1	10
Arrowroot—Findlater's Finest West India ...	per lb.	1	6
Finest quality St. Vincent	per lb.	1	2
Genuine	per lb.	0	8
Asparagus—	per tin	0	11
Baking Powder—			
Findlater's ...	¼ lb. tin 3½d., ½ lb. tin 6½d., 1 lb. tin	0	11
Borwick's	per 1s. tin 7½d., per 6d. tin	0	4
Borwick's ...	... per doz. 1d. packets 7½d., 2d. packets	1	3
Royal (American)	per tin 7d., 1s., and	1	11
Yeatman's Yeast Powder	per tin 4d. and	0	7½
Barley—Finest Pearl	per lb. 2½d., per stone	2	8
Second Quality	per lb. 2d., per stone	2	2
Robinson's Patent Prepared ...	per 6d. tin 4d., per 1s. tin	0	7½
Bath Bricks—	... each 1d., per doz.	0	10
Beans—Finest Haricot	per lb. 3½d., per stone	4	0
Fine Haricot, smaller size	per lb. 2d., per stone	2	2
Haricot Verts	per pint tin 5½d., per quart tin	0	10
Baked (Heinz)	per tin 9d. and	1	1
Blacking and Boot Creams—			
Findlater's Liquid	per 1s. 6d. jar	0	9
Everett's Liquid	per 1s. 6d. jar	0	10
Meltonian "	per jar	0	10½
Day & Martin's Liquid ...	per 1s. 6d. jar 9½d., per 1s. jar 7½d., per 6d. jar	0	3½
Carr's Liquid	per 1s. 6d. jar 9½d., per 1s. jar 7½d., per 6d. jar	0	3½
Browne's Satin Polish	per bottle	0	4
Browne's Satin Polish ...	...per bottle in cardboard box	0	4½
Carr's Kid Reviver	per bottle	0	4
Premier Paste (in skins) ...	...per packet of 1 doz. 3d., per half-gross box	1	6
Carr's Imperial White Cream	per bottle	0	4½
Carr's Imperial Brown Cream	per bottle	0	4½
Carr's Imperial Black Cream	per bottle	0	4½
Carr's Meta Black Boot Polish	per bottle	0	4½
D. & M's. Russet Cream	per bottle	0	4½
A. F. & Co.'s Brown Cream	per bottle	0	4½
A. F. & Co.'s White Cream	per bottle	0	4½
A. F. & Co.'s Black Cream	per bottle	0	4½
Brown's Meltonian Cream (Black or White)	...per bottle 8½d. and	1	1
Propert's Royal Navy Dressing ...	per wide-mouthed bottle	0	5
Propert's Universal Cream (White) ...	per wide-mouthed bottle	0	5
Propert's Universal Cream (Black) ...	per wide-mouthed bottle	0	5

		s.	d.
Beef—Libby's Corned Beef ...	per No. 2 tin 1s. 1d, per No. 1 tin	0	7
Roast Beef (New York)	per No. 2 tin	1	1
Essence of Beef—**Brand's**	... 2 oz. and 4 oz., 1s. 2d. and	2	3
Extract of Beef—see Extract of Meat			
Beef Suet—Hugon's Atora Brand	per lb.	0	9
Bird Seed	per packet 2d., 4d. and	0	6
" Sand	per packet 1d. and	0	3

Biscuits.

W. & R. Jacob & Co.'s, Huntley & Palmer's, Carr's, Gray Dunn's, etc.

	Per lb. s. d.	Per small tin, from 2 to 3 lbs. s. d.	Per tin of about 1 lb s. d.
Alexandra Nuts	0 7	—	—
American Crackers	0 5	—	—
American Ginger Wafers	—	—	0 11½
Abernethy (Thin)	0 6	—	—
Arrowroot (Thin)	0 8	1 8½	—
Arrowroot	0 7	1 8½	—
Bath Oliver (Jacob's)...	—	1 4	—
Bath Oliver (H. & P.)	—	1 8	—
Braemar	0 8	—	—
Breakfast	0 8½	—	—
Canadian Crackers	0 6½	1 10	0 11
Cafe Noir	0 6½	—	—
Clifton	0 7	—	—
Cocoa Nut	1 6	—	—
Coffee Biscuits	0 10	—	—
Cracknels	1 0	—	—
Cream Crackers	0 6	—	0 11
Dessert	1 4	—	—
Erin	0 5½	—	—
Fairy	0 8	—	—
Florador Fingers	1 0	—	1 0½
German Rusks	0 10	—	—
German Rusks (Schick's), a speciality ...	—	—	2 6
Ginger Nuts	0 6½	1 7½	—
Hovis Biscuits	—	2 2	—
Hubbard's Rusks	—	3 0	1 6
Iced Cherry Cakes	0 8	—	—
Ice Creams	—	—	1 0
Ice Creams, Raspberry Flavoured ..	—	—	1 0
Lunch (Huntley & Palmer's)	0 4	·	—
Lunch (Jacob & Co.)	0 3½	—	—
Macaroons	1 5	2 9½	—
Marie	0 8	—	—
Mellin's Food Biscuits	—	2 0	—
Milk	0 5	1 5	—
Mixed, Rich	0 10	2 2	—
Naples	1 0½	—	—
Oaten	0 8½	2 2½	—
Osborne	0 7½	1 8	—
Oval Thin Captains	0 5	—	—
Parmena Biscuits	—	1 10	—
People's Mixed	0 5½	—	—
Petit Beurre	0 6½	—	—
Rock Cakes	1 0	—	—
Savoy	1 4	—	—
Sponge Rusks	—	—	1 11
Sugar Wafers	—	—	0 10½
Sugar Wafers, Raspberry flavoured ...	—	—	0 10½
Sugar Wafers, Lemon flavoured ..	—	—	0 10½
Torrance's Shortbread	—	2 2	1 2
Torrance's Oatcakes	—	1 6	0 10
Water	0 5	1 5½	—
Wheatmeal	0 8½	—	—
Wheaten (M'Kenzie's)	—	2 5	—
Windsor Wafers	1 0	—	—

And many other kinds too numerous to list.

Findlater Grocery Prices in 1904—the year of Bloomsday.
1 shilling in 1904 = £3.90 in 2000 and 1 penny = 0.33p; 12 pennies in 1 shilling, 20 shillings in 1 pound.

Article	Terms	s.	d.
Black Lead—Findlater's ...	... per half doz. box	0	4
Nixey's	per tablet 1d, per packet	0	6
Dome	per box of half doz.	0	4
Rising Sun Stove Polish	per packet 1d., per doz.	0	10½
Zebra Grate Polish	per packet 1d, per half doz. 5½d, per doz.	0	10½
" " "	... per tin	0	2½
Blanc Mange Powder—			
Bird's Blanc Mange Powder ...	per 6d. packet 4d, 1s. packet	0	8
Bloater Paste—Lazenby's	per tin or pot 5d. and	0	10
Plumtree's	per flat pot	0	6
Blue—Findlater's	... per doz. squares	0	6
Ball, finest (Findlater's)	per lb.	0	8
Reckitt's Paris	... per doz. squares	0	8½
Boar's Head—			
In Glass Shapes, with Pistachio Kernels ...	per shape	1	0
Bottled Fruits— TART FRUITS.			
Red Plums	per bottle	0	7½
Gooseberries	per bottle	0	8
Yellow Plums	per bottle	0	8
Red Currants	per bottle	0	10
Greengages	per bott'e	0	10
Black Currants	per bottle	0	11
Kentish Cherries	per bottle	0	11
Morella Cherries	per bottle	1	0
Raspberries and Currants	per bottle	1	0
Raspberries	per bottle	1	1
FRUITS IN RICH SYRUP.			
Apricots, Peaches	per bottle 1s. 2d. and	1	9
Pears	per bottle	1	9
Strawberries, Cherries ...	per bottle 1s. 2d. and	1	10
Pine Apple Chunks...	per bottle	1	2
Damsons, Greengages, Red Plums, Golden Plums	per bottle	0	11½
Raspberries, Red Currants, Black Currants ...	per bottle	0	8½
Borax—Starch Glaze	1d. packets, per doz.	0	10
Bovril ...	per bottle—1 oz., 2 oz., 4 oz., 8 oz., 16 oz., 6½d., 11½d., 1s. 9d., 2s. 11d., and	4	10
Bovril	per bottle for 1 cup	0	2½
Invalid Bovril	per 2 oz.	1	3
Brass Polish—Harris'	per tin	0	4
Pynka	per tin 1d. and	0	2
Buttercup Metal Polish...	per tin 1d. and	0	4
Globe Metal Polish	per 4d. tin	0	3½
Matchless Metal Polish	per tin	0	4
Enameline	per tin	0	2½
Putz Pomade	per tin	0	3½
Brawn—Matterson's	per lb. tin 8½d., 2 lb.	1	4
Oxford, in Glass	per shape	1	0
Breton's Colouring for Vegetables	per bottle	0	10
Brunswick Black	per jar 4d. and	0	7½
Brushes—			
Hair Brushes ...	11d., 1s. 3d., 1s. 5d., 1s. 9d., 2s., 2s. 3d., 2s. 9d., 3s. 3d., 3s. 9d., and	4	9
Tooth Brushes	4½d., 5½d., 9d., and	0	11
Cloth Brushes	10d., 1s. 2d., 1s. 3d., and	1	6
Hat Brushes	5½d., 9d., and	0	10
Shaving Brushes	7½d., 11d., 1s. 6d., 2s. 3d. and	3	0
Nail Brushes	1d., 2d., 3½d., 7½d., 9½d., 11d., and	1	10
Browning—Lazenby's Sauce	per bottle	0	9½
Gravy Browning—Tomlinson's	per bottle	0	9½
Parisian Essence	per bottle	0	9
Brand's Specialities—			
Essence of Beef	... 2 oz. and 4 oz., 1s. 2d. and	2	3
Essence of Chicken...	... 2 oz.	1	9
Brand's Own Sauce	per bottle	0	8
Brand's A 1 Sauce	per bottle	0	8
Brand's Indian Chutnee	per bottle	0	5½
Butter—See Provisions.			
Cakes—See Confectionery.			
Calves' Feet Jelly—See Jellies.			
Candles—			
PRICE'S Gold Medal Palmitine—Sizes, 4's, 6's, 8's, and 12's	per 3lb. pkt.	2	4½
PRICE'S Gold Medal Palmitine—with self-fitting ends	per 1 lb. box	0	10
PRICE'S Belmont Paraffin—Sizes, 4's, 6's, 8's, and 12's	per 3 lb. packet	1	9
PRICE'S Belmont Paraffin—with self-fitting ends	per 1 lb. box	0	8½
PRICE'S Standard Paraffin—Sizes, 4's, 6's, 8's, and 12's	per 3 lb. packet	1	7½
PRICE'S Standard Paraffin—with self-fitting ends	per 1 lb. box	0	8
PRICE'S Coloured Paraffin—Sizes, 8's and 12's	per 3 lb. packet	2	4½
PRICE'S Coloured Paraffin—with self-fitting ends	per 1 lb. box	0	10
PRICE'S Primrose Paraffin—Sizes, 4's, 6's, 8's & 12's	per 3 lb. pkt.	1	5½
PRICE'S Cowslip Wax—Sizes, 4's, 6's, 8's, and 12's	per 3 lb. pkt.	1	2½
PRICE'S National Wax—Sizes, 6's, 8's, and 12's	per 3 lb. pkt.	1	1
PRICE'S Composite, Best Patent—Sizes, 4's, 6's, 8's, and 12's	per 3 lb. packet	2	0
PRICE'S Composite, OrdinaryBest—Sizes, 4's, 6's, 8's, and 12's	per 3 lb. packet	1	10½
PRICE'S Snuffless Dipts—Sizes, 8's and 12's	per 3 lb. packet	1	2
PRICE'S Carriage Candles—Palmitine Moons—Sizes, 6's and 8's	per 2 lb. box	1	8

Article	Terms	s.	d.
Candles—*Continued.*			
PRICE'S Wax Tapers, in boxes (Thick)	1 lb., 22 inches white	1	1
PRICE'S Wax Tapers, in boxes (Thin)	¼ lb., 11 inches, coloured	0	5½
FINDLATER'S Iverna Wax 4's, 6's, 8's, and 12's	per 3lb. packet	1	3
A variety of Fancy Candles for decorative purposes.			
Candied Peel—			
Mixed	in ½ lb. and 1 lb. boxes, 3½d. and	0	6½
Lemon	per lb.	0	5½
Orange	per lb.	0	5½
Citron	per lb.	0	8
Candy—Sugar Candy	per lb.	0	4
Capers—Findlater's, Lazenby's, &c., Finest	12 oz. bot. 1s. 2d., 6 oz. bot. 7d., 2 oz. bot.	0	4
Carbonate of Soda	per lb.	0	1½
Carbolic Powder—			
Calvert's Carbolic Disinfectant Powder (15%) ...	per 1s. tin	0	8
Carlsbad Plums	per box, 1s. and	1	9
Carraway Seeds—Finest Dressed	per lb.	0	6
Caviare—Noel's	per tin	2	1
Celery Salt	per bottle	0	5
Chillies	per lb.	1	0
Chamois Leathers	each 4d., 7d., 1s., 1s. 3d., 1s. 7d., 2s. 2d.,	2	10
Cheese—See Provision Department.			
Imperial Cream Cheese	per pot	1	0
Parmesan Cheese	per pot	0	9
Chicory—Powder, Loose	per lb.	0	6
Powder	per ¼ lb. packet 2d., ½ lb.	0	3½
Chicken Meal	... per 3½ lb. packet	0	9
Chicken, Essence of—Brand's	per 2 oz. tin	1	9
Chocolate— **Plain Chocolate.**			
CHOCOLAT-MENIER, Grand Prix, Paris, 1878. — Yellow Wrapper ...	... 1s. 8d. per lb. for	1	2½
Green Wrapper ...	... 2s. 6d. per lb. for	1	11
Pink Wrapper .	... 3s. 0d. per lb. for	2	6
Bronze Wrapper ..	... 3s. 6d. per lb. for	3	0
White Wrapper ...	... 4s. 0d. per lb. for	3	8
Chocolate Powder ...	... per ½ lb. tin for	0	8½
SUCHARD'S FABRIQUE DE CHOCOLAT — Chocolate, Des Indes, in 5 lb. packets,	per lb.	1	2½
" Des Caravanes, in 5lb. packets,	per lb.	1	4
" Economique	per lb.	1	6
" Caravanes Vanille	per lb.	1	8
" Dessert Saute	per lb.	2	3
" Swiss Croquettes, Dessert,	per packet 5½d. and	0	11
Chocolate Cigarettes (loose)	per doz.	0	3
Fancy Creams, various flavours { Larger sizes at proportionate prices }	1s. box for	0	11
	6d box for	0	5
Fancy Boxes, Baskets, Tins, etc., at all prices	from 3d. to	12	6
Cadbury's Mexican Chocolate	per packet	0	5
Fry's Soluble Chocolate ...	per lb. 1/-, per ¼ lb. packet	0	3
Peters' Swiss Milk Chocolate	per packet 1d, 3d, and	0	6
Mazawattee Chocolates—Unsurpassed for purity and Flavour.			
Mazawattee Chocolate Cream in Medallion Tins, assorted designs	per tin	0	1
Mazawattee Solid Eating Chocolate in "Shell" Tins	per tin	0	1
Mazawattee Bundles Solid Eating Chocolate (five bars to packet)	per packet	0	1
Mazawattee Solid Eating Chocolate (Cimbrosa)	per packet	0	3
Mazawattee Milk Chocolate (Latariba)	...per tin 1d., 3d. and	0	6
Mazawattee Nalesta Assorted Chocolates	in boxes ¼-lb. 3½d.; ½-lb. 6d.; 1-lb.	1	0
Mazawattee Solid Eating Chocolate (Salvaro)	per packet 4d. and	0	6
Mazawattee " " " (Latariba)	per tin 6d. and	0	9
Mazawattee Assorted Varieties (Naconda) Tins,	per tin 6d., 9d., and	1	6
Mazawattee Croquettes (Latariba) Tins ...	per tin	0	6
Mazawattee Chocolate Cream Balls (Naconda)	per lb.	1	0
Mazawattee Chocolate Drops, plain	per lb.	1	2
Mazawattee Chocolate Drops with Nonpariels	per lb.	1	2
Mazawattee Seashore Shell Tins, containing assorted Chocolates	per tin 1s. 6d. and	2	6
Mazawattee Peacock Tins	1s. 6d. and	2	6
Mazawattee Salvaro Chocolates (popular local views on lids of tins)	6d., 1s., and	1	6
Mazawattee handsome decorated cabinet, containing 12 tins of Assorted (Latariba) Chocolate Creams	per cabinet	3	0
Mazawattee Latariba Chocolates— Assorted Chocolates, Ginger; Assorted Fruit Creams, Valencia; Almonds, Vanilla, Creme aux Fleurs, Caramel, Coffee, Apricot; Amandes, Nougat, Walnuts	per lb	1	10
Mazawattee Chocolate Peppermint Cream ...	1/4 and	1	10
" " Drops with Walnuts on top	per lb.	1	8
Chutney—			
Bengal Club (Lazenby's)	per bottle	0	8
Tirhoot	per bottle	0	9
Colonel Skinner's	per bottle	1	3
Green Mangoe—quarts	per bottle	1	2
Brand's Indian	per bottle	0	5½
Indian Mangoe	per bottle	1	1
Heinz's Tomato Gem	per bottle	1	2
Heinz's Keystone	per bottle	0	10

Cigars and Cigarettes—All the leading brands at lowest prices.

Item	Price	s.	d.
Citrates—			
Bishop's Citrate of Caffeine ...	per bottle 11½d. and	1	7
Bishop's Citrate of Magnesia ...	per bottle 8½d. and	1	6
Bishop's Effervescent Saline ...	... per bottle	0	11½
Bishop's Citrate of Lithia ...	per bottle 11½d. and	1	7
Cinnamon—			
Whole and Ground	per oz. 2½d., per lb.	2	6
Citric Acid—			
Nelson's	per 3d. packet 2½d., per 6d. packet	0	4½
Cloves—			
Finest Amboyna (whole or ground) ..	per oz. 2½d., per lb.	2	6
Cock's Combs	per bot.	3	0
Cocoa—			
Findlater's Trinidad Selected Shell ...	per lb. packet	0	5
" " " " ...	per ½-lb. packet	0	2½
Finest selected Shell	per stone	5	6
Fine selected Shell	per lb. 2d. and	0	4
Cocoa Nibs	per lb.	1	3½
Cadbury's	per 6d. packet, 3 oz.	0	5½
Cadbury's ...	per 9d. tin 4 oz. 8d., per 1s. 6d. tin 9½ oz.	1	4½
Epps' Homœopathic	per ½ lb. 7d., per lb.	1	2
Schweitzer's Cocoatina ...	per ¼ lb. tin 10½d., ½ lb. 1s. 7½d., 1 lb. tin	3	1
Van Houtens Cocoa	¼ lb., 9½d.; ½ lb., 1s. 6d.; 1 lb.	2	10

BEST AND GOES FARTHEST.

The Lancet, 1897, says:—"Van Houten's Cocoa yields a maximum proportion of the valuable food constituents of the bean, and, what is of more importance still, these are presented in a condition more easy of assimilation and digestion than in cocoa not so prepared."

VAN HOUTEN'S IS THE ORIGINAL PURE SOLUBLE COCOA.

Item	Price	s.	d.
Rowntree's Elect Cocoa	per ¼ lb. tin	0	8
Van Raan's Cocoa	per ¼ lb. tin 9d., ½ lb. tin	1	5½
Findlater's Pure Cocoa ...	per ¼ lb. packet 8d., ½ lb. 1s. 3d., 1 lb.	2	6
Fry's Concentrated	per ¼ lb tin 8d., ½ lb.	1	3½
Fry's Malted Cocoa	per 1s. tin	0	9
Peptonised Cocoa and Milk (Savory & Moore's)	1s. 5d. and	2	2
Dr. Tibble's Vi-Cocoa	per packet 5½d.; per tin 8½d. and	1	4½
Mazawattee Latariba Cocoa ...	per tin 6d., 9d., 1s. 6d., and	3	0
Mazawattee Cimbrosa Cocoa ...	per tin 5d., 7½d., 1s. 3d., and	2	6
Coffee—			
Mazawattee Coffee and Chicory	per lb.	1	4
Mazawattee Pure Coffee	per lb.	2	0

Packed in ¼ lb., ½ lb., and 1 lb. air-tight tins, which preserve the delicate aroma and full flavour of this Coffee of Coffees.

Item	Price	s.	d.
FINDLATER'S Finest Coffee, in berries or ground	per lb.	1	10

A combination of the finest mountain growths.

This Coffee is also supplied in ½-lb. and 1-lb. air-tight canisters.

Item	Price	s.	d.
FINDLATER'S Breakfast Coffee	per lb.	1	6
" " " mixed with Chicory	per lb.	1	4
FINDLATER'S "Cafe Francais," per ½-lb. tin, 10d	per lb. tin	1	8

The latter is a Coffee prepared in the same manner as that for which the French people are so celebrated. It is a mixture of the finest Coffee berries, with a small quantity of Chicory. Its strength, delicacy and flavour cannot be surpassed.

Raw or Unroasted Coffee, 3d. per lb. less.

Item	Price	s.	d.
Coffee Essence—			
Paterson's Coffee Essence ...	per 6d. bottle 5d., 1s. bottle	0	9
New I.D.A. Liquid Coffee... ...	... per bottle 5d. and	0	9
Branson's	per 6d. bottle 4½d., 1s. bottle	0	8½
Symington's (Edinburgh)	... per bottle 6d. and	1	0
Coffee and Milk—			
Anglo-Swiss	per tin	0	9½
Cocoanut (Desiccated)	per tin	0	6
Combs—			
Hair Combs ...	... each 4½d., 5d., 7d., 9d., 11d., 1s. 2d., 1s. 6d., and	2	0
Fine Tooth Combs	each	0	4½
Condy's Fluid—	per 1s. bottle	0	11
Condensed Milk—			
Anglo-Swiss Full Cream Milks: Milkmaid—Swiss ...	per tin	0	5½
Milkmaid—English ...	in ½ lb tin	0	2½
Milkmaid—Ideal Milk (unsweetened)	per tin	0	4½
Milkmaid—Fourpenny Brand	per tin	0	4
Nestle's Milk	per tin	0	5½
Cup Milk	per tin	0	3
Cocoa and Milk (Anglo-Swiss Milkmaid) ...	per tin	0	8
Coffee and Milk (Anglo-Swiss Milkmaid) ...	per tin	0	9½
Corn Flour—			
Findlater's Superior Corn Flour	1 lb. packet 5d., ½ lb. 2½d.; per 4 lb. tin	1	8
William Polson's Indian ...	... per lb. 3½d., 6 lb. packet	1	8
Brown & Polson's ...	... per ½ lb. packet 3d.; 1 lb.	0	6
Colman's Corn Flour ...	... per 1 lb. packet	0	5
Coving Stones	... each 1d.; per doz.	0	11

Confectionery.

Cakes.—Manufactured in our own factory in Thomas Street, and guaranteed made only from finest quality flour, choicest fruit, best creamery butter, and fresh eggs.

No Butter or Egg substitutes whatever used in the manufacture. The Cakes are totally different from the so-called "grocer's" cakes—being equal to the finest home-made article. Cakes are delivered fresh three days weekly to our branch houses

		s.	d
Cakes for Cutting—			
Rich Almond ...	per lb.	1	2
Rainbow ...	per lb.	1	2
Marble ...	per lb.	1	2
Royal ...	per lb.	1	0
Italian, Extra Rich Fruit Cake, with Almond Paste ...	per lb.	1	0
Victoria Light Sultana Cake ...	per lb.	1	0
Cherry Cake ...	per lb.	1	0
Seed Cake ...	per lb.	0	10
Battenburg Cake ...	per lb.	0	10
Madeira Cake ...	per lb.	0	10
Chesterfield, Extra Rich Fruit ...	per lb.	0	8
Chancellor ...	per lb.	0	8
Crystallised Ginger ...	per lb.	0	8
Fig Cake—with Almond Icing ...	per lb.	0	8
Oxford Lunch ...	per lb.	0	8
Ginger Cake ...	per lb.	0	6
Grafton Madeira ...	per lb.	0	6
Grafton Seed ...	per lb.	0	6
Grafton Fruit ...	per lb.	0	6
Rice Cake ...	per lb.	0	6
Small Cakes—			
Cherry Cake, with Almond Paste ...	each	1	6
Cherry Cake ...	each	1	0
Oxford Lunch (3 lb.) ...	each	2	0
Oxford Lunch (2 lb.) ...	each	1	4
Oxford Lunch (1¼ lb.) ...	each	0	10
Bristol ...	each	0	10
Fig Cake (plain) ...	each 10d. and	1	0
Genoa ...	each	0	10
Madeira ...	each	0	10
Rich Almond Cake ...	each	0	10
Sultana ...	each	0	10
Seed ...	each	0	10
Sponge ...	each	0	10
School, large ...	each	0	11
School, small ...	each	0	6
Ginger ...	each	0	6
Cottage, Fruit ...	each	0	6
Cottage, Seed ...	each	0	6
Cottage, Swiss ...	each	0	6
Jam Sandwiches ...	each	0	8
Sponge Cakes ...	each	0	2
Sponge Cakes ...	each	0	1

And others too numerous to specify. Also a large assortment of **1d. Cakes** at all our Establishments.

Sweet Department.

Sugar Boilings, etc., manufactured in our Sweet Factory in Thomas Street from finest materials—pure sugar, and finest flavourings and colourings.

Some of our assortments are—

Item	Price	s.	d.
Lemon Drops, Acid Squares, Raspberries, Crystal Mixed Drops, Black Bull's Eyes, Clear Bull's Eyes, Rainbow Drops, Fruit Drops, Peppermint Cushions, Cocoa Chips, Almonds and Raisins, Chopped Rock, Chocolate Balls, Hawthorn Drops, Mixed Drops, Fruit Squares, Irish Kisses, Toffee Squares, Rose Drops, Strawberries, Clove Balls, Pine Apple Drops, Mixed Raspberries, Orange Drops, Sugar Plums, Pear Drops, Peppermint Squares, Peaches	per lb.	0	6
Butter Drops, Extra Strong Acid, Gooseberries, Cough Drops, Cocoa Drops, Blackberries	per tin	0	6
Barley Sugar, Lemon Plait, Raspberry Rock, Rose Rock, Clove Rock, Brown and Black Rock	per lb.	0	6
Almond Toffee, Real Brown Toffee, Pink, White, and Brown Cocoanut	per lb.	0	8

Sugar Sticks, each ¼d., ½d., 1d.

Item	Price	s.	d.
Mixed Sweets and Creams	per lb. 1s. 10d., 1s. 2d., 1s., 10d., 8d.,	0	6
Sugar Candy ...	per lb.	0	4
Peppermint Lozenges, Extra Strong ...	per lb. 8d. and	0	10
Lozenges, Musk, Cayenne, Cough, and Cachous ...	per lb.	1	0
Sugar Almonds ...	per lb.	1	0
Burnt Almonds ...	per lb.	1	0
Silk Bonbons or Satines ...	per lb.	1	6
Creams and Fondants, best ...	per lb. 1s. 4d., 2s. and	2	6
Creams and Fondants, second ...	per lb.	0	8
Edinburgh Rock ...	per tin 11d. and	0	5½
Bath Pipe ...	per lb.	1	0
Butter Scotch ...	per packet 3d., and	0	5
Nougat ...	per packet 3d. and	0	5
Chinese Figs ...	per drum	1	0
Caramels ...	(eight)	1	0
Caramels, Opera Cream ...	per lb.	1	4
Caramels, Anvil ...	per lb.	1	6

		s.	d.
Cream—Fresh daily	per jar 5½d. and	0	10
Cleeve's	per tin	0	8
Cream of Tartar—98 per cent. B.P.	per lb.	1	4
Crystallised and Glace Fruits—			
Angelica, Finest	per lb.	1	4
Assorted Fruits, First Choice	per lb. 1s. 8d.; per 4 lb. box	5	6
Apricots, Finest	per lb.	1	10
Cherries, Finest	per lb.	1	6
Greengages, Finest	per lb.	1	6
Pears, White and Red, Finest	per lb.	1	6
Pine Apple	per lb. 1s. and	1	6
Metz Fruits	per box 5d., 9d., and	1	5
Crystallised Ginger	per lb. 10d., 1s. 2d., and	1	5
Currants—			
Finest Vostizzas (cleaned and free from stalks)	per lb.	0	5
Finest Patras (cleaned and free from stalks)	per lb.	0	4
Fine	per lb.	0	3
Currie—			
Cook's Currie Paste	per pot	1	2½
Findlater's India Currie Powder	per half bottle 5½d.; bottle	0	10
Halford's Powder	per tin	0	6½
Curried Fowls, &c.—			
Halford's Fowl	per tin 1s. 3d., 2s. 2d., and	3	5
Halford's Rabbit	per tin 1s. 2d., 1s. 11d., and	3	2
Halford's Prawns	per tin	1	4
Halford's Lobster	per tin	1	2
Halford's Sauce	per tin	0	9
Custard Powder—			
Bird's	per 6d. packet 4d.; 1s. packet	0	8
Damsons—Finest	per large tin	1	1
In Rich Syrup	per bottle	0	11
Dates	per lb.	0	4
Dates Cartoons	each	0	6
Dessert	per 3 lb. box.	2	0
Disinfectants—Calvert's Disinfecting Powder	per 1s. tin	0	8
Condy's Fluid (red)	per bottle	0	11
Sanitas	per tin 11½d.; per bottle	0	11½
Dog Biscuits—			
Old Calabar	per stone 1s. 9d.; per cwt.	14	0
Spratt's	per stone 2s. 4d.; per cwt.	18	8
Puppy—Pet—Toy Pet Dog Biscuits	per packet	0	6
Dog Food (Clarke's Melox)	per 5 lb. bag	1	0
Rodnim Dog Food (Spratt's)	per 7 lb. bag	1	3
Dried Fruits—See under Apples, Apricots, Currants, Figs, Dates, Raisins, Plums, Pears, etc.			
Dried Herbs—Specially prepared and packed for A. F. & Co., for Soups, &c.			
Celery Seed, Basil, Marjoram, Mint, Parsley, Sage, Thyme, Mixed Herbs	per bottle	0	6
Eau De Cologne—			
No. 4711	per bottle	1	9
No. 54	per bottle	1	7
Crown Perfumery, long green bottle		1	0½
Jersey	per bottle 10½d., 1s. 9d., and	4	0
Egg Powder—			
Bird's	per 6d. packet	0	4
Ovo (Desiccated Eggs)	per tin of 1 doz. eggs	1	0
Emery Cloth—O. F. F. F.—Nos. 1, 2, and 3	per sheet 1d., per doz.	0	9
Enameline	per tin	0	2½
Ermco—See Plate Powders.			
Essences (Flavouring)—Bitter Almonds, Celery, Cinnamon, Claret Cup, Cloves, Cochineal, Ginger, Lemon Peel, Orange, Raspberry, Ratafia, Strawberry, Vanilla — FINDLATER'S Quintessence.	per bottle	0	4
	per bottle	0	7
	per 6 oz. bottle	2	6
	per 16 oz. bottle	5	6
Essence of Beef (Brand's)	per 2 oz. and 4 oz. tin 1s. 2d. and	2	3
,, ,, **Chicken**	per 2 oz. tin	1	9

		s.	d.
Extract of Meat—			
E. Lazenby & Son's (Liebig)	per ½ oz. jar 5d., 1 oz. 8d., 2 oz. 1s. 1d., 4 oz.	1	10
Armour's	per 1 oz. pot 8½d., 2 oz. 1s. 2½d., 4 oz. 2s. 3d., 8 oz.	4	3
Lemco (Liebig Company)	per 2 oz. jar 1s. 2½d.; 4 oz. 2s. 3d; 8 oz.	4	3
Oxo	per 2 oz. jar 10d.; per 4 oz.	1	6
Vigoral (Armour's)	per 2 oz. jar 11d.; 4 oz. 1s. 8d.; 8 oz.	2	11
Bovril,	per 1 oz. 6½d.; 2 oz. 11½d.; 4 oz. 1s. 9d; 8 oz. 2s. 11d.; 16 oz.	4	10
Extract of Soap—			
Hudson's	per doz.	0	9
Farola (Marshall's)—Large, Medium, or Fine	per packet	0	6
Figs—			
Extra Choice Dessert Layers	per lb.	0	10
Finest Layers	per lb.	0	8
Fine Quality Layers	per lb.	0	6
Finest Quality Layers	per box 10d., 1s., 2s. 6d.	3	9
Finest Pulled Loucooms	per box 1s. 6d., 3s. 4d., and	4	0
Finest Pulled Loucooms	per lb. 8d., 10d., and	1	0
Fish in Tins—			
Bloaters	per tin	0	5½
Findon Haddocks	per tin	0	7
Herring Roes in butter	per tin	0	8
Fresh Herrings	per tin	0	4
Kippered Herrings	per tin	0	6
Herrings in Tomato Sauce	per tin	0	6
Lobster (flat)	per half-tin 10d., per tin	1	6
Oysters	per tin	0	6
Prawns	per tin	1	2
Salmon	tall tins each 7d.; flat tins 10d.; ½-tins	0	5½
Sardines, Louis Edelin—Lazenby's	small tin 8½d.; large tin	1	2
Sardines—Philippe and Canaud	small tin 10½d.; large tin	1	4
Sardines—Peneaus	per large tin	1	2
Bouvais Flou, special value	per 18-oz. tin	1	0
Sardines in Tomatoes	per 18-oz. tin	0	10
Norwegian Smoked Sardines, a great delicacy	per tin 5d. and	0	9
Royans à la Bordelaise	per tin	0	6
Sardines, good quality	per large tin 6d. and	0	10
Sardines in glass	per shape	1	4
Florador Food—Large, Medium, or Fine	per packet	0	6
Florence Cream	per bottle 5½d. and	0	10
Flour—			
Findlater's Economo, in 5 lb. linen bags	each	1	0
Finest Flour Hungarian	per stone	2	6
Fine Quality Flour	per stone, 1s. 8d. and	1	10
Self-raising Flour	per packet 4d. and 8d.; per 7 lb. linen bag	1	3
Paisley Flour	per packet	0	6½
Foods—			
Neaves' Food	per tin	0	8
Nestle's Milk Food	per tin 8d. and	1	4
Benger's Food	per tin 1s. 3d. and	1	11
Mellin's Food	per bottle 1s. 1d. and	1	9½
Force	per packet	0	6
Frame Food Diet	per 1 lb.	0	11
Phœnix Food	per tin	1	0
Grape Nuts	per packet	0	7
Du Barry's Revalenta	½ lb. tin 1s. 7½d., 1 lb.	2	10
Horlick's Malted Milk	per bottle 1s. 4½d. and	2	5
Savory & Moore's Infant's Food	per 1s. size 8½d., per 2s. size	1	5
Shredded Wheat	per packet	0	6½
French Plums—We only stock the finest quality fruit, which is specially selected and packed for A. F. & Co., Ltd.			
Finest Imperial, our usual standard of very Large Soft Fruit	per 1 lb. bottle	1	6
Finest Imperial, our usual standard of very Large Soft Fruit	per 2 lb. bottle	2	9
Finest Imperial, our usual standard of very Large Soft Fruit	per 4 lb. bottle	4	9
Loose, Fine Bold Fruit, suitable for Dessert	per lb.	1	0
Loose, Fine Bold Fruit	per lb.	0	10
Fruits—ENGLISH TART FRUITS (BOTTLES).—*Purity and Extra Quality Guaranteed.*			
Red Plums	per bottle	0	7½
Gooseberries	per bottle	0	8
Yellow Plum	per bottle	0	8
Greengages	per bottle	0	10
Red Currants	per bottle	0	10
Black Currants	per bottle	0	11
Kentish Cherries	per bottle	0	11
Morella Cherries	per bottle	1	0
Raspberries and Currants	per bottle	1	0
Raspberries	per bottle	1	1

Fruits—*Continued.*

FRUITS IN RICH SYRUP (BOTTLES).

		s.	d.
Apricots, Peaches, Pears	per ½ bottle 1s. 2d., per bottle	1	9
Strawberries, Cherries	1s. 2d. and	1	10
Pine Apple Chunks	per bottle	1	2
Damsons, Greengages, Red Plums, Golden Plums	per bottle	0	11½
Raspberries, Red Currants, Black Currants ...	per bottle	0	8½
Macedoines of Fruits	per bottle	1	10

FRUITS IN TINS.

		s.	d.
Apples	gallon tins, each	1	1
Apricots	per tin 9d., 1s., and	1	6
Blackberries (Irish)	per tin	0	8
Damsons	per tin	1	1
Greengages	per tin	1	0
Golden Plums	per tin	1	0
Red Plums	per tin	1	0
Pine Apples	per tin 8d., 10d., and	1	0
Pine Apple Chunks	per tin	1	0
Peaches	per tin 9d., 1s., and	1	6
Pears	per tin 9d., 1s., and	1	6
Fruit Syrups—			
Raspberry Syrup	per bottle 5½d. and	0	10
Strawberry Syrup	per bottle 5½d. and	0	10
Lemon Syrup	per bottle 4½d. and	0	7
Fruit Saline, Salt, etc.			
Fruit Saline (Dunn's)	per bottle	1	3
Eno's Fruit Salt	per bottle	1	11
Concentrated Fruit Juices	per bottle	0	4½
Cambridge Lemonade	per pkt.	0	5½
Furniture Polish—			
A. F. & Co.'s	per bottle 4½d., 6d., and	0	9
A. F. & Co.'s "Perfection"	... per bottle 6d. and	1	0
Adams'	... per bottle 5d. and	0	10
Stephenson's Furniture Cream ...	... per bottle 5d. and	0	10
Jackson's Wax Polish	per tin	0	5½
Ronuk Furniture Polish	3d., 5½d., and	0	10½
Gelatine—			
Cox's Amber Brilliant ...	6d. packets 3½d., 1s. packets	0	7
Nelson's	6d. packets 3½d., 1s. packets	0	7
Loose Amber, finest	per lb.	2	6
French Leaf, finest	per lb.	1	9
" Extra—a speciality	per lb.	3	0
Gelatine Lozenges (Nelson's)	per lb.	1	4
Mixed Gelatines and Jujubes	per lb.	0	7
Ginger—			
Preserved, Genuine Chyloong Season's Crop, in jars, 8½d., 1s. 6d., and		2	5
Preserved (Finest) in glass	each	1	4
Crystallised Ginger	per lb. 10d., 1s. 2d., and	1	6
Finest White Bleached, Whole	per lb.	1	6
Finest Ground ... in 1 oz. tins 1½d., 2 oz. 2½d., 4 oz. 4½d.;	per lb.	1	6
Essence for Flavouring	... per bottle 7d. and	0	4
Glaze—			
Glaze for Tongues, Hams, &c.	per lb.	2	2
Glaze for Tongues, Hams, &c. (Lazenby) ...	per bottle	0	6½
Golden Syrup—(A. F. & Co.'s) per 16 oz. pot and 2 lb. jar, 3½d. and		0	7
Lyle's	per 1 lb. tin 4½d., 2 lb.	0	8
Glycerine—Price's	... per bottle 2d. and	0	5
Lever's	per bottle	0	2
Grape Nuts	per packet	0	7
Groats—			
Robinson's Prepared	per 6d. tin 4d., 1s. tin	0	7½
Groult's Preparations—			
Tapioca du Brésil	per packet	0	8
Sagou des Indes	per packet	0	7
Crême de Riz	per packet	0	4½
Potato Fécule	per packet	0	2½
Orge d'Allemagne	per packet	0	6
Greengages—Extra quality, in rich Syrup	per tin	1	0
" " " ...	per bot.	0	11½
Guava—Jelly	per glass jar	0	9
Haddocks—Findon	per tin	0	7
Halford's Preparations—See under Currie.			
Ham—Potted	per tin or pot 5d. and	0	10
Haricot Beans—			
Finest Giant, Hand-picked	per lb. 3½d., per stone	4	0
Fine Small Size	per lb. 2d., per stone	2	2
Verts, Finest	per pint tin 5½d., quart tin	0	10
Harness Composition—(Harris's)	per tin	0	7
Heinz's Specialities—			
Tomato Gem Chutney	per bottle	1	2
Keystone Chutney	per bottle	0	10
Tomato Ketchup	per 8 oz. 7½d., per 12 oz.	1	0
Tomato Soup	per tin 9d. and	1	1
Sweet Pickles	per bottle	0	11
Beans, Baked	per tin 9d. and	1	1
Indian Relish	per bottle	1	2
Keystone Mustard Dressing	per bottle	0	8
Evaporated Horse Radish	per bottle	1	0

		s.	d.
Herbs Dried—Specially prepared and packed for A. F. & Co., for Soups, &c.—			
Celery Seed	per bottle	0	6
Basil	per bottle	0	6
Marjoram	per bottle	0	6
Mint	per bottle	0	6
Parsley	per bottle	0	6
Sage	per bottle	0	6
Thyme	per bottle	0	6
Mixed Herbs	per bottle	0	6
Herrings—Fresh, very fine	per tin	0	4
Herrings, Kippered	per tin	0	6
Herrings, in Tomato	per tin	0	6
Hominy—American Pearl	per 5 lb. pkt.	0	9
Honey—Strained	per glass jar	0	11
Pure Irish, Guaranteed	per glass jar	0	10
Sections. Picked (Finest Maiden)	each, 10d. and	1	0
Californian Honey, Lazenby's	per glass jar	0	10
Housemaids' Gloves—Chamois	per pair	0	9
Tanned	per pair	0	11
Gauntlets, Chamois	per pair	1	2
Gauntlets, Tanned	per pair	1	4½
Hugon's Suet—Refined, Atora Brand	per lb.	0	9
Ink—			
Dichroic Ink (Draper's) per 6d. bottle 4½., 1s. bottle 9d.,	2s. bottle	1	5
Invalids' and Infants' Food—			
Benger's Food	...per tin 1s. 3d. and	1	11
Du Barry's Revalenta	½ lb. tin 1s. 7½d., 1 lb.	2	10
Force Food	per packet	0	6
Frame Food Diet	per 1 lb.	0	11
Grape Nuts	per packet	0	7
Horlick's Malted Milk	per bottle 1s. 4½d. and	2	5
Hubbard's Rusks	per tin 3s. and	1	6
Mellin's Food	per bottle 1s. 1d. and	1	9½
Neave's Food	per tin	0	8
Nestle's Milk Food...	per tin 8d. and	1	4
Phœnix Food	per tin	1	0
Ridge's Food	per tin	0	11½
Robinson's Patent Prepared Barley, per 1s. tin 7½d.;	per 6d. tin	0	4
Robinson's Patent Prepared Groats, per 1s. tin 7½d.;	per 6d. tin	0	4
Savory & Moore's Infant Food per 1s. size 8½d.;	per 2s. size	1	5
Isinglass (Swinborne's) ... per 8d. packet 6d.;	per 1s. packet	0	8
Italian Paste	finest assorted shapes, per lb.	0	7
Jackson's Wax Polish	per tin	0	5½

Jams—

Findlater's Guaranteed Whole Fruit Jams, in the manufacture of which only Pure Lump Sugar has been used :—

	per 4 oz.	per 8 oz. (s. d.)	Per 3 lb. Jar (s. d.)	Per 16 oz. pot (s. d.)	Per 2 lb. glass jar (s. d.)	Per 7 lb. stone jar (s. d.)
Strawberry		—	1 4	0 6½	0 11	3 2
Raspberry		—	1 4	0 6½	0 11	3 2
Black Currant		—	—	0 7	1 0	3 5
Apricot		—	—	0 6½	0 11	3 2
Greengage		—	—	0 6	0 10	2 10
Blackberry		—	—	0 6	0 10	2 10
Red Currant		—	—	0 6	0 10	—
Damson		—	—	0 6	0 10	—
Gooseberry		—	—	0 5½	0 9	2 8
Golden Plum		—	1 0	0 5	0 8	2 4
Plum			1 0	0 5	0 8	2 4
Black Currant Jelly	4½d.	6½d.		0 10	—	—
Red Currant Jelly	4½d.	6½d.		0 10	—	—
Apple Jelly		—	—	0 6	—	—
Bramble or Blackberry Jelly		—	—	0 7	0 11	—

Jams made expressly of perfectly fresh Fruit and Pure Cane Sugar upon the plantations of the Right Hon. Lord Sudeley :—

	Per 1 lb. glass pot. (s. d.)	Per 2 lb. glass jar. (s. d.)
Strawberry	0 8	1 3
Raspberry	0 8	1 3
Black Currant	0 8	1 3
Apricot	0 8	1 3

Jams manufactured in Ireland specially for ourselves, from Fruit grown in Ireland :—

	Per 1 lb. (s. d.)	Per 2 lb. (s. d.)	Per 7 lb. (s. d.)
Strawberry	0 6	0 10	2 8
Raspberry	0 6	0 10	2 8
Plum	0 5	0 8	3½ lb. 1 3
Mixed Fruit	0 4½	0 7½	3½ lb. 1 1

s. d.

Jellies—Lazenby's, Chivers', &c.—

Calves' Feet, Lemon, Orange, Aspic, &c. } Not flavoured with wine. { per quart 1 9; per pint 0 11½; per half pint 0 6½
Madeira, Noyeau, &c., Port, Maraschino, Punch, Champagne, Pine Apple, Vanilla } Flavoured with wine. { per quart 2 3; per pint 1 4; per half pint 0 9
Jellies in tablets (all flavours) ... ... each 0 3½
Frame Food Jelly ... ... per 1 lb. jar 0 8½

Julienne—For Soups ... ... per lb. packet 0 10

Ketchup—

Findlater's Mushroom, Warranted per half bottle 7d.; bottle 1s.; reputed quart 1 9
Tomato Ketchup, Gordon and Dilworth's ... per bottle 6d. and 0 11½
" " Heinz ... ... per bottle 7½d. and 1 0

Kid Reviver—Carr's ... ... per bottle 0 4

Knives—

Sardine ... ... each 0 1½
Various Patterns for opening tins ... ... each 0 6

Knife Powder—

Nixey's "Cervus" ... ... 6d. tins 4d., 1s. tins 0 7½
Oakey's "Wellington" ... ... per tin 4d. and 0 7½

Lard—Finest, in Bladders ... . per lb. 0 8

Lavender Water—

Whitaker's, per 1s bottle 8½d., 1s. 6d. bottle 1s. 0½d., 2s. 6d. bottle 1 9
Musk Lavender Water ... ... per bottle 4½d. and 1 1
Lavender Water, Crown Perfumery, long green bottle, per bottle 1 0½

Lemon Curd, ... per pot 0 11

Lemon Juices and Syrups—

Lemon Syrup, Lazenby's . ... per bottle 7d. 0 4½
Lemon Syrup, Carter's ... . per large bottle 1 2
Lemon Syrup, Rose's ... ... per bottle 1 1
Concentrated Fruit Juices, Eiffel Tower, etc. ... per bottle 0 4½
Concentrated Fruit Juices, Cambridge Lemonade per bottle 0 5½

Lemon Squash—

Findlater's ... ... per square bottle 0 10½

This is the finest Lemon Squash obtainable, and is guaranteed to be the product of Pure Lemon Juice and Cane Sugar.

Yeatman's ... ... per square bottle 0 9
Lazenby's ... ... per square bottle 0 9
Stower's Concentrated ... ... per bottle 1 2

Lentils—

German ... ... per lb. 0 4
Egyptian ... ... per lb. 0 3

Lime Juice—

Lime Juice, Findlater's .. .. per bottle 0 10
Lime Juice, Rose's ... ... per bottle 1 0
Lime Juice Cordial, Findlater's ... ... per bottle 0 11
Lime Juice Cordial, Rose's ... ... per bottle 1 2
Lime Juice Cordial, Stower's .. ... per bottle 1 1½
Lime Juice Syrup, Findlater's ... ... per bottle 0 11½
Lime Juice Syrup, Rose's ... ... per bottle 1 2

Liquorice—Finest Corigliano Juice, in sticks .. per lb. 1 6

Lobster—

Lobster Paste ... ... per half-tin 5d., per tin or pot 0 10
Cook's Lobster ... ... per half-tin, 10d.; per tin 1 6
Halford's Curried Lobster ... ... per tin 1 2

Lunch Tongues—Very delicate, Fairbank's per 1 lb. tin 1 3½

Macaroni—

Finest Genoa ... ... per lb. 5d., per box 1 8
Naples ... ... per lb. 0 4
"Raycel's" ... ... per packet 0 6

Mace—Whole or Ground ... ... per oz. 3½d., per lb. 4 2

Macedoines de Legumes, Finest ... ... per pint tin 0 7½
Finest .. .. per bottle 0 11½

Magnesia—

Murray's Fluid Magnesia ... per 1s. bottle 7d., 2s. 6d bottle 1 6
Citrate of Magnesia ... ... per 8½d. and 1 6

Malted Milk—

Malted Milk, Horlick's per large bottle 2s. 5d., per small bottle 1 4½

Marmalade—

Findlater's, Dundee make per 1 lb. pot 4½d.; per 2 lb. jar 7½d.; per 7 lb. jar 2 0
Findlater's (home made) ... ... per 1 lb. pot 6d., 2 lb. jar 0 11
Keiller's per 1 lb. pot 5½d.; per 2 lb. jar 10d.; per 4 lb. jar 1 5
Cairn's ... ... per 1 lb. pot 7d., 2 lb. jar 1 2
Tangerine ... ... per 1 lb. pot 8d., 2 lb. jar 1 3
Pine Apple ... ... per 1 lb. pot 8d., 2 lb. jar 1 3
Ginger and Pine Apple ... ... per 1 lb. pot 8d., 2 lb. jar 1 3
Ginger ... . per 1 lb. pot, 8d.; per 2 lb. jar 1 3
Lemon ... ... per 1 lb. pot 0 5

Matches—

Bryant & May's Patent Safety ... ... per doz. 0 7
Findlater's Safety ... . per doz. 0 6½
Small Sized Safety ... ... per doz. 2½d., per gross 2 0

Meat Juice—

Valentine's ... ... per bottle 3 0
See also Extract of Meat.

Meats—

Ham and Chicken, Potted—Lazenby's ... }
Strasburg Meat ... ... } per tin or pot 0 10; per ½ tin 0 5
Tongue, Game, etc. ... ... }

Plumtree's Fresh Potted Meats, "specially recommended," in white earthenware flat jars.

Beef, Tongue, Tongue and Ham, Tongue, Ham, and Chicken, Strasburg, Shrimp and Salmon Paste, &c., &c. } per jar 0 6

Libby's Corned Beef ... per No. 1 tin 7d., per No. 2 tin 1 1
Roast Beef (New York) .. .. per No. 2 tin 1 1
Matterson's Brawn ... ... per 1 lb. tin 8½d., 2 lb. tin 1 4
Matterson's Sausages 0 9½
Assorted Glencairn Pates, Chicken and Ham, &c. (C. & De Fourier) ... ... per tin 1s. 4d. and 2 4
Assorted Pies—Yachting, Camp, Pic-nic, &c. (C. & De Fourier) 1 4
Napier Oval Pates—Game, Lunch, Pic-nic, &c. (C. & De Fourier) 0 11½
Conway Household Pates, Turkey and Tongue, Chicken and Ham (C. & De Fourier) ... ... 6d. and 1 0
Galantine of Wild Boar's Head and Pistachio Kernels (C. & De Fourier) 1 5
Calves' Tongues (C. & De Fourier) ... ... 1s. 6d. and 2 6
Boiled Rabbit (C. & De Fourier) 0 11
Boar's Head, in glass shapes ... ... each 1 0
Oxford Brawn, in glass shapes ... ... each 1 0
Home Brand Ox Tongues, large size ... each 1 11

Metal Polish—

Buttercup Metal Polish ... ... per tin 1d. and 0 4
Globe Metal Polish ... ... per 4d. tin 0 3½
Matchless Metal Polish ... ... per tin 0 4
Harris's Brass Polish ... ... per tin 0 4
Pynka .. .. per tin 1d. and 0 2
Enameline ... ... per tin 0 2½
Putz Pomade ... ... per tin 0 3½

Mellin's Food ... per 1s. 6d. bottle 1s. 1d., 2s. 6d. bottle 1 9½

Metz Fruits—Finest, various shapes in ¼ lb., ½ lb., and 1 lb boxes 5d., 9d., and 1 5

Milk (Condensed)—

Anglo-Swiss Full Cream Milks. { Milkmaid—Swiss ... ... per tin 0 5½
Milkmaid—English ... ... in ½ lb. tin 0 2½
Milkmaid—Ideal Milk (unsweetened) per tin 0 4½
Milkmaid—Fourpenny Brand ... per tin 0 4
Nestle's Milk ... ... per tin 0 5½
Cup Milk ... ... per tin 0 3
Cocoa and Milk (Anglo-Swiss, Milkmaid) ... per tin 0 8
Coffee and Milk (Anglo-Swiss, Milkmaid) ... per tin 0 9½

Milk Food—Nestle's ... ... per tin 8d. and 1 4
Horlick's Malted Milk ... ... per tin 1s. 4½d. and 2 5

Mince Meat ... ... per 1 lb. glass jar 0 10

Mulligatawny Paste (Cook's) ... ... per pot 1 2½

Muscatels (See Raisins).

Mushrooms—

Mushrooms—Extra Champignons (finest only) per pint tin 0 11½
Mushrooms—Extra Champignons per half bottle 11½d., per bottle 1 4½

		s.	d.
Mustard—			
Findlater's D. S. F.	1 lb. tins, per lb.	1	3
Findlater's D. S. F.	½ lb. tins, per lb.	1	3
Findlater's D. S. F.	¼ lb. tins, per lb.	1	5
Findlater's Mustard, F.	in 5 lb. tins, per lb.	0	9½
Findlater's Mustard, S. F.	in 5 lb. tins, per lb.	1	1
Findlater's Mustard, D. S. F.	in 5 lb. tins, per lb.	1	2½
Colman's D. S. F.	1 lb. tins, per lb.	1	3
Colman's D. S. F.	½ lb. tins, per lb.	1	4
Colman's D. S. F.	¼ lb. tins, per lb.	1	6
Colman's	in 4 lb. tins, per lb., F., 10d.; S. F., 1s. 1½d.; D. S. F.	1	3
Moutarde de Maille	per pot	0	9
Night Lights—			
Clarke's Pyramids, 9 hours (8 lights in box)	per box	0	7½
Price's Child's	per box	0	5
Price's New Patent	per box	0	5½
Red Cross	per box	0	5
Nitre	per lb.	0	4
Nutmegs—			
Whole or Ground	per oz. 3½d., per lb.	4	2
Oatflour—Scott's Midlothian	per 1 lb. tin	0	8
White's "Red Star"	per 1 lb. tin	0	6
Oatmeal—			
Findlater's Finest Quality	in 5 lb. linen bags	1	2
Findlater's Finest Flake	in 5 lb. linen bags	1	2
Finest Flake (White's Wafer)	per stone	2	4
Finest Pin Head	per stone	2	4
Quaker Oats	per 2 lb. packet	0	5½
White's Wafer Flake Oats	per 2 lb. packet	0	5½
Oils for Salads and Cooking—			
Findlater's Finest Olive Oil, imported by ourselves from Leghorn, guaranteed absolutely pure, no admixture of Cotton Seed Oils, preserves all the full flavours of the Olives	large bottle	1	10
	half bottle	1	0
	quarter bot.	0	6½
Lazenby's Salad Oil	quarter bottle 7d., half bottle 1/1, large bottle	1	10
Fourche's Superfine Olive	per half bottle 1s. 3d., per bottle	2	2
Sweet Oil, in Pyramid Wicker Flasks	per bottle	0	7
Olives—			
Lazenby's French	per bottle 7d. and	1	1
Lazenby's Spanish	per bottle 7d. and	1	0
Ox Tongues—			
Lunch Tongues, very delicate	per 1 lb. tin	1	3½
Paysandu Ox Tongues	per 2¼ lb. tin	3	2
Home Brand Ox Tongues, large size	each	1	11
Oysters—Best Brand	per tin	0	6
Parisian Essence	per Imperial half-pint bottle	0	9
Parmesan Cheese—Grated for Macaroni	per bottle	0	9
Parrot Food	per packet 2d., 4d. and	0	6
Pastilles de Legumes—Carpenter's, for Colouring Soups	per tin	0	5½
Pate de Foie Gras	per tin 4s., 2s. 3d., and	1	3
Paté de Foie Gras (Noel's)	in terrines 2s. 3d. and	1	3
Paté façon Foie Gras aux trufles (Cunningham's)	per tin 5½d. and	0	10½
Peaches—			
A. F. & Co.'s extra quality, dessert	per tin	1	6
Extra quality, A. F. & Co.'s	per tin	1	0
First Standard quality	per tin	0	9
In glass	bottles 1s. 9d. and	1	2
Pears—			
A. F. & Co.'s Bartlett, dessert	per tin	1	6
Extra quality, A. F. & Co.'s	per tin	1	0
First Standard quality	per tin	0	9
Fruit in glass	bottles	1	9
Dried, Finest	per lb.	0	10
Pea Flour—			
Symington's Prepared	per 4d. packet 3d., per 6d. tin	0	4½
Peas—			
Finest Marrow-fats (hand-picked)	per 1 lb. pkt. 3d.; 2nd Qual., per lb.	0	2
Finest Split	per lb. 2d., per stone	1	10
Finest Green Split	per lb.	0	4
Young Peas, highly recommended	per pint tin 8d., quart tin	1	0
Young Peas, highly recommended	per bottle	1	0
Fine quality	per pint tin 5½d., quart tin 8d. and	0	10
Fine quality	per bottle	0	10

		s.	d.
Pepsalia	per bottle	0	11
Perfumery—			
Lime Tree, Lilac, Wall Flower, Wood Violet, Opoponax, Parma Violets, Jockey Club, Lily of the Valley, Millifleurs, White Rose, &c.	per 2s. 6d. bottle	1	6
	per 1s. 6d. bottle	1	0
Crab Apple Blossom (Crown Perfumery Co.)	per bottle 1s. 9d. and	3	6
Violette de Parme	per bottle	1	10
Rhine Violet	per 3s. 6d. bottle	3	0
Eau de Cologne, No. 4711	per bottle	1	9
Eau de Cologne, No. 54	per bottle	1	7
Eau de Cologne, Crown Perfumery	long green bottle	1	0½
Eau de Cologne, Jersey	per bottle 10½d., 1s. 9d., and	4	0
Lavender Water (Whitaker's)	per 1s. bottle 8½d., 1s. 6d. bottle 1s. 0½d., 2s. 6d. bottle	1	9
Musk Lavender Water	per bottle 4½d. and	1	1
Lavender Water, Crown Perfumery, long green bottle	per bottle	1	0½
Invigorating Lavender Salts (Crown Perfumery Co)	per bottle	1	6
Trotter Oil	4½d. and	0	9
American Bay Rhum		0	4½
Rose, Orange Flower, and Elder Flower Waters, triple strength	per bottle	0	10
Perfumed Sachets	each	0	4
Fuller's Earth Powder (Cleaver's)	per box	0	4½
Violet Powder (Cleaver's)	per box	0	4½
Oatmeal Powder (Cleaver's)	per box	0	4½
Juvenia Cream (Cleaver's)	per box	0	9½
Vinolia Cream	per box, 9½d., and	1	4
Vinolia Toilet Powder, white, pink, or cream	per box 10d. and	1	6
Vinolia Brilliantine, for hair or moustachios	per bottle	0	9
Brilliantine (Crown Perfumery Co.)	per bottle	1	0
Toilet Vinegar (Crown Perfumery Co.)	per bottle 8d. and	1	5
Toilet Vinegar (Rimmel's)	per bottle 9½d. and	1	8
Peel (Candied)—Mixed	in ½ lb. and 1 lb boxes 3½d. and	0	6½
Lemon	per lb.	0	5½
Orange	per lb.	0	5½
Citron	per lb.	0	8
Pepper—			
Black, Finest Whole	per lb.	0	9
Black, Finest Ground, loose	per lb.	0	9
Black, Finest Ground	per ¼ lb. tin 3½d., ½ lb. tin 6d., 1 lb. tin	0	11
Black, Finest Ground	per 1 oz. tin 1½d., 2 oz. tin	0	2½
White, Finest Whole	per lb.	1	2
White, Finest Ground, loose	per lb.	1	5
White, Finest Ground	per ¼ lb. tin 5d., ½ lb. tin 9d., 1 lb. tin	1	6
White, Finest Ground	per 1 oz. 1½d., 2 oz.	0	3
Cayenne Pepper	per lb.	1	6
Cayenne Pods (Chillies)	per lb.	1	0
Cayenne (Castors)	per bottle	0	3
Nepaul (Castors)	per bottle	0	4
Coraline Pepper	per bottle	1	0

LAZENBY'S, FINDLATER'S, &c.

Item		s.	d.
Pickles—			
Mixed, Piccalilli, Cauliflower, Chow Chow, Walnuts, Gherkins, Onions, White Onions, Red Cabbage	per half-bottle	0	5½
	per bottle	0	9½
	per half-gallon jar	2	4
Mixed Pickles, Piccalilli	in patent lever-top bottles	0	11
Captain White's Oriental	per ½ bottle 10d., per bottle	1	4
West India	per bottle	0	10½
Mango Relish	per bottle	0	10½
Nabob, Hot or Mild	per bottle	0	11½
Pickle Forks—Lazenby's	each	1	6
Pimento—			
Finest Pimento or Jamaica Pepper	per lb.	0	8
Pine Apples—			
Singapore (Whole) – A. F. & Co.'s Special Pack	per 3 lb. tin	1	0
Singapore (Whole)—A. F. & Co.'s first standard quality,	per 2½ lb. tin	0	10
Singapore Pines, special value	per 2½ lb. tin	0	8
Pine Apple Chunks, very fine	per tin 1s., per bottle	1	2
" " Cubes, crystallised	per lb. 1s. and	1	6
Pistachio Kernels—Finest	per lb.	8	0
Plate Powder—			
Goddard's	per packet	0	7½
Ermco Liquid Silver Polish	per bottle 5d. and	0	10
Plum Puddings—In Cloths	each 2s. 6d. and	3	6
Plum Puddings (in Bowls)	each	2	6

Item		s.	d.
Plums—Red Plums (Chivers')	per tin	1	0
Golden Victoria, in Rich Syrup	per tin	1	0
Greengages, finest	per tin	1	0
Damsons, finest	per tin	1	1

See also Fruits in Bottles.

Plums, French—

We only stock the finest quality fruit, which is specially selected and packed for A. F. & Co.

Item		s.	d.
Finest Imperial, our usual standard of very Large Soft Fruit,	per 1 lb. bottle	1	6
Finest Imperial, our usual standard of very Large Soft Fruit,	per 2 lb. bottle	2	9
Finest Imperial, our usual standard of very Large Soft Fruit,	per 4 lb. bottle	4	9
Loose, Fine Bold Fruit, suitable for Dessert	per lb.	1	0
Loose, Fine Bold Fruit	per lb.	0	10
Plums, Californian—	per lb., 6d. and	0	8
Plums, Carlsbad—per box	1s. and	1	9
Potato Flour—	per packet	0	2½

Potted Meats and Fish—LAZENBY'S and PLUMTREE'S—

Item		s.	d.
Anchovy Paste, Beef, Bloater Paste, Game, Ham	per tin or pot	0	10
Ham and Chicken, Lobster, Strasbourg Meats, Tongue	per half-tin or small pot	0	5
Sardine Paste (Cunningham)	per tin 5½d. and	0	10½
Plumtree's Fresh Potted Meat	per jar	0	6

See also under Meats.

Item		s.	d.
Poultry Meal	per 3½ lb. bag	0	9
Prawns—Barataria Prawns	per tin	1	2
Halford's Curried Prawns	per tin	1	4

Propert's Preparations—

Item		s.	d.
Propert's Royal Navy Dressing, in wide-mouthed bottles,	per bot.	0	5
Propert's Universal Cream, White or Black, „ „	per bot.	0	5

Provisions.

We have opened Provision Departments at our Head Offices, and at the Leinster Street, Rathmines, Howth, Sandymount, Blackrock, Dalkey, and Bray Branches.

We stock only the finest quality goods, and guarantee everything to be as described.

It is impossible to quote prices, as they are constantly changing with the fluctuation of the market. Latest quotations will be sent immediately on receipt of an enquiry.

Amongst other goods we stock :—

Matterson's Hams and Bacon.	Best Cool Butter.
Shaw's Hams and Bacon.	Cooking Butter.
Canadian Hams and Bacon.	New-laid Eggs.
American Hams.	Matterson's Sausages.
Boiled Hams.	Black and White Puddings.
Spiced Hams.	Palethorpe's Sausages.
Picnic Hams.	London Brawn.
Limerick Hams.	Finest Gloucester Cheese.
Jowls.	Cheddar, Gorgonzola, and other varieties of Home and Colonial Cheese, etc., etc.
Cleeve's Creamery Butter.	

Canadian Pea-fed Bacon—a Speciality.

Special Irish Bacon Cured and Smoked for ourselves—a Monopoly.

Item		s.	d.
Prunes (French)— Extra Choice	per lb.	0	6
Putz Pomade	per tin	0	3½

Raisins—

Item		s.	d.
Selected Dehesa, extra quality Imperial Layers	per lb.	1	4
Finest Imperial Clusters	per lb.	1	2
Finest Royal Clusters	per lb.	1	0
Finest Loose Muscatels	per lb.	0	8
Good Loose Muscatels	per lb.	0	6
Sultanas, Finest	per lb. 8d. and	0	7
Sultanas, Good	per lb.	0	6
Valencias, Finest	per lb. 6d. and	0	7
Valencias, Good	per lb.	0	5
Valencias, Stoned	per packet	0	8

Rabbit—

Item		s.	d.
Curried	per tin 1s. 2d., 1s. 11d., and	3	2
Boiled (C. & De Fourier)	per tin	0	11

Raspberry Vinegar—

Item		s.	d.
Raspberry Vinegar	per gal. 10s.; per doz.	20	0

Relish—See Sauces.

Item		s.	d.
Rennet (Essence of)—Lazenby's	per bottle	0	8½
Warren's Sweet	per bottle	0	8
Findlater's	per bottle	0	6
Rennet Tablets (Lazenby's)	per tube	0	5½
„ Powder (Lorimer's)	per bottle	0	5

Revalenta—

Item		s.	d.
Du Barry's Revalenta	½ lb. tin 1s. 7½d., 1 lb. tin	2	10

Rice—

Item		s.	d.
Java, Finest	per lb. 3½d., stone 4s., cwt.	31	0
Java, Good	per lb. 2½d., stone 2s. 6d., cwt.	19	0
Japan, Finest	per lb. 3d., stone 3s. 3d., cwt.	24	0
Patna, Finest	per lb. 2½d., stone 2s. 6d., cwt.	19	0
Rangoon	per lb. 1½d., stone 1s. 8d., cwt.	13	0
Ground	per lb. 2½d., stone 2s. 8d., cwt.	20	0
Fairy Flake Rice	per packet	0	3
Rice Flour	per lb. 2d., stone	2	2

Ronuk—

Item		s.	d.
No. 1 Household (Universal)	per tin 3d., 5½d., and	0	10½
Saffron—Finest	per oz.	4	3
Sago—Large Grain	per lb. 3d.; per stone	3	3
Small	per lb. 2½d., per stone	2	9
Salad Cream—Florence Cream	per bottle 5½d. and	0	10
Lazenby's	per bottle 5½d. and	0	10

Salad Oil—

Item		s.	d.
FINDLATER'S (Finest Olive)	quarter bottle 6½d., half bottle 1s., large bottle	1	10
Lazenby's	quarter bottle 7d., half bottle 1s. 1d., large bottle	1	10
Fourche's Superfine Olive	half bottle 1s. 3d., large bottle	2	2
Salmon—Tall Tins	per tin	0	7
Flat Salmon, Triumph Brand	per tin	0	10
Flat Salmon	per half tin	0	5½

Salt—

Item		s.	d.
Finest Eclipse, in packets	each	0	2
Bumsted's (Jars)	each	0	4½
Falk's	per packet	0	1
Alvina Patent Table Salt	per tin	0	3
Blocks, for Kitchen use	each 5d. and	0	10
Kitchen Salt	per stone	0	6
Oriental	per bottle	0	8½
Celery	per bottle	0	5
Cerebos Salt	per tin	0	5½
Dunn's Fruit Saline	per bottle	1	3
Eno's Fruit Salt	per bottle	1	11
Brill's Sea Salt for the Bath	per box	1	2
Pepsalia Table Salt	per bottle	0	11
Natural Health Salt	per tin	0	4
Saltpetre	per lb.	0	4
Sand for Birds	per packet, 1d. and	0	3
Sanitas	per tin or bottle	0	11½
Sanitary Rolls	each 3½d., per doz.	3	0

Sardines—

Item		s.	d.
Louis Edelin Sardines (**Lazenby's**)	small tin 8½d., large tin	1	2
Philippe and Canaud Sardines	small tin 10½d., large tin	1	4
Peneaus	per large tin	1	2
Bouvais Flon (special value)	per 18 oz. tin	1	0
Sardines Aux Tomatoes	18 oz. tin	0	10
Norwegian Smoked Sardines, in oil, a great delicacy	per tin 5d. and	0	9
Royans a la Bordelaise	per tin	0	6
Sardines, good quality	per large tin 6d. and	0	10
Sardines in glass	per shape	1	4
Sardine Knives (Ordinary)	each	0	1½
Knight's Patent	each	0	6

Sauces, Relish, etc.— s. d.

FINDLATER'S & LAZENBY'S.

Essence of Anchovies ... ... per bottle 5½d., 9½d., and 1 4½
Brand's Own Sauce ... ... per bottle 0 8
Brand's A1 Sauce ... ... per bottle 0 8
Browning (Lazenby's) ... ... per bottle 0 9½
Gravy Browning (Tomlinson & Co.'s) ... per bottle 0 9½
China Soy ... ... per bottle 4d. and 0 6½
Celery Salt ... ... per bottle 0 5
Chef Sauce (Lazenby's) ... . per bottle 0 9
Gentleman's Relish (Patum Peperium) ... per jar 0 10
Harvey (Lazenby's) ... ... per bottle 8½d. and 1 4
Halford's Curry Sauce ... ... per bottle 0 9
Horse Radish and Mustard ... ... per bottle 0 9
Hoe's Sauce ... ... per bottle 0 6
India Soy (Lazenby's) ... ... per bottle 4d. and 0 6½
India Relish (Heinz) ... ... per bottle 1 2
Keystone Mustard Dressing (Heinz) .. ... per bottle 0 8
Mango Relish ... ... per bottle 0 10½
Mellor's Worcester ... ... per bottle 4½d. and 0 9
Nabob ... ... per bottle 0 5½
Oriental Salt ... ... per bottle 0 8½
Parisian Essence ... ... per bottle 0 9
Reading ... ... per bottle 0 10
Sauce de Tomate ... ... per pint tin 6d., per quart tin 0 10
Sauce de Tomates (D. & G.) ... ... per bottle 0 6
Tomato Sauce **Lazenby's** ... ... per bottle 9d. and 1 3½
Tabasco ... ... per bottle 1 9
Wild Cherry Sauce ... ... per bottle 0 6
Worcester (Lea & Perrin's) ... ... per bottle 10d. and 1 6
Worcester (**Holbrook**) ... per Imperial half-pint bottle 0 6
Yorkshire Relish ... ... per bottle 4½d. and 0 9
Household ... ... per large bottle 0 6

Sausages—

Matterson's ... ... per lb. tin 0 9½
Fresh—See Provisions.

Semolina—Finest ... ... per lb. 0 3

Shrimps ... ... per tin 1 2

Soap (Household)—

Extra Tallow Crown ... ... per stone 3s. 9d., cwt. 29 0
Tallow Crown ... . per stone 2s. 8d., cwt. 21 0
Brown ... ... per stone 3s., cwt. 22 0
Household ... per lb. 2½d., stone 2s. 9d., half cwt. box 11 0
Titan Soap ... ... per packet 1 0
Sunlight ... ... per box of 3 bars 0 7½
Lifebuoy (Carbolic) ... ... per box of 3 bars 0 8½
Lux (Soap Flakes) ... ... per packet 1d., per doz. 1 0
Price's Carbolic Soap ... ... per lb. 0 3½
Sapolio ... ... per bar 0 3½
Maypole Soap ... ... (Black, 6d.), per tablet 0 3½
Barilla Soap ... ... per lb. 6d., per 14 lbs. 6 6
Hudson's Extract of Soap ... ... per doz. 0 9
Fels Naptha Soap ... ... per bar 0 2½
Buttermilk Soap (A. F. & Co.'s.) in boxes of 12 tablets, per tablet 0 2
Monkey Brand Soap ... ... per bar 0 3
Abbot Polishing Soap ... . per bar 0 3

Soaps (Toilet)—

Brown Windsor (Whitaker's)
Honey ... . } per tablet, new ovals ... 0 2
Almond and Glycerine ... } per tablet, magnum squares 0 4
Glycerine ... ... } per 1 lb. bar 0 9
Oatmeal ... ...
Pure White Glycerine (Whitaker's) ... per box of 3 tablets 1 0
Juvenia (Cleaver's) ... ... per tablet 0 5
Juvenia (Cleaver's) ... per box of 3 tablets, 1st quality 1 7
Juvenia (Cleaver's) ... per box of 3 tablets, "Family" 0 10½
Glycerine and Cucumber (Cleaver's) in boxes of 12 tablets, per tablet 0 3
White Rose and Cucumber (Cleaver's) in boxes of 12 tablets, per tablet 0 3
Unscented Transparent (Cleaver's) in boxes of 12 tablets, per tablet 0 3
Terebene (Cleaver's) ... ... per box of 3 tablets 1 1
Oatmeal and Glycerine (Cleaver's) ... per box of 3 tablets 0 8½
Brown Windsor (Cleaver's) ... ... per box of 3 tablets 0 8½
Oatmeal (Cleaver's) ... ... per box of 3 tablets 0 8½
Lavender Salt Soap (Crown Perfumery Co.) per box of 3 tablets 0 10½
Crown Violet Soap (Crown Perfumery Co.) per box of 3 tablets 1 4
Royal Castle (**Price's**) ... ... per box of 8 tablets 1 2
Glycerine Cream (**Price's**) ... per box of 3 tablets 1 0
Visitors (**Price's**) ... ... per box of 4 tablets 0 6
Armour's Toilet Soaps, assorted ... ... per tablet 0 2
" " " " ... ... per box of 3 tablets 1 0
Court (Price's) ... ... in boxes of 12 tablets, per tablet 0 2
Premier—Vinolia Co. ... in boxes of 3 tablets, per tablet 0 3½
Sulphur, Carbolic, Terebene or Coal Tar—Vinolia Co., per tablet, 3½d., per box of 3 tablets 0 10
Liril Violettes de Parme Soap ... ... per tablet 0 3½
Floral—Vinolia Co. ... in boxes of 3 tablets, per tablet 0 5

s. d.

Medical (Balsamic)—Vinolia Co., in boxes of 3 tablets, per tablet 7d., per box 1 9
Toilet (Otto)—Vinolia Co., in boxes of 3 tablets, per tablet, 9d., per box 2 3
Vestal—Vinolia Co. per tablet 2s. 2d., per box of 3 tablets 6 3
Toilet Soaps—Lever's ... ... per tablet 1d., 1½d., 3d. and 0 4
Unscented (Transparent)—Pears' ...in boxes of 3 doz., per tablet 0 3½
Scented (Transparent)—Pears' ... ... per tablet 0 7
Wash Balls—Pears' ... ... per tablet 0 7
Ivory Soap, Floating, Toilet size ... ... per tablet 0 2
Albion Milk and Sulphur Soap in boxes of 3 tablets, per box 0 10½
Fieira ... ... per tablet 2½d., per box of 12 tablets 2 3
Barilla Toilet Soap ... ... per tablet 0 2
Viardot Freres Complexion Soap, per tablet, 2d., per box of 12 tablets 1 11
Carbolic Toilet Soap—Calvert's ... per 1s. 6d. box of 3 tablets 1 0
Coal Tar Toilet Soap—Wright's, per tablet 4d., per box of 3 tablets 1 0
Cuticura Soap ... ... per tablet 11d., per box of 3 tablets 2 8

Shaving Soaps—

Terebene Shaving Foam—Cleaver's ... ... per tube 0 8½
Vinolia (Premier) Shaving Sticks ... ... per stick 0 5
Vinolia Shaving Soap (Premier), Flat Cakes ... ... per cake 0 10
Shaving Sticks—Pears' ... ... per stick 0 7

Soft Soap—

Imperial (Odourless) ... 2lb. tins 9d., 7 lb. tins 2 0
A. F. & Co.'s (for household use) ... 2lb tins 8½d., 7 lb. tins 1 10
Soft Soap in 28 lb. buckets ... ... per bucket 6 6

Soda—Carbonate of ... ... per lb. 0 1½
Washing... ... ... per stone 7d., cwt. 4 6

Soups— CROSS & BLACKWELL'S, LAZENBY'S, &c.

Grouse ... ...
Game ... ... } per tin 0 10½
Oyster ... ...
Hare ... ...

Giblet ... ...
Ox Cheek ... ...
Chicken Broth ... ...
Tomato ... ...
Hotch Potch ... ... } per tin 0 9½
Kidney ... ...
Mock Turtle ... ...
Mulligatawny ... ...
Ox Tail ... ...

Gravy ... ...
Green Pea ... ... } per tin 0 7½
Mutton Broth ... ...
Julienne ... ...

Ox Tail ... ... per quart tin 1 5
Gravy ... ... per quart tin 1 1
Tomato, Heinz's ... . per tin 1s. 1d., and 0 9
Soups in Bottle, Hare ... ...
Soups in Bottle, Mulligatawny ... ... } per bottle 1 3
Soups in Bottle, Ox Tail ... ... } ½ bottle 0 10
Soups in Bottle, Mock Turtle ... ...
Soups in Bottle, Gravy ... ... { per bottle 1 1
Soups in Bottle, Julienne ... ... } ½ bottle 0 9
Solidified Soups in Squares (Lazenby's), per packet 5d., per box of 1 doz. 4 10
Dried Turtle for Soups ... ... per lb. 8 0
Edwards' Desiccated, red, white, etc., per doz. 1d., squares 10d., per ¼ lb. packets 0 4
Edwards' Desiccated, Tomato ... per ¼ lb. tin 0 7
Gravy Browning, Tomlinson & Co.'s ... ... per bottle 0 9½
Raycel's Soup Pastes ... ... per packet 0 6

MAGGI'S SOUPS.

Consomme (clear soup) in gelatine tubes, each tube sufficient for two persons, boxes containing 10 tubes 1 8
French Soups, in boxes of 12 tablets, each tablet sufficient for two persons. Ordinary sorts, 29 varieties, per tablet 0 2½
French Soups, extra qualities, 6 varieties ... ... per tablet 0 3
French Soups, assorted, Series A to F ... ... per doz. 2 6
French Soups, assorted, Series G ... ... per doz. 3 0

Spratt's Specialities—

Dog Biscuits ... ... per stone 2s. 4d., per cwt. 18 8
Pet—Toy Pet—Puppy Dog Biscuits ... ... per pkt. 0 6
Chicken Meal ... ... per 3½ lb. pkt. 0 9
Bird Seed ... ... per pkt. 2d., 4d., and 0 6
Parrot Food ... ... per pkt. 2d., 4d., and 0 6
Sand for Birds ... ... per pkt. 1d and 0 3
Rodnim Dog Food ... ... per 7 lb. bag 1 3

Spices—

It is so important that Spices should be free from adulteration that we quote the finest qualities only. They will be found much more economical to use.

Item	Price	s.	d.
Allspice—Finest Pimento (Whole or Ground)	per lb.	0	8
Carraway Seeds—Finest Dressed	per lb.	0	6
Chillies—Red Pods	per lb.	1	0
Cinnamon—Whole or Ground	per oz. 2½d., per lb.	2	6
Cloves—Finest Amboyna (Whole or Ground)	per oz. 2½d., per lb.	2	6
Ginger—Finest White Bleached	per lb.	1	6
Ginger—Finest Ground	per lb.	1	6
Ginger—Finest Ground,	in 1 oz. tins 1½d., 2 oz. tins 2½d., 4 oz. tins	0	4½
Mace—Whole or Ground	per oz. 3½d., per lb.	4	2
Mixed Spice—Finest	per 1 oz. tin 1d., 2 oz. tin 2d., lb. tin	1	0
Nutmegs—Whole or Ground	per oz. 3½d., lb.	4	2
Pepper—Black, Finest Whole	per lb.	0	9
Pepper—Black, Finest Ground, loose	per lb.	0	9
Pepper, Black, Finest Ground	per tin 3½d., 6d., and	0	11
Pepper, Black, Finest Ground	per 1 oz. 1½d., per 2 oz.	0	2½
Pepper, White, Finest Whole	per lb.	1	2
Pepper, White, Finest Ground, loose	per lb.	1	5
Pepper, White, Finest Ground	per tin 5d., 9d., and	1	6
Pepper, White, Finest Ground	per 1 oz. 1½d., per 2 oz.	0	3
Cayenne Pepper	per lb.	1	6
Cayenne Pods (Chillies)	per lb.	1	0
Cayenne Pepper in Castors	per bottle	0	3
Nepaul Pepper in Castors	per bottle	0	4
Pistachio Kernels—Finest	per lb.	8	0
Saffron—Finest	per oz.	4	3
Vanilla Pods—Finest	per pod	0	8
Liquorice—Finest Corigliano Juice, in sticks	per lb.	1	6

Item	Price	s.	d.
Spinach (Epinards)	per tin	0	11
Spiritine	per tin 3d. and	0	5
Travelling Saucepan and Stand	each	1	6
Curling Stoves	each	1	3
Folding Stands	each	0	9
Sponges	each from 3d. to	7	6

Starch—

Item	Price	s.	d.
Findlater's Finest Superfine,	per ½ lb. 2½d., per lb. 4d., packet	1	4½
Robin Starch	per packet 1d., 3d., and	0	6
Borax Starch Glaze	...1d. packets per doz.	0	10
Colman's Starch	per packet about 4½ lbs.	1	6
Colman's Cream Starch	per packet	0	6

Suet—

Item	Price	s.	d.
Hugon's Refined Atora Brand	per lb.	0	9

Sugars—

Item	Price	s.	d.
Finest Lump Cubes	per lb. 2d. and	0	2½
Preserving Lump	per lb. 2d. and	0	2¼
Lump Dust (Castor Sugar)	per lb.	0	3
Icing	per lb.	0	4
Crystallised, Demerara Style	per lb.	0	2½
Finest White Crystal	per lb. 1¾d., 2d., and	0	2½
Coffee Crystals	per lb.	0	3
Crushed Sugars	per lb.	0	2
Barbadoes Style	per lb.	0	2½
Yellow Sugar, for Cooking	1½d. and	0	2

NOTE.—Above subject to market variations.

Item	Price	s.	d.
Sugar Candy	per lb.	0	4
Sugar Corn, American Sweet	per tin	0	9

Sweets, Sugar Boilings, etc.—See Confectionery.

Syrup—

Item	Price	s.	d.
Golden Syrup (A. F. & Co.'s)	per 16 oz. pot 3½d., 2 lb. jar	0	7
Golden Syrup, Lyle's	per 1 lb. tin 4½d., 2 lb. tin	0	8
Raspberry Syrup	per bottle 5½d., and	0	10
Strawberry Syrup	per bottle 5½d., and	0	10
Lemon Syrup	per bottle 4½d., and	0	7

Tamarinds—

Item	Price	s.	d.
Lazenby's West India Preserved	per pot	0	5½

Tapers—

Item	Price	s.	d.
Price's Wax Tapers, in boxes (Thick)	white 22 in. long	1	1
Price's Wax Tapers, in boxes (Thin)	coloured 11 in. long	0	5½

Tapioca—

Item	Price	s.	d.
Finest Rio kind	per lb. 5d., per stone	5	3
Good quality	per lb. 3d., per stone	3	3
Finest Seed Pearl Tapioca	per lb. 3d., per stone	3	3
Finest Bullet Tapioca	per lb. 3d., per stone	3	3
Groults for thickening soup	per packet	0	8
Snowflake Tapioca (White's)	per packet	0	4

Item	Price	s.	d.
Tartaric Acid—Ground or Crystallised	per lb.	1	8

Tomatoes—

Item	Price	s.	d.
Crown Brand	per tin	0	6
Whole (in long tins)	per tin	0	6½
Conserve or Puree	per pint tin 6d., per quart tin	0	10
Sauce de Tomates	per bottle	0	6
Tomato Gem Chutney (Heinz)	per bottle	1	2
Tomato Ketchup (Heinz)	per 8 ozs. 7½d.. 12 oz.	1	0
Do. do. (Gordon & Dilworth, Rowat's)	per bot. 6d. and	0	11½
Tomato Soup (Heinz)	per tin 1s. 1d. and	0	9

Tongues in Tins—

Item	Price	s.	d.
Lunch Tongues, very delicate	per No. 1 tin	1	3½
Paysandu Ox Tongues	per 2¼ lb. tin	3	2

Tooth Washes and Powders—

Item	Price	s.	d.
Cherry Tooth Paste	per pot	0	4½
White Rose Tooth Paste	per pot	0	8½
Fraisine Tooth Powder	per box	1	0
Carbolic Tooth Powder (Calvert's),	...per 1s. box 8d., per 6d. box	0	4
Dento Phenolene (Calvert's)	per 1s. 6d. bottle	1	0
Vinolia Dentifrice Premier	per pot 5d. and	0	10
Vinolia Dentifrice American	per pot	1	3
Vinolia Dentifrice English	per pot	2	2

Item	Price	s.	d.
Tooth Brushes	each 4½d., 5½d., 9d.	0	11
Treacle	1 lb. pot 3½d., 2 lb. jar	0	6½
Truffles	per bottle 7s., half-bottle 3s. 6d., and quarter bottle	1	11
Vanilla Pods (Finest)	per pod	0	8

Vegetable Colouring (Breton's)—For Jellies, Blanc Manges, &c.

Item	Price	s.	d.
Carmine Colouring (Warranted to contain no injurious ingredients)	per bottle	0	10
Red ,, ,, ,, ,,	per bottle	0	10
Green ,, ,, ,, ,,	per bottle	0	10
Yellow ,, ,, ,, ,,	per bottle	0	10

Item	Price	s.	d.
Vaseline	per bottle 2d., 4d., and	0	6

Vermicelli—

Item	Price	s.	d.
Finest Genoa	... per lb. 5d., per box	1	8
Vigoral (Armour's), per 2 oz. pot 11d., 4 oz. pot 1s. 8d.,	8 oz. pot 2s. 11d , 16 oz. pot	4	9

Vinegar—

Item	Price	s.	d.
Choicest Wine Vinegar (a speciality)	per bottle	0	8
Finest White	per quart 9d., per pint 5d., half-pint	0	3
Finest Brown	per quart 9d., per pint 5d., half-pint	0	3
Tarragon (Lazenby's)	per half-bottle 5½d., per bottle	0	9
Chili	per half-bottle 5½d., per bottle	0	9
Pure Malt Table Vinegar	per pint 5d., per quart	0	9
White Distilled Crystal Malt Vinegar	per pint 6d., per quart	0	10½

Vinolia Preparations—(See Perfumery and Soaps).

Wheaten Meal—

Item	Price	s.	d.
James Best & Son's	per 7 lb. bag 1s., 14 lb. bag	2	0
Shredded Wheat	per packet	0	6½

Item	Price	s.	d.
Wax—Best Yellow	per lb.	1	6
Wax Polish (Jackson's)	per tin	0	5½

Yeast Powder—

Item	Price	s.	d.
Yeatman's, The Perfection of Baking Powder	6d. tin 4d., 1s. tin	0	7½
Zebra Grate Polish,	per doz. 10½d., per pkt. of half-doz. 5½d., per pkt.	0	1
,, ,, ,, Paste	per tin	0	2½

AMERICA	Frog's Leap C.K.Mondavi Opus One Seghesio Sequoia Grove Seven Peaks
ARGENTINA	Trivento
AUSTRALIA	Penfolds Cape Mentelle Coldstream Hills Rouge Homme Wynns Seaview
CHILE	Concha y Toro Mapa, Baron Philippe de Rothschild
GERMANY	Bend in the River
HUNGARY	Royal Tokaji
ITALY	Araldica Badia a Coltibuono Lungarotti Candido Villa di Vetrice
NEW ZEALAND	Cloudy Bay Esk Valley Pelorus
PORTUGAL	Quinta do Noval Port
SOUTH AFRICA	Arniston Bay De Wetshof Kanonkop Koopmanskloof Mooiplaas Estate Neil Ellis
SPAIN	Marqués de Riscal C.V.N.E Bodegas Piedmonte

FRANCE	
Champagne	Veuve Clicquot Krug Ayala
Alsace	Schlumberger
Beaujolais	Bouchard Père et Fils Chateau de Raousset
Bergerac	Chateau de la Colline
Bordeaux	Baron Philippe de Rothschild Chateau Meaume Chateau de Fieuzal
Burgundy	Bouchard Père et Fils Henri Boillot Comte Lafon Chateau de la Saule Dujac Tollot-Beaut
Chablis	Bouchard Père et Fils Louis Michel Daniel Etienne Defaix
Chateauneuf	Dom. du Vieux Telegraphe
Gascogne	Plaimont
Languedoc	Baron Philippe de Rothschild Domaine Virginie Chateau Pech Celeyran
Loire	Jean Max Roger Jean Claude Chatelain Henri Pelle Jean Beauquin
Rhone	Caves des Papes Domaine Raspail-Ay Chateau de Grand Moulas Dom. de Coyeux
Armagnac	Chateau de Cassaigne
Cognac	Lheraud

Index

Page numbers in italic refer to illustrations.
Numbers followed by n indicate footnotes.

H

Y